Engaging Videos explore a variety of business topics related to the theory students are learning in class. **Exercise Quizzes** assess students' comprehension of the concepts in each video.

"I feel like MyLab Intro to Business helped me achieve a higher grade because of the excellent resources such as the flashcards and study plan to show me my areas of improvement."

— Lisa Morris, Student, Alamance Community College

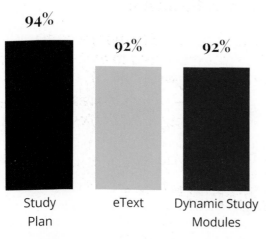

94%

92%

92%

Study Plan

eText

Dynamic Study Modules

% of students who found learning aid helpful

Dynamic Study Modules use the latest developments in cognitive science and help students study chapter topics by adapting to their performance in real time.

Pearson eText enhances student learning both in and outside the classroom. Accessible anytime, anywhere via MyLab or the app.

92%

of students would tell their instructor to keep using MyLab Intro to Business

For additional details visit: www.pearson.com/mylab/Intro-to-Business

Dedication

This book is dedicated to the many thousands of instructors and students who use Bovée and Thill texts to develop career-enhancing business skills. We appreciate the opportunity to play a role in your education, and we wish you the very best with your careers.

Courtland L. Bovée

John V. Thill

Business in Action

Courtland L. Bovée

Professor of Business
C. Allen Paul Distinguished Chair
Grossmont College

John V. Thill

Chairman and Chief Executive Officer
Global Communication Strategies

Pearson

Harlow, England • London • New York • Boston • San Francisco • Toronto • Sydney • Dubai • Singapore • Hong Kong
Tokyo • Seoul • Taipei • New Delhi • Cape Town • São Paulo • Mexico City • Madrid • Amsterdam • Munich • Paris • Milan

Vice President, Business, Economics, and UK Courseware: Donna Battista
Director of Portfolio Management: Stephanie Wall
Editorial Assistant: Alyson Grindall
Senior Project Editor, Global Edition: Daniel Luiz
Assistant Acquisitions Editor, Global Edition: Rosemary Iles
Assistant Project Editor, Global Edition: Aditi Chatterjee
Vice President, Product Marketing: Roxanne McCarley
Product Marketer: Kaylee Carlson
Product Marketing Assistant: Marianela Silvestri
Manager of Field Marketing, Business Publishing: Adam Goldstein
Field Marketing Manager: Nicole Price
Vice President, Production and Digital Studio, Arts and Business: Etain O'Dea
Director, Production and Digital Studio, Business and Economics: Ashley Santora
Managing Producer, Business: Melissa Feimer
Content Producer: Yasmita Hota

Content Producer, Global Edition: Pooja Aggarwal
Operations Specialist: Carol Melville
Design Lead: Kathryn Foot
Senior Manufacturing Controller, Global Edition: Caterina Pellegrino
Manager, Learning Tools: Brian Surette
Learning Tools Strategist: Michael Trinchetto
Managing Producer, Digital Studio and GLP: James Bateman
Managing Producer, Digital Studio: Diane Lombardo
Digital Studio Producer: Monique Lawrence
Digital Studio Producer: Alana Coles
Manager, Media Production, Global Edition: Vikram Kumar
Managing Editor, Media Production, Global Edition: Gargi Banerjee
Full Service Project Management: SPi Global
Full Service Project Manager: Rajakumar Venkatesan, SPi Global
Cover Design: Lumina Datamatics
Cover Art: ImageFlow/Shutterstock

Pearson Education Limited
KAO Two
KAO Park
Hockham Way
Harlow
Essex
CM17 9SR
United Kingdom

and Associated Companies throughout the world

Visit us on the World Wide Web at: www.pearsonglobaleditions.com

© Bovée and Thill LLC. All Rights Reserved 2020

ISBN 10: 1-292-33096-1
ISBN 13: 978-1-292-33096-9

British Library Cataloguing-in-Publication Data
A catalogue record for this book is available from the British Library

1 20

Typeset in Albertina MT Pro by SPi Global
Printed and bound by Vivar in Malaysia

Contents in Brief

Contents

CHAPTER 3

The Global Marketplace 110

CHAPTER 4

Business Ethics and Corporate Social Responsibility 136

PART 4

Supporting the Workforce: Motivation and Human Resources 295

CHAPTER 10

Employee Motivation 296

CHAPTER 11

Human Resources Management 319

PART 5

Satisfying the Customer: Marketing, Sales, and Customer Support 353

CHAPTER 12

The Art and Science of Marketing 354

CHAPTER 13

Product Management and Pricing Strategies 381

CHAPTER 14

Customer Communication and Product Distribution 410

PART 6

Managing the Money: Accounting and Financial Resources   447

Appendixes

Streamlined Coverage of Essential Business Topics

The Introduction to Business course is tasked with such a wide range of topics that fitting them all in is an endless challenge. To better align the textbook with your course curriculum, the 9th Edition of *Business in Action* has been streamlined from 20 chapters to 16—without losing any essential coverage.

New Learning and Career-Development Features

Three new activities in every chapter help students prepare for today's workplace challenges:

- **Growing as a Professional.** These activities encourage students to apply the business concepts they are learning about in each chapter to facets of their academic and personal lives right now. By developing professional behaviors now, they will impress interviewers and be ready to succeed from day one.

- **Resolving Ethical Dilemmas.** Enlightened companies expect their employees to navigate today's complex business environment with clear ethical thinking. These exercises challenge students with realistic ethical dilemmas that require thoughtful analysis and decision-making.

- **Intelligent Business Technology.** Recruiters are impressed when students show awareness and curiosity regarding the challenges and opportunities in contemporary business. These research activities help students grasp the benefits of the smart systems that their future employers are likely to be using.

Preparing Students to Thrive in the Digital Enterprise

The *digital transformation* is reshaping every functional area in business, and more than three-quarters of executives say that digital technology will have a "major" or "transformative" impact on their industries. Alert companies are scrambling to reinvent themselves by implementing new business models or optimizing existing models. In fact, students will encounter the digital enterprise before they even land a job, because many firms now use artificial intelligence and other smart tools throughout the recruiting and hiring process.

Business in Action, 9/e, is the only textbook in this market that helps students appreciate the full scope of this transformation. To give students a competitive advantage, every chapter has a new learning objective that focuses on a key aspect of thriving in the digital enterprise. These nontechnical overviews explain the business implications of innovations that students are hearing about in the media and that they will likely be expected to use on the job.

Extensive Content Enhancements

All new *Behind the Scenes* vignette/case study pairs. These chapter-opening vignettes and end-of-chapter case studies show students how professionals apply the same skills and concepts they are reading about in the chapter. All 16 vignette/case study pairs are new in this edition.

Nearly 30 new exhibits. *Business in Action*'s visual presentation features nearly 150 *Exhibits That Teach*—diagrams, graphs, quick-reference tables, and other exhibits that address the challenge of getting students to read long passages of text by presenting vital concepts visually. The emphasis throughout is on productive learning—on helping students minimize the time they spend reading while maximizing their learning outcome.

More than 275 new questions and student activities. Every chapter has fresh project ideas and evaluation questions.

Numerous revisions and updates. Dozens of chapter sections are new, updated, or substantially revised to reflect the latest research and practices in business; here is a partial list:

The Social Environment
The Technological Environment
The Economic Environment
The Market Environment
Thriving in the Digital Enterprise: Disruptive
 Technologies and Digital Transformation
The Spectrum of Economic Systems
Fiat Money and Cryptocurrency
The Money Supply
The Fed's Major Responsibilities
Banking's Role in the Economy
 The Too-Big-to-Fail Dilemma
 Time for Another Wall?
Thriving in the Digital Enterprise: Fintech
 Making Financial Services More Inclusive
 Improving the Efficiency of Financial
  Activities
 Strengthening the Security of Financial
  Systems
 Improving the Customer Experience in
  Financial Services
 Enhancing Financial Decision-Making
Thriving in the Digital Enterprise:
 AI-Assisted Translation
Forces That Promote Unethical Behavior
 Management Pressure and Corporate
  Culture
 A Willful Blindness to Harm
 A Sense of Impunity
Strategies for Supporting Ethical Behavior
The Proactive Stance: Moving Beyond CSR
Resolving the CSR Dilemma
The Right to Digital Security
Thriving in the Digital Enterprise: The Ethics of
 Artificial Intelligence
 Human Biases Embedded in AI Systems
 The Efforts to Make AI a Force for Good
Shareholders
Joint Ventures
Thriving in the Digital Enterprise: Big Data and
 Analytics
The Big World of Small Business
Innovating Without Leaving: Intrapreneurship
The New-Business Failure Rate
Pivoting: When a Better Idea Comes Along
Business Incubators and Accelerators
The Franchise Alternative
Thriving in the Digital Enterprise: Machine
 Learning and Deep Learning
Defining the Company's Purpose and Values
Managing Change
Building a Positive Organizational Culture
Thriving in the Digital Enterprise: Cognitive
 Automation
Rethinking Organization in the Age of Agility
Cross-Functional Teams
Virtual Teams
Characteristics of Effective Teams
Team Development
Sources of Team Conflict

Thriving in the Digital Enterprise: Taskbots and
 Robotic Process Automation
Extending Organizations with Value Webs
Supply Chain Systems and Methods
Lean Systems
Strategies for Ensuring Product Quality
Thriving in the Digital Enterprise: Industry 4.0
 and the Smart Factory
Motivating with Challenging Goals
Addressing Workplace Negativity
Thriving in the Digital Enterprise:
 Performance Management Systems
Guiding the Human Side of Business
Aligning the Workforce with Business
 Requirements
Creating Safe Workplaces
Ensuring Fair Treatment and Equal Opportunity
The Evolving Role of HR
Diversity and Inclusion Initiatives
Managing the Employment Life Cycle
Appraising Employee Performance
Understanding the Role of Labor Unions in
 Today's Business World
Thriving in the Digital Enterprise: Workforce
 Analytics
The Marketing Concept
Involving the Customer in the Marketing Process
Making Data-Driven Marketing Decisions
Marketing as Part of a Sustainable Business
 Strategy
Creating Satisfying Customer Experiences
The Consumer Decision Process
Thriving in the Digital Enterprise: Marketing
 Analytics
Algorithmic Pricing
Subscription Pricing
Thriving in the Digital Enterprise: Virtual and
 Augmented Reality
Inbound Versus Outbound Marketing
Communication Laws and Ethics
Advertising Media
Direct Response Marketing
Personal Selling
Consumer Promotions
Trade Promotions
Marketing Communication Strategies for Social
 Media
Social Customer Care
Retailing's Role in the Buying Process
The Challenging Economics of Retailing
The Outlook for Retailing: Innovation,
 Disruption, and the Great Divide
Thriving in the Digital Enterprise: Augmented and
 Automated Writing
Thriving in the Digital Enterprise: Distributed
 Ledgers and Blockchain
Types of Budgets
Venture Capital and Other Private Equity
Thriving in the Digital Enterprise: Smart Contracts

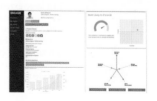

Solving Teaching and Learning Challenges

To improve student results, we recommend pairing this text content with **MyLab Intro to Business,** which is the teaching and learning platform that empowers you to reach every student. By combining trusted author content with digital tools and a flexible platform, MyLab personalizes the learning experience and will help your students learn and retain key course concepts while developing skills that future employers are seeking in their candidates. MyLab Intro to Business helps you teach your course, your way. Learn more at www.pearson.com/mylab/intro-to-business.

High-Efficiency, Objective-Driven Learning. Every chapter is divided into seven concise segments, each focused on its own learning objective and offering a comprehensive checkpoint to help students review and reinforce what they've learned. With this approach, each learning objective segment is treated as a mini-chapter within the chapter, letting students pace their intake and memorization, rather than trying to review an entire chapter at once.

1 **LEARNING OBJECTIVE**

Explain the concept of adding value in a business, and identify four useful ways to categorize businesses.

✔ **CHECKPOINT**

LEARNING OBJECTIVE 1: Explain the concept of adding value in a business, and identify four useful ways to categorize businesses.

SUMMARY: Businesses add value by transforming lower-value inputs to higher-value outputs. In other words, they make goods and services more attractive from the buyer's perspective, whether it's creating products that are more useful or simply making them more convenient to purchase. Companies can be categorized by product types and ranges, company size, geographic reach, and ownership.

CRITICAL THINKING: (1) What inputs does a musical group use to create its outputs? (2) Can not-for-profit organizations benefit from practices used by for-profit companies? Why or why not?

IT'S YOUR BUSINESS: (1) Think back to the last product you purchased; how did the companies involved in its creation and sale add value in a way that benefited you personally? (2) Can you see yourself working for a not-for-profit organization after you graduate? Why or why not?

KEY TERMS TO KNOW: business, revenue, business model, profit, competitive advantage, not-for-profit organizations

---

Interpreting and Summarizing the Changes in Contemporary Business. The world of business continues to evolve at a dizzying pace. *Business in Action* prepares students for these changes with thoughtful interpretations on subjects ranging from inclusiveness in financial services to the ethics of artificial intelligence.

Thriving in the Digital Enterprise: Disruptive Technologies and Digital Transformation

To a large extent, business strategy revolves around change—whether creating change, capitalizing on change, or surviving change. The basic concept of business is fixed: It's always going to be a question of adding value to satisfy customers in a way that generates a sustainable level of profit. However, the *way* that companies go about adding value and satisfying customers is always evolving, and the business world is currently going through an extra FIAT MONEY AND CRYPTOCURRENCY years to come.

The U.S. dollar and other modern currencies are often called **fiat money,** because they are issued and maintained through government *fiat,* or proclamation, and their value isn't tied to a physical asset such as gold. The dollar is *legal tender* in the United States, which means it can be used for any financial obligation. (This doesn't mean that every seller or lender must accept it or accept every *form* of it. Individuals and companies can accept or refuse to accept credit cards, large bills, coins, cash of any kind, and so on.[24])

Although each country has an official legal tender, this situation doesn't prevent parties

Chapter Warm-Ups

Assessment helps you hold your students accountable for **READING** and demonstrating their knowledge on key concepts in each chapter before coming to class.

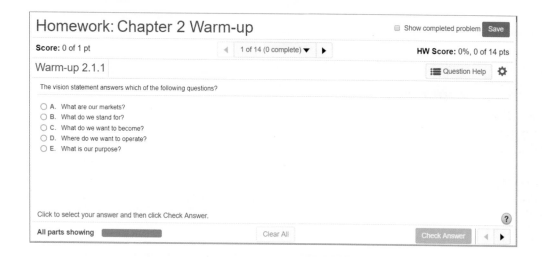

Chapter Quiz

Every chapter has quizzes written by our authors so you can assess your students' understanding of chapter learning objectives.

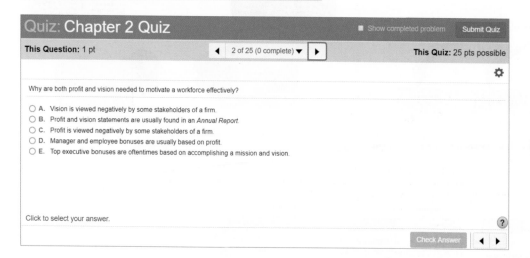

Visual Learning for a New Generation of Students.

Business in Action takes efficiency and student-friendly design to an entirely new level, with nearly 150 *Exhibits That Teach*. With these unique diagrams, infographics, and other exhibits, the emphasis throughout is on productive learning—on helping students minimize the time they spend reading while maximizing their learning outcome.

EXHIBIT 4.4 Perspectives on Corporate Social Responsibility

The perspectives on CSR can be roughly divided into four categories, from minimalist to proactive. Companies that engage in CSR can pursue either generic *philanthropy* or *strategic CSR*.

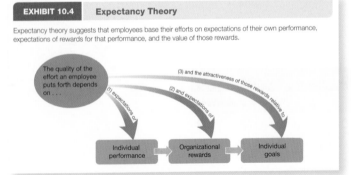

EXHIBIT 10.4 Expectancy Theory

Expectancy theory suggests that employees base their efforts on expectations of their own performance, expectations of rewards for that performance, and the value of those rewards.

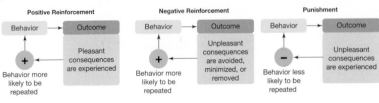

EXHIBIT 5.4 Types of Mergers

A *vertical merger* occurs when a company purchases a complementary company at a different stage or level in an industry, such as a furniture maker buying a lumber supplier. A *horizontal merger* involves two similar companies at the same level; companies can merge to expand their product offerings or their geographic market coverage. In a *conglomerate merger*, a parent company buys one or more companies in unrelated industries, often to diversify its business to protect against downturns in specific industries.

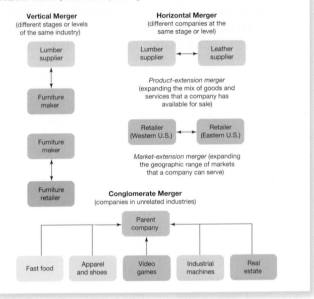

EXHIBIT 7.1 The Strategic Planning Process

Specific firms have their own variations of the strategic planning process, but these six steps offer a good general model. The circular arrangement is no coincidence, by the way. Strategic planning should be a never-ending process as you establish strategies, measure outcomes, monitor changes in the business environment, and make adjustments as needed.

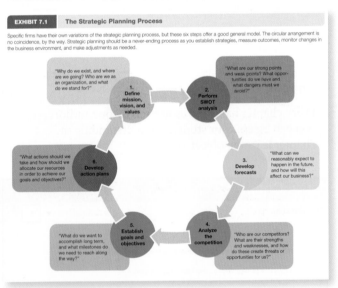

EXHIBIT 10.6 Reinforcement and Punishment

The terminology of reinforcement theory can be confusing because the terms are used differently in everyday speech than in psychology. Three points will help you keep the terms straight in your mind. First, both positive and negative reinforcement encourage a behavior to be repeated—they *reinforce* it, in order words. The difference is in how they work. Second, punishment (not negative reinforcement) is the opposite of positive reinforcement. Third, positive reinforcement can encourage undesirable behaviors, so it isn't necessarily a good thing, despite the "positive" label.

Positive Reinforcement	Negative Reinforcement	Punishment
Behavior → Outcome: Pleasant consequences are experienced. (+) Behavior more likely to be repeated	Behavior → Outcome: Unpleasant consequences are avoided, minimized, or removed. (+) Behavior more likely to be repeated	Behavior → Outcome: Unpleasant consequences are experienced. (−) Behavior less likely to be repeated

Vignettes and Case Studies That Bring Business Concepts to Life. Every chapter is bookended with a vignette/case study pair that help students grasp the principles covered in the chapter. The chapter-opening vignette introduces a company faced with a major strategic challenge or opportunity and encourages students to imagine how they would address that challenge. The chapter-closing case study describes the strategic choices the company's leaders made, including how they applied the concepts students just learned in the chapter. Three critical thinking questions require students to apply the concepts covered in the text.

REAL-TIME UPDATES
Learn More by Reading These Articles

The evolving relationship between us and our robot colleagues

This special series on GeekWire looks at the many facets of human-robot collaboration. Go to **real-timeupdates.com/bia9** and select Learn More in the Students section.

REAL-TIME UPDATES
Learn More by Exploring This Interactive Website

Find the best place to launch your career

For more than 20 years, *Fortune* magazine has been ranking the best 100 companies to work for in the United States. Go to **real-timeupdates.com/bia9** and select Learn More in the Students section.

Adding Value with Unique Resources. The unique *Real-Time Updates-Learn More* feature connects students with dozens of carefully selected online media items that complement the text's coverage with additional examples and valuable insights. Media items range from interactive websites and online videos to infographics, presentations, and podcasts.

In addition, students can explore thousands of curated media items in the Real-Time Updates system and subscribe to weekly updates.

Visit Real-Time Updates at **real-timeupdates .com/bia9**.

Developing Employability Skills

With its comprehensive coverage of contemporary business topics and a broad array of student activities, *Business in Action* helps students develop the skills that experts say are vital for success in the 21st-century workplace:

TEST YOUR KNOWLEDGE

Questions for Review

3-4. What is economic globalization?
3-5. What is the balance of trade, and how is it related to the balance of payments?
3-6. What is a floating exchange rate?
3-7. What is free trade?
3-8. How can protectionist moves create conflict within a country?

EXPAND YOUR KNOWLEDGE

Discovering Career Opportunities

If global business interests you, consider working for a U.S. government agency that supports or regulates international trade. Search the USAJobs website at www.usajobs.gov for an opening in international trade administration, such as an *international trade specialist*. Study the job description and answer the following questions:

PRACTICE YOUR SKILLS

Resolving Ethical Dilemmas

You're excited by the possibility of expanding your company internationally, and you have engaged the services of a consultant to help guide you into some promising new markets. While discussing the difficulty of getting government approval to sell your products in one particular country, the consultant advises you to be prepared to "spend a little cash to make things happen—be ready to wine and dine 'em."

- **Communication.** The Sharpening Your Communication Skills activity in every chapter is an opportunity to practice communication skills while exploring real-life business issues and challenges.
- **Critical thinking.** In many assignments and activities, students need to define and solve problems and make decisions or form judgments.
- **Collaboration.** The Building Your Team Skills activity in each chapter provides students with multiple opportunities to work with classmates on reports, presentations, and other projects.
- **Knowledge application and analysis.** The five diverse Practice Your Skills activities in every chapter let students put their developing business skills to work right away.
- **Business ethics and social responsibility.** Ethical choices are stressed from the beginning of the book, and the Resolving Ethical Dilemmas activity in every chapter encourages students to be mindful of the ethical implications that they could encounter in similar projects on the job.
- **Information technology skills.** Projects and activities in every chapter help students build skills with technology, and the Intelligent Business Technology research activity in each chapter encourages students to explore the major tools in use today.
- **Data literacy.** Many of the activities require students to develop data literacy skills, including the ability to access, assess, interpret, manipulate, summarize, and communicate data.

Instructor Teaching Resources

This program comes with the following teaching resources.

Supplements available to instructors at www.pearsonglobaleditions.com	Features of the Supplement
Instructor's Manual authored by Maureen Steddin	• Chapter summary • Chapter outline • Teaching notes • Suggested classroom exercises • Test Your Knowledge answers • Expand Your Knowledge answers • Practice Your Skills answers
Test Bank authored by Susan Schanne from Eastern Michigan University	• Over 1,500 multiple-choice, true/false, and essay questions • Answer explanations • Keyed by learning objective • Classified according to difficulty level • Classified according to learning modality: conceptual, application, critical thinking, or synthesis • Learning outcomes identified • AACSB learning standard identified (Ethical Understanding and Reasoning; Analytical Thinking Skills; Information Technology; Diverse and Multicultural Work Environments; Reflective Thinking; and Application of Knowledge)
Computerized TestGen	TestGen allows instructors to • customize, save, and generate classroom tests. • edit, add, or delete questions from the Test Item Files. • analyze test results. • organize a database of tests and student results.
PowerPoints authored by Jeffrey Anderson from Ohio University	Slides include all the graphs, tables, and equations in the textbook. PowerPoints meet accessibility standards for students with disabilities. Features include: • Keyboard and screen reader access • Alternative text for images • High contrast between background and foreground colors

About the Authors

Court Bovée

John Thill

Courtland L. Bovée and John V. Thill have been leading textbook authors for more than two decades, introducing millions of students to the fields of business and business communication. Their award-winning texts are distinguished by proven pedagogical features, extensive selections of contemporary case studies, hundreds of real-life examples, engaging writing, thorough research, and the unique integration of print and digital resources. Each new edition reflects the authors' commitment to continuous refinement and improvement, particularly in terms of modeling the latest practices in business and the use of technology.

Professor Bovée has 22 years of teaching experience at Grossmont College in San Diego, where he has received teaching honors and was accorded that institution's C. Allen Paul Distinguished Chair. Mr. Thill is a prominent communications consultant who has worked with organizations ranging from Fortune 500 multinationals to entrepreneurial start-ups. He formerly held positions with Pacific Bell and Texaco.

Courtland Bovée and John Thill were recently awarded proclamations from the Governor of Massachusetts for their lifelong contributions to education and for their commitment to the summer youth baseball program that is sponsored by the Boston Red Sox.

Acknowledgments

The Ninth Edition of *Business in Action* reflects the professional experience of a large team of contributors and advisors. A very special acknowledgment goes to George Dovel, whose superb writing and editing skills, distinguished background, and wealth of business experience assured this project of clarity and completeness. Also, we recognize and thank Jackie Estrada for her outstanding skills and excellent attention to details.

The supplements package for *Business in Action* has benefited from the able contributions of numerous individuals. We would like to express our thanks to them for creating a superb set of instructional supplements. We'd like to sincerely thank the following contributors for taking the time to create new content for MyLab Intro to Business for this edition: Susan Leshnower, Patricia Buhler, Storm Russo, Susan Schanne, Chris Parent (accuracy checker), and Kerri Tomasso (copyeditor).

We want to extend our warmest appreciation to the devoted professionals at Pearson Higher Education for their commitment to producing high-value, student-focused texts, including Donna Battista, Vice President, Business Publishing; Stephanie Wall, Director of Portfolio Management; Melissa Feimer, Managing Producer, Business; Yasmita Hota, Content Producer; Ashley Santora, Director of Production, Business; Becky Brown, Product Marketer; and Nicole Price, Field Marketing Manager. We are also grateful to Nicole Suddeth and Liz Kincaid of SPi Global, Angela Urquhart and Andrea Archer of Thistle Hill Publishing, and Melissa Pellerano.

Courtland L. Bovée

John V. Thill

Global Edition Acknowledgments

Pearson would like to thank the following people for their work on the Global Edition:

CONTRIBUTORS

Jon Sutherland

REVIEWERS

Benjamin Bader, Newcastle University Business School

Magda Sylwestrowicz, IUBH University of Applied Sciences

Kitty Szeto, The Chinese University of Hong Kong

Helen Yeh, The Hong Kong Polytechnic University

Using This Course to Launch Your Business Career

Have you already chosen a business profession or field of concentration? If so, this course will help you see how that specialty fits within the larger environment of business. If you haven't chosen a particular field, this course will introduce you to the wide range of professional specialties within business and help you explore the possibilities. And even if you're not planning a career in business, this course will help you put the functions of business in a broader social and economic context and show you how business practices can be put to productive use in not-for-profit, government, and community organizations.

SUCCEEDING IN THIS COURSE

In addition to the study and test-taking skills you've developed in your other courses, here are a few specific tips to help you succeed in this course:

- **Get organized.** This course covers a lot of territory, touching on every aspect of business. Make sure you have a system in place to take notes and study for exams, and schedule enough time for required readings, assignments, and team projects.
- **Focus on important themes and concepts.** If you find yourself getting overwhelmed by the details of a topic, back up and revisit the introduction to that section. The accounting chapter, for example, presents a number of terms you might be unfamiliar with. If things get confusing, refresh your memory of the basic categories of assets versus liabilities and revenues versus costs.
- **Relate what you're learning to your own experience.** As a consumer and an employee, you already know a lot about business, and one of the primary goals of this course is to help you leverage that knowledge by seeing business concepts from the other side—from the perspective of an owner or a manager. As you encounter each new concept, such as how companies set the prices of products, think about the question from both sides. In the case of pricing, for example, think about the *value* a product offers you as a consumer and about the *costs* that go into its production and distribution.
- **Pay attention to business and economic news, and relate it to course content.** Whenever you catch a bit of business or economic news, figure out how it relates to what you're learning in the course. If you read about a store closing, for instance, think about the possible reasons, from broader shifts in the economy to specific issues that affected the company. As the store's owner or manager, could you have done anything to prevent its closure?

Use this course as the first step in your business career—or as the next step in your new career, if you're a returning student.

- **Practice professional behavior.** A vital part of becoming a business professional is leaning how to conduct yourself professionally. You'll have opportunities throughout the course (and in every course) to demonstrate the qualities of professionalism that are described in Chapter 1.
- **Develop your business skills as you learn.** You don't have to wait until you're on the job to hone your business skills. At the end of each chapter, you'll find an activity called *Growing as a Professional*. Use this activity to apply the concepts you studied in the chapter.

REAL-TIME UPDATES
Learn More by Visiting This Website

Advice for every phase of the job-search process

From an introduction to job-search strategies to details on résumé writing, you'll find advice from career counseling professionals. Go to **real-timeupdates.com/bia9** and select Learn More in the Students section.

GETTING THE MOST FROM YOUR TEXTBOOK

This book and its supporting media are designed to help you absorb and retain all the fundamental concepts of business.

- **Objective-driven structure.** Each chapter is divided into seven sections, each with its own learning objective and checkpoint. The first six sections focus on various fundamentals of business, and the seventh is a special section that explores the digital transformation that is reshaping virtually every aspect of business today. Each section functions as a self-contained "mini" chapter, so you can study it on its own, without getting overwhelmed by the entire chapter all at once.
- **Learning objectives.** The learning objectives at the beginning of the chapter give you an idea of what you'll be studying. Each objective is tied to a major section heading, so it's easy to navigate through the chapter to study specific sections.
- **Checkpoints.** The checkpoints are a major feature to help you confirm what you've learned. Read the *Summary* to get a quick rundown on the learning objective, then ponder the *Critical Thinking* and *It's Your Business* questions to strengthen your understanding. If you need a quick refresher on any chapter, simply browse the checkpoints for a reminder of important concepts and key terms.
- **Behind the Scenes vignette and case study.** Each chapter opens with a brief story about a challenge or opportunity that a real-life professional or company faced. Read this short vignette to get a sense of the subject matter you'll be exploring in the chapter. At the end of the chapter, you'll see a more in-depth *Behind the Scenes* case study that describes how the person or firm applied the concepts you studied in the chapter.
- **Exhibits.** The many diagrams and illustrations throughout the book summarize essential information covered within each chapter. Particularly if you are a visual learner, use the exhibits to understand and confirm important concepts.
- **Key terms.** The book offers several ways to learn the most important terms in each chapter. Key terms are in bold type within the chapter, and you'll see a definition beside each one in the margin. By scanning the margins in each chapter, you can get a quick refresher on these terms. The Key Terms list at the end of the chapter shows the page number where each term is defined and discussed, and the Glossary at the end of the book compiles all the key terms in alphabetical order.
- **Test Your Knowledge.** These 20 questions in each chapter help you review information, analyze implications, and apply concepts. The questions include ethical considerations and concept integration from other chapters.
- **Expand Your Knowledge.** *Discovering Career Opportunities* gives you the chance to learn about various career paths and business specialties. *Intelligent Business Technology* is a brief research challenge involving technologies that are in widespread use in business or on their way to being widely adopted. Knowing about these tools and systems can give you an advantage in job interviews.

- **Practice Your Skills.** Enlightened employers expect you to make ethical choices, and the *Resolving Ethical Dilemmas* activity gives you practice in every chapter. *Growing as a Professional* lets you apply chapter concepts now to develop important analysis skills you can use on the job. *Sharpening Your Communication Skills* lets you practice listening, writing, and speaking in a variety of real-life scenarios. *Building Your Team Skills* teaches important team skills, such as brainstorming, collaborative decision making, developing a consensus, debating, role playing, and resolving conflict. *Developing Your Research Skills* familiarizes you with a wide variety of business reference materials and offers practice in developing research skills.
- **Real-Time Updates.** This free online service connects you with hundreds of media items that supplement your textbook, including articles, interactive websites, info-graphics, videos, and presentations. Plus, you'll see *Real-Time Updates Learn More* highlights throughout the book; these are linked to a special set of media items that expands on specific points in each chapter. Visit **real-timeupdates.com/bia9** for more information.
- **MyLab Intro to Business.** If your instructor uses MyLab, see page 16 for more information.

Finding Your Place in the World of Business

The field of business offers a rich and diverse range of opportunities, whether you're a generalist or someone with specific technical or creative interests. Chapter 1 offers an overview of the primary functions within business, and most of the remaining chapters focus on specific functional areas. To help put all this in context, the following discussions identify what employers look for in new hires and help you find your ideal fit in the world of business.

UNDERSTANDING WHAT EMPLOYERS LOOK FOR IN NEW HIRES

An important first step in finding your ideal place in the business world is understanding why companies choose some applicants and reject others. Companies take risks with every hiring decision—the risk that the person hired won't meet expectations and the risk that a better candidate slipped through their fingers. Many companies judge the success of their recruiting efforts by *quality of hire*, a measure of how closely new employees meet the company's needs. Given this perspective, what steps can you take to present yourself as the low-risk, high-reward choice?

Of course, your perceived ability to perform the job is an essential part of your potential quality as a new hire. However, hiring managers consider more than just your ability to handle the job. They want to know if you'll be reliable and motivated—if you're somebody who "gets it" when it comes to being a professional in today's workplace. Exhibit 1 lists the attributes companies list most frequently when looking for new employees.

Chapter 1 discusses many of these attributes in more detail in the sections on professionalism (pages 64–67) and career skills (pages 71–72).

FINDING YOUR BEST FIT

Figuring out where and how you can thrive professionally is a lifelong quest. You don't need to have all the answers now, and your answers will no doubt change in the coming years. However, start thinking about it now so that you can bring some focus to your job search. Organize your strategic planning with three questions: What do you want to do? What do you have to offer? How can you make yourself more valuable?

EXHIBIT 1	Attributes That Will Help You Stand Out in the Job Market

Employers judge their hiring efforts with a metric known as *quality of hire*. Develop these attributes, and you'll stand out as a quality hire in any field.

Core Business Skills	Personal Qualities
• Oral and written communication	• Committed to excellence; dissatisfied with mediocrity
• Communication with diverse audiences	• Dependable and accountable
• Information technology skills	• Committed to something greater than oneself
• Data literacy	• Confident but not brash
• Collaboration	• Curious, driven to learn
• Situation analysis and problem solving	• Flexible, adaptable, and open to change
• Time and resource management	• Respectful and inclusive
• Project management	• Ethical; lives and works with integrity
• Leadership	• Positive, resilient, able to roll with the punches and recover from setbacks
• Critical thinking	• Sensitive to expectations of etiquette
	• Self-reliant
	• Proactive; taking initiative without waiting to be told
	• Ambitious and goal-oriented

Sources: Based in part on Alison Doyle, "The Top Skills Employers Seek in College Grads," *The Balance*, 17 April 2018, www .thebalance.com; "Career Readiness Defined," National Association of Colleges and Employers, accessed 19 April 2018, www .naceweb.org; Penny Loretto, "The Top 10 Work Values Employers Look For," *The Balance Careers*, 15 March 2018, www.the balancecareers.com; Liz Ryan, "12 Qualities Employers Look for When They're Hiring," *Forbes*, 2 March 2016, www.forbes.com.

What Do You Want to Do?

Economic necessities and the dynamics of the marketplace will influence much of what happens in your career, and you may not always have the opportunity to do the kind of work you would really like to do. Even if you can't get the job you want right now, though, start your job search by examining your values and interests. Doing so will give you a better idea of where you want to be eventually, and you can use those insights to learn and grow your way toward that ideal situation. Consider these factors:

The day-to-day activities of different professions can vary widely. Do as much research as you can before you choose a career path to make sure it's the right path for you.

EXHIBIT 2	Career Planning Self-Assessment

Consider these questions to help identify the type of work you want to pursue in your career.

Activity or Situation	Strongly Agree	Agree	Disagree	No Preference
1. I want to work independently.	_____	_____	_____	_____
2. I want variety in my work.	_____	_____	_____	_____
3. I want to work with people.	_____	_____	_____	_____
4. I want to work with technology.	_____	_____	_____	_____
5. I don't want to be stuck in an office all day.	_____	_____	_____	_____
6. I want mentally challenging work.	_____	_____	_____	_____
7. I want to work for a large organization.	_____	_____	_____	_____
8. I want to work for a not-for-profit organization.	_____	_____	_____	_____
9. I want to work for a small business.	_____	_____	_____	_____
10. I want to work for a service business.	_____	_____	_____	_____

- **What would you like to do every day?** Research occupations that interest you. Find out what people really do every day. Ask friends, relatives, alumni from your school, and contacts in your social networks. Read interviews with people in various professions to get a sense of what their careers are like.
- **How would you like to work?** Consider how much independence you want on the job, how much variety you like, and whether you prefer to work with products, systems, people, ideas, words, figures, or some combination thereof.
- **How do your financial goals fit with your other priorities?** For instance, many high-paying business jobs involve a lot of stress, sacrifices of time with family and friends, and frequent travel or relocation. If other factors, such as stability, location, lifestyle, or intriguing work, are more important to you, you may have to sacrifice some level of pay to achieve them.
- **Have you established some general career goals?** For example, do you want to pursue a career specialty such as finance or manufacturing, or do you want to gain experience in multiple areas with an eye toward general management or entrepreneurship?
- **What sort of work culture are you most comfortable with?** Would you be happy in a formal hierarchy with clear reporting relationships? Or do you prefer less structure? Do you prefer teamwork or individualism? Do you prefer a competitive environment or a more cooperative culture?

You might need some time in the workforce to figure out what you really want to do, but it's never too early to start thinking about where you want to be. Filling out the assessment in Exhibit 2 can help you get a clearer picture of the nature of work you would like to pursue.

Activity or Situation	Strongly Agree	Agree	Disagree	No Preference
11. I want to start or buy a business someday.	_____	_____	_____	_____
12. I want regular, predictable work hours.	_____	_____	_____	_____
13. I want to work in a city location.	_____	_____	_____	_____
14. I want to work in a small town or suburb.	_____	_____	_____	_____
15. I want to work in another country.	_____	_____	_____	_____
16. I want to work from home, even if I'm employed by someone else.	_____	_____	_____	_____
17. I want to work in a highly dynamic profession or industry, even if it's unstable at times.	_____	_____	_____	_____
18. I want to have as much career stability as possible.	_____	_____	_____	_____
19. I want to enjoy my work, even if that means making less money.	_____	_____	_____	_____
20. I want to become a high-level corporate manager.	_____	_____	_____	_____

What Do You Have to Offer?

Knowing what you want to do is one thing. Knowing what companies or clients are willing to pay you to do is another thing entirely. You may already have a good idea of what you can offer employers. If not, some brainstorming can help you identify your skills, interests, and characteristics. Start by listing achievements you're proud of and experiences that were satisfying, and identify the skills that enabled those achievements. For example, leadership skills, speaking ability, and artistic talent may have helped you coordinate a successful class project. As you analyze your achievements, you may begin to recognize a pattern of skills. Which of these would be valuable to potential employers?

Next, look at your educational preparation, work experience, and extracurricular activities. What do your knowledge and experience qualify you to do? What have you learned from volunteer work or class projects that could benefit you on the job? Have you held any offices, won any awards or scholarships, or mastered a second language? What skills have you developed in nonbusiness situations that could transfer to a business position?

Take stock of your personal characteristics. Are you assertive, a born leader? Or are you more comfortable contributing under someone else's leadership? Are you outgoing, articulate, and comfortable around people? Or do you prefer working alone? Make a list of what you believe are your four or five most important qualities. Ask a relative or friend to rate your traits as well.

If you're having difficulty figuring out your interests, characteristics, or capabilities, consult your college career center. Many campuses administer a variety of tests that can help you identify interests, aptitudes, and personality traits. These tests won't reveal your "perfect" job, but they'll help you focus on the types of work best suited to your personality.

How Can You Make Yourself More Valuable?

While you're figuring out what you want from a job and what you can offer an employer, you can take positive steps toward building your career. First, look for opportunities to develop skills, gain experience, and expand your professional network. This might involve internships, volunteer work, freelance projects, part-time jobs, or projects that you initiate on your own. You can look for freelance projects on Craigslist and numerous other websites; some of these jobs have only nominal pay, but they do provide an opportunity for you to display your skills. Also consider applying your talents to *crowdsourcing* projects, in which companies and not-for-profit organizations invite the public to contribute solutions to various challenges. Look for ways to expand your *employment portfolio* and establish your *personal brand* (see the following sections).

Second, learn more about the industry or industries in which you want to work, and stay on top of new developments. Join networks of professional colleagues and friends who can help you keep up with trends and events. Follow the leading voices in a profession on social media. Many professional societies have student chapters or offer students discounted memberships. Take courses and pursue other educational or life experiences that would be difficult while working full time.

BUILDING YOUR NETWORK

Networking is the process of making informal connections with mutually beneficial business contacts. Networking takes place wherever and whenever people talk: at industry functions, at social gatherings, at alumni reunions—and all over the internet, from LinkedIn to Twitter to Facebook. In addition to making connections through social media tools, you might get yourself noticed by company recruiters.

Networking is more essential than ever because the vast majority of job openings are never advertised to the public. To avoid the time and expense of sifting through thousands of applications and the risk of hiring complete strangers, many companies start by asking their employees for recommendations—and these referrals are one of the most important sources of new employees.[1] The more people who know you, the better chance you have of being recommended for one of these hidden job openings.

Creative Ways to Build Your Network

Start building your network now. Your classmates could end up being some of your most valuable contacts, if not right away then possibly later in your career. Then branch out by identifying people with similar interests in your target professions, industries, and companies. Read news sites, blogs, and other online sources. Follow industry leaders on Twitter. You can also follow individual executives at your target companies to learn about their interests and concerns. Connect with people on LinkedIn and Facebook, particularly in groups dedicated to your career interests.

Participate in student business organizations, especially those with ties to professional organizations. Don't overlook volunteering; you not only meet people but also demonstrate your ability to solve problems, manage projects, and lead others. You can do some good while creating a network for yourself.

Keys to Being a Valued Networker

Remember that networking is about people helping each other, not just about other people helping you. Pay close attention to networking etiquette:[2]

- Be polite in every exchange. Not only is this the professional way to behave, but people are more inclined to help those who are positive and respectful.
- Don't speak poorly of your current employer or any past employers. Doing so is off-putting to other people, and it harms your reputation.

- Respect other people's time. Don't inundate people with messages, questions, or requests for help.
- Stay away from politics and other volatile topics. Remember that you're building a business network, not a circle of friends.
- Follow through on your promises. If you agree to make an introduction or provide information, make sure you do so.
- Follow up after meeting people. If you meet someone with shared interests, send a brief message within a day or two to solidify the connection you've made.

To become a valued network member, you need to be able to help others in some way. You may not have any influential contacts yet, but because you're researching industries and trends as part of your own job search, you probably have valuable information you can share via your online and offline networks. Or you might simply be able to connect one person with another who can help. The more you network, the more valuable you become in your network—and the more valuable your network becomes to you.

Finally, be aware that your online network reflects on who you are in the eyes of potential employers, so exercise some judgment in making connections and giving recommendations on LinkedIn.

Developing Your Personal Brand

You have probably heard the advice to develop a "personal brand" but might not know how to proceed or might not be comfortable with the concept of "branding" yourself. This section offers five steps that can make the task easier and more authentic.

Note that the process outlined here isn't about coming up with three or four words that are supposed to describe you, such as *Visionary, Creator, Problem Solver*, or things like that, as you may come across in some discussions of personal branding. This is a much more practical and comprehensive process that identifies the specific qualifications you can bring to the job, backs them up with solid evidence, and makes sure you are ready with a concise answer when an employer asks, "So, tell me about yourself."

DON'T CALL IT PERSONAL BRANDING IF YOU DON'T CARE FOR THE TERM

Some people object to the term *personal branding*, with its associations of product marketing, the implied need to "get out there and promote yourself," and perhaps the unseemly idea of reducing something as complex as yourself to an advertising slogan. If you are just starting your career, you might also wonder how to craft a meaningful brand when you don't have any relevant work experience.

Moreover, although personal branding makes obvious sense for professional speakers, authors, consultants, entrepreneurs, and others who must promote themselves in the public marketplace, those who aspire to professional or managerial positions in a corporate structure may rightly wonder why they need to "brand" themselves at all.

However, the underlying concept of branding as a *promise* applies to everyone, no matter the career stage or trajectory. A brand is fundamentally a promise to deliver on a specific set of values. For everyone in business, that promise is critical, whether it extends to a million people in the online audience for a TED Talk or a half-dozen people inside a small company. And even if you never think about your personal brand, you are continuously creating and re-creating it by the way you conduct yourself as a professional. In other words, even if you reject the idea of personal branding, other people will form an opinion of you and your "brand" anyway, so you might as well take charge and help create the impression that you want others to have of you.

As an alternative to a personal brand, think of your *professional promise*. Frame it this way: When people hear your name, what do you want them to think about you and your professional attributes and qualifications?

WRITE THE "STORY OF YOU"

When it's time to write or update your résumé, step back and think about where you've been in your life and your career and where you'd like to go. Helpful questions include *Do you like the path you're on, or is it time for a change? Are you focused on a particular field, or do you need some time to explore?*

This is also a great planning tool for developing a personal brand. Outline your story in three sections:

- **Where I have been**—the experiences from my past that give me insight into where I would like to go in the future
- **Where I am now**—where I currently stand in terms of education and career, and what I know about myself (including knowledge and skills, personal attributes, and professional interests)
- **Where I want to be**—the career progress and experiences I want to have, areas I want to explore, and goals I want to achieve

Think in terms of an image or a theme you'd like to project. *Am I academically gifted? A daring innovator? A well-rounded professional with wide-ranging talents? A technical wizard? A dependable, "go-to" problem solver that people can count on? A "connector" who can bring people and resources together?*

Writing this story arc is a valuable planning exercise that helps you think about where you want to go in your career. In essence, you are clarifying who you are professionally and defining a future version of yourself—and these are the foundations of the personal brand or professional promise. Another important benefit is that it makes the personal branding effort authentic, because it is based on your individual interests and passions.

CONSTRUCT YOUR BRAND PYRAMID

With your professional story arc as a guide, the next step is to construct a *brand pyramid* that has all the relevant support points needed to build a personal brand message (see Exhibit 3).

Start by compiling a *private inventory* of skills, attributes, experience, and areas for improvement. This should be a positive but realistic assessment of what you have to offer now and a "to-grow" list of areas where you want to develop or improve. Obviously, this inventory isn't for public consumption. As much as possible, provide evidence to back up each quality you list. If you are diligent and detail oriented, for instance, identify a time that you saved a project by methodically analyzing the situation to find a problem that others had overlooked. If you are a creative thinker, identify a time when you came up with an

---

EXHIBIT 3	**Your Personal Brand Pyramid**

Build your personal brand at three levels: a *private inventory* of your skills and assets, a *public profile* based on that inventory and how you want to present yourself to the world, and a *headline* that encapsulates what you can do for employers or clients.

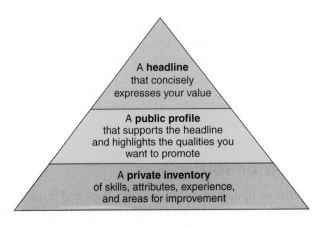

unusual new idea at work. Employers want to know *how* you can apply your skills, attributes, and experience; the more evidence you can provide, the better.

Next, select the appropriate materials from your inventory to develop a *public profile* that highlights the qualities you want to promote. As "Put Your Promise to Work" explains, this profile can take on a variety of forms for different communication platforms.

Finally, distill your professional promise down to a single, brief headline, also known as a *tagline* or *elevator pitch*. The headline should be a statement of compelling value, not a generic job title. Instead of "I'm a social media specialist," you might say, "I help small companies get the same reach on social media as giant corporations."

Of course, many students won't have the relevant job experience to say something like this, and your personal brand might be more an expression of potential. Even if you have no relevant professional experience, you still have personal attributes and educational qualifications that are the foundations of your brand.

Whether you call it your personal brand or your professional promise, figure out what you want to be as a professional and how you should communicate that to others.

The key is to make sure it's realistic and suggests a logical connection between the present and the future. Someone pursuing an MBA in finance can reasonably claim to have a strong toolset for financial analysis, but someone with no corporate work experience can't claim to be a bold, high-impact executive.

Here's a good example: "I am a data science major ready to make numbers come alive through leading-edge techniques in deep learning, data mining, and visualization."

Note that both your public profile and your headline should use relevant *keywords* from target job descriptions.

REDUCE OR ELIMINATE FACTORS THAT COULD DAMAGE YOUR BRAND

Every brand, no matter how popular and powerful, can be damaged by negative perceptions or performance issues. After identifying all the positives, do an objective analysis of areas that could undermine your career building efforts. For example, someone who tends to overpromise and underdeliver is going to develop a reputation for unreliability that could outweigh whatever positive qualities he or she can bring to the job. Other concerns might be related to specific skills that you need to develop in order to progress toward your career goals.

Be constantly mindful of the "multimedia you" that the world sees—your online presence, your personal appearance, your conduct in business and social settings, the way you sound on the phone, your mannerisms, your vocabulary, and anything else that shapes your reputation. Careers can be derailed by a single misjudged social media post, so always be putting the best "you" on display.

PUT YOUR PROMISE TO WORK

Now it's time to put the branding message to work. Your public profile could be expressed in a variety of ways—as a conventional résumé, the summary section on LinkedIn, an infographic résumé, or the introductory section of a personal webpage or e-portfolio.

The headline can be adapted and used in multiple ways as well, including in the headline field on LinkedIn, the qualifications summary on your résumé, and your Twitter profile, and as a ready answer to the common interview question "So, tell me about yourself."

Naturally, your brand message should be consistent across all the platforms and conversations where it used. For instance, an employer reviewing your résumé is likely to visit your LinkedIn profile as well, so it's important that the messages match. If you complete your branding pyramid first, it'll be easy to adapt it to a variety of different purposes while keeping your message consistent.

As you progress through your career, bear in mind that all this planning and communication is of no value if you fail to deliver on your brand promise. Remember that branding is only a *promise*—it's your *performance* that ultimately counts. When you deliver quality results time after time, your talents and professionalism will speak for you.

Lastly, your branding pyramid should be a "living document" that is updated whenever you acquire new skills or job experiences or want to move in a different direction. In addition, periodically revisiting it can be a good way to recapture the passion that initially launched you on your career path.

Crafting Your Résumé, LinkedIn Profile, and Employment Portfolio

Now that you have a clear idea of where you'd like to go in your career and what you have to offer, you're ready to craft three communication vehicles that will take you there: your résumé, your LinkedIn profile, and your employment portfolio.

WRITING AN EFFECTIVE RÉSUMÉ

Although you will create many messages during your career search, your résumé will be the most important document in this process. You will be able to use it directly in many instances, adapt it to a variety of uses such as an e-portfolio, and reuse pieces of it in social networking profiles and online application forms. Even if you apply to a company that doesn't request résumés, the process of developing your résumé will prepare you for interviewing and preemployment testing.

Developing a résumé is one of those projects that really benefits from multiple sessions spread out over several days or weeks. You are trying to summarize a complex subject (yourself!) and present a compelling story to strangers in a brief document.

Planning an effective résumé starts with understanding its true function—as a brief, persuasive business message intended to stimulate an employer's interest in meeting you and learning more about you. In other words, the purpose of a résumé is not to get you a job but rather to get you an interview.[3]

Organizing Your Résumé Around Your Strengths

Although a résumé can be organized in a number of ways, most are some variation of chronological organization, functional organization, or a combination of the two. The right choice depends on your background and your goals:

- In a *chronological résumé*, the work experience section dominates and is placed immediately after your contact information and introductory statement. The chronological approach is the most common way to organize a résumé, and many employers prefer this format because it presents your professional history in a clear, easy-to-follow arrangement.[4]

- A *functional résumé*, sometimes called a *skills résumé*, emphasizes your skills and capabilities, identifying employers and academic experience in subordinate sections. This arrangement stresses individual areas of competence rather than job history, and it can help you deemphasize periods of unemployment career stagnation. However, you should be aware that because the functional résumé can obscure your work history, some employment professionals are suspicious of it.[5]

- A *combination résumé* meshes the skills focus of the functional format with the job history focus of the chronological format. The chief advantage of this format is that it allows you to highlight your capabilities and education when you don't have a long or steady employment history, without raising concerns that you might be hiding something about your past.

Exhibits 4 through 6 on the following pages show how a job applicant adapted the combination format to work in three job-search scenarios, each of which you might face in your career as well.

| EXHIBIT 4 | Crafting Your Résumé, Scenario 1: Positioning Yourself for an Ideal Opportunity |

Even in an ideal job-search scenario, where your academic and professional experiences and interests closely match the parameters of the job opening, you still need to adapt your résumé content carefully to "echo" the specific language of the job description.[6]

The Scenario

You are about to graduate and have found a job opening that is in your chosen field. You don't have any experience in this field, but the courses you've taken in pursuit of your degree have given you a solid academic foundation for this position.

The Opportunity

The job opening is for an associate market analyst with Living Social, the rapidly growing advertising and social commerce service that describes itself as "the online source for discovering valuable local experiences." (A market analyst researches markets to find potentially profitable business opportunities.)

The Communication Challenge

You don't have directly relevant experience as a market analyst, and you might be competing against people who do. Your education is your strongest selling point, so you need to show how your course work relates to the position.

Don't let your lack of experience hold you back; the job posting makes it clear that this is an entry-level position. For example, the first bullet point in the job description says "Become an expert in market data . . .," and the required skills and experience section says that "Up to 2 years of experience with similar research and analysis is preferred." The important clues here are *become* (the company doesn't expect you to be an expert already) and *preferred* (experience would be great if you have it, but it's not required).

Keywords and Key Phrases

You study the job posting and highlight the following elements:

1. Working in a team environment
2. Research, including identifying trendy new businesses
3. Analyzing data using Microsoft Excel
4. Managing projects
5. Collaborating with technical experts and sales staff
6. Creating new tools to help maximize revenue and minimize risks
7. Bachelor's degree is required
8. Natural curiosity and desire to learn
9. Detail oriented
10. Hands-on experience with social media

Emma Gomes
(847) 555–2153
emma.gomes@mailsystem.net
emmawrites.blogspot.com

| **Address:** | **Permanent Address:** |
| 860 North 8th Street, Terre Haute, IN 47809 | 993 Church Street, Barrington, IL 60010 |

Summary of Qualifications

- In-depth academic preparation in marketing analysis techniques
- Intermediate skills with a variety of analytical tools, including Microsoft Excel and Google Analytics
- Front-line experience with consumers and business owners
- Multiple research and communication projects involving the business applications of social media

Education

B.S. in Marketing (Marketing Management Track), Indiana State University, Terre Haute, IN, anticipated graduation: May 2014

Program coursework

- 45 credits of core business courses, including Business Information Tools, Business Statistics, Principles of Accounting, and Business Finance
- 27 credits of marketing and marketing management courses, including Buyer Behavior, Marketing Research, Product and Pricing Strategy, and seminars in e-commerce and social media

Special projects

- "Handcrafting a Global Marketplace: The Etsy Phenomenon," in-depth analysis of how Etsy transformed the market for handmade craft items by bringing e-commerce capabilities to individual craftspeople
- "Hybrid Communication Platforms for Small Businesses," team service project for five small businesses in Terre Haute, recommending best practices for combining traditional and social-media methods of customer engagement and providing a customized measurement spreadsheet for each company

Work and Volunteer Experience

Independent math tutor, 2009-present. Assist students with a variety of math courses at the elementary, junior high, and high school level; all clients have achieved combined test and homework score improvements of at least one full letter grade, with an average improvement of 38 percent

Volunteer, LeafSpring Food Bank, Terre Haute, IN (weekends during college terms, 2012–present). Stock food and supply pantries; prepare emergency baskets for new clients; assist director with public relations activities, including website updates and social media news releases

Customer care agent, Owings Ford, Barrington, IL (summers, 2011–2013). Assisted the service and sales managers of this locally owned car dealership with a variety of customer-service tasks; scheduled service appointments; designed and implemented improvements to service-center waiting room to increase guest comfort; convinced dealership owners to begin using Twitter and Facebook to interact with current and potential customers.

Professional Engagement

- Collegiate member, American Marketing Association; helped establish the AMA Collegiate Chapter at Indiana State
- Participated in AMA International Collegiate Case Competition, 2011-2012

Awards

- Dean's List: 2012, 2013
- Forward Youth award, Barrington Chamber of Commerce, 2010

Gomes includes phone and email contacts, along with a blog that features academic-oriented writing.

Using a *summary of qualifications* for her opening statement lets her target the résumé and highlight her most compelling attributes.

Her education is a much stronger selling point than her work experience, so she goes into some detail—carefully selecting course names and project descriptions to echo the language of the job description.

She adjusts the descriptions and accomplishments of each role to highlight the aspects of her work and volunteer experience that are relevant to the position.

The final sections highlight activities and awards that reflect her interest in marketing and her desire to improve her skills.

Notice how Gomes adapts her résumé to "mirror" the keywords and phrases from the job posting:

1. Offers concrete evidence of teamwork (rather than just calling herself a "team player," for example)
2. Emphasizes research skills and experience in multiple instances
3. Calls out Microsoft Excel, as well as Google Analytics, a key online tool for measuring activity on websites
4. Indicates the ability to plan and carry out projects, even if she doesn't have formal project management experience
5. Indicates some experience working in a supportive or collaborative role with technical experts and sales specialists (the content of the work doesn't translate to the new job, but the concept does)
6. Suggests the ability to work with new analytical tools
7. Displays her B.S. degree prominently
8. Demonstrates a desire to learn and to expand her skills
9. Tracking the progress of her tutoring clients is strong evidence of a detail-oriented worker—not to mention someone who cares about results and the quality of her work
10. Lists business-oriented experience with Facebook, Twitter, and other social media

EXHIBIT 5 — Crafting Your Résumé, Scenario 2: Positioning Yourself for Available Opportunities

If you can't find an ideal job opening, you'll need to adjust your plans and adapt your résumé to the openings that are available. Look for opportunities that meet your near-term financial needs while giving you the chance to expand your skill set so that you'll be even more prepared when an ideal opportunity does come along.[7]

The Scenario

You are about to graduate but can't find job openings in the field you'd like to enter. However, you have found an opening that is in a related field, and it would give you the chance to get some valuable work experience.

The Opportunity

The job opening is for a seller support associate with Amazon, the online retail giant. Employees in this position work with merchants that sell products through the Amazon e-commerce system to make sure merchants are successful. In essence, it is a customer service job, but directed at these merchants, not the consumers who buy on Amazon.

The Communication Challenge

This isn't the job you ultimately want, but it is a great opportunity with a well-known company.

You note that the position does not require a college degree, so in that sense you might be a bit over-qualified. However, you also see a strong overlap between your education and the responsibilities and required skills of the job, so be sure to highlight those.

Keywords and Key Phrases

You study the job posting and highlight the following elements:

1. Be able to predict and respond to merchant needs; good business sense with the ability to appreciate the needs of a wide variety of companies
2. Strong written and oral communication skills
3. High degree of professionalism
4. Self-starter with good time management skills
5. Logically analyze problems and devise solutions
6. Comfortable with computer-based tools, including Microsoft Excel
7. Desire to expand business and technical skills
8. Customer service experience
9. Collaborate with fellow team members to resolve difficult situations
10. Record of high performance regarding quality of work and personal productivity

---

Emma Gomes
(847) 555–2153
emma.gomes@mailsystem.net
emmawrites.blogspot.com

Address:
860 North 8th Street, Terre Haute, IN 47809

Permanent Address:
993 Church Street, Barrington, IL 60010

Summary of Qualifications

- Front-line customer service experience with consumers and business owners
- Strong business sense based on work experience and academic preparation
- Intermediate skills with a variety of software tools, including Microsoft Excel and Google Analytics
- Record of quality work in both business and academic settings

Education

B.S. in Marketing (Marketing Management Track), Indiana State University, Terre Haute, IN, expected graduation May 2014

Program coursework

- 45 credits of core business courses, including Business Information Tools, Business Statistics, Principles of Accounting, and Business Finance
- 27 credits of marketing and marketing management courses, including Marketing Fundamentals, Buyer Behavior, Marketing Research, Retail Strategies and seminars in e–commerce and social media

Special projects

- "Handcrafting a Global Marketplace: The Etsy Phenomenon," in-depth analysis of how the Etsy e-commerce platform helps craftspeople and artisans become more successful merchants
- "Hybrid Communication Platforms for Small Businesses," team service project for five small businesses in Terre Haute, recommending best practices for combining traditional and social–media methods of customer engagement and providing a customized measurement spreadsheet for each company

Work and Volunteer Experience

Independent math tutor, 2009-present. Assist students with a variety of math courses at the elementary, junior high, and high school level; all clients have achieved combined test and homework score improvements of at least one full letter grade, with an average improvement of 38 percent

Volunteer, LeafSpring Food Bank, Terre Haute, IN (weekends during college terms, 2012–present). Stock food and supply pantries; prepare emergency baskets for new clients; assist director with public relations activities, including website updates and social media news releases

Customer care agent, Owings Ford, Barrington, IL (summers, 2011–2013). Assisted the service and sales managers of this locally owned car dealership with a variety of customer-service tasks; scheduled service appointments; designed and implemented improvements to service-center waiting room to increase guest comfort; convinced dealership owners to begin using Twitter and Facebook to interact with current and potential customers

Professional Engagement

- Collegiate member, American Marketing Association; helped establish the AMA Collegiate Chapter at Indiana State
- Participated in AMA International Collegiate Case Competition, 2011-2012

Awards

- Dean's List: 2012, 2013
- Forward Youth award, Barrington Chamber of Commerce, 2010

Gomes modified her summary of qualifications to increase emphasis on customer service.

She adjusts the selection of highlighted courses to reflect the retail and e-commerce aspects of this particular job opening.

She adjusts the wording of this Etsy project description to closely mirror what Amazon is—an e-commerce platform serving a multitude of independent merchants.

She provides more detail regarding her customer support experience.

The final sections are still relevant to this job opening, so she leaves them unchanged.

Notice how Gomes adapts her résumé to "mirror" the keywords and phrases from the job posting:

1. Suggests strong awareness of the needs of various businesses
2. Examples of experience with written business communication; she can demonstrate oral communication skills during phone, video, or in-person interviews
3. Results-oriented approach to tutoring business suggests high degree of professionalism, as do the two awards
4. The ability to work successfully as an independent tutor while attending high school and college is strong evidence of self-motivation and good time management
5. Indicates ability to understand problems and design solutions
6. Suggests the ability to work with a variety of software tools
7. Demonstrates a desire to learn and to expand her skills
8. Highlights customer service experience
9. Offers concrete evidence of teamwork (rather than just calling herself a "team player," for example)
10. Tracking the progress of her tutoring clients is strong evidence of someone who cares about results and the quality of her work; Dean's List awards also suggest quality of work; record of working while attending high school and college suggests strong productivity

| **EXHIBIT 6** | Crafting Your Résumé, Scenario 3: Positioning Yourself for More Responsibility |

When you have a few years of experience under your belt, your résumé strategy should shift to emphasize work history and accomplishments. Here is how Emma Gomes might reshape her résumé if she had held the two jobs described in Exhibits 3 and 4 and is now ready for a bigger challenge.[8]

The Scenario

Moving forward from Exhibits 3 and 4, let's assume you have worked in both those positions, first for two years as a seller support associate at Amazon and then for almost three years an associate market analyst at LivingSocial. You believe you are now ready for a bigger challenge, and the question is how to adapt your résumé for a higher-level position now that you have some experience in your chosen field. (Some of the details from the earlier résumés have been modified to accommodate this example.)

The Opportunity

The job opening is for a senior strategy analyst for Nordstrom. The position is similar in concept to the position at Living Social, but at a higher level and with more responsibility.

The Communication Challenge

This job is an important step up; a senior strategy analyst is expected to conduct in-depth financial analysis of business opportunities and make recommendations regarding strategy changes, merchandising partnerships with other companies, and important decisions.

You worked with a wide variety of retailers in your Amazon and Living Social jobs, including a number of fashion retailers, but you haven't worked directly in fashion retailing yourself.

Bottom line: You can bring a good set of skills to this position, but your financial analysis skills and retailing insights might not be readily apparent, so you'll need to play those up.

Keywords and Key Phrases

You study the job posting and highlight the following elements:

1. Provide research and analysis to guide major business strategy decisions
2. Communicate across business units and departments within Nordstrom
3. Familiar with retail analytics
4. Knowledge of fashion retailing
5. Qualitative and quantitative analysis
6. Project management
7. Strong communication skills
8. Bachelor's required; MBA preferred
9. Advanced skills in financial and statistical modeling
10. Proficient in PowerPoint and Excel

Emma Gomes
(847) 555–2153
emma.gomes@mailsystem.net
Twitter: www.twitter.com/emmagomes
1605 Queen Anne Avenue North, Seattle, WA 98109

Market and Strategy Analyst

- Five years of experience in local and online retailing, with three years of focus on market opportunity analysis
- Strong business sense developed through more than 60 marketing programs across a range of retail sectors, including hospitality, entertainment, and fashion
- Recognized by senior management for ability to make sound judgment calls in situations with incomplete or conflicting data
- Adept at coordinating research projects and marketing initiatives across organizational boundaries and balancing the interests of multiple stakeholders
- Advanced skills with leading analysis and communication tools, including Excel, PowerPoint, and Google Analytics

Professional Experience

Associate Market Analyst, LivingSocial, Seattle, WA (July 2011-present). Analyzed assigned markets for such factors as consumer demand, merchandising opportunities, and seller performance; designed, launched, and managed marketing initiatives in 27 retailing categories, including fashions and accessories; met or exceeded profit targets on 90 percent of all marketing initiatives; appointed team lead/trainer in recognition of strong quantitative and qualitative analysis skills; utilized both established and emerging social media tools and helped business partners use these communication platforms to increase consumer engagement in local markets.

Seller support associate, Amazon, Seattle, WA (July 2009–June 2011). Worked with more than 300 product vendors, including many in the fashion and accessories sectors, to assure profitable retailing activities on the Amazon e-commerce platform; resolved vendor issues related to e-commerce operations, pricing, and consumer communication; anticipated potential vendor challenges and assisted in the development of more than a dozen new selling tools that improved vendor profitability while reducing Amazon's vendor support costs by nearly 15 percent.

Education

Evening MBA program, University of Washington, Seattle, WA; anticipated graduation: May 2015. Broad-based program combining financial reporting, marketing strategy, competitive strategy, and supply chain management with individual emphasis on quantitative methods, financial analysis, and marketing decision models.

B.S. in Marketing (Marketing Management Track), Indiana State University, Terre Haute, IN, May 2009. Comprehensive coursework in business fundamentals, accounting and finance, marketing fundamentals, retailing, and consumer communications.

Professional Engagement

- Member, American Marketing Association
- Member, International Social Media Association
- Active in National Retail Federation and Retail Advertising & Marketing Association

Awards

- Living Social Top Ten Deals (monthly employee achievement award for designing the most profitable couponing deals); awarded seven times, 2011—2013
- Social Commerce Network's Social Commerce Innovators: 30 Under 30; 2012

Gomes stays with a summary of qualifications as her opening statement but gives it a new title to reflect her experience and to focus on her career path as a market analyst.

Work experience is now her key selling point, so she shifts to a conventional chronological résumé that puts employment ahead of education. She also removes the part-time jobs she had during high school and college.

She updates the Education section with a listing for the MBA program she has started (selecting points of emphasis relevant to the job opening) and reduces the amount of detail about her undergraduate degree.

She updates the Professional Engagement and Awards section with timely and relevant information.

Notice how Gomes adapts her résumé to "mirror" the keywords and phrases from the job posting:

1. Highlights her experience in market and business analysis and her continuing education in this area
2. Mentions skill at coordinating cross-functional projects
3. Lists experiences that relate to the collection and analysis of retail data
4. Emphasizes the work she has done with fashion-related retailing and retailing in general
5. Identifies experience and education that relates to quantitative and qualitative analysis (this point overlaps #1 and #3 to a
6. degree)
7. Mentions project management experience
8. Lists areas that suggest effective communication skills
9. Lists education, with emphasis on coursework that relates most directly to the job posting
10. Mentions work experience and educational background related to these topics

Includes these programs in the list of software tools she uses

Composing Your Résumé

Write your résumé using a simple and direct style. Use short, crisp phrases instead of whole sentences, and focus on what your reader needs to know. Avoid using the word *I*, which can sound both self-involved and repetitious by the time you outline all your skills and accomplishments. Instead, start your phrases with strong action verbs such as *created*, *managed*, and *transformed*. Whenever you can, quantify the results with carefully selected evidence that confirms your abilities, such as "Led the department in customer acquisition three years in a row."

Most résumés are now subjected to *keyword searches* in an applicant tracking system (ATS), in which a recruiter searches for résumés most likely to match the requirements of a particular job. Résumés that don't closely match the requirements may never be seen by a human reader, so it is essential to use the words and phrases that a recruiter is most likely to search for. Identifying these keywords requires some research, but you can uncover many of them while you are researching various industries and companies. In particular, study job descriptions carefully.

The following sections offer brief tips on composing each section of your résumé.

Name and Contact Information

Your name and contact information constitute the heading of your résumé; include the following:

- Name
- Address (both permanent and temporary, if you're likely to move during the job-search process)
- Email address (something simple and professional, such as deborahwhite@gmail.com)
- Phone number(s)
- The URL of your LinkedIn profile

Introductory Statement

You have three options for a brief introductory statement that follows your name and contact information:[9]

- **Career objective.** A career objective identifies either a specific job you want to land or a general career track you would like to pursue. Some experts advise against including a career objective because it can categorize you too narrowly, and it is essentially about fulfilling your desires, not about meeting the employer's needs. However, if you have little or no work experience in your target profession, a career objective might be your best option. If you do opt for an objective, word it in a way that relates your aspirations to employer needs.
- **Qualifications summary.** A qualifications summary offers a brief view of your key qualifications. The goal is to let a reader know within a few seconds what you can deliver. You can title this section generically as "Qualifications Summary" or "Summary of Qualifications," or, if you have one dominant qualification, you can use that as the title. Consider using a qualifications summary if you have one or more important qualifications but don't yet have a long career history. Also, if you haven't been working long but your college education has given you a dominant professional "theme," such as multimedia design or statistical analysis, you can craft a qualifications summary that highlights your educational preparedness.
- **Career summary.** A career summary offers a brief recap of your career with the goal of presenting increasing levels of responsibility and performance (see Exhibit 6 on the previous page for an example). A career summary is particularly good for people who have demonstrated the ability to take on increasing levels of responsibility in their chosen field and who want to continue in that field.

Whichever option you choose, make sure it includes the most essential keywords you identified in your research—and adapt these words and phrases to each job opportunity as needed.

Education

If you are early in your career, education is probably your strongest selling point. Present your educational background in depth, choosing facts that support your professional theme. Under the heading "Education," list the name and location of each school you have attended, the month and year of your graduation (say "anticipated graduation: _____" if you haven't graduated yet), your major and minor fields of study, significant skills and abilities you've developed in your coursework, and the degrees or certificates you've earned. List courses that are most relevant to each job opening, and indicate any scholarships, awards, or academic honors you've received.

Work Experience, Skills, and Accomplishments

Like the education section, the work experience section should focus on your overall theme in a way that shows how your past can contribute to an employer's future. Use keywords to call attention to the skills you've developed on the job and to your ability to handle responsibility. Emphasize what you accomplished in each position, not just the generic responsibilities of the job.

List your jobs in reverse chronological order, starting with the most recent. Include military service and any internships and part-time or temporary jobs related to your career objective. Include the name and location of the employer, and if readers are unlikely to recognize the organization, briefly describe what it does. When you want to keep the name of your current employer confidential, you can identify the firm by industry only ("a large video game developer"). If an organization's name or location has changed since you worked there, state the current name and location and include the old information preceded by "formerly . . ." Before or after each job listing, state your job title and give the years you worked in the job; use the phrase "to present" to denote current employment. Indicate whether a job was part-time.

Activities and Achievements

You can use this optional section to highlight activities and achievements outside of a work or educational context—but only if they make you a more attractive job candidate. For example, traveling, studying, or working abroad and fluency in multiple languages could weigh in your favor with employers that do business internationally.

Because many employers are involved in their local communities, they tend to look positively on applicants who are active and concerned members of their communities as well. Consider including community service activities that suggest leadership, teamwork, communication skills, technical aptitude, or other valuable attributes.

Personal Data

In most cases, your résumé should not include any personal data beyond the information described in the previous sections. When applying to U.S. companies, never include any of the following: physical characteristics, age, gender, marital status, sexual orientation, religious or political affiliations, race, national origin, salary history, reasons for leaving jobs, names of previous supervisors, names of references, Social Security number, or student ID number. Expectations differ in other countries, so research the job application process in specific countries if you need more information.

References

For professional and managerial positions, nearly all employers ask for and check references, so you need to be prepared with a list of people who are willing to speak on your behalf.[10] (The availability of references is assumed, so you don't need to put "References available upon request" at the end of your résumé.)

Plan to gather three types of references as you begin your job search:[11]

- *Professional references* are people who have had the opportunity to evaluate the knowledge and skills that you can bring to the jobs you are applying for. Professors and instructors, supervisors, colleagues, and even customers are all good candidates to approach for serving as professional references.

- Some employers may ask for *personal references*, people who are willing to vouch for your character. Good candidates here include people outside your family who have interacted with you in meaningful ways, including coaches, volunteer coordinators, and religious leaders. As appropriate, you may also ask any of your professional references to serve as personal references.
- To complete your LinkedIn profile, you will also need *LinkedIn recommendations* (see the next page).

Producing Your Résumé

Leave yourself plenty of time to finalize your résumé by revising it for clarity and conciseness, producing it in one or more formats, and proofreading it carefully. Your résumé is one of the most important documents you will ever write, and it must reflect a high level of care and quality. Recruiters and hiring managers want to find key pieces of information about you, including your top skills, your current job, and your education, in a matter of seconds. Don't make them work to find or decode this information. Weed out minor details until your résumé is tight, clear, and focused. Above all else, your résumé must be easy to read and easy for recruiters to skim quickly.[12]

You'll find a wide range of résumé designs in use today, from text-only documents that follow a conventional layout to full-color infographics with unique designs. Don't choose a style just because it seems trendy, flashy, or different. For example, you can find some eye-catching infographic résumés online, but many of those are created by graphic designers applying for visually oriented jobs in advertising, fashion, web design, and other areas in which graphic design skills are a must. In other words, the intended audience expects an applicant to have design skills, and the résumé is a good opportunity to demonstrate those. In contrast, a colorful, graphically intense résumé might just look odd to recruiters in finance, engineering, or other professions—and it's almost guaranteed to get rejected by an ATS. You can certainly supplement your conventional résumé with an infographic, a video, or other media elements, but don't submit one of these in place of a résumé.

The sample résumés in Exhibits 4 through 6 use a classic, conservative design that will serve you well for most business opportunities. Notice how they feature simplicity, an easy-to-read layout, effective use of white space, and clear typefaces. Recruiters can pick out the key pieces of information in a matter of seconds.

REAL-TIME UPDATES
Learn More by Exploring This Interactive Website

Design inspiration and easy-to-use templates

Canva is one of many online services that let you create a nicely designed résumé. Go to **real-timeupdates.com/bia9** and select Learn More in the Students section.

Writing Application Letters

Whenever you email a résumé to a recruiter or other contact in a company, use the body of your email message as an *application letter*, also known as a *cover letter*. (Even though this message is often not a printed letter anymore, many professionals still refer to it as a letter.) Note that not all recruiters take the time to read application letters, particularly at companies that receive a high volume of applications.[13] However, if you are emailing someone directly, it's good practice to include one anyway. It might catch the recruiter's eye, and the hiring manager who eventually gets your résumé may be interested in reading it.[14] (Some online application systems allow you to upload an application message, but many don't, so when you apply online, you might not have the opportunity to include an application letter.)

An application letter has three goals: to introduce your résumé, to persuade an employer to read it, and to request an interview. Recognize that this message is a great opportunity, too: You can communicate in a more personal and conversational way than you can with your résumé, you can show that you understand what an employer is looking for, and you can demonstrate your writing skills. Another key opportunity here involves soft skills such as interpersonal communication, which are difficult to quantify in a meaningful way on your résumé. In the letter, you can briefly describe a situation in which you used these skills to reach a measurable business result, for example, which is more compelling than simply listing skills.[15]

If the name of an individual manager is at all findable, address your letter to that person rather than to something generic such as "Dear Hiring Manager." Search LinkedIn, the company's website, industry directories, Twitter, and anything else you can think of to locate an appropriate name. Ask the people in your network if they know a name. If another applicant finds a name and you don't, you're at a disadvantage.

Remember that your reader's in-box is probably overflowing with résumés and application letters, and respect his or her time. Avoid gimmicks, and don't repeat information that already appears in your résumé. Keep your letter straightforward, fact based, short, upbeat, and professional.

DEVELOPING A COMPELLING LINKEDIN PROFILE

LinkedIn (www.linkedin.com) is the most important website to incorporate in your job search. Employment recruiters search LinkedIn for candidates far more than any other social network, and companies doing background checks on you are almost certain to look for your LinkedIn profile.[16]

You can think of LinkedIn as a "socially networked multimedia résumé." An effective LinkedIn profile includes all the information from your conventional résumé, plus some additional features that help you present yourself in a compelling way to potential employers. Here are nine tips for building an effective profile:[17]

1. **Photo.** Add a photo that says "professional" without being overly formal. You don't need to hire a professional photographer, but the photo needs to be clear and lit well enough so that your face isn't in shadow. Stand against a visually "quiet" background that won't distract viewers, dress appropriately for the jobs you are pursuing, and remember to smile.

2. **Headline.** Write a headline that expresses who you are or aspire to be as a professional, such as "Data science major ready to make data come alive through leading-edge techniques in data mining, visualization, and AI." Include keywords that target employers are likely to be searching for. As with other text fields on LinkedIn, you have a limited number of characters to work with here, so focus on your most valuable attributes. Erica Baker, for instance, establishes herself as a technically astute, creative problem solver with her LinkedIn headline: "I like to slay big problems and puzzles. My weapons of choice are logic, data, curiosity, and code."[18]

3. **Summary.** Write a summary that captures where you are and where you are going. Imagine that you are talking to a hiring manager in a personal and conversational tone, telling the story of where you've been and where you would like to go—but expressed in terms of meeting an employer's business needs. Highlight your job experience, education, skills, accomplishments, target industry, and career direction. Unlike the introductory statement on your conventional résumé, which you can fine-tune for every job opportunity, your LinkedIn summary offers a more general picture of who you are as a professional. Be sure to work in as many of the keywords from your research as you can, while keeping the style natural. Employers can use a variety of search tools to find candidates, and they'll look for these keywords.

4. **Experience.** Fill out the experience section using the material from your conventional résumé. Make sure the details of your employment match your résumé, as employers are likely to cross-check. However, you can expand beyond those basics, including linking to photos and videos of work-related accomplishments.

5. **Recommendations.** Ask for recommendations from people you know on LinkedIn. You may have a limited number of connections as you start out, but as your network expands you'll have more people to ask. A great way to get recommendations is to give them to the people in your network.

6. **Featured skills.** List your top skills and areas of expertise. As you expand your network, endorse the skills of people you know; many users will endorse your skills in return.

7. **Education.** Make sure your educational listing is complete and matches the information on your conventional résumé.

8. **Accomplishments.** LinkedIn offers a variety of categories that let you highlight academic achievements, special projects, publications, professional certifications, important coursework, honors, patents, and more. If you don't have an extensive work

history, use this section to feature academic projects and other accomplishments that demonstrate your skills.

9. **Volunteer experience and causes.** Add volunteering activities and charitable organizations that you support.

For the most current instructions on performing these tasks, visit the LinkedIn Help center at **www.linkedin.com/help/linkedin**. Remember that the more robust you make your profile, the better your chances are of catching the eye of company recruiters.

BUILDING AN EMPLOYMENT PORTFOLIO

Employers want proof that you have the skills to succeed on the job, which can be challenging if you don't have a lot of relevant work experience in your target field. Fortunately, you can use your college classes, volunteer work, and other activities to assemble compelling proof by creating an *employment portfolio*, a collection of projects that demonstrate your skills and knowledge.

Your portfolio is likely to be a multimedia effort, with physical work samples (such as reports, proposals, or marketing materials), digital documents, web content, blog posts, photographs, video clips, and other items. As appropriate, you can include these items in your LinkedIn profile, bring them to interviews, and have them ready whenever an employer, client, or networking contact asks for samples of your work.

You have a variety of options for hosting a portfolio online. Your LinkedIn profile can function as your portfolio home, your college may offer portfolio hosting, or you might consider one of the many commercial portfolio hosting services. To see a selection of student e-portfolios from colleges around the United States, go to **real-timeupdates.com/bia9**, select Student Assignments, and locate the link to student e-portfolios.

Your portfolio is also a great resource for writing your résumé, because it reminds you of all the great work you've done over the years. Moreover, you can continue to refine and expand your portfolio throughout your career; many independent professionals use portfolios to advertise their services.

As you assemble your portfolio, collect anything that shows your ability to perform, whether it's in school, on the job, or in other venues. However, you *must* check with employers before including any items that you created while you were an employee and also check with clients before including any *work products* (anything you wrote, designed, programmed, and so on) they purchased from you. Many business documents contain confidential information that companies don't want distributed to outside audiences.

For each item you add to your portfolio, write a brief description that helps other people understand the meaning and significance of the project. Include such details as these:

- **Background.** Why did you undertake this project? Was it a school project, a work assignment, or something you did on your own initiative?
- **Project objectives.** Explain the project's goals, if relevant.
- **Collaborators.** If you worked with others, be sure to mention that and discuss team dynamics, if appropriate. For instance, if you led the team or worked with others long distance as part of a virtual team, point that out.
- **Constraints.** Sometimes the most impressive thing about a project is the time or budget constraints under which it was created. If such constraints apply to a project, consider mentioning them in a way that doesn't sound like an excuse for poor quality. If you had only one week to create a website, for example, you might say that "One of the intriguing challenges of this project was the deadline; I had only one week to design, compose, test, and publish this material."
- **Outcomes.** If the project's goals were measurable, what was the result? For example, if you wrote a letter soliciting donations for a charitable cause, how much money did you raise?
- **Learning experience.** If appropriate, describe what you learned during the course of the project.

Assume that potential employers will find your e-portfolio site, even if you don't tell them about it, so don't include anything that doesn't represent you at your professional best.

Interviewing with Potential Employers

An employment interview is a meeting during which you and a potential employer ask questions and exchange information. The employer's objective is to find the best talent to fill available job openings, and your objective is to find the right match for your goals and capabilities.

The interview process can vary from company to company, but most firms interview candidates in stages as they narrow down the list of possibilities. The process usually starts with a *screening stage* designed to filter out applicants who lack the desired qualifications or who might not be willing to accept the salary range or other parameters of the position. Study the job description carefully, and be ready to respond to questions about the major qualifications of the position, using key points from your résumé. Bear in mind that you're not going to win the job at this point; your goal is to make it past the filter and on to the next stage. Note that in some cases you may be required to pass an assessment before you are allowed to begin the application process, so be prepared to do some online testing.[19]

Candidates who make it past screening are invited to more in-depth interviews in the selection stage that help the company select the person who is most likely to succeed in the position. Employers take various approaches to the selection stage, but a typical next step is a telephone interview with the hiring manager. The manager will want to dig a little deeper into your qualifications and start to determine your fit with the company's culture. This conversation also gives you the opportunity to see whether you can build rapport with your future boss. During these interviews, show keen interest in the job, relate your skills and experience to the organization's needs, listen attentively, and ask questions that show you've done your research. The most promising applicants are usually invited to visit the company for in-person interviews with a variety of staff and managers.

REAL-TIME UPDATES

Learn More by Exploring This Interactive Website

How much are you worth?

Find real-life salary ranges for a wide variety of jobs. Go to **real-timeupdates.com/bia9** and select Learn More in the Students section.

Be prepared to encounter a variety of interviewing approaches, often within the same interview or set of interviews. These approaches can be distinguished by the way they are structured, the number of people involved, and the purpose of specific questions.

- In a *structured interview*, the interviewer (or an app or online system) asks a set series of questions in a fixed order. By asking every candidate the same set of questions, the structured format helps ensure fair interviews and makes it easier for an employer to compare and rank candidates.[20] In contrast, an *unstructured interview* doesn't follow a predetermined sequence. It is likely to feel more conversational and personal, as the interviewer adapts the line of questioning based on your answers. Even though it may feel like a conversation, remember that it's still an interview, so keep your answers focused and professional.

- Interviews can also vary by the number of people involved. Most of your interviews are likely to be one-on-one conversations, but you may encounter a *panel interview*, where you answer questions from two or more interviewers in the same session. In a *group interview*, one or more interviewers meet with several candidates simultaneously. These sessions can involve group discussions and problem-solving activities. In addition to being an efficient way to interview a number of candidates, group interviews let employers see how individuals function in a group or team setting.[21]

- Effective interviewers use a variety of question types to elicit specific types of answers. *Behavioral interview questions,* such as "Tell me about a time you had to deal with a teammate who refused to do his or her share of the work," require you to craft answers based on your own experiences and attributes.[22] Effective answers to behavioral questions have three parts: (1) a brief summary of the situation or task, (2) the approach you took to solve the problem or meet the challenge, and (3) the results you achieved. The acronym STAR can help you remember the sequence: **S/T** for situation or task, **A** for approach, and **R** for results.[23] *Situational interview questions* are similar to behavioral questions except they focus on how you would handle various situations that could arise on the job. The situations will relate closely to the job you're applying for, so the more you know about the position and the company, the better prepared you'll be.

Interviews give employers the chance to go beyond the basic data of your résumé to get to know you better and to answer two essential questions. First, can you handle the responsibilities of the position? Naturally, the more you know about the demands of the position, and the more you've thought about how your skills match those demands, the better you'll be able to respond.

Second, will you be a good fit with the organization and the target position? All good employers want people who are confident, dedicated, positive, curious, courteous, ethical, and willing to commit to something larger than their own individual goals. Companies also look for fit with their individual cultures. Just like people, companies have different personalities. Some are intense; others are more laid back. Some emphasize teamwork; others expect employees to forge their own way and even compete with one another. Expectations also vary from job to job within a company and from industry to industry. An outgoing personality is essential for sales but less so for research, for instance.

Beyond these two general questions, most employers look for the qualities of professionalism described in Chapter 1. Throughout the interview process, look for opportunities to show your commitment to excellence, dependability, teamwork, etiquette, communication skills, and ethical decision-making.

REAL-TIME UPDATES
Learn More by Visiting This Website

Prepare for your next interview using these Pinterest pins

The Pinterest pinboard maintained by St. Edward's University offers dozens of helpful resources. Go to **real-timeupdates.com/bia9** and select Learn More in the Students section.

Succeeding in Your First Job

Your first job sets the stage for your career and gives you an opportunity to explore how you want to position yourself for the long term. If you are already working or are changing careers, you can combine these skills with the professional perspective you already have to take your career to a new level.

If the first job you land isn't quite as exciting as you'd hoped for, don't make the mistake of treating it as an "entry-level" position that is beneath your talents. Instead, view it as an opportunity to learn new skills, expand your business acumen, and demonstrate your professionalism. Remember that most people can succeed in jobs that are easy or fun, but it takes a real pro to succeed when things are difficult or uninspiring.

As you progress along your career path, the time and energy you have invested in this and other business courses will continue to yield benefits year after year. As you tackle each new challenge, influential company leaders—the people who decide how quickly you'll get promoted and how much you'll earn—will be paying close attention to how well you communicate and collaborate. They will observe your interactions with colleagues, customers, and business partners to see how you treat people and take advantage of opportunities to learn. They'll take note of how well you can collect data, find the essential ideas buried under mountains of information, and convey those points to other people. They'll observe your ability to adapt to different audiences and circumstances. They'll be watching when you encounter tough situations that require careful attention to ethics and etiquette. The good news: Every insight you gain and every skill you develop in this course will help you shine in your career.

Endnotes

1. Amy Segelin, "3 Steps to Cracking the Hidden Job Market," *Fortune*, 4 March 2017, fortune.com.

2. Richie Frieman, "Proper Networking Etiquette," Quickand DirtyTips.com, 1 May 2016, www.quickanddirtytips.com; Kevin Daum, "12 Rules of Highly Effective Networkers," *Inc.*, 10 November 2014, www.inc.com; Debra Wheatman, "Five Keys to Networking Etiquette for Your Career," Glassdoor blog, 25 May 2011, www.glassdoor.com/blog/.

3. Randall S. Hansen and Katharine Hansen, "What Résumé Format Is Best for You?" QuintCareers.com, accessed 7 August 2010, www.quintcareers.com.

4. Hansen and Hansen, "What Résumé Format Is Best for You?"

5. "Resume Red Flags to Watch For," Robert Half, 25 April 2017, www.roberthalf.com; Katharine Hansen, "Should You Consider a Functional Format for Your Resume?" QuintCareers.com, accessed 7 August 2010, www.quintcareers.com.

6. Job description keywords and key phrases quoted or adapted in part from "Associate Market Analyst" job opening posted on LivingSocial website, accessed 9 July 2012, corporate.livingsocial.com.

7. Job description keywords and key phrases quoted or adapted in part from "Seller Support Associate" job opening posted on Amazon website, accessed 12 July 2012, us-amazon.icims.com/jobs.

8. Job description keywords and key phrases quoted or adapted in part from "Senior Strategy Analyst" job opening posted on Nordstrom website, accessed 17 July 2012, careers.nordstrom.com.

9. Anthony Balderrama, "Resume Blunders That Will Keep You from Getting Hired," CNN.com, 19 March 2008, www.cnn.com; Michelle Dumas, "5 Resume Writing Myths," Distinctive Documents blog, 17 July 2007, blog.distinctiveweb.com; Kim Isaacs, "Resume Dilemma: Recent Graduate," Monster.com, accessed 26 March 2008, career-advice.monster.com.

10. Alison Doyle, "Will Employers Check Your References," *The Balance Careers*, 21 November 2017, www.thebalancecareers.com.

11. Alison Doyle, "How to Select and Use Job References," *The Balance*, 31 January 2018, www.thebalance.com.

12. Madeleine Burry, "What Do Employers Look for in a Résumé?" *The Balance Careers*, 13 July 2017, www.thebalancecareers.com.

13. Stephanie Vozza, "Cover Letters Are Dead: Do This Instead," *Fast Company*, 16 February 2016, www.fastcompany.com.

14. Ambra Benjamin, "Do Recruiters Read Cover Letters?" Ladders, 14 April 2018, www.theladders.com.

15. Alison Doyle, "Interpersonal Skills List and Examples," *The Balance Careers*, 28 November 2017, www.thebalancecareers.com.

16. Quentin Fottrell, "How Job Recruiters Screen You on LinkedIn," *MarketWatch*, 16 June 2016, www.marketwatch.com.

17. Alison Doyle, "The Most Effective Ways to Use LinkedIn," *The Balance Careers*, 9 April 2018, www.thebalancecareers.com; Alison Doyle, "Learn How to Make a Better LinkedIn Profile," *The Balance Careers*, 13 December 2017, www.thebalancecareers.com; "How to Build the Perfect LinkedIn Profile," Link Humans, accessed 28 April 2017, linkhumans.com; Carly Okyle, "18 Tips to Create Your Perfect LinkedIn Profile," *Entrepreneur*, 4 April 2016, www.entrepreneur.com; Lindsay Kolowich, "How to Craft the Perfect LinkedIn Profile: A Comprehensive Guide," *HubSpot*, 25 January 2016, blog.hubspot.com; Quentin Fottrell, "How Job Recruiters Screen You on LinkedIn," *MarketWatch*, 16 June 2016, www.marketwatch.com; Ed Han, "How to Write a Good LinkedIn Summary with Examples," *The Balance Careers*, 5 April 2018, www.thebalancecareers.com.

18. Erica Baker profile on LinkedIn, accessed 22 April 2018, www.linkedin.com/ericajoy.

19. Ryan Craig, "Startups Are Making the Rejection Letter a Thing of the Past," *TechCrunch*, 9 January 2017, techcrunch.com.

20. Michelle Silverstein, "Structured vs. Unstructured Interviews: The Verdict," Criteria Corp blog, accessed 2 May 2017, blog.criteriacorp.com; Alison Doyle, "What Is a Structured Job Interview?" *The Balance*, 16 July 2016, www.thebalance.com.

21. Alison Doyle, "Group Interview Questions and Interviewing Tips," *The Balance*, 6 January 2017, www.thebalance.com; Pamela Skillings, "Acing the Group Interview," Big Interview, accessed 2 May 2017, biginterview.com.

22. Pamela Skillings, "Behavioral Interview: Tips for Crafting Your Best Answers," Big Interview, accessed 2 May 2017, biginterview.com.

23. Skillings, "Behavioral Interview: Tips for Crafting Your Best Answers."

PART 1

Setting the Stage:
The Business of Business

Start your exploration of business by understanding how companies create value to generate revenue and profits, then continue with a look at disruptive forces in business and life in the digital enterprise. Learn the basics of supply and demand, the definition of money, and the role of contemporary banking. Expand your horizons with an overview of global business strategies. Finish this part by considering the role of business in society and the dimensions of business ethics.

Stefan Dahl Langstrup/Alamy Stock Photo

Developing a Business Mindset

LEARNING OBJECTIVES   After studying this chapter, you will be able to

1.   Explain the concept of adding value in a business, and identify four useful ways to categorize businesses.

2.   List three steps you can take to help make the leap from consumer to business professional.

3.   Discuss the five major environments in which every business operates.

4.   Explain the purpose of the six major functional areas in a business enterprise.

5.   Summarize seven of the most important business professions.

6.   Identify six components of professionalism.

7.   Describe the concepts of disruptive innovation and digital transformation.

8.   Identify seven essential business skills that you will have the opportunity to develop during this course.

MyLab Intro to Business
Improve Your Grade!
If your instructor is using MyLab Intro to Business, visit **www.pearson.com/ mylab/intro-to-business**.

BEHIND THE SCENES   Can Software That Reads Faces Create a New Business?

As a university student, Rana el Kaliouby was fascinated by the possibility of using artificial intelligence to identify emotional states by measuring facial expressions.

Affectiva

www.affectiva.com

Like many college students, Rana el Kaliouby pursued her education with an important life goal in mind. In her case, it was developing computer programs that could "read" people's faces, a goal she pursued from her undergraduate studies in Egypt to a PhD program at the University of Cambridge in England to her work as a research scientist in the Media Lab at the Massachusetts Institute of Technology (MIT).

She had become fascinated by the possibility of using artificial intelligence (AI) to identify emotional states by measuring facial expressions. Her motivation was to help people on the autism spectrum who can struggle to pick up emotional cues when communicating with others. Could a system detect those cues and provide information to help people have richer social interactions?

After el Kaliouby created software at MIT that could track emotional responses by comparing facial movements with a catalog of common expressions, she was surprised by how many of the lab's corporate sponsors were interested in it. The inquiries ranged from Toyota, which wanted to know if it might help detect when drivers were getting drowsy, to Fox television studios, which wanted to use it for audience-testing new shows.

If you were el Kaliouby, what would be your next step? What kind of company could you and your partners create? How would you deal with the ethical questions associated with AI in general and something as personal as emotion measurement in particular? How would you transform something as esoteric as an artificial intelligence algorithm into a commercially viable product, and how would you communicate its value to potential customers?[1]

INTRODUCTION

Rana el Kaliouby's introduction to business (see the chapter-opening Behind the Scenes) was unusual in that she didn't set out to create a company. However, as you'll read at the end of the chapter, she now heads one of the most intriguing companies in the exploding field of artificial intelligence. This chapter prepares you for the whirlwind tour of the business world you'll get in this course, starting with a quick overview of what businesses do and then some advice on making the leap from consumer to business professional.

Understanding What Businesses Do

The term *business* is used in multiple ways:

- As a label for the overall field of business concepts, as in "I plan to major in business."
- As a collective label for the activities of many companies, as in "This legislation is viewed as harmful to American business."
- As a way to indicate specific activities or efforts, as in "Our furniture business earned record profits last year, but our housewares business has lost money for the third year in a row."
- As a synonym for *company*, as in "Apple is a successful business." Other common synonyms here are *firm* and *enterprise*.

In this last sense, a **business** is any profit-seeking organization that provides goods and services designed to satisfy customers' needs.

ADDING VALUE: THE BUSINESS OF BUSINESS

A good way to understand what any business does is to view it as a system for satisfying customers by transforming lower-value inputs into higher-value outputs (see Exhibit 1.1 on the next page). If you want a loaf of bread, for instance, a silo full of wheat isn't of much value to you. After that wheat is milled into flour, it gets one step closer but is valuable only if you want to bake your own bread. A bakery can take care of the baking, but that helps only if you're willing to travel to the bakery instead of going to the supermarket where you normally shop. At every stage, a company adds value to create the product in a way that makes it appealing to the next customer in the chain.

Each company in this chain has made certain choices about what it will do to generate **revenue**, which is money the company brings in through the sale of goods and services. The result of these decisions is a company's **business model**, which is a clearly stated outline of how the business generates or intends to generate revenue. Of course, generating revenue isn't enough. The business model must also indicate how the company is going to realize **profit**, the amount of money left over after *expenses*—all the costs involved in doing business—have been deducted from revenue.

Competing to Attract and Satisfy Customers

As businesses create value-added products and offer them for sale to customers, they obviously don't do so in a vacuum. Other companies are also trying to sell their products to those same customers, and the result is *competition*. Competition gives customers a wider range of options, and it tends to increase quality, improve customer service, and lower prices.

---

1 LEARNING OBJECTIVE

Explain the concept of adding value in a business, and identify four useful ways to categorize businesses.

business
Any profit-seeking organization that provides goods and services designed to satisfy customers' needs.

revenue
Money a company brings in through the sale of goods and services.

business model
A concise description of how a business generates or intends to generate revenue.

profit
Money left over after all the costs involved in doing business have been deducted from revenue.

EXHIBIT 1.1	Adding Value to Satisfy Customers

Every company in this chain adds value for the next customer and for the ultimate consumer.

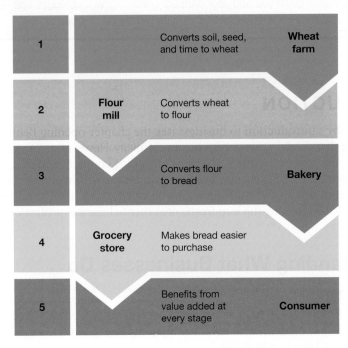

1	Converts soil, seed, and time to wheat	**Wheat farm**
2	**Flour mill**	Converts wheat to flour
3	Converts flour to bread	**Bakery**
4	**Grocery store**	Makes bread easier to purchase
5	Benefits from value added at every stage	**Consumer**

In a free-market economy, companies usually have a lot of flexibility in deciding which customers they want to focus on and how they want to compete. For instance, one bakery might decide to compete on price and thus structure its business model in such a way as to mass-produce bread at the lowest possible cost. Another might decide to compete on quality or uniqueness and structure its business model around handcrafted "artisan" bread that costs two or three times as much as the mass-produced bread. Each company seeks a **competitive advantage** that makes its products more appealing to its chosen customers. Consumers benefit from better products and more choices, and companies get to focus on what they do best.

competitive advantage
Some aspect of a product or company that makes it more appealing to target customers.

Accepting Risks in the Pursuit of Rewards

Take another look at Exhibit 1.1. Notice how every company from the farmer to the grocery store must accept some level of risk in order to conduct its business. Bad weather or disease could destroy the wheat crop. A shift in consumer behavior, such as cash-strapped families in a recession switching to bakery outlet stores instead of regular grocery stores, could leave some bakers, distributors, and retailers with bread nobody wants to buy. Businesses take these risks in anticipation of future rewards.

This linking of risk and reward is critical for two reasons. The first and more obvious is that without the promise of rewards, businesses would have no incentive to take on the risks. And without entrepreneurs and companies willing to accept risk, little would get done in the economy. The second reason that the risk associated with business decisions needs to "stay attached" to those decisions is to encourage smart and responsible decision making. If individuals and companies believe they can pursue rewards without facing the risks that should be attached to those pursuits, they are more likely to engage in irresponsible and even unethical behavior—a situation known as *moral hazard* (see Exhibit 1.2).

not-for-profit organizations
Organizations that provide goods and services without having a profit motive; also called *nonprofit organizations*.

IDENTIFYING MAJOR TYPES OF BUSINESSES

The driving forces behind most businesses are the prospects of earning profits and building *assets*, which are anything of meaningful value, from patents and brand names to real estate and company stock. In contrast, **not-for-profit organizations** (also known as *nonprofit organizations*)

EXHIBIT 1.2	Risk, Reward, and Moral Hazard

The relationship between risk and reward is fundamental to every modern economy. A company needs to see some promise of reward before it will decide to accept the risks involved in creating and selling products. However, to ensure responsible behavior, these risks need to stay attached to those decisions, meaning that if the decisions turn out badly, that company should suffer the consequences. If the risk gets disconnected from a decision—meaning someone else will suffer from a bad decision—a situation known as *moral hazard* is created. A significant recent example of this problem involved mortgage companies lending money to home-owners who were practically guaranteed to default on their loans, but then selling those loans as investments and thereby transferring the risk of nonpayment to someone else.

Healthy connection between risk and reward

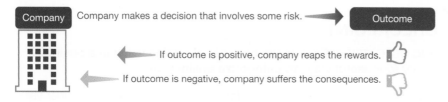

Moral hazard: Link between risk and reward is broken

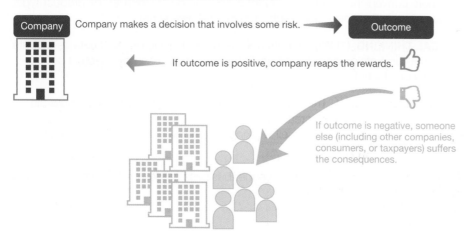

such as museums, most universities, and charities do not have a profit motive. However, they must operate efficiently and effectively to achieve their goals, and successful nonprofits apply many of the business-management principles you'll learn in this course.

Throughout this book, you'll encounter a diverse range of businesses, from independent freelancers to gargantuan corporations that generate more economic activity than many countries. To get a sense of this diversity and to envision where you might want to take your career, here are four helpful ways to categorize businesses:

- **Product types and ranges.** In everyday usage, people tend to divide the output of companies into "products and services." However, as Chapter 13 explains, from a business perspective it's more useful to view all outputs of business as products and divide these into *goods* and *services*. Most goods are *tangible*, meaning they have a physical presence. Other goods, such as software and downloadable music files, are *intangible*. Some companies offer only goods, and others offer only services; many firms offer a combination of the two. Companies also vary widely in the number and range of products they offer, from those with a single product to those with thousands of products in dozens of product lines, sometimes in completely unrelated industries.

- **Company size.** Big companies are truly big: The companies you see in the news most frequently tend to have hundreds or thousands of employees, and several of the largest companies in the world now employ more than a million people.[2] However, roughly three-quarters of the businesses in the United States are single-person operations with no employees. And of the 5 million or so companies that have employees, three-quarters of them have fewer than 10 workers.[3]

- **Geographic reach.** Companies can do business locally, regionally, nationally, or internationally. Thanks to the internet and global transportation services, geography is no longer the limitation it used to be, and even small companies can now serve customers around the world.
- **Ownership.** Firms can be owned and structured in a variety of ways, from sole proprietorships (one owner) to partnerships (typically several owners) to public corporations (which can have thousands of owners). Chapter 5 looks at company ownership in more detail.

 CHECKPOINT

LEARNING OBJECTIVE 1: Explain the concept of adding value in a business, and identify four useful ways to categorize businesses.

SUMMARY: Businesses add value by transforming lower-value inputs to higher-value outputs. In other words, they make goods and services more attractive from the buyer's perspective, whether it's creating products that are more useful or simply making them more convenient to purchase. Companies can be categorized by product types and ranges, company size, geographic reach, and ownership.

CRITICAL THINKING: (1) What inputs does a musical group use to create its outputs? (2) Can not-for-profit organizations benefit from practices used by for-profit companies? Why or why not?

IT'S YOUR BUSINESS: (1) Think back to the last product you purchased; how did the companies involved in its creation and sale add value in a way that benefited you personally? (2) Can you see yourself working for a not-for-profit organization after you graduate? Why or why not?

KEY TERMS TO KNOW: business, revenue, business model, profit, competitive advantage, not-for-profit organizations

---

2 LEARNING OBJECTIVE

List three steps you can take to help make the leap from consumer to business professional.

Making the Leap from Buyer to Seller

Even if this course is your first formal exposure to the business world, you already know a lot about business, thanks to your experiences as a consumer. You understand the impact of poor customer service, for example. You have a sense of product value and why some products meet your needs and others don't. In fact, you're an expert in the entire experience of searching for, purchasing, and using products.

SEEING BUSINESS FROM THE INSIDE OUT

As you progress through this course, you'll begin to look at things through the eyes of a business professional rather than those of a consumer. Instead of thinking about the cost of buying a particular product, you'll start to think about the cost of making it, promoting it, and distributing it. You'll think about what it takes to make a product stand out from the crowd and recognize the importance of finding opportunities in the marketplace. You'll begin to see business as an integrated system of inputs, processes, and outputs. As Rana el Kaliouby did when she cofounded Affectiva (see page 72), you'll start to develop a **business mindset** as you gain an appreciation for the many decisions that must be made and the many challenges that must be overcome before companies can deliver products that satisfy customer needs (see Exhibit 1.3).

business mindset
Adopting an insider's view of business with an appreciation for the decisions to be made and challenges that managers face.

EXHIBIT 1.3	The Business Mindset

Your experiences as a consumer have taught you a great deal about business already. Now the challenge is to turn those experiences around and view the world from a manager's perspective. Here are a few examples of how a business professional approaches some of the questions you've asked as a consumer.

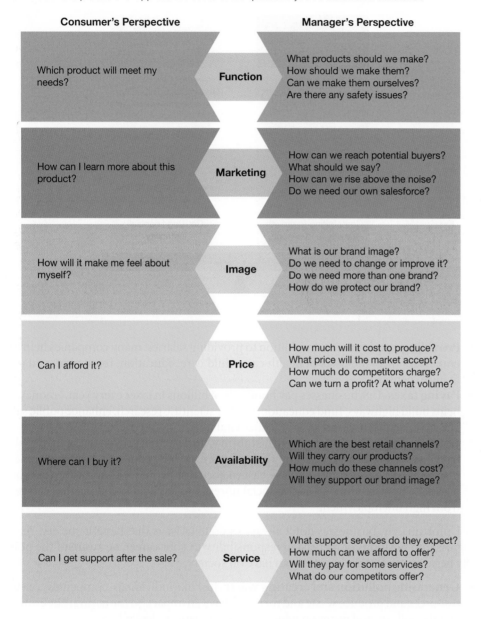

Consumer's Perspective　　　　　　**Manager's Perspective**

Function
Which product will meet my needs?
What products should we make?
How should we make them?
Can we make them ourselves?
Are there any safety issues?

Marketing
How can I learn more about this product?
How can we reach potential buyers?
What should we say?
How can we rise above the noise?
Do we need our own salesforce?

Image
How will it make me feel about myself?
What is our brand image?
Do we need to change or improve it?
Do we need more than one brand?
How do we protect our brand?

Price
Can I afford it?
How much will it cost to produce?
What price will the market accept?
How much do competitors charge?
Can we turn a profit? At what volume?

Availability
Where can I buy it?
Which are the best retail channels?
Will they carry our products?
How much do these channels cost?
Will they support our brand image?

Service
Can I get support after the sale?
What support services do they expect?
How much can we afford to offer?
Will they pay for some services?
What do our competitors offer?

APPRECIATING THE ROLE OF BUSINESS IN SOCIETY

Your experiences as a consumer, an employee, and a taxpayer have also given you some insights into the complex relationship between business and society. Chapter 4's discussion of *corporate social responsibility* digs deeper into this important topic, but for now, just consider some of the major elements of this relationship. Business has the potential to contribute to society in many useful ways, including the following (see Exhibit 1.4 on the next page):

- **Offering valuable goods and services.** Most of the goods and services you consider essential to your quality of life were made possible by someone with a profit motive.

| **EXHIBIT 1.4** | **Positive and Negative Effects of Business** |

The relationship between business and society is complex and far reaching. Individuals, communities, and entire nations benefit in multiple ways from the efforts of businesses, but even responsibly managed companies can at times have negative impacts on society.

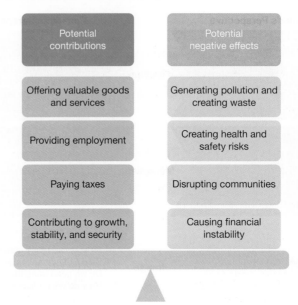

- **Providing employment.** In addition to providing salaries, many companies help their employees meet the costs of health care, child care, education, retirement, and other living expenses.
- **Paying taxes.** U.S. businesses pay hundreds of billions in taxes every year,[4] money that helps build highways, fund education, further scientific research, enhance public safety and national defense, and support other vital functions of government.
- **Contributing to national growth, stability, and security.** Beyond the mere dollars from taxes paid, a strong economy helps ensure a strong country. As one example, by providing job opportunities to the vast majority of people who want to work, businesses help the country avoid the social unrest and family disruptions that can result from high unemployment.

Unfortunately, businesses don't always operate in ways that benefit society. As you progress into positions of increasing responsibility in your career, be aware of the potentially negative effects that business can have on society:

- **Generating pollution and creating waste.** Just like individuals, companies consume resources and produce waste and therefore have an impact on the natural environment and the soil, air, and water on which all living creatures depend.
- **Creating health and safety risks.** Many business operations involve an element of risk to the health and safety of employees and surrounding communities. For instance, some of the products you use every day, including phones and computers, contain toxic materials. If these materials are not created, handled, and disposed of properly, they can cause serious illness or death.
- **Disrupting communities.** From occupying land to displacing existing businesses to overloading schools and roads with employees and their children, growing businesses can disrupt communities even as they provide employment and other benefits. And when businesses fall into decline, they can disrupt communities that have been depending on them.
- **Causing financial instability.** Irresponsible or poorly managed companies can become a liability to society if they are unable to meet their financial obligations and need assistance from the government, for example.

The potential negative effects of business are serious matters, but the good news is that you have a say in how business operates. Even as an employee early in your career, you can conduct yourself in ways that balance the profit motive with society's shared interests. And as you climb the corporate ladder or perhaps launch your own business, you'll be in a position to make decisions that help your company prosper in an ethical and sustainable manner.

USING THIS COURSE TO JUMP-START YOUR CAREER

No matter where your career plans take you, the dynamics of business will affect your work and life in innumerable ways. If you aspire to be a manager or an entrepreneur, knowing how to run a business is vital, of course. If you plan a career in a professional specialty such as law, engineering, or finance, knowing how businesses operate will help you interact with clients and colleagues more effectively. Even if you plan to work in government, education, or some other noncommercial setting, business awareness can help you; many of these organizations look to business for new ideas and leadership techniques. *Social entrepreneurs,* people who apply entrepreneurial strategies to enable large-scale social change, use business concepts as well.

As you progress through this course, you'll develop a fundamental business vocabulary that will help you keep up with the latest news and make better-informed decisions. By participating in classroom discussions and completing the chapter exercises, you'll gain some valuable critical-thinking, problem-solving, team-building, and communication skills that you can use on the job and throughout your life.

This course will also introduce you to a variety of jobs in business fields such as accounting, economics, human resources, management, finance, and marketing. You'll see how people who work in these fields contribute to the success of a company. You'll gain insight into the types of skills and knowledge these jobs require, and you'll discover that a career in business today is fascinating, challenging, and often quite rewarding.

In addition, a study of business management will help you appreciate the larger context in which businesses operate and the many legal and ethical questions managers must consider as they make business decisions. Government regulators and society as a whole have numerous expectations regarding the ways businesses treat employees, shareholders, the natural environment, other businesses, and the communities in which they operate.

 **CHECKPOINT**

LEARNING OBJECTIVE 2: List three steps you can take to help make the leap from consumer to business professional.

SUMMARY: To accelerate your transition from consumer to professional, develop a business mindset that views business from the inside out rather than the outside in, recognize the positive and negative effects that business can have on society, and use this course to develop a business vocabulary and explore the wide variety of jobs in the field of business.

CRITICAL THINKING: (1) How can consumer experiences help a business professional excel on the job? (2) If organized businesses didn't exist and the economy were composed of individual craftspeople, would the result be more or less pollution? Explain your answer.

IT'S YOUR BUSINESS: (1) How might you contribute to society as a business professional? (2) What is your view of business at this point in your life? Negative? Positive? A mixture of both? What experiences have shaped your view?

KEY TERM TO KNOW: business mindset

[3] **LEARNING OBJECTIVE**

Discuss the five major environments in which every business operates.

Recognizing the Multiple Environments of Business

The potential effects of business, both positive and negative, highlight the fact that no business operates in a vacuum. Every company operates within several interrelated environments that affect and are affected by business (see Exhibit 1.5).

THE SOCIAL ENVIRONMENT

social environment
Trends and forces in society at large.

All business activities take place within the broad **social environment**—the trends and forces in society at large. The social environment influences business in two important ways. First, social trends can affect the composition of the workforce and demand for goods and services. For example, if young adults wait longer to move out of their parents' homes, or if young couples wait longer to have children, this situation can influence the number of people in the workforce and the demand for everything from housing to cars to health care.

stakeholders
Internal and external groups affected by a company's decisions and activities.

Second, business has a huge impact on society, and various segments of society have expectations about the appropriate ways for businesses to operate. The responsibility of a company to its **stakeholders**—all those groups affected by its activities, from employees to local communities to advocacy groups—is a subject of ongoing controversy. A growing number of employees and company leaders believe that a company should strive for something more than just making money, giving rise to the concept of the *purpose-driven business*. You can read more about these issues in Chapter 4's discussion of corporate social responsibility.

EXHIBIT 1.5	The Multiple Environments of Business

Every business operates in an overlapping mix of dynamic environments that continuously create both opportunities and constraints.

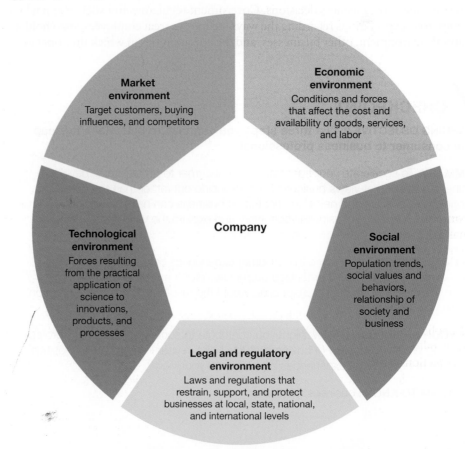

THE TECHNOLOGICAL ENVIRONMENT

The **technological environment** stems from the practical application of science to innovations, products, and processes. It's difficult to find a business these days that doesn't rely on technology, even if it's only using mobile communication to stay in touch with customers. Most of the biggest and most influential companies in the world today are firms that either make advanced technologies or use these innovations to achieve market dominance.

Technology is essential to business today, but it can also be an extremely disruptive force. This chapter's "Thriving in the Digital Enterprise" section (page 67), looks at *disruptive innovations*, developments that are powerful enough to create or destroy entire companies and industries.

technological environment
Forces resulting from the practical application of science to innovations, products, and processes.

> **REAL-TIME UPDATES**
> **Learn More by Reading This Article**
>
> **The future of work in a world of automation**
>
> Explore the changes that are needed to help the workforce adapt to a new age of AI and robotic automation. Go to **real-timeupdates .com/bia9** and select Learn More in the Students section.

THE ECONOMIC ENVIRONMENT

Directly or indirectly, virtually every decision a company makes is influenced by the **economic environment**, the conditions and forces that affect the cost and availability of goods, services, and labor and thereby shape the behavior of buyers and sellers. For example, a growing economy can help companies by increasing demand and supporting higher prices for their products, but it can also raise the costs of labor and materials the companies need. A shrinking economy, on the other hand, can damage even well-run, financially healthy companies by limiting demand for their products or the availability of loans or investments needed to expand operations.

The economic and technological environments are closely intertwined, partly because many innovations aim to reduce the costs of various business operations. Labor is typically one of a company's biggest expenses, for instance, so companies keep an eye out for new technologies that can reduce labor costs or improve labor productivity. Doing so can be good for business, but it can be bad for the workforce if fewer workers are needed. You'll be hearing a lot of discussion in the coming years about the potential for workers at every skill level to be displaced by artificial intelligence (AI), robotics, and other advanced technologies.

At the same time, technology can create economic opportunities for workers. Many people now work in jobs that didn't exist before the internet came into being, for example. In addition, millions of people now work full- or part-time in the **gig economy**, composed of people who work as independent contractors on a series of short-term projects or tasks (colloquially known as "gigs"). Much of the work in the gig economy is either technology based or enabled by technologies such as website services and mobile apps. Work in the gig economy varies widely, from household tasks to software development to the *sharing economy* of home- and ride-share services such as Airbnb and Lyft.

economic environment
The conditions and forces that affect the cost and availability of goods, services, and labor and thereby shape the behavior of buyers and sellers.

gig economy
Portion of the economy composed of people who work as independent contractors on a series of short-term projects or tasks.

legal and regulatory environment
Laws and regulations at local, state, national, and even international levels.

THE LEGAL AND REGULATORY ENVIRONMENT

Every business is affected by the **legal and regulatory environment**, the sum of laws and regulations at local, state, national, and even international levels. Some businesses, such as electricity and other basic utilities, are heavily regulated, even to the point of government agencies determining how much companies can charge for their services. The degree to which various industries should be regulated remains a point of contention year in and year out.

The policies and practices of government bodies also establish an overall level of support for businesses operating within their jurisdictions. Taxation, fees, efforts to coordinate multiple regulatory agencies, the speed of granting permits and licenses, labor rules, environmental restrictions, protection for assets such as patents and brand names, roads and other infrastructure, and the transparency and consistency of decision making all affect this level of support.

Millions of people work full- or part-time in the gig economy, taking on short-term tasks and projects as independent contractors rather than as employees.

nd3000/Shutterstock

THE MARKET ENVIRONMENT

market environment
A company's target customers, the buying influences that shape the behavior of those customers, and competitors that market similar products to those customers.

Within the various other environments just discussed, every company operates within a specific **market environment** composed of three important groups: (1) its *target customers*, (2) the *buying influences* that shape the behavior of those customers, and (3) *competitors*—other companies that market similar products to those customers.

The nature of the market environment varies widely from industry to industry, from markets that are relatively stable with clearly defined boundaries to markets that are shifting and dynamic. The commercial airplane market, for instance, is fairly stable. There are a handful of well-established competitors (Boeing, Airbus, and a few others), there is very little risk that a new type of product will appear and threaten to replace airliners, and customers (airlines) behave in predictable ways.

barriers to entry
Resources or capabilities a company must have before it can start competing in a given market.

Much of this stability comes from high **barriers to entry**, which are resources or capabilities a company must have before it can start competing in a given market. Airline manufacturing is a *capital-intensive* business that requires enormous amounts of money, huge facilities, and complex production equipment. Other barriers to entry include government testing and approval, tightly controlled distribution, strict licensing procedures, limited supplies of raw materials, and highly skilled employees.

In contrast, markets with low barriers to entry can be highly dynamic, with new suppliers appearing almost overnight. The music industry used to have high barriers to entry because a small number of record companies controlled the recording and distribution of music. With the advent of low-cost digital recording and online distribution, however, virtually anyone can now produce and distribute music.

Lowering barriers to entry and leaping over the boundaries that separate and define markets are two recurring themes of business innovation and disruption. Given the rate of change in today's business world, companies can find themselves under attack from competitors they never imagined. Google and Amazon illustrate this in startling ways. Google started out as a search engine, but the conglomerate of companies it grew into (called Alphabet) now competes or plans to compete in such diverse areas as operating systems, home automation, driverless cars, health care, and retailing. Amazon started out as a bookstore and now competes in just about every sector of retailing and is also a major player in cloud computing services (essentially renting computing capacity to other companies), television and movie production, and consumer electronics. It has built a vast network of ocean, air, and truck transport capacity for its own use, leading some to speculate that it could soon start competing with the likes of UPS and FedEx.[5]

✓ CHECKPOINT

LEARNING OBJECTIVE 3: Discuss the five major environments in which every business operates.

SUMMARY: Business influences and is influenced by (1) the social environment—the trends and forces in society at large; (2) the technological environment and its ability to create and destroy markets and alter business processes; (3) the economic environment—the conditions and forces that affect the cost and availability of goods, services, and labor and thereby shape the behavior of buyers and sellers; (4) the legal and regulatory environment, comprising all the rules and regulations relating to business activities; and (5) the market environment, composed of target customers, buying influences, and competitors.

CRITICAL THINKING: (1) Is it wise for cities and states to compete with each other to be more business friendly, specifically with regard to lower tax rates on businesses? Why or why not? (2) Even though it never sells directly to consumers, does a company such as Boeing need to pay attention to population trends? Why or why not?

IT'S YOUR BUSINESS: (1) How has technology made your educational experience in college different from your experience in high school? (2) In what ways are you a market influencer? Do your buying choices and recommendations affect the decisions of other consumers?

KEY TERMS TO KNOW: social environment, stakeholders, technological environment, economic environment, gig economy, legal and regulatory environment, market environment, barriers to entry

Identifying the Major Functional Areas in a Business Enterprise

Throughout this course, you'll have the opportunity to learn more about the major functional areas within a business enterprise. In the meantime, the following sections offer a brief overview to help you see how all the pieces work together (see Exhibit 1.6).

RESEARCH AND DEVELOPMENT

Products are conceived and designed through **research and development (R&D)**, sometimes known as *product design* or *engineering*. Of course, not all companies have an R&D function; many companies simply resell products that other firms make, for example. However, for companies that do develop products, R&D is essential to their success because it

4 **LEARNING OBJECTIVE**
Explain the purpose of the six major functional areas in a business enterprise.

research and development (R&D)
Functional area responsible for conceiving and designing new products.

EXHIBIT 1.6   **Major Functional Areas in a Business Enterprise**

The functional areas in a business coordinate their efforts to understand and satisfy customer needs. Note that this is a simplified model, and that various companies organize their activities in different ways.

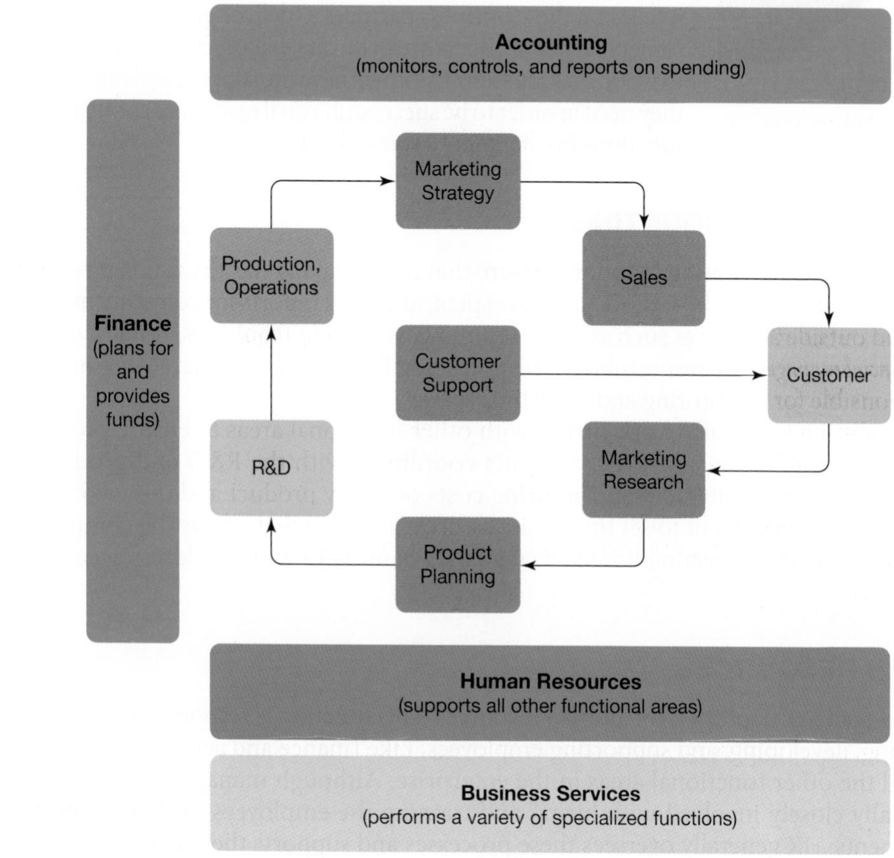

provides the ideas and designs that allow these firms to meet customer needs in competitive markets. Companies that rely heavily on science and technology must devote considerable resources to ongoing R&D. Firms can also engage in *process* R&D to design new and better ways to run their operations.

MANUFACTURING, PRODUCTION, AND OPERATIONS

Variously called *manufacturing, production,* or *operations,* this function concerns whatever the company makes (for goods-producing businesses) or does (for service businesses). In addition to supervising the actual production activity, operations managers are responsible for a wide range of other strategies and decisions, including *purchasing* (arranging to buy the necessary materials for manufacturing), *logistics* (coordinating the incoming flow of materials and the outgoing flow of finished products), and *facilities management* (everything from planning new buildings to maintaining them). Chapter 9 explores operations management in more detail.

MARKETING, SALES, DISTRIBUTION, AND CUSTOMER SUPPORT

Christine Langer-Pueschel/Shutterstock

Work in marketing encompasses a wide range of strategic and tactical activities, from defining new products to generating creative ideas for advertising.

Your experience as a consumer probably gives you more insight into marketing, sales, distribution, and customer support than any other functional area in business. Although the lines separating these three activities are often blurry, generally speaking, *marketing* is charged with identifying opportunities in the marketplace, working with R&D to develop products to address those opportunities, creating branding and advertising strategies to communicate with potential customers, and setting prices. The *sales* function develops relationships with potential customers and persuades customers to buy the company's goods and services. The *distribution* function is responsible for delivering products to customers (if a company sells directly to its customers) or to *intermediaries* such as retailers (if it relies on these business partners to deliver products to end customers). After products are in buyers' hands, *customer support* goes to work, making sure customers have the support and information they need in order to be successful. You'll read more about all these functions in Chapters 12 through 14.

FINANCE AND ACCOUNTING

The finance and accounting functions ensure that the company has the funds it needs in order to operate, control how those funds are spent, and draft reports for company management and outside audiences such as investors and government regulators. Roughly speaking, *financial managers* are responsible for planning and funding, whereas *accounting managers* are responsible for monitoring and reporting.

Accounting specialists work closely with other functional areas to ensure profitable decision making. For instance, accountants coordinate with the R&D and production departments to estimate the manufacturing costs of a new product and then work with the marketing department to set the product's price at a level that allows the company to be competitive while meeting its financial goals. Chapters 15 and 16 address accounting and finance.

HUMAN RESOURCES

As you'll read in Chapter 11, the human resources (HR) function is responsible for recruiting, hiring, developing, and supporting employees. Like finance and accounting, HR supports all the other functional areas in the enterprise. Although managers in other areas are usually closely involved with hiring and training the employees in their respective departments, HR generally oversees these processes and supports the other departments as needed. The HR department is also charged with making sure the company is in compliance with the many laws concerning employee rights and workplace safety.

BUSINESS SERVICES

In addition to these core functions, a wide variety of *business services* exist to help companies with specific needs in law, banking, real estate, and other areas. These services can be performed by in-house staff, external firms, or a combination of the two. For example, a company might have a small permanent legal staff to handle routine business matters such as writing contracts but then engage a specialist law firm to help with a patent application or a major lawsuit. Similarly, all but the smallest companies have accounting professionals on staff to handle routine matters, but companies that sell shares of stock to the public are required to have their financial records *audited* (reviewed) by an outside accounting firm.

 CHECKPOINT

LEARNING OBJECTIVE 4: Explain the purpose of the six major functional areas in a business enterprise.

SUMMARY: (1) Research and development (R&D) creates the goods and services that a company can manufacture or perform for its customers. (2) Manufacturing, production, or operations is the part of the company where the firm makes whatever it makes or performs whatever services it performs. (3) The related group of functions in marketing, sales, distribution, and customer support are responsible for identifying market opportunities, crafting promotional strategies, and making sure customers are supplied and satisfied with their purchases. (4) Finance and accounting plan for the company's financial needs, control spending, and report on financial matters. (5) Human resources recruits, hires, develops, and supports employees. (6) Various business services provide expertise in law, real estate, and other areas.

CRITICAL THINKING: (1) Do companies that deliver services rather than creating tangible goods ever need to engage in research and development? Why or why not? (2) Why is good customer support essential to the success of marketing and sales activities?

IT'S YOUR BUSINESS: (1) Think of a strongly positive or strongly negative experience you've had with a product or company. What feedback would you like to give the company, and to which functional area would you direct your feedback? (2) Have you already chosen the functional area where you want to work after graduation? If so, what led you to that choice?

KEY TERMS TO KNOW: research and development (R&D)

Exploring Careers in Business

Whether you're getting ready to start your career or you've been in the workforce for a while, use this course as an opportunity to explore the many career track options in the world of business. To help stimulate your thinking, this section offers a quick overview of seven major business fields.[6] However, don't limit yourself to these seven by any means. For just about any professional interest you might have, you can probably find a business-related career to pursue, from entertainment and sports to health care and sciences and everything in between. Also, pay attention to employment trends; as the business environment evolves, employment opportunities in various fields grow and shrink at different rates.

 LEARNING OBJECTIVE

Summarize seven of the most important business professions.

OPERATIONS MANAGER

Operations management encompasses all the people and processes used to create the goods and perform the services that a company sells. The work can involve a wide range of tasks and disciplines, including production engineering, assembly, testing, scheduling,

operations management
Management of the people and processes involved in creating goods and services.

quality assurance, information technology, forecasting, finance, logistics, and customer support. Some degree of technical acumen is always required, and many operations managers begin their careers in technical positions such as industrial engineering.

The work can be demanding as the organization deals with fluctuating demand levels and with process and supply problems. On the other hand, if you want to balance your business interests with being involved in creating a company's products, one of these management positions might be perfect for you.

HUMAN RESOURCES SPECIALIST

HR specialists and managers plan and direct personnel-related activities, including recruiting, training and development, compensation and benefits, employee and labor relations, and health and safety. HR managers develop and implement systems and practices to accommodate a firm's strategy and to motivate and manage diverse workforces. HR also oversees *talent management* efforts, making sure the company can attract, develop, and retain people with the types of talent the company needs in order to compete in its chosen markets.

INFORMATION TECHNOLOGY MANAGER

information technology (IT)
A functional area of business as well as the systems responsible for gathering, processing, and distributing information where needed throughout an organization.

Every company relies on timely, accurate information across all functional areas, and getting information to the right people via computer and communication systems is the job of the **information technology (IT)** function. IT is such an important function in today's business environment that many corporations have a top-ranking executive known as a *chief technology officer* (CTO) or *chief information officer* (CIO) in charge of IT strategy. Jobs in IT typically require a degree in a technical field, but an understanding of business processes, finance, and management is also important, particularly as you move up through the ranks of IT management. A master of business administration (MBA) is expected for IT managers in many organizations.

MARKETING SPECIALIST

A wide range of career opportunities exist in the interrelated tasks of identifying and understanding market opportunities and shaping the product, pricing, and communication strategies needed to pursue those opportunities. Whether your interests lie in branding strategy, online retailing, advertising, public relations, creative communication, interpersonal relations, or social media, chances are you can find a good fit somewhere in the world of marketing.

Many small companies and virtually all midsize and large companies have a variety of marketing positions, but many of these jobs are also found in advertising agencies, public relations (PR) firms, and other companies that offer specialized services to clients. Some marketing jobs are highly specialized (advertising copywriter and e-commerce architect, for instance), whereas others encompass many aspects of marketing (brand managers, for example, deal with a variety of marketing and sales functions).

Oleksiy Mark/Shutterstock

Information technology managers are responsible for the systems that collect, process, and distribute vital information throughout the organization.

SALES PROFESSIONAL

If you thrive on competition, enjoy solving problems, and get energized by working with a wide range of people, you should definitely consider a career in sales, becoming one of the professionals responsible for building relationships with customers and helping them make purchase decisions. As a consumer, your exposure to sales might be limited to the retail sector of professional selling, but the field is much more diverse. Salespeople sell everything from design services to pharmaceuticals to airliners.

Many salespeople enjoy a degree of day-to-day freedom and flexibility not usually found in office-bound jobs. On the other hand, the pressure can be intense; few jobs have the immediate indicators of success or failure that sales has, and most salespeople have specific targets, or *quotas*, they are expected to meet.

ACCOUNTANT

If working at the intersection of mathematics and business sounds appealing, a career in accounting or finance could be just right for you. Accounting tasks vary by job and industry, but in general, *management accountants* are responsible for collecting, analyzing, and reporting on financial matters, such as analyzing budgets, assessing the manufacturing costs of new products, and preparing state and federal tax returns. *Internal auditors* verify the work of the company's accounting effort and look for opportunities to improve efficiency and cost-effectiveness. *Public accountants* offer accounting, tax preparation, and investment advice to individuals, companies, and other organizations. *External auditors* verify the financial reports of public companies as required by law, and *forensic accountants* investigate financial crimes.

Accounting professionals need to have an affinity for numbers, analytical minds, and attention to detail. Their work can have wide-ranging effects on investors, employees, and executives, so accuracy and timeliness are critical. Communication skills are important in every accounting function. Computer skills are also increasingly important, particularly for accountants involved with the design or operation of financial information systems.

FINANCIAL MANAGER

Financial managers perform a variety of leadership and strategic functions. *Controllers* oversee the preparation of income statements, balance sheets, and other financial reports; they frequently manage accounting departments as well. *Treasurers* and *finance officers* have a more strategic role, establishing long-term financial goals and budgets, investing the firm's funds, and raising capital as needed. Other financial management positions include *credit managers*, who supervise credit accounts established for customers, and *cash managers*, who monitor and control cash flow.

Unlike accounting tasks, for which there is a long tradition of outsourcing, the work of financial managers is generally kept in-house, particularly in midsize and large companies. The work of a financial manager touches every part of the company, so a broad understanding of the various functional areas in business is a key attribute for this position. The ability to communicate with people who aren't financial experts is also vital. Moreover, awareness of information technology developments is important for *chief financial officers* (CFOs) and other top financial managers so that they can direct their companies' investments in new or improved systems as needed.

REAL-TIME UPDATES
Learn More by Exploring This Interactive Website

Figure out your next move

My Next Move helps you identify careers that involve the kinds of work you like to do. Go to **real-timeupdates.com/bia9** and select Learn More in the Students section.

Young couple choosing a car in a showroom

Blue Jean Images/Alamy Stock Photo

CHECKPOINT

LEARNING OBJECTIVE 5: Summarize seven of the most important business professions.

SUMMARY: (1) Operations managers oversee all the people and processes involved in creating the goods and services that a company sells. (2) HR specialists and managers plan and direct HR activities such as recruiting, training and development, compensation and benefits, employee and labor relations, and health and safety. (3) IT managers oversee the design, implementation, and maintenance of systems that help deliver the right information at the right time to the right people in the organization. (4) Marketing specialists perform one or more tasks involved in identifying and understanding market opportunities and shaping the product, pricing, and promotional strategies needed to pursue those opportunities. (5) Sales professionals build relationships with customers and help them make purchase decisions. (6) Accountants collect, analyze, and report on financial matters; they also perform audits to verify financial reports or find ways to lower costs. (7) Financial managers plan for the company's financial needs, invest funds, and raise capital.

CRITICAL THINKING: (1) Why are communication skills essential in all seven of the functional areas discussed in this section? (2) Why would financial managers be in a good position to rise up the company ladder?

IT'S YOUR BUSINESS: (1) Which of these seven general career areas appeals to you the most? Why? (2) If you eventually plan to start your own company but want to gain experience working in a corporation first, which of these career paths would you choose? Why?

KEY TERM TO KNOW: operations management, information technology (IT)

---

[6] **LEARNING OBJECTIVE**

Identify six components of professionalism.

professionalism
The quality of performing at a high level and conducting oneself with purpose and pride.

Achieving Professionalism

As you map out your career, think about what kind of businessperson you want to be. Will you be someone who just puts in the hours and collects a paycheck? Or will you be someone who performs on a higher plane, someone who wants to make a meaningful contribution and be viewed as a true professional? **Professionalism** is the quality of performing at a high level and conducting oneself with purpose and pride. True professionals exhibit six distinct traits: striving to excel, being dependable and accountable, being a team player, demonstrating a sense of etiquette, communicating effectively, and making ethical decisions (see Exhibit 1.7).

STRIVING TO EXCEL

Pros are good at what they do, and they never stop improving. No matter what your job might be at any given time—even if it is far from where you aspire to be—strive to perform at the highest possible level. Not only do you have an ethical obligation to give your employer and your customers your best effort, but excelling at each level in your career is the best way to keep climbing upward to new positions of responsibility. Plus, being good at what you do delivers a sense of satisfaction that is hard to beat.

In many jobs and in many industries, performing at a high level requires a commitment to continuous learning and improvement. The nature of the work often changes as markets and technologies evolve, and expectations of quality tend to increase over time as well. View this constant change as a positive thing, as a way to avoid stagnation and boredom.

BEING DEPENDABLE AND ACCOUNTABLE

Develop a reputation as somebody people can count on. This means meeting your commitments, including staying on schedule and staying within budgets. These are skills that take some time to develop as you gain experience with the amount of time and money required to accomplish various tasks and projects. With experience, you'll learn to be careful with

EXHIBIT 1.7 | Elements of Professionalism

To develop a reputation as a true professional, develop these six attributes—and keep improving all the way through your career.

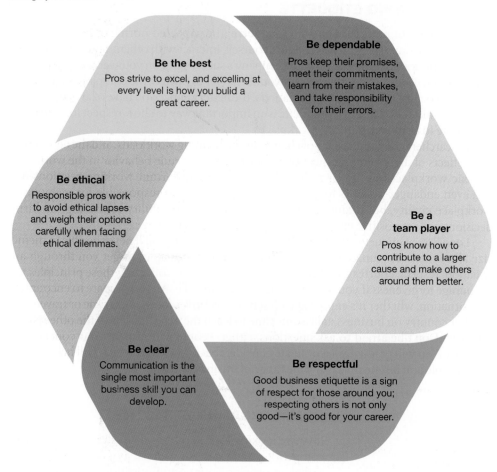

Be the best
Pros strive to excel, and excelling at every level is how you bulid a great career.

Be dependable
Pros keep their promises, meet their commitments, learn from their mistakes, and take responsibility for their errors.

Be ethical
Responsible pros work to avoid ethical lapses and weigh their options carefully when facing ethical dilemmas.

Be a team player
Pros know how to contribute to a larger cause and make others around them better.

Be clear
Communication is the single most important business skill you can develop.

Be respectful
Good business etiquette is a sign of respect for those around you; respecting others is not only good—it's good for your career.

your commitments. You don't want to be known as someone who overpromises and underdelivers.

Being accountable also means owning up to your mistakes and learning from failure so that you can continue to improve. Pros don't make excuses or blame others. When they make mistakes—and everybody does—they face the situation head on, make amends, and move on.

BEING A TEAM PLAYER

Professionals know that they are contributors to a larger cause, that it's not all about them. Just as in athletics and other team efforts, being a team player in business is something of a balancing act. On the one hand, you need to pay enough attention to your own efforts and skills to make sure you're pulling your own weight. On the other hand, you need to pay attention to the overall team effort to make sure the team succeeds. Remember that if the team fails, you fail, too.

Great team players know how to make those around them more effective, whether it's lending a hand during crunch time, sharing resources, removing obstacles, making introductions, or offering expertise. In fact, the ability to help others improve their performance is one of the key attributes executives look for when they want to promote people into management.

Being a team player also means showing loyalty to your organization and protecting your employer's reputation—one of the most important assets any company has. Pros don't

REAL-TIME UPDATES
Learn More by Watching This Video

Battle through anything with advice from a champion endurance racer

Amelia Boone is one of the toughest people on Earth, with the trophies to prove it. Hear why she chooses to face adversity head on. Go to **real-timeupdates.com/bia9** and select Learn More in the Students section.

trash their employers in front of customers or on social media. When they see a problem, they solve it; they don't share it.

DEMONSTRATING ETIQUETTE

etiquette
The expected norms of behavior in any particular situation.

A vital element of professionalism is **etiquette**, the expected norms of behavior in any particular situation. The way you conduct yourself, interact with others, and handle conflict can have a profound influence on your company's success and on your career. When executives hire and promote you, they expect your behavior to protect the company's reputation. The more you understand such expectations, the better chance you have of avoiding career-damaging mistakes. Moreover, etiquette is an important way to show respect for others and contribute to a smooth-running workplace.

Researchers cite the fast pace of change, overwhelming workloads, and the depersonalizing effects of digital communication as key reasons for rude behavior in the workplace. A toxic workplace can lower productivity, damage important working relationships, and even endanger people's long-term health.[7] Everyone is responsible for maintaining workplace civility, but managers have a particular responsibility to make good hiring decisions and set positive examples through their own behavior.

Long lists of etiquette "rules" can be overwhelming, and you'll never be able to memorize all of them. Fortunately, you can count on three principles to get you through any situation: respect, courtesy, and common sense. Moreover, following these principles will encourage forgiveness if you do happen to make a mistake. As you prepare to encounter a new situation, whether it's engaging with senior executives for the first time or traveling to another country on business, take some time to learn the expectations of the other people involved. Don't be afraid to ask questions, either. People will respect your concern and curiosity. You will gradually accumulate considerable knowledge, which will help you feel comfortable and be effective in a wide range of business situations.

JL-Pfeifer/Shutterstock

No other business skill can help you in as many ways as communication—in writing and in person.

REAL-TIME UPDATES

Learn More by Exploring This Interactive Website

Find the best place to launch your career

For more than 20 years, *Fortune* magazine has been ranking the best 100 companies to work for in the United States. Go to **real-timeupdates.com/bia9** and select Learn More in the Students section.

COMMUNICATING EFFECTIVELY

If you're looking for a surefire way to stand out from your competition and establish yourself as a competent professional, improving your communication skills may be the most important step you can take. Follow these guidelines to improve your effectiveness as a communicator:

- **Listen actively.** Active listening means making a conscious effort to turn off your own filters and biases to truly hear and understand what someone else is saying.
- **Provide practical information.** Give people useful information that is adapted to their specific needs.
- **Give facts rather than vague impressions.** Use concrete language, specific detail, and supporting information that is clear, convincing, accurate, and ethical.
- **Don't present opinions as facts.** If you are offering an opinion, make sure the audience understands that.
- **Present information in a concise, efficient manner.** Audiences appreciate—and respond more positively to—high-efficiency messages.
- **Clarify expectations and responsibilities.** Clearly state what you expect from your readers or listeners and what you can do for them.
- **Offer compelling, persuasive arguments and recommendations.** Make it clear to people how they will benefit from responding to your messages the way you would like them to.

MAKING ETHICAL DECISIONS

True professionals conduct themselves with a clear sense of right and wrong. They avoid committing *ethical lapses,* and they carefully weigh all the options when confronted with *ethical dilemmas.* Chapter 4 discusses these situations in more detail.

 CHECKPOINT

LEARNING OBJECTIVE 6: Identify six components of professionalism.

SUMMARY: Professionalism is the quality of performing at a high level and conducting yourself with purpose and pride. Six key traits of professionalism are striving to excel, being dependable and accountable, being a team player, demonstrating a sense of etiquette, communicating effectively, and making ethical decisions.

CRITICAL THINKING: (1) How much loyalty do employees owe to their employers? Explain your answer. (2) Would it be unethical to maintain a positive public persona if you have private doubts about the path your company is pursuing? Why or why not?

IT'S YOUR BUSINESS: (1) In what ways do you exhibit professionalism as a student? (2) You can see plenty of examples of unprofessional business behavior in the news media and in your own consumer and employee experiences. Why should you bother being professional yourself?

KEY TERMS TO KNOW: professionalism, etiquette

Thriving in the Digital Enterprise: Disruptive Technologies and Digital Transformation

7 **LEARNING OBJECTIVE**
Describe the concepts of disruptive innovation and digital transformation.

To a large extent, business strategy revolves around change—whether creating change, capitalizing on change, or surviving change. The basic concept of business is fixed: It's always going to be a question of adding value to satisfy customers in a way that generates a sustainable level of profit. However, the *way* that companies go about adding value and satisfying customers is always evolving, and the business world is currently going through an extraordinary set of changes that are likely to influence your career path for years to come.

These changes all revolve around digital technology and involve connectivity, communication (including mobile devices and social media), and AI. A **digital enterprise** is any company that uses these technologies as one of the foundations of its value-creation processes, regardless of what industry it is in or what products it makes.

digital enterprise
Any company that uses digital systems as one of the foundations of its value-creation processes, regardless of what industry it is in or what products it makes.

As you get ready to enter or reenter the workforce or continue to advance in your career if you're already working, it's important to be aware of this concept of the digital enterprise. Executives across many industries are wrestling with how to apply digital technologies in their companies, and they'll be looking for employees who are comfortable working in a digital environment. And, as you near graduation and begin your job search, you'll want to be able to recognize which companies are succeeding at this complex effort and which are still struggling with it.

To help you prepare, the final section in each chapter of this book explores aspects of life in the digital enterprise, with an emphasis on knowledge you can use to thrive in this dynamic business environment. In this chapter, we look at two important concepts that will give you a better perspective on all these changes: *disruptive innovations* and *digital transformation.*

A digital enterprise relies on a variety of digital tools and systems to maximize productivity and customer satisfaction.

DISRUPTIVE INNOVATIONS

Some changes in the business environment happen gradually and often predictably, such as when an aging consumer population increases or decreases demand for particular goods and services or when a particular brand or type of product falls out of fashion. Companies need to anticipate and respond to such changes, but they don't fundamentally alter the way businesses operate.

disruptive innovation
Development so fundamentally different and far reaching that it can create new professions, companies, or even entire industries while damaging or destroying others.

Other types of changes, however, can be downright traumatic—or exciting, depending on whether you're benefiting from a change or getting steamrolled by it. Online retailing, digital music, mobile communication, and social media are examples of changes that permanently shifted the way many consumers behave and many businesses operate. Each of these is a **disruptive innovation**, a development so fundamentally different and far reaching that it can create new professions, companies, or even entire industries while damaging or destroying others.

As one measure of the power of technology-driven disruption, half the companies on the Fortune 500 list (the largest corporations in the United States) in 2000 had disappeared from the list 15 years later.[8] They had gone bankrupt, had shrunk off the list, had been left in the dust by faster-growing firms, or were acquired by or merged into other companies. And the future doesn't look any more stable to some observers. Former Cisco CEO John Chambers, whose career essentially spanned the rise of digital technology, famously predicted that 40 percent of large corporations will not adapt quickly enough to digital disruption and "will not exist in a meaningful way" by the year 2025.[9]

Disruptive technologies are an intriguing phenomenon, for several reasons. First, predicting whether a new technology will be truly disruptive is difficult. In many cases, multiple other forces from the technological, economic, social, and legal regulatory environments need to converge before an innovation has a major impact. For instance, without broadband wireless networks, a digital communication infrastructure, data encryption methods, a vast array of free and low-cost apps, mobile-friendly web services, and more computing power than computers used to have, a smartphone would just be an expensive way to make phone calls. With the combined impact of all these innovations, mobile phones have changed the way many people live and the way many businesses operate. Keep this in mind if you're considering joining a company with a promising new product that hasn't caught on yet—what other changes need to occur before the product and the company will succeed?

Second, predicting *when* the disruption will happen is just as difficult. Many promising technologies can take years to have an impact. Mobile phones and handheld computers had been around for two or three decades before all the pieces fell into place and the smartphone era took off. Intriguing new inventions can generate a lot of interest, press coverage, and "hype" long before they have any real impact on business, and expectations sometimes outpace what the technology can deliver. This pattern repeats so often that the management consulting firm Gartner has modeled a five-stage roller-coaster curve it calls the Hype Cycle (see Exhibit 1.8).

Third, predicting the eventual impact of a disruption is also challenging. AI is finally going mainstream as a business tool after many decades of hopes and hype, but its long-term impact is difficult to gauge at this point. Millions of jobs involve tasks and decisions that AI could conceivably do (and is now doing in many cases), but it's impossible to pin down how disruptive it will be to the job market. AI will redefine many jobs, eliminate some, and create some—and people in most professions should be prepared to learn new skills and adapt as opportunities and expectations change.[10]

The best advice you can move forward with is to keep your eyes and ears open to innovations that could affect your career and your company. Carefully consider the predictions you hear, but before you make any major career decisions, ask yourself what will have to happen for those predictions to come true. Predicting the future is always a dicey proposition, but with a skeptical approach, you have a better chance of separating reasonable projections from pie-in-the-sky wishful thinking.

DIGITAL TRANSFORMATION

The first and broadest disruptive technology to consider is related to this notion of the digital enterprise. Companies such as Amazon, Facebook, and Affectiva, the company that

EXHIBIT 1.8	The Gartner Hype Cycle

The consulting firm Gartner devised this visual model to map the evolution of technological innovations over time. The cycle starts when an innovation begins to capture attention, even if no practical business uses have been proven yet. Media coverage then builds expectations, often above and beyond what the technology is currently capable of delivering. Almost inevitably, these expectations are dashed, and a backlash of disillusionment sets in when the technology can't meet those inflated expectations. However, if the technology truly has potential, customers gradually gain experience with it and get a more accurate sense of what it can do, and it eventually becomes a productive business resource.

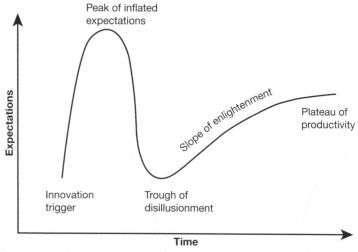

Courtesy of Gartner, Inc.

Rana el Kaliouby cofounded to commercialize her AI software (see page 72), started out "digital," but many others have roots in the so-called brick-and-mortar world of manufacturing, retailing, and other industries. Many of these companies are going through a **digital transformation** to become digital enterprises. Businesses as diverse as car companies, grocery stores, oil and gas producers, pharmaceutical companies, heavy equipment manufacturers, and banks are adopting *digital strategies* to serve customers better, operate more efficiently, and stave off new competitive threats. Many executives now believe it is imperative to "disrupt themselves" through digital transformation rather than waiting until other companies force disruption on them.[11]

digital transformation
Process of reimagining a company's business model and operations to become a digital enterprise.

Digital transformation can incorporate a variety of technologies, including *big data*, the Internet of Things, cloud computing, social media, mobile apps, AI, robotics, and robotic process automation (see Exhibit 1.9 on the next page).[12] Most of these innovations are covered in future chapters and Appendix C, Information Technology.

The speed at which this phenomenon hit the business world is rather amazing. In a 2015 cross-industry survey, fewer than 1 percent of executives believed that digital technology would disrupt their industries. Only two years later, more than 75 percent said it would have a "major" or "transformative" impact, and half the companies in another survey said they were already working on digital transformations.[13]

In industry after industry, companies are scrambling to transform themselves by implementing new business models or optimizing existing models. With a product portfolio consisting of locomotives, ship engines, oil drilling motors, and other heavy equipment, GE Transportation might seem far removed from the digital world of cloud computing and smartphone apps. However, the company has reinvented itself as a digital solutions provider to help customers operate more efficiently and more safely. Its innovations range from real-time monitoring systems that feed data into AI systems to tell when an engine needs maintenance to *digital twins*—detailed, continuously updated digital models of locomotives and other machines that can be used for such purposes as troubleshooting their physical counterparts and simulating usage scenarios.[14]

REAL-TIME UPDATES
Learn More by Reading These Articles

The evolving relationship between us and our robot colleagues

This special series on GeekWire looks at the many facets of human-robot collaboration. Go to **real-timeupdates.com/bia9** and select Learn More in the Students section.

EXHIBIT 1.9	Elements of Digital Transformation and Optimization

Companies can use a wide range of techniques and technologies to optimize specific aspects of their operations or to completely transform their business models. In addition to the technologies listed here, social media and mobile computing and communication also play key roles in many digitization efforts.

Business model reimagination	Rethinking what value a company should create for its customers and how it should create that value
Process optimization	Redesigning or refining existing business processes to make them more effective and more efficient
Big data and analytics	*Big data* refers to the massive flows of data coming from customer records, social media, process sensors, financial transactions, and many other sources; *analytics* encompasses a variety of computer-driven efforts to extract meaning from all those data, often using forms of artificial intelligence
Internet of Things (IoT)	Refers to the many billions of devices now connected to the internet, from simple sensors to complex machinery; the goal of IoT is to make systems smarter, more autonomous, and more responsive to user needs
Cloud computing	An on-demand approach to computing in which companies essentially rent online computing capacity and software from a service provider, rather than buying and maintaining the assets themselves ("cloud" here refers somewhat vaguely to the internet, since cloud computing is accessed via the internet)
Robotic process automation	Aims to do for knowledge work what robots do for manufacturing and other physical processes; targets the high-volume "paperwork" aspects of business and can automate some of the routine communication that this sort of work typically involves
Artificial intelligence	The application of computing power to replicate one of more aspects of human intelligence; generally speaking, it's a three-stage process: collecting data or information, analyzing or processing that input to make decisions, then applying the results of that decision-making activity
Digital twins	Accurate, detailed digital models of equipment that update in real time using data from their physical counterparts; can aid in troubleshooting, predictive maintenance, and design improvement
Low-code app development	Systems that allow subject-matter experts to create apps without having in-depth programming knowledge or skills

Sources: Based in part on Laura Cox, "At a Glance—Digital Twins," *Disruption*, 11 December 2017, disruptionhub.com; "Big Data: What It Is and Why It Matters," SAS, accessed 23 January 2018, www.sas.com; Steve Ranger, "What Is the IoT? Everything You Need to Know About the Internet of Things Right Now," *ZDNet*, 19 January 2018, www.zdnet.com; Eric Knorr, "What Is Cloud Computing? Everything You Need to Know Now," *InfoWorld*, 10 July 2017, www.infoworld.com.

Digital transformation can be difficult and complex, and not all companies are seeing a positive outcome from the effort. True transformation means rethinking how a company creates value and how it is managed, making the human element as important as the technical elements. Transformation can require people to give up control and step out of their comfort zones. At a less-comprehensive level, companies can benefit from optimizing existing processes, although it's important to make sure they're not just getting better at doing the wrong things. However a firm approaches it, experts say companies that are best at digital transformation will reap the lion's share of the business benefits, so transformation itself has become a vital management skill.[15]

For more perspective on developing a business mindset and becoming a successful professional, visit **real-timeupdates.com/bia9** and select Chapter 1.

CHECKPOINT

LEARNING OBJECTIVE 7: Describe the concepts of disruptive innovation and digital transformation.

SUMMARY: A disruptive innovation is a development so fundamentally different and far reaching that it can create new professions, companies, or even entire industries while damaging or destroying others. Digital transformation is the process of reimagining a company's business model and operations to become a digital enterprise—any company that uses advanced digital technologies as one of the foundations of its value-creation processes.

CRITICAL THINKING: (1) Consider a local coffee shop or café that doesn't sell anything digital. Can it still become a digital enterprise? Explain your answer. (2) How many of the technologies and services you routinely use in your daily life were once disruptive innovation?

IT'S YOUR BUSINESS: (1) If you don't have much interest in technology and are instead intrigued by finance, sales, or some other aspect of business, how can you still thrive in a digital enterprise? (2) Would you consider going to work for a company that is betting its future on a potentially disruptive innovation that hasn't yet taken hold in the marketplace? Why or why not?

KEY TERMS TO KNOW: digital enterprise, disruptive innovation, digital transformation

Developing Skills for Your Career

In addition to giving you insights into every major aspect of business, this course offers multiple opportunities to develop essential skills in seven areas:

- **Communication.** "Communicating Effectively" on page 66 highlights how important communication skills are at every stage in your career. For hands-on practice, you can complete the Sharpening Your Communication Skills activity at the end of every chapter.
- **Critical thinking.** In many of the assignments and activities, you will need to define and solve problems and make decisions or form judgments about a particular situation or set of circumstances. To give you plenty of practice, you'll find Critical Thinking questions in the Checkpoints within each chapter, three more Critical Thinking questions in the Behind the Scenes case wrap-up at the end of each chapter, and several Questions for Analysis in the Test Your Knowledge section at the end of each chapter.
- **Collaboration.** Depending on the configuration of your course, you will have various opportunities to work with classmates on reports, presentations, and other projects. The Building Your Team Skills projects are great opportunities to practice collaboration while solving realistic business challenges.
- **Knowledge application and analysis.** The ability to learn a concept and then apply that knowledge to other challenges is a skill that employers value highly. The Questions for Application at the end of every chapter will help you practice. The It's Your Business questions in the Checkpoints within each chapter and Growing as a Professional section at the end of each chapter also provide the chance to engage in reflective thinking related to knowledge you will acquire throughout the course.
- **Business ethics and social responsibility.** As you work on projects throughout the course, be mindful of the ethical implications you could encounter in similar projects on the job. To practice, look for questions labeled Ethical Considerations in the Test Your Knowledge section and the Ethical Dilemmas activity in the Practice Your Skills section.

⑧ LEARNING OBJECTIVE

Identify seven essential business skills that you will have the opportunity to develop during this course.

- **Information technology skills.** Your instructor may ask you to use a variety of digital media as you work on the various exercises and activities throughout the course. Use projects and activities to build your skills with technology, including word-processing apps, spreadsheets, presentation software, blogging, and messaging systems.
- **Data literacy.** You'll have multiple opportunities to fine-tune your data literacy skills, which include the ability to access, assess, interpret, manipulate, summarize, and communicate data. Many of the activities throughout the book involve practicing your research and information analysis skills, including Discovering Career Opportunities and Intelligent Business Technology in the Expand Your Knowledge section and Developing Your Research Skills in the Practice Your Skills section in each chapter.

BEHIND THE SCENES

An Unexpected Turn Launches an Innovative New Company

Rana el Kaliouby had her career plan in place: Conduct research in artificial intelligence aimed at helping people on the autism spectrum. Together with professor Rosalind Picard, her mentor at the MIT Media Lab who pioneered the field of *affective computing* (computing that involves human emotion), she was able to demonstrate how computers can be trained to recognize and respond to human emotion.

However, that career trajectory took an unexpected turn when their AI tools began to catch the attention of the lab's various corporate sponsors, who besieged them for advice and assistance on applying this technology to business problems. With so many potential opportunities to pursue, the lab's management decided the best move was to spin out the project as its own company, and el Kaliouby and Picard became the cofounders of Affectiva. El Kaliouby was reluctant to leave her work in academia and dilute her focus on helping people with autism, but the lab's director convinced her that commercializing the software and applying it in multiple ways would improve the AI techniques it relies on.

Like many young companies, Affectiva encountered some conflicts as it found its footing. The firm's original CEO, a sales executive the founders brought on board to help launch the company, wanted to focus on marketing the software for advertising testing, not on health care or assistive technologies such as the autism tool el Kaliouby had envisioned. The demand for advertising applications took precedence, and the company achieved early success in this market.

Businesses spend billions of dollars on advertising every year, and the managers spending that money are understandably curious to know whether their ads are triggering the emotional responses they are designed to elicit. Affectiva partnered with Millward Brown, a major market research company, which became an investor in the company and continues to use its primary product, Affdex, to test thousands of ads every year.

Part of any start-up experience is clarifying organizational values, which Affectiva did on multiple occasions when potential customers wanted to do things with the technology that Picard and el Kaliouby did not support. Picard described how difficult it can be for a company to turn away opportunities, particularly when it is new and trying to build revenue. However, Affectiva is adamant that its products will not be used to spy on people or measure anyone's emotional state without their consent, so the company continues to turn away potential customers who don't share its values in this regard.

Start-ups often go through leadership changes as well. Picard served as Affectiva's chief scientist until 2013, when she left to cofound a company that makes smart, wearable medical devices, including one for people with epilepsy. El Kaliouby stepped into the CEO's role in 2016.

Since that initial move into advertising testing, el Kaliouby and her team have been applying the technology in many other areas. More than a thousand companies use it in such diverse efforts as education, health care, television and movies, gaming, legal depositions, and human resources. In fact, don't be surprised if you encounter an online video interview during your job search that uses Affectiva's system, or something similar, to measure your emotional reactions. Affectiva has also expanded into voice analysis, giving businesses another way to assess their communication efforts. "Emotion AI," as Affectiva refers to its technology, is likely to play a role in the next generation of automobiles as well, such as by monitoring driver attention and emotion levels in self-driving cars during the critical "hand-off" moments when the car takes control from the driver and vice versa.

The original dream of helping people with autism hasn't been forgotten, either. A company called Brain Power incorporates Affectiva's capabilities in Google Glass eyeglasses, creating a system that provides children and adults on the autism spectrum with real-time feedback that helps them develop skills needed to navigate social situations. Another company uses the technology to help stroke victims recover and rebuild cognitive skills.

Beyond these specific applications, el Kaliouby wants people to understand how important it is for AI systems to have empathy, both to be more effective and to make sure that AI becomes a positive force in people's lives, rather than a negative one. AI is reaching deeper into just about every aspect of business, and the better that computers can get along with us, the better we'll be able to get along with them.[16]

Critical Thinking Questions

1-1. Rana el Kaliouby refers to herself as the "chief evangelist" for Affectiva. What do you think this means in a business context, and how important is this activity for a CEO?

1-2. How does Affectiva add value in the markets where it does business?

1-3. How might the social environment influence Affectiva's growth in the future?

Learn More Online

Explore Affectiva and its products at **www.affectiva.com**. If you're curious, you can try the Emotion AI technology yourself, either on the company's website or through its mobile app. Read the explanation of how the company's software works. Do you find the descriptions and explanations convincing? If you were an advertiser, would you be intrigued enough to test your ads this way?

End of Chapter

KEY TERMS

barriers to entry (58)
business (49)
business mindset (52)
business model (49)
competitive advantage (50)
digital enterprise (67)
digital transformation (69)
disruptive innovation (68)
economic environment (57)
etiquette (66)
gig economy (57)
information technology (IT) (62)

legal and regulatory environment (57)
market environment (58)
not-for-profit organizations (50)
operations management (61)
professionalism (64)
profit (49)
research and development (R&D) (59)
revenue (49)
social environment (56)
stakeholders (56)
technological environment (57)

TEST YOUR KNOWLEDGE

Questions for Review

1-4. What is the difference between revenue and profit?

1-5. What are some examples of risk?

1-6. How would you describe a business mindset?

1-7. What are four potential ways that business activity can cause harm?

1-8. Why does a business have a responsibility to its stakeholders?

1-9. What do operations managers do? What are their additional responsibilities?

1-10. How does the role of a marketing specialist differ from that of a sales professional?

1-11. What is professionalism?

1-12. What is a digital enterprise?

1-13. What is digital transformation?

Questions for Analysis

1-14. Would you consider a job offer from a company if the company's recruiters have trouble describing the firm's business model? Why or why not?

1-15. Does a downturn in the economy hurt all companies equally? Provide several examples to support your answer.

1-16. **Ethical Considerations.** Is managing a business in ways that reflect society's core values always ethical? Explain your answer.

1-17. How can business knowledge and skills help social entrepreneurs reach their goals?

1-18. Why is it so difficult to predict whether an innovation might disrupt an industry and when it could happen?

Questions for Application

1-19. How will you be able to apply your experience as a consumer of educational services to the challenges you'll face in your career after graduation?

1-20. If you were planning to launch an AI-related company like Affectiva, which elements of the social environment should you be aware of?

1-21. What are some of the ways in which a company in the health-care industry could improve its long-term planning by studying population trends?

1-22. Identify three ways in which the principles of professionalism described in this chapter can make you a more successful student.

1-23. What are some of the ways a locally owned retail store could become a digital enterprise?

EXPAND YOUR KNOWLEDGE

Discovering Career Opportunities

Today, there are several ways to seek advice and access resources that can help you find your career. Consider the different ways you might be able to find such help. Select one of these methods and create a poster that explains its uses and advantages.

Intelligent Business Technology: Text Mining

Text mining, a type of data analytics, uses natural language processing to extract meaning from textual sources. For instance, companies can use it for *social listening* to identify themes (such as prevailing customer sentiment or threats to a company's reputation) hidden in mountains of written information, from Twitter and Facebook posts to customer emails and surveys. Research one current business application of text mining and write a one-paragraph summary of how companies are using it and how it helps them compete or satisfy customers more effectively.

PRACTICE YOUR SKILLS

Resolving Ethical Dilemmas

Imagine that you have travelled to many countries and have developed a taste for and interest in street food. Now that you have completed your degree program, you are in a position to obtain sufficient funding to set up one small food outlet in your local neighborhood. You feel that street food is a vital part of anyone's travel experience, as authentic cuisine can instantly provide customers with the feel of a particular place. Globally, street food is growing in popularity as compared to celebrity-endorsed brands since it is considered honest and wholesome. Your street food will be vegan and based on South Asian *aloo chaat* (potato with spices and chutney). It is easy to prepare and serve.

You need to find talented employees who will buy into the concept and successfully sell the food at the new outlet. However, there is no guarantee that the business will be successful. In a brief report, identify some general steps you could take to reduce the risk for employees and how you would communicate the ways you would add value for customers when you pitch the idea.

Growing as a Professional

Don't wait until you're on the job to develop your professionalism. College gives you multiple opportunities to hone your approach to work, which will help you hit the ground running after you graduate. The sooner you can get in sync with the professional work environment, the sooner you are likely to succeed in your first job and position yourself for a promotion. If you are already working or have worked in a business setting, think about the ways you could make an even stronger impression, and fine-tune those skills.

Communication is the single most important skill you can have in business, so use every interaction with your instructors as a chance to practice. If you have ever started an email message to an instructor with "Yo, prof," now would be a good time to up your game. Imagine that you are communicating with a high-level executive or someone else whose opinion of you will have a huge impact on your career advancement. You don't have to be stiff and overly formal; read the situation based on how each instructor communicates with you. Use a respectful greeting (ask your instructors how they would like to be greeted in person and in writing, if they haven't already told you), complete sentences, and standard punctuation.

How would you rate the quality of your interactions with your instructors? What could you do to improve communication? Do you feel awkward when communicating at a more formal level than you are accustomed to in your personal or social life? What steps can you take to get comfortable with "professional-grade" communication before you graduate?

Sharpening Your Communication Skills

Identify a service-based company you are familiar with and answer the following questions: What identifies this company as a service provider? What role do the customers play? Why are they important to your chosen company? What could the company do to attract more customers? Present your analysis to the rest of the class.

Building Your Team Skills

In teams assigned by your instructor, each member should first identify one career path (such as marketing or accounting) that he or she might like to pursue and share that choice with the rest of the team. Each team member should then research the others' career options to find at least one significant factor, positive or negative, that could affect someone entering that career. For example, if there are four people on your team, you will research the three careers identified by your three teammates. After the research is complete, convene an in-person or online meeting to give each member of the team an informal career counseling session based on the research findings.

Developing Your Research Skills

Gaining a competitive advantage in today's marketplace is critical to a company's success. Research any company that sounds interesting to you, and identify the steps it has taken to create competitive advantages for individual products or the company as a whole.

1-24. What goods or services does the company manufacture or sell?

1-25. How does the company set its goods or services apart from those of its competitors? Does the company compete on price, quality, service, innovation, or some other attribute?

1-26. How do the company's customer communication efforts convey those competitive advantages?

Writing Assignments

1-27. If individual accountability is an essential element of professionalism, why is it also important to be an effective team player? Explain your answer.

1-28. Do laws and regulations always restrict or impede the efforts of business professionals, or can they actually help businesses? Explain your answer.

ENDNOTES

1. Todd Wasserman, "5 Questions with Affectiva's Rana el Kaliouby," *DeeplyAI*, 2 January 2018, deeplyai.com; Rana el Kaliouby profile, LinkedIn, accessed 1 January 2018, www.linkedin.com/in/kaliouby; David Pring-Mill, "Tech Is Becoming Emotionally Intelligent, and It's Big Business," *SingularityHub*, 2 November 2017, singularityhub.com; Raffi Khatchadourian, "We Know How You Feel," *New Yorker*, 19 January 2015, www.newyorker.com; Khari Johnson, "Affectiva CEO: AI Needs Emotional Intelligence to Facilitate Human-Robot Interaction," *VentureBeat*, 9 December 2017, venturebeat.com; Brain Power campaign page on Indeigogo, accessed 1 January 2018, www.indiegogo.com; Affectiva website, accessed 1 January 2018, www.affectiva.com; Bernard Marr, "The Next Frontier of Artificial Intelligence: Building Machines That Read Your Emotions," *Forbes*, 15 December 2017, www.forbes.com; Rana el Kaliouby, "After a Year as a CEO, I've Learned 4 Things Matter More Than Anything Else," *Inc.*, 30 August 2017, www.inc.com.

2. "The World's 50 Largest Companies Based on Number of Employees in 2016," Statista, www.statista.com.

3. "Firm Data Size," U.S. Small Business Administration, accessed 18 January 2018, www.sba.gov.

4. "Amount of Revenue by Source," Tax Policy Center, 15 February 2017, www.taxpolicycenter.org.

5. Zvi Schreiber, "Is Logistics About to Get Amazon'ed?" *TechCrunch*, 29 January 2016, techcrunch.com.

6. Career profiles in this section based in part on *Occupational Outlook Handbook*, U.S. Bureau of Labor Statistics, www.bls.gov/ooh.

7. "Why We Need to Kick Incivility Out of the Office," *Knowledge@Wharton*, 30 June 2017, knowledge.wharton.upenn.edu.

8. Pierre Nanterme, "Digital Disruption Has Only Just Begun," World Economic Forum, 17 January 2016, www.weforum.org.

9. "Cisco's John Chambers on the Digital Era," McKinsey, March 2016, www.mckinsey.com.

10. Arwa Mahdawi, "What Jobs Will Still Be Around in 20 Years? Read This to Prepare Your Future," *Guardian*, 26 June 2017, www.theguardian.com.

11. Chris Preimesberger, "KPMG Survey of CEOs Shows Serious Issues with Digital Transformations," *eWeek*, 21 August 2017, 5.

12. "A Crisis in Digital Transformation," Wipro Digital presentation, 1 June 2017, www.slideshare.net.

13. Alex Moore, "Digitizing the Organization," *TD*, June 2017, 18–21; Andy Noronha, "How Companies Are Fighting Threats from Amazon and Digital Disruption," *CNBC*, 11 September 2017, www.cnbc.com.

14. GE Transportation website, accessed 23 January 2018, www.getransportation.com; Sarah Lukens, "A Digital Twin Approach for Designing Cost-Effective Maintenance Strategies," GE, accessed 23 January 2018, www.ge.com; Charles Babcock, "GE Plans Software Platform for Creating 'Digital Twins,'" *InformationWeek*, 20 July 2016, www.informationweek.com.

15. Tom Puthiyamadam, "How the Meaning of Digital Transformation Has Evolved," *Harvard Business Review*, 29 May 2017, hbr.org; Sam Del Rowe, "Digital Transformation Needs to Happen Now," *Customer Relationship Management*, October 2017, 30–33; Jacques Bughin, Tanguy Catlin, Martin Hirt, and Paul Willmott, "Why Digital Strategies Fail," *McKinsey Quarterly*, January 2018, www.mckinsey.com; Jacques Bughin, Laura LaBerge, and Anette Mellbye, "The Case for Digital Reinvention," *McKinsey Quarterly*, February 2017, www.mckinsey.com; Jacques Bughin and Nicholas Van Zeebroeck, "6 Digital Strategies, and Why Some Work Better Than Others," *Harvard Business Review*, 31 July 2017, hbr.org; "A Crisis in Digital Transformation," Wipro Digital.

16. See note 1.

2 Economics, Money, and Banking

LEARNING OBJECTIVES   After studying this chapter, you will be able to

1 Define *economics*, explain why scarcity is central to economic decision making, and identify the major ways of measuring economic activity.

2 Define *economic system*, and explain the government's role in a free-market economy.

3 Explain the interaction between demand and supply.

4 Identify four macroeconomic issues that are essential to understanding the behavior of the economy.

5 List the four financial functions of money, and define two key measures of the money supply.

6 Explain the role of the Federal Reserve System, list the major types of banking institutions, and summarize banking's role in the economy.

7 Define *fintech*, and discuss five ways that financial institutions are innovating with digital technology.

MyLab Intro to Business
Improve Your Grade!
If your instructor is using MyLab Intro to Business, visit **www.pearson.com/ mylab/intro-to-business**.

BEHIND THE SCENES | JPMorgan Chase: Racing to Reinvent Banking

JPMorgan Chase CEO Jamie Dimon guides the company's business strategy amid an ongoing technological revolution.

Kristoffer Tripplaar/Alamy Stock Photo

www.jpmorganchase.com

"Silicon Valley is coming."

Throughout history, keeping a sharp lookout for hostile invaders has been an essential survival skill. In today's banking business, firms need to fend off competitive threats not only from each other, but also from a wave of invaders from outside the realm of banking.

These hungry hordes are armed with cloud computing, mobile apps, artificial intelligence, and other technologies—and the intention to disrupt the banking sector with new services and new ways to deliver existing services.

Jamie Dimon, CEO of the bank holding company JPMorgan Chase, knows all about the threat that his bank and others like it face from the digital invaders. When he warned shareholders that "Silicon Valley is coming," he pointed out that "there are hundreds of startups with a lot of brains and money working on various alter-natives to traditional banking." In other words, these newcomers are creating alternatives to the banking services that JPMorgan Chase has been providing in one form or another since 1799.

If you were leading JPMorgan Chase, how would you respond to this digital threat? Would you do more of the same with traditional banking functions and relationships? Shift your focus entirely to mobile and digital to confront the invaders head on? Or perhaps try a blended strategy, combining the best of the old with the best of the new?[1]

INTRODUCTION

Economic forces affect every aspect of running a business, whether it's a local coffee shop or a global giant such as JPMorgan Chase (profiled in the chapter-opening Behind the Scenes). This chapter offers a brief introduction to economics from a business professional's perspective, including the interaction of supply and demand and the macro view of the economy. The second half explores money, banking, and the digital revolution known as *fintech*.

What Is This Thing Called the Economy?

The **economy** is the sum of all economic activity within a given region, from a city to a country to the entire world. The economy can be a difficult thing to wrap your mind around because it is complex, constantly in motion, a subject of heated dispute, and at times hard to see—even though it's everywhere around us. People who devote their lives to studying it can have a hard time agreeing on how the economy works, when it might be "broken," or how to fix it if it is broken. However, business leaders need to understand and pay attention to some key principles.

Economics is the study of how a society uses its scarce resources to produce and distribute goods and services. Economics is roughly divided into a small-scale perspective and a large-scale perspective. The study of economic behavior by consumers, businesses, and industries that collectively determine the quantity of goods and services demanded and supplied at different prices is termed *microeconomics*. The study of larger economic issues, such as unemployment, the effect of government policies, and how a country maintains and allocates its scarce resources, is termed *macroeconomics*.[2]

Although microeconomics looks at the small picture and macroeconomics looks at the big picture, understanding the economy at either scale requires an understanding of how the small and large forces interact. For instance, numerous macro forces and policies determine whether families can afford to buy or redecorate homes. In turn, the aggregate behavior of all those homeowners at the micro level affects the vitality and direction of the overall economy.

FACTORS OF PRODUCTION

Each society must decide how to use its economic resources, or **factors of production** (see Exhibit 2.1). *Natural resources* are things that are useful in their natural state, such as land, forests, minerals, and water. *Human resources* are people and their individual talents and capacities. *Capital* includes money, machines, tools, and buildings that a business needs in order to produce goods and services. *Entrepreneurship* is the spirit of innovation, the initiative, and the willingness to take the risks involved in creating and operating businesses. *Knowledge* is the collective intelligence of an organization. *Knowledge workers*, employees whose primary contribution is the acquisition and application of business knowledge, are a key economic resource for businesses in today's economy.

Traditionally, a business or a country was considered to have an advantage if its location offered plentiful supplies of natural resources, human resources, capital, and entrepreneurs. In today's global marketplace, however, intellectual assets are often the key. Companies can easily obtain capital from one part of the world, purchase supplies from another, and locate production facilities in still another. They can relocate some of their operations to

1 LEARNING OBJECTIVE
Define *economics*, explain why scarcity is central to economic decision making, and identify the major ways of measuring economic activity.

economy
The sum of all economic activity within a given region.

economics
The study of how a society uses its scarce resources to produce and distribute goods and services.

factors of production
Economic resources, including natural resources, human resources, capital, entrepreneurship, and knowledge.

EXHIBIT 2.1   **Factors of Production**

Every good or service is created from some combination of these five factors of production.

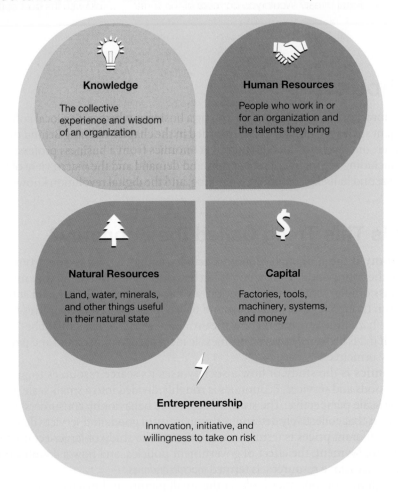

wherever they find a steady supply of affordable workers, or they can assemble virtual teams of knowledge workers from anywhere on the planet. Chapter 3 discusses this issue of economic globalization in more detail.

THE ECONOMIC IMPACT OF SCARCITY

scarcity
A condition of any productive resource that has finite supply.

The impact of **scarcity**, meaning that a given resource has a finite supply, is fundamental to understanding economics.[3] By looking back over the factors of production, you can see that the supply of all these resources is limited. Even entrepreneurial energy is limited in the sense that there are only so many entrepreneurs in the economy, and each entrepreneur can accomplish only so much during a given time span.

Scarcity has two powerful effects: It creates competition for resources, and it forces trade-offs on the part of every participant in the economy. First, at every stage of economic activity, people and organizations compete for the resources they need. Businesses and industries compete with each other for materials, employees, and customers. As a consumer, you compete with other consumers. If you were the only person in town who needed a loaf of bread, you would have tremendous power over the bakeries and grocery stores as the only customer. However, because you compete with thousands of other consumers for a limited supply of bread, you have far less control over the bread market.

Second, this universal scarcity of resources means that consumers, companies, and governments are constantly forced to make *trade-offs*—giving up one thing to get something else. You have to decide how to spend the 24 hours you have every day, and every choice involves a trade-off: The more time you spend on one activity means less time for every other activity you could possibly pursue. Businesses must make similar trade-offs, such as deciding how much money to spend on advertising a new product versus how much to spend on the materials used to make it, or deciding how many employees to have in sales versus in customer support. Just like you, businesses never have enough time, money, and other resources to accomplish what they'd like to, so success in life and in business is largely a matter of making smart trade-offs.

By the way, economists have a name for the most attractive option not selected when making a trade-off. *Opportunity cost* refers to the value of the most appealing alternative from all those that weren't chosen.[4] In other words, opportunity cost is a way to measure the value of what you gave up when you pursued a different opportunity.

ECONOMIC MEASURES AND MONITORS

Economic indicators are statistics such as interest rates, unemployment rates, housing data, and industrial productivity that let business and political leaders measure and monitor economic performance (see Exhibit 2.2). *Leading indicators* suggest changes that may happen to the economy in the future and are therefore valuable for planning. In contrast, *lagging indicators* provide confirmation that something has occurred in the past.

Housing starts, for example, are a leading indicator showing where several industries are headed. When housing starts drop, the construction industry contracts, and the effect soon ripples through other sectors of the economy, from the manufacture of plumbing fixtures, carpet, and appliances to a variety of services, including furniture retailing, real estate sales, and other areas that are dependent on housing-related transactions.

Another key leading indicator is *durable-goods orders*, or orders for goods that typically last more than three years (which can mean everything from desk chairs to airplanes). A rise in durable-goods orders is a positive indicator that business spending is turning around. In addition to these indicators, economists closely monitor several *price indexes* and the nation's economic output to get a sense of how well the economy is working.

In contrast, corporate profits and unemployment are among the key lagging indicators.[5] For example, companies tend to reduce their workforces after the economy has slowed down and sales revenues have dropped. Although they don't have the predictive power of leading indicators, lagging indicators give policymakers insights into how the economy is functioning and whether corrective steps might be needed.

economic indicators
Statistics that measure the performance of the economy.

EXHIBIT 2.2	Key Economic Indicators

Here are some of the key indicators that help policymakers and business leaders assess the state of the economy.

Indicator	Implications
Housing starts	Housing is a major component of the economy, and each new house built triggers a cascade of demand for related goods and services, so a rise or fall in the number of new houses under construction suggests that demand for all those related goods and services will expand or shrink as well.
Durable-goods orders	Similar to housing starts, sales of durable goods such as cars, appliances, and machinery suggest the economic health and confidence of consumers and businesses; if orders are declining, for instance, it indicates that buyers could have a pessimistic outlook on the economy.
Price indexes	The various consumer and producer price indexes indicate whether the economy is heating up or cooling off.
Unemployment rate	As a lagging indicator, unemployment rates don't have the predictive power of other indicators, but they can confirm the direction in which the economy has moved.
Gross domestic product (GDP)	As a measure of the total output of the economy, a rising or falling GDP suggests trends in the overall health of business.

Price Indexes

Price changes, especially price increases, are a significant economic indicator. *Price indexes* offer a way to monitor the inflation or deflation in various sectors of the economy. An index is simply a convenient way to compare numbers over time and is computed by dividing the current value of some quantity by a baseline historical value and then multiplying by 100. Rather than saying something has increased by 28 percent, for example, economists would say the index is at 128.

Government statisticians compute a wide variety of price indexes, each designed to monitor a particular aspect of economic activity. The best known of these, the **consumer price index (CPI)**, measures the rate of inflation by comparing the change in prices of a representative "basket" of consumer goods and services, such as clothing, food, housing, and transportation. The CPI has always been a hot topic because of its many uses. For example, the federal government uses it to adjust Social Security payments, businesses use it to calculate cost-of-living increases for employees, and many use it to gauge how well the government is keeping inflation under control.[6]

consumer price index (CPI)
A monthly statistic that measures changes in the prices of a representative collection of consumer goods and services.

In contrast to the CPI, the **producer price index (PPI)** measures prices at the producer or wholesaler level, reflecting what businesses are paying for the products they need. (Like the CPI, the PPI is often referred to as a single index, but it is actually a family of more than 600 industry-specific indexes.) In addition to monitoring economic activity, PPIs have a number of managerial uses, from helping companies place an accurate value on inventories to protecting buyers and sellers with *price-escalation clauses* in long-term purchasing contracts.[7]

producer price index (PPI)
A statistical measure of price trends at the producer and wholesaler levels.

National Economic Output

The broadest measure of an economy's health is the **gross domestic product (GDP)**. The GDP measures a country's output—its production, distribution, and use of goods and services—by computing the sum of all goods and services produced for *final* use in a country during a specified period (usually a year). The products may be produced by either domestic or foreign companies as long as the production takes place within a nation's boundaries. Sales from a Honda assembly plant in Ohio, for instance, would be included in the U.S. GDP, even though Honda is a Japanese company. Monitoring GDP helps a nation evaluate its economic policies and compare current performance with prior periods or with the performance of other nations.

gross domestic product (GDP)
The value of all the final goods and services produced by businesses located within a nation's borders; excludes outputs from overseas operations of domestic companies.

GDP has largely replaced a previous measure called the *gross national product (GNP)*, which excludes the value of production from foreign-owned businesses within a nation's boundaries and includes receipts from the overseas operations of domestic companies. GNP considers *who* is responsible for the production; GDP considers *where* the production occurs.

 CHECKPOINT

LEARNING OBJECTIVE 1: Define *economics*, explain why scarcity is central to economic decision making, and identify the major ways of measuring economic activity.

SUMMARY: Economics is the study of how individuals, companies, and governments use scarce resources to produce the goods and services that meet a society's needs. Scarcity is a crucial concept in economics because it creates competition for resources and forces everyone to make trade-offs. Economic activity is monitored and measured with statistics known as *economic indicators*; leading indicators help predict changes, and lagging indicators confirm changes that have already occurred. Two major indicators are *price indexes*, which track inflation or deflation over time for a fixed "basket" of goods and services, and *gross domestic product (GDP)*, which is the total value of the goods and services produced for final use in a country during a specified period.

CRITICAL THINKING: (1) Why is entrepreneurship considered a factor of production? (2) Why is GDP considered a more accurate measure of a country's economic health than GNP?

IT'S YOUR BUSINESS: (1) Did you consider opportunity cost when you chose the college or university you are currently attending? (2) What trade-offs did you make in order to read this chapter at this exact moment in your life? (Think about the decisions you made to get to a point in your life where you're taking a business course.)

KEY TERMS TO KNOW: economy, economics, factors of production, scarcity, economic indicators, consumer price index (CPI), producer price index (PPI), gross domestic product (GDP)

Economic Systems

The roles that individuals, businesses, and governments play in allocating a society's resources depend on the society's **economic system**, the basic set of rules for allocating resources to satisfy its citizens' needs. Any economic system must address several fundamental questions: *What* will be produced and in what quantities, *how* will these goods and services be produced, and *who* should be able to acquire which products?[8]

THE SPECTRUM OF ECONOMIC SYSTEMS

How a given country answers those fundamental questions determines what kind of economic system it has. At one extreme, the government could make all the decisions about production, pricing, and distribution, and at the other extreme, it could leave all those decisions in the hands of individuals and companies. Various countries have reached different conclusions about what is best for their citizens (see Exhibit 2.3).

In a **planned system**, also called a *command system* or a *command-and-control system*, government controls the allocation of resources, including decisions regarding which

2 **LEARNING OBJECTIVE**

Define *economic system*, and explain the government's role in a free-market economy.

economic system
The policies that define a society's particular economic structure; the rules by which a society allocates economic resources.

planned system
Economic system in which the government controls most of the factors of production and regulates their allocation.

EXHIBIT 2.3	World's Healthiest Economies

Judging the health of an economy is not a simple matter, given the number of variables involved. Some of the people in a country might be doing very well while many others aren't, for example, or a country could be doing well in the short term but isn't positioned for long-term economic growth. The Legatum Institute in London ranks the world's economies through a comprehensive analysis of more than 100 separate factors. Here are its rankings of the top 10 healthiest economies, starting with a broad measure of *prosperity* that includes quality of governance, education, personal freedom, natural environment, and other quality-of-life factors, followed by narrower assessments of *economic quality* and *business environment*.

Rank (2017)	Overall Prosperity	Economic Quality	Business Environment
1	Norway	Sweden	United States
2	New Zealand	Singapore	New Zealand
3	Finland	New Zealand	Hong Kong
4	Switzerland	Netherlands	Canada
5	Sweden	Denmark	United Kingdom
6	Netherlands	Switzerland	Singapore
7	Denmark	United Kingdom	Australia
8	Canada	Norway	Norway
9	Australia	Germany	Switzerland
10	United Kingdom	United States	Finland

Source: "The Legatum Prosperity Index 2017," Legatum Institute, www.prosperity.com.

free-market system
Economic system in which decisions about what to produce and in what quantities are decided by the market's buyers and sellers.

capitalism
Economic system based on economic freedom and competition.

products are produced and in what quantities.[9] Planned economies are often equated with *socialism*, which in its most developed theoretical form involves collective ownership of the means of production.

In contrast, a country that leaves most of the decisions in the hands of private enterprise is said to have a **free-market system**, sometimes called a *market system* or a *price system*. Individuals and companies own the factors of production and are largely free to decide what products to make, how to make them, where to sell them, and what price to charge. **Capitalism** and *private enterprise* are the terms most often used to describe business in a free-market system, where private parties own and operate most businesses and where competition, supply, and demand determine which goods and services are produced.

Although you will hear references to "free-market economies" or "socialist economies," neither of them exists in a pure form (except in North Korea, perhaps). All modern economies combine elements of the free-market and socialist models, and no economy is truly "free" in the sense that anyone can do whatever he or she wants to do. Local, state, national, and even international governments such as the European Union intervene in the economy to accomplish goals that leaders deem socially or economically desirable. This practice of limited intervention is characteristic of a *mixed economy* or *mixed capitalism*, which is the economic system in the United States and most other countries.[10]

For example, government bodies intervene in the U.S. economy in a variety of ways, such as by influencing allocations of resources through tax incentives, prohibiting or restricting the sale of certain goods and services, setting limits on how products can be produced (to minimize pollution, for example), or setting *price controls*. Price controls can involve maximum allowable prices (such as limiting rent increases or capping the cost of insurance) and minimum allowable prices (such as supplementing the prices of agricultural goods to ensure producers a minimum level of income or establishing minimum wage levels).[11]

REAL-TIME UPDATES
Learn More by Exploring This Interactive Website

The world's most prosperous countries

This sortable list weighs eight other variables in addition to economic strength. Go to **real-timeupdates.com/bia9** and select Learn More in the Students section.

Moreover, although free-market capitalism remains the foundation of the U.S. economy, some important elements of the U.S. economy are socialized and have been for many years. Public schools, much of the transportation infrastructure, various local and regional utilities, and several major health-care programs all fit the economic definition of socialism. Socialism and capitalism are competing philosophies, but they are not mutually exclusive, and each approach has strengths and weaknesses, which is why modern economies combine aspects of both.

Nationalization and Privatization

The line between socialism and capitalism isn't always easy to define, and it doesn't always stay in the same place, either. Governments can change the structure of the economy by *nationalizing*—taking ownership of—selected companies or in extreme cases even entire industries. They can also move in the opposite direction, *privatizing* services once performed by the government by allowing private businesses to perform them instead.

In recent years, governments of various countries have done both, for different reasons and in different industries. For example, private companies now own or operate a number of highways, bridges, ports, prisons, airports, and other infrastructure elements in the United States and other countries. A major argument made in favor of privatizing these services is that profit-seeking companies are more motivated to operate efficiently than government agencies are. However, these operations often happen in the absence of direct competition, which removes one of the key motivations for companies to innovate and to serve customers satisfactorily.

GOVERNMENT'S ROLE IN A FREE-MARKET SYSTEM

As with many issues in economics, the debate over privatization takes place against the backdrop of a philosophical dispute about what government's role in society should be. For as long as the United States has been in existence, people have been arguing over just how free the free market should be. In the broader view, this argument springs from profound philosophical differences over the role government should play in society as a whole. More narrowly, even professional economists don't always agree on what role the government should play in the economy.

Much of the debate about the government's role can be framed as a question of **regulation** versus **deregulation**—having more rules in place to govern economic activity versus having fewer rules in place and relying more on the market to prevent excesses and correct itself over time. Generally speaking, the argument for more regulation asserts that companies can't always be counted on to act in ways that protect stakeholder interests and that the market can't be relied on as a mechanism to prevent or punish abuses and failures. The argument for deregulation contends that government interference can stifle innovations that ultimately help everyone by boosting the entire economy and that some regulations burden individual companies and industries with unfair costs and limitations.

Four major areas in which the government plays a role in the economy are protecting stakeholders, fostering competition, encouraging innovation and economic development, and stabilizing and stimulating the economy.

regulation
Relying more on laws and policies than on market forces to govern economic activity.

deregulation
Removing regulations to allow the market to prevent excesses and correct itself over time.

Protecting Stakeholders

Chapter 1 points out that businesses have many stakeholders, including colleagues, employees, supervisors, investors, customers, suppliers, and society at large. While serving one or more of these stakeholders, a business may sometimes neglect, or at least be accused of neglecting, the interests of other stakeholders in the process. For example, managers who are too narrowly focused on generating wealth for shareholders might not spend the funds necessary to create a safe work environment for employees or to minimize the business's impact on the community.

In an attempt to balance the interests of stakeholders and protect those who might be adversely affected by business, the U.S. federal government has established numerous regulatory agencies (see Exhibit 2.4), and state and local governments have additional agencies. Chapter 4 takes a closer look at society's concerns for ethical and socially responsible behavior and the ongoing debate about business's role in society.

EXHIBIT 2.4	Major Government Agencies and What They Do

Government agencies protect stakeholders by developing and promoting standards, regulating and overseeing industries, and enforcing laws and regulations.

Government Agency or Commission	Major Areas of Responsibility
Consumer Financial Protection Bureau (CFPB)	Educates consumers about and supervises providers of consumer financial services
Consumer Product Safety Commission (CPSC)	Regulates and protects public from unreasonable risks of injury from consumer products
Environmental Protection Agency (EPA)	Develops and enforces standards to protect the environment
Equal Employment Opportunity Commission (EEOC)	Protects and resolves discriminatory employment practices
Federal Aviation Administration (FAA)	Sets rules for the commercial airline industry
Federal Communications Commission (FCC)	Oversees communication by telephone, telegraph, radio, and television
Federal Energy Regulatory Commission (FERC)	Regulates rates and sales of electric power and natural gas
Federal Highway Administration (FHA)	Regulates vehicle safety requirements
Federal Trade Commission (FTC)	Enforces laws and guidelines regarding unfair business practices and acts to stop false and deceptive advertising and labeling
Food and Drug Administration (FDA)	Enforces laws and regulations to prevent distribution of harmful foods, drugs, medical devices, and cosmetics
Interstate Commerce Commission (ICC)	Regulates and oversees carriers engaged in transportation between states: railroads, bus lines, trucking companies, oil pipelines, and waterways
Occupational Safety and Health Administration (OSHA)	Promotes worker safety and health
Securities and Exchange Commission (SEC)	Protects investors and maintains the integrity of the securities markets
Transportation Security Administration (TSA)	Protects the national transportation infrastructure

Fostering Competition

Based on the belief that fair competition benefits the economy and society in general, governments intervene in markets to preserve competition and ensure that no single enterprise becomes too powerful. For instance, if a company has a monopoly, it can potentially harm customers by raising prices or stifling innovation and harm potential competitors by denying access to markets. Numerous laws and regulations have been established to help prevent individual companies or groups of companies from taking control of markets or acting in other ways that restrain competition or harm consumers.

Antitrust Legislation   *Antitrust* laws limit what businesses can and cannot do, to ensure that all competitors have an equal chance of succeeding. Some of the earliest government moves in this arena produced such landmark pieces of legislation as the Sherman Antitrust Act, the Clayton Antitrust Act, and the Federal Trade Commission Act, which generally sought to rein in the power of a few huge companies that had financial and management control of a significant number of other companies in the same industry.[12] Usually referred to as *trusts* (hence the label *antitrust legislation*), these huge companies controlled enough of the supply and distribution in their respective industries, such as Standard Oil in the petroleum industry, to muscle smaller competitors out of the way. Governments remain active in antitrust activities to this day, with tech giants such as Google, Facebook, Amazon, and Microsoft getting hit with antitrust lawsuits and penalties that sometimes run into the billions of dollars.[13]

Merger and Acquisition Approvals   To preserve competition and customer choice, governments occasionally prohibit companies from combining through mergers or acquisitions (see Chapter 5). In other cases, they may approve a combination but only with conditions, such as *divesting* (selling) some parts of the company or making other concessions.

Encouraging Innovation and Economic Development

Governments can use their regulatory and policymaking powers to encourage specific types of economic activity. A good example is encouraging the development and adoption of innovations that governments consider beneficial in some way, such as promoting the growth of alternative energy sources through economic incentives for producers and customers. In the interest of boosting employment, governments can also attract companies to build in certain locales by offering land grants or tax relief.

REAL-TIME UPDATES

Learn More by Exploring This Interactive Website

Explore the world through economic trends

GeoFRED adds mapping capabilities to economic data, making it easy to visualize differences across counties, states, and nations. Go to **real-timeupdates.com/bia9** and select Learn More in the Students section.

Stabilizing and Stimulating the Economy

In addition to the specific areas of regulation and policy just discussed, governments have two sets of tools they can use to stabilize and stimulate the national economy: monetary policy and fiscal policy. **Monetary policy** involves adjusting the nation's *money supply*, the amount of "spendable" money in the economy at any given time. In the United States, monetary policy is controlled primarily by the Federal Reserve Board (see page 96).[14]

    Fiscal policy involves changes in the government's revenues and expenditures to stimulate a slow economy or dampen a growing economy that is in danger of overheating and causing inflation. On the revenue side, governments can adjust the revenue they bring in by changing tax rates and various fees collected from individuals and businesses (see Exhibit 2.5). When the federal government lowers the income tax rate, for instance, it does so with the hope that consumers and businesses will spend and invest the money they save from lower tax bills.

    On the expenditure side, local, state, and federal government bodies constitute a huge market for goods and services, with billions of dollars of collective buying power. Governments can stimulate the economy by increasing their purchases, sometimes even to the point of creating *stimulus programs* with the specific purpose of expanding employment opportunities and increasing demand for goods and services.

monetary policy
Government policy and actions taken by the Federal Reserve Board to regulate the nation's money supply.

fiscal policy
Use of government revenue collection and spending to influence the business cycle.

EXHIBIT 2.5	Major Types of Taxes

Running a government is an expensive affair. Here are the major types of taxes that national governments, states, counties, and cities collect to fund government operations and projects.

Type of Tax	Levied On
Income taxes	Income earned by individuals and businesses. Income taxes are the government's largest single source of revenue.
Real property taxes	Assessed value of the land and structures owned by businesses and individuals.
Sales taxes	Retail purchases made by customers. Sales taxes are collected by retail businesses at the time of the sale and then forwarded to state governments. Disputes continue over taxes on e-commerce sales made across state lines.
Excise taxes	Selected items such as gasoline, tobacco, and liquor. Often referred to as "sin" taxes, excise taxes are implemented in part to help control potentially harmful practices.
Payroll taxes	Earnings of individuals to help fund Social Security, Medicare, and unemployment compensation. Corporations match employee contributions.

 CHECKPOINT

LEARNING OBJECTIVE 2: Define *economic system*, and explain the government's role in a free-market economy.

SUMMARY: An economic system encompasses the roles that individuals, businesses, and the government play in allocating a society's resources. Modern economies exist on a spectrum from *free market* to *planned*. In free-market systems, individuals and companies are largely free to make economic decisions; in planned systems, government administrators make the major decisions regarding production. All modern economies incorporate elements of both models. Four major areas in which the government plays a role in a free-market economy are protecting stakeholders, fostering competition, encouraging innovation and economic development, and stabilizing and stimulating the economy.

CRITICAL THINKING: (1) Why are no economies truly free, in the sense of having no controls or restrictions? (2) What are some possible risks of privatizing basic services such as prisons or the transportation infrastructure?

IT'S YOUR BUSINESS: (1) What are your emotional reactions to the terms *capitalism* and *socialism*? Explain why you feel the way you do. (2) Would you rather pay lower taxes and accept the fact that you need to pay for many services such as health care and education, or pay higher taxes with the assurance that the government will provide many basic services for you? Why?

KEY TERMS TO KNOW: economic system, planned system, free-market system, capitalism, regulation, deregulation, monetary policy, fiscal policy

The Forces of Demand and Supply

 LEARNING OBJECTIVE

Explain the interaction between demand and supply.

At the heart of every business transaction is an exchange between a buyer and a seller. The buyer wants or needs a particular service or good and is willing to pay the seller in order to obtain it. The seller is willing to participate in the transaction because of the anticipated financial gains. **Demand** refers to the amount of a good or service that customers will buy at a given time at various prices. **Supply** refers to the quantities of a good or service that

demand
Buyers' willingness and ability to purchase products at various price points.

supply
A specific quantity of a product that a seller is able and willing to provide at a particular date at various prices.

demand curve
A graph of the quantities of a product that buyers will purchase at various prices.

producers will provide on a particular date at various prices. The two forces work together to impose a kind of dynamic order on the market.

UNDERSTANDING DEMAND

The airline industry offers a helpful demonstration of supply and demand. A **demand curve** is a graph that shows the amount of product that buyers will purchase at various prices, all other factors being equal. Demand curves typically slope downward, implying that as price drops, more people are willing to buy. The black line labeled *Initial demand* in Exhibit 2.6 shows a possible demand curve for the monthly number of economy tickets on a hypothetical airline's Chicago-to-Denver route. You can see that as price decreases, demand increases, and vice versa. If demand is strong, airlines can keep their prices consistent or perhaps even raise them. If demand weakens, they can lower prices to stimulate more purchases. (Airlines and other service providers use sophisticated *yield management* software to constantly adjust prices in order to keep average ticket prices as high as possible while also keeping their planes as full as possible.)

This movement up and down the demand curve is only part of the story, however. Demand at all price points can also increase or decrease in response to a variety of factors. If overall demand for air travel decreases, the entire demand curve moves to the left (the orange line in Exhibit 2.6). If overall demand increases, the curve moves to the right (the green line). The bulleted lists in Exhibit 2.6 indicate how various factors can cause overall demand to increase or decrease:

- Customer income
- Customer preferences toward the product (fears regarding airline safety, for example)
- The price of *substitute products* (products that can be purchased instead of air travel, including rail tickets, automobile travel, or web conferencing)
- The price of *complementary products* (such as hotel accommodations or restaurant dining for the airline industry)

EXHIBIT 2.6	**Demand Curve**

The demand curve (black line) for economy seats on a hypothetical airline's Chicago-to-Denver route shows that the higher the ticket price, the smaller the quantity of seats demanded, and vice versa. Overall demand is rarely static; however, market conditions can shift the entire curve to the left (decreased demand at every price, orange line) or to the right (increased demand at every price, green line).

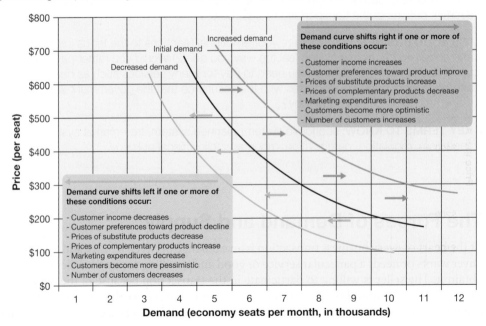

- Marketing expenditures (for advertising and other promotional efforts)
- Customer expectations about future prices and their own financial well-being

For example, if the economy is down and businesses and consumers have less money to spend, overall demand for air travel is likely to shrink. Businesses will seek less expensive substitutes, such as videoconferencing and online meetings, and consumers may vacation closer to home so they can travel by car. Conversely, if customers have more money to spend, more of them are likely to travel, thereby increasing overall demand.

UNDERSTANDING SUPPLY

Demand alone is not enough to explain how a company sets its prices or production levels. In general, a firm's willingness to produce and sell a product increases as the price it can charge and its profit potential per item increase. In other words, as the price customers are willing to pay goes up, the quantity supplied generally goes up (within the constraints of a given company or industry, naturally). The relationship between prices and quantities that sellers will offer for sale, regardless of demand, is illustrated with a **supply curve**.

Movement along the supply curve typically slopes upward: As prices rise, the quantity that sellers are willing to supply also rises. Similarly, as prices decline, the quantity that sellers are willing to supply declines. Exhibit 2.7 shows a possible supply curve for the monthly number of economy seats available on the airline's Chicago-to-Denver route at different prices. The graph shows that increasing prices for economy tickets on that route should increase the number of seats an airline is willing to offer for that route, and vice versa.

As with demand, supply is dynamic and is affected by a variety of internal and external factors. They include the cost of inputs (such as wages, fuel, and airport gate fees for the airlines), the number of competitors in the marketplace, and advancements in technology that allow companies to operate more efficiently. A change in any of these variables can

supply curve
A graph of the quantities of a product that sellers will offer for sale, regardless of demand, at various prices.

| EXHIBIT 2.7 | Supply Curve |

This supply curve for economy seats on the Denver-to-Chicago route shows that the higher the price, the more tickets (seats) the airline would be willing to supply, all else being equal. As with demand, however, the entire supply curve can shift to the left (decreased supply) or the right (increased supply) as producers respond to internal and external forces.

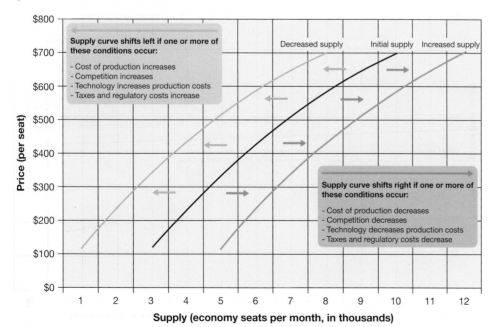

shift the entire supply curve, either increasing or decreasing the amount offered at various prices, as Exhibit 2.7 suggests.

UNDERSTANDING HOW DEMAND AND SUPPLY INTERACT

equilibrium price
The point at which quantity supplied equals quantity demanded.

Buyers and sellers clearly have opposite goals: Buyers want to buy at the lowest possible price, and sellers want to sell at the highest possible price. Neither side can "win" this contest outright. Customers might want to pay $10 for a ticket from Chicago to Denver, but airlines aren't willing to sell many, if any, at that price. Conversely, the airlines might want to charge $1,000 for a ticket, but customers aren't willing to buy many, if any, at that price. So, the market in effect arranges a compromise known as the **equilibrium price**, at which the demand and supply curves intersect (see Exhibit 2.8).[15] At the equilibrium price point, customers are willing to buy as many tickets as the airline is willing to sell.

Because the supply and demand curves are dynamic, so is the equilibrium point. As variables affecting supply and demand change, so will the equilibrium price. For example, increased concerns about airline safety could encourage some travelers to choose alternatives such as automobile travel or web conferencing, thus reducing the demand for air travel at every price and moving the equilibrium point as well. Suppliers might respond to such a reduction in demand by either cutting the number of flights offered or lowering ticket prices in order to restore the equilibrium level.

Questions of supply, demand, and equilibrium pricing are among the toughest issues managers and entrepreneurs face. For example, imagine you're a concert promoter planning for next year's summer season. You have to balance the potential demand for each performer across a range of prices, in the hope of matching the supply you can deliver (the seating capacity of each venue and the number of shows). And, you must make these predictions months in advance and make financial commitments based on your predictions. Predict well, and you'll make a tidy profit. Predict poorly, and you could lose a pile of money.

REAL-TIME UPDATES

Learn More by Exploring This Interactive Website

The national warehouse of economic data

The U.S. Commerce Department's Bureau of Economic Analysis is your one-stop shop for economic data. Go to **real-timeupdates. com/bia9** and select Learn More in the Students section.

EXHIBIT 2.8	**The Relationship Between Supply and Demand**

The equilibrium price is established when the amount of a product that suppliers are willing to sell at a given price equals the amount that consumers are willing to buy at that price.

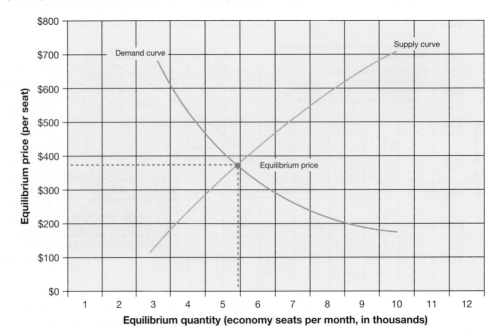

CHECKPOINT

LEARNING OBJECTIVE 3: Explain the interaction between demand and supply.

SUMMARY: *Demand* is the amount of a good or service that customers will buy at a given time at various prices; it can be shown visually as a *demand curve*. The entire demand curve can shift as market conditions change. Similarly, *supply* is the amount of a good or service that producers will provide on a particular date at various prices; it can be shown with a *supply curve*, which can also shift in response to market forces. In the simplest sense, demand and supply affect price in the following manner: When the price goes up, the quantity demanded goes down, but the supplier's incentive to produce more goes up. When the price goes down, the quantity demanded increases, but the quantity supplied may (or may not) decline. The point at which the demand and supply curves intersect—the point at which demand and supply are equal—is the *equilibrium price*.

CRITICAL THINKING: (1) How does the interaction of demand and supply keep a market in balance, at least approximately and temporarily? (2) If the prices of complementary products for a given product go up, what effect is this increase likely to have on demand for that product?

IT'S YOUR BUSINESS: (1) Are there any products or brands you are so loyal to that you will purchase them at almost any price? Will you accept less expensive substitutes? (2) Have you ever purchased something simply because it was on sale? Why or why not?

KEY TERMS TO KNOW: demand, supply, demand curve, supply curve, equilibrium price

The Macro View: Understanding How an Economy Operates

 LEARNING OBJECTIVE

Identify four macroeconomic issues that are essential to understanding the behavior of the economy.

All the individual instances of supply and demand and all the thousands and millions of transactions that take place over time add up to the economy. This section explores four "big-picture" issues that are essential to understanding the overall behavior of the economy: competition in a free-market system, business cycles, unemployment, and inflation.

COMPETITION IN A FREE-MARKET SYSTEM

Competition is the situation in which two or more suppliers of a product are rivals in the pursuit of the same customers. The nature of competition varies widely by industry, product category, and geography (see Exhibit 2.9). At one extreme is **pure competition**, in which there are multiple suppliers and none of them are dominant enough to be able to control prices. At the other extreme, in a **monopoly**, one supplier so thoroughly dominates a market that it can control prices and essentially shut out other competitors. Monopolies can happen "naturally," as companies innovate or markets evolve (a *pure monopoly*), or by government mandate (a *regulated monopoly*). However, the lack of competition in a monopoly situation is considered so detrimental to a free-market economy that monopolies are often prohibited by law (see "Merger and Acquisition Approvals" on page 84).

Most of the competition in advanced free-market economies is **monopolistic competition**, in which numerous sellers offer products that can be differentiated from one another and new suppliers can enter the market.[16] The risk/reward nature of capitalism promotes constant innovation in pursuit of competitive advantage, rewarding companies that do the best job of satisfying customers.

When the number of competitors in a market is quite small, and the competitors influence each other through their production and pricing decisions, a situation known as

competition
Rivalry among businesses for the same customers.

pure competition
A situation in which so many buyers and sellers exist that no single buyer or seller can individually influence prices.

monopoly
A situation in which one company dominates a market to the degree that it can control prices.

monopolistic competition
A situation in which many sellers differentiate their products from those of competitors in at least some small way.

EXHIBIT 2.9	**Categories of Competition**

Markets vary widely in the nature of competition they exhibit and the choices that buyers have. Here are five major categories of competition and the factors that distinguish them.

 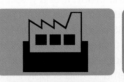 

Pure Competition	**Monopolistic Competition**	**Oligopoly**	**Pure Monopoly**	**Regulated Monopoly**
Characteristics: • Many small suppliers • Virtually identical products • Low barriers to entry	**Characteristics:** • Can have few or many suppliers, of varying size • Products can be distinguished but are similar enough to be replacements • Variable barriers to entry but market open to all	**Characteristics:** • Small number of suppliers, even as few as just two (a *duopoly*) • Products can be distinguished in important ways, but replacements are still available • Barriers to entry tend to be high, making entering the market difficult	**Characteristics:** • Only one supplier in a given market • Monopoly achieved without government intervention, by innovation, specialization, exclusive contracts, or a simple lack of competitors • Products are unique, with no direct replacements available • Barriers to entry are extremely high, making entering the market difficult or impossible	**Characteristics:** • Only one supplier in a given market • Monopoly granted by government mandate, such as a license to provide cable TV and internet service • No product competition is allowed • Barriers to entry are infinitely high; new competitors are not allowed
Price competition: • No single firm can grow large enough to influence prices across the market	**Price competition:** • Firms that excel in one or more aspects can gain some control over pricing	**Price competition:** • Individual firms can have considerable control over pricing	**Price competition:** • Suppliers can charge as much as they want, at least until people stop buying	**Price competition:** • Prices are set by government mandate
Buyers' choices: • Extensive	**Buyers' choices:** • Extensive	**Buyers' choices:** • Limited	**Buyers' choices:** • None	**Buyers' choices:** • None

oligopoly
A market situation in which a small number of suppliers, sometimes only two, provide a particular good or service.

oligopoly is created. In an oligopoly, customers have some choice, unlike in a monopoly, but not as many choices as in monopolistic competition. From a buyer's point of view, oligopolies can behave much like monopolies if the suppliers act in parallel ways. For example, if you can choose from four mobile phone carriers but they all charge about the same price, and the others raise or lower their prices whenever one of them does, there isn't much competition in this market.[17] Many industries in the United States have become more concentrated (meaning they have fewer suppliers) over the past two decades, raising concerns about the decline of competition.[18]

BUSINESS CYCLES

The economy is always in a state of change, expanding or contracting in response to the combined effects of technological breakthroughs, changes in investment patterns, shifts in consumer attitudes, world events, and other forces. *Economic expansion* occurs when the economy is growing and consumers are spending more money, which stimulates higher employment and wages, which then stimulate more consumer purchases. *Economic contraction* occurs when such spending declines, employment drops, and the economy as a whole slows down.

If the period of downward swing is severe, the economy may enter a **recession**. There are no official definitions of what constitutes a recession, but a common benchmark is

recession
A period during which national income, employment, and production all fall; often defined as at least six months of decline in the GDP.

a decline in GDP for two consecutive quarters. The National Bureau of Economic Research, a widely quoted independent research organization, uses the more general definition of "a significant decline in economic activity spread across the economy, lasting more than a few months, normally visible in real GDP, real income, employment, industrial production, and wholesale-retail sales."[19] A deep and prolonged recession can be considered a *depression*, which also doesn't have an official definition but is generally considered to involve a catastrophic collapse of financial markets. When a recession or depression is particularly deep or long, the news media and others sometimes give it an informal name, such as the Great Depression of the 1930s or the Great Recession of 2007–2009.

When a downward swing or recession is over, the economy enters a period of recovery. These up-and-down swings are commonly known as **business cycles**, although this term is somewhat misleading because economies do not expand and contract in regular and predictable "cycles." *Economic fluctuations* is a more accurate way to characterize the economy's real behavior (see Exhibit 2.10).[20]

business cycles
Fluctuations in the rate of growth that an economy experiences over a period of several years.

UNEMPLOYMENT

Unemployment is one of the most serious effects of economic contraction. In addition to the personal trauma it poses to workers and their families, unemployment can be part of a vicious circle of economic pain as these consumers have less money to spend, which reduces revenue for companies and tax revenues for governments, which may in turn lead to even higher unemployment.

The **unemployment rate** indicates the percentage of the *labor force* currently without employment. The labor force consists of people ages 16 and older who are either working or looking for jobs.[21] Not all cases of unemployment are the same, however. As Exhibit 2.11 on page 92 explains, each of the four types of unemployment—*frictional, structural, cyclical,* and *seasonal*—has unique implications for business and political leaders.

unemployment rate
The portion of the labor force (those ages 16 and older who have or are looking for a job) currently without a job.

INFLATION

Like almost everything else in the economy, prices of goods and services rarely stay the same for very long. **Inflation** is a steady rise in the average prices of goods and services throughout the economy. **Deflation**, on the other hand, is a sustained fall in average prices.

inflation
An economic condition in which prices rise steadily throughout the economy.

EXHIBIT 2.10   **Fluctuations in the U.S. Economy**

The U.S. economy has a long history of expansion and contraction. This chart shows the year-to-year change (as a percentage of the previous year) in GDP (see page 80). All the bars above zero represent years of economic expansion, and all the bars below zero represent years of contraction.

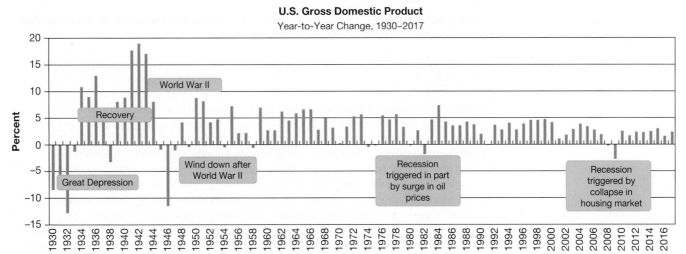

U.S. Gross Domestic Product
Year-to-Year Change, 1930–2017

Source: Data from U.S. Bureau of Economic Analysis, National Income and Product Accounts Tables, 13 March 2018, www.bea.gov.

EXHIBIT 2.11   Types of Unemployment

Economists identify four types of unemployment, each with unique causes and concerns.

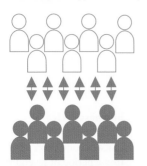 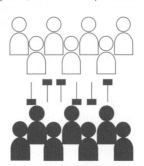 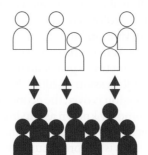 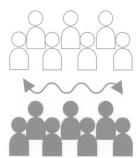

Frictional Unemployment	**Structural Unemployment**	**Cyclical Unemployment**	**Seasonal Unemployment**
• The "natural" flow of workers into and out of jobs, such as when a person leaves one job without first lining up a new job • Always some level of frictional unemployment in the economy	• A mismatch between workers' skills and current employer needs • Workers can't find jobs that match their qualifications, and employers can't find employees with the skills their job openings require • A never-ending concern as changes in the external environments of business make some skills obsolete and create demand for new skills	• Caused by economic fluctuations • Occurs when demand for goods and services drops, businesses reduce production, thereby requiring fewer workers • An increasing number of people who want to work can't find jobs • During catastrophic depressions, can run as high as 20 or 25 percent	• Predictable increases and decreases in the need for workers in industries with seasonal fluctuations in customer demand • Common in agriculture, leisure and entertainment, retailing, and accounting services

Sources: Data from Roger LeRoy Miller, *Economics Today*, 19th ed. (New York: Pearson, 2018), 147–148, 375.

deflation
An economic condition in which prices fall steadily throughout the economy.

Inflation is a major concern for consumers, businesses, and government leaders because of its effect on *purchasing power,* or the amount of a good or service you can buy for a given amount of money. When prices go up, purchasing power goes down. Runaway inflation is such an unsettling prospect that the Federal Reserve devotes much of its attention to monitoring inflation and using monetary controls to keep the economy from overheating.

✔ CHECKPOINT

LEARNING OBJECTIVE 4: Identify four macroeconomic issues that are essential to understanding the behavior of the economy.

SUMMARY: First, competition in a free-market system occurs on a spectrum from *pure competition* to *monopolies*; most competition in free-market economies is *monopolistic competition*, meaning that the number of sellers is large enough that none can dominate the market and products can be distinguished in at least some small way. Second, the economy expands and contracts, or fluctuates over time; this activity is commonly called the *business cycle*, although the fluctuations do not follow a regular cyclical pattern. Third, unemployment is a vitally important issue in economics because of the serious effects it has on individuals, families, communities, and the economy as a whole. The types of unemployment include cyclical (from reduced labor needs during an economic contraction), frictional (from the normal inflow and outflow of workers as people change jobs), structural (from the skills workers possess not aligning with the skills employers need), and seasonal (from the ebb and flow of labor demand in certain industries over the course of a year). Fourth, inflation affects every aspect of economic activity because of the effects it has on the prices of goods, services, and labor.

Money's Role in Business

Almost every aspect of business—from the basic economics of supply and demand to paying employees, pricing products, and buying advertising—involves money. Now it's time to explore money itself, along with the organizations that influence how much money is available in the economy, how much it costs to borrow it, and what services these organizations provide to consumers and businesses.

The $20 bill you're carrying around in your pocket and the billions of dollars that a megabank moves around the world are all part of a vast collection known as the *money supply*. The nature of this supply potentially affects every aspect of your financial life, from the size of your car payments to how soon you'll be able to retire.

THE MEANING OF MONEY

Money is anything generally accepted as a means of paying for goods and services. Although you're accustomed to coins and paper bills, societies through the ages have used a wide variety of things for money. Every country has its own system of money, or *currency*, except for those that share a currency such as the *euro* used in the European Union and those that use another country's currency because it is more stable.

Money performs four essential functions:[22]

- **A medium of exchange.** Money simplifies transactions, because a buyer can exchange money for a good or service rather than trying to exchange another good or product for it. Of course, you don't necessarily need money to make an exchange. You could *barter* one thing or service for another, and there are *barter exchanges* where consumers or businesses can trade goods and services without using cash. However, for most transactions, money is simply easier and more efficient.
- **A unit of accounting.** Money is a measure of value, meaning that buyers and sellers don't have to negotiate the relative worth of dissimilar items with every transaction.
- **A temporary store of value.** Holding money, whether it's physical cash, a value in a bank account, or some other storage mechanism, is a way of accumulating wealth until it is needed.
- **A standard of deferred payment.** Money can also function as a means of exchange over time, such as when you purchase something using a credit card but don't actually pay for it at that point. The credit card issuer pays the merchant at the time of the transaction, and you promise to pay the credit card issuer at some point in the future.

LEARNING OBJECTIVE 5
List the four financial functions of money, and define two key measures of the money supply.

money
Anything generally accepted as a means of paying for goods and services; serves as a medium of exchange, a unit of accounting, a store of value, and a standard of deferred value.

To be truly useful, any form of money needs to serve as a medium of exchange, as a unit of accounting, as a store of value, and as a standard of deferred payment.

imageBROKER/Alamy Stock Photo

The practical value of money stems from two key properties: liquidity and trust.[23] Money is the most *liquid* asset because it can be exchanged easily and often instantly for something else of value. In contrast, if you own a million-dollar house but have no money come dinner time, you'll go hungry because your wealth is *illiquid*—you may be "house rich," but you can't very easily exchange part of your house for food.

If you do have a $20 bill to hand over to a pizza delivery person, what exactly are you using as payment? A paper rectangle with a bit of ink splashed on it? The only reason the pizza seller will relinquish your dinner is because he or she trusts that the bill you're handing over in exchange represents $20 worth of real economic value. At one point in U.S. history, the value of that paper rectangle would've been tied to the price of gold, and you could have exchanged your bills for a specific amount of gold, but the value of money is no longer linked to gold. Instead, there is basically an agreement that the bill represents a certain amount of exchangeable value, so the pizzeria can take your $20 and use it to pay its bills, and so on through the entire economy.

FIAT MONEY AND CRYPTOCURRENCY

fiat money
Official currencies issued and maintained through government *fiat*, or proclamation.

The U.S. dollar and other modern currencies are often called **fiat money**, because they are issued and maintained through government *fiat*, or proclamation, and their value isn't tied to a physical asset such as gold. The dollar is *legal tender* in the United States, which means it can be used for any financial obligation. (This doesn't mean that every seller or lender must accept it or accept every *form* of it. Individuals and companies can accept or refuse to accept credit cards, large bills, coins, cash of any kind, and so on.[24])

Although each country has an official legal tender, this situation doesn't prevent parties in a transaction from using their own forms of money by private agreement. Just about anything that can perform the functions listed in the previous section can serve as money. In the past, all kinds of physical goods have been used as money. Today, a new wave of alternative money is happening in the form of **cryptocurrencies**, digital tokens that rely on cryptography for security.[25] Bitcoin is the best-known of these, but more than a thousand such currencies now exist.

cryptocurrency
Currency represented by digital tokens.

Sergiy Palamarchuk/Shutterstock

Legal tender means a currency can be used for any financial obligation.

Cryptocurrency is a revolution-in-progress, so its ultimate impact is impossible to predict, but it has the potential to influence business and economics in at least four ways:

- **As an alternative to fiat currency.** Cryptocurrency appeals to many people because of its anonymity and because its value can't be manipulated by central banks in the same way fiat currencies can. However, for any currency to come into wide use, it will need to have low transaction costs and fairly stable value. Purchasers will be reluctant to use it if they think its value could increase, and suppliers will be reluctant to accept it if they think its value could decrease.

- **As a disruptive force in global economics and politics.** Cryptocurrency could end up playing an interesting role in global politics. For example, one of the strongest ways that countries can influence the behavior of other countries, non-state entities, or even individual companies is through the threat of *economic sanctions*, which reduce the target's ability to participate in the global economic system. Several types of sanctions involve currency, including freezing bank accounts and blocking use of the international communication systems for money transfers.[26] If a country wanted to sidestep sanctions or the threat of sanctions, it could create its own official cryptocurrency.[27] Cryptocurrency could also help "de-dollarize" the global economy, reducing the influence the U.S. dollar has in international trade and diplomacy.[28]

- **As a speculative investment.** After Bitcoin's market value skyrocketed in 2014 and again in 2017, many people began seeing cryptocurrency as an intriguing investment opportunity. Bitcoin and other digital coins got swept up in a speculative frenzy.[29] However, because crypto-currencies have no inherent value and aren't backed by a country's central banks, investing in them is risky.

- **As a driver of potentially disruptive technologies.** Cryptocurrency's most far-reaching impact might come from the technologies that are required for their creation and use, including *blockchain* (see page 467 in Chapter 15) and *smart contracts* (see page 499 in Chapter 16).

REAL-TIME UPDATES
Learn More by Watching This Video

What is the future of money?

Currency futurist Neha Narula explores the potential ramifications of cryptocurrency. Go to **real-timeupdates.com/bia9** and select Learn More in the Students section.

Governments around the world are grappling with how to regulate cryptocurrencies, and their decisions will shape the future of these new currencies. Responses so far range from outlawing cryptocurrencies in a few instances to exploring official cryptocurrencies, with many countries adopting a wait-and-see approach before taking regulatory action.[30]

THE MONEY SUPPLY

Every economy has a certain amount of money in circulation at any given time, a quantity known as the **money supply**, or the *money stock*. The money supply can be measured in several ways. Economists focus on two aggregates known as *M1* and *M2* (see Exhibit 2.12). M1 consists of cash held by the public and money deposited in a variety of checking accounts. M2 is a broader measure, incorporating M1 plus savings accounts, balances in retail money-market mutual funds, and small *time deposits*—money held in interest-paying accounts such as certificates of deposit that may restrict the owner's right to withdraw funds on short notice.[31] In simple terms, M1 is money that is spendable now, and M2 adds money that could be spendable fairly soon.

money supply
The amount of money in circulation at any given time.

The implications of the money supply in terms of interest rates, prices, and other economic variables are not entirely clear. Economists used to be able to point to a predictable relationship between the money supply and interest rates, with increases in the money supply leading to lower interest rates and therefore potentially more business activity, for example. Because of this close relationship, the Federal Reserve and other nations' central banks could reliably use the money supply to guide monetary policy. However, over the past couple of decades, that relationship has become murkier, and the Federal Reserve uses a wider array of variables to set policy.[32]

EXHIBIT 2.12   The Money Supply

Both M1 and M2 have risen in recent years, which by conventional thinking suggests the risk of inflation. However, inflation has remained under control, so the causal link with inflation must not be quite so simple.

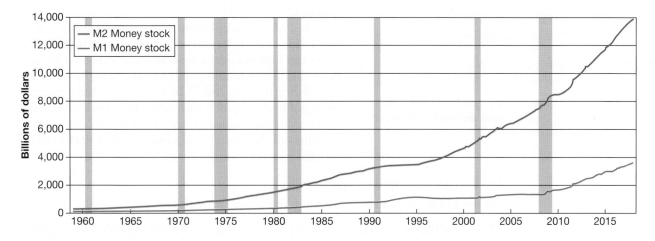

Source: "M1 and Components," Federal Reserve Bank of St. Louis, accessed 13 March 2018, fred.stlouisfed.org. Used courtesy of the Federal Reserve Bank of St. Louis.

CHECKPOINT

LEARNING OBJECTIVE 5: List the four financial functions of money, and define two key measures of the money supply.

SUMMARY: Money, anything generally accepted as a means of paying for goods and services, performs four financial functions: as a medium of exchange, as a unit of accounting, as a temporary store of value, and as a standard of deferred payment. The money supply is the amount of money in circulation at any given point in time. The aggregate M1 is cash held by the public and money deposited in a variety of checking accounts; M2 includes M1 plus savings accounts, balances in retail money-market mutual funds, and small time deposits such as certificates of deposit.

CRITICAL THINKING: (1) What might happen if people lose trust in their country's currency? (2) Why couldn't you buy your groceries using an amount of gold of equal value to the cost of the items you want to purchase?

IT'S YOUR BUSINESS: (1) What actions have you had to take in your own life to overcome liquidity problems? (2) Did those actions negatively affect your financial health later on? Explain your answer.

KEY TERMS TO KNOW: money, fiat money, cryptocurrency, money supply

---

[6] **LEARNING OBJECTIVE**

Explain the role of the Federal Reserve System, list the major types of banking institutions, and summarize banking's role in the economy.

Federal Reserve System
The central banking system of the United States; responsible for regulating banks and implementing monetary policy.

Banking Institutions and Services

Business is supported and served by a wide variety of financial institutions in both government and the private sector. This section offers a brief overview of the Federal Reserve and the various banks that work with businesses.

THE FEDERAL RESERVE

In response to repeated financial panics in the late 19th and early 20th centuries, Congress created a national central bank, the **Federal Reserve System**, in 1913 to help stabilize the U.S. banking industry (see Exhibit 2.13). The "Fed," as the system is commonly known, has two main components: a network of 12 regional banks that oversee the nation's banks and a board of governors that determine policy. All *national banks* (those authorized, or *chartered*, by the U.S. Department of the Treasury) must become members of the Fed system, and *state banks* (those chartered by individual state banking regulators) may choose to join. Together, about one-third of the commercial banks in the United States are members of the Fed system, although this group holds the vast majority of bank deposits.[33]

The Fed is an independent body in the sense that its decisions do not have to be ratified by Congress or the president. However, Congress does have indirect influence because the Fed is legally bound to pursue the economic priorities established by Congress.[34] To help ensure independence from political influence, members of the Fed's policymaking board are appointed to staggered 14-year terms, and no members of the presidential administration or any elected officials may serve on the board.[35]

REAL-TIME UPDATES
Learn More by Reading This PDF

An in-depth look at the purposes and functions of the Federal Reserve

The Fed is a complicated and sometimes controversial institution; find out what it really does. Go to **real-timeupdates.com/bia9** and select Learn More in the Students section.

The Fed's Major Responsibilities

The work of the Fed can be divided into five broad categories:[36]

- Conducting monetary policy as required by Congress, with three objectives: maximizing employment, keeping prices stable, and keeping inflation under control
- Maintaining the stability of the financial system by minimizing *systemic* risks (financial risks that extend beyond any single bank or other company)

EXHIBIT 2.13   Federal Reserve System

The U.S. Federal Reserve System is a complex organization designed to prohibit any political faction or region of the country from exerting undue influence over the bank's decisions.

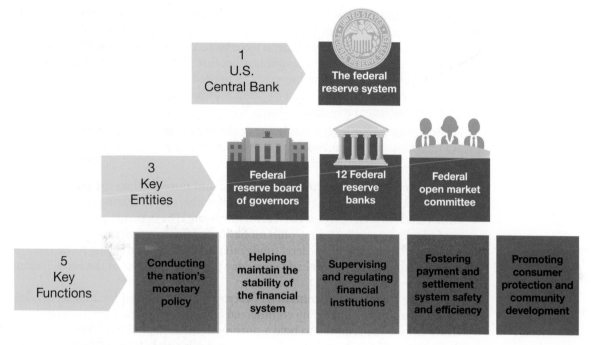

Sources: *The Federal Reserve System: Purposes & Functions*, 10th ed. (Washington, D.C.: Board of Governors of the Federal Reserve System, 2016), 1.

- Supervising and regulating individual financial institutions
- Ensuring a secure and efficient payment system to support financial transactions, including providing an adequate supply of currency and processing checks and electronic payments
- Protecting consumers and promoting community development by ensuring fair lending, fair housing, and community reinvestment.

As the "bank for banks," the Fed provides many of the services that a commercial bank provides to businesses and consumers, including holding deposits and making loans. It also operates two electronic systems for transferring money between banks, one for large amounts of cash and the smaller *automated clearing house (ACH)* system for routine payments made by check.[37]

As a supervisory and regulatory body, the Fed monitors the operation of state banks that are members of the Fed system, all *bank holding companies* (companies than own multiple banks), and the U.S. operations of foreign banks. The Fed's key objectives in this respect are making sure that banks are financially sound and that customers' accounts are safe, and it has the authority to take formal or informal action against banks that are out of compliance with Fed guidelines. Two other important aspects of the Fed's regulatory mandate are approving bank mergers and acquisitions and implementing finance-related consumer protection laws.[38]

Monetary policy is decided by the Federal Open Market Committee (FOMC), which includes the Fed's board of governors, the president of the New York City Fed, and 4 of the other 11 regional presidents. The Fed's three primary objectives are sometimes in conflict, so the FOMC faces a constant balancing act as it tries to optimize the overall results.[39]

The Fed's Tools for Implementing Monetary Policy

The Fed has several tools for implementing monetary policy, although "tool" suggests a stronger degree of control than it actually has. The Fed can't force banks to raise or lower the interest rates they charge their customers or flip a switch to make the economy heat up or slow down. Instead, it works indirectly, making changes in the economic variables it does control in the hope that those changes will nudge banks and other players in the economy in the desired direction.

federal funds rate
The interest rate that member banks charge each other to borrow money overnight from the funds they keep in their Federal Reserve accounts.

The Federal Funds Rate Much of the Fed's influence is exerted through the **federal funds rate**, which is the rate that member banks charge each other to borrow money from the funds they keep in their Federal Reserve accounts (see Exhibit 2.14). (You'll often hear this rate referred to as the *overnight rate*, because banks typically borrow these funds overnight to adjust their required reserves as needed.) The federal funds rate is a fundamental driver of economic behavior because it influences short- and long-term interest rates, foreign exchange rates, and inflation.[40]

As important as the federal funds rate is, the Fed doesn't set this rate directly. Instead, it sets a target rate and then tries to push the federal funds rate as close as possible to that target using three mechanisms:[41]

- **Buying and selling Treasury bonds, bills, and notes.** When the Fed buys Treasuries, this action injects money into the economy, thereby increasing the money supply, which tends to then decrease the federal funds rate. The opposite effect happens when the Fed sells Treasuries: Selling pulls money out of the economy, decreasing the money supply and increasing the federal funds rate. This buying and selling is the Fed's most powerful tool and is used nearly every day to adjust the level of the Fed's Treasuries holdings.
- **Adjusting reserve requirements.** All *depository institutions* (those that accept deposits from customers), including commercial banks, savings and loan associations, and credit unions, are required to hold a portion of those deposits in *reserve* to make sure they can provide cash on demand to customers who wish to withdraw it. By changing the reserve percentage, the Fed allows these institutions to lend out more or less of their deposited amounts, thereby affecting the size of the money supply. In contrast to the frequently used open-market operations, however, the Fed does not change the reserve ratio frequently, because doing so is costly to implement and a small change can have a drastic effect.
- **Lending through the discount window.** The Fed's *discount window* (no longer an actual window) is a process for making short-term loans to depository institutions when they are unable to get funds through normal interbank borrowing. This situation can happen when the overall supply of funds available has dropped (such as in a credit

EXHIBIT 2.14	Federal Funds Rate

The federal funds rate is adjusted in response to prevailing economic conditions as the Fed tries to balance economic growth with inflation control.

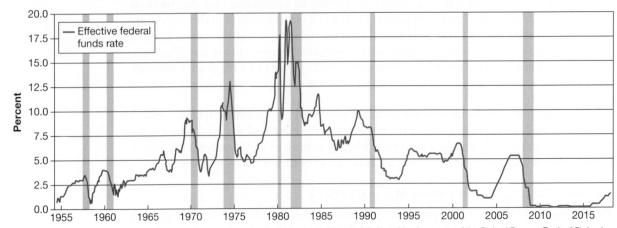

Source: "Effective Federal Funds Rate," Federal Reserve Bank of St. Louis, accessed 13 June 2018, fred.stlouisfed.org. Used courtesy of the Federal Reserve Bank of St. Louis.

crunch), an institution did not receive an expected loan from another institution, or a smaller bank needs to even out seasonal fluctuations in its deposits. The volume of lending through the discount window is relatively low, but these loans often play an important role in relieving money supply shortages that might push the federal funds rate up.

Even with these mechanisms at its disposal, however, there are limits to how much the Fed can "move the needle" by changing the federal funds target rate.

The Discount Rate The Fed's other key interest rate is the **discount rate**, which is the rate that member banks pay when they borrow funds through the discount window. Unlike with the federal funds rate, the Fed does set the discount rate directly. When the Fed changes the discount rate, each member bank generally changes its **prime rate**, which is the rate a bank charges its customers with the best credit ratings. Many other interest rates are also based on banks' prime rates, including some variable rate loans and credit cards that adjust their rates over time as the prime rate fluctuates. Raising the discount rate discourages loans and therefore tends to tighten the money supply; lowering it encourages lending and expands the money supply.

discount rate
The interest rate that member banks pay when they borrow funds from the Fed.

prime rate
The interest rate a bank charges its best loan customers.

Other Government Banking Agencies and Institutions

The Fed shares responsibility for banking oversight and financial activities with a number of other agencies and semi-independent institutions. Here are several of the most significant at the federal level:

- **FDIC.** After thousands of banks failed in the United States during the Great Depression, the government established the Federal Deposit Insurance Corporation (FDIC), www.fdic.gov, to protect money in customer accounts and to manage the transition of assets whenever a bank fails. Banks pay a fee to join the FDIC network, and in turn, the FDIC guarantees to cover any losses from bank failure up to a maximum of $250,000 per account.[42]
- **NCUA.** The National Credit Union Administration (NCUA), www.ncua.gov, provides regulatory supervision and account protection for credit unions.
- **Fannie Mae and Freddie Mac.** These two quasi-public companies operate under the close supervision of the federal government with a mandate to support home ownership for low- and moderate-income buyers by making mortgage funding more readily available. (The two companies' unusual names come from the acronyms of their original official names, the Federal National Mortgage Association—*FNMA*—and the Federal Home Loan Mortgage Corporation—*FHLMC*.) Fannie Mae and Freddie Mac don't extend home loans themselves but rather purchase and guarantee loans made by banks and other primary lenders, thus helping to ensure the availability of funds for home buyers. In this *secondary market*, individual loans are often pooled together and transformed into investment products known as *mortgage-backed securities*. (Although buying, selling, and investing in loans might sound like an odd concept, every loan represents a stream of future cash flow—the sum of all the payments due from the borrower—and therefore has an identifiable value and can be sold as an asset.)

INVESTMENT BANKS

Investment banks offer a variety of investing and advisory services to organizational customers, including corporations, other financial institutions, pension funds, and governments. Some also cater to very wealthy individuals, but they don't provide services to the general public. Investment banks provide some combination of the following services:[43]

- Facilitating mergers, acquisitions, sales, and spin-offs of companies
- Underwriting *initial public offerings* (when a company sells shares of stock to the public for the first time)
- Managing and advising on investments

investment banks
Firms that offer a variety of services related to initial public stock offerings, mergers and acquisitions, and other investment matters.

- Raising capital (such as by selling bonds) on behalf of corporate or government clients
- Advising on and facilitating complex financial transactions
- Investing in or lending money to companies
- Providing risk management advice
- "Making markets" for clients, which involves acting as an interim buyer or seller to help clients acquire or divest assets

COMMERCIAL BANKS

commercial banks
Banks that accept deposits, offer various checking and savings accounts, and provide loans; note that this label is often applied to banks that serve businesses only, rather than consumers.

Commercial banks are financial institutions that, generally speaking, accept deposits, offer various types of checking and savings accounts, and provide loans. The terminology can be confusing because some of these institutions don't call themselves banks, and some people use the term *commercial bank* to refer to banks that serve businesses only, not consumers. However, "commercial banking" is a good way to distinguish this class of services from both investment banking and nonbanking financial services. Here are the major types of commercial banks:

Consumers and businesses can use a variety of financial institutions for their banking needs.

- *Retail banks* serve consumers with checking and savings accounts, debit and credit cards, and loans for homes, cars, and other major purchases.
- *Merchant banks* offer financial services to businesses, particularly in the area of international finance. *Merchant banking* is sometimes more narrowly defined as the management of private equity investments, making it more akin to investment banking.[44]
- *Thrift banks*, also called *thrifts*, or *savings and loan associations*, offer deposit accounts and focus on offering home mortgage loans.
- *Credit unions* are not-for-profit, member-owned cooperatives that offer deposit accounts and lending services to consumers and small businesses. Note that thrifts and credit unions do not refer to themselves as banks, but the broad definition of banking used here distinguishes them from investment banks.
- *Private banking* refers to a range of services for wealthy individuals and families, such as managing real estate and other investments, setting up trust funds, and planning philanthropic giving.[45]

OTHER FINANCIAL SERVICES

In addition to commercial banks of all shapes and sizes, various other types of firms provide essential financial services to consumers and businesses. Some complement services offered by banks; others compete with banks in one or more areas. For example, *independent mortgage companies* originate mortgages using their own funds, and *mortgage brokers* initiate loans on behalf of a mortgage lender in exchange for a fee.

A variety of nonbank institutions lend money to consumers and businesses for vehicles, home improvements, expansion, purchases, and other purposes. Some of these *finance companies* are independent; others are affiliated with retailers or manufacturers. For example, Toyota Financial Services, a wholly owned subsidiary of Toyota Motor Corporation, offers car loans to drivers buying Toyota vehicles.[46] Credit cards are another major category of lending; some cards are issued by banks, whereas others are issued by retailers and credit card companies such as American Express.

Credit rating agencies offer opinions about the credit worthiness of borrowers and of specific investments, such as corporate bonds. Moody's, Standard & Poor's, and Fitch are the major rating agencies of businesses and securities; Equifax, Experian, and TransUnion are the major agencies that rate consumer credit worthiness. Before any bank or finance company will give you a loan, it will check your *credit rating* to judge the level of risk you represent as a borrower.

BANKING'S ROLE IN THE ECONOMY

It's impossible to overstate the importance of banking in the economy. Business as we know it simply couldn't exist without the many services that financial institutions provide. Moreover, many conveniences and possibilities of modern consumer life, including school loans, credit cards, savings accounts, and home mortgages, are made possible through banking services.

For all the benefits banking provides, however, its role in the economy hasn't always been without harm or controversy. For example, financial firms of all types and sizes played central roles in the interconnected housing and credit crises that triggered the Great Recession of 2007–2009. As business activity slowed down, millions of people who had no involvement in the risky and often fraudulent behavior that caused the meltdown lost their jobs or were otherwise affected. Modern society needs banking, to be sure, but it really needs safe and stable banking. As JPMorgan Chase's Jamie Dimon puts it, "We have a huge obligation to society—not only must we never fail, but we need to be steadfast."[47]

The Too-Big-to-Fail Dilemma

Banking activities raise a lot of potential concerns, but two in particular have been sources of controversy for years and will continue to be into the future. The first involves the influence of a small number of very large banks. The banking industry has consolidated dramatically in recent years, and the United States now has roughly one-third of the banks it had three decades ago. As a consequence, the largest banks, such as JPMorgan Chase, are *huge*, and they hold a staggering portion of the country's cash accounts. Of the 5,000 banks now in operation, the 10 largest hold half of all deposits, and the three largest hold more than a third.[48] In addition, major financial companies are often contractually linked to each other through short-term loans and credit guarantees (in which one company guarantees to cover another's losses in the event of credit defaults).[49]

Given their size and interconnectedness, the failure of just one of these big banks could cause tremendous strain on the government and the economy. You will hear these colossal firms referred to as being "too big to fail." However, this doesn't mean a bank *can't* fail because it is too big; it means a bank's presence in the economy is so big that regulators will take special action to make sure it *doesn't* fail.[50] This is an aspect of the containment of systemic risk mentioned on page 96 as one of the Fed's major responsibilities, but some people question whether it is wise to leave such risks active in the economy and ask whether these giant firms should be broken up.[51]

The Boundaries of Investment Banking and Commercial Banking

The second source of controversy is related to the first and involves the boundary between investment banking and commercial banking. Some experts blamed risky investment activity by commercial banks (using depositors' funds, in some cases) for the stock market crash that triggered the Great Depression. In response, the Glass-Steagall Act of 1933 (which also established the FDIC) aimed to restore confidence in U.S. financial firms by prohibiting investment banks and commercial banks from crossing into each other's businesses and potentially abusing their fiduciary duties at the expense of customers. Another

Along with JPMorgan Chase, these three banking firms are in the trillion-dollar club of giant U.S. banks.

key objective of Glass-Steagall was to ensure that a catastrophic failure in one part of the financial services industry would not invade every other part, as it did in 1929.[52]

Beginning in 1980, several waves of deregulation dramatically reshaped the banking and financial services industries—and in the eyes of some observers, helped create the conditions that led to the financial meltdown that triggered the Great Recession. After several decades of lobbying by the banking industry, piecemeal exemptions to the law, and regulatory changes that chipped away at the wall between commercial and investment banking, the Financial Services Modernization Act of 1999 effectively removed the Glass-Steagall wall.[53] As a result of this legislation and several other regulatory changes over the past 30 years, many of the barriers that once separated various kinds of banking, investing, and insurance services are now gone, paving the way for colossal, multifaceted firms such as today's JPMorgan Chase and Bank of America. Debate continues about whether some form of the Glass-Steagall wall should be reinstated, which would "re-compartmentalize" investment banking and probably reduce the size of the largest financial firms.[54]

 CHECKPOINT

LEARNING OBJECTIVE 6: Explain the role of the Federal Reserve System, list the major types of banking institutions, and summarize banking's role in the economy.

SUMMARY: The Fed is active in five major areas: (1) conducting monetary policy with the objectives of maximizing employment, keeping prices stable, and managing inflation; (2) maintaining the stability of the financial system by minimizing systemic risks; (3) supervising and regulating individual financial institutions; (4) ensuring a secure and efficient payment system to support financial transactions, including providing an adequate supply of currency; and (5) protecting consumers and promoting community development. The two major types of banking institutions are *investment banks*, which help companies with mergers and acquisitions, initial public offerings, and other major financial issues, and *commercial banks*, which include retail banks and a variety of similar firms. Banking plays an essential role in the modern economy, but safe and stable banking is a vital social need. Two major concerns are the concentration of deposits among a handful of "too-big-to-fail" banks and the possible need to reinstate the wall separating investment banking from commercial banking.

CRITICAL THINKING: (1) Why would a company's financial managers want to pay attention to the federal funds rate? (2) Rather than promising to support any too-big-to-fail banks, could the federal government instead simply warn everyone that doing business with one of these firms is risky? Why or why not?

IT'S YOUR BUSINESS: (1) If you are hoping to get a loan to expand your business, will you welcome the news that the Fed is raising the discount rate? Why or why not? (2) Would you put any of your life savings into cryptocurrency? Why or why not?

KEY TERMS TO KNOW: Federal Reserve System, federal funds rate, discount rate, prime rate, investment banks, commercial banks

---

7 **LEARNING OBJECTIVE**

Define *fintech*, and discuss five ways that financial institutions are innovating with digital technology.

fintech
Technologies with the potential to improve or disrupt financial services.

Thriving in the Digital Enterprise: Fintech

Financial institutions have been using technology for decades, but over the past few years the attention to technology has ramped up dramatically. The term **fintech** is used as a label for a wide range of innovations that have the potential to improve financial services—and in some instances, radically disrupt them. At least 10,000 companies are active in fintech, so advances are taking place in just about every corner of banking, investing, and insurance.[55]

Fintech involves a variety of technologies, including artificial intelligence (AI), cloud computing, and mobile apps, with both *customer-facing* and *back-office* technologies.[56] This section explores five major areas that are seeing benefits from new fintech. (Note that many of the innovations contribute more than one type of benefit, so there is a lot of overlap in these categories.)

MAKING FINANCIAL SERVICES MORE INCLUSIVE

A number of fintech initiatives aim to give more people easier access to financial services by lowering costs and other barriers, such as minimum account levels. In some cases, this means offering banking services to consumers and small-business owners whose needs haven't been met by traditional banks.[57]

In other cases, fintechs innovate by bypassing intermediaries in the conventional banking system. For example, banks essentially gather money from people who want to store it somewhere safe and lend that money back out to other people. *Crowdfunding* and *peer-to-peer lending* services make this happen without the bank as the intermediary. At LendingClub, for example, consumers and small-business owners can apply for loans online, the system quickly evaluates their credit worthiness, and then investors (individuals or institutions) can choose to fund loans that meet their risk/reward criteria. Borrowers whose financial situations might disqualify them from traditional bank loans can sometimes get financed through peer-to-peer lending, and the process is much faster and cheaper than conventional loan applications.[58]

Other fintech platforms give more people access to the stock market and other investment opportunities by making it possible to invest smaller amounts than is possible with traditional stock brokerages. Conventional brokerages charge a commission of anywhere from $5 to $30 or more every time you want to buy or sell. If you tried to invest a modest amount every week, for instance, these transaction costs could eat up all your potential gains. In addition, many traditional investments have minimum required amounts that are beyond the reach of many beginning investors. New, highly automated fintech brokerages such as Robinhood, Stash, and Acorns (see Exhibit 2.15) eliminate per-trade commissions and let you invest in the stock market for as little as $5 at a time.[59]

EXHIBIT 2.15	Fintech Apps

Innovative fintech services such as Betterment give even beginning investors access to automated investing tools that produce better results with less time and effort.

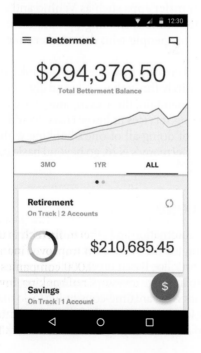

Adam Radosavljevic/Shutterstock

Fintech companies that serve customers through mobile apps are challenging the established banking industry.

IMPROVING THE EFFICIENCY OF FINANCIAL ACTIVITIES

Another group of fintech activities aim to lower the costs, delays, and complexity associated with traditional banking activities. For example, transferring money internationally has long been a slow, expensive, and sometimes aggravating procedure with intermediaries taking a cut and customers getting surprised by costs hidden in the form of marked-up exchange rates. In TransferWise's radically simpler approach, the money never actually crosses borders. Instead, the company maintains its own bank accounts in countries all over the world and pays out of its local accounts whenever a transfer is initiated. TransferWise uses the same exchange rate that banks use, which is the best possible rate available anywhere, promising up to 90 percent lower costs for customers.[60]

Banks and other financial services companies are also applying fintech to reduce their own costs. For example, JPMorgan Chase is using AI to review commercial loan agreements. This task used to consume up to 360,000 hours of staff time a year, but the AI-enabled system now does it in a matter of seconds and with fewer errors.[61]

STRENGTHENING THE SECURITY OF FINANCIAL SYSTEMS

The financial services sector is constantly under siege by cybercriminals, with massive data breaches becoming frustratingly common. Even when a company is equipped with comprehensive safeguards, the sheer number of intrusion alerts can overwhelm security staff. Fintech innovators are now applying automated, AI-based threat intelligence to help identify intrusions and plug vulnerabilities more quickly. Intelligent systems also work to spot suspicious transactions correctly, both to protect customers and to catch illegal activity. Unfortunately, criminals continue to innovate with smarter and faster malware, creating an AI arms race when it comes to financial security.[62]

IMPROVING THE CUSTOMER EXPERIENCE IN FINANCIAL SERVICES

The ability to accomplish an ever-growing array of tasks via mobile apps and online services has conditioned consumers to expect the same from financial services. Popular fintech apps include mobile banking apps, peer-to-peer cash transfer apps such as Venmo and Zelle, and financial planning services such as Mint. Metromile is shaking up auto insurance by offering pay-by-mile policies that are cheaper for people who drive fewer miles per year than average.[63]

neobanks
Banks that provide services entirely through mobile and digital channels.

Mobile and cloud technologies have also helped create a new category of banks, often referred to as **neobanks**, which provide services entirely through mobile and digital channels. Without large staffs and physical branches to maintain, these companies have much lower cost structures and therefore can offer banking services at lower costs. In addition, these banks offer the simplicity and convenience of doing all of one's banking within a single app. The most innovative neobanks, such as Germany's N26, go beyond basic banking to offer insurance and investing services as well.[64]

ENHANCING FINANCIAL DECISION-MAKING

A final group of fintech innovations apply cognitive automation and other tools to help investors make better financial decisions without paying for the services of a financial adviser. These so-called *robo advisers* assemble investment portfolios based on each client's risk tolerance, resources, and objectives. These systems aim to improve investors' returns by removing emotion-driven decision-making and automating tasks that are time-consuming to do manually, such as rebalancing portfolios over time and tax-loss harvesting (selling an investment that has declined in value to use the loss as a tax write-off and then buying back into the market).[65]

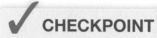

✔ CHECKPOINT

LEARNING OBJECTIVE 7: Define *fintech*, and discuss five ways that financial institutions are innovating with digital technology.

SUMMARY: Fintech refers to a wide range of technological innovations that have the potential to improve financial services—and in some instances, radically disrupt them. Five major categories of fintech innovations include making financial services more inclusive, improving efficiency of financial activities, strengthening security of financial systems, improving the customer experience in financial services, and enhancing financial decision making.

CRITICAL THINKING: (1) If a substantial portion of the public has been underserved by conventional banks, as many in fintech assert, why shouldn't the Fed or other regulatory bodies step in and require banks to serve these customers? (2) What questions should anyone ask before moving personal funds from a conventional bank to a neobank?

IT'S YOUR BUSINESS: (1) Do you use a mobile banking app now? If so, what are its advantages and disadvantages compared to doing your banking in person at a physical bank branch? (2) Would you be comfortable leaving your retirement portfolio in the hands of a robo adviser? Why or why not?

KEY TERMS TO KNOW: fintech, neobanks

BEHIND THE SCENES

Responding to the Digital Invaders at JPMorgan Chase

When it comes to the banking establishment, you can't get much more establishment than JPMorgan Chase. Through its various incarnations and acquisitions that can be traced as far back as 1799, the New York financial giant now has the corporate DNA of more than 1,200 predecessor banks. With annual revenue in the neighborhood of $100 billion, $2.5 trillion in assets, more than $1 trillion in customer deposits, and a quarter of a million employees, it is one of the country's largest financial services firms and an integral part of the U.S. economy. (A bank's assets include its own cash and government securities such as Treasury bills, plus the current value of all the mortgages and other loans it has extended to its customers.)

No company can grow this big without paying attention to its competitors, and CEO Jamie Dimon is obsessive about the competition. As he put it when discussing the digital invaders from Silicon Valley, "we analyze all of our competitors in excruciating detail—so we can learn what they are doing and develop our own strategies accordingly." That deep analysis told him that JPMorgan Chase needed to adapt and adapt quickly, because fintech innovators are able to lure customers away with new services, lower costs, and greater convenience.

After sizing up the competitive threat, Dimon and his team crafted a multipronged response that includes investing heavily in its own fintech, establishing partnerships with selected fintech innovators, and making banking more inclusive. In other words, it's a combination of competition and cooperation, designed to blunt the threat of digital innovators encroaching into its markets and positioning the bank for a vastly changed business landscape.

Dimon has directed billions of dollars into expanding the company's technological capabilities, including developing many of the same capabilities that fintech start-ups are bringing to market, such as all-in-one mobile banking services. However, recognizing that no company can or should try to do it all in such a complex business environment, Dimon also emphasizes partnering with fintech start-ups to integrate their products and technologies with JPMorgan Chase's systems and customer offerings. The bank has been able to add peer-to-peer payments and digital loan applications for both home mortgages and small-business funding, for example.

The effort to make banking more inclusive is a combination of good corporate citizenship and smart business strategy. Through its Financial Solutions Lab, the bank partners with the not-for-profit Center for Financial Services Innovation to develop financial tools for people who are underserved by current banking services. Millions of people lack the resources to weather hardships such as illnesses or accidents as well as the ability to build a stable financial base for improving their lives. Many don't use regular banks at all and instead rely on costly check-cashing services, payday lenders, and other alternatives. These underserved populations are a key target of neobanks, with their low costs and low entry barriers. The Financial Solutions Lab invests in neobanks and other fintech innovators that can help more people develop stronger financial foundations, including saving more and improving their credit ratings. In addition to providing vital help to millions, the initiative helps JPMorgan Chase gather intelligence about a market segment that historically it hasn't been active in and potentially develop relationships with a new population of customers.

The strategy is certainly paying off so far. The bank continues to rack up increasing levels of revenue and profits, even as competitive threats multiply. Just as important, with its forward-looking viewpoint, it is positioned to continue innovating and staying in front of customer expectations.[66]

Critical Thinking Questions

2-1. If JPMorgan Chase is doing well serving its current customer segments, why would it bother with the added effort of targeting lower-income clients?

2-2. Would it make sense for the company to market its most basic banking services under a different brand name to avoid diluting its higher-end J.P. Morgan brand? Why or why not?

2-3. Which of the various kinds of competition identified in the chapter does JPMorgan Chase engage in? Explain your answer.

Learn More Online

Visit JPMorgan Chase online at **www.jpmorganchase.com** and explore the two halves of the company, J.P. Morgan (which offers investment banking, private banking, and similar services) and Chase (which offers consumer and business banking). Look into any of the service areas that you find interesting or relevant to your financial needs. Do you find the presentation of the various services to be clear and compelling?

End of Chapter

KEY TERMS

business cycles (91)
capitalism (82)
commercial banks (100)
competition (89)
consumer price index (CPI) (80)
cryptocurrency (94)
deflation (92)
demand (86)
demand curve (86)
deregulation (83)
discount rate (99)
economic indicators (79)
economic system (81)
economics (77)
economy (77)
equilibrium price (88)
factors of production (77)
federal funds rate (98)
Federal Reserve System (96)
fiat money (94)
fintech (102)
fiscal policy (84)

free-market system (82)
gross domestic product (GDP) (80)
inflation (91)
investment banks (99)
monetary policy (84)
money (93)
money supply (95)
monopolistic competition (89)
monopoly (89)
neobanks (104)
oligopoly (90)
planned system (81)
prime rate (99)
producer price index (PPI) (80)
pure competition (89)
recession (90)
regulation (83)
scarcity (78)
supply (86)
supply curve (87)
unemployment rate (91)

TEST YOUR KNOWLEDGE

Questions for Review

2-4. What are the five primary factors of production?

2-5. Why is the economic concept of scarcity a crucial one for businesspeople to understand?

2-6. Does China have a purely planned economic system? Explain your answer.

2-7. What is the argument for regulation and deregulation in a free-market system?

2-8. What is the difference between the prime rate and the discount rate?

2-9. How does a government stimulate its economy through fiscal policy?

2-10. What does it mean when a bank is labeled "too big to fail"?

Questions for Analysis

2-11. Why do governments intervene in free-market systems?

2-12. What would happen if scarcity did not exist in economies?

2-13. How does inflation affect the economy of a country?

2-14. How do sellers compete in monopolistic competition and in monopoly competition?

2-15. If risk is a part of doing business, why should the Fed be concerned with systemic risk?

2-16. Why might a central bank use monetary policy as a control tool?

2-17. What are the benefits of a fintech company's ability to bypass traditional intermediaries in a financial system?

2-18. If a particular fintech company is likely to disrupt any aspect of the country's financial system, should the government take steps to prevent it from doing so? Why or why not?

2-19. **Ethical Considerations.** The risk of failure is an inherent part of free enterprise. Does society have an obligation to come to the aid of entrepreneurs who try but fail? Why or why not?

Questions for Application

2-20. How can the government stimulate the economic performance of its leading businesses or industries?

2-21. What would be the impact of introducing a minimum allowable price on a highly desirable product? Explain your answer.

2-22. When a budget airline releases flight tickets, the initial selling price is below cost. By the day of the flight itself, the tickets are generating over 300 percent profit. How does this work?

2-23. **Concept Integration.** What effect might the technological environment, discussed on page 57 in Chapter 1, have on the equilibrium price in a given market?

EXPAND YOUR KNOWLEDGE

Discovering Career Opportunities

Thinking about a career in economics? Find out what economists do by reviewing the *Occupational Outlook Handbook* in your library or online at **www.bls.gov/ooh**. This is an authoritative resource for information about all kinds of occupations. Search for "economists" and then answer these questions:

2-24. Briefly describe what economists do and their typical working conditions.

2-25. What is the job outlook for economists? What is the average salary for starting economists?

2-26. What training and qualifications are required for a career as an economist? Are the qualifications different for jobs in the private sector than for those in the government?

Intelligent Business Technology: Fintech in Indonesia

Research the new advances in fintech in Indonesia. In a brief report, describe the challenges and opportunities for fintech start-ups in Indonesia.

PRACTICE YOUR SKILLS

Resolving Ethical Dilemmas

Assume you're launching a new business, but you have a low credit score and no real track record. You will find it difficult to raise funds by approaching a financial institution and securing a loan. You have resolved to use social media to promote your new business and to apply to a peer-to-peer lending service to raise the necessary funds. There is no guarantee that the business will succeed.

Your business has enormous potential appeal for the 22–30 age group. In a brief memo, outline how crowdfunding might be appropriate. What is the degree of risk for potential investors?

Growing as a Professional

Just as you are in college, in the workplace you will be judged by the quality of your work. Use your various assignments and projects to hone your ability to create high-quality reports, presentations, and other work products. Focus on both *content quality* and *production quality*. Content quality involves the thoroughness of your research, the logic of your conclusions, and the effectiveness of your communication efforts. Production quality encompasses the look and feel of what you deliver. Unprofessional documents and presentations can diminish the impact of all your great work on content quality, so pay attention to design and production issues. Learn the basic principles of page layout and visual design to make sure you can create documents that are attractive and easy to read. Study slide design to make sure you know how to create presentation slides that are effective, attractive, and appropriate for a professional environment. A business communication course will cover these topics, but don't wait until you take that course to learn the basics. Search online for tips on "document design" or "presentation design," then practice these techniques on all your assignments and you'll be a step ahead when you enter (or reenter) the job market.

Sharpening Your Communication Skills

Identify a crowdfunding platform. What is its target market for lenders? What are the features and user benefits that make it an attractive investment platform? Assume that you are reviewing personal finance for young adults. Use the information you found to make a five-minute video presentation about this platform for YouTube.

Building Your Team Skills

Zidisha is an online peer-to-peer lending platform that connects investors with some of the world's most impoverished and isolated entrepreneurs. Find out more at www.zidisha.org. As of 2019, the platform has attracted funding for over 230,000 projects. It largely caters to smaller entrepreneurs in Africa, providing loans to marginalized borrowers who do not have Internet access via local intermediary micro-finance organizations. The founder, Julia Kurnia, has been operating this microlending platform since 2008, when she was working in Niger and realized that connectivity in developed countries could be leveraged to attract micro-investment in developing countries.

Does Zidisha or similar peer-to-peer lending platforms already exist in your country? If so, how do they work in your country? What are their features and mission? What reasons does Julia Kurnia give for setting up Zidisha? Is this the right way to handle micro-financing? Discuss these issues with your team and explain how these platforms might offer an alternative to more formal and traditional loans and financing.

Developing Your Research Skills

In small groups, research examples of privatization in different industries, such as energy and transport, around the world. Consider the impact of privatization on these industries and economies. Find out about the kinds of difficulties that may be involved when governments try to privatize industries. Summarize your findings in a one-page report.

Writing Assignments

2-27. When the needs of various stakeholders conflict, how should legislators and regulators approach these dilemmas?

2-28. How might the word *free* affect public and political discussions of free-market systems?

ENDNOTES

1. "Bank Data & Statistics," Federal Deposit Insurance Corporation, 31 December 2017, www.fdic.com; "Our History," JPMorgan Chase, accessed 13 March 2018, www.jpmorganchase.com; "JPMorgan's Fintech Strategy," *Business Insider*, 6 April 2017, www.businessinsider.com; Jamie Dimon, "Letter to Shareholders," *JPMorgan Chase 2014 Annual Report*, 16; Jamie Dimon, "Letter to Shareholders," *JPMorgan Chase 2016 Annual Report*, 9–10.

2. Roger LeRoy Miller, *Economics Today*, 19th ed. (New York: Pearson, 2018), 3; Robin Bade and Michael Parkin, *Foundations of Macroeconomics*, 8th ed. (New York: Pearson, 2018), 3.

3. Miller, *Economics Today*, 28.

4. Miller, *Economics Today*, 30.

5. "Lagging Indicator," *Investopedia*, accessed 5 March 2018, www.investopedia.com.

6. "Consumer Price Index," U.S. Bureau of Labor Statistics, accessed 5 March 2018, www.bls.gov.

7. "Producer Price Indexes," U.S. Bureau of Labor Statistics, accessed 5 March 2018, www.bls.gov.

8. Miller, *Economics Today*, 4.

9. Miller, *Economics Today*, 4–5.

10. Miller, *Economics Today*, 5.

11. Miller, *Economics Today*, 82.

12. "The Antitrust Laws," U.S. Federal Trade Commission, accessed 7 March 2018, www.ftc.gov.

13. "The Techlash Against Amazon, Facebook and Google—And What They Can Do," *Economist*, 20 January 2018, www.economist.com; Mark Scott, "Google Fined Record $2.7 Billion in E.U. Antitrust Ruling," *New York Times*, 27 June 2017, www.nytimes.com.

14. "Monetary Policy," U.S. Federal Reserve, accessed 7 March 2018, www.federalreserve.gov.

15. Bade and Parkin, *Foundations of Macroeconomics*, 96.

16. Miller, *Economics Today*, 560.

17. Tim Wu, "The Oligopoly Problem," *New Yorker*, 25 April 2013, www.newyorker.com.

18. David Wessel, "Is a Lack of Competition Strangling the U.S. Economy?" *Harvard Business Review*, March–April 2018, 106–114.

19. "US Business Cycle Expansions and Contractions," National Bureau of Economic Research, accessed 8 March 2018, www.nber.org.

20. Miller, *Economics Today*, 155.

21. "Glossary," U.S. Bureau of Labor Statistics, accessed 8 March 2018, www.blg.gov.

22. R. Glenn Hubbard and Anthony Patrick O'Brien, *Money, Banking, and the Financial System*, 3rd ed. (New York: Pearson, 2018), 27.

23. Miller, *Economics Today*, 325–326.

24. "Legal Tender Status," U.S. Department of the Treasury, accessed 11 March 2018, www.treasury.gov.

25. "Cryptocurrency," Investopedia.com, accessed 11 March 2018, www.investopedia.com.

26. "Compliance," SWIFT, accessed 11 March 2018, www.swift.com; Jonathan Masters, "What Are Economic Sanctions?" Council on Foreign Relations, 7 August 2017, www.cfr.org.

27. Max Seddon and Martin Arnold, "Putin Considers 'Cryptorouble' as Moscow Seeks to Avoid Sanctions," *Financial Times*, 1 January 2018, www.ft.com.

28. Oscar Jonsson, "Why Cryptocurrencies Could Push the Dollar from World Reserve Currency Status," *Forbes*, 7 November 2017, www.forbes.com.

29. John W. Schoen, "This Chart Shows Bitcoin's Meteoric Rise over the Last 6 Years," CNBC, 29 November 2017, www.cnbc.com; Yifan Yu, "Despite Soaring Bitcoin Value, It's Unclear How Many Millionaires Have Been Minted as a Result," *Barron's*, 11 January 2018, www.barrons.com.

30. Brad Stephenson, "5 Countries Where Bitcoin Is Illegal," *Lifewire*, 22 December 2017, www.lifewire.com; Seddon and Arnold, "Putin Considers 'Cryptorouble' as Moscow Seeks to Avoid Sanctions."

31. Hubbard and O'Brien, *Money, Banking, and the Financial System*, 38.

32. "What Is the Money Supply? Is It Important?" U.S. Federal Reserve, accessed 8 March 2018, www.federalreserve.gov.

33. *The Federal Reserve System: Purposes & Functions*, 10th ed. (Washington, D.C.: Board of Governors of the Federal Reserve System, 2016), 74; Hubbard and O'Brien, *Money, Banking, and the Financial System*, 435.

34. *The Federal Reserve System: Purposes & Functions*, 15.

35. "How Is the Federal Reserve System Structured?" Federal Reserve System, accessed 26 November 2013, www.federalreserve.gov.

36. *The Federal Reserve System: Purposes & Functions*, 1–2, 119, 153–154.

37. "What We Do," Federal Reserve Bank of New York, accessed 26 November 2013, www.newyorkfed.org.

38. *The Federal Reserve System: Purposes & Functions*, 74–79.

39. *The Federal Reserve System: Purposes & Functions*, 15–16.

40. *The Federal Reserve System: Purposes & Functions*, 16–17.

41. *The Federal Reserve System: Purposes & Functions*, 38–44; Joao Santos and Stavros Peristiani, "Why Do Banks Have Discount Windows?" Federal Reserve Bank of New York, 30 March 2011, www.newyorkfed.org.

42. "Deposit Insurance," FDIC, 9 March 2018, www.fdic.gov.

43. Goldman Sachs, accessed 9 March 2018, www.goldmansachs.com; J.P. Morgan, accessed 9 March 2018, www.jpmorgan.com.

44. "Piper Jaffray Merchant Banking," Piper Jaffray, accessed 10 March 2018, www.piperjaffray.com.

45. "Private Wealth Management," UBS, accessed 10 March 2018, www.ubs.com.

46. Toyota Financial Services, accessed 9 March 2018, www.toyotafinancial.com.

47. Dimon, "Letter to Shareholders," 2014.

48. Hubbard and O'Brien, *Money, Banking, and the Financial System*, 331.

49. David C. Wheelock, "Too Big to Fail: The Pros and Cons of Breaking Up Big Banks," *Regional Economist*, October 2012, www.stlouisfed.org.

50. Hubbard and O'Brien, *Money, Banking, and the Financial System*, 408.

51. Wheelock, "Too Big to Fail: The Pros and Cons of Breaking Up Big Banks."

52. Stephan Labaton, "Accord Reached on Lifting Depression-Era Barriers Among Financial Industries," *New York Times*, 23 October 1999, A1, B4.

53. "The Long Demise of Glass-Steagall," *PBS Frontline*, accessed 27 September 2009, www.pbs.org.

54. Hubbard and O'Brien, *Money, Banking, and the Financial System*, 357–358.

55. Lucas Mearian, "What Is FinTech (and How Has It Evolved)?" *Computerworld*, 18 September 2017, www.computerworld.com.

56. Edward Robinson, "Fintech, the Buzzword Finance Loves and Hates: QuickTake Q&A," *Bloomberg*, 23 February 2017, www.bloomberg.com.

57. Mary Wisniewski, "Is Small Business Banking Next in Line for Disruption?" *American Banker*, 3 November 2015, www.americanbanker.com.

58. "How Does an Online Credit Marketplace Work?" LendingClub, accessed 12 March 2018, www.lendingclub.com; "Fintech," *Investopedia*, accessed 12 March 2018, www.investopedia.com.

59. Robinhood, accessed 12 March 2018, www.robinhood.com; Acorns, accessed 12 March 2018, www.acorns.com.

60. Jordan Bishop, "TransferWise Review," 16 November 2017, *How I Travel* blog, www.howitravel.co.

61. Debra Cassens Weiss, "JPMorgan Chase Uses Tech to Save 360,000 Hours of Annual Work by Lawyers and Loan Officers," *ABA Journal*, 2 March 2017, www.abajournal.com.

62. Penny Crosman, "AI as New Tool in Banks' Crime-Fighting Bag?" *American Banker*, 12 March 2018, www.americanbanker.com; Bill Hogan, "Why the Financial Sector Needs to Focus on Automating Threat Intelligence," Fortinet, 12 September 2017, www.fortinet.com; Derek Manky, "Byline: Artificial Intelligence: Cybersecurity Friend or Foe?" Fortinet, 22 May 2017, www.fortinet.com.

63. Ainsley Harris, "5 Fintech Startups to Watch in 2017," *Fast Company*, 26 December 2016, www.fastcompany.com.

64. Robert Barba, "5 Questions to Ask Before Trying a Neobank," Bankrate, 14 February 2018, www.bankrate.com; N26, accessed 12 March 2018, next.n26.com/en-de/.

65. Arielle O'Shea and Anna-Louise Jackson, "Best Robo-Advisors: 2018 Top Picks," NerdWallet, 9 January 2018, www.nerdwallet.com; Dan Egan, "Get All the Returns You Deserve," Betterment, 26 June 2017, www.betterment.com.

66. See note 1.

3

The Global Marketplace

LEARNING OBJECTIVES   After studying this chapter, you will be able to

1 Explain why nations trade, and describe how international trade is measured.

2 Discuss the nature of conflicts in global business, including free trade and government interventions in international trade.

3 Identify the major organizations that facilitate international trade and the major trading blocs around the world.

4 Discuss the importance of understanding cultural and legal differences in the global business environment.

5 Define the major forms of international business activity.

6 Discuss the strategic choices that must be considered before entering international markets.

7 Describe the current state of AI-assisted translation and its value to international businesses.

MyLab Intro to Business
Improve Your Grade!
If your instructor is using MyLab Intro to Business, visit **www.pearson.com/mylab/intro-to-business**.

BEHIND THE SCENES | Airbnb: From Making a Few Bucks to Disrupting the Global Travel Industry

Airbnb cofounders Brian Chesky, Joe Gebbia, and Nathan Blecharczyk faced the intriguing challenge of expanding the home-sharing service internationally.

www.airbnb.com
Entrepreneurs launch companies for a variety of reasons, sometimes grand and ambitious reasons. For San Francisco roommates and design-school graduates Brian Chesky and Joe Gebbia, the goal was slightly less lofty: They couldn't afford to pay their rent and needed to leverage whatever they could to make some quick money.

What they had was a bit of extra space in their apartment and the knowledge that a major design conference was coming to town. Hotel rooms would be scarce—and expensive for other young designers like themselves. They bought three air mattresses and launched their humble venture as Air Bed and Breakfast, a play on the established lodging category of "bed and breakfast." In addition to offering an inexpensive place to sleep and breakfast during the conference, they planned to make additional money serving as tour guides for visiting designers—establishing the themes of community and personalized experiences that would later prove to be guiding values.

After selling out their three air beds for the conference, they realized they might be on to something with this room-sharing idea and brought in a former roommate, software engineer Nathan Blecharczyk, as a third cofounder. Proving their instinct about a business opportunity took several years and several failed launches, but when they finally got the right pieces in place, the phenomenon now known as Airbnb took off. Airbnb started as a low-cost, community-driven alternative to hotels, but before long it became a mainstream choice for many travelers. More property owners began to view Airbnb as a way to supplement their incomes, and more travelers began to view it as a legitimate alternative to hotels.

Travel is an international adventure, of course, and it didn't take long to recognize that the entire world was a potential market for the service. If you were leading Airbnb, how would you pursue markets outside the United States? How would you structure the company to balance the need for centralized planning with localized market responses? How would you transplant a successful model from your home country to dozens and dozens of countries, each with unique cultures, languages, and business practices?[1]

INTRODUCTION

The experience of Airbnb (profiled in the chapter-opening Behind the Scenes) is a great example of the opportunities and challenges of global expansion. International business has grown dramatically in recent years, and it's no stretch to say that this growth affects virtually every company in some way, even those that never reach beyond their own borders.

Fundamentals of International Trade

Wherever you're reading this, stop and look around for a minute. You might see cars that were made in Japan running on gasoline from Russia or Saudi Arabia, mobile phones made in South Korea, food grown in Canada or Mexico or Chile, a digital music player made in China, clothing made in Vietnam or Italy, industrial equipment made in Germany—and dozens of other products from every corner of the globe. Conversely, if you or a family member works for a midsize or large company, chances are it gets a significant slice of its revenue from sales to other countries. In short, we live and work in a global marketplace. Moreover, although the United States remains one of the world's most competitive countries, dozens of other countries compete for the same employees, customers, and investments (see Exhibit 3.1 on the next page).

> **1   LEARNING OBJECTIVE**
>
> Explain why nations trade, and describe how international trade is measured.

WHY NATIONS TRADE

Commerce across borders has been going on for thousands of years, but advances in transportation and communication in the past few decades have transformed the global business landscape. One significant result is **economic globalization**, the increasing integration and interdependence of national economies around the world. Six reasons help explain why countries and companies trade internationally:

- **Focusing on relative strengths.** The classic theory of *comparative advantage* suggests that each country should specialize in those areas where it can produce goods and services most efficiently and trade for goods and services that it can't produce as economically.[2] The basic argument is that such specialization and exchange will increase a country's total output and allow trading partners to enjoy a higher standard of living.
- **Expanding markets.** Many companies have ambitions too large for their own backyards. Well-known U.S. companies such as Microsoft and Boeing would be a fraction of their current size if they were limited to the U.S. marketplace. Similarly, companies based in other countries, from giants such as Toyota, Shell, and Nestlé to thousands of smaller but equally ambitious firms, view the U.S. consumer and business markets as a vast opportunity.
- **Pursuing economies of scale.** All this international activity involves more than just sales growth, of course. By expanding their markets, companies can benefit from **economies of scale**, which enable them to produce goods and services at lower costs by purchasing, manufacturing, and distributing higher quantities. For instance, Boeing and the European consortium Airbus spend enormous amounts of money designing new airliners and creating the tooling, facilities, and systems need to manufacture them.

economic globalization
The increasing integration and interdependence of national economies around the world.

economies of scale
Savings from buying parts and materials, manufacturing, or marketing in large quantities.

EXHIBIT 3.1	The World's Most Competitive Economies

According to the World Economic Forum (WEF), these are the 10 most competitive economies in the world, based on their ability to sustain economic growth. (Hong Kong, a Special Administrative Region of the People's Republic of China, is evaluated separately by the WEF.) Note that other ranking approaches can produce different results. For example, the Swiss business college IMD currently ranks the United States, Hong Kong SAR, and Singapore as the top three countries.

■ 1. Switzerland   ■ 6. Hong Kong SAR
■ 2. United States   ■ 7. Sweden
■ 3. Singapore   ■ 8. United Kingdom
■ 4. Netherlands   ■ 9. Japan
■ 5. Germany   ■ 10. Finland

Source: Data from "The Global Competitiveness Report 2017–2018," World Economic Forum, www.weforum.org; "IMD World Competitive Ranking 2018," IMD, www.imd.org.

By selling internationally, they can expand their sales volumes and increase the chances of turning a profit on every plane sold.

- **Acquiring materials, goods, and services.** No country can produce everything its citizens want at prices they're willing to pay, so companies and consumers alike reach across borders to find what they need.
- **Keeping up with customers.** In some cases, companies have to expand in order to keep or attract multinational customers. For example, suppose a retailer with stores in 20 countries wants to hire a single advertising agency to manage all its ad campaigns. Any agency vying for the account might need to open offices in all 20 countries in order to be considered.
- **Keeping up with competitors.** If a firm begins to see benefits from selling internationally, such as gaining economies of scale from higher sales volumes, its competitors may have no choice but to start expanding internationally as well.

HOW INTERNATIONAL TRADE IS MEASURED

Chapter 2 discusses how economists monitor certain key economic indicators to evaluate how well a country's economic system is performing, and several of these indicators measure international trade. Two key measurements of a nation's level of international trade are the *balance of trade* and the *balance of payments*. The total value of a country's exports minus the total value of its imports, over some period of time, determines its **balance of trade**. In years when the value of goods and services exported by a country exceeds the value of goods and services it imports, the country has a positive balance of trade, or a **trade surplus**. The opposite is a **trade deficit**, when a country imports more than it exports.

The **balance of payments** is the broadest indicator of international trade. It is the total flow of money into the country minus the total flow of money out of the country over some period of time.[3] For example, when a U.S. company buys all or part of a company based in

balance of trade
Total value of the products a nation exports minus the total value of the products it imports, over some period of time.

trade surplus
A favorable trade balance created when a country exports more than it imports.

trade deficit
An unfavorable trade balance created when a country imports more than it exports.

balance of payments
The sum of all payments one nation receives from other nations minus the sum of all payments it makes to other nations, over some specified period of time.

another country, that investment is counted in the balance of payments but not in the balance of trade. Similarly, when a foreign company buys a U.S. company or purchases U.S. stocks, bonds, or real estate, those transactions are part of the balance of payments.

FOREIGN EXCHANGE RATES AND CURRENCY VALUATIONS

When companies buy and sell goods and services in the global marketplace, they complete the transaction by exchanging currencies. The process is called *foreign exchange*, the conversion of one currency into an equivalent amount of another currency. The number of units of one currency that must be exchanged for a unit of the second currency is known as the **exchange rate** between the currencies.

Most international currencies operate under a *floating exchange rate system*, meaning that a currency's value or price fluctuates in response to the forces of global supply and demand.[4] The supply and demand of a country's currency are determined in part by what is happening in the country's own economy. Moreover, because supply and demand for a currency are always changing, the rate at which it is exchanged for other currencies may change a little each day.

A currency is called *strong* relative to another when its exchange rate is higher than what is considered normal and called *weak* when its rate is lower than normal ("normal" is a relative term here). Note that "strong" isn't necessarily good, and "weak" isn't necessarily bad when it comes to currencies, as Exhibit 3.2 illustrates. Exchange rates can dramatically affect a company's financial results by raising or lowering the cost of supplies it imports and raising or lowering the price of goods it exports.

exchange rate
The rate at which the money of one country is traded for the money of another.

REAL-TIME UPDATES
Learn More by Exploring This Interactive Website

Do a deep dive into balance of trade data
Explore the overall U.S. balance of trade for any time period and compare trade balances with any other country. Go to **real-timeupdates.com/bia9** and select Learn More in the Students section.

EXHIBIT 3.2	Strong and Weak Currencies: Who Gains, Who Loses?

A strong dollar and a weak dollar aren't necessarily good or bad; each condition helps some people and hurts others.
Sources: Based in part on John J. Wild and Kenneth L. Wild, *International Business: The Challenges of Globalization*, 8th ed. (New York: Pearson, 2016), 253; Rebecca Patterson, "A Weak Dollar Hurts More than It Helps," CNBC, 26 January 2018, www.cnbc.com.

✓ CHECKPOINT

LEARNING OBJECTIVE 1: Explain why nations trade, and describe how international trade is measured.

SUMMARY: Nations and companies trade internationally for any of six reasons: focusing on their relative strengths (producing the goods and services in which they excel and trading for other products they need); expanding into new markets to increase sales revenues; pursuing economies of scale to achieve lower production costs; acquiring materials, goods, and services not available at home; tending to the needs of multinational customers; and keeping up with competitors that are expanding internationally. Two primary measures of a country's international trade are its balance of trade, which is exports minus imports, and its balance of payments, a broader measure that includes all incoming payments minus all outgoing payments.

CRITICAL THINKING: (1) Would it be wise for an advertising agency to open offices in Europe and Asia to service a single multinational client? Why or why not? (2) If IBM invests $40 million in a joint venture in China, would that amount be counted in the U.S. balance of trade or the balance of payments?

IT'S YOUR BUSINESS: (1) In the last major purchase you made, did you take into consideration whether the product was made in the United States or another country? (2) Does country of origin matter to you when you shop?

KEY TERMS TO KNOW: economic globalization, economies of scale, balance of trade, trade surplus, trade deficit, balance of payments, exchange rate

---

<table><tr><td>2</td><td>**LEARNING OBJECTIVE**</td></tr></table>

Discuss the nature of conflicts in global business, including free trade and government interventions in international trade.

free trade
International trade unencumbered by restrictive measures.

protectionism
Government policies aimed at shielding a country's industries from foreign competition.

Conflicts in International Trade

Just as employees compete for jobs and companies compete for customers, countries compete with one another for both. Naturally, the U.S. government promotes and protects the interests of U.S. companies, workers, and consumers. Other countries are trying to do the same thing for their stakeholders. As a consequence, international trade is a never-ending tug of war.

FREE TRADE

The economic tug of war between countries is often framed in the debate over **free trade**, when international trade takes place without government intervention on either side. The flip side of free trade is **protectionism**, when a government institutes policies to protect its own industries or workers. Like free-market capitalism, though, no international trade is completely free in the sense that it takes place without regulations of any kind. Instead, international trade should be viewed along a continuum from "more free" to "less free."

The debate over free trade is complicated, and it will never be solved in any permanent sense because countries, industries, and companies are constantly maneuvering in search of advantages in the global marketplace. While it's easy to get bogged down in the particular details of whatever trade spats are currently grabbing the headlines, any discussion of free trade should consider five essential ideas:

- **Conflict between nations.** Trade agreements are often intertwined with international politics and foreign policy decisions. Trade has been fundamental in helping countries rebuild from wars and in preventing hostilities.[5] At the same time, even strong allies can engage in trade disputes as each side seeks to maximize its economic advantages.
- **Conflict within nations.** The conflict over free trade can be just as bitter inside a country as between countries, because trade policy decisions can simultaneously help one segment and hurt another. For example, steel imported into the United States is a continuing source of consternation, because the country now produces less steel than it did in years past, the steel industry employs far fewer workers than it once did,

and imported steel is often cheaper than domestically pro-duced steel. The instinct to help domestic steel producers by protecting them from lower-cost imports sounds both sensible and sensitive. However, the industries in the United States that use steel in their products benefit from lower steel prices—as do their customers—and these industries employ many times more workers than the steel industry does.[6] Across a variety of industries, protectionist measures to save jobs have often come at a high cost to consumers.[7]

International trade agreements are often controversial, with various parties concerned about the effects on jobs, the environment, and other issues.

- **Asymmetrical wins and losses.** Free trade is credited with lifting millions out of poverty around the world, but gains in one place often come at the expense of losses elsewhere. Supporters of free trade generally acknowledge that it produces winners and losers but that the winners gain more than the losers lose, so the net effect is positive.[8] However, when one group wins at the expense of another, it's difficult to convince those who are harmed that free trade is beneficial.

- **Short-term effects versus long-term effects.** As in most aspects of business and government, some decisions can appear to be beneficial in the short term but have negative long-term consequences. For example, instead of protecting jobs in an industry that is no longer competitive on a global scale, a more sensible long-term plan might be to help those workers, companies, and regions transition to new and more economically viable activities.

- **The broader business environment.** Trade takes place within the broader economic, social, and technological environments, making it difficult at times to isolate the effects of trade policy decisions. For instance, the U.S. steel industry is now five times more productive than it was in the 1980s, meaning it needs only one-fifth the workers to produce the same amount of steel.[9] In other words, job losses in the industry can't all be attributed to foreign competition; many have been lost to automation and other process improvements.

GOVERNMENT INTERVENTION IN INTERNATIONAL TRADE

When a government believes that free trade is not in the best interests of its national security, domestic industries, workforce, or consumers, it can intervene in several ways:

- **Tariffs.** Taxes, surcharges, or duties levied against imported goods are known as **tariffs**. Tariffs can be levied to generate revenue, to restrict trade, or to punish other countries for disobeying international trade laws.

- **Quotas. Import quotas** limit the amount of particular goods that countries allow to be imported during a given year.

- **Embargoes.** An **embargo** is a complete ban on the import or export of certain products or even on all trade between certain countries.

- **Restrictive import standards.** Countries can assist their domestic producers by establishing restrictive import standards, such as requiring special licenses for doing certain kinds of business and then making it difficult or expensive for foreign companies to obtain such licenses.[10]

- **Export subsidies.** In addition to intervening on imported goods, countries can also intervene to help domestic industries export their products to other countries. **Export subsidies** are a form of financial assistance in which producers receive enough money from the government to allow them to lower their prices in order to compete more effectively in the world market.

- **Antidumping measures.** The practice of exporting large quantities of a product at a price lower than the cost of production or below what the company would charge in its home market is called **dumping**. This tactic is most often used to try to win customers overseas or to reduce product surpluses. If a domestic producer can demonstrate that low-cost imports are damaging its business, it can appeal to its government to seek relief through international trade organizations.

tariffs
Taxes levied on imports.

import quotas
Limits placed on the quantity of imports a nation will allow for a specific product.

embargo
A total ban on trade with a particular nation (a sanction) or of a particular product.

export subsidies
A form of financial assistance in which producers receive enough money from the government to allow them to lower their prices in order to compete more effectively in the global market.

dumping
Charging less than the actual cost or less than the home-country price for goods sold in other countries.

- **Sanctions.** Sanctions are politically motivated embargoes that revoke a country's normal trade relations status; they are often used as forceful alternatives short of war. Sanctions can include arms embargoes, foreign-assistance reductions and cutoffs, trade limitations, tariff increases, import-quota decreases, visa denials, air-link cancellations, and more.

 CHECKPOINT

LEARNING OBJECTIVE 2: Discuss the nature of conflicts in global business, including free trade and government interventions in international trade.

SUMMARY: The root cause of trade conflict is that every country has a natural interest in protecting its own security and supporting its industries, workers, and consumers. The result is that countries often deviate from the notion of free trade by intervening in various ways, including the use of tariffs, import quotas, embargoes, restrictive import standards, export subsidies, antidumping measures, and sanctions.

CRITICAL THINKING: (1) What would happen to U.S. workers if all international trade suddenly became free, in the sense of there being no government intervention anywhere in the world? (2) What would be the effect on U.S. consumers?

IT'S YOUR BUSINESS: (1) Would you be willing to pay more for your clothes in order to keep more apparel manufacturing in the United States? Why or why not? (2) Do you or would you consider purchasing "fair trade" products, for which prices are set high enough to ensure a living wage for everyone involved in their production, even though these higher prices can make them less competitive in world markets?

KEY TERMS TO KNOW: free trade, protectionism, tariffs, import quotas, embargo, export subsidies, dumping

---

3 **LEARNING OBJECTIVE**

Identify the major organizations that facilitate international trade and the major trading blocs around the world.

International Trade Organizations

With international trade such a huge part of the world's economies, organizations that establish trading rules, resolve disputes, and promote trade play important roles in global business.

ORGANIZATIONS FACILITATING INTERNATIONAL TRADE

In an effort to ensure equitable trading practices and to iron out the inevitable disagreements over what is fair and what isn't, governments around the world have established a number of important agreements and organizations that address trading issues, including the World Trade Organization, International Monetary Fund, and World Bank.

The World Trade Organization

The World Trade Organization (WTO), **www.wto.org**, is a permanent forum for negotiating, implementing, and monitoring international trade procedures and for mediating trade disputes among its 160-plus member countries. The organization's work is guided by six principles:[11]

- Preventing discriminatory policies that favor some trading partners over others or a country's own products over those of other countries
- Reducing trade barriers between countries
- Making trade policies more predictable and transparent
- Promoting fair competition by discouraging unfair practices
- Promoting economic progress in the world's less-developed countries
- Ensuring that countries don't use environmental or public health policies as a disguise for protectionism

The WTO attempts to hammer out major agreements in "rounds," marathon negotiating sessions that take years to work out details and disagreements. The difficulty is not surprising—a trade agreement between just two countries can be extremely complicated, so attempts at global agreements are immense undertakings and are not always successful. The most recent, called the Doha round because it took place in Doha, Qatar, started in 2001 and was terminated in 2015 without achieving its goals.[12]

The International Monetary Fund

The International Monetary Fund (IMF), **www.imf.org**, was established after World War II to foster international financial cooperation and increase the stability of the international economy. Now with 189 member countries, the IMF's primary functions are monitoring global financial developments, offering technical advice and training to help countries manage their economies more effectively, and providing short-term loans to member countries. These loans can be made for a variety of reasons, from helping a country deal with a natural disaster to stabilizing a country's economy in order to limit the spread of a financial crisis beyond its borders.[13]

The World Bank

The World Bank, **www.worldbank.org**, is a group of five financial institutions whose primary goals are eradicating the most extreme levels of poverty around the world and raising the income of the poorest people in every country as a way to foster shared prosperity for everyone. Although it is not as directly involved in international trade and finance on the same scale as the WTO and IMF, the World Bank does indirectly contribute to trade by working to improve economic conditions through investing in education, health care, and other concerns in developing countries.[14]

TRADING BLOCS

Trading blocs, or *common markets*, are regional organizations that promote trade among member nations (see Exhibit 3.3 on the next page). Although specific rules vary from group to group, their primary objective is to ensure the economic growth and benefit of members. As such, trading blocs generally promote trade inside the region while creating uniform barriers against goods and services entering the region from nonmember countries.

North American Free Trade Agreement

In 1994, the United States, Canada, and Mexico formed the North American Free Trade Agreement (NAFTA), paving the way for freer flow of goods, services, and capital within the bloc through the phased elimination of tariffs and quotas.[15] NAFTA was controversial when first implemented, and it has remained controversial ever since.[16] Assessing the treaty's full impact is difficult because so many economic factors are involved, and a variety of other forces have affected all three countries' economies over the past two decades.

NAFTA also illustrates the challenge of analyzing international economic activity and linking measurable effects to specific causes. And, as is often the case with economic change, gains for some groups come at the expense of losses for other groups. The authors of a congressional report issued on NAFTA's 20th anniversary summarized its overall impact this way: "NAFTA did not cause the huge job losses feared by the critics or the large economic gains predicted by supporters."[17] Other analyses point to losses of up to a million U.S. jobs, but many of those were likely lost to automation, the Great Recession, and China's rising role in the global economy.[18]

The European Union

One of the largest trading blocs is the European Union (EU), **europa.eu**, whose membership now encompasses more than two dozen countries and half a billion people. Viewed as a whole, the EU now constitutes the world's largest economy.

trading blocs
Organizations of nations that remove barriers to trade among their members and that establish uniform barriers to trade with nonmember nations.

REAL-TIME UPDATES
Learn More by Exploring This Interactive Website

Get an interactive look at global economic data

This interactive Data Mapper tool from the International Monetary Fund makes it easy to explore and compare key economic data for countries around the world. Go to **real-timeupdates.com/bia9** and select Learn More in the Students section.

REAL-TIME UPDATES
Learn More by Visiting This Website

A deep look at important global business matters

The World Economic Forum publishes in-depth studies on a wide range of global business topics, from food production to health care to sustainable energy. Go to **real-timeupdates.com/bia9** and select Learn More in the Students section.

EXHIBIT 3.3   Members of Major Trading Blocs

As the economies of the world become increasingly linked, many countries have formed powerful regional trading blocs that trade freely with one another but place restrictions on trade with other countries and blocs. (The United Kingdom may be out of the European Union by the time you read this.)

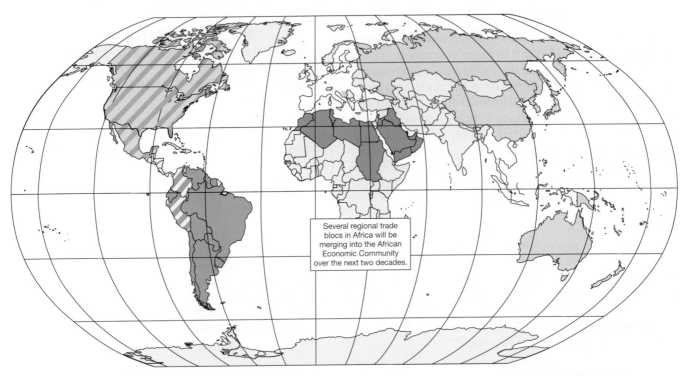

Several regional trade blocs in Africa will be merging into the African Economic Community over the next two decades.

European Union (EU)	North American Free Trade Agreement (NAFTA)	Association of Southeast Asian Nations (ASEAN)	Union of South American Nations (UNASUR)	Asia-Pacific Economic Cooperation (APEC)	Greater Arab Free Trade Area (GAFTA)
Austria	Canada	Brunei Darussalam	Argentina	Australia	Algeria
Belgium	Mexico	Cambodia	Bolivia	Brunei Darussalam	Bahrain
Bulgaria	United States	Indonesia	Brazil	Canada	Egypt
Croatia		Laos	Chile	Chile	Iraq
Cyprus		Malaysia	Colombia	China	Jordan
Czech Republic		Myanmar	Ecuador	Hong Kong	Kuwait
Denmark		Philippines	Guyana	Indonesia	Lebanon
Estonia		Singapore	Paraguay	Japan	Libya
Finland		Thailand	Peru	Republic of Korea	Morocco
France		Vietnam	Suriname	Malaysia	Oman
Germany			Uruguay	Mexico	Palestine
Greece			Venezuela	New Zealand	Qatar
Hungary				Papua New Guinea	Saudi Arabia
Ireland				Peru	Sudan
Italy				Philippines	Syria
Latvia				Russia	Tunisia
Lithuania				Singapore	United Arab Emirates
Luxembourg				Chinese Taipei	Yemen
Malta				Thailand	
Netherlands				United States	
Poland				Vietnam	
Portugal					
Romania					
Slovakia					
Slovenia					
Spain					
Sweden					
United Kingdom					

Sources: Member lists as of 17 March 2018: europa.eu; www.asean.org; www.unasursg.org; www.apec.org; www.economy.gov.lb.

EU nations have eliminated hundreds of local regulations, variations in product standards, and protectionist measures that once limited trade among member countries. Trade now flows among these countries in much the same way it does among states in the United States. And the EU's reach extends far beyond the borders of Europe; to simplify design and manufacturing for world markets, many companies now create their products to meet EU specifications. If you've seen the "CE" marking on any products you may own, that stands for Conformité Européene and indicates that the product has met EU standards for safety, health, and environmental responsibility.[19]

The EU has taken a significant step beyond all other trading blocs in the area of money by creating its own currency, the *euro*, which has been adopted by more than half its member states. By switching to a common currency, these countries have made financial transactions simpler and less expensive. According to EU leadership, the euro has simplified commerce for consumers and businesses, lowered inflation and interest rates, improved transparency in pricing, provided a more stable currency, and given the EU a stronger presence in global financial markets.[20]

As you might expect with an international organization comprising so many countries with diverse cultures and economies, the EU wrestles with a variety of internal controversies and upheavals. The most significant in recent years was a 2016 vote in the United Kingdom to withdraw from the EU, an event referred to as *Brexit* (for British exit).

The Asia-Pacific Economic Cooperation

The Asia-Pacific Economic Cooperation (APEC), **www.apec.org**, is an organization of 21 countries working to liberalize trade in the Pacific Rim (the land areas that surround the Pacific Ocean). Member nations represent 40 percent of the world's population and more than 50 percent of the world's gross domestic product. Like other trade blocs, APEC has a long-term goal of encouraging trade and investment among member countries and helping the region achieve sustainable economic growth.[21]

 CHECKPOINT

LEARNING OBJECTIVE 3: Identify the major organizations that facilitate international trade and the major trading blocs around the world.

SUMMARY: Major organizations that facilitate trade include the World Trade Organization (WTO), the International Monetary Fund (IMF), and, at least indirectly, the World Bank. Major regional trading blocs include NAFTA (Canada, Mexico, and the United States), the European Union (more than two dozen countries across Europe), and APEC (21 countries around the Pacific Rim).

CRITICAL THINKING: (1) Why do trade disputes sometimes take years to resolve? (2) If a country currently benefits from high tariffs on imports, why might it consider joining a trading bloc that requires it to lower or eliminate those tariffs?

IT'S YOUR BUSINESS: (1) Can you identify any ways in which your life as an employee or a consumer has been affected by U.S. membership in trading blocs such as NAFTA and APEC? (2) How can you confirm that the effect was caused by trading bloc membership?

KEY TERM TO KNOW: trading blocs

The Global Business Environment

 LEARNING OBJECTIVE

Discuss the importance of understanding cultural and legal differences in the global business environment.

Doing business internationally can be a boon for many companies, but it also presents many challenges. Every country has unique laws, customs, consumer preferences, ethical standards, and political and economic forces. Understanding cultural and legal differences is an essential first step for any business contemplating international operations.

CULTURAL DIFFERENCES IN THE GLOBAL BUSINESS ENVIRONMENT

culture
A shared system of symbols, beliefs, attitudes, values, expectations, and norms for behavior.

Culture is a shared system of symbols, beliefs, attitudes, values, expectations, and norms for behavior. Culture shapes business practices in multiple ways, including communication practices, social norms and customs, and the way that people in a society respond to differences in gender, religion, age, and other aspects of diversity. One of the most important adjustments that businesspeople need to make when working internationally is to step out of their own cultural mindsets and adapt to the cultures of the places in which they do business.

ethnocentrism
Judging all other groups according to the standards, behaviors, and customs of one's own group.

stereotyping
Assigning a wide range of generalized and often false attributes to an individual based on his or her membership in a particular culture or social group.

cultural pluralism
The practice of accepting multiple cultures on their own terms.

Specifically, it's important to avoid **ethnocentrism**, the tendency to judge other groups according to the standards, behaviors, and customs of one's own culture, and **stereotyping**, assigning a wide range of generalized and often false attributes to an individual on the basis of membership in a particular culture or social group. To show respect for others and to interact successfully around the globe, adopt the more positive viewpoint of **cultural pluralism**—the practice of accepting multiple cultures on their own terms. A few simple habits can help:

- **Avoid assumptions.** Don't assume that others will act the same way you do, use language and symbols the same way you do, or even operate from the same values and beliefs.
- **Avoid judgments.** When people act differently, don't conclude that they are in error or that their way is invalid or inferior. As with assumptions, doing so requires conscious effort, such as not letting someone's appearance or accent influence your perceptions.[22]
- **Acknowledge distinctions.** Don't ignore the differences between another person's culture and your own.

Successful international businesspeople embrace other cultures on their own terms and work to avoid the distortions of an ethnocentric outlook.

Horizon International Images Limited/Alamy Stock Photo

Unfortunately, overcoming ethnocentrism and stereotyping is not a simple task, even for people who are highly motivated to do so. Moreover, research suggests that people often have beliefs and biases they're not even aware of—and that may even conflict with the beliefs they *think* they have.[23]

Effectively adapting your communication efforts to another culture requires knowledge about the culture and the ability and motivation to change your personal habits as needed.[24] Fortunately, you don't need to learn about the whole world all at once. Many companies appoint specialists for countries or regions, giving employees a chance to focus on just one culture at a time. And if your employer conducts business internationally, it may offer training and support for employees who need to learn more about specific cultures.

Even a small amount of research and practice will help you get through many business situations. In addition, most people respond positively to honest effort and good intentions, and many business associates will help you along if you show an interest in learning more about their cultures. Don't be afraid to ask questions. People will respect your concern and curiosity. You will gradually accumulate considerable knowledge, which will help you feel comfortable and be effective in a wide range of business situations.

Numerous websites and books offer advice on traveling to and working in specific cultures. Also try to sample newspapers, magazines, and even the music and movies of another country. For instance, a movie can demonstrate nonverbal customs even if you don't grasp the language. However, be careful not to rely solely on entertainment products. If people in other countries based their opinions of U.S. culture only on some of the silly comedies and violent action movies that the United States exports around the globe, what sort of impression do you imagine they'd get?

REAL-TIME UPDATES
Learn More by Exploring This Interactive Website

Get detailed information about any country

The *CIA World Factbook* has information on everything from ethnic groups to government structures. Go to **real-timeupdates.com/bia9** and select Learn More in the Students section.

For some of the key issues to research before doing business in another country, refer to Exhibit 3.4.

EXHIBIT 3.4	Checklist for Doing Business Abroad

Use this checklist as a starting point when planning business activity in another country.

Action	Details to Consider
Understand social customs	• How do people react to strangers? Are they friendly? Hostile? Reserved? • How do people greet each other? Should you bow? Nod? Shake hands? • How do you express appreciation for an invitation to lunch, dinner, or someone's home? Should you bring a gift? Send flowers? Write a thank-you note? • Are any phrases, facial expressions, or hand gestures considered rude? • How do you attract the attention of a waiter? Do you tip the waiter? • When is it rude to refuse an invitation? How do you refuse politely? • What topics may or may not be discussed in a social setting? In a business setting? • How do social customs dictate interaction between men and women? Between younger people and older people?
Learn about clothing and food preferences	• What occasions require special attire? • What colors are associated with mourning? Love? Joy? • Are some types of clothing considered taboo for one gender or the other? • How many times a day do people eat? • How are hands or utensils used when eating? • Where is the seat of honor at a table?
Assess political patterns	• How stable is the political situation? • Does the political situation affect businesses in and out of the country? • Is it appropriate to talk politics in social or business situations?
Understand religious and social beliefs	• To which religious groups do people belong? • Which places, objects, actions, and events are sacred? • Do religious beliefs affect communication between men and women or between any other groups? • Is there a tolerance for minority religions? • How do religious holidays affect business and government activities? • Does religion require or prohibit eating specific foods? At specific times?
Learn about economic and business institutions	• Is the society homogeneous or heterogeneous? • What languages are spoken? • What are the primary resources and principal products? • Are businesses generally large? Family controlled? Government controlled? • What are the generally accepted working hours? • How do people view scheduled appointments? • Are people expected to socialize before conducting business?
Appraise the nature of ethics, values, and laws	• Is money or a gift expected in exchange for arranging business transactions? • Do people value competitiveness or cooperation? • What are the attitudes toward work? Toward money? • Is politeness more important than factual honesty?

Source: Courtland L. Bovée and John V. Thill, *Business Communication Today,* 14th ed. © 2018 p. 82. Reprinted and electronically reproduced by permission of Pearson Education, Inc. Upper Saddle River, New Jersey.

LEGAL DIFFERENCES IN THE GLOBAL BUSINESS ENVIRONMENT

As you conduct business around the world, you'll find that legal systems and expectations of ethical behavior can vary across countries and cultures. Differences in national legal systems may not be as immediately obvious as cultural differences, but they can have a profound effect on international business efforts. For instance, the legal systems in the United States and the United Kingdom are based on *common law*, in which tradition, custom, and judicial interpretation play important roles. In contrast, the systems in countries such as France and Germany are based on *civil law*, in which legal parameters are specified in detailed legal codes. A third type of legal system, *theocratic law*, or law based on religious principles, predominates in countries such as Iran and Pakistan.[25] Beyond the differences in legal philosophies, the business of contracts, copyrights, employee rights, consumer protection, product labeling, and other legal matters can vary considerably from one country to another.[26]

Tax havens and bribery are two serious issues that highlight the challenges and complexities of international business law.

Tax Havens

tax haven
A country whose favorable banking laws and low tax rates give companies the opportunity to shield some of their income from higher tax rates in their home countries or other countries where they do business.

A **tax haven** is a country whose favorable banking laws and low tax rates give companies the opportunity to shield some of their income from higher tax rates in their home countries or other countries where they do business. The amount of money involved is difficult to pin down because so much of the activity is secret, but estimates run well into the trillions of dollars.[27]

Although a vast amount of criminal money moves through or is sheltered in certain tax havens, using tax havens isn't necessarily illegal. However, it can be a highly controversial practice, particularly in the case of multinational corporations that use internal transfers or other processes to lower their tax burdens. Critics charge that being able to move funds around the world to minimize taxes gives multinational companies an unfair advantage over local competitors and allows them to avoid the shared responsibility of supporting infrastructure, education, and other public resources. The United States alone is estimated to lose $150 billion a year from overseas tax havens used by U.S. corporations.[28]

Cracking down on illegal use of tax havens and changing the laws that allow legal use of tax havens is not easy, because their beneficiaries are some of the richest and most powerful countries, corporations, and individuals in the world. Plus, the countries that serve as tax havens often do so because it's one of the few ways they have to generate economic activity.[29] However, individual countries and the European Union do occasionally force changes. Apple and Google are among the multinational companies that have recently been forced to pay more taxes by restricting their ability to move profits through tax havens.[30]

Bribery

An enduring dilemma for many companies is the question of making payments to government officials in some countries in order to secure contracts or otherwise gain a business advantage. These practices discourage much-needed investment in developing countries, undermine democratic processes and weaken trust in government, raise prices for consumers by inflating business costs, potentially create environmental degradation by letting companies skirt regulations, and can even present security risks by essentially putting officials' actions up for the highest bid.[31]

Although the practice is so common in some locations that it's considered a standard way of doing business, paying bribes is broadly illegal for U.S. companies under the Foreign Corrupt Practices Act (FCPA). The FCPA allows common business considerations such as hosting officials at social functions and giving modest gifts. However, if anything of value is offered to government officials with the intent to get them to break the laws of their own countries, the action is illegal and subject to heavy penalties under the FCPA.[32]

REAL-TIME UPDATES
Learn More by Visiting This Website

Working to eradicate corruption around the world

Learn more about the work of Transparency International. Go to **real-timeupdates.com/bia9** and select Learn More in the Students section.

CHECKPOINT

LEARNING OBJECTIVE 4: Discuss the importance of understanding cultural and legal differences in the global business environment.

SUMMARY: Elements of culture include language, social values, ideas of status, decision-making habits, attitudes toward time, use of space, body language, manners, religions, and ethical standards. Awareness of and respect for cultural differences is essential to avoiding communication breakdowns and fostering positive working relationships. Understanding differences in legal systems and specific laws and regulations in other countries is another vital aspect of successful international business. Tax havens and bribery of government officials are two recurring and complex issues in international business.

CRITICAL THINKING: (1) What steps could you take to help someone from another country adapt to U.S. business culture? (2) How can you convey respect for another person's culture even if you don't agree with it or even understand it?

IT'S YOUR BUSINESS: (1) When you encounter someone whose native language is different from yours, what steps do you take to make sure communication is successful? (2) How does another person's "foreignness" influence your perceptions of his or her abilities?

KEY TERMS TO KNOW: culture, ethnocentrism, stereotyping, cultural pluralism, tax haven

Forms of International Business Activity

Beyond cultural and legal concerns, companies that plan to go international also need to think carefully about the right organizational approach to support these activities. The five common forms of international business are importing and exporting, licensing, franchising, strategic alliances and joint ventures, and foreign direct investment. Each has varying degrees of ownership, financial commitment, and risk (see Exhibit 3.5).

IMPORTING AND EXPORTING

Importing involves buying goods or services from a supplier in another country, whereas **exporting** is the selling of products outside the country in which they are produced. Exporting is one of the least risky forms of international business activity. It allows a firm

5 **LEARNING OBJECTIVE**

Define the major forms of international business activity.

importing
Purchasing goods or services from another country and bringing them into one's own country.

exporting
Selling and shipping goods or services to another country.

EXHIBIT 3.5 | **Forms of International Business Activity**

Depending on their goals and resources and the opportunities available, companies can choose from five different ways to conduct business internationally.

Importing and exporting
Buying and selling goods and services across national borders, without establishing a physical or legal business presence in other countries

International licensing
Licensing intellectual property such as a design patent to a company in another country, which then produces the product and sells it locally

International franchising
Selling the rights to use an entire business system, such as a fast-food restaurant, including the brand name and internal processes

International strategic alliances and joint ventures
Forming a long-term business partnership with a local company in a new market or creating a new company with a local partner

Foreign direct investment
Buying an established company or launching a new company in another country

to enter a foreign market gradually, assess local conditions, and then fine-tune its product offerings to meet the needs of local markets. In most cases, the firm's financial exposure is limited to the costs of researching the market, advertising, and compensating sales channel intermediaries. A variety of intermediaries exist to help companies, even the smallest businesses, get started with exporting.

Many countries now have foreign trade offices to help importers and exporters. Other helpful resources include professional agents, local businesspeople, and the International Trade Administration of the U.S. Department of Commerce (www.export.gov), which offers several services, including political and credit-risk analysis, advice on entering foreign markets, and financing tips.[33] Companies without the resources to manage export activities themselves also have the option of exporting indirectly through agents and export management companies.[34]

INTERNATIONAL LICENSING

licensing
Agreement to produce and market another company's product in exchange for a royalty or fee.

Licensing is another popular approach to international business. License agreements entitle one company to use some or all of another firm's intellectual property (patents, trademarks, brand names, copyrights, or trade secrets) in return for a royalty payment. The potential benefits of licensing as an international expansion strategy include quicker market entry, lower financial commitment, lower risks, and in some cases the ability to get around import/export restrictions or tariffs.[35]

INTERNATIONAL FRANCHISING

Some companies choose to expand into foreign markets by *franchising* their operations. Chapter 6 discusses franchising in more detail, but briefly, franchising involves selling the right to use a *business system*, including brand names, business processes, trade secrets, and other assets. Franchising is an attractive option for many companies because it reduces the costs and risks of expanding internationally while leveraging their investments in branding and business processes.

INTERNATIONAL STRATEGIC ALLIANCES AND JOINT VENTURES

Strategic alliances (discussed in Chapter 5), which are long-term partnerships between two or more companies to jointly develop, produce, or sell products, are another important way to reach the global marketplace. Alliance partners typically share ideas, expertise, resources, technologies, investment costs, risks, management, and profits. In some cases, a strategic alliance might be the only way to gain access to a market.

A *joint venture*, in which two or more firms join together to create a new business entity that is legally separate and distinct from its parents, is an alternative to a strategic alliance. In some countries, foreign companies are prohibited from owning facilities outright or from investing in local business, so establishing a joint venture with a local partner may be the only way to do business there.[36]

FOREIGN DIRECT INVESTMENT

foreign direct investment (FDI)
Investment of money by foreign companies in domestic business enterprises.

multinational corporations (MNCs)
Companies with operations in more than one country.

Many firms prefer to enter international markets through partial or whole ownership and control of business operations in foreign countries, an approach known as **foreign direct investment (FDI)**. FDI typically gives companies greater control, but it carries much greater economic and political risk and is more complex than any other form of entry in the global marketplace. Companies that establish a physical presence in multiple countries through FDI are called **multinational corporations (MNCs)**. MNCs can approach international markets in a variety of ways; see "Organizational Strategies for International Expansion" in the next section.

CHECKPOINT

LEARNING OBJECTIVE 5: Define the major forms of international business activity.

SUMMARY: The major forms of international business activity are importing and exporting (buying and selling across national boundaries), licensing (conferring the rights to create a product), franchising (selling the rights to use an entire business system and brand identity), strategic alliances and joint ventures (forming partnerships with other companies), and foreign direct investment (buying companies or building facilities in another country).

CRITICAL THINKING: (1) Can a company successfully export to other countries without having staff and facilities in those countries? Why or why not? (2) Why would a company decide on foreign direct investment, even though it is more expensive and riskier than other options?

IT'S YOUR BUSINESS: (1) What connotations does the word *imported* have for you? (2) On what do you base your reaction?

KEY TERMS TO KNOW: importing, exporting, foreign direct investment (FDI), multinational corporations (MNCs)

Strategic Approaches to International Markets

[6]   **LEARNING OBJECTIVE**

Discuss the strategic choices that must be considered before entering international markets.

Expanding internationally is obviously not a decision any business can take lightly. The rewards can be considerable, but the costs and risks must be analyzed carefully. This section offers a brief look at overall organizational strategies for international expansion, followed by strategic questions in the various functional areas of the business.

ORGANIZATIONAL STRATEGIES FOR INTERNATIONAL EXPANSION

When a firm decides to establish a presence in another country, it needs to consider its long-term objectives, the nature of its products, the characteristics of the markets into which it plans to expand, and the management team's ability to oversee a geographically dispersed operation. These considerations can lead to one of several high-level organizational strategies: multidomestic, global, and transnational (see Exhibit 3.6 on the next page):[37]

- In the **multidomestic strategy**, a company creates highly independent operating units in each new country, giving local managers a great deal of freedom to run operations as they see fit. Although this strategy can help a company respond more quickly and effectively to local market needs, it doesn't always deliver the economy-of-scale advantages that other strategies can bring. In addition, the lack of centralized control can lead to situations in which local managers act in ways contrary to corporate strategy or guidelines.
- In the **global strategy**, a company embraces the notion of economic globalization by viewing the world as a single integrated market. This approach is essentially the opposite of the multidomestic strategy. Managerial control in the global strategy is highly centralized, with headquarters in the home country making all major decisions.
- In the **transnational strategy**, a company uses a hybrid approach as it attempts to reap the benefits of international scale while being responsive to local market dynamics. This is the essence of the often-heard advice to "think globally, act locally." (You may hear it referred to as acting "glocally.") With this approach, major strategic decisions, product planning, and business systems such as accounting and purchasing are centralized, but local business units are given the freedom to make "on-the-ground" decisions that are most appropriate for local markets. As you'll see in the Behind the Scenes wrap-up at the end of the chapter, this is the approach Airbnb uses for its international operations.

multidomestic strategy
A decentralized approach to international expansion in which a company creates highly independent operating units in each new country.

global strategy
A highly centralized approach to international expansion, with headquarters in the home country making all major decisions.

transnational strategy
A hybrid approach that attempts to reap the benefits of international scale while being responsive to local market dynamics.

EXHIBIT 3.6   Organizing for Global Business

Multinational companies can choose from several different ways to organize their operations.

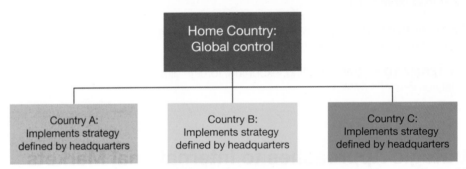

Multidomestic: Decentralized control, with individual divisions or subsidiaries in various countries free to pursue strategies that align with local markets

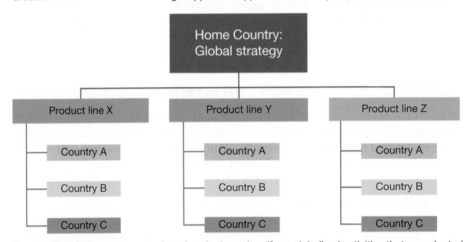

Global: Centralized control and single approach, applied as uniformly as possible around the world

Transnational: Pursues economies of scale through uniform globalized activities that are adapted as needed to local conditions

Source: Based on Stephen P. Robbins and Mary Coulter, *Management*, 14th ed. (New York: Pearson, 2018), 118.

FUNCTIONAL STRATEGIES FOR INTERNATIONAL EXPANSION

Choosing the right form of business to pursue is the first of many decisions that companies need to make when moving into other countries. Virtually everything you learn about in this course, from human resources to marketing to financial management, needs to be reconsidered carefully when going international. Some of the most important decisions involve products, customer support, promotion, pricing, and staffing:

- **Products.** International businesses face two primary questions regarding products. First, which products should they try to sell in each market? Second, should they *standardize* their products, selling the same product everywhere in the world, or *customize* their products to accommodate the lifestyles and habits of local target markets? Customization seems like an obvious choice, but it can increase costs and operational complexity, so the decision to customize is not automatic. The degree of customization can also vary. A company may change only a product's name or packaging, or it can modify a product's components, size, and functions. Understanding a country's regulations, culture, and local competition is essential to making smart product design and branding decisions.

- **Customer support.** Cars, computers, and other products that require some degree of customer support add another layer of complexity to international business. Customers may be reluctant to buy foreign products that don't offer some form of local support, whether it's a local dealer, a manufacturer's branch office, or a third-party organization that offers support under contract to the manufacturer.

- **Promotion.** Advertising, public relations, and other promotional efforts also present the dilemma of standardization versus customization. In addition to language differences, companies need to consider nonverbal symbols (the significance of colors and hand gestures, for example), local competition, and a variety of cultural differences.

- **Pricing.** Even a standardized strategy adds to the cost of doing business, from transportation to communication, and customized international strategies add even more. Before moving into other countries, businesses need to make sure they can cover all these costs and still be able to offer competitive prices.

- **Staffing.** Depending on the form of business a company decides to pursue in international markets, staffing questions can be major considerations. Many companies find that a combination of U.S. and local personnel works best, mixing company experience with local connections and lifelong knowledge of the working culture.

Starbucks maintains consistent brand imagery around the world while adapting to local languages.

Given the number and complexity of the decisions to be made, you can see why successful companies plan international expansion with great care—and adapt quickly if their strategies and tactics aren't working. The consequences of not planning carefully or adapting quickly to missteps can be high.

For the latest information on international business, visit **real-timeupdates.com/bia9** and select Chapter 3.

 CHECKPOINT

LEARNING OBJECTIVE 6: Discuss the strategic choices that must be considered before entering international markets.

SUMMARY: The strategic choices a business must make include the basic organizational strategy that defines what kind of company the firm will be in each country and a variety of functional strategies involving such aspects as products, customer support, promotion, pricing, and staffing. Organizational strategies include multidomestic (a highly decentralized approach), global (a highly centralized approach), and transnational (a hybrid approach).

CRITICAL THINKING: (1) If a multidomestic approach gives local managers the most flexibility for responding to local market conditions, why wouldn't every international company use this strategy? (2) How might the choice of overall organizational strategy affect a company's staffing plans in each country?

IT'S YOUR BUSINESS: (1) How does Apple's "Designed in California" product label influence your perceptions of product quality? (2) Do you think it helps counter negative public opinion about U.S. companies that manufacture products in other countries as a way to reduce labor costs? Why or why not?

KEY TERMS TO KNOW: multidomestic strategy, global strategy, transnational strategy

<table>
<tr><td>

7 **LEARNING OBJECTIVE**

Describe the current state of AI-assisted translation and its value to international businesses.

machine translation
Any form of computer-based, automated language translation.

</td></tr>
</table>

Thriving in the Digital Enterprise: AI-Assisted Translation

Language is one of the many practical challenges of conducting international business when multiple languages are involved. **Machine translation**, as automated translation has historically been called, has been one of the long-standing goals of artificial intelligence (AI).

The latest generation of AI-assisted translation tools are getting accurate enough to be useful in many basic communication scenarios. However, they must be used with caution. Bear in mind that they are processing language, not reading for understanding in the same way that humans do.[38] The more that a piece of text leans toward abstraction or involves word play, complex phrasing, idiomatic expressions, or subtle shades of meaning, the less likely it will translate correctly using one of these systems. And if you're not familiar with the second language, you might not be able to tell that the translation is faulty.

For concrete, straightforward language, though—the style used in many business communication scenarios—Google Translate and other services can help you get at least the basic gist of text written in another language. For example, for translating company overviews, product descriptions, operating guides, and similar content, the tools can be quite helpful. The translation probably won't be 100 percent correct, but you can usually work out the meaning. Whenever you need to translate contracts or other documents in which complete accuracy is critical, however, the services of a professional translator are well worth the cost.

For translating your own writing into another language, the question of using machine translation depends on the situation and the audience.[39] If you are writing email messages to a coworker, for instance, the occasional language glitch won't matter too much. For public content such as websites and marketing materials, though, it's best to use a translator to ensure accuracy and natural tone.

TEXT TRANSLATION

Translation tools can work at several levels: translating written text (that you type or copy into the system), translating text within images, and translating spoken language. Working with written text is the simplest of these because the system doesn't need to convert sounds to text and then convert text back to sound, in addition to performing the translation. Two useful applications of text translation are the translation features of common web browsers (see Exhibit 3.7) and mobile apps that can translate text as you type it in.

Translating text within images adds a layer of complexity to the process, because the system must be able to recognize words from within an image. However, *optical character recognition* is now refined enough to handle text that is clearly visible and in standard type fonts. For international travel, a particularly handy smartphone feature is the ability to aim your phone's camera at a sign or other printed material and let the translation app tell you what it says.

Hey Google, help me speak Japanese

Real-time voice translation addresses the multiple challenges of recognizing speech, converting it to text in the original language, translating it to a second language, and then synthesizing voice output in that language.

REAL-TIME VOICE TRANSLATION

The trickiest translation job of all is translating spoken language in real time or close to real time so that people can carry on a conversation or participate in a presentation. Doing so requires multiple layers of technology, including *speech recognition* and *synthesis* to "hear" and "speak" the language, *natural language processing* and *natural language generation* to understand the incoming language and output sensible language, and the translation capability in the middle.

EXHIBIT 3.7   **Automated Website Translation**

Although they haven't reached the proficiency of human translators, AI-enabled translation tools such as Google Translate have improved dramatically in recent years. For example, you can usually get at least the gist of a website published in another language.

SELECT YOUR TEXTBOOK:

Business Communication Today

Excellence In Business Communication

Business Communication Essentials

Business In Action

SÉLECTIONNEZ VOTRE MANUEL :

Communication d'entreprise aujourd'hui

Excellence en communication d'entreprise

Principes de la communication d'entreprise

Affaires en action

Even with all these challenges, though, systems such as Skype Translator and Google Translate are getting remarkably adept. Google's Pixel Buds earbuds offer nearly instantaneous translation across dozens of languages, making it theoretically possible to travel much of the world and converse with anyone who is similarly equipped, at least for basic conversations.[40]

A variety of other smartphone and smartwatch apps offer translation without the need for each party to have identical equipment; speakers take turns talking to the device, then listen as it outputs the translated speech. Microsoft's PowerPoint Presentation Translator adds real-time translation for presenters, making it easier for global professionals to connect with their audiences.[41]

These tools can't replace human translators or interpreters in every scenario, but when you don't have those options and need to reach across a language barrier, they can help you make essential business connections.

 CHECKPOINT

LEARNING OBJECTIVE 7: Describe the current state of AI-assisted translation and its value to international businesses.

SUMMARY: Translation technologies have made great strides in recent years and are now useful tools for many basic business communication situations. However, they must be used with some caution; if you're not familiar with the other language, you might not be able to tell if you're getting a faulty translation. For important documents or situations, it's best to hire a translator or interpreter, but for everyday communication when you can live without 100 percent accuracy, AI-assisted translation is a useful and cost-effective alternative.

CRITICAL THINKING: (1) Do you think real-time translation, even if it gets close to the quality of human translators, will ever eliminate the need to learn other languages in order to communicate effectively with diverse, global audiences? Why or why not? (2) Would it be worth the effort to learn at least a few basic words and phrases in the language of a foreign business partner if the other party speaks your language? Why or why not?

IT'S YOUR BUSINESS: (1) Have you ever translated a website, email message, or other document using automated translation? Were the results satisfactory, and were you able to confirm the quality of the translation? (2) Find a partner who speaks another language and try one of these translations apps or services in a live conversation. How would you characterize the translation quality and the experience overall?

KEY TERM TO KNOW: machine translation

BEHIND THE SCENES

Airbnb Succeeds with Global Vision but Local Touch

Brian Chesky, Joe Gebbia, and Nathan Blecharczyk knew they were on to something with the idea of playing matchmaker between people with extra rooms or vacant homes to rent and travelers looking for cheaper or more interesting alternatives to hotels. However, in those early days they might not have realized they were setting a course to disrupt the global travel industry and become a major force in what is now known as the *sharing economy*.

Among other things, Airbnb's growth is a story of dogged persistence. Despite multiple rejections from investors and several failed attempts at launching the company, the trio kept at it. They learned, adapted, and in the parlance of entrepreneurship, *pivoted* multiple times in search of the right product–market fit.

Many companies view international expansion as an opportunity to grow. Airbnb saw it as a necessity. The *network effect* is crucial to its success; that is, the larger the network of hosts and guests, the more valuable the system is to everyone. Potential hosts will be more inclined to join the community if they believe there will be enough business to make it worthwhile, and travelers will be more inclined to search for accommodation on Airbnb if they believe they will find lodgings that suit their needs. As the company's vice president in charge of product development, Joe Zadeh, puts it, "for Airbnb to work we have to be everywhere."

Of course, there are many different ways to operate internationally, and these decisions can make or break a company's expansion plans. Airbnb's choices were defined on one side by its reliance on technology and strong company values and on the other by the extremely diverse range of local market dynamics around the world. To make sure it maximizes the return on its investment in web and mobile technologies and upholds those core values while responding to local conditions, the company uses the transnational strategy described on page 125. In other words, it is a model of thinking globally while acting locally.

The company's values and operating standards include a strong sense of community for hosts and guests, high standards of cleanliness and safety, and respect for government authority. Regardless of where they are in the world, hosts and guests alike are expected to treat each other and surrounding neighborhoods with respect. The company offers extensive guidance to hosts, for instance, to make sure guests have a safe and enjoyable experience and that property owners stay in compliance with real estate laws, tax regulations, and other expectations. To make sure these global values are implemented appropriately on a local level, Airbnb gives hosts specific city-by-city advice on how to follow regulations.

The willingness to work with government regulators is crucial to the company's success, now and in the future. (In this regard, Airbnb's approach from the beginning was starkly different from that of Uber, another major player in the sharing economy, which under its original leadership earned a reputation for crossing ethical and legal barriers.) Property sharing is a more pervasively disruptive enterprise than ride sharing, so this cooperative approach might be viewed as enlightened self-interest. Many cities around the world suffer from a housing shortage, with rents so high in desirable central locations that even people with midrange incomes can't afford to live there. When property owners choose to rent their spaces to short-term visitors, they keep these accommodations out of the general housing supply and thereby make choices even more limited for people who want to live in those areas. With its global mandate to respond to local authorities individually, rather than trying to impose its business model on the world, Airbnb is better positioned to succeed in the face of occasional opposition.

Promotion and communication are other key ways that Airbnb implements the global-local model. All aspects of branding and communication strategy are defined at a high level but adapted to local conditions country by country. In Airbnb's role as an intermediary, it has double the marketing challenges of a typical company: It needs to attract hosts willing to share their properties with complete strangers *and* travelers willing to forgo the predictability of hotels for the unique experience of staying in someone else's home. Connecting with people on a local, individual basis is therefore crucial.

With a presence in nearly 200 countries, content translation is a huge and never-ending task for Airbnb as new listings are continuously added to the site. Airbnb uses a semi-automated approach to translating the website into more than two dozen languages, including a custom translation tool that detects when new phrases are added to listings and sends them to the company's translators, who can then fine-tune the wording.

Airbnb also adapts its account management and payment systems to accommodate local needs. For example, customers in many countries can sign up using a Facebook or Google account. However, in China and other parts of Asia, the mobile messaging services Weibo and WeChat are much more popular, so Airbnb lets people sign up using their accounts on those systems. Payment options are also highly localized, such as a method for getting around the lack of credit cards in Cuba.

The business has grown unimaginably since those early air-mattress days, and the company's smart approach to international operations deserves much of the credit. As Airbnb confronts new challenges from competitors and local market conditions, Chesky, Gebbia, and Blecharczyk are sure to keep thinking globally and acting locally with continued success.[42]

Critical Thinking Questions

3-1. Would licensing the Airbnb business system to other companies have been a better way to establish the brand in various countries? Why or why not?

3-2. Should Airbnb consider changing its name to something more locally meaningful in each country? Why or why not?

3-3. Why does the sense of community as a strategic theme work better for Airbnb than it would for a ride-sharing company such as Uber or Lyft?

Learn More Online

Visit **www.airbnb.com** and peruse some of the lodging available in three countries that interest you as a traveler. Do you find any significant difference in the way the rooms, homes, or experiences are presented? Do the listings make you more interested in visiting these places? How does this compare to searching for hotel rooms in the same locations?

End of Chapter

KEY TERMS

balance of payments (112)
balance of trade (112)
cultural pluralism (120)
culture (120)
dumping (115)
economic globalization (111)
economies of scale (111)
embargo (115)
ethnocentrism (120)
exchange rate (113)
export subsidies (115)
exporting (123)
foreign direct investment (FDI) (124)
free trade (114)

global strategy (125)
import quotas (115)
importing (123)
licensing (124)
machine translation (128)
multidomestic strategy (125)
multinational corporations (MNCs) (124)
protectionism (114)
stereotyping (120)
tariffs (115)
tax haven (122)
trade deficit (112)
trade surplus (112)
trading blocs (117)
transnational strategy (125)

TEST YOUR KNOWLEDGE

Questions for Review

3-4. What is economic globalization?

3-5. What is the balance of trade, and how is it related to the balance of payments?

3-6. How can international trade be measured?

3-7. What is free trade?

3-8. How can protectionist moves create conflict within a country?

3-9. What is the purpose of the International Monetary Fund?

3-10. Why are tax havens controversial?

3-11. Why might a business choose to opt for a multidomestic strategy when it launches its products or services globally?

Questions for Analysis

3-12. Why might a global business favor foreign direct investment as a means of expansion?

3-13. Which do you think offers the lowest degree of potential expansion risk to a global brand, licensing or franchising? Explain your answer.

3-14. How can governments intervene in international trade? Is this considered a positive action?

3-15. How can small businesses benefit from trading internationally?

3-16. Why is the transnational strategy considered a hybrid of the multidomestic and global strategies?

3-17. How might social media and popular culture affect a company's functional strategies for international expansion, particularly regarding products and promotion?

3-18. What is machine translation?

3-19. **Ethical Considerations.** Is it ethical for major grocery chains to import food products at lower prices from overseas rather than buy higher-cost products from domestic producers? Why or why not?

Questions for Application

3-20. Suppose you own a small company that manufactures baseball equipment. You are aware that Russia is a large market, and you are considering exporting your products there. However, you know you need to learn more about Russian culture before making contact with potential business partners. What steps could you take to improve your cultural awareness?

3-21. Identify two companies in your country that have successfully expanded abroad. Why do the two companies trade internationally? Research information from newspapers (print or online editions) to support your answer.

3-22. A European snack manufacturer wants to set up manufacturing plants in Asia and South America. How should the manufacturer go about initiating the proposed changes? What form of business activity do you think is the right choice for him? Why or why not?

3-23. **Concept Integration.** You just received notice that a large shipment of manufacturing supplies that one of your factories in another country has been waiting for has been stuck in customs for two weeks. A local business associate in that country tells you that you are expected to give customs agents some "incentive money" to see that everything clears easily. How will you handle this situation? Evaluate the ethical merits of your decision by considering the approaches listed in Exhibit 4.4 on page 146.

EXPAND YOUR KNOWLEDGE

Discovering Career Opportunities

If global business interests you, consider working for a U.S. government agency that supports or regulates international trade. Search the USAJobs website at **www.usajobs.gov** for an opening in international trade administration, such as an *international trade specialist*. Study the job description and answer the following questions:

3-24. On the basis of this job description, what education and skills (personal and professional) would you need to succeed in this job?

3-25. How well does this job description fit your qualifications and interests?

3-26. How important would interpersonal skills be in this position? Why?

Intelligent Business Technology: Automated Translation

The automated translation capabilities discussed on pages 128–130 give business professionals a valuable tool for communicating with global reach. However, the tools are still not 100 percent accurate, nor do they really understand meaning in the same way that human translators do.

Research the current state of automated translation and write a one- or two-paragraph summary of its accuracy and dependability as a business communication tool, along with your advice to business professionals who want to use these tools.

PRACTICE YOUR SKILLS

Resolving Ethical Dilemmas

You're excited by the possibility of expanding your company internationally, and you have engaged the services of a consultant to help guide you into some promising new markets. While discussing the difficulty of getting government approval to sell your products in one particular country, the consultant advises you to be prepared to "spend a little cash to make things happen—be ready to wine and dine 'em."

Download *A Resource Guide to the U.S. Foreign Corrupt Practices Act* from **www.justice.gov/criminal-fraud/fcpa-guidance**, and read the section titled "Gifts, Travel, Entertainment, and Other Things of Value," including the hypothetical examples. Compile a list of steps you could take that would be permissible under the FCPA.

Growing as a Professional

Chapter 1 highlighted dependability as one of the most important qualities to develop as a professional. Life on the job is going to be a lot like life in college in the sense that you'll have a continuous stream of deadlines that require you to keep multiple projects on schedule. Use the opportunity you have now to develop the estimating skills you'll need in order to pull together accurate schedules.

For example, keep track of how long it takes you to write one page of a paper, on average. Time requirements vary with the amount of research involved and other factors, of course, but after a while you'll get a sense of how long it takes to accomplish various types and sizes of projects.

Gaining insight into how long various tasks take will also help you to *scope* projects more accurately. For instance, when you have some leeway regarding the length or the production quality of a paper or presentation, you can adjust the magnitude of the work to fit your available time. This will help you meet schedule commitments and avoid the unpleasant discovery that you've spent 70 or 80 percent of your available time but have completed only 20 or 30 percent of the project.

Sharpening Your Communication Skills

Languages never translate on a word-for-word basis. When doing business in the global marketplace, choose words that communicate a single idea clearly. Avoid using slang or idioms (words that can have meanings far different from their individual components when translated literally). For example, if a U.S. executive tells an executive unfamiliar with baseball or cricket that a change in plans "really threw us a curve ball," chances are that communication will fail.

Team up with two other students and list 10 examples of slang (in your native language) that would probably be misinterpreted or misunderstood during a business conversation with someone from another culture. Next to each example, suggest other words you might use to convey the same message. Make sure the alternatives mean exactly the same as the original slang or idiom. Compare your list with those of your classmates.

Building Your Team Skills

With a team assigned by your instructor, research four violations of the FCPA that resulted in fines of $100 million or more. (Note that although this chapter focused on the anti-bribery provisions in the FCPA, the act also includes provisions that prohibit "off the books" accounting in order to ensure financial reporting transparency.) What common threads can you find in these four cases? What advice would you give to international dealmakers to help them avoid the fates of these companies?

Developing Your Research Skills

In today's global environment, companies both small and large need to be aware of the global marketplace and its demands. With more and more companies choosing to trade and compete internationally, trading in only one nation can be considered a risk for many companies. Research examples of companies that trade internationally and consider the questions below:

3-27. While conducting your research, did you find examples of companies operating in trading blocs? Explain the benefits of trading blocs using one of your companies as an example.

3-28. Based on your research, what risks might a company be exposed to if it chooses not to trade internationally? Use specific examples to illustrate your answer.

3-29. List some of the other examples of companies that trade internationally. What strategies have these companies adopted for international trade?

Writing Assignments

3-30. How does free trade create situations in which companies can pit the workers of one country against the workers of another?

3-31. Should the U.S. government promote trade policies that benefit some companies or industries while potentially harming others? Why or why not?

ENDNOTES

1. "About Us," Airbnb, accessed 18 March 2018, www.airbnb.com; Patrick Yip, "How to Grow a Business in 190 Markets: 4 Lessons from Airbnb," OneSky blog, 16 January 2017, www.oneskyapp.com; Biz Carson, "How 3 Guys Turned Renting an Air Mattress in Their Apartment into a $25 Billion Company," *Business Insider*, 23 February 2016, www.businessinsider.com; "Airbnb's Aggressive International Expansion," *Marketing Strategy International*, 6 February 2017, marketingstrategyinternational.com; Artur Kornienko, "Global Marketing Done Right. Learn from Airbnb," GFluence, 8 December 2016, gluence.com; Shayna Fowler, "Airbnb's Localization Strategy," United Language Group, 4 August 2017, daily.unitedlanguagegroup.com; Harriet Taylor, "How Airbnb Is Growing a Far-Flung Global Empire," *CNBC*, 8 June 2016, www.cnbc.com; "Among Private Tech Firms, Airbnb Has Pursued a Distinct Strategy," *Economist*, 27 May 2017, www.economist.com; Brian Solomon, "How Airbnb Expanded to 190 Countries by Thinking 'Glocal,'" *Forbes*, 3 May 2016, www.forbes.com.

2. John J. Wild and Kenneth L. Wild, *International Business: The Challenges of Globalization*, 8th ed. (New York: Pearson, 2016), 143.

3. "Balance of Payments," Federal Reserve Bank of New York, accessed 16 March 2018, www.newyorkfed.org.

4. Reem Heakel, "Currency Exchange: Floating Rate Vs. Fixed Rate," *Investopedia*, accessed 16 March 2018, www.investopedia.com.

5. I. M. Destler, "America's Uneasy History with Free Trade," *Harvard Business Review*, 28 April 2018, hbr.org.

6. Justin Fox, "Steel and Aluminum Jobs Don't Add Up to Much," *Bloomberg*, 2 March 2018, www.bloomberg.com.

7. Peter Buxbaum, "What's the Cost of Trade Protectionist Policies?" *Global Trade*, 10 February 2017, www.globaltrademag.com; David G. Tarr and Morris E. Morkre, "Aggregate Costs to the United States of Tariffs and Quotas on Imports," U.S. Federal Trade Commission, December 1984, www.ftc.gov.

8. Uwe E. Reinhardt, "How Convincing Is the Case for Free Trade?" blog post, *New York Times*, 18 February 2011, www.nytimes.com.

9. "Steel Industry Profile," American Iron and Steel Institute, accessed 16 March 2018, www.steel.org.

10. "Common Trade Concerns and Problems Experienced by U.S. Textile/Apparel/Footwear/Travel Goods Exporters," U.S. Department of Commerce, International Trade Administration, Office of Textiles and Apparel, accessed 1 August 2011, web.ita.doc.gov.

11. "What We Stand For," World Trade Organization, accessed 16 March 2018, www.wto.org.

12. "The Doha Round Finally Dies a Merciful Death," *Financial Times*, 21 December 2015, www.ft.com.

13. "About the IMF," International Monetary Fund, accessed 16 March 2018, www.imf.org.

14. "What We Do," World Bank Group, accessed 16 March 2018, www.worldbank.org.

15. "North American Free Trade Agreement (NAFTA)," USDA Foreign Agricultural Service, accessed 29 June 2007, www.fas.usda.gov.

16. Julián Aguilar, "Twenty Years Later, NAFTA Remains a Source of Tension," *New York Times*, 7 December 2012, www.nytimes.com.

17. M. Angeles Villarreal and Ian F. Fergusson, "NAFTA at 20: Overview and Trade Effects," *Congressional Research Service*, 28 April 2014, www.crs.gov.

18. "NAFTA's Legacy," The Week, 19 February 2017, theweek.com.

19. "Facts and Figures," European Union, accessed 16 March 2018, europa.eu.

20. "The Euro," European Union, accessed 16 March 2018, europa.eu.

21. "About APEC," Asia-Pacific Economic Cooperation, accessed 16 March 2018, www.apec.org.

22. Richard D. Bucher, *Diversity Consciousness: Opening Our Minds to People, Cultures, and Opportunities*, 4th ed. (New York: Pearson, 2015), 140.

23. Project Implicit, accessed 6 March 2018, implicit.harvard.edu/implicit.

24. P. Christopher Earley and Elaine Mosakowsi, "Cultural Intelligence," *Harvard Business Review*, October 2004, 139–146.

25. Wild and Wild, *International Business: The Challenges of Globalization*, 88.

26. Richard L. Daft, *Management*, 13th ed. (Boston: Cengage, 2018), 120.

27. Nicholas Shaxson, "How to Crack Down on Tax Havens," *Foreign Affairs*, March/April 2018, 94–107.

28. Shaxson, "How to Crack Down on Tax Havens."

29. Shaxson, "How to Crack Down on Tax Havens."

30. Nick Statt, "Google Still Exploiting Tax Loopholes to Shelter Billions in Overseas Ad Revenue," *The Verge*, 2 January 2018, www.theverge.com.

31. "What Are the Costs of Corruption?" Transparency International, accessed 17 March 2018, www.transparency.org; *A Resource Guide to the U.S. Foreign Corrupt Practices Act*, U.S. Department of Justice and U.S. Securities and Exchange Commission, 14 November 2012.

32. *A Resource Guide to the U.S. Foreign Corrupt Practices Act*.

33. Export.gov, accessed 16 March 2018, www.export.gov.

34. Wild and Wild, International Business: The Challenges of Globalization, 324.

35. "Technology Licensing," Export.gov, accessed 16 March 2018, www.export.gov.

36. "Joint Ventures," Export.gov, accessed 16 March 2018, www.export.gov.

37. Stephen P. Robbins and Mary Coulter, *Management*, 14th ed. (New York: Pearson, 2018), 118.

38. Douglas Hofstader, "The Shallowness of Google Translate," *The Atlantic*, 30 January 2018, www.theatlantic.com.

39. Bill Swallow, "Is Google Translate Good Enough?" Scriptorium, January 2018, www.scriptorium.com.

40. "Skype Translator," Skype, accessed 6 March 2018, www.skype.com; iTranslate Voice, accessed 6 March 2018, itranslatevoice.com; Laura Cox, "Artificial Intelligence & Business Communication," *Disruption*, 22 May 2017, disruptionhub.com.

41. "Presentation Translator, a Microsoft Garage Project," Microsoft, accessed 6 March 2018, www.microsoft.com.

42. See note 1.

4 Business Ethics and Corporate Social Responsibility

LEARNING OBJECTIVES   After studying this chapter, you will be able to

1 Discuss what it means to practice good business ethics, and highlight the forces that can influence ethical decision-making.

2 Define corporate social responsibility (CSR), and explain the difference between philanthropy and strategic CSR.

3 Distinguish among the four perspectives on corporate social responsibility.

4 Discuss the role of business in protecting the natural environment, and define sustainable development.

5 Identify five fundamental consumer rights and the responsibility of business to respect them.

6 Explain the responsibilities businesses have toward their employees.

7 Identify two categories of ethical concerns with artificial intelligence.

MyLab Intro to Business
Improve Your Grade!
If your instructor is using MyLab Intro to Business, visit **www.pearson.com/ mylab/intro-to-business**.

BEHIND THE SCENES   Unilever: Pursuing a New Idea That's 150 Years Old

Unilever CEO Paul Polman carries on the company's purpose-driven tradition.

www.unilever.com

As you'll read in this chapter, the *purpose-driven business* has become a significant topic in today's business world as more leaders and employees look for ways to create meaning beyond the pursuit of profits. However, the concept of a purpose-driven business dates back many decades.

About the time that Sherlock Holmes began to leave fictional footprints around Victorian London, William Lever came up with the idea for Sunlight Soap. He envisioned much more than a product he could sell profitably—he aimed to make life better for the people who bought his products. As he put it: "To make cleanliness commonplace; to lessen work for women; to foster health and contribute to personal attractiveness, that life may be more enjoyable and rewarding . . . " Those are certainly goals worthy of the best efforts a company can put forth.

Lever's interest in making the world a better place extended to his workforce, too. As demand grew for Sunlight Soap, he built an entire village in Liverpool to provide employees with safe, quality housing and leisure-time activities. Other popular products and international expansion followed. In 1930, the company merged with the Dutch company Margarine Unie to become Unilever.

The merger created one of the biggest companies in the world at the time, and Unilever continued to grow decade after decade and today remains one of the giants of consumer goods with sales of more than $50 billion every year. Chances are you buy at least one of the brands in its wide product portfolio, which includes Axe body spray, Ben & Jerry's, Dove soap, Klondike bars, Lipton tea, Noxzema, and Q-tips.

The commitment to going beyond the basic expectations of making products and turning a profit continues, even as Unilever battles in the global marketplace with other consumer goods giants and a new wave of digital- and social-savvy rivals. If you were Unilever CEO Paul Polman, how would you maintain and expand the ethos of doing well by doing good? How would you balance the demands of stakeholders, including investors who want to see the stock grow and employees who want their work to mean more than just pumping out products? How would you keep the spirit of William Lever alive in a business world that demands constant growth and short-term profits?[1]

INTRODUCTION

Like Unilever's Paul Polman (profiled in the chapter-opening Behind the Scenes), managers in every industry today must balance the demands of running a profitable business with the expectations of running a socially responsible company. As a future business leader, you will face some of the challenges discussed in this chapter, and your choices won't always be easy. You may struggle to find ethical clarity in some situations or even to understand what your choices are and how each option might affect your company's various stakeholders. You may need to muster the courage to stand up to colleagues, bosses, or customers if you think ethical principles are being violated. Fortunately, by having a good understanding of what constitutes ethical behavior and what society expects from business today, you'll be better prepared to make these tough choices.

Ethics in Contemporary Business

Assessing the ethics of contemporary business is no simple matter, partly because of disagreement over what constitutes responsible behavior and partly because the behavior of individual companies runs the gamut from positive to neutral to negative. However, it is safe to say that there is significant concern about the ethics of today's business leaders. Harvard Business School professor Rakesh Khurana probably speaks for many when he says, "One way of looking at the problem with American business today is that it has succeeded in assuming many of the appearances and privileges of professionalism, while evading the attendant constraints and responsibilities."[2] By and large, the public seems to agree (see Exhibit 4.1 on the next page).

The news is not all bad, of course. Most businesses are run by ethical managers and staffed by ethical employees whose positive contributions to their communities are overshadowed at times by headline-grabbing scandals. As you will read about Unilever at the end of the chapter and in various examples throughout the chapter, companies around the world help their communities in countless ways, from sponsoring youth sports teams to raising millions of dollars for building hospitals.

Moreover, even when companies are simply engaged in the normal course of business—and do so ethically—they contribute to society by making useful products, providing employment, and paying taxes. Business catches a lot of flak these days, some of it deserved, but overall, its contributions to the health, happiness, and well-being of society are beyond measure.

DEFINING ETHICAL BEHAVIOR

Ethics are the principles and standards of moral behavior that are accepted by society as right and wrong. Practicing good business ethics involves, at a minimum, competing fairly and honestly, communicating truthfully, and not causing harm to others:

- **Competing fairly and honestly.** Businesses are expected to compete fairly and to not knowingly deceive, intimidate, or misrepresent themselves to customers, competitors, clients, employees, the media, or government officials.
- **Communicating truthfully.** Communicating truthfully is a simple enough concept: Tell the truth, the whole truth, and nothing but the truth. However, matters sometimes

1 LEARNING OBJECTIVE
Discuss what it means to practice good business ethics, and highlight the forces that can influence ethical decision-making.

ethics
The rules or standards governing the conduct of a person or group.

| EXHIBIT 4.1 | **Public Perceptions of Business Ethics** |

One can argue whether public perceptions of business ethics accurately reflect the behavior of the entire community of business professionals or simply mirror the behavior of businesses and individuals who make headlines. This graph shows the percentage of Americans who rate the honesty and ethics of particular professions as either "high" or "very high." Several business professions are shown, along with several nonbusiness professions for comparison.

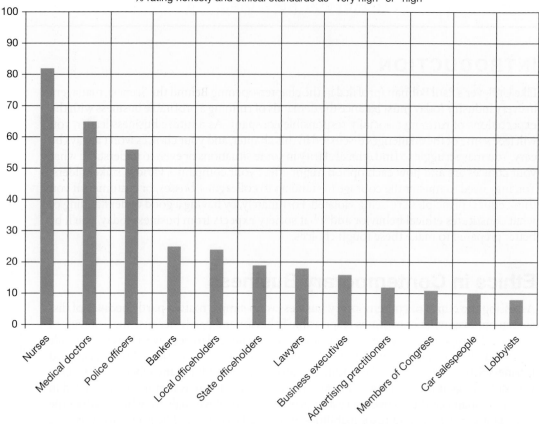

U.S. Public Opinion of Selected Professions
% rating honesty and ethical standards as "very high" or "high"

Source: Data from Megan Brenan, "Nurses Keep Healthy Lead as Most Honest, Ethical Profession," Gallup, 26 December 2017, www.gallup.com.

aren't so clear. For instance, if you plan to introduce an improved version of a product next year, do you have an obligation to tell customers who might buy the existing product this year? Suppose you do tell them, and so many decide to delay their purchases that you end up with a cash flow problem that forces you to lay off several employees. Would that be fair for customers but unfair for your employees?

- **Not causing harm to others.** All businesses have the capacity to cause harm to employees, customers, other companies, their communities, and investors. Problems can start when leaders make decisions that put their personal interests above those of other stakeholders, underestimate the risks of failure, or neglect to consider or control negative effects on other people and organizations. For example, **insider trading**, in which company insiders use confidential information to gain an advantage in stock market trading, harms other investors. (Insider trading is illegal, in addition to being unethical.) Of course, harm can also result even when managers have acted ethically—but they are still responsible for these negative outcomes.

insider trading
The use of unpublicized information that an individual gains from the course of his or her job to benefit from fluctuations in the stock market.

FORCES THAT PROMOTE UNETHICAL BEHAVIOR

Some cases of unethical behavior occur simply because people in a company are greedy or unprincipled and apparently believe that the potential rewards of unethical behavior outweigh the risks of getting caught. Other cases, however, aren't quite as straightforward.

This section explores three recurring areas of unethical behavior that share greed and self-preservation as root causes but differ in how those causes can affect decision-making.

Management Pressure and Corporate Culture

Employees who might not consider violating ethical guidelines or breaking the law on their own can find themselves swept up in dysfunctional corporate cultures that pressure them to step over the line. For example, unrealistic expectations and pressure from management have been cited as major factors in two recent cases of unethical behavior on an epic scale, one in banking and one in automobiles.

Under pressure to meet sales quotas, thousands of employees at Wells Fargo signed up customers for phony bank accounts and other fee-bearing services.

Millions of Phony Bank Accounts Under pressure to meet unrealistic sales targets, employees at Wells Fargo signed up customers for new bank accounts, credit cards, and insurance policies without the customers' knowledge. The scandal was massive by any measure: Thousands of employees were involved over the course of many years, and they set up more than 2 million phony accounts and charged more than a half-million customers for unnecessary car insurance. Customers wound up paying fees on accounts opened in their names that they didn't know about, and many suffered significant financial damage.[3]

Falsified Pollution Data In an attempt to get around pollution laws, engineers at the German carmaker Volkswagen installed "defeat devices" in the software that controlled the diesel engines in as many as 11 million cars sold worldwide. The software could manipulate the engine's performance while cars were undergoing emissions testing in order to lower the measurable output of harmful nitrous oxides, then return the engines to normal operation as soon as they passed the tests and got out onto the highway—where they would emit up to 40 times the legal U.S. limit for nitrous oxide emissions.[4]

A Willful Blindness to Harm

Financial pressures and career aspirations can lead people into what one might call a willful blindness to harm—they simply don't want to see that their companies or the products they sell might be causing harm. Convincing the interdependent members of an organization to face reality isn't always easy, unfortunately. In the words of University of Michigan management professor Noel Tichy, "Bureaucracies love to lie to themselves."[5] Two cases involving *intermediaries* highlight this problem.

The Opioid Crisis The United States is suffering from an epidemic of prescription drug addiction that claims the lives of tens of thousands of people every year. These aren't "street drugs" made and sold by criminal organizations but legitimate medical products manufactured and distributed by some of the biggest corporations in the country. The problem is a staggering oversupply made possible by a lack of control in the distribution chain.

For example, over an eight-year period, more than 20 million hydrocodone and oxycodone pills were shipped to Williamson, West Virginia—a town of fewer than 3,200 people. The abuse originates with doctors who overprescribe and patients who get prescriptions from more than one doctor, and the manufacturers and distributors defend themselves by saying they are following all applicable laws and regulations. However, critics point to the outlandish numbers of pills reaching some communities and say distributors should be doing a better job of monitoring and controlling the product flow.[6]

The Destructive Downside of Social Media Social media platforms promoted the idea of bringing people together but have instead, in their role as information intermediaries, been accused of tearing society apart by enabling online abuse and the spread of false information.

Social media have brought numerous benefits to business and society, but many people are now concerned about the negative consequences of these communication technologies.

Keith Weed, Unilever's chief marketing officer, sums up the problem that many perceive: "Fake news, racism, sexism, terrorists spreading messages of hate, toxic content directed at children—parts of the internet we have ended up with [are] a million miles from where we thought it would take us."[7]

Twitter, Facebook, and Google (partly in its role as the owner of YouTube) have all come under intense scrutiny for the abusive behavior of some users and the way in which all three systems have been used to spread hoaxes, false rumors, and political disinformation. Some of these criticisms have even come from people who helped create the systems.[8]

For example, Twitter users continue to complain that the company doesn't do enough to shut down accounts that violate its terms of service, and many women continue to be subjected to appalling amounts of abuse, including death threats. Twitter has a team dedicated to stopping trolls, but critics inside and outside the company claim that despite early warnings, company leaders ignored advice to build a more robust system that would make it easier to fight abuse.[9]

Facebook has had problems with abuse, misinformation, and privacy violations practically since its founding.[10] For instance, after asserting that it wasn't a media company and therefore wasn't responsible for the content posted by its users and then claiming that "fake news" on the network wasn't a widespread problem, Facebook admitted that it had been manipulated by organizations and foreign interests trying to influence the 2016 U.S. presidential election. University of North Carolina professor Zeynep Tufekci called it "a systematic failure of responsibility."[11] Like Twitter, Facebook has been accused of not doing enough to shore up vulnerabilities in its systems.[12]

Twitter, Facebook, and YouTube are under pressure from government bodies, advocacy groups, investors, and advertisers to improve the integrity of their networks and the online safety of their users. As one of the largest advertisers in the world, for instance, Unilever has a lot of financial influence over digital media and said it will "not invest in platforms that do not protect children or which create division in society."[13] And Salesforce.com CEO Marc Benioff, a high-profile figure in Silicon Valley, said, "Companies like Facebook and Twitter . . . don't know how they're being used and they don't even know who's using them. Well, that's unacceptable. These companies have to take full responsibility for the technology that they've created and to make sure that it's being used in a proper way with the right morals and values that we would expect any corporation to be led by."[14]

A Sense of Impunity

The entrepreneurial spirit can be an inspiring source of creative energy and is responsible for many of the advances that contribute to modern life. Perhaps no part of the global economy embodies this energy more than Silicon Valley—both the actual technology-centric valley in California and other locales around the world where tech entrepreneurs have that "Silicon Valley" attitude of rapid innovation. Facebook's former motto of "move fast and break things" sums up the attitude of many start-ups, although one can trace a hint of that mindset back more than a century to the inventor Thomas Edison, who was quoted as saying, "There ain't no rules around here! We're trying to accomplish something!"[15]

Uber CEO Dara Khosrowshahi is working to reform the company's culture and repair its reputation after a series of ethical missteps under previous leadership.

However, this scrappy mindset that the normal rules don't apply to them can tempt some entrepreneurs and managers into believing that *laws* don't apply to them. Uber, for example, developed a reputation in its early years for ignoring laws that it didn't agree with and pushing the limits of others. Uber's current CEO, Dara Khosrowshahi, acknowledges that the company was "guilty of hubris" under its original leadership.[16] He is working hard to repair the company's reputation, but the firm could be in for an expensive few years, as it faces multiple criminal probes and dozens of civil lawsuits.[17]

Unethical behavior isn't limited to high-profile cases such as these, of course. Other frequently reported instances of unethical behavior in business settings include accepting kickbacks, stealing company property, and sexual harassment (addressed in Chapter 11).[18]

STRATEGIES FOR SUPPORTING ETHICAL BEHAVIOR

With so much pressure and temptation to bend or break the rules, ensuring ethical behavior in their organizations must be a top priority for all business leaders. Here are six steps every company can take:

- **Start from the top.** Ethical behavior must start at the highest levels of the organization, and everyone in the organization needs to see that top executives behave ethically.
- **Define expectations and set an example.** Companies with strong ethical practices create cultures that reward good behavior—and don't intentionally or unintentionally reward bad behavior.[19] At United Technologies (**www.utc.com**), a diversified manufacturer based in Hartford, Connecticut, managers and supervisors have specific ethical norms they are expected to follow in order to set positive examples for employees and business partners.[20]
- **Craft a code of ethics with visible consequences.** A **code of ethics** is a formal policy document that defines an organization's guiding values, complete with advice for handling specific situations that could arise in the course of business.
- **Train and support employees.** Training in ethical issues and decision-making, coupled with support from managers, can help employees avoid ethical missteps and resolve ethical dilemmas.
- **Practice transparency.** Information is another key area in which stakeholders have differing expectations and demands. Businesses need to and have the right to withhold various types of information, including future product designs, strategic plans, competitive analyses, and more. However, employees, communities, customers, investors, and other groups have ethically and often legally legitimate claims to a wide range of other information. **Transparency**, which can be defined as "the degree to which information flows freely within an organization, among managers and employees, and outward to stakeholders," builds trust and helps prevent unethical cultures from taking root."[21]
- **Provide feedback channels.** An important aspect of transparency is two-way communication, giving employees and other parties a safe and confidential way to share questions and concerns with management. Such communication can range from informal meetings with a supervisor to *ethics hotlines* that employees can call to report concerns. Reporting unethical or illegal behavior is known as **whistle-blowing**, and smart companies make sure employees have a way to express concerns internally so that issues can be brought to management's attention and resolved quickly. Otherwise, employees may be forced to take their concerns public through the news media, government regulators, or the social media. For internal feedback mechanisms to work, however, employees need to know their concerns are addressed and that they won't suffer retaliation for blowing the whistle. Unfortunately, retaliation appears to be widespread. In the Wells Fargo case, employees had been reporting the phony accounts scandal for years. The bank not only didn't act on the reports but in some cases allegedly fired employees who raised concerns.[22]

code of ethics
A written statement that sets forth the principles that guide an organization's decisions.

transparency
The degree to which affected parties can observe relevant aspects of transactions or decisions.

whistle-blowing
The disclosure by a company insider of information that exposes illegal or unethical behavior by others within the organization.

REAL-TIME UPDATES
Learn More by Visiting This Website

Tackling the growing problem of technology addiction

The Center for Humane Technology works to address the problem of technologies deliberately designed to hijack human attention. Go to **real-timeupdates.com/bia9** and select Learn More in the Students section.

GUIDELINES FOR MAKING ETHICAL DECISIONS

When the question of what is right and what is wrong is clear, ethical decisions are easy to make: You simply choose to do the right thing. (At least *making* the decision is simple; *implementing* the decision may be another story.) If you choose the wrong course, such as cheating on your taxes or stealing from your employer, you commit an **ethical lapse**. The choices were clear, and you made the wrong one.

ethical lapse
A situation in which an individual or a group makes a decision that is morally wrong, illegal, or unethical.

EXHIBIT 4.2	Stakeholders' Rights: A Difficult Balancing Act

Balancing the individual needs and interests of a company's stakeholders is one of management's most difficult tasks. Consider how these three examples could affect each of five stakeholder groups in a different way. (Note that some people may fall into multiple groups. Employees, for example, are taxpayers and members of the local community, and they may also be shareholders. Also, these scenarios and outcomes offer a simplified view of what is likely to happen in each case, but they illustrate the mixed effects that can result from management decisions.)

Decision	Shareholders (entrust money to the company in anticipation of a positive return on their investment)	Employees (devote time, energy, and creativity to the company's success)	Customers (expect to receive quality products and maximum value for prices paid)	Local Community (can be affected both positively and negatively by the company's presence and actions)	Taxpayers (affected indirectly by the amount of tax revenue that local, state, and federal governments get from the company)
Company decides to *offshore* some of its production to another country with lower labor costs; lays off significant number of employees	▲ Stand to benefit from lower production costs, which could increase sales, profits, or both, probably leading to increases in share price	▼ Some employees lose their jobs; morale likely to suffer among those who keep theirs	▲ Benefit from lower prices	▼ Suffers from loss of spendable income in the local economy and taxes paid to local government; exodus of employees can drive down home values	▼▲ Might be hurt or helped by the move, depending on whether loss of income tax paid by U.S. employees is offset by increased income tax paid by the company, for example
Company institutes a generous pay and benefits increase to improve employee morale	▼▲ Might be hurt in the short term as the stock market punishes the company for increasing its cost structure and diverting funds away from development; could help over the long term if the move boosts employee productivity	▲ Benefit from higher pay and more valuable benefits	▼▲ Could be hurt by higher prices if prices are raised to cover the added costs; could benefit from higher levels of employee satisfaction, leading to improved customer service	▲ Benefits from more spendable income in the local economy and taxes paid to local government; better employee benefits could also mean less drain on community resources such as health clinics	▲ Benefit from more money paid into government treasuries through higher income taxes
Company installs a multimillion-dollar waste water recirculation system that surpasses regulatory requirements; system will pay for itself in lower water bills, but not for 10 years	▼▲ Probably hurt as stock market punishes an investment with no immediate payback; increased goodwill and long-term cost savings help in years ahead	▼▲ Probably hurt in the short term as less money is available for raises and benefits; likely to benefit in the long term as the costs are recovered	▼ Hurt as higher costs are passed along as higher prices	▲ Helped by the company's efforts to conserve a shared natural resource	▼ Hurt as the company writes off the cost of the system, thereby lowering the taxes it pays to the government

ethical dilemma
A situation in which more than one side of an issue can be supported with valid ethical arguments.

However, you will encounter situations in which choices are not so clear. An **ethical dilemma** is a situation in which you must choose between conflicting but arguably valid options, or even a situation in which all your options are unpleasant. As Exhibit 4.2 suggests, stakeholders' needs often conflict, requiring managers to make tough decisions about resource allocation.

Consider the following points to help find the right answer whenever you face an ethical dilemma:

- Make sure you frame the situation accurately, taking into account all relevant issues and questions.
- Identify all parties who might be affected by your decision, and consider the rights of everyone involved.

- Be as objective as possible. Don't make a decision just to protect your own emotions, and don't automatically assume you're viewing a situation fairly and objectively.
- Don't assume that other people think the way you do. The time-honored "Golden Rule" of treating others the way you want to be treated can cause problems when others don't *want* to be treated the same way you do.
- Watch out for **conflicts of interest**, situations in which competing loyalties can lead to ethical lapses. For instance, if you are in charge of selecting an advertising agency to handle your company's next campaign, you would have an obvious conflict of interest if your spouse or partner works for one of the agencies under consideration.

conflicts of interest
Situations in which competing loyalties can lead to ethical lapses, such as when a business decision may be influenced by the potential for personal gain.

Exhibit 4.3 identifies six well-known approaches to resolving ethical dilemmas.

EXHIBIT 4.3	**Approaches to Resolving Ethical Dilemmas**

These approaches can help you resolve ethical dilemmas you may face on the job. Be aware that in some situations, different approaches can lead to different ethical conclusions.

Approach	Summary
Justice	Treat people equally or at least fairly in a way that makes rational and moral sense.
Utilitarianism	Choose the option that delivers the most good for the most people (or protects the most people from a negative outcome).
Individual rights	To the greatest possible extent, respect the rights of all individuals, particularly their right to control their own destinies.
Individual responsibilities	Focus on the ethical duties of the individuals involved in the situation.
The common good	Emphasize qualities and conditions that benefit the community as a whole, such as peace and public safety.
Virtue	Emphasize desirable character traits such as integrity and compassion.

Sources: Manuel Velasquez, Claire Andre, Thomas Shanks, S.J., and Michael J. Meyer, "Thinking Ethically: A Framework for Moral Decision Making," Markkula Center for Applied Ethics, Santa Clara University, accessed 3 June 2009, www.scu.edu; Ben Rogers, "John Rawls," *Guardian,* 27 November 2002, www.guardian.co.uk; Irene Van Staveren, "Beyond Utilitarianism and Deontology: Ethics in Economics," *Review of Political Economy,* January 2007, 21–35.

 CHECKPOINT

LEARNING OBJECTIVE 1: Discuss what it means to practice good business ethics, and highlight the forces that can influence ethical decision-making.

SUMMARY: Three essential components of good business ethics are competing fairly and honestly, communicating truthfully, and not causing harm to others. Various forces can lead professionals toward or away from unethical decisions. Aside from simple greed, forces that promote unethical behavior include management pressure and corporate culture, a willful blindness to harm, and a sense of impunity. Strategies for supporting ethical behavior include starting from the top to establish an ethical culture, defining expectations and setting examples for employees, crafting and enforcing a code of ethics, training and supporting employees, practicing transparency, and providing feedback channels.

CRITICAL THINKING: (1) If you go to work tomorrow morning and your boss asks you to do something you consider unethical, what factors will you take into consideration before responding? (2) How can you balance the business need to inspire employees to compete aggressively with the moral need to avoid competing unethically?

IT'S YOUR BUSINESS: (1) In your current job (or any previous job you've held), in what ways does your employer contribute to society? (2) Have you ever encountered an ethical dilemma in your work? If so, how did you resolve it?

KEY TERMS TO KNOW: ethics, code of ethics, transparency, whistle-blowing, ethical lapse, ethical dilemma, conflicts of interest

Define corporate social responsibility (CSR), and explain the difference between philanthropy and strategic CSR.

corporate social responsibility (CSR)
The idea that business has obligations to society beyond the pursuit of profits.

Corporate Social Responsibility

Corporate social responsibility (CSR) is the notion that business has obligations to society beyond the pursuit of profits. There is widespread—although not universal—agreement that CSR is both a moral imperative for business and a good thing for society, but the issues aren't quite as clear as they might seem at first glance.

THE RELATIONSHIP BETWEEN BUSINESS AND SOCIETY

What does business owe society, and what does society owe business? Any attempt to understand and shape this relationship needs to consider four essential truths:

- Consumers in contemporary societies enjoy and expect a wide range of benefits, from education and health care to the use of credit and products that are safe to use. Most of these benefits share an important characteristic: They require money.
- Profit-seeking companies are the economic engine that powers modern society; they generate the vast majority of the money in a nation's economy, either directly (through their own taxes and purchases) or indirectly (through the taxes and purchases made by the employees they support).
- Much of what we consider when assessing a society's standard of living involves goods and services created by profit-seeking companies.
- Conversely, companies cannot hope to operate profitably without the many benefits provided by a stable, functioning society: talented and healthy employees, a legal framework in which to pursue commerce, a dependable transportation infrastructure, stable financial markets, opportunities to raise money, and customers with the ability to pay for goods and services, to name just some of them.

Profit-seeking companies provide many of the comforts and conveniences of modern life.

Business and society clearly need each other—and each needs the other to be healthy and successful.

Business leaders have been involved in governmental affairs for about as long as companies have existed, usually with an eye toward encouraging regulatory changes that benefit businesses. Traditionally, CEOs have tended to stay out of the limelight when it comes to social, environmental, and other issues. Over the past couple of decades, however, business leaders have taken more visible stands on issues that affect their employees, their customers, and their communities at large. Some of this activity stems from stakeholder pressure and some from a growing consensus that government lacks the will or the ability to address issues on which people are demanding action. Leaders from companies as diverse as Disney, JPMorgan Chase, Walmart, Salesforce.com, AT&T, and Merck have all taken public stands on divisive issues in recent years, and there's every indication they will continue to be more involved in the public square than in years past.[23]

PHILANTHROPY VERSUS STRATEGIC CSR

philanthropy
The donation of money, time, goods, or services to charitable, humanitarian, or educational institutions.

Companies that engage in CSR activities can choose between two broad courses of action: general philanthropy or strategic CSR. **Philanthropy** involves donating money, employee time, or other resources to various causes without regard for any direct business benefits for the company. This can range from narrow goals such as supporting an arts group to broad programs such as JPMorgan Chase's multiyear, $100 million investment to help Detroit rebuild its economy.[24] Through a combination of free products, employee time, use of company facilities, and cash contributions, U.S. companies donate billions of dollars every year.[25]

strategic CSR
Social contributions that are directly aligned with a company's overall business strategy.

In contrast to generic philanthropy, **strategic CSR** involves social contributions that are directly aligned with a company's overall business strategy. In other words, the company helps itself and society at the same time. This approach can be followed in a variety of ways. A company can help develop the workforce by supporting job training efforts or use volunteering programs to help train employees. For example, in UPS's Community Internship Program, management candidates volunteer in community programs to help them understand the needs and challenges of various population groups while developing essential skills.[26]

Exactly how much can or should businesses contribute to social concerns? This is a difficult decision because all companies have limited resources that must be allocated to a number of goals, such as upgrading facilities and equipment, developing new products, marketing existing products, and rewarding employee efforts, in addition to contributing to social causes. Regardless of the level of contribution that is right for any particular company, expectations in general are clearly changing. Employees, customers, and communities expect today's companies to take a stand on important issues and contribute to the greater good. Thousands of businesses are responding, using their financial clout and other resources in positive ways.

 CHECKPOINT

LEARNING OBJECTIVE 2: Define corporate social responsibility (CSR), and explain the difference between philanthropy and strategic CSR.

SUMMARY: Corporate social responsibility (CSR) is the notion that business has obligations to society beyond the pursuit of profits. However, there is no general agreement on what those responsibilities are or which elements of society should determine those obligations or benefit from them. Philanthropy involves donating time, money, or other resources, without regard for any direct business benefits. In contrast, strategic CSR involves contributions that are aligned with the company's business needs and strategies.

CRITICAL THINKING: (1) Given that "society" is not an organized entity, how can society decide what the responsibilities of business are in a CSR context? (2) Is philanthropy morally superior to strategic CSR? Why or why not?

IT'S YOUR BUSINESS: (1) How do a company's philanthropic or CSR efforts influence your purchasing behavior? (2) Is it ethical for companies to invest in your college or university in exchange for publicity? Why or why not?

KEY TERM TO KNOW: corporate social responsibility (CSR), philanthropy, strategic CSR

Perspectives on Corporate Social Responsibility

3 | LEARNING OBJECTIVE

Distinguish among the four perspectives on corporate social responsibility.

To encourage ethical behavior and promote a mutually beneficial relationship between business and society, it is clearly necessary to establish expectations about how businesses should conduct themselves. Approaches to CSR can be roughly categorized into four perspectives, from minimalist to proactive (see Exhibit 4.4 on the next page).

MINIMALIST CSR

According to what might be termed the *minimalist view*, the only social responsibility of business is to pay taxes and obey the law. In 1970, Nobel Prize–winning economist Milton Friedman articulated this view by saying, "There is only one social responsibility of business: to use its resources and engage in activities designed to increase its profits so long as it stays within the rules of the game, which is to say, engages in open and free competition without deception or fraud."[27] However, very few business leaders still agree with this perspective; in a recent poll of Fortune 500 CEOs, only 4 percent agreed with what Friedman wrote.[28]

Friedman's view, which tends to reject the stakeholder concept described in Chapter 1, might seem selfish and even antisocial, but it raises a couple of important issues. First, any

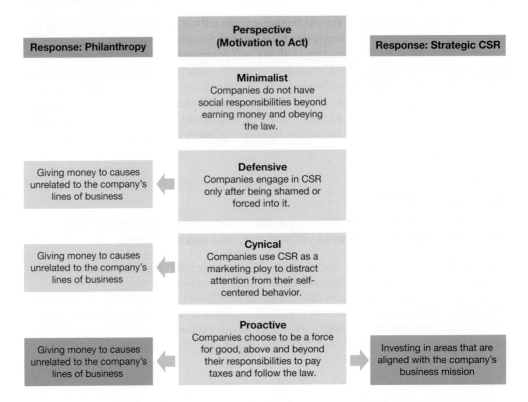

EXHIBIT 4.4   **Perspectives on Corporate Social Responsibility**

The perspectives on CSR can be roughly divided into four categories, from minimalist to proactive. Companies that engage in CSR can pursue either generic *philanthropy* or *strategic CSR*.

Response: Philanthropy

Perspective (Motivation to Act)

Response: Strategic CSR

Minimalist
Companies do not have social responsibilities beyond earning money and obeying the law.

Defensive
Companies engage in CSR only after being shamed or forced into it.

Giving money to causes unrelated to the company's lines of business ◄

Cynical
Companies use CSR as a marketing ploy to distract attention from their self-centered behavior.

Giving money to causes unrelated to the company's lines of business ◄

Proactive
Companies choose to be a force for good, above and beyond their responsibilities to pay taxes and follow the law.

Giving money to causes unrelated to the company's lines of business ◄   ► Investing in areas that are aligned with the company's business mission

business that operates ethically and legally provides society with beneficial goods and services at fair prices. This is a positive contribution, regardless of one's stance on CSR.

Second—and this is a vital point to consider even if you reject the minimalist view—should businesses be in the business of making social policy and spending the public's money? Proponents of the minimalist view claim that this is what happens when companies make tax-deductible contributions to social causes. For example, assume that in response to pressure from activists, a company makes a sizable contribution that nets it a $1 million tax break. That's $1 million taken out of the public treasury, where voters and their elected representatives can control how money is spent, and put into whatever social cause the company chooses to support. In effect, the corporation and the activists are spending the public's money, and the public has no say in how it is spent. Would it be better for society if companies paid full taxes and let the people (through their elected representatives) decide how their tax dollars are put to work?

DEFENSIVE CSR

nongovernmental organizations (NGOs)
Not-for-profit groups that provide charitable services or promote social and environmental causes.

Many companies today face pressure from a variety of activists and **nongovernmental organizations (NGOs)**, not-for-profit groups that provide charitable services or that promote causes, from workers' rights to environmental protection. One possible response to this pressure is to engage in CSR activities as a way to avoid further criticism. In other words, the company may take positive steps to address a particular issue only because it has been embarrassed into action by negative publicity.

Note that companies can engage in proactive CSR and still receive criticism from advocacy groups. A company and an NGO might disagree about responsibilities or outcomes, or in some cases, an NGO might target a company for a problem that the company has already been working on. In other words, it can't immediately be concluded that a company is simply being defensive when it engages in CSR while in the glare of public criticism.

CYNICAL CSR

Another possible approach to CSR is purely cynical, in which a company accused of irresponsible behavior promotes itself as being socially or environmentally responsible without making substantial improvements in its business practices. For example, environmental activists use the term *greenwash* (a combination of *green* and *whitewash*, a term that suggests covering something up) as a label for publicity efforts that portray companies as being environmentally friendly when their actions speak otherwise.

THE PROACTIVE STANCE: MOVING BEYOND CSR

In the fourth approach, proactive CSR, company leaders believe they have responsibilities beyond making a profit, and they back up their beliefs and proclamations with actions taken on their own initiative. In a sense, this is moving beyond CSR, because it involves leaders and their employees asking, "How can we be a force for good?" and not just, "How can we avoid being bad?" (In fact, some people now reject CSR as a label on the grounds that it has been rendered meaningless by too many cynical CSR moves. Unilever's Paul Polman banned the term's use within the company, for example.[29])

This proactive mindset is the foundation of being a **purpose-driven business**, a company that aspires to accomplish more than just making money for owners and investors, just as William Lever did back in 19th-century England. This mindset doesn't mean these companies don't have a profit motive, but rather that they seek profitable opportunities to pursue a social or environmental goal. Being a purpose-driven business used to be something of a fringe idea, but it has rapidly become mainstream. Larry Fink is CEO of Black-Rock, one of the largest investment firms in the world, managing more than $6 trillion in client assets—much of which is invested in corporate stocks. This gives the company tremendous leverage over corporations and gives Fink a formidable platform. In one of his recent annual letters to the CEOs of the companies in which BlackRock invests, he had this to say:[30]

> Society is demanding that companies, both public and private, serve a social purpose. To prosper over time, every company must not only deliver financial performance, but also show how it makes a positive contribution to society. Companies must benefit all of their stakeholders, including shareholders, employees, customers, and the communities in which they operate.

purpose-driven business
A company that aspires to accomplish more than just making money for owners and investors.

REAL-TIME UPDATES
Learn More by Exploring This Interactive Website

Connecting businesses with sustainable opportunities

The Global Opportunity Explorer presents companies and entrepreneurs with hundreds of sustainable business opportunities. Go to **real-timeupdates.com/bia9** and select Learn More in the Students section.

RESOLVING THE CSR DILEMMA

So, what's the right answer? Of the four perspectives on CSR, we can instantly eliminate the cynical approach simply because it is dishonest and therefore unethical. The minimalist view will continue to have its proponents, although they are becoming rarer. Many companies will likely engage in defensive CSR in some areas, perhaps even while they take a more proactive stance in others.

A two-tiered approach to CSR can yield a practical, ethical answer to this complex dilemma. At the first tier, companies must take responsibility for the consequences of their actions and limit the negative impact of their operations. This approach can be summarized as "do no harm," and it is not a matter of choice. Just as a society has a right to expect certain behavior from all citizens, it has a right to expect a basic level of responsible behavior from all businesses, including minimizing pollution and waste, minimizing the depletion of shared natural resources, being honest with all stakeholders, offering real value in exchange for prices asked, and avoiding exploitation of employees, customers, suppliers, communities, and investors. Some of these issues are covered by laws, but others aren't, thereby creating the responsibility of ethical decision-making by all employees and managers in a firm.

At the second tier, moving beyond "do no harm" and defensive CSR to a more proactive stance becomes a matter of choice. Companies can choose to help in whatever way their investors, managers, and employees see fit. However, as Larry Fink's message to corporate

REAL-TIME UPDATES
Learn More by Visiting This Website

Companies that are making positive changes

Fortune's Change the World list highlights companies that are investing in solutions to a wide variety of societal challenges. Go to **real-timeupdates.com/bia9** and select Learn More in the Students section.

leaders suggests, what was once considered voluntary is becoming expected by many. These expectations make up the *social license to operate*, the minimum level of business practices that society demands from companies.[31] (This is not a license in the literal sense, but an expression of what society demands from business.) Companies that fail to conduct themselves in a way that society expects may find themselves facing an uphill battle of activism and increased regulation in the future.

For more insights on CSR, visit **real-timeupdates.com/bia9** and select Chapter 4.

✔ CHECKPOINT

LEARNING OBJECTIVE 3: Distinguish among the four perspectives on corporate social responsibility.

SUMMARY: The spectrum of viewpoints on CSR can be roughly divided into minimalist (business's only obligation is to compete to the best of its abilities without deception or fraud), defensive (in which businesses engage in CSR efforts only in response to social pressure), cynical (in which businesses engage in CSR as a public relations ploy), and proactive, or going beyond CSR (in which businesses contribute to society based on a belief that they have an obligation to do so).

CRITICAL THINKING: (1) Do you agree that giving companies tax breaks for charitable contributions distorts public spending by indirectly giving companies and activists control over how tax revenues are spent? Why or why not? (2) If Company A takes a cynical approach to CSR and Company B takes a proactive approach, but they make identical contributions to society, is one company "better" than the other? Why or why not?

IT'S YOUR BUSINESS: (1) Have you ever suspected a company of engaging in greenwashing or other disingenuous CSR activities? How would you prove or disprove such a suspicion? (2) If you were the head of a small company and wanted to give back to society in some way, how would you select which organizations or causes to support?

KEY TERMS TO KNOW: nongovernmental organizations (NGOs), purpose-driven business

 LEARNING OBJECTIVE

Discuss the role of business in protecting the natural environment, and define sustainable development.

CSR: The Natural Environment

Environmental concerns of pollution, resource depletion, and waste are other important aspects of the relationship between business and society. Unfortunately, these issues occasionally get politicized and polarized. Environmentalists and their political allies sometimes portray business leaders as heartless profiteers who would strip the Earth bare for a few bucks. Their political opponents, on the other hand, sometimes cast environmentalists as "tree huggers" who care more about bunnies and butterflies than about jobs and other human concerns. As is often the case, the shouting match between these extreme positions obscures real problems—and opportunities for real solutions.

To reach a clearer understanding of this situation, keep three important points in mind. First, the creation, delivery, use, and disposal of products that society values virtually always generate pollution and consume natural resources. For instance, it's tempting to assume that web-based and digital businesses are "clean" because there is no visible pollution. However, the internet and all the devices and services associated with it, from Google searches to bitcoin mining, have a voracious appetite for electricity, and the generation of electricity seriously affects the environment. Although the share of the electricity generated by renewable means in the United States is increasing, about 60 percent of the country's electricity is still generated by burning coal or natural gas (see Exhibit 4.5).

EXHIBIT 4.5	Sources of Electrical Power in the United States

Natural gas is now the top source of electricity generation in the United States, but renewable energy sources (driven by dramatic gains in solar and wind) are growing faster. Together, renewables and hydropower supplied as much electricity as nuclear in 2017. Exhibit 4.5a shows the five major sources of electricity; Exhibit 4.5b breaks out the most significant types of renewable sources.

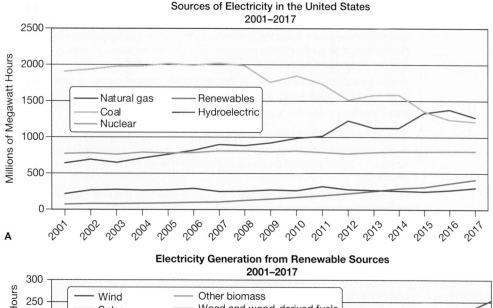

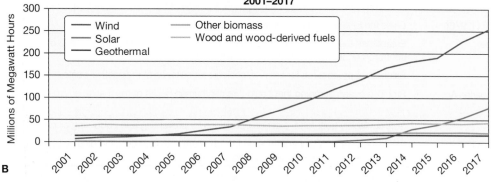

Note: *Doesn't include petroleum and other minor sources or hydroelectric pumped storage, which is used for load balancing. The data lines for renewables in Exhibit 4.5a and for solar in Exhibit 4.5b include only utility-scale solar prior to 2014; they include both utility-scale and small-scale solar from 2014 onward.*
Source: Data from Electricity Data Browser, U.S. Energy Information Administration, www.eia.gov.

Second, "environmental" issues are often as much about human health and safety as they are about forests, rivers, and wildlife. The availability of clean air, clean water, and healthy soil affects everyone, not just people concerned with wild spaces.

Third, many of these issues are neither easy nor simple. They often require tough trade-offs, occasional sacrifice, disruptive change, and decision-making in the face of uncertainty. Meeting these challenges will require people to be clear-headed, open-minded, adaptable, and courageous.

EFFORTS TO CONSERVE RESOURCES AND REDUCE POLLUTION

Concerns over pollution and resource depletion have been growing since the dawn of the Industrial Age in the 19th century. However, widespread concern for the environment really dates to the 1960s, when *ecology*, the study of the relationship between organisms and the natural environment, entered mainstream discussion. In 1963, federal, state, and local governments began enacting laws and regulations to reduce pollution (see Exhibit 4.6 on the next page). Many states and cities have also passed their own tough clean-air laws.

You've no doubt heard the slogan "reduce, reuse, recycle" as advice for conserving resources and minimizing pollution. Google offers a great example of what businesses

EXHIBIT 4.6	Major Federal Environmental Legislation

Since the early 1960s, major federal legislation aimed at protecting the environment and human health has focused on providing cleaner air and water and reducing toxic waste. (Many of these laws have been amended since their original dates of passage.)

Legislation	Key Provisions
Clean Air Act (1963) Clean Air Act (1967) Clean Air Act (1970)	Assist states and localities in formulating control programs; set federal standards for auto-exhaust emissions; set maximum permissible pollution levels; authorize nationwide air-pollution standards and limitations to pollutant discharge; require scrubbers in new coal-fired power plants; direct the Environmental Protection Agency (EPA) to prevent deterioration of air quality in clean areas; set schedule and standards for cutting smog, acid rain, hazardous factory fumes, and ozone-depleting chemicals
Solid Waste Disposal Act (1965)	Authorizes research and assistance to state and local control programs; regulates treatment, storage, transportation, and disposal of hazardous waste
National Environmental Policy Act (1969)	Establishes a structure for coordinating all federal environmental programs
Resource Recovery Act (1970)	Subsidizes pilot recycling plants; authorizes nationwide control programs
Clean Water Act (1972) Clean Water Act (1977)	Authorize grants to states for water-pollution control; give federal government limited authority to correct pollution problems; authorize EPA to set and enforce water-quality standards
Noise Control Act (1972)	Requires EPA to set standards for major sources of noise and to advise Federal Aviation Administration on standards for airplane noise
Endangered Species Act (1973)	Establishes protections for endangered and threatened plants and animals
Safe Drinking Water Act (1974)	Sets standards of drinking-water quality; requires municipal water systems to report on contaminant levels; establishes funding to upgrade water systems
Toxic Substances Control Act (1976)	Requires chemicals testing; authorizes EPA to restrict the use of harmful substances
Resource Conservation and Recovery Act (1976)	Gives the EPA authority to control hazardous waste
Comprehensive Environmental Response, Compensation, and Liability Act (1980)	Establishes the "Superfund" program to oversee the identification and cleanup of uncontrolled or abandoned hazardous-waste sites
Nuclear Waste Policy Act (1982)	Establishes procedures for creating geologic repositories of radioactive waste
Marine Protection, Research, and Sanctuaries Act (1988)	Prohibits ocean dumping that could threaten human health or the marine environment
Oil Pollution Act (1990)	Sets up liability trust fund; extends operations for preventing and containing oil pollution
Energy Independence and Security Act (2007)	Aims to reduce U.S. dependence on foreign energy sources by expanding energy production options and improving energy efficiency

Sources: U.S. Environmental Protection Agency, accessed 22 March 2018, www.epa.gov; "Overview: Key Federal Environmental Laws," FindLaw, accessed 22 March 2018, www.findlaw.com.

can do in this regard. Its *data centers* house the estimated 2.5 million computer servers that power Google searches, stream YouTube videos, and deliver Gmail—and make Google one of the world's biggest consumers of electricity. The company devotes considerable research and engineering effort to run its data centers as efficiently as possible and thereby limit its resource consumption. These efforts including recycling and repurposing old computers, investing in renewable energy sources to help make them economically viable and more widely available, redesigning servers to make them more energy efficient, and applying artificial intelligence to reduce the energy needed to cool data centers. Because of this effort, Google is much more energy efficient than typical data center owners, and it shares this knowledge with other companies to help them reduce consumption as well.[32]

REAL-TIME UPDATES

Learn More by Visiting This Website

See how Google is helping to reduce the internet's electricity appetite

Google has made significant progress in becoming more energy efficient, and it shares these insights with other big electricity users. Go to **real-timeupdates.com/bia9** and select Learn More in the Students section.

sustainable development
Operating business in a manner that minimizes pollution and resource depletion, ensuring that future generations will have vital resources.

THE TREND TOWARD SUSTAINABILITY

Efforts to minimize resource depletion and pollution are part of a broader effort known as *sustainability*, or **sustainable development**, which the United Nations has defined as development that "meets the needs of the present without compromising the ability of future generations to meet their own needs."[33] Notice how this idea expands the stakeholder concept from Chapter 1 by including stakeholders from the future, not just those with an immediate interest in what a company does.

Sustainable development can certainly require changes to the way companies conduct business, but paying attention to a broader scope of stakeholders and managing for the longer term doesn't automatically mean that companies have to take a financial hit to "go green." As you'll read at the end of the chapter, for example, Unilever's emphasis on sustainable strategies and practices makes it more economically efficient as well.

By taking a broad and long-term view of their companies' impact on the environment and stakeholders throughout the world, managers can ensure the continued availability of the resources their organizations need and be better prepared for the future.

 CHECKPOINT

LEARNING OBJECTIVE 4: Discuss the role of business in protecting the natural environment, and define sustainable development.

SUMMARY: As major users of natural resources and generators of waste products, businesses play a huge role in conservation and pollution-reduction efforts. Many businesses are making an effort to reduce, reuse, and recycle. All these efforts are part of a trend toward sustainable development, which can be defined as meeting the needs of the present without compromising the ability of future generations to meet their own needs.

CRITICAL THINKING: (1) Should all industries be required to meet the same levels of pollution control? Why or why not? (2) What do stakeholders of the present owe to stakeholders of the future?

IT'S YOUR BUSINESS: (1) In what ways could your employer (or your college, if you're not currently working) take steps to reduce resource depletion? (2) How did you dispose of the last electronic product you stopped using?

KEY TERMS TO KNOW: sustainable development

CSR: Consumers

The 1960s activism that awakened business to its environmental responsibilities also gave rise to **consumerism**, a movement that put pressure on businesses to consider consumer needs and interests. (Note that some people use *consumerism* in a negative sense, as a synonym for *materialism*.) Consumerism prompted many businesses to create consumer affairs departments to handle customer complaints. It also prompted state and local agencies to set up bureaus to offer consumer information and assistance. At the federal level, President John F. Kennedy announced a "bill of rights" for consumers, laying the foundation for a wave of consumer-oriented legislation (see Exhibit 4.7 on the next page).

THE RIGHT TO BUY SAFE PRODUCTS

As mentioned previously, doing no harm is one of the foundations of social responsibility. The United States and many other countries go to considerable lengths to ensure the safety of the products sold within their borders. The U.S. government imposes many safety standards that are enforced by the Consumer Product Safety Commission (CPSC), as well as by other federal and state agencies. Companies that don't comply with these rules are forced to take corrective action, and the threat of product-liability suits and declining sales motivates companies to meet safety standards.

⑤ LEARNING OBJECTIVE

Identify five fundamental consumer rights and the responsibility of business to respect them.

consumerism
A movement that pressures businesses to consider consumer needs and interests.

EXHIBIT 4.7	Major Federal Consumer Legislation

Major federal legislation aimed at consumer protection has focused on food and drugs, false advertising, product safety, and credit protection.

Legislation	Major Provisions
Food, Drug, and Cosmetic Act (1938)	Puts cosmetics, foods, drugs, and therapeutic products under Food and Drug Administration's jurisdiction; outlaws misleading labeling
Cigarette Labeling and Advertising Act (1965)	Mandates warnings on cigarette packages and in ads
Fair Packaging and Labeling Act (1966, 1972)	Requires honest, informative package labeling; labels must show origin of product, quantity of contents, uses or applications
Truth in Lending Act (Consumer Protection Credit Act) (1968)	Requires creditors to disclose finance charge and annual percentage rate; limits cardholder liability for unauthorized use
Fair Credit Reporting Act (1970)	Requires credit-reporting agencies to set process for assuring accuracy; requires creditors to explain credit denials
Consumer Product Safety Act (1972)	Creates Consumer Product Safety Commission
Magnuson-Moss Warranty Act (1975)	Requires complete written warranties in ordinary language; requires warranties to be available before purchase
Alcohol Beverage Labeling Act (1988)	Requires warning labels on alcohol products, saying that alcohol impairs abilities and that women shouldn't drink when pregnant
Children's Online Privacy Protection Act (1988)	Gives parents control over the collection or use of information that websites can collect about children
Nutrition Education and Labeling Act (1990)	Requires specific, uniform product labels detailing nutritional information on every food regulated by the Food and Drug Administration (FDA)
American Automobile Labeling Act (1992)	Requires carmakers to identify where cars are assembled and where their individual components are manufactured
Deceptive Mail Prevention and Enforcement Act (1999)	Establishes standards for sweepstakes mailings, skill contests, and facsimile checks to prevent fraud and exploitation
Controlling the Assault of Non-Solicited Pornography and Marketing Act (2003)	Known as CAN-SPAM, attempts to protect online consumers from unwanted and fraudulent email
Consumer Product Safety Improvement Act (2008)	Strengthens standards for lead in children's products; mandates safety testing for imported children's products; creates a searchable database for reporting accidents, injuries, and illnesses related to consumer products
Dodd-Frank Wall Street Reform and Consumer Protection Act (2010)	Amends a number of earlier acts and regulations in an attempt to improve the stability of the banking and investment industries; establishes the Consumer Financial Protection Bureau

Source: www.fda.gov; uscode.house.gov; www.ftc.gov; www.cpsc.com; www.ttb.gov; www.consumerfinance.gov.

THE RIGHT TO BE INFORMED

Consumers have a right to know what they're buying, how to use it, and whether it presents any risks to them. They also have a right to know the true price of goods or services and the details of purchase contracts. Accordingly, numerous government regulations have been put in place to ensure buyers get the information they need in order to make informed choices. Of course, buyers share the responsibility here, at least morally if not always legally. Not bothering to read labels or contracts or not asking for help if you don't understand them is no excuse for not being informed.

Fortunately, both consumers and businesses can turn to a wide range of information sources to learn more about the goods and services they purchase. The spread of social media and their use in *social commerce* (see page 358), in which buyers help educate one another, has helped shift power from sellers to buyers. For just about every purchase you consider these days, you can find independent information about it before you choose.

THE RIGHT TO CHOOSE WHICH PRODUCTS TO BUY

Especially in the United States, the number of products available to consumers is staggering, even sometimes overwhelming. But how far should the right to choose extend? Are we entitled to choose products that are potentially harmful, such as cigarettes, alcoholic beverages, guns, sugary soft drinks, or fatty fried foods? Should the government make such products illegal or discourage purchasing by making them expensive to buy, or should consumers always be allowed to decide for themselves what to buy? These are not always simple questions, because the impact of consumer choices often spreads beyond the people making the choices.

THE RIGHT TO BE HEARD

The fourth component of consumer rights is the right to be heard. Social media have created a revolution in terms of giving consumers a voice they never had, providing them with numerous ways to ask questions, voice concerns, provide feedback, and demand attention. Savvy companies monitor Twitter, blogs, and other online venues to catch messages from dissatisfied customers. Companies that fail to respond or that respond in defensive, inward-looking ways are likely to lose business to competitors that embrace social media and the power they give today's consumers.

Hackers breached the network of the credit agency Equifax and stole sensitive financial data on 150 million people.

THE RIGHT TO DIGITAL SECURITY

Advances in digital technology have not been all positive for consumers, however. Any company that collects information on or about consumers has a clear ethical obligation to keep it safe and secure, but the growing number of massive data-security breaches in recent years indicates how poorly many companies are meeting this obligation.

For example, the credit agency Equifax failed to stop hackers from stealing the sensitive financial data of 150 million people—nearly half the population of the United States. And, following a troubling pattern among companies that have been hacked, Equifax failed to take steps to secure its network, even after it was warned about vulnerabilities.[34] This breach was particularly galling to many consumers because they have no control over whether credit agencies such as Equifax can collect and use their financial data.

Digital security breaches raise the risk of **identity theft**, in which criminals steal personal information and use it to take out loans, request government documents and tax refunds, get expensive medical procedures, and commit other types of fraud. Millions of U.S. consumers are victims of identity theft every year, and the effects can be financially devastating.[35]

Digital security is a difficult challenge in the United States, because U.S. law offers no comprehensive legal rights to privacy, and data protection policy is a patchwork of hundreds of industry-specific regulations and state and local laws that leave much up to the responsibility of individual companies.[36] In contrast, the European Union's General Data Protection Regulations (GDPR) provide a single set of regulations across industries, with a number of important elements to protect consumers, such as "the right to be forgotten" by having all of one's data erased. The GDPR also mandates stiff penalties—up to 4 percent of a company's annual revenue—for violations. Although these are EU regulations, they affect many U.S. companies because they apply to any companies that sell to EU residents or process data on these residents.[37]

identity theft
A crime in which thieves steal personal information and use it to take out loans and commit other types of fraud.

REAL-TIME UPDATES
Learn More by Visiting This Website

Get help if you've been a victim of identity theft

See how to report identify theft and get started on a recovery plan. Go to **real-timeupdates.com/bia9** and select Learn More in the Students section.

 CHECKPOINT

LEARNING OBJECTIVE 5: Identify five fundamental consumer rights and the responsibility of business to respect them.

SUMMARY: Five fundamental consumer rights in the United States are the right to safe products, the right to be informed, the right to choose, the right to be heard, and the right to digital security. Many specific aspects of these rights are embodied in government regulations, but others rely on business professionals to practice ethical and responsive decision-making.

CRITICAL THINKING: (1) Is there a point at which responsibility for product safety shifts from the seller to the buyer? Explain your answer. (2) If providing full information about products raises prices, should businesses still be required to do so? Why or why not?

IT'S YOUR BUSINESS: (1) How do social media influence your behavior as a consumer? (2) Have you ever lodged a complaint with a business? If so, what was the outcome?

KEY TERM TO KNOW: consumerism, identity theft

---

⑥ **LEARNING OBJECTIVE**
Explain the responsibilities businesses have toward their employees.

CSR: Employees

The past few decades have brought dramatic changes in the composition of the global workforce and in the attitudes of workers. These changes have forced businesses to modify their recruiting, training, and promotion practices, as well as their overall corporate values and behaviors. This section discusses some key responsibilities that employers have toward their employees.

THE PUSH FOR EQUALITY IN EMPLOYMENT

discrimination
In a social and economic sense, denial of opportunities to individuals on the basis of some characteristic that has no bearing on their ability to perform in a job.

The United States has always stood for economic freedom and the individual's right to pursue opportunity. Unfortunately, in the past, many people were targets of economic **discrimination**, being relegated to low-paying, menial jobs and prevented from taking advantage of many opportunities solely on the basis of their race, gender, disability, or religion.

The Civil Rights Act of 1964 established the Equal Employment Opportunity Commission (EEOC), the regulatory agency that addresses job discrimination. The EEOC is responsible for monitoring hiring practices and for investigating complaints of job-related discrimination. It has the power to file legal charges against companies that discriminate and to force them to compensate individuals or groups that have been victimized by unfair practices. The Civil Rights Act of 1991 amended the original act in response to a number of Supreme Court decisions that had taken place in the intervening quarter-century. Among its key provisions are limiting the amount of damage awards, making it easier to sue for discrimination, giving employees the right to have a trial by jury in discrimination cases, and extending protections to overseas employees of U.S. companies.[38]

Affirmative Action

affirmative action
Activities undertaken by businesses to recruit and promote members of groups whose economic progress has been hindered through either legal barriers or established practices.

In the 1960s, **affirmative action** programs were developed to encourage organizations to recruit and promote members of groups whose past economic progress has been hindered through legal barriers or common practices. (College admissions have also been influenced by affirmative action laws, but the focus here is on business practices.) The "affirmative" part of affirmative action indicates laws that go beyond outlawing discrimination to actively helping people in groups whose historical status may leave them at a disadvantage in the contemporary job market.

For example, companies with contracts to sell goods or services to the federal government may be required to establish programs that focus on hiring and enabling career advancement for women, members of nonwhite ethnic groups, and military veterans with disabilities. Many states have similar requirements for companies that wish to pursue government contracts.[39]

The concept of affirmative action was controversial when it was introduced and remains so to this day, with disagreements over whether it is fair, whether it was or still is needed, and whether various efforts have successfully addressed the issues. Policy debates aside, however, well-managed companies are finding that embracing diversity in the richest sense is good for business. You'll read more about diversity and inclusion in Chapter 11.

People with Disabilities

In 1990, people with a wide range of physical and mental difficulties got new workplace protections with the passage of the Americans with Disabilities Act (ADA), which guarantees equal opportunities in housing, transportation, education, employment, and other areas. As defined by the 1990 law, *disability* is a broad term that refers not only to those with physical handicaps but also to those with cancer, heart disease, diabetes, epilepsy, HIV/AIDS, drug addiction, alcoholism, emotional illness, and other conditions. In most situations, employers cannot legally require job applicants to pass a physical examination as a condition of employment. Employers are also required to make reasonable accommodations to meet the needs of employees with disabilities, such as by modifying workstations or schedules.[40]

WORKPLACE SAFETY

Employers have an ethical and legal responsibility to ensure the safety of their employees in the workplace. Every year, several thousand U.S. workers lose their lives on the job, and many thousands more are injured (see Exhibit 4.8).[41] During the 1960s, mounting concern about workplace hazards resulted in the passage of the Occupational Safety and Health Act of 1970, which set mandatory standards for safety and health and also established the Occupational Safety and Health Administration (OSHA) to enforce them. These standards govern a range of concerns, including exposure to hazardous materials, noise levels, fire protection, and *ergonomics,* the study of how people interact with computers and other machines.[42] (Employers also have a responsibility to prevent *hostile workplaces*; sexual harassment is addressed in Chapter 11.)

   Concerns for employee safety can extend beyond a company's own workforce, and this concern is particularly acute for the many U.S. companies that contract out production to factories in Asia, Latin America, and other parts of the world to make products under their brand names. Often responding to pressure from advocacy groups such as United Students Against Sweatshops (usas.org), Nike and other manufacturers are taking steps to monitor and improve working conditions in these factories, including working to eliminate forced labor, slavery, and human trafficking.[43] And nearly 200 U.S. colleges have joined the Fair Labor Association (www.fairlabor.org) to help ensure that school-logo products are manufactured in an ethical manner.[44]

EXHIBIT 4.8	Fatal Occupational Injuries

Transportation accidents are the leading cause of death on the job in the United States. Overall, U.S. workers suffer fatal on-the-job injuries at a rate of 3.2 deaths per 100,000 full-time employees per year.

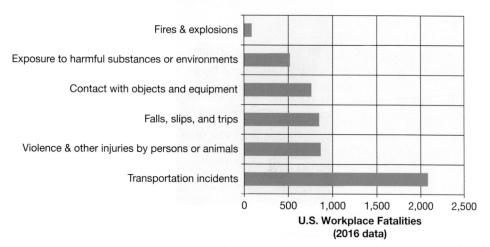

U.S. Workplace Fatalities
(2016 data)

Source: "Census of Fatal Occupational Injuries," U.S. Bureau of Labor Statistics, www.bls.gov.

✔ CHECKPOINT

LEARNING OBJECTIVE 6: Explain the responsibilities businesses have toward their employees.

SUMMARY: In addition to the impact a company has on its external stakeholders, CSR applies within the company as well, to the way employees are treated. Major issues include the push for equal opportunity, which includes affirmative action programs and regulations to protect the rights of people with disabilities, occupational safety and health, and workplace harassment.

CRITICAL THINKING: (1) Does affirmative action seem like a fair approach? Why or why not? (2) Should employees automatically get paid more to work in hazardous jobs? Why or why not?

IT'S YOUR BUSINESS: (1) Have you ever experienced or observed discrimination on the job? If so, how did you handle the situation? (2) Has this chapter changed your perspective about the relationship between business and society? Why or why not?

KEY TERMS TO KNOW: discrimination, affirmative action

[7]   LEARNING OBJECTIVE

Identify two categories of ethical concerns with artificial intelligence.

Thriving in the Digital Enterprise: The Ethics of Artificial Intelligence

As one of the most powerful technologies ever developed, artificial intelligence (AI) is already influencing human life in multiple ways and promises to do so even more in the future. Although many of these developments are positive (see Exhibit 4.9), AI shares the two-sided nature of every major technology: The power that enables it to be a positive force can also let it become a negative force. Moreover, even with good intentions, it is impossible to foresee and control all the consequences that AI could unleash.

EXHIBIT 4.9	Augmented Ability Technologies

Augmented ability tools help people across a wider spectrum of physical or cognitive ability interact with devices and their immediate environments in more complete and fulfilling ways. For example, Microsoft's Seeing AI app can help people with limited vision by reading texts, recognizing currency, identifying people, scanning barcodes, and identifying objects in a room or on the street. The app speaks to the user to describe whatever it thinks it sees, and it can be trained to recognize family members, friends, and colleagues.

Two issues of particular concern from an ethical perspective are embedded biases and a lack of transparency and accountability.

HUMAN BIASES EMBEDDED IN AI SYSTEMS

Like all human creations, AI reflects the intentions and beliefs of its creators—sometimes consciously and sometimes subconsciously. Simplifying greatly, AI systems incorporate algorithms, or instructions, and data that those instructions operate upon. If either the algorithms or the data reflect human biases, the AI system will likely exhibit those same biases.

For instance, facial recognition systems, which are increasingly being used for security and identification purposes, are "trained" using large collections of photographs. What they learn depends to a large degree on the photos in those collections. When African American AI researcher Joy Buolamwini discovered that some of the most widely used facial recognition systems had much higher error rates on female and nonwhite faces, she traced the problem to the photo sets they were trained on, which were composed of mostly white, male faces. The only way she could get some of the systems to recognize her face as a face at all was to wear a white mask.[45]

The developers of these systems are making improvements, but the fact that the problems existed in the first place could reflect the lack of diversity in AI research. As Buolamwini put it, "You can't have ethical AI that's not inclusive. And whoever is creating the technology is setting the standards."[46]

Another area in which AI systems can exhibit bias is language processing, because they learn from human language usage, which can have patterns of bias that range from overt to deeply buried. For instance, in a test where otherwise identical résumés were presented to some employers displaying a European American name and to other employers displaying an African American name, the résumé with the European American name drew 50 percent more interview invitations.[47] If AI systems take on biased behaviors from language usage, their ability to automate decision-making at lightning speed can propagate biases throughout business and society as a whole.

Other areas where AI systems can potentially exhibit bias include risk-assessment systems that purport to predict an individual's likelihood of committing a crime and automated applicant-evaluation systems used to make lending and hiring decisions. However, these automated approaches can be *less* biased than human decision-makers if they are programmed to focus on objective factors.[48] In an important sense, we don't want AI that can think like humans; we want AI that can think better than humans do.

AI researcher Joy Buolamwini discovered that some widely used facial recognition systems literally couldn't see her until she put on a white mask.

LACK OF TRANSPARENCY AND ACCOUNTABILITY

One of the most unnerving aspects of some advanced decision-making systems is the inability of even their creators—much less the general public—to understand why the systems make some of the decisions they do. For example, an AI system called Deep Patient is uncannily effective at predicting diseases by studying patients' medical data. In some instances, doctors don't know how it reached its decisions, and the system can't tell them, either.[49]

This lack of insight has troubling implications for law enforcement, medicine, hiring, and just about any other field where AI might be used. For instance, if a risk-assessment system says that a prisoner is likely to reoffend and therefore shouldn't be paroled, should the prisoner's lawyers be able to cross-examine the AI? What if even the AI system can't explain how it reached that decision?[50]

THE EFFORTS TO MAKE AI A FORCE FOR GOOD

AI unquestionably has the potential to benefit humankind in many ways, but only if it is directed toward beneficial applications and applied in ethical ways. How can society make sure that the decisions made and the actions taken by AI systems reflect the values and priorities of the people who are affected? How can we ensure that people retain

Courtesy of Terah Lyons, Partnership on AI

As executive director of the Partnership on AI, Terah Lyons works with a wide range of technology companies, research institutions, and advocacy groups to ensure the ethical and beneficial application of artificial intelligence.

REAL-TIME UPDATES
Learn More by Visiting This Website

Working to make AI a force for good

The Partnership on AI addresses major ethical and social questions raised by AI. Go to **real-timeupdates.com/bia9** and select Learn More in the Students section.

individual dignity and autonomy even as intelligent systems take over many tasks and decisions? And how can we make sure that the benefits of AI aren't limited to those who have access to the science and technology behind it? For example, a high percentage of the available AI talent is currently concentrated in a handful of huge tech companies that have the money necessary to buy up promising AI start-ups. While this benefits Google, Amazon, and Facebook in their business pursuits, potential applications in other industries, agriculture, medicine, and other fields might be lagging behind for want of talent.[51]

Recognizing how important it is to get out in front of these questions before the technology outpaces our ability to control it, a number of organizations are wrestling with these issues. One of the largest is the Partnership on AI, whose membership includes many of the major corporate players in AI and dozens of smaller companies, research centers, and advocacy organizations. Its areas of focus include ensuring the integrity of *safety-critical* AI in transportation and health care; making AI fair, transparent, and accountable; minimizing the disruptive effect of AI on the workforce; and collaborating with a wide range of organizations to maximize the social benefits of AI.[52]

Individual companies are also helping in significant ways. Microsoft, for instance, is directing $50 million and some of its considerable AI talent to AI for Earth, a program that uses AI to improve outcomes in agriculture, water resources, education, and other important areas.[53]

The spread of AI throughout business highlights the importance of ethical awareness and ethical decision-making. Only by building ethical principles into these systems can we expect them to generate ethically acceptable outputs.

 CHECKPOINT

LEARNING OBJECTIVE 7: Identify two categories of ethical concerns with artificial intelligence.

SUMMARY: Two major categories of ethical concerns are the potential for embedding human biases in AI systems and the potential lack of transparency and accountability. Bias concerns stem from potential bias embedded in language and the lack of diversity in research efforts. The transparency and accountability concerns revolve around the inability to understand how some AI systems make decisions.

CRITICAL THINKING: (1) What are the dangers of having so much AI talent concentrated in so few companies? (2) Should companies use AI systems if they can't entirely explain how the systems make decisions?

IT'S YOUR BUSINESS: (1) Would you ever refuse to go through the interviewing process with a company if you knew you would be evaluated at some point by an AI system? Why or why not? (2) If your employer announced it was instituting AI-assisted performance evaluation, what are some of the questions you might want to ask your superiors?

BEHIND THE SCENES

Unilever Has a Plan for Sustainable Business, But Will Investors Have the Patience?

In his wildest dreams, William Lever probably couldn't have imagined what his 19th-century soap enterprise would grow into by the 21st century. Unilever is now a massive global entity. On any day of the year, one-third of the world's population is using a Unilever product.

Even if he couldn't have imagined what the company would grow into, if he were alive today, he surely would be proud of how his successors have carried on his founding purpose of creating products and running a company for the benefit of people, beyond the mere pursuit of profits. Today, his legacy lives on in Unilever's Sustainable Living Plan. The company describes it as "driving growth through brands with purpose, taking out costs from our business, reducing risks, and helping us to build trust—creating long-term value for the multiple stakeholders we serve."

Many companies set goals to make a positive impact on their communities. But few go as far as Unilever, which is fundamentally placing a bet that one of the world's largest companies can do well by doing good. The Sustainable Living Plan is based on three audacious goals: helping 1 billion people worldwide improve their health and well-being, cutting the company's environmental footprint in half, and enhancing the livelihoods of millions of people who work for the company either directly as employees or indirectly as suppliers and partners.

All over the globe, Unilever works toward these goals through a variety of programs, including working to eliminate deforestation, helping farmers switch to sustainable growing practices, assisting communities with clean water and sanitation, and creating job opportunities to allow more women in developing countries to enter the workforce. And its efforts to manage its own operations in sustainable ways are producing impressive results. By reducing waste and resource usage, it cut three-quarters of a billion dollars from its costs over the past decade. More than half of its agricultural raw materials are now sustainably sourced.

Unilever not only runs its own business according to its values, but also is trying to shape other facets of the business environment in positive ways. As one of the world's largest advertisers, with an annual budget in the neighborhood of $10 billion, Unilever has a lot of influence over all forms of media. One of its top priorities is cleaning up the *digital supply chain*, the systems that deliver online advertising on various websites and social media platforms. Chief marketing officer Keith Weed has challenged Google, Facebook, and others to solve the problems of anonymous parties being able to post objectionable content all over the internet: "We cannot continue to prop up a digital supply chain—one that delivers over a quarter of our advertising to our consumers—which at times is little better than a swamp in terms of its transparency."

Of course, to accomplish any of its broader social and environmental goals, Unilever must continue to be a strong and profitable company. As it pursues its inspired purpose, Unilever faces two serious financial challenges. First, consumer goods companies tend to run on very thin profit margins. Price competition is intense in most categories, so any company in this industry needs to run a tight, efficient ship and be able to justify major expenditures.

Second, publicly traded corporations (those that sell shares of stock to the public) are under tremendous pressure to "hit the numbers" every quarter, which has created a climate of *short-termism* that can distort financial decision-making. Impatient investors might sell off shares if prices don't rise quickly enough. Stock prices are driven primarily by earnings, and companies are often pressured to improve quarterly earnings by cutting costs as low as possible—including on such things as social outreach efforts. In addition, major investors who grow dissatisfied with a company's performance can sometimes buy up enough stock and the voting power that comes with it to put their own representatives on the board of directors—and in some cases, get enough control to oust a company's CEO. Unilever's CEO Paul Polman and the Unilever board had to fend off just such a challenge in 2017, when U.S. competitor Kraft Heinz launched a hostile takeover bid. They survived this attempt, but others are likely to come.

Despite the challenges, Unilever continues to succeed at following its purpose and living the ideals of the Sustainable Living Plan. As more and more consumers and workers embrace the principles of sustainability, Unilever stands to benefit as a preferred supplier and employer. It has identified 18 of its products as "sustainable living" brands, each identified with a social or environmental purpose. Consumers appear to be responding; this group of products is now responsible for 60 percent of the company's growth. Plus, an increasing number of workers want to be associated with companies such as Unilever. In 34 countries around the world, college graduates identify Unilever as the number-one employer of choice.

Polman is getting ready to turn the controls over to a successor, and no matter what the future holds for Unilever, he will go down in history as an executive who backed up inspiring talk about social and environmental principles with unflinching commitment and bold action.[54]

Critical Thinking Questions

4-1. Not all consumers care about the social and environmental goals that Unilever embraces; is it a mistake for the company to align itself so visibly with these goals? Why or why not?

4-2. How does helping small farmers in developing countries benefit Unilever?

4-3. Why wouldn't Unilever just donate a portion of its profits to social and environmental causes, rather than integrating them with the company's operations?

Learn More Online

Visit **www.unilever.com** and explore the Sustainable Living section. What measures of progress does the company now list? How does this information influence your perceptions as a consumer of Unilever and its products? Would you consider going to work for Unilever after reading this information?

End of Chapter

KEY TERMS

affirmative action (154)
code of ethics (141)
conflicts of interest (143)
consumerism (151)
corporate social responsibility (CSR) (144)
discrimination (154)
ethical dilemma (142)
ethical lapse (141)
ethics (137)

identity theft (153)
insider trading (138)
nongovernmental organizations (NGOs) (146)
philanthropy (144)
purpose-driven business (147)
strategic CSR (144)
sustainable development (150)
transparency (141)
whistle-blowing (141)

TEST YOUR KNOWLEDGE

Questions for Review

4-4. How does ethics differ from corporate social responsibility?

4-5. What is whistle-blowing? Why would it be used?

4-6. What is cynical CSR? Give an example.

4-7. What is a purpose-driven business?

4-8. What are the two extreme positions in which business owners and environmentalists are portrayed?

4-9. What are the two conflicting interpretations of consumerism?

4-10. Why might AI be inherently biased?

Questions for Analysis

4-11. Why can't legal considerations resolve every ethical question?

4-12. How do individuals use philosophical principles in making ethical business decisions?

4-13. In what sense does proactive CSR move beyond the usual concept of CSR?

4-14. Why might a business choose to be unethical regardless of the risks involved and the moral issues at stake?

4-15. Why are more business leaders speaking out on public and social issues than in years past?

4-16. Why is it important for a company to balance its social responsibility efforts with its need to generate profits?

4-17. **Ethical Considerations.** Is it ethical for companies to benefit from their efforts to practice CSR? Why or why not? How can anyone be sure that CSR efforts aren't just public relations ploys?

4-18. What effects have social media had on CSR?

4-19. To what extent do you agree with the proposition that all ethical dilemmas are simply conflicts of interest?

4-20. Why is a lack of transparency a concern in AI?

Questions for Application

4-21. Based on what you've learned about CSR, what effect will CSR considerations have on your job search?

4-22. **Concept Integration.** Chapter 2 identified knowledge workers as a key economic resource of the 21st century. If an employee leaves a company to work for a competitor, what types of knowledge would be ethical for the employee to share with the new employer, and what types would be unethical to share?

4-23. **Concept Integration.** Is it ethical for state and city governments to entice specific businesses to relocate their operations to that state or city by offering them special tax breaks that are not extended to other businesses operating in that area?

EXPAND YOUR KNOWLEDGE

Discovering Career Opportunities

Businesses, government agencies, and not-for-profit organizations offer numerous career opportunities related to ethics and social responsibility.

- Search the *Occupational Outlook Handbook* at **www.bls.gov/ooh** for "occupational health and safety specialists and technicians," jobs concerned with a company's responsibility toward its employees. What are the duties and qualifications of the jobs you have identified? Are the salaries and future outlooks attractive for all these jobs?
- Select one job from the *Handbook* and search blogs, websites, and other sources to learn more about it. Try to find real-life information about the daily activities of people in this job. Can you find any information about ethical dilemmas or other conflicts in the duties of this position? What role do you think people in this position play within their respective organizations?
- What skills, educational background, and work experience do you think employers are seeking in applicants for the specific job you are researching? What keywords do you think employers would search for when reviewing résumés submitted for this position?

Intelligent Business Technology: Assistive Technologies

The term *assistive technologies* covers a broad range of devices and systems that help people with physical or cognitive impairments perform activities that might otherwise be difficult or impossible. These include technologies that help people communicate orally and visually, interact with computers and other equipment, and enjoy greater mobility, along with myriad other specific functions.

Assistive technologies create a vital link for thousands of employees with disabilities, giving them opportunities to pursue a greater range of career paths and giving employers access to a broader base of talent. Plus, the economy and society benefit when everyone who can contribute is able to, and assistive technologies are an important part of the solution.

Research several assistive technologies now on the market. Choose one assistive technology that interests you, and in a brief email message to your instructor, explain how this technology can help companies support employees or customers with disabilities.

PRACTICE YOUR SKILLS

Resolving Ethical Dilemmas

One of your closest friends has just started working in a smartphone store, and you are shocked at what she has told you about in-house sales training at her store. She has been asked to inform customers that once they sign a contract, their new phone will be delivered within 48 hours even though the delivery time is usually a week, and she has also been instructed not to discuss clauses in the contract. Cheaper options are not to be offered and customers are to be told that they must commit immediately to take advantage of deals.

Your friend has a strong code of honor but she also does not want to ignore the training and disobey her manager. To help her, write some persuasive arguments that she can present to her manager to convince him/her how the brand's reputation might be damaged if staff follow the instructions given during in-house sales training.

Growing as a Professional

Spend a few minutes around successful people in any field, and chances are you'll notice how optimistic they are. They believe in what they're doing, and they believe in themselves and their ability to solve problems and overcome obstacles.

Being positive doesn't mean displaying mindless optimism or ignoring bad news. It means acknowledging that things may be difficult but then buckling down and getting the job done anyway. It means no whining and no slacking off, even when the going gets tough. We live in an imperfect world, no question.

Jobs can be boring or difficult, customers can be unpleasant, and bosses can be unreasonable. But when you're a pro, you find a way to power through.

This quality will serve you well throughout your career, and it will make your career and your life much more enjoyable. If you're not naturally upbeat and positive, use your college experience as an opportunity to practice developing this mindset. You might be surprised at how you can talk yourself into a more positive frame of mind, even when you're in a tough patch. The next time you get frustrated or feel overwhelmed with a class or an assignment, view it as a challenge to power through. And when you do power through, celebrate it as an accomplishment. After you string together a few of these successes, you'll start to develop the attitude that nobody can get you down or stand in your way.

Sharpening Your Communication Skills

Imagine you are working as part of a team in a large sales department. In recent weeks, you have become increasingly concerned with the behavior of one of your senior colleagues. You suspect that he is putting pressure on potential customers to sign up for expensive contracts that they cannot afford. As yours is a high-pressure, target-driven department, jobs are at risk if people do not meet their targets. This might be one of the reasons for your colleague's behavior. You are, however, uncomfortable about talking to your colleague about his unethical behavior and think it best to discuss the matter with your manager instead.

In a brief email to your manager, outline your concerns regarding the behavior of your colleague in an appropriate and professional manner.

Building Your Team Skills

Every organization can benefit from having a code of ethics to guide decision-making. But whom should a code of ethics protect, and what should it cover? In this exercise, you and the rest of your team are going to draft a code of ethics for your college or university.

Start by thinking about who will be protected by this code of ethics. What stakeholders should the school consider when making decisions? What negative effects might decisions have on these stakeholders? Then think about the kinds of situations you want your school's code of ethics to cover. One example might be employment decisions; another might be disclosure of confidential student information.

Next, draft your school's code of ethics. Start by identifying general principles and then provide specific guidelines. Write a general introduction explaining the purpose of the code and who is being protected. Next, write a positive statement to guide ethical decisions in each situation you identified previously in this exercise. Your statement about promotion decisions, for example, might read: "School officials will encourage equal access to job promotions for all qualified candidates, with every applicant receiving fair consideration."

Compare your code of ethics with the codes drafted by your classmates. Did all the codes seek to protect the same stakeholders? What differences and similarities do you see in the statements guiding ethical decisions?

Developing Your Research Skills

Articles on corporate ethics and social responsibility regularly appear in business journals and newspapers. Find one or more articles that discuss one of the following ethics or social responsibility challenges faced by a business:

- Environmental issues, such as pollution, acid rain, or hazardous-waste disposal
- Employee or consumer safety measures
- Consumer information or education
- Employment discrimination or diversity and inclusion initiatives
- Investment ethics
- Industrial spying and theft of trade secrets
- Fraud, bribery, and overcharging
- Company codes of ethics

What is the nature of the ethical challenge or social responsibility issue presented in the article? Does the article report any wrongdoing by a company or agency official? Was the action illegal, unethical, or questionable? What course of action would you recommend the company or agency take to correct or improve matters now?

Which stakeholder groups were affected? What lasting effects will be felt by the company and by these stakeholders?

Writing Assignments

4-24. What steps could a bookstore take to engage in strategic CSR?

4-25. Why would a company want to make it easy for its own employees to engage in whistle-blowing, even if doing so could subject the firm to legal penalties?

ENDNOTES

1. Unilever website, accessed 22 March 2018, www.unilever .com; Julia Kollewe, "Marmite Maker Unilever Threatens to Pull Ads from Facebook and Google," *Guardian*, 12 February 2018, www.guardian.com; Vivienne Walt, "Unilever CEO Paul Polman's Plan to Save the World," *Fortune*, 17 February 2017, www .fortune.com; Thomas Buckley and Matthew Campbell, "If Unilever Can't Make Feel-Good Capitalism Work, Who Can?" *Bloomberg Businessweek*, 30 August 2017, www.bloomberg.com; Thomas Buckley, "Unilever CEO Loses Cool with Goldman Analyst at Investor Day," *Bloomberg*, 1 December 2017, www .bloomberg.com.

2. Rakesh Khurana, "The Future of Business School," *BusinessWeek*, 26 May 2009, www.businessweek.com.

3. Donna Borak and Danielle Bronner-Wiener, "Wells Fargo Will Be Fined $1 Billion," *CNN Money*, 19 April 2018, money.cnn .com; Bethany McLean, "How Wells Fargo's Cutthroat Corporate Culture Allegedly Drove Bankers to Fraud," *Vanity Fair*, Summer 2017, www.vanityfair.com; Lucinda Shen, "Wells Fargo Has Been Fined $185 Million for Opening Unauthorized Accounts,"

Fortune, 8 September 2016, www.fortune.com; "Wells Fargo: What It Will Take to Clean Up the Mess," *Knowledge@Wharton*, 8 August 2017, knowledge.wharton.upenn.edu.

4. Jeff S. Bartlett, Michelle Naranjo, and Jeff Plungis, "Guide to the Volkswagen Emissions Recall," *Consumer Reports*, 23 October 2017, www.consumerreports.com; Roger Parloff, "How VW Paid $25 Billion for 'Dieselgate'—and Got Off Easy," *Fortune*, 6 February 2018, www.fortune.com; "Volkswagen 'Misused' Me, Accused Executive Tells Judge," *Reuters*, 3 December 2017, www.reuters.com.

5. Geoff Colvin, "Inside Wells Fargo's Plan to Fix Its Culture Post-Scandal," *Fortune*, 11 June 2017, www.fortune.com.

6. Lindsey Bever, "A Town of 3,200 Was Flooded with Nearly 21 Million Pain Pills as Addiction Crisis Worsened, Lawmakers Say," *Washington Post*, 31 January 2018, www.washingtonpost .com; Laurel Wamsley, "Drug Distributors Shipped 20.8 Million Painkillers to West Virginia Town of 3,000," *NPR*, 30 January 2018, www.npr.org.

7. Kollewe, "Marmite Maker Unilever Threatens to Pull Ads from Facebook and Google."

8. David Meyer, "Facebook Is 'Ripping Apart' Society, Former Executive Warns," *Fortune*, 12 December 2017, www.fortune.com; Amy B. Wang, "Former Facebook VP Says Social Media Is Destroying Society with 'Dopamine-Driven Feedback Loops,'" *Washington Post*, 12 December 2017, www.washingtonpost.com.

9. Maya Kosoff, "'Just an Ass-Backward Tech Company': How Twitter Lost the Internet War," *Vanity Fair*, 19 February 2018, www.vanityfair.com.

10. Harry McCracken, "A Brief History of Mark Zuckerberg Apologizing (or Not Apologizing) for Stuff," *Fast Company*, 21 March 2018, www.fastcompany.com.

11. Adam Entous, Elizabeth Dwoskin, and Craig Timberg, "Obama Tried to Give Zuckerberg a Wake-Up Call over Fake News on Facebook," *Washington Post*, 24 September 2017, www.washingtonpost.com; Steve Kovach, "Sheryl Sandberg Got Everything Wrong About Facebook's Role as a Media Company," *Business Insider*, 12 October 2017, www.businessinsider.com.

12. Nate Lanxon, "Former Facebook Employee Tells U.K. Lawmakers His Warnings Were Ignored," *Bloomberg*, 21 March 2018, www.bloomberg.com; Sarah Frier and Max Chafkin, "Under Fire and Losing Trust, Facebook Plays the Victim," *Bloomberg Businessweek*, 21 March 2018, www.bloomberg.com.

13. Sarah Vizard, "Unilever Threatens to Pull Ad Spend from Platforms That 'Breed Division,'" *Marketing Week*, 12 February 2018, www.marketingweek.com.

14. Nicole Sinclair, "Facebook and Twitter Must Take 'Full Responsibility' for What They've Created," *Yahoo! Finance*, 6 November 2017, finance.yahoo.com.

15. Quote Investigator, 19 April 2012, quoteinvestigator.com.

16. Maya Kosoff, "Uber's New C.E.O. Says Travis Kalanick Was 'Guilty of Hubris'," *Vanity Fair*, 23 January 2018, www.vanityfair.com.

17. Eric Newcomer, "Uber Pushed the Limits of the Law. Now Comes the Reckoning." *Bloomberg*, 11 October 2017, www.bloomberg.com.

18. Vincent Ryan, "More Whistleblowing, but Also More Retaliation," *CFO*, 19 March 2018, www.cfo.com.

19. James O'Toole and Warren Bennis, "What's Needed Next: A Culture of Candor," *Harvard Business Review*, June 2009, 54–61.

20. "United by Values," United Technologies, accessed 18 March 2018, www.utc.com.

21. Neil Patel, "Why a Transparent Culture Is Good for Business," *Fast Company*, 9 October 2014, www.fastcompany.com; O'Toole and Bennis, "What's Needed Next: A Culture of Candor," 59.

22. Ann Marsh, "Wells Fargo Ends Fight with a Whistleblower in Fake-Accounts Scandal," *Financial Planning*, 20 January 2018, www.financial-planning.com.

23. David Gelles, "The Moral Voice of Corporate America," *New York Times*, 19 August 2017, www.nytimes.com; Alan Murray, "The CEO's Role in Society," *Fortune CEO Daily* (newsletter), 6 June 2017; Alan Fleischmann, "With CEO Statesmanship Ascendant in 2017, What's Ahead in 2018?" *Forbes*, 30 December 2017, www.forbes.com.

24. Kathy Bloomgarden, "Why Companies Can't Just Write Checks to Do Good," *Fortune*, 6 October 2017, www.fortune.com.

25. "Corporate Giving Restored Since Pre-Global Recession; Non-Cash Contributions Dominate," press release, 16 September 2013, The Conference Board, www.conferenceboard.org.

26. "Community Internship Program," UPS, accessed 23 March 2018, www.ups.com; Susan Ladika, "The Responsible Way," *Workforce*, 16 July 2013, www.workforce.com.

27. Milton Friedman, "The Social Responsibility of Business Is to Increase Its Profits," *New York Times Magazine*, 13 September 1970, SM17.

28. Murray, "The CEO's Role in Society."

29. Buckley and Campbell, "If Unilever Can't Make Feel-Good Capitalism Work, Who Can?"

30. Larry Fink, "A Sense of Purpose (Larry Fink's Annual Letter to CEOs)," Blackrock, accessed 23 March 2018, www.blackrock.com.

31. "Social License (SLO)," *Investopedia*, accessed 24 March 2018, www.investopedia.com.

32. "DeepMind AI Reduces Google Data Centre Cooling Bill by 40%," DeepMind blog, 20 July 2016, deepmind.com; "Google Data Centers," Google, accessed 24 March 2018, www.google.com/about/datacenters; "Google Data Center FAQ," *Data Center Knowledge*, 16 March 2017, www.datacenterknowledge.com.

33. "Report of the World Commission on Environment and Development," United Nations General Assembly, 96th Plenary Meeting, 11 December 1987, www.un.org.

34. Dell Cameron, "Report: Equifax Warned of Vulnerability Six Months Before Attack, Took No Action," Gizmodo, 26 October 2017, gizmodo.com; Tom McKay, "Report: Equifax Lost Even More Information on Consumers Than It Told the Public," Gizmodo, 10 February 2018, gizmodo.com; Brian Fung, "Equifax's Massive 2017 Data Breach Keeps Getting Worse," *Washington Post*, 1 March 2018, www.washingtonpost.com.

35. "Identify Theft: The Aftermath 2016," Identity Theft Resource Center, www.idtheftcenter.org.

36. "Data Protection Laws of the World: United States," DLA Piper, accessed 24 March 2018, www.dlapiperdataprotection.com; "Data Protection Law," HG.org, accessed 24 March 2018, www.hg.org.

37. "GDPR Key Changes," EUGDPR.org, accessed 24 March 2018, www.eugdpr.org; Danny Palmer, "What Is GDPR? Everything You Need to Know About the New General Data Protection Regulations," ZDNet, 16 November 2017, www.zdnet.com.

38. "The Civil Rights Act of 1991," U.S. Equal Employment Opportunity Commission, accessed 26 March 2018, www.eeoc.gov.

39. "Affirmative Action: General: When Would My Company Need to Have an Affirmative Action Program?" Society for Human Resource Management, 9 November 2015, www.shrm.org.

40. "Disability Discrimination," U.S. Equal Employment Opportunity Commission, accessed 26 March 2018, www.eeoc.gov.

41. "Injuries, Illnesses, and Fatalities," Bureau of Labor Statistics, accessed 31 May 2009, www.bls.gov/iif.

42. "OSHA Law & Regulations," U.S. Department of Labor, Occupational Safety and Health Administration, accessed 26 March 2018, www.osha.gov.

43. Katherine Long, "New UW Contract with Nike That Allows Inspections of Overseas Factories Is First of Its Kind," *Seattle Times*, 8 November 2017, www.seattletimes.com; "Nike Supply Chain Disclosure: Nike, Inc. Statement on Forced Labor, Human Trafficking and Modern Slavery for Fiscal Year 2017," Nike, www.nike.com; "Slavery & Human Trafficking Statement," Focusrite, 19 October 2016, www.focusrite.com.

44. Fair Labor Association, accessed 24 March 2018, www.fairlabor.org.

45. Steve Lohr, "Facial-Recognition Technology Works Best If You're a White Guy," *New York Times*, 12 February 2018, www.nytimes.com; "About This Project," Algorithmic Justice League, accessed 15 March 2018, www.ajlunited.org.

46. Lohr, "Facial-Recognition Technology Works Best If You're a White Guy."

47. Hannah Devlin, "AI Programs Exhibit Racial and Gender Biases, Research Reveals," *Guardian*, 13 April 2017, www.theguardian.com.

48 Tobias Baer and Vishnu Kamalnath, "Controlling Machine-Learning Algorithms and Their Biases," McKinsey, November 2017, www.mckinsey.com; Finale Doshi-Velez and Mason Kortz, "AI Is More Powerful Than Ever. How Do We Hold It Accountable?" *Washington Post*, 20 March 2018, www.washingtonpost.com.

49 Will Knight, "The Dark Secret at the Heart of AI," *Technology Review*, 11 April 2017, www.technologyreview.com.

50 Doshi-Velez and Kortz, "AI Is More Powerful Than Ever. How Do We Hold It Accountable?"

51 Ryan Kottenstette, "Silicon Valley Companies Are Undermining the Impact of Artificial Intelligence," *TechCrunch*, 15 March 2018, techcrunch.com.

52 "Thematic Pillars," Partnership on AI, accessed 26 March 2018, www.partnershiponai.org.

53 Nat Levy, "Microsoft Doubles Down on Its 'AI for Earth' Initiative, Pledging $50M at Paris Climate Event," *GeekWire*, 11 December 2017, www.geekwire.com.

54 See note 1.

Building the Framework: Business Ownership and Entrepreneurship

This part opens with a look at how businesses are structured and governed, from sole proprietorships to partnerships to public corporations, followed by options for joining forces: mergers, acquisitions, strategic alliances, and joint ventures. Chapter 6 then explores the world of entrepreneurship and small-business ownership, including business plans, financing, and franchising.

iStock/Getty Images

Forms of Ownership

LEARNING OBJECTIVES   After studying this chapter, you will be able to

1   Define *sole proprietorship*, and explain the six advantages and six disadvantages of this ownership model.

2   Define *partnership*, and explain the six advantages and three disadvantages of this ownership model.

3   Define *corporation*, and explain the four advantages and six disadvantages of this ownership model.

4   Explain the concept of *corporate governance*, and identify the three groups responsible for ensuring good governance.

5   Identify the potential advantages of pursuing mergers and acquisitions as a growth strategy, along with the potential difficulties and risks.

6   Define *strategic alliance* and *joint venture*, and explain why a company would choose these options over a merger or an acquisition.

7   Explain how companies can use *big data* and *analytics* to create value and find competitive advantages.

MyLab Intro to Business
Improve Your Grade!
If your instructor is using MyLab Intro to Business, visit **www.pearson.com/mylab/intro-to-business**.

BEHIND THE SCENES   Saba: Exploring the Opportunity to Grow

If Saba Software opted to expand by acquiring another company, it would face a variety of strategic and tactical decisions, including how to integrate personnel from the other company into its current workforce.

Monkey Business Images/Shutterstock

www.saba.com

Companies that want to expand their sales have two basic options: sell more of their existing products or develop more products to sell. This choice is complicated enough on its own, but it's only the start, because this decision triggers a whole new set of decisions. If a firm decides to develop new products, it must figure out how to design, create, and market them and whether to target them toward the firm's existing customer base or go in search of new customers.

From its headquarters near San Francisco, Saba pioneered the concept of a *learning management system* that companies could use to streamline employee training. In the 20 years since its founding, that focus has expanded into the more comprehensive *talent management* arena, which includes *workforce planning* (identifying the talents a company needs in order to meet its business objectives), *recruiting* (finding, hiring, and onboarding new employees), and *succession planning* (identifying and preparing the employees who can fill management slots as executives retire).

As it expanded its offering toward a fully integrated system that could help companies keep employees productive and engaged throughout the entire employee life cycle, Saba recognized the need to provide a key piece of the puzzle: *performance management*, which encompasses establishing performance goals and monitoring progress.

If you were leading Saba, how would you go about adding performance management capabilities to the company's product offerings? Would you develop this new product in-house? Partner with a company that already sells performance management software? Or perhaps take the full leap and buy another company outright?[1]

INTRODUCTION

One of the most fundamental decisions you must make when starting a business is selecting a form of business ownership. This decision can be complex and have far-reaching consequences for owners, employees, and customers. Picking the right ownership structure involves knowing your long-term goals and how you plan to achieve them. The choice also depends on your desire for control and your tolerance for risk. Then as the business evolves over time, you may need to modify the original structure or join forces with other companies (see Saba in the chapter-opening Behind the Scenes). Even if you have no plans to start a business, knowing the legal structure of the companies where you might work is vital information to have.

The three most common forms of business ownership are sole proprietorships, partnerships, and corporations. Each form has its own characteristic internal structure, legal status, size, and fields to which it is best suited. Each also has key advantages and disadvantages for the owners (see Exhibit 5.1 on the next page).

Sole Proprietorships

A **sole proprietorship** is a business owned by one person (although it may have many employees). Many farms, retail establishments, and small service businesses are sole proprietorships, as are many home-based businesses, such as those operated by caterers, consultants, and freelance writers. Many of the local businesses you frequent around your college campus are likely to be sole proprietorships, and you may be a sole proprietor yourself if you work as a freelancer, as an Uber driver, or in any other independent money-making capacity.

1 **LEARNING OBJECTIVE**
Define *sole proprietorship*, and explain the six advantages and six disadvantages of this ownership model.

sole proprietorship
A business owned by a single person.

ADVANTAGES OF SOLE PROPRIETORSHIPS

Operating as a sole proprietorship offers six key advantages:

- **Simplicity.** A sole proprietorship is easy to establish and requires far less paperwork than other structures. About the only legal requirement for establishing a sole proprietorship is obtaining the necessary business licenses and permits required by the city, county, and state. Otherwise, simply by starting business operations without creating a partnership or a corporation, you legally establish yourself as a sole proprietor.[2]
- **Single layer of taxation.** Income tax is a straightforward matter for sole proprietorships. The federal government doesn't recognize the company as a taxable entity; all profit "flows through" to the owner, where it is treated as personal income and is taxed accordingly.
- **Privacy.** Beyond filing tax returns and certain other government reports that may apply to specific businesses, sole proprietors generally aren't required to report anything to anyone. Your business is your business. Of course, if you apply for a loan or solicit investors, you will need to provide detailed financial information to these parties.

Sole proprietorship can entail significant risks and a lot of work, but the potential rewards entice millions of people to consider it every year.

CREATISTA/Shutterstock

EXHIBIT 5.1	Forms of Business Ownership

Each of the major forms of business ownership has distinct advantages and disadvantages.

Structure	Control	Profits and Taxation	Liability Exposure	Ease of Establishment
Sole proprietorship	One owner has complete control	Profits and losses flow directly to the owners and are taxed at individual rates	Owner has unlimited personal liability for the business's financial obligations	Easy to set up; typically requires just a business license and a form to register the company name
General partnership	Two or more owners; each partner is entitled to equal control unless agreement specifies otherwise	Profits and losses flow directly to the partners and are taxed at individual rates; partners share income and losses equally unless the partnership agreement specifies otherwise	All partners have unlimited liability, meaning their personal assets are at risk to mistakes made by other partners	Easy to set up; partnership agreement not required but strongly recommended
Limited partnership	Two or more owners; one or more general partners manage the business; limited partners don't participate in the management	Same as for general partnership	Limited partners have limited liability (making them liable only for the amount of their investment); general partners have unlimited liability	Same as for general partnership
Corporation	Unlimited number of shareholders; no limits on stock classes or voting arrangements; ownership and management of the business are separate (shareholders in public corporations are not involved in management decisions; in private or closely held corporations, owners are more likely to participate in managing the business)	Profits are taxed at corporate rates; profits are taxed again at individual rates when (or if) they are distributed to investors as dividends	Investor's liability is limited to the amount of his or her investment	More complicated and expensive to establish than a sole proprietorship; requirements vary from state to state

- **Flexibility and control.** As a sole proprietor, you aren't required to get approval from a business partner, a boss, or a board of directors to change any aspect of your business strategy or tactics. You can make your own decisions, from setting your own hours to deciding how much of the work you'll do yourself and how much you'll assign to employees. It's all up to you (within the limits of whatever contractual obligations you might have, of course, such as a franchising agreement—see page 207). Also, as the sole owner, whatever financial value exists in the business is yours. You can keep the business, sell it, give it away, or bequeath it to your children.
- **Fewer limitations on personal income.** As a partner in a partnership or an employee in a corporation, your income is established by various agreements and compensation policies. As a sole proprietor, you keep all the after-tax profits the business generates; if the business does extremely well, you do extremely well. Of course, if the business doesn't generate any income, you don't get a paycheck.
- **Personal satisfaction.** For many sole proprietors, the main advantage is the satisfaction of working for themselves—of taking the risks and enjoying the rewards. If you work hard, make smart decisions, and have a little bit of luck, you get to see and enjoy the fruits of your labor.

REAL-TIME UPDATES

Learn More by Visiting This Website

Get help from a Small Business Development Center

Are you thinking of starting a business or already running one? Find out where to get help from a local adviser. Go to **real-timeupdates .com/bia9** and select Learn More in the Students section.

DISADVANTAGES OF SOLE PROPRIETORSHIPS

For all its advantages, sole proprietorship also has six significant disadvantages:

- **Financial liability.** In a sole proprietorship, the owner and the business are legally inseparable, which gives the proprietor **unlimited liability**: Any legal damages or debts incurred by the business are the owner's personal responsibility. If you aren't covered by appropriate insurance and run into serious financial or legal difficulty, such as getting sued for an accident that happened on your premises, you could lose not only the business but all your personal assets as well.

- **Demands on the owner.** There's quite a bit of truth to the old joke that working for yourself means you get to set your own hours—you can work whichever 80 hours a week you want. In addition to the potential for long hours (certainly, not all sole proprietors work long hours), you often have the stress of making all major decisions, solving all major problems, and being tied so closely to the company that taking time off is sometimes impossible. Plus, solo business owners can feel isolated and unable to discuss problems with anyone.[3] Fortunately, social media sites have been a blessing for sole proprietors in this and many other respects. Small-business owners can reach out for advice, fresh ideas, useful contacts, or simply the socializing opportunities that are often missing.

- **Limited managerial perspective.** Running even a simple business can be a complicated effort that requires expertise in accounting, marketing, information technology (IT), business law, and many other fields. Few individual owners possess enough skills and experience to make consistently good decisions. To get broader input for important decisions, small-business owners can turn to a variety of sources, including networks and support groups designed specifically for sole proprietors to counsel each other on key decisions.[4]

- **Resource limitations.** Because they depend on a single owner, sole proprietorships usually have fewer financial resources and fewer ways to get additional funds from lenders or investors. This lack of capital can hamper a small business in many ways, limiting its ability to expand, to hire the best employees, and to survive rough economic periods.

- **No employee benefits for the owner.** Moving from a corporate job to sole proprietorship can be a shock for employees accustomed to paid vacation time, sick leave, health insurance, and other benefits that many employers offer. Sole proprietors get none of these perks without paying for them out of their own pockets.

- **Finite life span.** Although some sole proprietors pass their businesses on to their heirs, the owner's death may mean the demise of the business. And even if the business does transfer to an heir, the founder's unique skills may have been crucial to its successful operation.

unlimited liability
A legal condition under which any damages or debts incurred by a business are the owner's personal responsibility.

✓ CHECKPOINT

LEARNING OBJECTIVE 1: Define *sole proprietorship*, and explain the six advantages and six disadvantages of this ownership model.

SUMMARY: A sole proprietorship is a business owned by a single individual and legally inseparable from that person. The six advantages of this structure are simplicity, a single layer of taxation, privacy, flexibility and control, fewer limitations on personal income, and personal satisfaction. The six disadvantages are unlimited financial liability, demands on the owner, limited managerial perspective, resource limitations, no employee benefits for the owner, and a finite life span.

CRITICAL THINKING: (1) How many sole proprietors do you know? Do they seem satisfied with the choice of working for themselves? Why or why not? (2) Would you ever consider going into business as a sole proprietor? Why or why not?

[2] **LEARNING OBJECTIVE**

Define *partnership*, and explain the six advantages and three disadvantages of this ownership model.

partnership
An unincorporated company owned by two or more people.

general partnership
A partnership in which all partners have joint authority to make decisions for the firm and joint liability for the firm's financial obligations.

limited partnership
A partnership in which one or more persons act as *general partners* who run the business and have the same unlimited liability as sole proprietors.

limited liability
A legal condition in which the maximum amount each owner is liable for is equal to whatever amount each invested in the business.

Partnerships

A **partnership** is a company that is owned by two or more people but is not a corporation. The partnership structure is appropriate for firms that need more resources and leadership talent than a sole proprietorship but don't need the fundraising capabilities or other advantages of a corporation. Many partnerships are small, with just a handful of owners, although a few are immense; the accounting and consulting firm PwC (**www.pwc.com**), for example, has more than 10,000 partners.[5] (Note that some companies refer to their employees as "partners," but that isn't the same thing as legal business partners.)

Partnerships come in two basic forms. In a **general partnership**, all partners have the authority to make decisions for the firm and *joint liability* for the firm's financial obligations.[6] If the partnership gets into financial trouble, all the partners must dig into their own pockets to pay the bills, just as sole proprietors must.

To minimize personal liability exposure, some organizations opt instead for a **limited partnership**. Under this type of partnership, one or more persons act as *general partners* who run the business and have the same unlimited liability as sole proprietors. The remaining owners are *limited partners*, investors who do not participate in running the business and who have **limited liability**—the maximum amount they are liable for is whatever amount each invested in the business.[7]

Two additional types of partnerships have been created in recent years to accommodate the needs of particular industries or professions. A *master limited partnership (MLP)* is allowed to raise money by selling *units* of ownership to the general public, in the same way corporations sell shares of stock to the public. This gives MLPs the fundraising capabilities of corporations without the double-taxation disadvantage (see "Disadvantages of Corporations" on page 173). Strict rules limit the types of companies that qualify for MLP status; most are in the energy industry.[8]

The *limited liability partnership (LLP)* form of business was created to help protect individual partners in certain professions from major mistakes (such as errors that trigger malpractice lawsuits) made by other partners in the firm. In an LLP, each partner has unlimited liability only for his or her own actions and at least some degree of limited liability for the partnership as a whole. Restrictions on who can form an LLP—and how much liability protection is offered under this structure—vary by jurisdiction.[9]

ADVANTAGES OF PARTNERSHIPS

Partnerships offer two of the same advantages as sole proprietorships plus four more that overcome some important disadvantages of being a sole owner:

- **Simplicity.** Strictly speaking, establishing a partnership is almost as simple as establishing a sole proprietorship: You and your partners simply say you're in business together, apply for the necessary business licenses, and get to work. Although this approach is legal, it is neither safe nor sensible. Partners need to protect themselves and the company with a partnership agreement (see "Keeping It Together: The Partnership Agreement" on the next page).
- **Single layer of taxation.** Income tax is straightforward for partnerships. Profit is split between or among the owners based on whatever percentages they have agreed to. Each owner then treats his or her share as personal income.
- **More resources.** One of the key reasons to partner with one or more co-owners is to increase the amount of money you have to launch, operate, and grow the business.

In addition to the money that owners invest themselves, a partnership can potentially raise more money because partners' personal assets support a larger borrowing capacity.

- **Cost sharing.** An important financial advantage in many partnerships is the opportunity to share costs. For example, a group of lawyers or doctors can share the cost of facilities and support staff while continuing to work more or less independently.
- **Broader skill and experience base.** Pooling the skills and experience of two or more professionals can overcome one of the major shortcomings of the sole proprietorship. If your goal is to build a business that can grow significantly over time, a partnership can be much more effective than trying to build a business as a sole owner.[10]
- **Longevity.** By forming a partnership, you increase the chances that the organization will endure, because new partners can be drawn into the business to replace those who die or retire.

One of the key advantages of forming a partnership is combining the talents and experience of two or more people.

DISADVANTAGES OF PARTNERSHIPS

Anyone considering the partnership structure needs to be aware of three potentially significant disadvantages:

- **Unlimited liability.** All owners in a general partnership and the general partners in a limited partnership face the same unlimited liability as sole proprietors. However, the risk of financial wipeout can be even greater because a partnership has more people making decisions that could end in catastrophe (unless the company is formed as an LLP).
- **Potential for conflict.** More bosses equal more chances for disagreement and conflict. Partners can disagree over business strategy, the division of profits (or the liability for losses), ethical principles, hiring and firing of employees, and other significant matters. Even simple interpersonal conflict between partners can hinder a company's ability to succeed. To minimize conflict and manage it when it does arise, partners should spell out decision-making authority in the partnership agreement and maintain an atmosphere of open, honest communication.[11]
- **Expansion, succession, and termination issues.** Partnerships need to consider how they will handle such issues as expanding by bringing in an additional partner, replacing a partner who wants to sell out or retire, and terminating a partner who is unable or unwilling to meet the expectations of his or her role in the organization. Such issues can destroy partnerships if the owners don't have clear plans and expectations for addressing them.

KEEPING IT TOGETHER: THE PARTNERSHIP AGREEMENT

A carefully written *partnership agreement* can maximize the advantages of the partnership structure and minimize the potential disadvantages. Although state laws (everywhere except Louisiana) specify some basic agreements about business partnerships, these laws are generic and therefore not ideal for many partnerships.[12] At a minimum, a partnership agreement should address investment percentages, profit-sharing percentages, management responsibilities and other expectations of each owner, decision-making strategies, succession and exit strategies (if an owner wants to leave the partnership), criteria for admitting new partners, and dispute-resolution procedures (including dealing with owners who aren't meeting their responsibilities).[13]

A clear and complete agreement is important for every partnership, but it can be particularly important when you are going into business with a friend, a spouse, or anyone else with whom you have a personal relationship. Although you might have a great personal partnership, the dynamics of that relationship could get in the way of a successful business partnership. For instance, a couple who are accustomed to sharing decisions and responsibilities equally in their personal relationship could struggle in a business relationship in which one of them is the clear leader of the company. In addition, stresses and strains in the business relationship can filter into the personal relationship. To protect both the personal and the professional partnerships, make sure you start with a clear understanding of what the business relationship will be.

 CHECKPOINT

LEARNING OBJECTIVE 2: Define *partnership,* **and explain the six advantages and three disadvantages of this ownership model.**

SUMMARY: Partnership is a business structure in which two or more individuals share ownership of the firm. The two basic forms of partnership are *general partnership*, in which all owners play an active role and have unlimited liability, and *limited partnership*, in which only the general partner or partners have active management roles and unlimited liability. Six key advantages of partnership are simplicity, a single layer of taxation, more resources, cost sharing, broader skill and experience base, and longevity. Three potential disadvantages are unlimited liability for general partners; potential for conflict; and expansion, succession, and termination issues.

CRITICAL THINKING: (1) Would you prefer going into a business with a seasoned professional you don't know well or with someone you know, like, and trust but who doesn't have a lot of business experience? Why? (2) What are the three most important qualifications you would look for in a potential business partner?

IT'S YOUR BUSINESS: (1) Would you consider entering into a business partnership with your best friend? Why or why not? (2) Now turn the question around: Would your best friend consider having *you* as a business partner?

KEY TERMS TO KNOW: partnership, general partnership, limited partnership, limited liability

3 **LEARNING OBJECTIVE**

Define *corporation*, and explain the four advantages and six disadvantages of this ownership model.

corporation
A legal entity, distinct from any individual persons, that has the power to own property and conduct business.

shareholders
Investors who purchase shares of stock in a corporation.

public corporation
A corporation in which stock is sold to anyone who has the means to buy it.

private corporation
A corporation in which all the stock is owned by only a few individuals or companies and is not made available for purchase by the public.

Corporations

A **corporation** is a legal entity, distinct from any individual persons, that has the power to own property and conduct business. It is owned by **shareholders**, investors who purchase shares of stock. The stock of a **public corporation** is sold to anyone who has the means to buy it—individuals, investment companies such as mutual funds, not-for-profit organizations, and other companies. Such corporations are said to be *publicly held* or *publicly traded*. In contrast, the stock of a **private corporation**, also known as a *closely held corporation*, is owned by only a few individuals or companies and is not made available for purchase by the public. Corporations can change from private to public ownership or from public to private ownership as their financial needs and strategic interests change.

With their unique ability to pool money from outside investors, corporations can grow to an enormous size. The annual revenues of the world's largest corporations, such as Walmart, Toyota, Royal Dutch Shell, Apple, and Sinopec Group, are larger than the entire economies of many countries.[14] However, many small firms and even individuals also take advantage of the unique benefits of corporate organization.

ADVANTAGES OF CORPORATIONS

Corporations have become a major economic force because this structure offers four major advantages over sole proprietorships and partnerships:

- **Ability to raise capital.** The ability to pool money by selling shares of stock to outside investors is the reason corporations first came into existence and remains one of the key advantages of this structure. (As Chapter 16 explains, corporations can also raise money by selling *bonds*.) Some firms have raised a billion dollars or more by selling stock to the public for the first time.[15] The potential for raising vast amounts gives corporations an unmatched ability to invest in research, marketing, facilities, acquisitions, and other growth strategies.

- **Liquidity.** The stock of publicly traded companies has a high degree of **liquidity**, which means that investors can easily and quickly convert their stock into cash by selling it on the open market. In contrast, *liquidating* (selling) the assets of a sole proprietorship or a partnership can be slow and difficult. Liquidity helps make corporate stocks an attractive investment, which increases the number of people and institutions willing to invest in such companies. In addition, because shares have value established in the open market, a corporation can use shares of its own stock to acquire other companies.

- **Longevity.** Liquidity also helps give corporations a long life span; when shareholders sell or bequeath their shares, ownership simply passes to a new generation, so to speak. Finding willing buyers for a corporation's stock is generally much easier than finding willing buyers for a sole proprietorship or stakes in a partnership.

- **Limited liability.** A corporation itself has unlimited liability, but the various shareholders who own the corporation face only limited liability—their maximum potential loss is only as great as the amount they've invested in the company. As with liquidity, limited liability offers protection that helps make corporate stocks an attractive investment.

> **liquidity**
> A measure of how easily and quickly an asset such as corporate stock can be converted into cash by selling it.

DISADVANTAGES OF CORPORATIONS

The advantages of the corporate structure are compelling, but six significant disadvantages must be considered carefully:

- **Cost and complexity.** Starting a corporation is more expensive and more complicated than starting a sole proprietorship or a partnership, and "taking a company public" (selling shares to the public) can be expensive and time-consuming for upper managers. For a large firm, the process can cost several million dollars and consume months of executive time.[16]

- **Reporting requirements.** To help investors make informed decisions about stocks, government agencies require publicly traded companies to publish extensive and detailed financial reports. These reports can eat up a lot of staff and management time, and they can expose strategic information that might benefit competitors or discourage investors who are unwilling to wait for long-term results.

- **Managerial demands.** In addition to reporting requirements, top executives must devote time and energy to meeting with shareholders, financial analysts, and the news media.

- **Possible loss of control.** Outside investors who acquire enough of a company's stock can gain seats on the board of directors and therefore begin exerting their influence on company management. In a *hostile takeover* (see page 179), outsiders can take complete control and even replace the company founders if they believe a change in leadership would benefit shareholders.

- **Double taxation.** A corporation must pay federal and state corporate income tax on its profits, and individual shareholders must pay income taxes on their share of the company's profits received as *dividends* (periodic payments that some corporations opt to make to shareholders).

- **Short-term orientation of the stock market.** Publicly held corporations release their financial results once

The board members and officers of a public corporation meet once a year with shareholders.

FABRICE COFFRINI/Getty Images

every quarter, and this seemingly simple requirement can have a damaging effect on the way companies are managed. The problem is that executives often feel the pressure to show earnings growth from quarter to quarter so that the stock price keeps increasing—even if smart, strategic reasons exist for sacrificing earnings in the short term, such as investing in new product development or retaining talented employees instead of laying them off during slow periods. Managers sometimes wind up zigzagging from one short-term fix to the next, trying to prop up the stock price for investors who don't have the patience to wait for strategic, long-term plans to bear fruit. When executive compensation is closely tied to stock prices, managers may have even more incentive to compromise the long-term health of the company in order to meet quarterly expectations.[17] To escape this pressure, corporate leaders sometimes choose to take their companies private, meaning they buy all the shares held by the public and convert the company to privately held status.

SPECIAL TYPES OF CORPORATIONS

S corporation
A type of corporation that combines the capital-raising options and limited liability of a corporation with the federal taxation advantages of a partnership.

limited liability company (LLC)
A structure that combines limited liability with the pass-through taxation benefits of a partnership; the number of shareholders is not restricted, nor is members' participation in management.

benefit corporation
A profit-seeking corporation whose charter specifies a social or environmental goal that the company must pursue in addition to profit.

As with the partnership structure, special types of corporations have been created to help the owners of small private corporations. An **S corporation**, or *subchapter S corporation*, combines the capital-raising options and limited liability of a corporation with the federal taxation advantages of a partnership (although a few states tax S corporations like regular corporations).[18] Corporations seeking "S" status must meet certain criteria, including a maximum of 100 investors.[19]

The **limited liability company (LLC)** structure offers the advantages of limited liability, along with the pass-through taxation benefits of a partnership. Furthermore, LLCs are not restricted in the number of shareholders they can have, and members' participation in management is not restricted as it is in limited partnerships. Given these advantages, the LLC structure is recommended for most small companies that aren't sole proprietorships.[20] However, LLCs do have some potential disadvantages. Employee benefits are not tax deductible as they are for other types of companies. And because an LLC has no stock to sell, it can't use stock options as an employee benefit, nor can it raise money via the stock market.[21]

Finally, an intriguing new type of corporate structure supports the goals of businesspeople who want their companies to pursue social and environmental goals while still pursuing profits as any other corporation does. A **benefit corporation** has most of the attributes of a regular corporation but adds the legal requirement that the company must also pursue a stated nonfinancial goal, such as hiring workers whose life histories make employment difficult to attain or reducing the environmental impact of particular products. The corporation's performance toward meeting that nonfinancial goal must be independently verified as well. Entrepreneurs who launch a corporation with social or environmental objectives in mind are assured that even if they give up or lose voting control of the corporation, the company is still legally required to pursue its social or environmental goal. In addition, the transparency offered by third-party verification provides assurance for customers who want to buy from companies that support causes they value. Roughly two-thirds of U.S. states now recognize benefit corporations.[22]

The labels applied to various types of corporations can be a bit confusing. The most important points to remember are the difference between privately and publicly held corporations and the basic features of S corporations and LLCs. Exhibit 5.2 summarizes these features, along with some other terms you may run across in the business media.

EXHIBIT 5.2	Corporate Structures

Different types of corporate structures serve different purposes for their owners. The first four terms are the most important to remember.

Structure	Characteristics
Public corporation (also known as *publicly held* or *publicly traded*)	Corporation whose stock is sold to the general public
Private corporation (also known as *closely held*)	Corporation whose stock is held by a small number of owners and is not available for sale to the public
S corporation (also known as *subchapter S corporation*)	Corporation allowed to sell stock to a limited number of investors while enjoying the pass-through taxation of a partnership
Limited liability company (LLC)	Corporate structure with benefits similar to those of an S corporation, without the limitation on the number of investors
Benefit corporation	Profit-seeking corporation whose charter also requires it to pursue a stated social or environmental goal
Subsidiary	Corporation primarily or wholly owned by another company
Parent company	Corporation that owns one or more subsidiaries
Holding company	Special type of parent company that owns other companies for investment reasons and usually exercises little operating control over those subsidiaries
Alien corporation	Corporation that operates in the United States but is incorporated in another country
Foreign corporation (sometimes called an *out-of-state corporation*)	Company that is incorporated in one state (frequently the state of Delaware, where incorporation laws are more lenient) but that does business in several other states where it is registered
Domestic corporation	Corporation that does business only in the state where it is chartered (incorporated)

 CHECKPOINT

LEARNING OBJECTIVE 3: Define *corporation*, and explain the four advantages and six disadvantages of this ownership model.

SUMMARY: A corporation is a legal entity with the power to own property and conduct business. The four primary advantages of this structure are the ability to raise capital by selling shares of ownership, liquidity (meaning it is easy to convert shares of ownership to cash), longevity, and limited liability for owners. Six disadvantages are start-up costs and complexity, ongoing reporting requirements, extra demands on top managers, potential loss of control, double taxation, and the short-term orientation of the stock market.

CRITICAL THINKING: (1) Why is the LLC structure recommended for most small companies that aren't sole proprietorships? (2) How can the demands of the stock market affect managerial decision-making?

IT'S YOUR BUSINESS: Assume you own stock in a large, publicly traded corporation that is hiring a new chief executive officer (CEO). All other things being equal, who would be a better choice: a brilliant strategic thinker who is a weak communicator with poor "people skills" or a gifted public speaker and motivator who is competent but perhaps not brilliant when it comes to strategy? Explain your answer.

KEY TERMS TO KNOW: corporation, shareholders, public corporation, private corporation, liquidity, S corporation, limited liability company (LLC), benefit corporation

Explain the concept of *corporate governance*, and identify the three groups responsible for ensuring good governance.

board of directors
A group of professionals elected by shareholders as their representatives, with responsibility for the overall direction of the company and the selection of top executives.

corporate governance
In a broad sense, all the policies, procedures, relationships, and systems in place to oversee the successful and legal operation of the enterprise; in a narrow sense, the responsibilities and performance of the board of directors specifically.

proxy
A document that authorizes another person to vote on behalf of a shareholder in a corporation.

shareholder activism
Activities undertaken by shareholders (individually or in groups) to influence executive decision-making in areas ranging from strategic planning to social responsibility.

Corporate Governance

Although a corporation's shareholders in theory own the business, few of them are typically involved in managing it, particularly if the corporation is publicly traded. Instead, shareholders who own *common stock* elect a **board of directors** to represent them, and the directors in turn select the corporation's top officers, who actually run the company (see Exhibit 5.3). The term **corporate governance** can be used in a broad sense to describe all the policies, procedures, relationships, and systems in place to oversee the successful and legal operation of the enterprise. However, media coverage and public discussion tend to define governance in a narrower sense, as the responsibilities and performance of the board of directors specifically. Because serious corporate blunders can wreak havoc on employees, investors, and the entire economy, effective corporate governance has become a vital concern for society as a whole, not just for individual companies themselves.

SHAREHOLDERS

Even though most don't have any direct involvement in company management, shareholders play a key role in corporate governance. All shareholders who own common stock are invited to an annual meeting at which top executives present the previous year's results and plans for the coming year and shareholders vote on various resolutions that may be before the board. Those who cannot attend the annual meeting in person can vote by **proxy**, authorizing management to vote on their behalf.

Because shareholders elect the directors, in theory they are the ultimate governing body of the corporation. However, a major corporation may have thousands or even millions of shareholders, so unless they own a large number of shares, individual shareholders usually have little influence. Notable exceptions are *institutional investors,* such as pension funds, insurance companies, mutual funds, religious organizations, and college endowment funds. Those with large holdings of stock can have considerable influence over management. For example, the 300-plus institutions that make up the Interfaith Center on Corporate Responsibility (ICCR) collectively control hundreds of billions of dollars in corporate stock, giving them a powerful voice.[23]

Shareholder activism, in which shareholders pressure management on matters ranging from executive pay to corporate social responsibility to overall company performance, has become an increasingly visible factor in corporate governance. BlackRock (see page 177) is one of several large investment firms that are active in what is commonly known as *ESG*—environmental, social, and governance issues.[24]

EXHIBIT 5.3	**Corporate Governance**

Shareholders of a corporation elect representatives to the board of directors, who hire the corporate officers who run the company and hire other employees to perform the day-to-day work. (Note that corporate officers are also employees.)

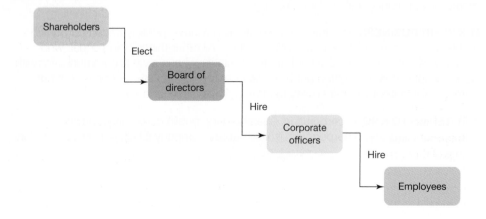

The governance role of shareholders, particularly influential activist shareholders, is complex and sometimes controversial. Two key issues are an emphasis on stock price over every other aspect of corporate performance—and the interests of other stakeholders—and a lack of accountability for the influence that shareholders can exert. Voting power, or at least the threat to use it, can pressure boards and executives into decisions that may be good for the short-term price of the stock but bad for employees, communities, the environment, or the long-term health of the company. This view of governance stems from the minimalist perspective on CSR (see page 145), which most executives and much of society as a whole now reject. Moreover, the pressure that shareholders can exert typically doesn't come with any legal accountability (because of their limited liability) for negative outcomes, so it is a classic example of moral hazard. Some scholars, executives, and influential investors such as BlackRock say it is time to replace the shareholder-centric model with a more comprehensive and sustainable view of corporate governance.[25]

Shareholder activism is one of the options available to people who want to influence the decisions and actions of public corporations.

Stephen Brashear/Getty Images

BOARD OF DIRECTORS

As the representatives of the shareholders, the members of the board of directors are responsible for selecting corporate officers, guiding corporate affairs, reviewing long-term plans, making major strategic decisions, and overseeing financial performance. Boards are typically composed of major shareholders (both individuals and representatives of institutional investors), philanthropists, and executives from other corporations. Directors are often paid a combination of an annual fee and *stock options*, the right to buy company shares at an advantageous price.

Much of the attention focused on corporate reform in recent years has zeroed in on boards, with various boards being accused of not paying close enough attention to what their companies were doing, approving management proposals without analyzing them carefully, being allied too closely with management to serve as the independent representatives of shareholders, or simply failing to add enough value to strategy planning. In response to both outside pressure and management's recognition of how important an effective board is, corporations are wrestling with a variety of board-related issues:

- **Composition.** Identifying the type of people who should be on the board can be a major challenge. The ideal board is a balanced group of seasoned executives, each of whom can "bring something to the table" that helps the corporation, such as extensive contacts in the industry, manufacturing experience, insight into global issues, and so on. The ratio of insiders (company executives) to outsiders (independent directors) is another hot topic. Federal law now requires that the majority of directors be independent, but to be effective these outsiders must have enough knowledge about the inner workings of the organization to make informed decisions. Diversity is also important, to ensure that boards address issues that apply to all their stakeholders, including diverse customer segments. Board diversity has been improving slowly, but as one indicator, men still hold about 80 percent of the seats on the boards of the 500 largest U.S. public corporations, and at the current rate of change it may take until 2025 or 2030 for boards to achieve gender parity.[26]
- **Education.** Overseeing a modern corporation is an almost unimaginably complex task. Board members are expected to understand everything from government regulations to financial management to executive compensation strategies—in addition to the inner workings of the corporation itself. Various companies offer special training programs or orientation sessions for directors in such areas as financial reporting (to make sure directors who aren't well versed in finance can understand their company's own financial statements), compliance challenges, product research, manufacturing, and human resources issues.[27]

- **Liability.** One of the more controversial reform issues has been the potential for directors to be held legally and financially liable for misdeeds of the companies they oversee and even for simply failing to investigate "red flags" in company financial reports.[28]
- **Independent board chairs.** The *board chair* (or *chairman*, as many companies refer to the position) oversees the other members of the board of directors—who are supposed to oversee the corporate officers who make up the top management team, while the CEO oversees the top management team. Historically, the CEO was also the board chair in many U.S. corporations, meaning that in a sense, the CEO was his or her own boss. The current trend is toward dividing these responsibilities with either an independent board chair or a *lead director*, an independent board member who guides the operation of the board and helps maintain its role as an independent voice in governance.[29]
- **Recruiting challenges.** Being an effective director in today's business environment is a tough job—so tough that good candidates may start to think twice about accepting directorships. Well-chosen board members are more vital than ever, though, so corporate and government leaders have no choice but to solve these challenges.

CORPORATE OFFICERS

corporate officers
The top executives who run a corporation.

The third and final group that plays a key role in governance is composed of **corporate officers**, the top executives who run the company. Because they implement major board decisions, make numerous other business decisions, ensure compliance with a dizzying range of government regulations, and perform other essential tasks, the executive team has the major influence on a company's performance and financial health. The highest-ranking officer is the **chief executive officer (CEO)**, and that person is aided by a team of other "C-level" or "C-suite" executives, such as the chief financial officer (CFO), chief information officer (CIO), chief technology officer (CTO), and chief operating officer (COO)—titles vary from one corporation to the next.

chief executive officer (CEO)
The highest-ranking officer of a corporation.

Corporate officers are hired by the board and generally have legal authority to conduct the company's business, in everything from hiring the rest of the employees to launching new products. The actions of these executives can make or break the company, so it is obviously in the board's interest to hire the best talent available, help them succeed in every way possible, and pay attention to what these managers are doing.

✔ CHECKPOINT

LEARNING OBJECTIVE 4: Explain the concept of *corporate governance*, and identify the three groups responsible for ensuring good governance.

SUMMARY: Corporate governance involves all the policies, procedures, relationships, and systems in place to oversee the successful and legal operation of the enterprise. More narrowly, it refers specifically to the responsibilities and performance of the board of directors. The three groups responsible for good governance are (1) the shareholders, who elect (2) the board of directors, who approve overall strategy and hire (3) the corporate officers, who run the company.

CRITICAL THINKING: (1) Why are some shareholder activists pressuring corporations to increase the number of board seats held by women and minorities? (2) Why do many corporations now divide board chair and CEO responsibilities between two people?

IT'S YOUR BUSINESS: Should the qualifications of the board of directors play a role in your decision of whether to buy the stock of a particular corporation? Why or why not?

KEY TERMS TO KNOW: board of directors, corporate governance, proxy, shareholder activism, corporate officers, chief executive officer (CEO)

Mergers and Acquisitions

If a company determines that it doesn't have the right mix of resources and capabilities to achieve its goals and doesn't have the time or inclination to develop them internally, it can purchase or partner with a firm that has what it needs. Businesses can combine permanently through either *mergers* or *acquisitions*. The two terms are often discussed together, usually with the shorthand phrase "M&A," or are used interchangeably (although they are technically different, and the legal and tax ramifications can be quite different, depending on the details of the transaction). As you'll read in the Behind the Scenes case wrap-up at the end of the chapter, Saba uses a combination of acquisitions and strategic alliances to expand the production solutions it can offer to customers.

In a **merger**, two companies join to form a single entity. Companies can merge either by pooling their resources or by one company purchasing the assets of the other.[30] Although not strictly a merger, a *statutory consolidation*, in which two companies create a new, third entity that then purchases the two original companies, is often lumped together with mergers and acquisitions.[31] (Adding to the confusion, businesspeople and the media often use the term *consolidation* in two general senses: to describe any combination of two companies, merger or acquisition, and to describe situations in which a wave of mergers and acquisitions sweeps across an entire industry, reducing the number of competitors.)

In an **acquisition**, one company buys a controlling interest in the voting stock of another company. In most acquisitions, the selling parties agree to be purchased; management is in favor of the deal and encourages shareholders to vote in favor of it as well. Because buyers frequently offer shareholders more than their shares are currently worth, sellers are often motivated to sell. However, in some situations, a buyer attempts to acquire a company against the wishes of management. In such a **hostile takeover**, the buyer tries to convince enough shareholders to go against management and vote to sell.

To finance an acquisition, buyers can offer sellers cash, stock in the acquiring company, or a combination of the two. Another option involves debt. A **leveraged buyout (LBO)** occurs when someone purchases a company's publicly traded stock primarily by using borrowed funds, sometimes using the target company's assets as collateral for these loans. The debt is expected to be repaid with funds generated by the company's operations and, often, by the sale of some of its assets.

An LBO is an aggressive move and can be quite risky if the buyer takes on so much debt that repayment demands deplete the cash the company has for operations and growth. In 2018, retailing icon Toys R Us was forced to close down after filing for bankruptcy the year before, in large part because it could no longer make the payments on the billions of dollars of debt it was saddled with from a 2005 LBO.[32]

ADVANTAGES OF MERGERS AND ACQUISITIONS

A merger or an acquisition is a rare event for many firms, but some other companies use acquisitions as a strategic tool to expand year after year. Companies pursue mergers and acquisitions for a variety of reasons: They might hope to increase their buying power because of their larger size, increase revenue by cross-selling products to each other's customers, increase market share by combining product lines to provide more comprehensive offerings, or gain access to new expertise, systems, and teams of employees who already know how to work together. In many cases, the primary goal is to reduce overlapping investments and capacities in order to lower ongoing costs. Exhibit 5.4 on the next page identifies the most common types of mergers.

DISADVANTAGES OF MERGERS AND ACQUISITIONS

Although the advantages can be compelling, joining two companies is a complex process because it involves virtually every aspect of both organizations. Here are just some of the daunting challenges that must be overcome:

- Executives must agree on how the merger will be financed—and then come up with the money to make it happen.

---

5 **LEARNING OBJECTIVE**

Identify the potential advantages of pursuing mergers and acquisitions as a growth strategy, along with the potential difficulties and risks.

merger
An action taken by two companies to combine as a single entity.

acquisition
An action taken by one company to buy a controlling interest in the voting stock of another company.

hostile takeover
Acquisition of another company against the wishes of management.

leveraged buyout (LBO)
Acquisition of a company's publicly traded stock, using funds that are primarily borrowed, usually with the intent of using some of the acquired assets to pay back the loans used to acquire the company.

EXHIBIT 5.4	**Types of Mergers**

A *vertical merger* occurs when a company purchases a complementary company at a different stage or level in an industry, such as a furniture maker buying a lumber supplier. A *horizontal merger* involves two similar companies at the same level; companies can merge to expand their product offerings or their geographic market coverage. In a *conglomerate merger*, a parent company buys one or more companies in unrelated industries, often to diversify its business to protect against downturns in specific industries.

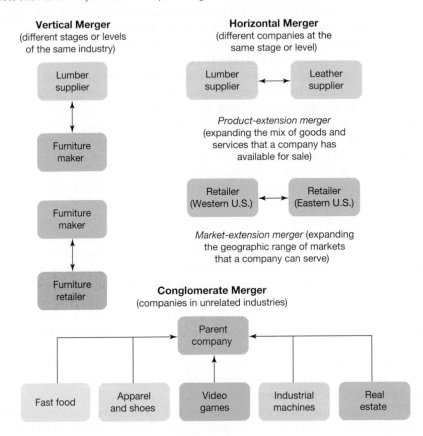

- Managers need to decide who will be in charge after the companies join forces.
- Marketing departments need to figure out how to blend product lines, branding strategies, and advertising and sales efforts.
- Incompatible information systems (including everything from email to websites to accounting software) may need to be rebuilt or replaced in order to operate together seamlessly.
- Companies must often deal with layoffs, transfers, and changes in job titles and work assignments.
- The *organizational cultures* (see page 228) of the two firms must be harmonized somehow; mergers can result in *culture clash* between different values, management styles, communication practices, workplace atmospheres, and approaches to managing the changes required to implement the merger.[33]

Moreover, while managers and employees are wrestling with all these challenges, they need to continue manufacturing products, satisfying customers, and tending to all the other daily details of business. Mergers can drive customers away if they feel neglected while the two companies are busy with all the internal chores of stitching themselves together.

Because of these risks and difficulties, most mergers fail to meet their stated business goals.[34] The worst deals can waste millions or billions of dollars and destroy massive amounts of *market valuation* (the total value of a company's stock). Even with the risks and long odds, though, managers continue to pursue mergers and acquisitions, and some companies have become quite proficient at the process. Companies that use acquisitions as a central element of their growth strategies usually develop comprehensive processes for evaluating and implementing acquisitions. In fact, "acquisition skill" can be considered a competitive advantage for the companies that do it frequently and do it well.[35]

MERGER AND ACQUISITION DEFENSES

Every corporation that sells stock to the general public is potentially vulnerable to takeover by any individual or company that buys enough shares to gain a controlling interest. However, as mentioned previously, most takeovers are friendly acquisitions welcomed by the acquired company. A hostile takeover can be launched in one of two ways: by tender offer or by proxy fight. In a *tender offer*, the buyer, or *raider*, as this party is sometimes called, offers to buy a certain number of shares of stock in the corporation at a specific price. The price offered is generally more, sometimes considerably more, than the current stock price, so that shareholders are motivated to sell. The raider hopes to get enough shares to take control of the corporation and to replace the existing board of directors and management. In a *proxy fight*, the raider tries to persuade other shareholders to vote the way it wants in the hope of compiling enough votes to oust the board and management.

Corporate boards and executives have devised a number of schemes to defend themselves against unwanted takeovers. With a *poison pill* defense (often labeled a *shareholder rights plan* by a company that uses it), a targeted company invokes some move that makes it less valuable to the potential raider, with the hope of discouraging the takeover. A common technique is to sell newly issued stock to current stockholders at prices below the market value of the company's existing stock, thereby increasing the number of shares the raider has to buy.[36] With the *white knight* tactic, a third company is invited to acquire a company that is in danger of being swallowed up in a hostile takeover.

 CHECKPOINT

LEARNING OBJECTIVE 5: Identify the potential advantages of pursuing mergers and acquisitions as a growth strategy, along with the potential difficulties and risks.

SUMMARY: Mergers and acquisitions can help companies reduce costs by eliminating redundancies and increasing buying power, increase revenue by cross-selling goods and services to each other's customers or expanding into new markets, and compete more effectively by adding new technologies or talented employees. However, the difficulties and risks are considerable: coming up with the money, deciding which managers will be in charge, merging marketing and sales efforts, reconciling information systems, dealing with redundant employees, and meshing different corporate cultures.

CRITICAL THINKING: (1) If you were on the board of directors at a company and the CEO proposed a merger with a top competitor, what types of questions would you want answered before you gave your approval? (2) If a CEO has an opportunity to merge with or acquire another company and is reasonably certain that the transaction will benefit shareholders, is the CEO obligated to pursue the deal? Why or why not?

IT'S YOUR BUSINESS: (1) Have you (or someone you know) ever experienced a merger or an acquisition as an employee? Was your job (or the job of the person you know) affected? (2) Have you ever experienced a merger or an acquisition as a customer? Did customer service suffer during the transition of ownership?

KEY TERMS TO KNOW: merger, acquisition, hostile takeover, leveraged buyout (LBO)

6 | **LEARNING OBJECTIVE**

Define *strategic alliance* and *joint venture*, and explain why a company would choose these options over a merger or an acquisition.

strategic alliance
A long-term partnership between companies to jointly develop, produce, or sell products.

joint venture
A separate legal entity established by two or more companies to pursue shared business objectives.

Strategic Alliances and Joint Ventures

Chapter 3 discusses strategic alliances and joint ventures from the perspective of international expansion, defining a **strategic alliance** as a partnership between companies to jointly develop, produce, or sell products, and a **joint venture** as a separate legal entity established by the strategic partners. Both of these options can be more attractive than a merger or an acquisition in certain situations, and companies are increasingly using them to pursue opportunities.[37]

STRATEGIC ALLIANCES

Strategic alliances can accomplish many of the same goals as a merger or an acquisition but with less risk and work than permanently integrating two companies.[38] They can help a company gain credibility in a new field, expand its market presence, gain access to technology, diversify offerings, and share best practices without forcing the partners to become permanently entangled. Alliances can be an attractive option for independent freelancers all the way up to the world's largest corporations.

JOINT VENTURES

Although strategic alliances avoid much of the work and risk of formal mergers, they don't create a unified entity that functions with a single management structure, information system, and other organizational elements. In contrast, a joint venture lets companies create an operation that is more tightly integrated than a strategic alliance but without disrupting the original companies to the extent that a merger or acquisition does. Over the past two decades, joint ventures have been growing faster than mergers and acquisitions, and the companies involved report a much higher success rate.[39]

Although both strategic alliances and joint ventures offer compelling alternatives to mergers and acquisitions, they must be planned carefully and entered into cautiously. When a company acquires another firm, it is free to make adjustments along the way if things don't pan out as hoped, because it has complete control over the operation. However, strategic alliances and joint ventures don't offer the same degree of flexibility, because both parties must agree

REAL-TIME UPDATES
Learn More by Reading This PDF

Discover the keys to success for strategic alliances and joint ventures

More companies are considering strategic alliances and joint ventures; find out what it takes to make them successful. Go to **real-timeupdates.com/bia9** and select Learn More in the Students section.

 CHECKPOINT

LEARNING OBJECTIVE 6: Define *strategic alliance* and *joint venture,* and explain why companies would choose these options over a merger or an acquisition.

SUMMARY: Strategic alliances can accomplish many of the same goals as a merger or an acquisition but with less risk and work than permanently integrating two companies. A joint venture lets companies create an operation that is more tightly integrated than a strategic alliance but without disrupting the original companies to the extent that a merger or acquisition does.

CRITICAL THINKING: Why are an increasing number of companies considering joint ventures rather than mergers and acquisitions?

IT'S YOUR BUSINESS: Assume that you've worked for years to build up a strong and independent company; would you be comfortable sharing power with another company in a strategic alliance or joint venture? Why or why not?

KEY TERMS TO KNOW: strategic alliance, joint venture

EXHIBIT 5.5	Options for Joining Forces

Companies can choose from a variety of ways to combine resources and capabilities.

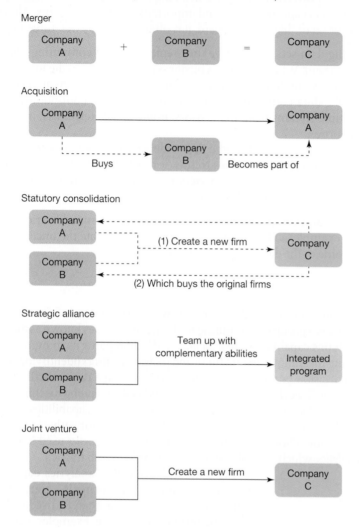

Merger

Acquisition

Statutory consolidation

Strategic alliance

Joint venture

on changes if things don't initially work out. As part of defining the new arrangement, the parties should establish change-management and conflict-resolution procedures so that they can deal with unexpected developments down the road.[40]

Exhibit 5.5 offers a quick graphical summary of the major ways businesses can join forces. For more information on company structure, corporate governance, and related issues, visit **real-timeupdates.com/bia9** and select Chapter 5.

Thriving in the Digital Enterprise: Big Data and Analytics

7   LEARNING OBJECTIVE

Explain how companies can use *big data* and *analytics* to create value and find competitive advantages.

In some important ways, the business of modern business is data, which in a broad sense includes everything from sensor readings and financial transactions to photographs and Twitter messages. Consumers generate data constantly. Online shopping, mobile app usage, package deliveries, Instagram posts, mass transit rides, phone calls—virtually every time you interact with any kind of technology, you generate data. Meanwhile, businesses also generate data in everything they do, and the billions of Internet of Things (IoT) devices attached to the internet are constantly adding to the pile as well.

BIG DATA

big data
The massive data sets that companies collect and analyze to find important trends and insights.

As a result of all this data generation, today's businesses often deal with a staggering flow of data, but they have powerful new tools to help. **Big data** is the term for the massive data sets that companies collect and analyze to find important trends and insights. Although there is no official definition of "big" in this regard, it is often defined by the "three Vs":[41]

- **Volume.** Big data sets are so large they require special computing systems to store and process them. When Walmart's business analysts want to dig into sales trends, for instance, the system they use can handle billions of transactions at once.[42]
- **Velocity.** Big data comes at you fast, so to speak, with continuous, real-time, and near- real-time streams from IoT sensors, point-of-sale terminals, internet shopping carts, and more.
- **Variety.** These data records come in a wide variety of formats from all manner of sources. To gain insight into sales trends, for instance, Walmart analyzes data from 200 separate sources, including transactions from its stores and websites, social media posts, weather, gas prices, and economic data.[43]

Some experts and companies that provide big data systems add various other dimensions. IBM, for example, adds a fourth V, for *veracity*, to indicate the uncertainty regarding the quality of some of the data that a system collects.[44]

ANALYTICS

analytics
Computing tools and techniques used to analyze big data; major types include data mining, text mining, and predictive analytics.

Those virtual mountains of data don't yield answers on their own, of course. The other half of the technology is a group of computing tools and techniques known as **analytics**. Three important analytics capabilities are *data mining* (finding patterns in numerical data), *text mining* (extracting meaning from text files), and *predictive analytics* (identifying the most likely outcomes of a decision or scenario). Big data analytics often use the artificial intelligence (AI) capabilities you'll see discussed throughout this book, including machine learning, deep learning, and natural language processing. All these analytics capabilities also come under the heading of *business intelligence*—systems and techniques for gathering and processing valuable information. (Note that you'll also see the term *analytics* used in other contexts, such as *web analytics*, which compiles statistical reports on web traffic.)

Big data and associated analytics capabilities are at the core of the digital transformation concept discussed in Chapter 1, and together they can be used to find answers across the business enterprise. Examples include analyzing sales patterns, finding potential customers, troubleshooting product and process failures, analyzing financial risks, allocating investments, detecting fraudulent transactions, maximizing crop yields, minimizing energy usage, finding customer dissatisfaction points, optimizing workforces, and predicting equipment failures before they occur.[45] Even if you're not interested in the nuts and bolts of big data, chances are you will use the tools at some point in your career. Many systems now offer *self-serve analytics*, so if you're a specialist in marketing or finance, for example, you can use the capabilities without being a data scientist or an IT expert (see Exhibit 5.6).

REAL-TIME UPDATES
Learn More by Visiting This Website

The latest on big data and analytics

IBM's Big Data & Analytics Hub has blog posts, videos, presentations, and more. Go to **real-timeupdates.com/bia9** and select Learn More in the Students section.

✓ CHECKPOINT

LEARNING OBJECTIVE 7: Explain how companies can use *big data* and *analytics* to create value and find competitive advantages.

SUMMARY: Big data sets and the associated analytics tools help companies harness the staggering amount of data that modern digital systems generate. The data collected include numerical quantities, visual elements such as photographs, and text. Three major analytics capabilities are data mining, text mining, and predictive analytics.

EXHIBIT 5.6	**Big Data and Analytics**

Companies use big data and analytics to collect, organize, and analyze the vast streams of data that modern consumer life and business activities generate. The Clarabridge text analytics system, for example, helps companies extract patterns of meaning from written communication.

 **CLARABRIDGE**   www.clarabridge.com

CRITICAL THINKING: Why might a company want to know that some production machinery is about to fail before it actually fails?

IT'S YOUR BUSINESS: As a consumer, could you remove yourself as a data source—that is, could you stop transmitting the data that businesses gather to analyze your behavioral patterns? Explain your answer.

KEY TERMS TO KNOW: big data, analytics

BEHIND THE SCENES

Saba Buys Its Way into the Performance Management Market

When Saba was ready to address the need to fill out its product portfolio with performance management software, it faced a decision that confronts many companies at some point: Build it or buy it. Specifically, should it (a) try to create that capability on its own, knowing that it could take months or even years to develop a full-featured, competitive offering, (b) buy a compatible product from another company that it could then integrate into its existing product suite, or (c) buy an entire company?

Under the direction of recently retired CEO Pervez Qureshi, Saba went with option c, spending $293 million to acquire Halogen Software, another industry-leading and highly respected developer of human resources systems. Halogen had a successful product that addressed the performance-management piece of the puzzle, an established customer base, several hundred experienced staffers, and some key executives who took high-level positions in Saba after the deal was signed.

Leaders of both firms emphasized not only the technical compatibility between the companies' products but also the firms' strategic and cultural compatibility. Most of the Halogen staff stayed onboard as their facility in Ottawa was rebranded with the Saba name. The employees marked the occasion by auctioning off the letters from the Halogen sign outside the building and donating the proceeds to a local charity. Several said that even as they looked forward to joining Saba, they had fond memories of their time at Halogen, so having the letters as mementos would keep that memory alive.

The acquisition appears to be a success so far, but acquisitions are not the only option Saba pursues to offer its customers more-complete solutions. It also establishes strategic alliances with a wide variety of companies that can bring in technical services to build turnkey solutions, expand a system with additional content such as training courses, provide ongoing customer service, or function as marketing affiliates in specific countries or regions. More than 80 other companies currently partner with Saba, giving customers a diverse range of options to get the unique solutions they need in order to manage human resources.

With the combined Halogen and Saba team under new CEO Phil Saunders, the company is confident it can pursue additional market opportunities and accelerate the launch of new talent-management solutions.[46]

Critical Thinking Questions

5-1. As part of this acquisition, the board chair of Halogen became the board chair of Saba. How might Saba executives feel about acquiring a company but then, in essence, reporting to someone from the company they had just purchased?

5-2. Assuming that most of the Halogen team stays in what was the company's home in Ottawa, what effect might this have on day-to-day operations, given that Saba's headquarters are in California? How might the company overcome any limitations of distance?

5-3. Human resources software can become a fundamental part of a company's central nervous system, tracking everything from hiring decisions to employee reviews to payroll. In an acquisition like Saba's purchase of Halogen, what steps should the companies take to assure their existing customers that the acquisition won't disrupt their daily operations?

Learn More Online

Visit **www.saba.com** and explore the Solutions, Industries, and Customers sections of the website. Read a few of the latest posts in the Saba blog. How well does the company present itself to potential customers? Are its marketing messages clear and compelling? Would you be interested in working for Saba after reading this material?

End of Chapter

KEY TERMS

acquisition (179)
analytics (184)
benefit corporation (174)
big data (184)
board of directors (176)
chief executive officer (CEO) (178)
corporate governance (176)
corporate officers (178)
corporation (172)
general partnership (170)
hostile takeover (179)
joint venture (182)
leveraged buyout (LBO) (179)
limited liability (170)

limited liability company (LLC) (174)
limited partnership (170)
liquidity (173)
merger (179)
partnership (170)
private corporation (172)
proxy (176)
public corporation (172)
S corporation (174)
shareholder activism (176)
shareholders (172)
sole proprietorship (167)
strategic alliance (182)
unlimited liability (169)

TEST YOUR KNOWLEDGE

Questions for Review

5-4. What is the role of a shareholder in a corporation?

5-5. What is the difference between a merger and an acquisition?

5-6. What are the key advantages of sole proprietorship?

5-7. What is a public corporation and why do some companies choose this form of ownership?

5-8. How does a holding company differ from a parent company?

5-9. What is the role of a company's board of directors?

5-10. What is a proxy fight?

5-11. What is big data?

Questions for Analysis

5-12. Why might unlimited liability be a major concern in a partnership?

5-13. To what extent do shareholders control the activities of a corporation?

5-14. How might a company benefit from having a diverse board of directors that includes representatives of several industries, countries, cultures, and demographic groups?

5-15. What issues should the board of directors address when a company is considering a merger or an acquisition?

5-16. Why might a board of directors decide to work with activist investors rather than against them?

5-17. **Ethical Considerations.** Why is leveraged buyout such a risky way of trying to finance an acquisition?

5-18. **Ethical Considerations.** Are poison pill defenses ethical? If a potential acquirer buys company stock legally, thereby becoming a part owner of the company, should management be allowed to entrench itself against the wishes of this owner? Explain your answer.

5-19. What kinds of competitive advantages could big data and analytics give a firm?

Questions for Application

5-20. Suppose you and some friends want to start a business that offers business culture training to foreign business representatives in your country. You all think the business will work but worry about being left with debts at such a young age if it fails. What form of ownership should you choose for your start-up and why?

5-21. According to the consultancy business Alvarez & Marsal, the United Kingdom accounts for 35 percent of all business targets of shareholder activism.[47] Why is shareholder activism becoming more common?

5-22. China's rapid economic development has been coupled with an increasing interest in and attention to the corporate governance of Chinese businesses. The China Securities Regulatory Commission released a Code of Corporate Governance for Listed Companies in 2019 covering basic principles, shareholder rights, codes of conduct, and ethics. Evaluate whether the current code is sufficient in terms of corporate governance.

5-23. **Concept Integration.** You've developed considerable expertise in setting up new manufacturing plants, and now you'd like to strike out on your own as a consultant who advises other companies. However, you recognize that manufacturing activity tends to expand and contract at various times during the business cycle (see Chapter 2). Do you think a single-consultant sole proprietorship or a small corporation with a half-dozen or more consultants would be better able to ride out tough times at the bottom of a business cycle?

EXPAND YOUR KNOWLEDGE

Discovering Career Opportunities

Are you best suited to working as a sole proprietor, as a partner in a business, or as an employee or a manager in a corporation? For this exercise, select three businesses with which you are familiar: one run by a single person, such as a web design consultant or a local landscaping firm; one run by two or three partners, such as a small accounting firm; and one that operates as a corporation, such as Target or Walmart.

- Write down what you think you would like about being the sole proprietor, one of the partners, the corporate manager, or an employee in the businesses you have selected. For example, would you like having full responsibility for the sole proprietorship? Would you like being able to consult with other partners in the partnership before making decisions? Would you settle for less autonomy to get the benefits of being a corporate employee?

- Now write down what you might dislike about each form of business. For example, would you dislike the risk of bearing all legal responsibility in a sole proprietorship? Would you dislike having to talk with your partners before spending the partnership's money? Would you dislike having to write reports for top managers and shareholders of the corporation?

- Weigh the pluses and minuses you have identified in this exercise. In comparison, which form of business most appeals to you?

Intelligent Business Technology: Data Mining

Data mining techniques are used in a wide variety of business functions. Research one current application in finance, marketing, network security, manufacturing, or any other area. Identify how it can help a company reduce costs, lower operational risks, enhance customer satisfaction, or otherwise improve competitiveness. In a brief email report, describe the application and its business benefits.

PRACTICE YOUR SKILLS

Resolving Ethical Dilemmas

You were flattered when two of your peers in the industry asked you to join them in a new business consulting partnership. They have admired the work you've done developing marketing strategies and new-product launches. You feel quite comfortable doing this work, but you know that consulting is not the same as being a corporate employee. The core of the work is the same, but consultants often need to function as salespeople, too—particularly in a start-up firm, where everyone will be expected to bring in new clients. You are much less confident in your ability to perform in this role. You expressed your reservations in a meeting with the two potential partners, but they told you not to worry about it, that you'll pick it up as you go. However, you have a sense that you're not cut out to handle sales. On the other hand, the promise of doing the strategy work you love for a variety of clients is immensely appealing.

Should you accept the partnership offer or not? Explain your answer, making up any details you need in order to craft a realistic scenario.

Growing as a Professional

You may find yourself wanting or needing to work as an independent contractor or freelancer at some point in your career. Independent contractors may work for a company in essentially every way that an employee does, but they don't have permanent status. Some work for a fixed duration; others work on a project-by-project basis. Freelancers work more as standalone entities, marketing their services to a variety of customers.

Thinking about how you would market your services is a good way to clarify the value you bring to the marketplace, and this exercise can help even if you spend your entire career as a full-time employee. Imagine that you have completed your degree and are ready to strike out on your own as an independent professional. Brainstorm your most-significant points of value, then write a headline that summarizes what you as a business entity have to offer.

Sharpening Your Communication Skills

You manage a small team that works for a local business. Recently, you have discovered that your firm will merge with another rival firm. To ensure transparency with your staff, prepare a short report that explains what a merger is and how it may affect your team.

Building Your Team Skills

Imagine that the leaders of the course you are enrolled in are considering making significant changes to manage and influence student groups as key stakeholders. The course leaders see themselves as supplying a product or service to the students of your course as a customer base and feel that students need to be more closely considered in all aspects of decision-making.

Your team must create a profile of the typical stakeholder groups or student groups in your course. As a team, consider the needs, wants, and expectations of each student group from the course program. Also, take into account the levels of interest and influence of these groups, and how would you go about ensuring that interest is maintained and improved and that the student groups are better informed and engaged.

Now suggest how the course leaders can meet with the key stakeholders. The purpose should be to have an exploratory conversation to understand their goals. What are the stakeholders looking for? How likely is it that the course will be able to meet their expectations? How can the course balance the competing demands and requirements of stakeholders? How might the project of reform go forward as a partnership between the institution, the course leaders, the student groups, and other stakeholders?

Select a spokesperson to deliver a brief presentation to the class, summarizing your team's ideas and the reasoning behind your suggestions. After all the teams have completed their presentations, discuss the differences and similarities in the proposed approach for the inclusion of student stakeholders. Do all teams agree on which stakeholders should be considered? Lead a classroom discussion on the course's responsibility to its stakeholders.

Developing Your Research Skills

Mergers and acquisitions are commonplace in the business world. Research well-known mergers and acquisitions about which plenty of information and data is available. Select one that interests you and consider the following questions.

- Write a short summary outlining your research on the chosen merger and acquisition.
- Why do you think the merger and the acquisition took place? What internal and external factors may have influenced the outcome? How do you think it was perceived by the employees of the firms in question?
- The after-effects of a merger or an acquisition can often be felt for extended periods of time. What impact did the merger and the acquisition have in the long term, both internally and externally? If your example is a more recent one, consider what you think the future impact will be on (a) the company, (b) consumers, and (c) the industry the company is part of.

Writing Assignments

5-24. Why are leveraged buyouts considered risky?

5-25. Is it ethical for special-interest groups to engage in shareholder activism? Explain your answer.

ENDNOTES

1. Saba website, accessed 30 March 2018, www.saba.com; "Halogen Software to Be Acquired by Saba Software," Saba, 23 February 2017, www.saba.com; "Gartner Names Halogen a Visionary in Magic Quadrant for Talent Management Suites for the Fourth Consecutive Year," Saba, 2 March 2017, www.saba.com; "Saba Completes Acquisition of Halogen Software," Saba, 1 May 2017, www.saba.com; "Old Halogen Software Sign Finds New Space in Employees' Homes," *Ottawa Business Journal*, 20 November 2017, www.obj.ca; "Ottawa's Halogen Sold to California Firm for $293M," *Ottawa Business Journal*, 27 February 2017, www.obj.ca; "Saba Software Announces CEO Succession," Saba, 21 February 2018, www.saba.com.

2. Beth Laurence, "Learn About Business Ownership Structures," Nolo, accessed 29 March 2018, www.nolo.com.

3. Norman M. Scarborough and Jeffrey R. Cornwall, *Essentials of Entrepreneurship and Small Business Management*, 8th ed. (New York: Pearson, 2016), 220.

4. "Join the Club," *Entrepreneur*, December 2008, 89.

5. "Facts and Figures,", PwC accessed 29 March 2018, www.pwc.com.

6. Laurence, "Learn About Business Ownership Structures."

7. Scarborough and Cornwall, *Essentials of Entrepreneurship and Small Business Management*, 223–225.

8. "MLP 101," MLP Association, accessed 29 March 2018, www.mlpassociation.org.

9. "Limited Liability Partnership," *Entrepreneur*, accessed 29 March 2018, www.entrepreneur.com.

10. Kelly K. Spors, "So, You Want to Be an Entrepreneur," *Wall Street Journal*, 23 February 2009, online.wsj.com.

11. Scarborough and Cornwall, *Essentials of Entrepreneurship and Small Business Management*, 225.

12. Beth Laurence, "Creating a Partnership Agreement," *Nolo*, accessed 29 March 2018, www.nolo.com.

13. Laurence, "Creating a Partnership Agreement."

14. "Fortune Global 500," *Fortune*, accessed 29 March 2018, fortune.com/global500/list; "GDP (current US$)," The World Bank, accessed 29 March 2018, data.worldbank.org.

15. "Largest Global IPOs," Renaissance Capital IPO Center, accessed 29 March 2018, www.renaissancecapital.com.

16. "Considering an IPO to Fuel Your Company's Future?" PwC, accessed 29 March 2018, www.pwc.com.

17. Sanford M. Jacoby and Sally Kohn, "Japan's Management Approaches Offer Lessons for U.S. Corporations," *Seattle Times*, 27 March 2009, www.seattletimes.com.

18. Scarborough and Cornwall, *Essentials of Entrepreneurship and Small Business Management*, 229–231; Beth Laurence, "S Corporations," Nolo, accessed 29 March 2018, www.nolo.com.

19. "S Corporations," U.S. Internal Revenue Service, accessed 29 March 2018, www.irs.gov.

20. Scarborough and Cornwall, *Essentials of Entrepreneurship and Small Business Management*, 232; "How to Choose the Right Legal Structure," *Inc.*, January–February 2009, www.inc.com.

21. Scarborough and Cornwall, *Essentials of Entrepreneurship and Small Business Management*, 232.

22. Benefit Corp, accessed 29 March 2019, www.benefitcorp.net; Alex Goldmark, "The Benefit Corporation: Can Business Be About More Than Profit?" *Good*, 1 July 2011, www.good.is; "Maryland First State in Union to Pass Benefit Corporation Legislation," B Corporation press release, 14 April 2010, www.crswire.com; B Corporation website, accessed 5 August 2011, www.bcorporation.net.

23. Interfaith Center on Corporate Responsibility, accessed 29 March 2018, www.iccr.org; William J. Holstein, "Unlikely Allies," *Directorship*, 3 October 2006, www.forbes.com.

24. Christopher P. Skroupa, "2017 And Beyond—Major Trends Shaping Shareholder Activism," *Forbes*, 31 October 2017, www.forbes.com.

25. Joseph L. Bower and Lynne S. Paine, "The Error at the Heart of Corporate Leadership," *Harvard Business Review*, May–June 2017, 50–60; Larry Fink, "A Sense of Purpose (Larry Fink's Annual Letter to CEOs)," BlackRock, accessed 23 March 2018, www.blackrock.com.

26. "The Heidrick & Struggles Board Monitor: Board Diversity at an Impasse?" 8 November 2017, www.heidrick.com; "Missing Pieces Report: The 2016 Board Diversity Census of Women and Minorities on Fortune 500 Boards," Deloitte, www.deloitte.com.

27. Susan Ellen Wolf, Robert J. Bertolini, Thomas J. Colligan, Fred Hassan, and Thomas J. Sabatino, Jr., "The Case for Customized Board Education," *The Corporate Governance Advisor*, January/February 2011, 1–6; Joann S. Lublin, "Back to School," *Wall Street Journal*, 21 June 2004, R3.

28. Bill Baker, Larry West, Brian Cartwright, and Brian Nysenbaum, "Liability of Outside Directors in SEC Enforcement Actions," *The Corporate Governance Advisor*, May/June 2011, 16–21.

29. "Trends in Independent Board Leadership Structures," EY, accessed 29 March 2018, www.ey.com; Jeffrey M. Stein and Parth S. Munshi, "The Changing Role of the Lead Director," *The Corporate Governance Advisor*, November/December 2008, 11–18.

30. "Mergers & Acquisitions Explained," *Thomson Investors Network*, accessed 8 April 2004, www.thomsoninvest.net.

31. "Business Consolidation," *Investopedia*, accessed 29 March 2018, www.investopedia.com.

32. Dawn McCarty, Tiffany Kary, and Daniela Wei, "Toys 'R' Us Collapses into Bankruptcy Thanks to Crushing Debt," *Bloomberg*, 18 September 2017, www.bloomberg.com.

33. Greta Roberts, "The Soft Things That Make Mergers Hard," *Harvard Business Review* blog network, 12 July 2011, blogs.hbr.org.

34. Chris Bargin, "The Three Reasons Why Tech M&A Deals Fail to Deliver Value," *Forbes*, 19 October 2017, www.forbes.com.

35. Tim Merrifield, "Six Tips for Succeeding with the Art of Acquisition," Cisco, accessed 5 August 2011, www.cisco.com.

36. "Poison Pill," *Investopedia*, accessed 29 March 2018, www.investopedia.com.

37. "Joint Ventures and Strategic Alliances: Examining the Keys to Success," PwC, accessed 29 March 2018, www.pwc.com.

38. Michael Hickins, "Searching for Allies," *Management Review*, January 2000, 54–58.

39. Arnaud Leroi and Philip Leung, "The Secrets to Successful Joint Ventures," *Forbes*, 11 April 2017, www.forbes.com; "Joint Ventures and Strategic Alliances: Examining the Keys to Success."

40. Leroi and Leung, "The Secrets to Successful Joint Ventures."

41. "Big Data: What It Is and Why It Matters," SAS, accessed 29 March 2018, www.sas.com.

42. Bernard Marr, "Really Big Data at Walmart: Real-Time Insights from Their 40+ Petabyte Data Cloud," *Forbes*, 23 January 2017, www.forbes.com.

43. Bernard Marr, "Walmart: Big Data Analytics at the World's Biggest Retailer," Bernard Marr & Co., accessed 29 March 2018, www.bernardmarr.com.

44. "The Four V's of Big Data," IBM, accessed 29 March 2018, www.ibmbigdatahub.com.

45. "How Companies Are Using Big Data and Analytics," McKinsey, April 2016, www.mckinsey.com; Lisa Morgan, "Big Data: 6 Real-Life Business Cases," *InformationWeek*, 26 May 2015, www.informationweek.com.

46. See note 1.

47. "Over 50 U.K. Companies at Significant Risk of Shareholder Activism," Alvarez & Marsal, accessed 12 August 2018, www.alvarezandmarsal.com.

6 Entrepreneurship and Small-Business Ownership

LEARNING OBJECTIVES
After studying this chapter, you will be able to

1 Highlight the contributions small businesses make to the U.S. economy.

2 List the most common reasons people start their own companies, and identify the common traits of successful entrepreneurs.

3 Explain the importance of planning a new business, and outline the key elements in a business plan.

4 Identify the major causes of business failures, explain what *pivoting* means, and identify sources of advice and support for business owners.

5 Discuss the principal sources of funding for small businesses.

6 Explain the advantages and disadvantages of franchising.

7 Define *machine learning* and *deep learning*, and describe their importance to contemporary business.

MyLab Intro to Business
Improve Your Grade!
If your instructor is using MyLab Intro to Business, visit **www.pearson.com/mylab/intro-to-business**.

BEHIND THE SCENES Alyza Bohbot: Carrying on One Tradition and Starting Another

Courtesy of Alyza Bohbot, City Girl Coffee

After Alyza Bohbot took over her parents' specialty coffee roasting company, her focus turned to using business as a means to help women in the global coffee trade.

www.citygirlcoffee.com

Alyza Bohbot was getting ready to start her second career, far from her childhood home in Duluth, Minnesota. After a brief stint in retail management, she had returned to college to get a second degree and now was all set to begin a new life as a school counselor. However, when her parents announced they were ready to retire and wanted to sell the family business, she paused. Her parents had devoted a quarter-century to building their specialty coffee company, Alakef Coffee Roasters, and although she had never entertained the idea of taking over, Bohbot couldn't make peace with the idea of the family business, which she described as "my whole life" while growing up, passing into a stranger's hands.

Parents who own companies are often keen to have an adult child take over when it's time to retire, but Bohbot's parents had mixed emotions. As much as they liked the idea of her stepping in, they didn't want her to be saddled with the responsibility if it wasn't her true passion. The family agreed to a six-month trial run to see if Bohbot could truly connect with the idea of running a coffee company.

Three years later, she was definitely connected—and about to dive even deeper into the global business of coffee. At a meeting of the International Women's Coffee Alliance, she learned about the economic challenges facing women who work in the world's coffee-growing regions. She had a "lightbulb moment," as she called it, and knew she had to act. Women do an estimated 70 percent of the work involved in coffee farming but often have little

opportunity for economic independence. In her view, "Women are such an integral part of the industry and the workforce, yet they don't have decision-making power or access to resources."

If you were in Bohbot's position, how would you act on this impulse to help? What steps could you take to use business as a force for change while meeting the responsibilities of running a profitable business?[1]

INTRODUCTION

Because you're studying business, chances are you've already had an idea or two for a new business. Are you ready to commit yourself fully to a business idea, as Alyza Bohbot (profiled in the chapter-opening Behind the Scenes) has done? Being an entrepreneur is one of the most exciting and important roles in business, but it requires high energy and some tough decision-making, as you'll discover in this chapter.

The Big World of Small Business

Except for operations that are spun off from existing companies, even the biggest corporations begin life as small businesses. It's no exaggeration to say the modern economy couldn't exist without small businesses.

Defining just what constitutes a small business is complicated but vitally important because billions of dollars are at stake when it comes to employment regulations (from which the smallest companies are often exempt) and government supply and service contracts reserved for small businesses. For research and reporting purposes, the U.S. Small Business Administration (SBA) defines a small business as any independent firm with fewer than 500 employees.[2]

To qualify for certain federal programs and compete for federal contracts, however, a company must meet criteria established by federal regulations and administered by the SBA. These include several general requirements, such as being independently owned and "not nationally dominant in its field," and specific limits on number of employees or annual revenues. In some industries, the SBA uses the number of employees as the limit, which ranges from 100 to 1,500 employees. In others, it uses annual revenue as the criterion, which ranges from as little as $750,000 to as much as $38.5 million.[3]

For general discussion, we can define a **small business** as an independent firm that has fewer than 500 employees and is not dominant in its market.

ECONOMIC ROLES OF SMALL BUSINESSES

From employing millions of people to creating essential products, small businesses play a vital role in the U.S. economy (see Exhibit 6.1 on the next page). Here are some of the major contributions small firms make:

- **They provide jobs.** Although most small businesses have no employees, those that do employ about half of the private-sector workforce in this country and create roughly two-thirds of all new jobs.[4]
- **They introduce new products.** The freedom to innovate that is characteristic of many small firms continues to yield countless advances: Among all firms that routinely apply for U.S. patents on new inventions, small businesses receive 16 times more patents per employee than larger firms do.[5]
- **They meet the needs of larger organizations.** Many small businesses act as distributors, servicing agents, and suppliers to larger corporations and to numerous government agencies.

1 LEARNING OBJECTIVE
Highlight the contributions small businesses make to the U.S. economy.

small business
A company that is independently owned and operated, is not dominant in its field, and employs fewer than 500 people.

EXHIBIT 6.1	The Economic Impact of Small Businesses in the United States

As these selected statistics show, small businesses (defined here as independent firms with fewer than 500 employees) are a major force in employment, economic activity, and global exports.

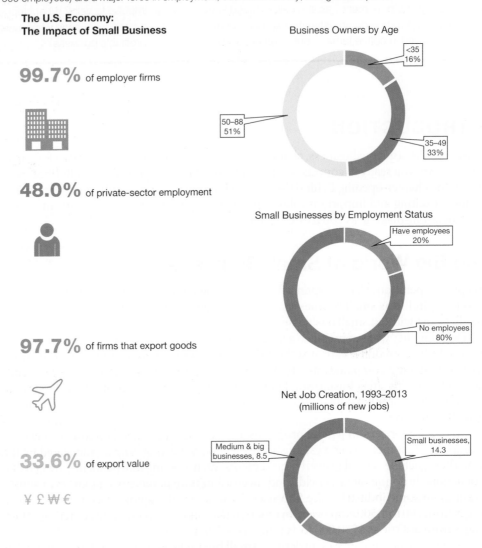

The U.S. Economy: The Impact of Small Business

99.7% of employer firms

48.0% of private-sector employment

97.7% of firms that export goods

33.6% of export value

Business Owners by Age
- <35 16%
- 50–88 51%
- 35–49 33%

Small Businesses by Employment Status
- Have employees 20%
- No employees 80%

Net Job Creation, 1993–2013 (millions of new jobs)
- Medium & big businesses, 8.5
- Small businesses, 14.3

Sources: *Annual Report of the Office of Economic Research, FY 2016*, U.S. Small Business Administration; "Frequently Asked Questions," U.S. Small Business Administration, June 2016, www.sba.gov.

- **They take risks that larger companies sometimes avoid.** Entrepreneurs play a significant role in the economy as risk takers—people willing to try new and unproven ideas.
- **They provide specialized goods and services.** Small businesses frequently spring up to fill niches that aren't being served by existing companies.
- **They provide economic opportunities for a diverse range of people.** For example, over the 20-year period from 1997 through 2017, the number of companies owned by women more than doubled, and the number owned by women of color more than quadrupled.[6]

CHARACTERISTICS OF SMALL BUSINESSES

Small businesses vary widely in terms of long-term objectives and growth potential. Most small businesses are single-person operations, and many have limited potential to grow beyond providing income for their independent owners. These are sometimes called *lifestyle businesses*, because they are built around the personal and financial needs of an individual or a family.

Other small businesses have strong potential to grow if their owners desire, such as by adding additional retail locations or designing new products. And some firms are small simply because they are still young but have ambitious plans to grow. These *high-growth ventures* are usually run by a team rather than by one individual, and they expand rapidly by obtaining a sizable supply of investment capital and by introducing new products or services to a large market.

Regardless of their primary objectives, small companies tend to differ from large ones in several important ways:

- Most small firms have a narrow focus, offering fewer goods and services to fewer market segments.
- Unless they are launched with generous financial backing, which is rare, small businesses must get by with limited resources.
- Smaller businesses often have more freedom to innovate and move quickly. As they grow larger, companies tend to get slower and more bureaucratic. In contrast, entrepreneurial firms usually find it easier to operate "on the fly," making decisions quickly and reacting swiftly to changes in the marketplace.

Small-business ownership provides economic opportunities for a wide range of people.

✓ CHECKPOINT

LEARNING OBJECTIVE 1: Highlight the contributions small businesses make to the U.S. economy.

SUMMARY: Small businesses provide jobs, employing about half the private-sector workforce. They introduce new and innovative products, they supply many of the needs of larger organizations, they inject considerable amounts of money into the economy, they often take risks that larger organizations avoid, and they provide many specialized goods and services.

CRITICAL THINKING: (1) Why do you think many companies grow more risk averse as they grow larger? (2) If they wanted to, could large businesses take the place of small businesses in the U.S. economy? For instance, could someone build a nationwide landscaping company? Why or why not?

IT'S YOUR BUSINESS: If you can't land the right job soon after graduation, would you consider starting a business? Why or why not?

KEY TERMS TO KNOW: small business

The Entrepreneurial Spirit

2 **LEARNING OBJECTIVE**
List the most common reasons people start their own companies, and identify the common traits of successful entrepreneurs.

entrepreneurial spirit
The positive, forward-thinking desire to create profitable, sustainable business enterprises.

To some people, working for themselves or starting a company seems like a perfectly natural way to earn a living. To others, the thought of working outside the structure of a regular company might seem too scary to even contemplate. However, every professional should understand the **entrepreneurial spirit**—the positive, forward-thinking desire to create profitable, sustainable business enterprises—and the role it can play in *every* company, not just small or new firms. The entrepreneurial spirit is vital to the health of the economy and to everyone's standard of living, and it can help even the largest and oldest companies become more profitable and competitive.

WHY PEOPLE START THEIR OWN COMPANIES

Starting a company is nearly always a difficult, risky, exhausting endeavor that requires significant sacrifice. Why do people do it? Some want more control over their future, some can't find corporate jobs that fit their interests or skill sets, and others are simply tired of working for someone else. Some have new product ideas that they believe in with such passion that they're willing to devote themselves to a start-up enterprise. Some start companies to pursue business goals that are important to them on a personal level, as you'll read about at the end of the chapter with Alyza Bohbot's decision to launch a new coffee company.

QUALITIES OF SUCCESSFUL ENTREPRENEURS

Although it's impossible to lump millions of people into a single category, successful entrepreneurs tend to share a number of characteristics (see Exhibit 6.2). If you have many of these traits, successful entrepreneurship could be in your future, too—if you're not already a hard-working entrepreneur.

INNOVATING WITHOUT LEAVING: INTRAPRENEURSHIP

The innovative, future-oriented spirit of entrepreneurship isn't limited to people who start or want to start companies. Many employees of existing firms have that same creative drive but for various reasons want to remain within the structure of an established organization. These *intrapreneurs*, employees who approach their work with the imagination and drive typical of entrepreneurs, can be essential sources of product and process innovation in almost any company.[7] In fact, as more firms face the threat of disruptive innovation in their

EXHIBIT 6.2	Qualities Shared by Successful Entrepreneurs

Although no single personality profile fits all successful entrepreneurs, here are the qualities that entrepreneurs tend to have.

Confidence
- Want to control their destiny
- Have a deep sense of responsibility for the outcome
- Decisive; willing to make decisions without full data
- Curious, creative, and eager to learn
- Want feedback and are highly adaptable
- Willing to take sensible risks but are not "gamblers"

Passion
- Love what they do
- Inspire others with their passion
- Visionary; not satisfied with the status quo
- Pursue goals with energy and commitment
- Confident and optimistic, with a long-term orientation
- Often value achievement as highly as money

Drive
- Not discouraged by failure; willing to grit it out
- Self-reliant and resourceful
- Willing to work hard for as long as it takes
- Extremely disciplined and self-motivated
- Willing to make sacrifices in other aspects of their lives

Sources: Norman M. Scarborough and Jeffrey R. Cornwall, *Essentials of Entrepreneurship and Small Business Management*, 8th ed. (New York: Pearson, 2016), 5—12; Sujan Patel, "10 Essential Characteristics of Highly Successful Entrepreneurs," *Inc.*, 2 September 2017, www.inc.com; Nina Zipkin, "Barbara Corcoran on the 5 Traits All Successful Entrepreneurs Share," *Entrepreneur*, 12 April 2017, www.entrepreneur.com.

industries, intrapreneurial employees can help companies "disrupt themselves" before they get outmoded by new competitors.

However, innovating within a larger organization is sometimes easier said than done, because companies tend to become more analytical, more deliberate, more structured, and more careful as they mature. Mechanisms put in place to prevent mistakes and protect existing business can also hamper innovative thinking by restricting people to tried-and-true methods. Organizations can develop habits based on behaviors and decisions that made sense in the past but that no longer aligned with a changed business environment. Companies sometimes need to take special steps to encourage, protect, and reward intrapreneurs.[8]

 CHECKPOINT

LEARNING OBJECTIVE 2: List the most common reasons people start their own companies, and identify the common traits of successful entrepreneurs.

SUMMARY: People start businesses for a variety of reasons, including gaining more control over their future, wanting to avoid working for someone else, having new product ideas that they are deeply passionate about, pursuing business goals that are important to them on a personal level, or seeking income alternatives when they can't find jobs that fit. The entrepreneurial spirit—the positive, forward-thinking desire to create profitable, sustainable business enterprises—is a good way to summarize the entrepreneurial personality. Specifically, successful entrepreneurs tend to love what they do and are driven by a passion to succeed at it, they are disciplined and willing to work hard, they are confident and optimistic, and they like to control their own destiny. Moreover, they relate well to others and are able to inspire others, are curious, learn from their mistakes without letting failure drag them down, are adaptable and tuned in to their environments, and are moderate but careful risk takers.

CRITICAL THINKING: (1) Would someone who excels at independent entrepreneurship automatically excel at an intrapreneurial effort? Why or why not? (2) Does the inability or unwillingness to work within the constraints of a typical corporation mean someone is naturally suited to entrepreneurship? Why or why not?

IT'S YOUR BUSINESS: (1) If you had to start a business right now and generate profit as quickly as possible, what kind of business would you start? Explain your answer. (2) How would you describe your level of entrepreneurial spirit?

KEY TERMS TO KNOW: entrepreneurial spirit

The Start-Up Phase: Planning and Launching a New Business

3 **LEARNING OBJECTIVE**

Explain the importance of planning a new business, and outline the key elements in a business plan.

The start-up phase is an exciting time because entrepreneurs and small-business owners love to roll up their sleeves and get to work, but it's also an exhausting time because a lot of work must be done. Focusing that start-up energy and making sure essential tasks are completed calls for careful decision-making and planning, starting with choosing the best ownership option and creating an effective business plan.

SMALL-BUSINESS OWNERSHIP OPTIONS

People who have an entrepreneurial urge sometimes jump to the conclusion that starting a new company is the best choice, but it's definitely not the only choice—and it's not always the right one. Before you decide, consider all three options: creating a new business, buying an existing business, or buying a franchise. Creating a new business has many advantages, but it can also be the most difficult option (see Exhibit 6.3 on the next page).

EXHIBIT 6.3	Business Start-Up Options

Creating an all-new, independent business can be an exciting prospect, but this brief comparison highlights how much work it requires and how many risks are involved. (You can read more about franchising on page 205.)

Start-Up Strategy	Financial Outlay at Start-Up	Possibilities for Attracting Outside Funding	Owner's Freedom and Flexibility	Business Processes and Systems	Support Networks	Workforce	Customer Base, Brand Recognition, and Sales
Create a new, independent business	Some businesses can be started with very little cash; others, particularly in manufacturing, may require a lot of capital	Usually very limited; most lenders and many investors want evidence that the business can generate revenue before they'll offer funds; venture capitalists invest in new firms, but only in a few industries	Very high, particularly during early phases, although low capital can severely restrict the owner's ability to maneuver	Must be designed and created from scratch, which can be time-consuming and expensive	Suppliers, bankers, and other elements of the network must be selected; the good news is that the owner can select and recruit ones that he or she specifically wants	Must be hired and trained at the owner's expense	None; must be built from the ground up, which can put serious strain on company finances until sales volume builds
Buy an existing independent business	Can be considerable; some companies sell for multiples of their annual revenue, for example	Banks are more willing to lend to established, profitable businesses, and investors are more likely to invest in them	Less than when creating a new business because facilities, work force, and other assets are already in place; more than when buying a franchise	Already in place, which can be a plus or a minus, depending on how well they work	Some elements will already be in place but may need to be upgraded	Already in place, which could be a positive or a negative, but at least there are staff to operate the business	Assuming the business is at least somewhat successful, it has a customer base with ongoing sales and some brand reputation (which could be positive or negative)
Buy into a franchise system	Varies widely, from a few thousand to several million dollars; most well-known franchises require low- to mid-six figures	Varies, but many franchisors do not allow franchisees to buy a franchise with borrowed funds, so they must have their own capital; many have minimum liquidity and net worth criteria	Low to very low; most franchisors require rigid adherence to company policies and processes	One of the key advantages of buying a franchise is that it comes with an established business system	Varies; some franchise companies specify which suppliers a franchisee can use	Must be hired and trained, but many franchisors provide training or training support	Customer base and repeat sales must be built, but one of the major advantages of a franchise is established brand recognition

Compared to starting a new business, buying an existing business can involve less work and less risk—provided, of course, that you check out the company carefully. When you buy a healthy business, you generally purchase an established customer base, functioning business systems, proven products or services, and a known location. In addition, financing an existing business is often much easier because lenders are reassured by the company's history and existing assets and customer base.

Still, buying an existing business is not without disadvantages and risks. You may need a considerable amount of financing to buy a fully functioning company, for example, and you will inherit any problems the company has, from unhappy employees to obsolete equipment to customers with overdue accounts. Thorough research is a must.[9]

The third option, buying a franchise (see page 205), combines many of the benefits of independent business ownership with the support that comes with being part of a larger organization.

BLUEPRINT FOR AN EFFECTIVE BUSINESS PLAN

Although some successful entrepreneurs claim to have done little formal planning, they all have at least *some* intuitive idea of what they're trying to accomplish and how they hope to do it. In other words, even if they haven't produced a formal printed document, chances are they've thought through the big questions, which is just as important. As FedEx founder Fred Smith put it, "Being entrepreneurial doesn't mean [you] jump off a ledge and figure out how to make a parachute on the way down."[10]

A **business plan** summarizes a proposed business venture, communicates the company's goals, highlights how management intends to achieve those goals, and shows how customers will benefit from the company's goods or services. Preparing a business plan serves three important functions. First, it guides the company operations and outlines a strategy for turning an idea into reality. Second, it helps persuade lenders and investors to finance your business if outside money is required. Third, it can provide a reality check in case an idea just isn't feasible.

business plan
A document that summarizes a proposed business venture, its goals, and plans for achieving those goals.

Business plans can be written before the company is launched, when the founders are defining their vision of what the company will be, when the company is seeking funding, and after the company is up and running, when the plan serves as a monitor-and-control mechanism to make sure operations are staying on track. At any stage, a business plan forces you to think about personnel, marketing, facilities, suppliers, distribution, and a host of other issues vital to a company's success. The specific elements to include in a business plan can vary based on the situation; here are the sections typically included in a plan written to attract outside investors:[11]

- **Summary.** In one or two paragraphs, summarize your business concept, particularly the business model, so investors can see how the company will generate revenue and produce a profit. The summary must be compelling, catching the investor's attention and giving him or her reasons to keep reading. Describe your product or service and its market potential. Highlight some things about your company and its leaders that will distinguish your firm from the competition. Summarize your financial projections and indicate how much money you will need from investors or lenders and where it will be spent.
- **Mission and objectives.** Explain the purpose of your business and what you hope to accomplish.
- **Company overview.** Give full background information on the origins and structure of your venture.
- **Products or services.** Concisely describe your products or services, focusing on their unique attributes and their appeal to customers.
- **Management and key personnel.** Summarize the background and qualifications of the people most responsible for the company's success.
- **Target market.** Provide data that will persuade an investor that you understand your target market. Be sure to identify the strengths and weaknesses of your competitors.
- **Marketing strategy.** Provide projections of sales volume and market share; outline a strategy for identifying and reaching potential customers, setting prices, providing customer support, and physically delivering your products or services. Whenever possible, include evidence of customer acceptance, such as advance product orders.
- **Design and development plans.** If your products require design or development, describe the nature and extent of what needs to be done, including costs and potential problems.
- **Operations plan.** Provide information on facilities, equipment, and personnel requirements.
- **Start-up schedule.** Forecast development of the company in terms of completion dates for major aspects of the business plan.
- **Major risk factors.** Identify all potential negative factors and discuss them honestly.
- **Financial projections and requirements.** Include a detailed budget of start-up and operating costs, as well as projections for income, expenses, and cash flow for the first three years of business. Identify the company's financing needs and potential sources.
- **Exit strategy.** Explain how investors will be able to cash out or sell their investment, such as through a public stock offering, sale of the company, or a buyback of the investors' interest.

REAL-TIME UPDATES

Learn More by Exploring This Interactive Website

Try the Lean Canvas yourself

Use this free tool to see how lean business planning works. Go to **real-timeupdates.com/bia9** and select Learn More in the Students section.

Veteran investors advise entrepreneurs to create a concise *executive summary* of their business plan to use when presenting their ideas to investors for the first time. Entrepreneurs often have as little as 20 minutes (and sometimes even less) to make these pitches, so a compelling presentation backed up by an executive summary no longer than 20 pages is ideal. The most important part of the entire package is "the grab," a one- or two-sentence statement that gets an investor's attention. If an investor is intrigued, he or she can then read the executive summary to get a better sense of the opportunity and then review the full business plan before deciding whether to provide funds.[12]

LEAN BUSINESS PLANNING

Not all start-up veterans and investors believe in the value of a conventional, in-depth business plan, at least in a company's early stages. Reasons for this skepticism include the amount of time and energy required to research and write a plan, the reluctance of many target readers to read such lengthy documents, the uncertainty of whether a new product or company idea will even work, and the difficulty of correctly anticipating all the circumstances and obstacles that a young company will encounter.

Particularly for companies that are developing new products or new business models before they can launch, some experts recommend that entrepreneurs devote most of their energy to getting a working product or service model in front of potential customers as quickly as possible so it can be verified and fine-tuned before proceeding to extensive business planning. Two popular alternatives to conventional business plans are high-level overviews known as the Business Model Canvas and the Lean Canvas. They are essentially one-page business plans that present only the essential ideas that make up an intended business model.[13]

 CHECKPOINT

LEARNING OBJECTIVE 3: Explain the importance of planning a new business, and outline the key elements in a business plan.

SUMMARY: Planning is essential because it forces you to consider the best ownership strategy for your needs and circumstances (creating a new company, buying an existing company, or buying a franchise) and it forces you to think through the factors that will lead to success. An effective business plan should include your mission and objectives, company overview, management, target market, marketing strategy, design and development plans, operations plan, start-up schedule, major risk factors, and financial projections and requirements.

CRITICAL THINKING: (1) Why is it important to identify critical risks and problems in a business plan? (2) Many experts suggest that you write the business plan yourself, rather than hiring a consultant to write it for you. Why is this a good idea?

IT'S YOUR BUSINESS: (1) Think of several of the most innovative or unusual products you currently own or have recently used (don't forget about services as well). Were these products created by small companies or large ones? (2) Optimism and perseverance are two of the most important qualities for entrepreneurs. On a scale of 1 (lowest) to 10 (highest), how would you rate yourself on these two qualities? How would your best friend rate you?

KEY TERMS TO KNOW: business plan

The Growth Phase: Nurturing and Sustaining a Young Business

④ **LEARNING OBJECTIVE**

Identify the major causes of business failures, explain what *pivoting* means, and identify sources of advice and support for business owners.

So far, so good. You've done your planning and launched your new enterprise. Now the challenge is to keep going and keep growing toward your goals. To ensure a long and healthy life for your business, start by understanding the reasons new businesses can fail.

THE NEW-BUSINESS FAILURE RATE

You may have heard some frightening "statistics" about the failure rate of new businesses, with various sources saying that 70, 80, or even 90 percent of new business ventures fail. Unfortunately, calculating a precise figure that represents all types of businesses across all industries is probably impossible.

First, the definition of "failure" can be hard to pin down and varies from one business owner to the next. For example, business owners may retire, return to the corporate workforce to get away from the grind of running a business alone, or simply decide to pursue a different path in life. All of these closures would count as failures in a typical survey, but they wouldn't count as failures to the business owners themselves.

Second, establishing a time frame is essential for a failure rate to have any meaning. For example, ill-conceived or undercapitalized businesses often don't survive the first year, so the early failure rate is quite high. However, after the bad ideas collide with reality and disappear, the rate of failure slows down, and the companies that fail do so for a wide variety of reasons, some internal and some external.

Third, structural changes in the economy or in a particular industry can cause business closures that don't reflect a general pattern that is applicable to all companies.

In other words, view every failure statistic with skepticism unless you can find out how it was calculated. For instance, "90 percent of new restaurants fail in the first year" is repeated so often that many people assume it must be true. However, a comprehensive study of 81,000 restaurants over a 20-year period showed that the failure rate at the one-year point was less than 20 percent.[14]

No matter what the percentage is in a given industry over a particular time frame, if your business fails, it's a 100 percent failure rate for you. To help make sure you don't become a statistic, start by understanding why businesses tend to fail (see Exhibit 6.4 on the next page) and figure out how to avoid making the same mistakes.

PIVOTING: WHEN A BETTER IDEA COMES ALONG

Many companies end up growing into a different place than the founders envisioned at the outset. Smart entrepreneurs monitor how their initial product offerings are received in the market and adapt if they see opportunities to be more successful, a move known as **pivoting**. This can range from adjusting the feature set of an individual product all the way up to taking the company in a completely new direction, and some companies pivot multiple times until they find the right product-market fit. Twitter, Pinterest, and PayPal are just a few of the well-known companies that pivoted to get to where they are today.[15]

pivoting
Adjusting a firm's business model when a better opportunity presents itself.

ADVICE AND SUPPORT FOR BUSINESS OWNERS

Keeping a business going is no simple task, to be sure. Fortunately, entrepreneurs can get advice and support from a wide variety of sources, and much of this help is free. To get started, a host of YouTube channels, podcasts, websites, magazines, and social media sources offer advice on every aspect of entrepreneurship and small-business ownership. For more formal coaching and support, you can turn to the various organizations discussed in this section.

REAL-TIME UPDATES
Learn More by Visiting This Website

Free advice for every stage of the start-up experience

Kauffman Entrepreneurs, sponsored by the Ewing Marion Kauffman Foundation, is a treasure trove of learning material on every aspect of starting and running a small business. Go to **real-timeupdates .com/bia9** and select Learn More in the Students section.

EXHIBIT 6.4	**Why New Businesses Fail**

Here are the most common reasons that new businesses fail.

Strategic Issues	Leadership Issues	Marketing and Sales Issues	Financial Issues
Little or no demand: Company introduced a product that few, if any, customers wanted.	**Managerial incompetence:** Owner didn't know how to plan, lead, control, or organize.	**Ineffective marketing:** Small companies—especially *new* small companies—face a tremendous challenge getting recognition in crowded markets.	**Inadequate funding:** Company lacked the funding needed to launch or scale up to the point of being self-funding.
Lack of strategic planning or a viable business model: Owners didn't think through all the variables needed to craft a viable business strategy.	**Lack of relevant experience:** Owner may be experienced in business but not in the particular markets or technologies that are vital to the new firm's success.	**Uncontrolled growth:** Company added customers faster than it could handle them, leading to chaos, or might have even "grown its way into bankruptcy" if it spent wildly to capture and support	**Poor cash management:** Company spent too much on nonessentials, failed to balance expenditures with incoming revenues, failed to use loan or investment funds wisely, or failed to budget enough to pay its bills.
Failure to pivot: Owners missed (or failed to take) a chance to purpose a better opportunity.	**Inability to make the transition from employee to entrepreneur:** Owner couldn't juggle the multiple and diverse responsibilities or survive the lack of support that comes with going solo.	customers. **Poor location:** For retailers and businesses that depend on easy customer access or visibility, a poor location limited sales potential.	**Excessive overhead:** Company created too many fixed expenses that weren't directly related to creating or selling products, leaving it vulnerable to any slowdown in the economy.
Overpowering competition: Company might have been on the right track, but the competition simply did things better.	**Motivational collapse:** Entrepreneur burned out before the business became self-sustaining.	**Customer neglect:** Company failed to support customers or respond to problems.	**Poor inventory control:** Company produced or bought too much inventory, raising costs too high—or it did the opposite and was unable to satisfy demand.

Sources: Jayson DeMers, "A New Study Reveals the 20 Factors That Predict Startup Failure: Do Any Apply to You?" *Entrepreneur*, 5 February 2018, www.entrepreneur .com; Norman M. Scarborough and Jeffrey R. Cornwall, *Essentials of Entrepreneurship and Small Business Management*, 8th ed. (New York: Pearson, 2016), 37–39; Brian Hamilton, "The 7 Biggest Financial Mistakes Businesses Make," *Inc.*, 9 August 2011, www.inc.com.

Government Agencies and Not-for-Profit Organizations

Numerous city, state, and federal government agencies offer business owners advice, assistance, and even financing in some cases. For instance, many cities and states have an office of economic development charged with helping companies prosper so that they might contribute to the local or regional economy. At the federal level, small businesses can apply for loans backed by the SBA, get management and financing advice, and learn about selling to the federal government at **www.sba.gov**. The Minority Business Development Agency (**www.mbda.gov**) offers advice and programs to minority-owned businesses.

Some of the best advice available to small businesses is delivered by thousands of volunteers from the Service Corps of Retired Executives (SCORE), a resource partner of the SBA. These experienced business professionals offer free advice and one-to-one counseling to entrepreneurs. You can learn more at **www.score.org**.

Many colleges and universities also offer entrepreneurship and small-business programs. Check with your college's business school to see whether resources are available to help you launch or expand a company. The U.S. Chamber of Commerce (**www.uschamber.com**) and its many local chambers offer advice and special programs for small businesses as well.

Business Partners

Banks, credit card companies, software companies, and other firms you do business with can also be a source of advice and support. For example, the Open Forum, hosted by American Express, offers a variety of videos, articles, and other resources to help small-business owners.[16] As you might expect, the resources provided by these companies are part of their marketing strategies and so include a certain amount of self-promotion, but don't let that stop you from taking advantage of all the free advice you can get.

Marius Venter/Alamy Stock Photo

Getting advice from seasoned entrepreneurs and executives is invaluable for new business owners.

Mentors and Advisory Boards

Many entrepreneurs and business owners take advantage of individual mentors and advisory boards. Mentoring can happen through both formal programs such as SCORE and informal relationships developed in person or online. In either case, the advice of a mentor who has been down the road before can be priceless.

An **advisory board** is a form of group mentoring in which you assemble a team of people with subject-area expertise or vital contacts to help review plans and decisions. Unlike a corporate board of directors, an advisory board does not have legal responsibilities, and you don't have to incorporate to establish an advisory board. The key to success with an advisory board is to be objective about your strengths and weaknesses so you can recruit advisers who will fill the gaps in your knowledge and experience. Many business owners with boards also "pay it forward" by serving on advisory boards for other companies.[17]

advisory board
A team of people with subject-area expertise or vital contacts who help a business owner review plans and decisions.

Many small-business owners assemble advisory boards made up of people who can fill in gaps in their knowledge and experience.

Networks and Support Groups

No matter what industry you're in or what stage your business is in, you can probably find a local or online network of people with similar interests. Many cities across the country have local networks; search online for "entrepreneur network." Some entrepreneurs meet regularly in small groups to analyze each other's progress month by month. Being forced to articulate your plans and decisions to peers—and to be held accountable for results—can be an invaluable reality check. Some groups focus on helping entrepreneurs hone their presentations to potential investors. In addition to local in-person groups, social networking technology gives entrepreneurs an endless array of opportunities to connect online.

Business Incubators and Accelerators

Business incubators and accelerators are centers that provide early-stage businesses with various combinations of advice, financial support, access to industry insiders and connections, office and manufacturing facilities, and other services a company needs to get started. Some are not-for-profit organizations affiliated with the economic development agencies of local or state governments or universities, some are for-profit enterprises, some are run by venture capitalists, and some companies have internal incubators to encourage new ventures.

The terms *incubator* and *accelerator* are sometimes used interchangeably, but they do have different requirements and expectations. In general, **business incubators** help an entrepreneurial team develop an idea into a workable business model and establish a company framework for commercializing products. Start-ups often stay in incubators for indefinite periods of time as they develop their business models. Most incubators are not-for-profit organizations focused on creating jobs to spur local economic development.[18]

Business accelerators work with existing companies with the primary goal of making them more attractive to investors. Accelerators usually take a small ownership share in the company in exchange for providing their services, and most provide a small amount of *seed money* (see page 202) to help the company through this stage. In contrast to the open-ended time frames of incubators, accelerators usually have a predefined development process that takes only a few months, and companies are expected to be "investor-ready" at the end of the program. Accelerators have rigorous application requirements and accept only a small fraction of companies that apply. As a result, the best accelerators have very high success rates.[19]

business incubators
Facilities that help early-stage entrepreneurial teams develop ideas into workable business models and establish company frameworks for commercializing products.

business accelerators
Organizations that work with existing companies with the primary goal of making them more attractive to investors.

REAL-TIME UPDATES
Learn More by Visiting This Website

Find an incubator or accelerator for your business

The International Business Innovation Association helps entrepreneurs connect with incubators and accelerators. Go to **real-timeupdates.com/bia9** and select Learn More in the Students section.

CHECKPOINT

LEARNING OBJECTIVE 4: Identify the major causes of business failures, explain what *pivoting* means, and identify sources of advice and support for business owners.

SUMMARY: The causes of business failure can be grouped into four categories: (1) strategic issues, including little or no demand, lack of strategic planning or a viable business model, a failure to pivot, and overpowering competition; (2) leadership issues, including managerial incompetence, lack of relevant experience, inability to make the transition from employee to entrepreneur, and motivational collapse; (3) marketing and sales issues, including ineffective marketing, uncontrolled growth, poor location, and customer neglect; and (4) financial issues, including inadequate funding, poor cash management, excessive overhead, and poor inventory control. Pivoting means to change direction when the initial business model isn't working or when a better opportunity appears. For help and advice, business owners can turn to a variety of government agencies, not-for-profit organizations, business partners, mentors and advisory boards, networks and support groups, and business incubators and accelerators.

CRITICAL THINKING: (1) Why would a state or local government invest taxpayer dollars in a business incubator? (2) Can you think of any risks of getting advice from other entrepreneurs?

IT'S YOUR BUSINESS: (1) Have you ever shopped at a store or eaten in a restaurant and said to yourself, "This place isn't going to make it"? What factors caused you to reach that conclusion? (2) Does your college have an entrepreneur program or participate in a business incubator? If you wanted to start a business, how might such services help you?

KEY TERMS TO KNOW: pivoting, advisory board, business incubators, business accelerators

---

[5] **LEARNING OBJECTIVE**

Discuss the principal sources of funding for small businesses.

Financing Options for Small Businesses

Figuring out *how much* you'll need in order to start a business requires good insights into the particular industry you plan to enter. Figuring out *where* to get the money is a creative challenge no matter which industry you're in. Financing a business enterprise is a complex undertaking, and chances are you'll need to piece together funds from multiple sources, possibly using a combination of *equity* (in which you give investors a share of the business in exchange for their money) and *debt* (in which you borrow money that must be repaid). You'll read more about equity and debt financing in Chapter 16. Exhibit 6.5 identifies, in broad terms, the major types of financing available to businesses at various stages in their life cycle.

PRIVATE FINANCING

Private financing covers every source of funding except selling stocks and bonds. Nearly all companies start with private financing to get **seed money**, their first infusion of capital. The range of private financing options is diverse, from personal savings to funds from an ongoing full- or part-time job to investment funds set up by large corporations looking for entrepreneurial innovations.

seed money
The first infusion of capital used to get a business started.

Four common categories of private financing are banks and microlenders, venture capitalists, angel investors, and personal credit cards and lines of credit.

Banks and Microlenders

Bank loans are one of the most important sources of financing for small business, although banks generally require a company to have an established track record, positive cash flow,

EXHIBIT 6.5	**Financing Possibilities over the Life of a Small Business**

The potential funding sources available to a business owner vary widely, depending on where the business is in its life cycle. Note that this is a general summary and covers only the most common funding sources. Individual lending opportunities depend on the specific business owner(s), the state of the economy, and the type of business and its potential for growth. For example, venture capital is available only to firms with the potential to grow rapidly and only in a few industries.

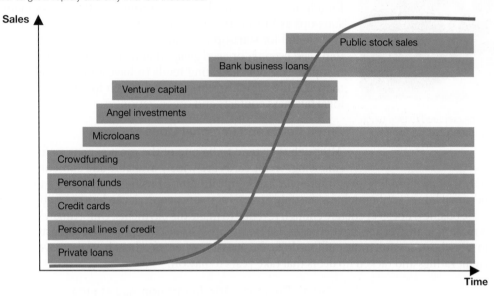

and some marketable *collateral*, such as buildings or equipment, to back the loan. In addition, as a small-business owner, your personal credit will affect whether you can get a business bank loan and at what interest rate—another good reason to manage your personal credit wisely.[20]

In response to the needs of entrepreneurs who don't qualify for standard bank loans or who don't need the amount of a regular loan, hundreds of not-for-profit organizations now serve as **microlenders**, offering loans as small as $100. Many of these are local organizations that want to support entrepreneurs and promote economic development in their communities.[21]

microlenders
Organizations, often not-for-profit, that lend smaller amounts of money to business owners who might not qualify for conventional bank loans.

REAL-TIME UPDATES
Learn More by Visiting This Website

Extending the reach of business funding through microfinancing

The Association for Enterprise Opportunity promotes the availability of vital financing for *microbusinesses*, those with up to five employees. Go to **real-timeupdates.com/bia9** and select Learn More in the Students section.

Venture Capitalists

At the other end of the funding scale are **venture capitalists (VCs)**, investment specialists who raise pools of capital from large private and institutional sources (such as pension funds) to finance ventures that have high growth potential and need large amounts of capital. VC funding provides a crucial stimulus to the economy by making risky, early-stage investments in firms that are likely to become major employers if their products succeed in the marketplace. Because one-third of VC-funded start-ups don't succeed, those that do succeed need to really pay off to compensate the VCs involved. VCs are therefore extremely focused and selective; they invest in only a few thousand companies in the United States every year.[22]

Given the amounts of money involved and the expectations of sizable returns, VCs usually invest in high-potential areas such as information technology, energy, biotechnology, and digital media. Unlike banks or most other financing sources, VCs do more than simply provide money. They also provide management expertise in return for a significant ownership interest in the business. Once the business becomes profitable, VCs reap the rewards by selling their interest to long-term investors, usually after the company goes public.

venture capitalists (VCs)
Investors who provide money to finance new businesses in exchange for a portion of ownership, with the objective of selling their shares at a significant gain.

When you pitch your business to investors, be prepared to face tough questions about how the company will compete successfully in your chosen markets.

angel investors
Private individuals who invest money in start-ups, usually earlier in a business's life and in smaller amounts than VCs are willing to invest or banks are willing to lend.

Angel Investors

Start-up companies that aren't good candidates for VC funding (or aren't far enough along to attract VC investment) often look for **angel investors**, private individuals who put their own money into start-ups, with the goal of eventually selling their interest at a gain. These individuals are willing to invest smaller amounts than VCs and often stay involved with the company for a longer time. Angels invest in roughly 10 times as many start-ups as VCs every year and provide 90 percent of the outside capital for start-up companies.[23] Many of these investors join *angel networks* or *angel groups* that invest together in chosen companies. Angel investing tends to have a more local focus than venture capitalism, so you can search for angels through local business contacts and organizations.

Credit Cards and Personal Lines of Credit

Although they tend to be one of the most expensive forms of financing, credit cards are widely available and sometimes the only source of funding an entrepreneur has. While funding a business with credit cards or a personal line of credit might be the only option for many people, it can be a risky approach if the business doesn't generate enough revenue to make the payments. Unfortunately, there is no simple answer about whether to use credit cards; some entrepreneurs have used them to launch successful, multimillion-dollar businesses, whereas others have destroyed their credit ratings and racked up debts that take years to pay off.

REAL-TIME UPDATES
Learn More by Visiting This Website

Venture capital that doesn't care where you came from

The investors behind the Hustle Fund don't care about your pedigree; they want to know if you have a good idea and know how to hustle. Go to **real-timeupdates.com/bia9** and select Learn More in the Students section.

REAL-TIME UPDATES
Learn More by Visiting This Website

Find your investing angel or become one yourself

The Angel Capital Association offers a wealth of guidance for early-stage investors and entrepreneurs. Go to **real-timeupdates.com/bia9** and select Learn More in the Students section.

Small Business Administration Assistance

The SBA offers several financing programs for small businesses. To get an SBA-backed loan, you apply to a regular bank or credit union, which actually provides the money. The SBA guarantees to repay most of the loan amount (the percentage varies by program) if you fail to do so. In addition to operating its primary loan guarantee program, the SBA also manages a microloan program in conjunction with not-for-profit, community-based lenders.[24]

The Small Business Investment Companies (SBICs) created by the SBA are another option for raising money. These firms offer loans, venture capital, or a combination of the two. SBICs have their own criteria for lending and investing, although most target established, profitable businesses.[25]

PUBLIC FINANCING

Companies with solid growth potential may also seek funding from the public at large, although only a small fraction of the companies in the United States are publicly traded. Whenever a corporation offers its shares of ownership to the public for the first time, the company is said to be *going public*. The shares

initial public offering (IPO)
A corporation's first offering of shares to the public.

offered for sale at this point are the company's **initial public offering (IPO)**. Going public is an effective method of raising needed capital, but it can be an expensive and time-consuming process with no guarantee of raising the amount of money needed.

CROWDFUNDING

crowdfunding
Soliciting project funds, business investment, or business loans from members of the public.

Crowdfunding is an intriguing twist to funding that combines elements of public and private financing in which a company gathers funds from members of the public by encouraging a large number of people to contribute to or invest in a new project or a new company. Kickstarter (**www.kickstarter.com**) is perhaps the best known of these web services that provide a way for people and organizations to seek money from the public. Crowdfunding services fall into two general categories. Kickstarter and similar sites focus on individual projects or charitable endeavors, and people provide money in exchange for the product being created or simply to help people and causes they believe in. In contrast, services such as Crowdfunder (www.crowdfunder.com) and Indiegogo (www.indiegogo.com) help business owners raise money to launch or expand companies, and the people who provide money are investing in or lending to the company.

 CHECKPOINT

LEARNING OBJECTIVE 5: Discuss the principal sources of funding for small businesses.

SUMMARY: Sources of *private financing* for small businesses include banks and microlenders, venture capitalists, angel investors, credit cards and personal lines of credit, and loan programs from the Small Business Administration. Companies that reach sufficient size with continued growth potential have the additional option of seeking *public financing* by selling shares. Crowdfunding gathers funds from members of the public by encouraging a large number of people to contribute to or invest in a new project or a new company.

CRITICAL THINKING: (1) Would a profitable small business with only moderate growth potential be a good candidate for venture capitalist funding? Why or why not? (2) Why would angel investors help finance companies privately, rather than buying shares of publicly traded companies?

IT'S YOUR BUSINESS: (1) Would you be willing to take on credit card debt in order to start a company? Why or why not? (2) What would it take to convince you to invest in or contribute to a crowdsourced start-up?

KEY TERMS TO KNOW: seed money, microlenders, venture capitalists (VCs), angel investors, initial public offering (IPO), crowdfunding

---

The Franchise Alternative

An alternative to creating or buying an independent company is to buy a **franchise**, which grants the buyer the rights to use various components of an established business. In these relationships, the **franchisor** is the company that founded the business, and a **franchisee** is an individual or company that buys the rights to use some aspect of that business. Franchising is a major component of the economy in terms of both product sales and employment, and many well-known companies in fast food, fitness, hotels, and other industries are operated as franchises.

TYPES OF FRANCHISES

Franchise arrangements come in two primary types. The type most people are thinking of when they talk about franchising is the *business-format franchise*. This is by far the most common model and is used by many well-known companies, including McDonald's, 7-Eleven, Dunkin' Donuts, and The UPS Store. This arrangement is also the most comprehensive. The franchisee gains the right to use an entire business system, including brand names, store designs, operating processes, and more.[26]

The second type of franchising allows independent business owners to affiliate with well-known brand names and sell popular products without the constraints of operating within a strictly defined business format. A *product-distribution franchise* gives the franchisee the right to sell products as part of a franchisor's distribution system. New cars, gasoline,

6 **LEARNING OBJECTIVE**

Explain the advantages and disadvantages of franchising.

franchise
A business arrangement in which one company (the franchisee) obtains the rights to sell the products and use various elements of a business system of another company (the franchisor).

franchisor
A company that licenses elements of its business system to other companies (franchisees).

franchisee
A business owner who pays for the rights to sell the products and use the business system of a franchisor.

Franchising is a popular route into small-business ownership. Many of the restaurants and service businesses you see across the country are franchises.

beverages, and home appliances are some of the common products that are often marketed via this model.[27] For example, Ford Motor Company manufacturers the cars and trucks that bear its name, but those vehicles are sold through independent dealers that purchase the right to sell the vehicles and use the Ford brand name.

THE MONEY SIDE OF FRANCHISING

Owning a business-format franchise involves both initial and ongoing costs. These costs vary widely, based on the complexity and popularity of the franchise.

Initial Franchising Costs

The initial costs of launching a franchise come in two parts. The first is a one-time payment called the *franchise fee*, which gives the franchisee access to the system along with a variety of start-up services that can include site-location studies, market research, training, initial advertising, and guidance on building or preparing a facility that meets the franchisor's standards. This fee typically ranges from $25,000 to $75,000.[28]

The second part involves all the costs associated with buying, building, and equipping a facility, as needed, and in some cases the supplies required to get going. This amount can range from a few thousand dollars for a simple home-based service business to a million dollars or more for a popular fast-food restaurant to tens of millions of dollars for luxury hotel chains.

All start-up costs, the franchise fee, and any required operating capital are summed up in an amount labeled the *initial investment*. In many cases, franchisees must also meet minimum levels of liquid assets (spendable cash, essentially) and personal net worth.

Ongoing Franchising Costs

Franchisees also incur one or two types of ongoing costs related to their franchise license (in addition to the usual business expenses of materials, rent, payroll, and so on). Most systems require *royalty payments* that are based on a percentage of revenue. These are paid at regular intervals, such as monthly or quarterly. Most royalty payments fall in the range of 4 to 9 percent, although they can run considerably higher.[29] Some franchise systems also require franchisees to make regular payments to an advertising fund. Together, these two recurring payments can add up to 10 to 12 percent of revenue.

ADVANTAGES OF FRANCHISING

Franchising is a popular option for many people because it combines some of the freedom of working for oneself with many of the advantages of being part of a larger, established organization. You can be your own boss, hire your own employees, and benefit directly from your own hard work. If you invest in a successful franchise, you know you are getting a viable business model, one that has worked many times before. If the franchise system is well managed, you get the added benefit of instant name recognition, national advertising programs, training, standardized quality of goods and services, a support network of other franchisees, financial assistance (in some systems), and a proven formula for success.[30]

DISADVANTAGES OF FRANCHISING

Although franchising offers many advantages, it is not the ideal vehicle for everyone. Perhaps the biggest disadvantage is the relative lack of control, at several levels:

- When you buy into a franchise system, particularly a business-format franchise, you agree to follow the business format, and franchisors can prescribe virtually every aspect of the business, from the color of the walls to the products you can carry. In fact, if your primary purpose in owning a business is the freedom to be your own boss, franchising probably isn't the best choice because you don't have a great deal of flexibility in many systems.

EXHIBIT 6.6	Key Questions to Ask Before Signing a Franchise Agreement

Before signing a franchise agreement, be sure to read the *franchise disclosure document*, which covers 21 aspects of the business arrangement. Here are some of the key questions to consider.

1. What are the total start-up costs? What does the initial franchise fee cover? Does it include a starting inventory of supplies and products?

2. Who pays for employee training?

3. How are the periodic royalties calculated, and when must they be paid?

4. Who provides and pays for advertising and promotional items? Do you have to contribute to an advertising fund?

5. Are all trademarks and names legally protected?

6. Who selects or approves the location of the business?

7. Are you restricted to selling certain goods and services?

8. Are you allowed to sell online?

9. How much control will you have over the daily operation of the business?

10. Is the franchise assigned an exclusive territory?

11. If the territory is not exclusive, does the franchisee have the right of first refusal on additional franchises established in nearby locations?

12. Is the franchisee required to purchase equipment and supplies from the franchisor or other suppliers?

13. Under what conditions can the franchisor and/or the franchisee terminate the franchise agreement?

14. Can the franchise be assigned to heirs?

Source: Buying a Franchise: A Consumer Guide, U.S. Federal Trade Commission, June 2015, www.ftc.gov.

- As a franchisee, you usually have little control over decisions the franchisor makes that affect the entire system. However, many systems have advisory councils that give franchisees the chance to share ideas and concerns.

- If the fundamental business model of the franchise system no longer works—or never worked well in the first place—or if customer demand for the goods and services you sell declines, you don't have the option of independently changing your business in response.

HOW TO EVALUATE A FRANCHISING OPPORTUNITY

With so much at stake, researching a franchising opportunity carefully is vital (see Exhibit 6.6). The U.S. Federal Trade Commission requires franchisors to disclose extensive information about their operations to prospective franchisees, including background information on the company and its executives, the company's financial status, the history of any litigation involving other franchisees, initial and ongoing costs, all restrictions put on franchisees, the availability and cost of training, procedures for ending the franchise agreement, earnings projections, and the names of current and former franchise owners. All this information is available in the *franchise disclosure document*. Study this document and talk to as many current and former franchise owners as you can before taking the plunge.[31]

 CHECKPOINT

LEARNING OBJECTIVE 6: Explain the advantages and disadvantages of franchising.

SUMMARY: Franchising appeals to many because it combines some of the advantages of independent business ownership with the resources and support of a larger organization. It can also be less risky than starting or buying an independent business because you have evidence that the business model works. The primary disadvantages are the lack of control and the costs, both the initial start-up costs and the monthly payments based on a percentage of sales.

CRITICAL THINKING: (1) Why might a business owner with a successful concept decide to sell franchises rather than expand the company under his or her own control? (2) Why might someone with strong entrepreneurial spirit be dissatisfied with franchise ownership?

IT'S YOUR BUSINESS: (1) Are you a good candidate for owning and operating a franchise? Why or why not? (2) Think about a small-business idea you've had or one of the small businesses you patronize frequently. Could this business be expanded into a national or international chain? Why or why not?

KEY TERMS TO KNOW: franchise, franchisee, franchisor

7 **LEARNING OBJECTIVE**

Define *machine learning* and *deep learning*, and describe their importance to contemporary business.

machine learning
The general capability of computers to learn.

deep learning
A type of machine learning that uses layers of neural networks to attack problems at multiple levels.

Thriving in the Digital Enterprise: Machine Learning and Deep Learning

For any artificial intelligence (AI) system to possess intelligence, it needs to be able to learn, which can include such scenarios as understanding text, converting spoken language to written text, and recognizing the content of photographs and videos. **Machine learning** refers to the general capability of computers to learn. Don't be thrown off by the "machine" part; it always refers to software running on a computer or other digital device, although that computer might be embedded in a machine such as a robot.

Intelligent systems learn by being trained through extensive exposure to vast numbers of images, text fragments, handwriting samples, recordings of human speech, email messages, or whatever types of data the system is designed to process. Not surprisingly, big data plays an important role in today's AI systems. (Note that any system will only be as accurate as the data it is trained on. Recall from page 157 the bias problem, Joy Buolamwini discovered when she realized that some facial recognition systems at the time couldn't "see" her dark-skinned, female face because they had been trained primarily on white, male faces.)

GOING DEEPER WITH DEEP LEARNING

Deep learning is a specific type of machine learning that uses layers of *artificial neural networks* to mimic the function of neurons and neural networks in the brain. Deep learning uses networks of computer processors working in parallel as artificial neurons, mirroring the brain's neural connections. Each of these neurons processes numerical inputs from multiple other neurons and outputs a value that other neurons can use. All these neurons interact and dynamically produce an answer in response to whatever inputs the system has received.[32]

For this process to work, all the neurons in the network need to know *how* to process the values they receive from other neurons, and they gain this capability by being trained on massive data sets. After each training pass, the neurons' numerical outputs are adjusted to reduce errors. The training process is repeated, millions of times in some cases, until the error rate is reduced to an acceptable level.[33]

Now for the "deep" part of deep learning. These systems solve problems using successive layers of neural networks, with each layer trained to figure out one piece of the puzzle. Exhibit 6.7 offers a conceptual view of how this works, in this case with image recognition. Deep learning systems can continuously adapt and teach themselves how to keep learning, so their potential extends beyond more basic machine learning systems.

These neural networks are "deep" in another way, too, in that the people who create and use them can't always explain how they work, which creates the concerns over transparency and accountability described in Chapter 4. Research into just how these networks function is an ongoing theoretical conversation.[34]

EXHIBIT 6.7	Deep Learning

As this simplified view of deep learning indicates, a system is first trained on millions of photos, video captures, word strings, or whatever content it is designed to analyze. The layers of neural networks are fine-tuned until they become increasingly accurate, and then the system is ready to use. It works in layers to decode whatever is presented to it, with each neural network layer analyzing a particular aspect. Note that the system doesn't "know" anything about horses or animals in the same way humans do. Instead, it concludes that the attributes it is seeing in this image match the attributes it has seen in other images of horses, so it also concludes that there is a high probability that this is a horse, too.

1. System is first trained on millions of images, words, or other objects, with the neural layers adjusted for increased accuracy.

2. An object (such as an image for an image-recognition system) is presented to the system.

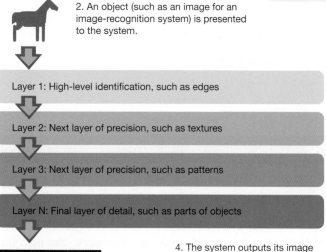

Layer 1: High-level identification, such as edges

Layer 2: Next layer of precision, such as textures

Layer 3: Next layer of precision, such as patterns

Layer N: Final layer of detail, such as parts of objects

3. Each layer analyzes a particular aspect of the object, starting from high-level identification down through increasing degrees of detail and precision.

Object: Purple horse

4. The system outputs its image identification, text translation, or whatever it is designed to produce.

Source: Based on information from Chris Olah, "Understanding the Inner Workings of Neural Networks," The Keyword blog, 12 March 2018, www.blog.google.

THE BUSINESS SIDE OF MACHINE LEARNING AND DEEP LEARNING

Why does any of this matter to a business professional? Thanks to several advances in methodology and technology that occurred more or less simultaneously a few years ago, machine learning and deep learning applications are exploding in the business world. Self-driving cars, automated image recognition on social media and on manufacturing production lines, real-time translation, virtual assistants on mobile devices, automated medical diagnosis, sentiment analysis that reads the emotional state of the Twittersphere, malware and intrusion threat analysis on computer networks, automated investing systems, product recommendations on Amazon, those uncannily accurate movie recommendations that show up in your Netflix account—all these rely on machine learning or deep learning.[35]

To be sure, deep learning has a lot of hype surrounding it, and not all the applications you hear about will become mainstream. In fact, in 2017, the research and consulting firm Gartner had deep learning at the very top of the "inflated expectations" peak in its hype cycle (see page 68).[36] However, with so many proven applications already and so much continuing research and development (Google alone is working on more than 1,000 deep learning projects), deep learning is here to stay. Venture capitalists are pouring billions of dollars into AI and deep learning start-ups, and over a few short years, deep learning has gone from a sci-fi curiosity to a feature that many VCs expect to see in new products.[37]

✓ CHECKPOINT

LEARNING OBJECTIVE 7: Define *machine learning* **and** *deep learning*,
and describe their importance to contemporary business.

SUMMARY: Machine learning refers to an AI system's ability to learn after being trained on massive sets of whatever types of data a system is designed to analyze, from photos to speech recordings. Deep learning is a type of machine learning that uses layers of artificial neural networks to process incoming data and dynamically learn how to become more accurate. Both categories are used widely in business today, with applications in virtually every functional area.

CRITICAL THINKING: If you were asked to invest in or take a job in a company that claims to be innovating in the deep learning arena, what steps could you take to separate the hype from the business reality?

IT'S YOUR BUSINESS: Would you be comfortable using a deep learning system in your job if you or the people who created it can't explain how it worked? Why or why not?

KEY TERMS TO KNOW: machine learning, deep learning

BEHIND THE SCENES

Alyza Bohbot Finds a New Purpose in Her Purpose-Driven Business

When Alyza Bohbot returned home to Duluth, Minnesota, and assumed ownership of Alakef Coffee Roasters, she fulfilled her mission of keeping her parents' company in the family. However, that proved to be only the beginning of her journey in the coffee business.

Many of the world's 25 million coffee farms are small, family-owned businesses. Overall, women perform an estimated 70 percent the work involved in growing, harvesting, and distributing coffee, but in many countries, cultural and legal constraints deny them fair compensation for their work or access to vital resources.

At a meeting of the International Women's Coffee Alliance (IWCA) not long after she had taken over as owner as Alakef, Bohbot heard the story of a widowed coffee farmer in Colombia who was unable to finance equipment she needed in order to keep her farm going. Her husband had been killed in the armed conflict that has flared up throughout the country for decades, and banks refused to lend money to a woman. Bohbot decided then that she had to do something to help.

Supporting women through organizations such as the IWCA and the Café Femenino Foundation, which helps women and families in coffee-growing regions, was an important step but not enough. Bohbot wanted an entire company whose mission was to balance the inequalities faced by women in the global coffee business. "I wanted to do something no one else is doing and genuinely make a difference."

While continuing to run Alakef, she started a second company to pursue this vision. From its name to a pink-centric brand design scheme that Bohbot calls "unapologetically feminine,"

there's no mistaking the intent of City Girl Coffee. She believes it is the only coffee roaster in the country that aims to source its beans entirely from farms that are owned or managed by women. And she gives a portion of the company's profits to the organizations helping women in the coffee business.

Her purpose-driven business approach isn't always easy. Working through the international web of coffee bean distributors to find beans grown by female farmers takes more time and effort, and it increases the risk of supply shortages. Consultants advised against creating a brand so decidedly feminine, and some competitors have sniped that the brand and the message are just a marketing ploy.

But Bohbot is committed to her cause and is winning fans. The digital media company Refinery29, which focuses on issues that affect young women and takes a dim view of products that are artificially gendered as a cynical marketing appeal to female consumers, applauds City Girl Coffee's authenticity and bold approach. And, with an insight that every smart marketing professional will recognize, Bohbot is totally comfortable with the fact that the brand won't resonate with all coffee drinkers—and it shouldn't try to.

City Girl Coffee is winning over customers, too. A growing number of consumers, across many product categories, want their purchases to align with their values, and the younger consumers Bohbot targets are responding. In the company's second year, sales increased 300 percent—the kind of growth that every start-up dreams about. Bohbot has her eye on the long game, though, and is being careful not to grow so fast she loses the ability to pursue the purpose that inspired her in the first place.[38]

Critical Thinking Questions

6-1. Some companies have been criticized for gendering products such as tools and toys in an attempt to appeal to girls and women. The phrase "pink it and shrink it" is sometimes used to describe what critics see as meaningless and cynical attempts to make products feminine. Alyza Bohbot enthusiastically and unapologetically branded City Girl Coffee in a feminine style. Why does this approach work so well for City Girl Coffee?

6-2. What are the business risks of Bohbot's product-sourcing and branding strategies?

6-3. Aside from the socially conscious element of sourcing coffee from women-owned farms, what are the marketing advantages of Bohbot's business model and branding strategy? (Feel free to look ahead to Chapter 12's discussions of segmentation and targeting to get more insights on this question.)

Learn More Online

Visit **www.citygirlcoffee.com** and explore the About and Buy Coffee sections. How does the design and content compare with other online commerce sites you visit frequently? If you drink coffee, does the website's presentation make you inclined to purchase from City Girl Coffee?

End of Chapter

KEY TERMS

advisory board (201)
angel investors (204)
business accelerators (201)
business incubators (201)
business plan (197)
crowdfunding (204)
deep learning (208)
entrepreneurial spirit (193)
franchise (205)

franchisee (205)
franchisor (205)
initial public offering (IPO) (204)
machine learning (208)
microlenders (203)
pivoting (199)
seed money (202)
small business (191)
venture capitalists (VCs) (203)

TEST YOUR KNOWLEDGE

Questions for Review

6-4. What contributions do small businesses make to the society?

6-5. What is meant by the term entrepreneurial spirit?

6-6. How do lean business plans differ from conventional business plans?

6-7. Why might buying an existing independent business sometimes be more efficient than starting a new one?

6-8. What are the advantages and disadvantages of owning a franchise?

6-9. What are the key reasons for most small-business failures?

6-10. Why should a business be willing to pivot?

6-11. How does venture capital investing differ from angel investing?

6-12. What is deep learning?

Questions for Analysis

6-13. Why is the entrepreneurial spirit vital to the health of the economy?

6-14. Could writing a conventional business plan ever cause more harm than good? Explain your answer?

6-15. Is pivoting a sign of failure for a young company? Why or why not?

6-16. What are the financing options for entrepreneurs looking to start their own business?

6-17. **Ethical Considerations.** You're thinking about starting your own chain of upscale, drive-through espresso stands. You have several ideal sites in mind, and you've analyzed the industry and all the important statistics. You have financial backing, and you really understand the coffee market. In fact, you've been a regular at a competitor's operation for more than a month.

The owner thinks you're his best customer, but you're not there because you love the espresso. No, you're actually spying. You're learning everything you can about the competition so you can outsmart them. Is this behavior ethical? Explain your answer.

Questions for Application

6-18. Intrapreneurship should be encouraged at the workplace. It can lead to new innovations and ideas as well as streamlining and cost cutting. How might an organization encourage intrapreneurs to flourish?

6-19. Based on your total life experience up to this point—as a student, consumer, employee, parent, and any other role you've played—what sort of business would you be best at running? Why?

6-20. If you wanted some assistance in setting up and running a new business, you might look at business incubators as a solution. What kind of assistance would you consider the most valuable?

6-21. You love building and fine-tuning business systems in order to figure out the best ways to create and deliver products, solve customer problems, and so on. After 10 years in a corporate job, you're ready to apply this passion to your own company. You're intrigued by the systematic approaches the world's most successful franchising operations use to multiply their market reach. Would buying a franchise be a good choice for you? Why or why not?

6-22. Concept Integration. Entrepreneurship is one of the five factors of production, as discussed in Chapter 2 (page 77). Review that material and explain why entrepreneurs are an important factor for economic success.

6-23. Concept Integration. Pick a local small business or franchise that you visit frequently and discuss whether that business competes on price, speed, innovation, convenience, quality, or any combination of those factors. Be sure to provide some examples.

EXPAND YOUR KNOWLEDGE

Discovering Career Opportunities

You have been inspired by Brian Chesky, Joe Gebbia, and Nathan Blecharczyk, the co-founders of Airbnb, to be an entrepreneur yourself. Starting a company is not easy, yet you are determined to own and operate your own business. You think this chapter will be the turning point in your life.

Read articles on Airbnb online. You consider Brian and Joe as your mentors. Which entrepreneurial characteristics determined their success? Which entrepreneurial characteristic will you be able to exhibit to run your own business? How have their business failures motivated you in your personal and professional networks? Besides Airbnb, what other business and social support could you possibly benefit from? You are also keen to reach out to local entrepreneurial support groups. Who are these groups, and in what ways could they offer advice?

Intelligent Business Technology: Deep Learning

Research a current business application of deep learning and write a one-paragraph summary of how companies are using it and how it helps them compete or satisfy customers more effectively.

PRACTICE YOUR SKILLS

Resolving Ethical Dilemmas

One of an entrepreneur's greatest gifts is the ability to see into the future, to see where things are heading, whether it's good or bad. Assume you lead a start-up that is in the meal-delivery business. Your team delivers ready-to-eat meals from local restaurants. Sales have been modest so far, enough to keep the company going but nothing spectacular. You are starting to think the company might do better by pivoting into the meal kit arena, where it would deliver ready-to-cook meals instead. These subscription-based services might be able to get around the biggest problem you have now: unpredictable demand from customers who use the service occasionally but may not use it for weeks at a time.

Here's the catch: A pivot like this would force a major change in your business model. Rather than maintaining relationships with restaurants, for example, you would have to develop relationships with farmers and food wholesalers. And here's the dilemma: You will need a couple of months to study the market and see how companies such as Plated and Blue Apron succeed in it. If you do decide to pivot, it will probably mean shaking up the team, with at least a few people losing their jobs. Should you tell your employees you are considering this pivot now, but won't have an answer for two months, or wait until you've completed your investigation? Explain your answer.

Growing as a Professional

Exhibit 1.3 on page 53 lists many of the ways that a business mindset differs from a consumer mindset . You can develop your business mindset by honing your entrepreneurial instincts. Whenever you see or hear about a product that intrigues you, imagine what it would take to design, produce, market, deliver, and service it. Think about what it would be like to lead a company through some or all these steps in the process. Imagine what would be needed to get started in that business. This sort of "useful daydreaming" can get you thinking about what it takes to build a company and whether you could be successful as an entrepreneur in that market.

Sharpening Your Communication Skills

To receive both financial and nonfinancial support, entrepreneurs need to be able to communicate their plan, vision, and ideas to others. Imagine that you want to start your own business.

In small groups or individually, come up with an idea for a business venture and devise a business plan that can be presented before potential investors. Make sure you include a clear vision for the business and your financial projections. Use specific examples to convince the investors.

Building Your Team Skills

The questions shown in Exhibit 6.6 cover major issues you should explore before investing money in a franchise. However, there are many more questions you should ask in the process of deciding whether to buy a particular franchise.

With your team, browse the franchise listings at **www .entrepreneur.com/business-opportunities** to find an interesting opportunity. Read the information on this site, then explore the franchising section of the chosen company's website for more information. Next, generate a list of at least 10 questions an interested buyer should ask about this potential business opportunity.

Choose a spokesperson to present your team's ideas to the class. After all the teams have reported, hold a class discussion to analyze the lists of questions generated by all the teams. Which questions were on most teams' lists? Why do you think those questions are so important? Can your class think of any additional questions that were not on any team's list but seem important?

Developing Your Research Skills

There are many opportunities for individuals to gain support and funding for their business ideas. Research the different sources of funding and support that would be available to you if you started your own business.

- As a university student, what opportunities have you found so far for your business idea? Discuss the different sources of support that may be available to you.
- Compare two of the sources of support. What do they offer? Why would each be beneficial to your idea?
- Why might now be a good time to start your own business?

Writing Assignments

6-24. Given the risks involved in starting any company, should an aspiring entrepreneur investigate all possible failure scenarios and develop action plans to avoid these potential outcomes? Explain your answer.

6-25. Is "I don't like having a boss tell me what to do" a good reason to start your own company? Explain your answer.

ENDNOTES

1. "About," City Girl Coffee, accessed 2 April 2018, www.city girlcoffee.com; "One Cup of Coffee, Two Spoons of Equality: City Girl Coffee Is on a Mission to Help Women Producers," *See Change*, 27 September 2017, www.seechangemagazine.com; Lissa Maki, "New Alakef CEO Launches City Girl Coffee," Perfect Duluth Day blog, 4 April 2016, www.perfectduluthday. com; Dan Hyman, "Family Business Gets a Jolt with Coffee That Empowers Women," *New York Times*, 21 December 2017,www .nytimes.com; Clint Rainey, "This 'Unapologetically Feminine' Coffee Brand Sources All Its Beans from Women," *Grubstreet*, 21 December 2017, www.grubstreet.com; Olivia Harrison, "City Girl Coffee Co. Is the Food Brand for Women We Actually Need," *Refinery29*, 22 December 2017, www.refinery29.com; Amy Rea, "City Girl Coffees from Alakef Coffee," Heavy Table, 16 November 2015, heavytable.com.
2. "Firm Size Data," U.S. Small Business Administration, accessed 1 April 2018,www.sba.gov.
3. "Size Standards," U.S. Small Business Administration, accessed 31 March 2018,www.sba.gov; "Table of Size Standards," U.S. Small Business Administration, effective 31 July 2018,www.sba .gov.
4. U.S. Small Business Administration, *Frequently Asked Questions: Advocacy the Voice of Small Business in Government*, September 2012.
5. U.S. Small Business Administration, *Frequently Asked Questions: Advocacy the Voice of Small Business in Government*.
6. "Number of Women-Owned Businesses Growing 2.5 Times Faster Than National Average," American Express, 8 November 2017,www.americanexpress.com.
7. David K. Williams, "The 4 Essential Traits of 'Intrapreneurs,'" *Forbes*, 30 October 2013,www.forbes.com; Murray Newlands, "10 Things Entrepreneurs Need to Know About Intrapreneurship," *Inc.*, 6 January 2015,www.inc.com.
8. Simone Ahuja, "What It Takes to Innovate Within Large Corporations," *Harvard Business Review*, 15 June 2015, hbr.org.
9. "Buy an Existing Business or Franchise," U.S. Small Business Administration, accessed 31 March 2018,www.sba.gov.
10. Joshua Hyatt, "The Real Secrets of Entrepreneurs," *Fortune*, 15 November 2004, 185–202.
11. Heidi Brown, "How to Write a Winning Business Plan," *Forbes*, 18 June 2010,www.forbes.com; Michael Gerber, "The Business Plan That Always Works," *Her Business*, May/June 2004, 23–25; J. Tol Broome, Jr., "How to Write a Business Plan," *Nation's Business*, February 1993, 29–30; Albert Richards, "The Ernst & Young Business Plan Guide," *R & D Management*, April 1995, 253; David Lanchner, "How Chitchat Became a Valuable Business Plan," *Global Finance*, February 1995, 54–56; Marguerita Ashby-Berger, "My Business Plan—And What Really Happened," *Small Business Forum*, Winter 1994–1995, 24–35; Stanley R. Rich and David E. Gumpert, *Business Plans That Win $$$* (New York: Harper & Row, 1985).

12. Bill Reichert, "Getting to Wow!" Garage Technology Ventures, accessed 31 March 2018, www.garage.com; "Writing a Compelling Executive Summary," Garage Technology Ventures, accessed 31 March 2018, www.garage.com.

13. Strategyzer, accessed 31 March 2018, www.strategyzer.com; "More About the Lean Canvas," Canvanizer, accessed 31 March 2018, canvanizer.com.

14. Adam Ozimek, "No, Most Restaurants Don't Fail in the First Year," *Forbes*, 29 January 2017, www.forbes.com.

15. Selcuk Atli, "The Startup Pivot Pyramid," 500 Startups, 24 May 2016, 500.co; Jason Nazar, "14 Famous Business Pivots," *Forbes*, 8 October 2013, www.forbes.com.

16. OPEN Forum, accessed 31 March 2018, www.americanexpress.com/us/small-business/openforum/explore.

17. Michele Lerner, "How to Choose the Best Advisory Board for Your Small Business," *Forbes*, 11 December 2015, www.forbes.com.

18. Martin Zwilling, "Every Startup Gains from an Incubator or Accelerator," *Entrepreneur*, 25 May 2016, www.entrepreneur.com.

19. Techstars website, accessed 31 March 2018, www.techstars.com; Hubert Zajicek, "Accelerator vs. Incubator: Which Is Right for You?" *Entrepreneur*, 26 May 2017, www.entrepreneur.com; Zwilling, "Every Startup Gains from an Incubator or Accelerator."

20. Norman M. Scarborough and Jeffrey R. Cornwall, *Essentials of Entrepreneurship and Small Business Management*, 8th ed. (New York: Pearson, 2016), 501–502.

21. Benjamin Pimentel, "Microloans: 13 Top U.S. Nonprofit Lenders," NerdWallet, 26 October 2016, www.nerdwallet.com.

22. National Venture Capital Association website, accessed 31 March 2018, www.nvca.org.

23. "Who Is the American Angel?" Angel Capital Association, accessed 31 March 2018, www.angelcapitalassociation.org; National Venture Capital Association website, accessed 31 March 2018, www.nvca.org.

24. U.S. Small Business Administration website, accessed 31 March 2018, www.sba.gov.

25. U.S. Small Business Administration website, accessed 31 March 2018, www.sba.gov.

26. Scarborough and Cornwall, *Essentials of Entrepreneurship and Small Business Management*, 252.

27. Michael Seid, "Product and Trade Name Franchising (Traditional Franchising)," *The Balance*, 25 February 2017, www.thebalance.com; Scarborough and Cornwall, *Essentials of Entrepreneurship and Small Business Management*.

28. "Franchise Hub," *Entrepreneur*, accessed 1 April 2018, www.entrepreneur.com.

29. Andrew Seid, "The Basics of Franchise Royalty Payments," *The Balance*, 27 July 2017, www.thebalance.com; Jeff Elgin, "Are Royalty Fees the Norm with Franchises?" *Entrepreneur*, 2 December 2013, www.entrepreneur.com.

30. Scarborough and Cornwall, *Essentials of Entrepreneurship and Small Business Management*, 256.

31. *Buying a Franchise: A Consumer Guide*, U.S. Federal Trade Commission, accessed 1 April 2018, www.ftc.gov.

32. Michael Copeland, "What's the Difference Between Artificial Intelligence, Machine Learning, and Deep Learning?" Nvidia blog, 29 July 2016, blogs.nvidia.com.

33. Nikola M. Živkovi?, "How Do Artificial Neural Networks Learn?" Code Project, 21 January 2018, www.codeproject.com; Chris Olah, "Understanding the Inner Workings of Neural Networks," The Keyword blog, 12 March 2018, www.blog.google; Copeland, "What's the Difference Between Artificial Intelligence, Machine Learning, and Deep Learning?"

34. Natalie Wolchover, "New Theory Cracks Open the Black Box of Deep Learning," *Quanta*, 21 September 2017, www.quantamagazine.org.

35. Christine Taylor, "Machine Learning vs. Deep Learning: In Apps and Business," *Datamation*, 10 January 2018, www.datamation.com; Bernard Marr, "The Top 10 AI and Machine Learning Cases Everyone Should Know About," *Forbes*, 30 September 2016, www.forbes.com; Copeland, "What's the Difference Between Artificial Intelligence, Machine Learning, and Deep Learning?"

36. Louis Columbus, "Gartner's Hype Cycle for Emerging Technologies, 2017 Adds 5G and Deep Learning for First Time," *Forbes*, 15 August 2017, www.forbes.com.

37. Roger Parloff, "Why Deep Learning Is Suddenly Changing Your Life," *Fortune*, 28 September 2016, fortune.com.

38. See note 1.

Guiding the Enterprise: Leadership, Organization, and Operations

Now it's time to look at the nature and role of management, the options managers have for organizing the workforce, and the systems that companies use to create goods and services. Chapter 7 introduces the four key functions of management and the essential skills that managers need. Chapter 8 explores the many ways to organize a company, from traditional command-and-control structures to new virtual forms. Chapter 9 looks at the systems mindset and how it relates to the production of goods, the performance of services, and attention to quality.

CHAPTER **7** **Management Roles, Functions, and Skills**

CHAPTER **8** **Organization and Teamwork**

CHAPTER **9** **Production Systems**

Cathy Yeulet/123RF

7

Management Roles, Functions, and Skills

LEARNING OBJECTIVES After studying this chapter, you will be able to

1 Explain the importance of management, and identify the three vital management roles.

2 Describe the planning function, and outline the strategic planning process.

3 Describe the organizing function, and differentiate among top, middle, and first-line management.

4 Describe the leading function, leadership style, and organizational culture.

5 Describe the controlling function, and explain the four steps in the control cycle.

6 Identify and explain four important types of managerial skills.

7 Discuss the potential of cognitive automation in management decision-making.

MyLab Intro to Business
Improve Your Grade!
If your instructor is using MyLab Intro to Business, visit **www.pearson.com/mylab/intro-to-business**.

BEHIND THE SCENES

AMD: An Innovative Company in Need of Innovative Business Management

When she took over as president and CEO of AMD, Dr. Lisa Su had to figure out how to turn around a company with a history of innovation but serious financial troubles.

www.amd.com

If you appreciate the gaming performance of your Microsoft Xbox One or Sony PS4, you have Dr. Lisa Su to thank. As senior vice president and general manager at Advanced Micro Devices (AMD), she led the effort to get the company's high-performance processors into these gaming consoles. Not long after, she was promoted to president and CEO, fulfilling an ambition to run a company after an impressive career in the semiconductor industry.

Being CEO of a semiconductor company might have been Su's dream job, but the scenario she took over at AMD in 2014 was closer to a nightmare. After years of running a distant second to industry leader Intel in the market for the processing chips that drive computers, game consoles, and other devices, AMD hadn't turned a profit since 2011. After multiple stumbles, including a major acquisition that didn't pan out, late product deliveries, and decisions to exit high-end segments of the market, the company was in such dire straits that some analysts wondered if it would survive much longer.

Even though AMD has been a perennial runner-up to Intel in terms of market share, it has always been a respected innovator that has advanced the state of the art in semiconductor design in multiple ways. And Su had the level of engineering chops that AMD has always been known for. Earlier in her career at IBM, she was chosen to be the special technical adviser to the CEO, and she is a fellow of the Institute of Electrical and Electronics Engineers with more than 40 published papers to her name.

Technical acumen wasn't the problem. The problem was on the business side of the equation. AMD was heavily in debt, sales and market share were dropping, and the company's strategic directions and resources weren't well aligned with the most promising market opportunities. Occasional successes such as the Xbox One and PS4 wins weren't enough. If you were in Lisa Su's position, what steps would you take to pull AMD back from the brink? How would you reshape strategy and redirect the company's talent? And critically, could you do it in time to prevent a total collapse?[1]

INTRODUCTION

Whether they are first-line supervisors or top executives such as Lisa Su (profiled in the chapter-opening Behind the Scenes), managers have tremendous influence over the success or failure of the companies they lead. If you aspire to become a manager, you can improve your chances of success by gaining a thorough understanding of what being a manager really entails. This chapter explores the roles that managers play, the functions they perform, and the essential skills they need.

The Roles of Management

Management comprises the interrelated tasks of planning, organizing, leading, and controlling in pursuit of organizational goals.[2] To perform these tasks effectively, managers engage in *interpersonal roles, information roles,* and *decisional roles.*

Lisa Su no longer designs circuits, but the decisions she makes, the organizational framework she establishes, the expectations she sets, the executives she hires to run various parts of the company, and the culture she establishes all have an enormous impact on the company's success. Likewise, the executives who report to her aren't directly engaged in the tasks of creating products and supporting customers. However, within the scope of his or her own responsibilities, each of these managers also has significant influence on the company's fortunes. Although managers don't usually do the hands-on work in an organization, they create the environment and provide the resources that give employees opportunities to excel in their work.

In addition, given the effect that managerial decisions and behaviors have on employees, customers, investors, and other stakeholders, it's no exaggeration to say that management is one of the most vital professions in the contemporary economy. The quality of management can make or break a company by inspiring and enabling employees—or by destroying morale and motivation. In fact, half of the employees in the United States report having left a job in order to escape an incompetent or toxic boss.[3]

Managers who effectively and ethically guide their companies contribute greatly to our standard of living and our economic security. By the same measure, managers who fail, through poor planning, misguided decisions, or questionable ethics, can create havoc that extends far beyond the walls of their own companies. In other words, management is one of the most important functions in society, not just within the sphere of business.

INTERPERSONAL ROLES

Management is largely a question of getting work accomplished through the efforts of other people, so a manager must play a number of interpersonal roles, including leading employees, building relationships, and acting as a liaison between groups and individuals both inside and outside the company (such as suppliers, government agencies, consumers, labor unions, and community leaders). Effective managers tend to excel at networking, fostering relationships with many people within their own companies and within the industries and communities where their companies do business.

1 **LEARNING OBJECTIVE**

Explain the importance of management, and identify the three vital management roles.

management
The process of planning, organizing, leading, and controlling to meet organizational goals.

Interpersonal roles are an essential aspect of management.

INFORMATIONAL ROLES

Managers spend a fair amount of time gathering information from sources both inside and outside an organization. The higher up they are, the more they rely on subordinates to collect, analyze, and summarize information—and the greater the risk that they will fall out of touch with what is happening on "the front lines," where the essential day-to-day work of the organization is performed.

Not surprisingly, listening is one of the most vital skills a manager can have. When Bill Sandbrook took over as CEO of U.S. Concrete, it was on perilous financial footing and in dire need of strategic guidance; he spent most of his first three months on the job simply listening. Even though he had decades of experience elsewhere in the industry, he knew he had much to learn from the firm's employees and customers.[4]

Managers also communicate information to employees, other managers, and other stakeholders. This communication involves virtually every form of information, from technical and administrative information to motivational speeches to strategic planning sessions. And it involves every form of media, from private conversations to digital messaging to videoconferences that connect managers with employees across the country or around the world.

The increasing use of social media for both internal and external communication is changing the nature of the manager's informational role in many companies. In the past, communication was often concentrated in formal channels that tended to flow in only one direction at a time, such as from a manager down to his or her subordinates or from "the company" to customers. With social media, a more conversational model is emerging, in which more people can participate and communication is more immediate and less formal. The smart use of social media is helping managers learn more from employees and customers and communicate with stakeholder groups more effectively.

DECISIONAL ROLES

Managers up and down the organizational ladder face an endless stream of decisions. Many of these decisions are fairly routine, such as choosing which of several job candidates to hire or setting the prices of new products. Other decisions, however, might occur only once or twice in a manager's career, such as responding to a product-tampering crisis or the threat of a hostile takeover. Some decisions are made after extensive information gathering and analysis; others must be made on the spot, with little else but judgment and intuition to guide the manager's choice.

REAL-TIME UPDATES
Learn More by Reading These Articles

Decision-making advice for leaders and aspiring leaders

The *Harvard Business Review* offers an extensive library of articles on all aspects of decision-making. Go to **real-timeupdates.com/bia9** and select Learn More in the Students section.

One of the most significant changes that has occurred in business management in recent years is the effort to push decision-making as far down the organizational pyramid as possible, giving whichever employees face a particular situation the authority to make decisions about it. This approach not only accelerates and improves work flow and customer service but also frees up higher-level managers to work on more strategic matters.

As you'll read on page 235, *cognitive automation* is another intriguing innovation in management decision-making. Many companies are exploring the use of AI to augment their managers' decision-making skills.

Being able to move among these roles comfortably while performing the basic management functions is just one of the many skills that managers must have. The following sections provide a closer look at those four basic functions—planning, organizing, leading, and controlling.

CHECKPOINT

LEARNING OBJECTIVE 1: Explain the importance of management, and identify the three vital management roles.

SUMMARY: Managers create the environment and provide the resources that give employees opportunities to excel in their work. Managerial responsibilities include creating the organizational framework, fostering a positive culture, and setting expectations. The three vital managerial roles are interpersonal (interacting with others), informational (receiving and sharing information), and decisional (making decisions).

CRITICAL THINKING: (1) How are social media changing the nature of a manager's information role? (2) Would managers get more respect from employees if they "rolled up their sleeves" and pitched in with the daily work more often? Why or why not?

IT'S YOUR BUSINESS: (1) Review the process you went through to choose the college you are currently attending. What lessons from your experience could someone apply to managerial decision-making? (2) Do you believe you have the right personality for management? If not, what areas would you work on?

KEY TERM TO KNOW: management

The Planning Function

Managers engage in **planning** when they develop strategies, establish goals and objectives for the organization, and translate those strategies and goals into action plans. **Strategic plans** outline the firm's long-range (often two to five years) organizational goals and set a course of action the firm will pursue to reach its goals. The *strategic planning process* consists of six interrelated steps: defining the organization's purpose and values, performing a SWOT analysis, developing forecasts, analyzing the competition, establishing goals and objectives, and developing action plans (see Exhibit 7.1 on the next page).

DEFINING THE COMPANY'S PURPOSE AND VALUES

To achieve any level of strategic clarity, planners first need to agree on why the company exists—its *purpose*—and how it will conduct itself as it pursues its goals—its *values*.

Companies use a variety of statements to articulate their purpose; unfortunately, there is no universal terminology for these, so the labels can get a bit confusing. The term **mission statement** is probably the most commonly used. Some companies use the term *vision statement* or *statement of purpose*. To add to the confusion, some companies use a *vision statement* to define an ideal future they wish to create or be a part of as well as a *mission statement* to express what they will do to make that future come into being.

Regardless of the terminology, defining a clear purpose is essential because it gives a company focus. For example, the medical device manufacturer Welch Allyn defines its mission as providing "superlative medical products, services and solutions which are used by health-care professionals at the point of care in acute and primary settings all around the world."[5] Note how this statement clearly defines the scope of the company's activities and its priorities in serving its target customers. Just as important, it eliminates activities the firm could pursue, such as creating medical products for consumers, which would give the company a distinctly different strategic focus.

To complement the mission statement, many companies develop a **values statement** that identifies the principles that guide the company's decisions and behaviors and establish expectations for everyone in the organization. For instance, in addition to such attributes as integrity, service, fun, and inclusiveness, Enterprise Holdings (the parent company of Enterprise Rent-A-Car, Alamo, and National Car Rental) identifies hard work as one of its values: "Running a successful business is hard work. Commit to your responsibilities and your future, and you'll receive the accolades and rewards you deserve."[6]

2 **LEARNING OBJECTIVE**

Describe the planning function, and outline the strategic planning process.

planning
Establishing objectives and goals for an organization and determining the best ways to accomplish them.

strategic plans
Plans that establish the actions and the resource allocation required to accomplish strategic goals; they're usually defined for periods of two to five years and developed by top managers.

mission statement
A brief statement of why an organization exists; in other words, what the organization aims to accomplish for customers, investors, and other stakeholders.

values statement
A brief articulation of the principles that guide a company's decisions and behaviors.

| EXHIBIT 7.1 | The Strategic Planning Process |

Specific firms have their own variations of the strategic planning process, but these six steps offer a good general model. The circular arrangement is no coincidence, by the way. Strategic planning should be a never-ending process as you establish strategies, measure outcomes, monitor changes in the business environment, and make adjustments as needed.

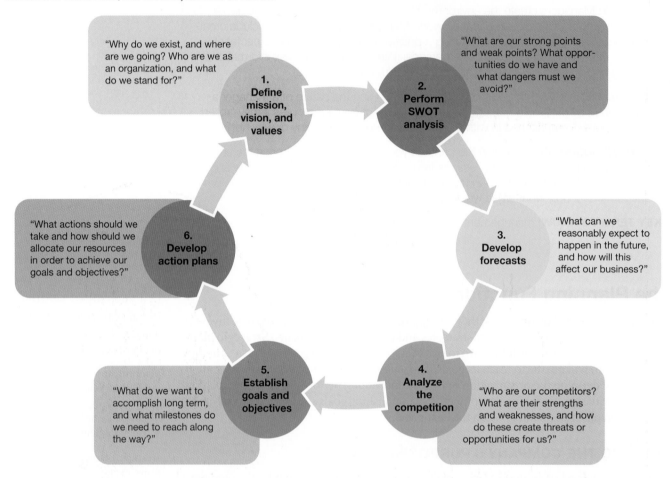

"Why do we exist, and where are we going? Who are we as an organization, and what do we stand for?"

1. Define mission, vision, and values

"What are our strong points and weak points? What opportunities do we have and what dangers must we avoid?"

2. Perform SWOT analysis

"What can we reasonably expect to happen in the future, and how will this affect our business?"

3. Develop forecasts

"Who are our competitors? What are their strengths and weaknesses, and how do these create threats or opportunities for us?"

4. Analyze the competition

"What do we want to accomplish long term, and what milestones do we need to reach along the way?"

5. Establish goals and objectives

"What actions should we take and how should we allocate our resources in order to achieve our goals and objectives?"

6. Develop action plans

ASSESSING STRENGTHS, WEAKNESSES, OPPORTUNITIES, AND THREATS

Before establishing long-term goals, a company needs to have a clear assessment of its strengths and weaknesses relative to the opportunities and threats it faces. This analysis is commonly referred to as SWOT (pronounced "swat"), which stands for strengths, weaknesses, opportunities, and threats.

Strengths are positive internal factors that contribute to a company's success, which can be anything from a team of expert employees to financial resources to unique technologies. *Weaknesses* are negative internal factors that inhibit the company's success, such as obsolete facilities, inadequate financial resources to fund growth, or lack of managerial depth and talent. Identifying a firm's internal strengths and weaknesses helps management understand its current abilities so it can set proper goals. When Lisa Su assessed the situation at AMD after taking over as CEO, for instance, she probably would have pegged engineering talent as a strength and debt as a weakness.

After taking inventory of the company's internal strengths and weaknesses, the next step is to identify the external opportunities and threats that might significantly affect the firm's ability to attain desired goals. *Opportunities* are positive situations that represent the

Enterprise Rent-A-Car clearly articulates its company values and expects managers and employees to uphold them in their work.

EXHIBIT 7.2	SWOT Analysis

Identifying a firm's strengths, weaknesses, opportunities, and threats is a common strategic planning technique. Here are some examples of the factors a company might identify during a SWOT analysis.

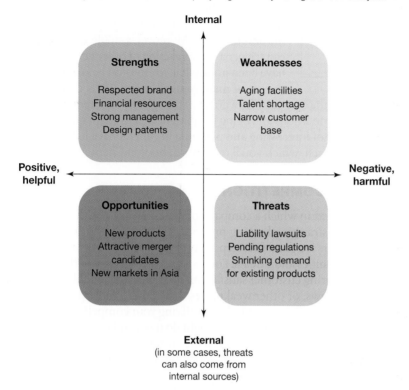

possibility of generating new revenue. Shrewd managers and entrepreneurs recognize opportunities before others do and then promptly act on their ideas.

Threats are negative forces that could inhibit a firm's ability to achieve its objectives, including such external factors as new competitors, new government regulations, economic contraction, changes in interest rates, disruptions in supply, technological advances that render products obsolete, theft of intellectual property, product liability lawsuits, and even the weather. Depending on the company and the industry, it can also be helpful to consider internal threats if they have the potential to disrupt business.

Exhibit 7.2 offers a handy visual to remember the four components of a SWOT analysis.

DEVELOPING FORECASTS

By its very nature, planning requires managers to make predictions about the future. Forecasting is a notoriously difficult and error-prone part of strategic planning. Managers need to predict not only *what* will (or will not) occur, but also *when* it will occur and *how* it will affect their business. Forecasting influences the decisions managers make regarding virtually every business activity, and misreading the future can damage or even destroy a company.

Managerial forecasts fall under two broad categories: *quantitative forecasts,* which are typically based on historical data or tests and often involve complex statistical computations, and *qualitative forecasts,* which are based more on intuitive judgments. Neither method is foolproof, but both are valuable tools and are often used together to help managers fill in the unknown variables that inevitably crop up in the planning process. For example, managers can make statistical projections of next year's sales based on data from previous years while factoring in their judgment about the impact of new competitors, changing regulations, or other external forces.

REAL-TIME UPDATES
Learn More by Reading This Article

Getting past the "hockey stick"

Forecasting too often succumbs to irrational optimism in which projected sales magically bend upward like a hockey stick. Go to **real-timeupdates.com/bia9** and select Learn More in the Students section.

As important as forecasting is, it represents a vexing paradox because, to a significant degree, the future is simply not predictable. Technology, fashion, and other influential forces often move forward in lurches and leaps that are difficult to predict. Extraordinary events—such as wars, economic meltdowns, or natural disasters—can play havoc with the best forecasts. Moreover, a single surprising development can trigger a chain reaction of other developments that might have been impossible to envision before. One key element in the art of management, therefore, is crafting plans that are solid enough to move the company forward in a strategically coherent direction while staying alert to changing conditions and being flexible enough to adapt quickly when things do change. The difficulty of forecasting and planning in general have led many organizations to adopt an *agile* approach, which you'll read more about in Chapter 8.

ANALYZING THE COMPETITION

The competitive context in which a company operates needs to be thoroughly understood and factored into the strategic planning process. Performing a SWOT analysis on each of your major competitors is a good first step. Identifying *their* strengths and weaknesses helps pinpoint *your* opportunities and threats. For instance, if you discover that one of your competitors has been suffering customer satisfaction problems, that could be a sign of financial difficulties, product flaws, or other weaknesses that could create opportunities for you to capture additional market share. Similarly, identifying your competitors' opportunities and threats can give you insight into what they might do next, and you can plan accordingly.

Competitive analysis should always keep the customer's perspective in mind. You may believe you have the best product, the best reputation, and the best customer service, but the only beliefs that matter are those of your target customers. Conversely, you might believe that a competitor's less expensive products are inferior, but those products might well be good enough to meet customers' needs—meaning that the higher cost of your higher-quality products puts you at a disadvantage.

ESTABLISHING GOALS AND OBJECTIVES

goal
A broad, long-range target or aim.

objective
A specific, short-range target or aim.

Although the terms are often used interchangeably, it helps to think of a **goal** as a broad, long-range accomplishment that the organization wants to attain and to think of an **objective** as a specific, short-range target designed to help reach that goal. For AMD, a *goal* might be to capture 15 percent of the market for smartphone processors over the next five years, and an *objective* in support of that goal might be to introduce a new and faster model every year.

Businesspeople are often advised to make their goals and objectives "SMART," as in *specific, measurable, attainable, relevant,* and *time limited.* For example, "substantially increase our sales" is a poorly worded statement because it doesn't define what *substantially* means or when it should be measured. This acronym can be a helpful reminder to set meaningful goals, but as with the paradox of forecasting, it's important to use good judgment and be flexible, too.[7] For example, you may not know whether a goal is attainable until you try to reach it, or you might reach it easily and realize you set your sights too low.

For more on the benefits and risks of goal setting, see pages 305–306.

DEVELOPING ACTION PLANS

With strategic goals and objectives in place, the next step is to develop a plan to reach them. Plans are often organized in a hierarchy, just as a company itself is. For instance, the overall strategic plan might be supported at the next level down by a research and development plan, a manufacturing plan, and a marketing plan, describing how each functional area will help the company reach its strategic goals and objectives.

The names and contents of these *tactical plans* or *operational plans* vary widely by industry, company, and business function. Some address all the actions required in a particular department or functional area over a recurring time frame, such as a quarter or a year, whereas others address all the tasks involved in a single project or event. For example, a *launch plan* for a new product might cover a period that begins several months or a year before the product is introduced to the public and extends several months after the launch. Such a plan would identify all the actions needed to coordinate the launch of the product, including the production ramp-up, promotional activities, sales training, physical distribution, and every other task and resource allocation decision needed to get the new product off to a successful start.

By the way, crafting a solid plan and carrying it through to completion are great ways to make a name for yourself early in your career, even for relatively simple projects. Demonstrate that you can figure out what needs to be done, coordinate all the resources, and then bring the project in on schedule and on budget. Upper managers will notice and keep you in mind when they need people to take on more challenging and important projects.

 CHECKPOINT

LEARNING OBJECTIVE 2: Describe the planning function, and outline the strategic planning process.

SUMMARY: Planning is the process of developing strategies, establishing goals and objectives for the organization, and translating those strategies and goals into action plans. Plans vary in their time frame and scope, from high-level, long-range strategic plans to lower-level, short-term tactical and operational plans. The strategic planning process consists of six interrelated steps: defining the organization's purpose and values, performing a SWOT analysis, developing forecasts, analyzing the competition, establishing goals and objectives, and developing action plans.

CRITICAL THINKING: (1) Would Boeing and Old Navy develop strategic plans over the same time horizon? Why or why not? (2) How does the mission statement guide the planning process?

IT'S YOUR BUSINESS: (1) What is your personal mission or vision statement for your career and your life? Have you ever thought about your future in this way? (2) Consider a career path that you might pursue upon graduation, and perform a quick SWOT analysis. What are some of your internal strengths and weaknesses and external opportunities and threats?

KEY TERMS TO KNOW: planning, strategic plans, mission statement, values statement, goal, objective

The Organizing Function

Organizing, the process of arranging resources to carry out an organization's plans, is the second major function of managers. To organize effectively, managers must think through all the activities that employees perform, as well as all the facilities and equipment employees need in order to complete those activities. Managers also give people the ability to work toward company goals by determining who will have the authority to make decisions, to perform or supervise activities, and to distribute resources. Chapter 8 discusses the organizing function in more detail; for now, it's sufficient to recognize the three levels of management in a typical corporate hierarchy—top, middle, and first-line. Together, they make up the **management pyramid** (see Exhibit 7.3 on the next page).

TOP MANAGERS

Top managers are the upper-level managers, such as Lisa Su, who have the broadest authority and who take overall responsibility for an organization. This tier includes corporate officers and usually the next layer or two of management beneath them, depending on

3 **LEARNING OBJECTIVE**
Describe the organizing function, and differentiate among top, middle, and first-line management.

organizing
The process of arranging resources to carry out the organization's plans.

management pyramid
An organizational structure divided into top, middle, and first-line management.

EXHIBIT 7.3	The Management Pyramid

Here are some of the typical jobs at the three basic levels of management.

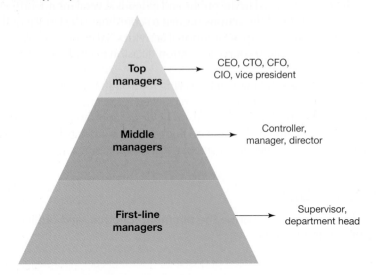

top managers
Those at the highest level of the organization's management hierarchy; they are responsible for setting strategic goals, and they have the most power and responsibility in the organization.

the size and structure of the company. The term *executive* applies to top managers. Typical job titles include the "C"-level positions, such as chief marketing officer (CMO) and chief financial officer (CFO), and vice presidents (the largest corporations may have dozens of vice presidents overseeing various divisions or functions).

Top managers establish the structure for the organization as a whole, and they select the people who fill the upper-level positions. Top managers also make long-range plans, establish major policies, and often represent the company to the media, the community, and other stakeholders. Two significant ways in which top management differs from lower management tiers are the long time frames executives must work with and the magnitude of the decisions they need to make. Given the difficulty and importance of these strategic decisions, the ability to make tough judgment calls is highly valued in top executives.

MIDDLE MANAGERS

middle managers
Those in the middle of the management hierarchy; they develop plans to implement the goals of top managers and coordinate the work of first-line managers.

Middle managers have similar responsibilities but on a smaller scale, such as for an individual division or facility. The term *middle management* is somewhat vague, but in general, managers at this level report upward to top executives, and first-line managers report to middle managers. In other words, they usually manage other managers, not workers. A smaller company might have a single layer of middle management (or none at all, in many cases), whereas a large corporation could have a half-dozen or more layers of middle managers. Typical titles at this level are department manager and business unit manager.[8]

The term *middle management* is sometimes used disparagingly, giving the impression that middle managers are "bureaucrats" who clog up the works without adding much value. Some observers have gone so far as to blame such managers for much that ails the modern corporation.[9] Many companies have also *flattened* their organizational structures by removing one or more layers of middle management.

However, middle managers play the essential role of translating strategic goals and objectives into the actions that allow the company to meet those targets. Although they may not do the actual day-to-day work, middle managers are the

REAL-TIME UPDATES
Learn More by Visiting This Website

Mistakes can be great teachers

Fortunately, you don't need to make the mistakes yourself. You can borrow the hard-won wisdom of dozens of entrepreneurs and executives. Go to **real-timeupdates.com/bia9** and select Learn More in the Students section.

ones who put the systems and resources in place so that front-line teams can work efficiently and with coordinated purpose. They also provide vital coaching and mentoring for first-line managers who are making the transition to management. As leadership consultant Steve Arneson emphasizes, "It's the leaders in the middle who must communicate and execute strategy, solve problems, create efficiencies, and manage performance."[10] In his analysis of the video game industry, Wharton management professor Ethan Mollick concluded that middle managers who oversaw new game development had a greater impact on company performance than the top managers who set strategy or the developers who designed and created the games.[11]

FIRST-LINE MANAGERS

At the bottom of the management pyramid are **first-line managers** (or *supervisory managers*). They oversee the work of nonmanagerial employees, and they put into action the plans developed at higher levels. Titles at this level include supervisor and office manager.[12] The types of employees these managers supervise vary widely, from entry-level workers with limited experience and education to advanced experts in engineering, science, finance, and other professional specialties.

first-line managers
Those at the lowest level of the management hierarchy; they supervise the operating employees and implement the plans set at the higher management levels.

Like managers at the levels above them, first-line managers face challenges unique to their position in the hierarchy. As the direct interface between "management" and the employees, they have the most immediate responsibility for ensuring that necessary work is done according to agreed-on performance standards. They must also deal with any friction that exists between employees and management. Supervisors are also usually quite involved in recruiting, hiring, and training of employees. In this role, they perform the vital task of making sure that employees acquire the skills they need and that they adapt to the organization's culture.

 CHECKPOINT

LEARNING OBJECTIVE 3: Describe the organizing function, and differentiate among top, middle, and first-line management.

SUMMARY: The organizing function involves arranging an organization's resources in the best way possible to help reach its goals and objectives. Top managers grapple with long-range, strategic issues and often must make decisions about events and conditions several years into the future. They also have important communication roles, representing the company to external stakeholders. Middle managers usually have responsibility over individual divisions or facilities and are charged with translating strategic plans into the tactical plans that will allow the company to reach its goals and objectives. First-line managers supervise nonmanagement employees; they have the shortest time horizons and greatest tactical perspective.

CRITICAL THINKING: (1) Why might a manager need to deemphasize skills honed in previous positions as he or she rises through the organizational hierarchy? (2) Would top managers or first-line managers typically have more or less of the information they'd like to have for the decisions they need to make? Why?

IT'S YOUR BUSINESS: (1) Based on your experience leading teams or supervising people at work, how would you rate your performance as a manager? (2) If you were suddenly promoted to manage the department you've been working in, would you change your "work" personality? Why or why not?

KEY TERMS TO KNOW: organizing, management pyramid, top managers, middle managers, first-line managers

4   **LEARNING OBJECTIVE**

Describe the leading function, leadership style, and organizational culture.

leading

The process of guiding and motivating people to work toward organizational goals.

The Leading Function

Leading is the process of influencing and motivating people to work willingly and effectively toward common goals. Managers with good leadership skills have greater success in influencing the attitudes and actions of others and motivating employees to put forth their best performance.

All managers must be effective leaders to be successful, but management and leadership are not the same thing. One way to distinguish between the two is to view management as the rational, intellectual, and practical side of guiding an organization and to view leadership as the inspirational, visionary, and emotional side. Both management and leadership involve the use of power, but management involves *position power* (so called because it stems from the individual's position in the organization), whereas leadership involves *personal power* (which stems from a person's own unique attributes, such as expertise or charisma).[13]

Successful leaders tend to share many of the same traits, but no magical set of personal qualities automatically destines someone for leadership. Nevertheless, in general, good leaders possess a balance of several types of intelligence:

- *Cognitive intelligence* involves reasoning, problem solving, memorization, and other rational skills. Obviously, leaders need a sufficient degree of cognitive intelligence to understand and process the information required for planning and decision-making in their jobs.
- *Emotional intelligence* is a measure of a person's awareness of and ability to manage his or her own emotions and to recognize emotional states in others. People with high emotional intelligence are tuned into their own emotional states and the effect those emotions have on others, and they are able to regulate their emotional responses in order to minimize the disruption caused by negative emotions and to use positive emotions to enhance the emotional well-being of people around them.[14]
- *Social intelligence* involves looking outward to understand the dynamics of social situations and the emotions of other people in addition to your own.[15] Socially adept managers have a knack for finding and building common ground with people of all kinds. Moreover, leaders, in a sense, "infect" their organizations with their own emotions, positive or negative.[16]

All three types of intelligence are essential to building the competencies that lead to success. In fact, various studies suggest that in both leadership and life in general, emotional and social intelligence play a far greater role in success than purely cognitive intelligence.[17]

REAL-TIME UPDATES

Learn More by Reading This Article

Company health is every bit as important as personal health

See the strong correlation between a company's "health" (basically, how well it does all the things you're learning in this course) and its long-term performance. Go to **real-timeupdates.com/bia9** and select Learn More in the Students section.

DEVELOPING AN EFFECTIVE LEADERSHIP STYLE

Leadership style can be viewed as finding the right balance between *what* the leader focuses on and *how* he or she makes things happen in the organization. Every manager has a definite style, although good leaders usually adapt their approach to match the requirements of the particular situation.[18] Across the range of leadership styles, you can find three basic types (see Exhibit 7.4). **Autocratic leaders** control the decision-making process in their organizations, often restricting the decision-making freedom of subordinates. Autocratic leadership generally has a bad reputation, and when it's overused or used inappropriately, it can certainly produce bad results or stunt an organization's growth. However, companies can find themselves in situations where autocratic leadership is needed to guide the firm through challenging situations or to bring uncooperative units in line.

Democratic leaders, in contrast, delegate authority and involve employees in decision-making. Also known as *collaborative* leaders, these managers invite and seek input from anyone in the organization who can add insight to the decision-making process. For example, after Salesforce.com installed an internal social networking application that gave everyone in the company the chance to share information, CEO Marc Benioff began monitoring the flow of insights and realized that some of the most valuable information about customers

autocratic leaders

Leaders who do not involve others in decision-making.

democratic leaders

Leaders who delegate authority and involve employees in decision-making.

EXHIBIT 7.4	Leadership Styles

Leadership styles fall on a continuum from autocratic (manager makes the decisions) to democratic (manager and subordinates make decisions together) to laissez-faire (subordinates make decisions on their own). Each style has strengths and weaknesses, and effective managers often adapt their style to suit specific situations.

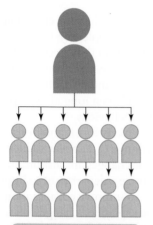
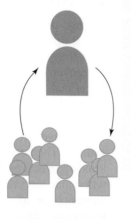
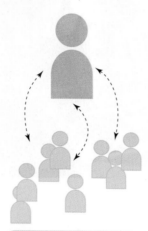

Autocratic Leadership

Manager makes the decisions and issues directives down the chain of command; subordinates have little or no freedom to make decisions, deviate from plans, or provide contrary input.

Democratic Leadership

Manager shares decision-making authority, seeking input and inviting subordinates to participate in a coordinated planning process; group can encourage a change of course if needed.

Laissez-faire Leadership

Manager acts as adviser and supporter, offering input when asked but generally letting subordinates chart and adjust their own course toward meeting agreed-on goals and objectives.

was coming from employees upper management didn't normally communicate with. Inspired by that discovery, he opened the annual strategic planning meeting to the entire company via social networking.[19] This style of offering greater involvement to employees is often called **participative management**.

The third leadership style takes its name from the French term *laissez-faire*, which can be translated roughly as "hands off." **Laissez-faire leaders** take the role of supporters and consultants, encouraging employees' ideas and offering insights or opinions when asked. After the overall strategic direction and priorities are in place, they emphasize **employee empowerment**—giving employees the power to make decisions that apply to their specific aspects of work.

COACHING AND MENTORING

Leaders have an important responsibility for education and encouragement, which may take the form of coaching and mentoring. **Coaching** involves meeting with employees to discuss any problems that may hinder their ability to work effectively and to offer suggestions and encouragement to help them find their own solutions to work-related challenges. (Note that the term *executive coaching* usually refers to hiring an outside management expert for one-on-one development work with senior managers.)

Mentoring is similar to coaching but is based on long-term relationships between senior and junior members of an organization. The mentor is usually an experienced manager or employee who can help guide other managers and employees through the corporate maze. Mentors have a deep knowledge of the business and can explain office politics, serve as role models for appropriate business behavior, and provide valuable advice about how to succeed within the organization. Mentoring programs are used in a variety of ways,

participative management
A philosophy of allowing employees to take part in planning and decision-making.

laissez-faire leaders
Leaders who leave most decisions up to employees, particularly those concerning day-to-day matters.

employee empowerment
Giving employees the power to make decisions that apply to their specific aspects of work.

coaching
Helping employees reach their highest potential by meeting with them, discussing problems that hinder their ability to work effectively, and offering suggestions and encouragement to overcome these problems.

mentoring
A process in which experienced managers guide less experienced colleagues in nuances of office politics, serving as role models for appropriate business behavior and helping to negotiate the corporate structure.

Dmitry Shironosov/123RF

Managers play an important role as coaches and mentors.

such as helping newly promoted managers make the transition to leadership roles and helping women and minorities prepare for advancement.

MANAGING CHANGE

Change presents a major leadership challenge for one simple reason: Many people don't like it, or at least they don't like being told they need to change. Moreover, even when change is clearly necessary and beneficial, it can be stressful and disruptive while the change is taking place and even long after as people settle into new roles and behaviors.

Change can come in many forms and from many sources. The need to change can appear suddenly or build up over time. Some changes are *proactive*, such as when managers reorganize a department to improve work flow or take steps to improve collaboration and teamwork. Many of these planned changes fall under the umbrella of *organizational development*, modifying the structure and dynamics of an organization to improve performance and employee well-being.[20] Other changes are *reactive*, such as when a new competitor jumps into the market or new government regulations appear, forcing companies to change.

Regardless of the factors driving a change, managing change successfully in an organization requires an active approach. A widely used model of change management introduced by psychologist Kurt Lewin advocates three stages: *unfreezing* the status quo, making the change, and *freezing* new behaviors and methods to help ensure that people don't slip back into the old ways of doing things.[21]

Making the actual change is often the easiest of the three steps, ironically enough. The biggest challenges usually occur before the change, when managers need to encourage employees to embrace the need for change, and after the change, when managers need to help employees settle into productive new modes of working. Both challenges are easier to meet when managers (1) carefully study the forces that will work for and against the upcoming change, (2) engage the people who will be affected by the change, and (3) listen to their inputs and accommodate their concerns as much as possible.[22]

REAL-TIME UPDATES

Learn More by Watching These Videos

The wisdom of successful leaders

The TED playlist on leadership offers dozens of presentations by leaders from across the spectrum of human endeavor. Go to **real-timeupdates.com/bia9** and select Learn More in the Students section.

BUILDING A POSITIVE ORGANIZATIONAL CULTURE

organizational culture
A set of shared values and norms that support the management system and that guide management and employee behavior.

Strong leadership is a key element in establishing a productive **organizational culture** (sometimes known as *corporate culture*)—the set of underlying values, norms, and practices shared by members of an organization (see Exhibit 7.5). Culture can be a negative or a positive force in an organization, and managers set the tone by establishing expectations, defining rules and policies that shape behavior, and acting as role models.

Positive cultures create an environment that encourages employees to make smart decisions for the good of the company and its customers. At companies with corporate cultures that support employees, employees routinely go the extra mile to make sure customers are treated well. In contrast, negative, dysfunctional cultures can lead to employee burnout, poor decision-making, and other problems. Microsoft CEO Satya Nadella is earning praise for reforming the tech giant's culture from a high-pressure, hyper-competitive environment to one that is more empathic and cooperative. Nadella emphasizes humility as well, saying he wants to change the company from "know it all" to "learn it all."[23] One key measure of his success is the increasing number of employees who are returning to the company after having left in exhaustion or frustration.[24]

EXHIBIT 7.5	Creating the Ideal Culture in Your Company

You can't create a culture directly, but you can establish the behaviors and values that in turn do create a culture. Use this list of questions to explore the many ways you can foster a positive culture—and avoid the growth of a negative culture.

Vision
- Have you articulated a compelling vision for the company?
- Based on that vision, have you defined a mission statement that employees understand and can implement?

Company Values
- Do employees know how their work relates to this mission?
- Is there a common set of values that binds the organization together?
- Do you and other executives or owners demonstrate these values day in and day out?

People
- How are people treated?
- Do you foster an atmosphere of civility and respect?
- Do you value and encourage teamwork, with all ideas welcomed?
- Do you acknowledge, encourage, and act upon (when appropriate) ideas from employees?
- Do you give employees credit for their ideas?
- Have you shown a positive commitment to a balance between work and personal life?

Community
- Have you clarified how the company views its relationship with the communities it affects?
- Do your actions support that commitment to community?

Communication
- Do you practice and encourage open communication?
- Do you share operating information throughout the company so that people know how the company is doing?
- Do you regularly survey employees on workplace issues and ask for their input on solutions?
- Is there an open-door policy for access to management?

Employee Performance
- Do you handle personnel issues with fairness and respect?
- Do employees receive feedback regularly?
- Are employee evaluations based on agreed-on objectives that have been clearly communicated?

Sources: John Coleman, "Six Components of a Great Corporate Culture," *Harvard Business Review*, 6 May 2013, hbr.org; Andrew Bird, "Do You Know What Your Corporate Culture Is?" *CPA Insight*, February/March 1999, 25–26; Gail H. Vergara, "Finding a Compatible Corporate Culture," *Healthcare Executive*, January/February 1999, 46–47; Hal Lancaster, "To Avoid a Job Failure, Learn the Culture of a Company First," *Wall Street Journal*, 14 July 1998, B1.

 CHECKPOINT

LEARNING OBJECTIVE 4: Describe the leading function, leadership style, and organizational culture.

SUMMARY: Leading is the art and science of influencing and motivating people to work toward common goals. Leaders can exhibit a range of styles in what they choose to focus on (strategic versus operational matters) and how they make things happen (forcing versus enabling). Three specific leadership styles are autocratic, democratic, and laissez-faire. Organizational culture is the set of underlying values, norms, and practices shared by members of an organization.

CRITICAL THINKING: (1) Are management and leadership the same thing? If not, why not? (2) Can a single individual be an autocratic, a democratic, and a laissez-faire leader? Why or why not?

> **IT'S YOUR BUSINESS:** (1) What is your natural inclination in terms of the three basic leadership styles—autocratic, democratic, or laissez-faire? Think about times in school, at work, or in social situations in which you played a leadership role. How did you lead? (2) Does leadership experience in school activities such as student government and athletics help prepare you for business leadership? Why or why not?
>
> **KEY TERMS TO KNOW:** leading, autocratic leaders, democratic leaders, participative management, laissez-faire leaders, employee empowerment, coaching, mentoring, organizational culture

[5] **LEARNING OBJECTIVE**
Describe the controlling function, and explain the four steps in the control cycle.

controlling
The process of measuring progress against goals and objectives and correcting deviations if results are not as expected.

The Controlling Function

Controlling is the management function of keeping a company's activities on track toward previously established goals. The nature of control varies widely, from directly intervening in a process to modifying policies or systems in a way that enables employees to reach their objectives. Traditionally, managers in many companies literally controlled the activities of their subordinates with detailed and exacting work rules. However, management in today's companies tends to emphasize enabling and supporting employees, more than controlling.[25] This is sometimes referred to as *servant leadership*, suggesting that mangers are there to meet the needs of employees, not the other way around.

THE CONTROL CYCLE

A good way to understand managerial control is to envision the *control cycle*, a four-step process of (1) establishing performance standards based on the strategic plan, (2) measuring performance, (3) comparing performance to standards, and (4) responding as needed (see Exhibit 7.6). Of course, the specific steps taken in any situation depend on the industry, the company, the functional area within the company, and the manager's leadership style. In some cases, the control cycle is a formal process with explicit measurements, reports, and other tools. In others, control is subtle.

Establishing Performance Standards

In the first step of the control cycle, managers set *standards*, the criteria against which performance will be measured. Top managers set standards for the organization as a whole, such as revenue and profitability targets. Then, for their individual areas of responsibility, middle and first-line managers set standards based on the overall organizational standards of performance.

Knowing which variables to use as standards and the values to set as performance targets can require a lot of experience and experimentation. Choosing variables that are truly meaningful rather than just easy to measure can also be a significant challenge. For example, *web analytics* software can deliver a lot of data about online traffic, but it might not answer crucial questions such as why website visitors abandon their online shopping carts without buying anything.

benchmarking
Collecting and comparing process and performance data from other companies.

A common approach to setting standards is **benchmarking**, comparing a company's key performance attributes with those of industry leaders.[26] For example, a company might discover that its average revenue per employee (total sales divided by the number of employees) is significantly lower than that of the best company in its industry. With this data point in hand, the company could look for ways to make its selling process more efficient, train salespeople to go after bigger deals, or find other ways to improve the cost-revenue ratio.

One of the most important performance variables that fall under managerial control is *quality*—a measure of how closely activities or outcomes conform to predetermined standards and customer expectations. You'll learn more about quality in such areas as product and process quality in manufacturing and operations management (see page 286) and quality of hire in human resources (see page 331).

EXHIBIT 7.6	**The Control Cycle**

The control cycle starts with setting strategic goals and then establishing performance standards that will tell managers and employers whether the company is on track to meet those goals. As the company goes about its business, performance is measured along the way and then compared against the standards. If performance meets or exceeds the standards, no corrective action is required. However, if performance is below the standards, management can either take steps to improve performance (if the standards are still considered achievable) or lower the standards and possibly reset the goals (if they are deemed to be unachievable).

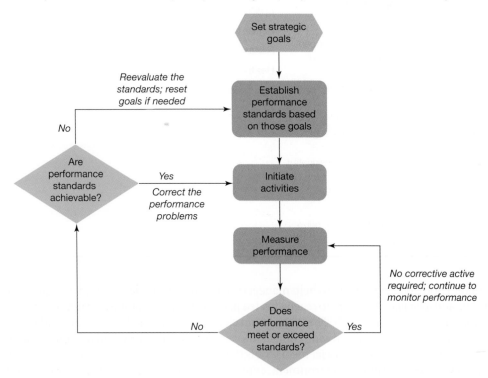

Measuring Performance and Responding as Needed

In the second step of the control cycle, managers assess performance, using both quantitative (specific, numerical) and qualitative (subjective) performance measures. For example, many companies use a **balanced scorecard**, which monitors performance from multiple perspectives, including finances, customers and other stakeholders, internal processes, and organizational capacity (which includes talent, technology, culture, and other components of productive capability).[27]

balanced scorecard
A method of monitoring the performance from four perspectives: finances, operations, customer relationships, and the growth and development of employees and intellectual property.

In the third step, managers compare performance with the established standards. If the level of performance falls short, the next step is usually to take corrective action to improve performance. However, in some cases, managers might decide that the level of performance originally hoped for is not realistic. For example, a sales department might have set aggressive goals for a new product at the beginning of the year, but then a tough competitor appeared out of nowhere three months later. The department manager may have no choice but to lower the sales target for the rest of the year.

CRISIS MANAGEMENT: MAINTAINING CONTROL IN EXTRAORDINARY CIRCUMSTANCES

No matter how well a company plans for its future, mistakes and catastrophes happen. And although not every specific crisis can be envisioned, managers can plan how the company should respond to each type of possible event. **Crisis management** involves the decisions and actions needed to keep a company functioning smoothly and to tend to stakeholder needs during and after an emergency.

crisis management
Procedures and systems for minimizing the harm that might result from some unusually threatening situations.

Successful crisis management requires clear thinking and quick action while a crisis is unfolding, but smart companies don't wait until a crisis hits. A *crisis management plan* needs to

EXHIBIT 7.7	**Communicating in a Crisis**

Crisis situations test a manager's ability to make decisions and communicate clearly.

When a Crisis Occurs:

Do	Don't
Prepare for trouble ahead of time by identifying potential problems, appointing and training a response team, and preparing and testing a crisis management plan.	Blame anyone for anything.
	Speculate in public.
Get top management involved immediately.	Refuse to answer questions.
Set up a news center for company representatives and the media that is equipped with phones, computers, and other digital tools for preparing news releases and online updates. At the news center, take the following steps:	Release information that will violate anyone's right to privacy.
	Use the crisis to pitch products or services.
• Issue frequent news updates, and have trained personnel available to respond to questions around the clock.	Play favorites with media representatives.
• Provide complete information packets to the media as soon as possible.	
• Prevent conflicting statements, and provide continuity by appointing a single person trained in advance to speak for the company.	
• Tell receptionists and other employees to direct all phone calls to the designated spokesperson in the news center.	
• Provide updates when new information is available via blog posts, Twitter updates, text messaging, Facebook, and other appropriate media.	
Tell the whole story—openly, completely, and honestly. If you are at fault, apologize.	
Demonstrate the company's concern by your statements and your actions.	

contain both *contingency plans* to help managers make important decisions in a limited time frame and *communication plans* to reach affected parties quickly and forestall rumors and false information (see Exhibit 7.7). The plan should clearly specify which people are authorized to speak for the company, provide contact information for all key executives, and include a list of the news outlets and social media tools that will be used to disseminate information. In today's media-saturated environment, companies need to begin communicating within minutes after a crisis occurs, to reach those who need information and to avoid the appearance of stonewalling or confusion.

 CHECKPOINT

LEARNING OBJECTIVE 5: Describe the controlling function, and explain the four steps in the control cycle.

SUMMARY: The controlling function consists of the activities and decisions involved in keeping a company's activities on track toward previously established goals. The four steps in the control cycle are establishing performance standards based on the strategic plan, measuring performance, comparing performance to standards, and responding as needed.

CRITICAL THINKING: (1) Why is it important to meet the needs of internal customers? (2) Is lowering performance standards in response to a failure to meet those standards necessarily a sign of "giving up"? Why or why not?

IT'S YOUR BUSINESS: (1) Do you benchmark your performance in any aspect of your personal or academic life? If yes, does it help you improve? If not, can you identify some aspects that could potentially benefit from benchmarking? (2) Think back over any crises you've faced in your life. How well did you respond? What would you do differently in a future crisis?

KEY TERMS TO KNOW: controlling, benchmarking, balanced scorecard, crisis management

Essential Management Skills

Managers rely on a number of skills to perform their functions and maintain a high level of quality in their organizations. These skills can be classified as *interpersonal, technical, conceptual,* and *decision-making.* As managers rise through an organization's hierarchy, they may need to deemphasize skills that helped them in lower-level jobs and develop different skills. For instance, staying closely involved with project details is often a plus for first-line supervisors, but it can lead to serious performance issues for higher-level managers who should be spending time on more strategic issues.[28]

6 **LEARNING OBJECTIVE**

Identify and explain four important types of managerial skills.

INTERPERSONAL SKILLS

The various skills required to communicate with other people, work effectively with them, motivate them, and lead them are **interpersonal skills**. Because managers mainly get things done through people at all levels of the organization, such skills are essential. Encouraging employees to work together toward common goals, interacting with employees and other managers, negotiating with partners and suppliers, developing employee trust and loyalty, and fostering innovation are all activities that require interpersonal skills.

interpersonal skills
Skills required to understand other people and to interact effectively with them.

Communication is the most important and pervasive interpersonal skill that managers use. Effective communication not only increases a manager's and an organization's productivity but also shapes the impressions made on colleagues, employees, supervisors, investors, and customers. In your role as a manager, communication allows you to perceive the needs of these stakeholders (your first step toward satisfying them), and it helps you respond to those needs. Moreover, as the workforce becomes more diverse—and as more companies recognize the value of embracing diversity in their workforces—managers need to adjust their interactions with others, communicating in a way that considers the different needs, backgrounds, experiences, and expectations of their workforces.

TECHNICAL SKILLS

A person who knows how to operate a machine, prepare a financial statement, or use a web content management system has **technical skills**, the knowledge and ability to perform the tasks required in a particular job. Technical skills are most important at lower organizational levels because managers at those levels work directly with employees who are using the tools and techniques.

technical skills
The ability and knowledge to perform the mechanics of a particular job.

However, in today's increasingly technology-driven business environment, managers often need to have a solid understanding of the processes they oversee. One obvious reason is that they need to grasp the technical matters if they are to make smart decisions regarding planning, organizing, leading, and controlling. Another key reason for understanding technical matters is that demonstrating a level of technical aptitude gives managers credibility in the eyes of their employees. They may not need to have the hands-on skills that their employees require, but they need to know enough about what their employees do to make insightful decisions.

Managers at all levels use **administrative skills**, which are the technical skills necessary to direct an organization, including scheduling, researching, analyzing data, and managing projects. Managers must know how to start a project or work assignment from scratch, map out each step in the process to its successful completion, develop project costs and timelines, and establish checkpoints at key project intervals.

administrative skills
The technical skills necessary to direct an organization, including scheduling, researching, analyzing data, and managing projects.

CONCEPTUAL SKILLS

Managers need **conceptual skills** to visualize organizations, systems, markets, and solutions—both as complete entities on their own and as interrelated pieces of a whole. For example, the most visible part of a company's accounting system is probably its accounting software and the reports it produces, but the entire system also includes procedures, policies, and the people who process and use financial information. At the same time, the accounting system is also part of an overall business system and needs to integrate seamlessly with sales, purchasing, production, and other functions.

conceptual skills
The ability to understand the relationship of parts to the whole.

Conceptual skills are especially important to top managers because they are the strategists who develop the plans that guide the organization toward its goals. Managers use their conceptual skills to acquire and analyze information, identify both problems and opportunities, understand the competitive environment in which their companies operate, and develop strategies and plans. The ability to conceptualize solutions that don't yet exist, to see things as they could be rather than simply as how they are, is a vital skill for executives.

DECISION-MAKING SKILLS

decision-making skills
The ability to identify a decision situation, analyze the problem, weigh the alternatives, choose an alternative, implement it, and evaluate the results.

Decision-making skills involve the ability to define problems and opportunities and select the best course of action. To ensure thoughtful decision-making, managers can follow a formal process such as the six steps highlighted in Exhibit 7.8:

1. **Recognize and define the problem or opportunity.** Most companies look for problems or opportunities by gathering customer feedback, conducting studies, or monitoring such warning signals as declining sales or profits, excess inventory build-up, or high customer turnover.
2. **Identify and develop options.** The goal of this step is to develop a list of alternative courses of action. A problem that is easy to identify, such as a steady decline in sales revenue, might not have any easy answers. This step requires solid conceptual skills. Managers may need to break old thinking habits and throw away long-held assumptions in order to find promising solutions to tough problems.
3. **Analyze the options.** Once the ideas have been generated, they need to be studied and compared using criteria such as cost, feasibility, availability of resources, market acceptance, potential for revenue generation, and compatibility with the company's mission and values. Some decisions present a simple yes-or-no choice, but others present multiple options that must be compared.

EXHIBIT 7.8	Steps in the Decision-Making Process

Following these six steps will help you make better decisions, particularly if you make a habit of applying what you learn from every decision outcome to the next decision you need to make.

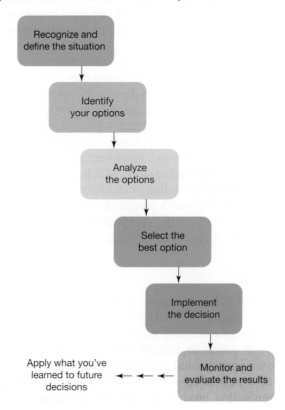

4. **Select the best option.** For some decisions, quantitative analysis can identify a clear choice from the available options. For other decisions, however, managers might have to rely on intuition and experience to point the way.

5. **Implement the decision.** After an option has been selected, it's time to implement the decision.

6. **Monitor the results.** Finally, managers monitor the results of decisions over time to see whether the chosen alternative works, whether any new problems or opportunities arise because of the decision, and whether the decision should be modified to meet changing circumstances.

Although this list presents a logical and comprehensive method for decision-making, it's important to realize that managers must frequently make decisions with incomplete or imperfect information and without as much time as they'd like to study their options.

In other cases, data can't help because there's nothing yet to measure or analyze, such as when a company is exploring uncharted territory with innovative products. These decisions rely more on vision and imagination.[29] They can be the riskiest decisions a manager ever makes, but they can also create entirely new industries when someone imagines a reality that doesn't exist and then moves forward to make it real.

For the latest information on managerial skills, visit **real-timeupdates.com/bia9** and select Chapter 7.

> **REAL-TIME UPDATES**
>
> **Learn More by Reading This Article**
>
> **The stunning decline of an American icon**
>
> See the veritable catalog of bad decisions that undermined General Electric. Go to **real-timeupdates.com/bia9** and select Learn More in the Students section.

 CHECKPOINT

LEARNING OBJECTIVE 6: Identify and explain four important types of managerial skills.

SUMMARY: Interpersonal skills are the abilities to communicate with, motivate, and lead others. Technical skills involve the "mechanics" of a particular job, including the administrative skills of project management. Conceptual skills are the abilities to visualize organizations, systems, markets, and solutions—even when they may not exist yet. Decision-making skills include defining problems and opportunities and selecting the best course of action to take in each case.

CRITICAL THINKING: (1) Why is trust a vital aspect of a manager's interpersonal skills? (2) What are the risks of poorly defining problems or opportunities before making decisions?

IT'S YOUR BUSINESS: (1) Would you succeed as a manager if you started a company right out of college, without having gained any experience as an employee in another company? Why or why not? (2) How would you rate your conceptual skills? Does "seeing the big picture" come easily to you? If not, how might you improve in this area?

KEY TERMS TO KNOW: interpersonal skills, technical skills, conceptual skills, decision-making skills

---

Thriving in the Digital Enterprise: Cognitive Automation

7 LEARNING OBJECTIVE
Discuss the potential of cognitive automation in management decision-making.

Most of us like to think we do a pretty good job of thinking. When we face a decision, we gather the data we need, process them rationally, and choose the best available alternative. If we need to hire someone, for instance, we pick the best candidate from everyone who applied. If we need to make a big sale, we pursue the most attractive prospect and say the right things at the right time.

THE COLD TRUTH ABOUT DECISION-MAKING

The reality is that our quality of thinking and decision-making can be all over the map, from brilliantly insightful to wildly misguided. The evidence of this is just about everywhere you look in the business arena: sure-fire new products that disappear without a trace when they hit the market, companies that ride a wave of customer enthusiasm but somehow stumble into bankruptcy, mergers and acquisitions that destroy millions or billions of dollars of shareholder value, people who quit jobs they were excited to take, and companies that hire hot new talent only to send it packing.

The primary reason people make unsatisfactory decisions is brutally simple: Decision-making is *difficult*. Professionals and managers sometimes have too little data and sometimes too much data. Conditions in the marketplace can change faster than managers can make and implement a decision. And for all its amazing creative capacity, the human mind is not always a finely tuned decision-making machine. We all are vulnerable to perceptual blind spots, logical fallacies, and emotional biases. To complicate matters, we often believe we are better at decision-making than we really are, which removes any incentive to improve.

AI TO THE (POSSIBLE) RESCUE

cognitive automation
AI technology that aims to help professionals and managers with complex questions that present some of the most daunting decision scenarios.

If there's a problem anywhere in the business universe, somebody is working on an artificial intelligence (AI)–based solution. **Cognitive automation** aims to help professionals and managers with complex questions that present some of the most daunting decision scenarios. (A related technology, *robotic process automation*, tackles narrower and more well-defined business tasks. You can read more about it on page 266.)

Unlike some AI techniques that replace human activities, cognitive automation is generally a more collaborative technology that divides decision-making into the components that humans can do well and those that computers can do well. Here are a few examples of cognitive automation capabilities in use today:[30]

- Assembling teams by matching people who are most likely to work together productively on team projects
- Matching individuals with project assignments based on their history of performance on previous projects
- Analyzing financial contracts
- Assessing staff and management performance
- Identifying sales prospects who are most likely to respond positively to a sales call and gathering the optimum set of information that salespeople need to interact with each potential customer (see Exhibit 7.9)

In each of these scenarios, computers take over the tasks they are better at, such as sorting through data files quickly or making personnel decisions based on actual measured performance rather than on "gut feel" or emotional inclination. With machine learning and deep learning, cognitive automation can tap into the vast stores of historical results to make more objective, data-driven decisions.

Salesforce.com, which makes the "Einstein" sales assistant shown in Figure 7.9, uses a version of the same technology itself for strategic analysis and decision-making. CEO Marc Benioff uses it live during executive team sessions to cross-check the information and predictions his managers give him, for instance. He says that by eliminating the human tendencies to skew the facts or tell the boss what people think he wants to hear, the system "has transformed me as CEO."[31]

If cognitive automation handles the data-intensive aspects of decision-making, it could free up managers for the more unstructured, creative, and interpersonal aspects of leadership. As with most aspects of AI, it will be an intriguing journey over the next few years to see how far the technology can or can't go.

EXHIBIT 7.9	**Cognitive Automation**

Cognitive automation helps professionals and managers make more informed decisions by applying predictive analytics and other techniques to characterize likely outcomes of various decision choices. In this example, the Einstein AI from Salesforce.com™ helps sales professionals prioritize which prospects to call on and what information to share with them.

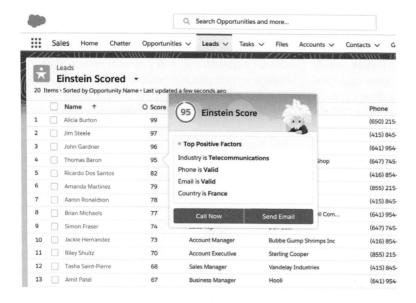

 CHECKPOINT

LEARNING OBJECTIVE 7: Discuss the potential of cognitive automation in management decision-making.

SUMMARY: The promise of cognitive automation is that it can take over the data-intensive aspects of high-level decision-making. Doing so could improve the quality of these decisions and free up managers for more creative and interpersonal work.

CRITICAL THINKING: (1) If cognitive automation takes over the decision-making roles of management, what will be left for managers to do? (2) If a cognitive automation system makes a poor decision, who should take the blame—the people who made it or the people who used it?

IT'S YOUR BUSINESS: As a manager or business owner, would you let an AI system overrule you when it comes to choosing which employees to hire? Why or why not?

KEY TERM TO KNOW: cognitive automation

BEHIND THE SCENES

Lisa Su Pulls Off the Impossible at AMD

When Lisa Su was handed the controls at AMD, fulfilling her ambition to become CEO of a semiconductor manufacturer, it might have looked like a case of "be careful what you wish for." The company had been stumbling badly, with missed opportunities, a failed acquisition that loaded it with billions in debt, unmet promises to customers, unclear and unstable product strategies, and a string of unprofitable years as its sales and share price sank. At one point, the company had gone through four CEOs in four years, leaving employees, customers, and investors with little sense of stability or optimism.

However, Su believed in the company's fundamental strengths and in her own vision to turn it around. Although this was her first stint as a CEO, she was well versed in what it took to lead large technology companies. Like most new CEOs, she had risen through the ranks by taking on increasing levels of responsibility and managing ever-larger organizations. Plus, she had enjoyed a unique opportunity during her stint at IBM, when she was appointed special technical adviser to IBM's new CEO at the time, Lou Gerstner. Gerstner had been brought in to lead a turnaround of the once-mighty king of computers. Su had a front-row seat from which to watch a seasoned CEO execute a major corporate turnaround, which undoubtedly served her well when she faced her own turnaround challenge at AMD.

In the years before Su stepped into the top office, AMD had more or less conceded the high-performance, high-profit segment of the market to Intel and others and was surviving by producing more basic computer chips and competing on low cost. However, even survival was no longer assured at that point, as AMD struggled to pay the interest on its debt amid a string of annual losses.

AMD needed a bold new strike, and Su delivered with a three-pronged strategy. The first element was to move the company back to its roots as a developer of high-end products. The company simplified its product strategy, focusing on a single processor platform that could be leveraged and scaled into a variety of products for specific customer needs, from video game consoles to the powerful server computers used in corporate data centers. And she made sure these priority projects got the resources and management attention they needed.

The second element was committing to deeper relationships with customers. This is vital in a business such as microprocessors, in which chip suppliers compete to score "design wins" where customers such as Sony, Lenovo, or Microsoft design a specific chip into their next new product. A single design win can result in millions of processor sales.

To support the refocused product development effort and the renewed commitment to customer relationships, the third element involved simplifying and focusing the organization. This has improved communication up and down and across the organization and rebuilt the trust and confidence that had ebbed during the years of struggle.

The swift and bold moves paid off—more dramatically and more quickly than many analysts considered possible. Su and her team are earning rave reviews for restoring AMD's "swagger," as one analyst put it, and delivering products that are strong competitors in growing and emerging market segments. Confidence in the company from customers and investors seems to be returning, too, although years of execution problems still leave some skeptical. Su doesn't express any doubts about where the company is heading, though, and is confident that she and her team "can return this company to making a lot of money."[32]

Critical Thinking Questions

7-1. Why might managers and executives fail to react more quickly when their companies begin to stumble?

7-2. What does a new CEO like Su have at stake when launching an ambitious turnaround?

7-3. What sort of internal resistance might Su have encountered when she proposed her turnaround plan?

Learn More Online

Visit AMD's website at **www.amd.com**. Which new products is the company currently highlighting? Which customer segments does it appear to be targeting with these products? If you're a gamer, look through the information the company offers the gaming community. How do these outreach efforts help a company like AMD increase sales?

End of Chapter

KEY TERMS

autocratic leaders (226)
administrative skills (233)
balanced scorecard (231)
benchmarking (230)

coaching (227)
cognitive automation (236)
conceptual skills (233)
controlling (230)

crisis management (231)
decision-making skills (234)
democratic leaders (226)
employee empowerment (227)
first-line managers (225)
goal (222)
interpersonal skills (233)
laissez-faire leaders (227)
leading (226)
management (217)
management pyramid (223)
mentoring (227)

middle managers (224)
mission statement (219)
objective (222)
organizational culture (228)
organizing (223)
**participative
    management** (227)
planning (219)
strategic plans (219)
technical skills (233)
top managers (224)
values statement (219)

TEST YOUR KNOWLEDGE

Questions for Review

7-4. Explain the difference between quantitative and qualitative forecasts, and outline their key advantages and disadvantages.

7-5. What is the purpose of a values statement?

7-6. How would you distinguish between a goal and an objective?

7-7. What is the purpose of a balanced scorecard?

7-8. What responsibilities are associated with management?

7-9. How do autocratic, democratic, and laissez-faire leadership styles differ?

7-10. Why is it likely that managers will fall out of touch with the day-to-day activities of the business as they are promoted to senior levels?

7-11. What is cognitive automation?

Questions for Analysis

7-12. What is the role of emotional intelligence in effective leadership?

7-13. Is it safe for managers to proceed with strategic planning if they haven't done a thorough SWOT analysis or similar assessment? Why or why not?

7-14. Who provides the leadership in a self-managed team or other organizational unit without an appointed manager? Explain your answer.

7-15. If leaders can't identify all the crises that a company might encounter, does it make sense to engage in crisis planning? Why or why not?

7-16. Is laissez-faire leadership equivalent to essentially no leadership at all? Why or why not?

7-17. What might managers need to "unlearn" as they move up the corporate hierarchy?

7-18. What are the possible consequences of reducing middle management positions?

7-19. **Ethical Considerations.** Apart from meeting the company's future talent needs, do managers have a personal ethical obligation to help their employees develop and advance in their careers? Explain your answer.

Questions for Application

7-20. Which would be more difficult to forecast 10 years from now: the number of 60-year-olds or their average disposable income? Why?

7-21. You're the youngest person in your department, and you just got promoted to department manager. What steps could you take to make sure all your employees have confidence in your management and leadership?

7-22. **Concept Integration.** How do mission, vision, and values relate to the notion of a purpose-driven business discussed in Chapter 4?

7-23. **Concept Integration.** What is the principal difference between a business plan (as discussed in Chapter 6) and a strategic plan?

EXPAND YOUR KNOWLEDGE

Discovering Career Opportunities

If you become a manager, how much of your day will be spent performing each of the four basic functions of management? This is your opportunity to find out. Arrange to shadow a manager (such as a department head, a store manager, or a shift supervisor) for a few hours. As you observe, categorize the manager's activities in terms of the four management functions and note how much time each activity takes. If observation is not possible, interview a manager in order to complete this exercise.

7-24. How much of the manager's time is spent on each of the four management functions? Is this the allocation you expected?

7-25. Ask whether this is a typical workday for this manager. If it isn't, what does the manager usually do differently? During a typical day, does this manager tend to spend most of his or her time on one particular function?

7-26. Of the four management functions, which does the manager believe is most important for good organizational performance? Do you agree?

PRACTICE YOUR SKILLS

Resolving Ethical Dilemmas

Imagine that you're a store manager in a large retail chain. Your boss, the regional manager, has just handed you your sales target for the following year. You're not sure whether to laugh or cry. The target is a 20 percent increase over this year—and you and your team are struggling mightily to hit this year's target. Your store's local market has suffered the double whammy of the loss of a major employer, which took a lot of well-paying jobs with it, *and* the appearance of a major competitor. You'll be thrilled if you can hit this year's target, but you don't see any way you'll be able to sell 20 percent more next year.

You explain this to your boss, to no avail. The boss is merely passing along a goal from corporate, and it's not negotiable.

What do you tell your employees? Will you be loyal to top management and press ahead with the goal, even though you know in your heart it is unattainable? Or will you open up to your employees and tell them you don't believe the goal is realistic but that you all have to pitch in and try your best?

Growing as a Professional

Even if you don't currently have any official leadership positions in your academic, athletic, volunteer, or work activities, look for opportunities to hone your leadership skills and develop your leadership style. Think about the type of leader you want to be. Practice coaching and mentoring. Evaluate your ability to manage change, even if it's only you going through a significant life change or other event. And build a positive culture for yourself and around yourself in every facet of your life. Be a positive and helpful presence for those around you, and don't tolerate negative or destructive people on your "team," whether that's a formal organizational unit or the people in your personal sphere.

Sharpening Your Communication Skills

Planning is an essential skill for any manager. However, managers should also be able to communicate their plans effectively to all

Intelligent Business Technology: Cognitive Automation

Research one of the cognitive automation solutions now on the market. Look for one that emphasizes managerial decision support, rather than more task-focused robotic process automation. (Note that cognitive automation might be offered as one capability within a system that is called something else.) Identify the major benefits and risks of using this tool, and summarize them in a short report or post for your class blog.

those concerned. Consider an activity, event, or a task that you are planning with others (or have planned recently). Develop an action plan that details how your event will move forward and assigns responsibilities for each area. Summarize your action plan in a brief, two-paragraph email to your team outlining your ideas.

Building Your Team Skills

With a team of fellow students, carry out the strategic planning process for a business or brand you are familiar with. Do not refer to its website or any other material; make judgments based on your own observations. Begin the strategic planning process by defining the company's mission, vision, and values. Present your team's ideas in a chart modeled after Exhibit 7.1. Then answer the following questions as a team: What have you learnt about the strategic planning process? What other information would have been valuable to complete this exercise?

Developing Your Research Skills

Find two articles in business journals or newspapers that profile two senior managers who lead a business organization.

7-27. What experience, skills, and business background do the two leaders have? Do you see any striking similarities or differences in their backgrounds?

7-28. What kinds of business challenges have these two leaders faced? What actions did they take to deal with those challenges? Did they establish any long-term goals or objectives for their company? Did the articles mention a new change initiative?

7-29. Describe the leadership strengths of these two people as they are presented in the articles you selected. Is either leader known as a team builder? A long-term strategist? A shrewd negotiator? What are each leader's greatest areas of strength?

Writing Assignments

7-30. How does the quality of business management affect society as a whole?

7-31. How will your experiences as an employee affect the leadership style you adopt when you become a manager?

ENDNOTES

1. Profile of Dr. Lisa Su, AMD, accessed 26 April 2018, www .amd.com; Therese Poletti, "AMD Earnings Cap a Stunning 2017, but There Is Still Plenty to Do," *MarketWatch*, 1 February 2018, www.marketwatch.com; Patrick Moorhead, "AMD CEO Lisa Su and the Art of a Turnaround," *Forbes*, 1 November 2016, www.forbes.com; Ryan Shrout, "AMD's Lisa Su: I 'Can Return This Company to Making a Lot of Money'," *MarketWatch*, 27 October 2017, www.marketwatch.com; Aaron Pressman, "Chipmaker AMD Makes a Big Bet on Brand-New Tech," *Fortune*, 28 June 2017, fortune.com; Aaron Pressman, "How AMD Seeks to Match Intel and Nvidia in Machine Learning," *Fortune*, 21 December 2016, fortune.com; Aaron Pressman, "AMD Avoids Plunging Cryptocurrency Prices, Stock Leaps 14%," *Fortune*, 26 April 2018, fortune.com; Aaron Pressman, "Inside AMD's Ryzen Revamp: Second Generation Chip Is Faster and Cheaper," *Fortune*, 19 April 2018, fortune.com; Paige Tanner, "What Is the Secret Behind AMD's Turnaround?" Market Realist, 10 July 2017, marketrealist.com.

2. Richard L. Daft, *Management*, 13th ed. (Boston: Cengage, 2018), 4.

3. Manfred F. R. Kets de Vries, "Managing Yourself: Do You Hate Your Boss?" *Harvard Business Review*, December 2016, hbr.org.

4. "What Leaders Gain by Listening Closely to Employees," *Knowledge@Wharton*, 29 June 2017, knowledge.wharton.upenn.edu.

5. Welch Allyn, accessed 27 April 2018, www.welchallyn.com.

6. "Our Company," Enterprise Holdings, accessed 26 April 2018, go.enterpriseholdings.com/our-company/our-values.

7. Alastair Dryburgh, "Don't You Believe It . . . It's Smart to Have SMART Objectives," *Management Today*, June 2011, 14.

8. Daft, *Management*, 17.

9. Dean Foust, "Speaking Up for the Organization Man," *BusinessWeek*, 9 March 2009, 78.

10. Steve Arneson, "Lead from the Middle," *Leadership Excellence*, March 2008, 19.

11. "Why Middle Managers May Be the Most Important People in Your Company," *Knowledge@Wharton*, 25 May 2011, knowledge.wharton.upenn.edu.

12. Daft, *Management*, 18.

13. Daft, *Management*, 518–519.

14. Andrew J. Dubrin, *Human Relations for Career and Personal Success*, 11th ed. (New York: Pearson, 2017), 92–93.

15. James G. Clawson, *Level Three Leadership: Getting Below the Surface*, 2nd ed. (Upper Saddle River, N.J.: Prentice Hall, 2003), 116.

16. Cary Cherniss, "Emotional Intelligence: What It Is and Why It Matters," Consortium for Research on Emotional Intelligence in Organizations, accessed 4 April 2009, www.eiconsortium.com.

17. Cherniss, "Emotional Intelligence: What It Is and Why It Matters."

18. Daniel Goleman, "Leadership That Gets Results," *Harvard Business Review*, March–April 2000, 78–90.

19. Herminia Ibarra and Morten T. Hansen, "Are You a Collaborative Leader?" *Harvard Business Review*, July/August 2011, 69–74.

20. Stephen P. Robbins and Timothy A. Judge, *Essentials of Organizational Behavior*, 14th ed. (New York: Pearson, 2018), 291.

21. Stephen Robbins, Mary Coulter, and David DeCenzo, *Fundamentals of Management*, 10th ed. (New York: Pearson, 2017), 241.

22. Robbins, Coulter, and DeCenzo, *Fundamentals of Management*, 242.

23. "Microsoft CEO Satya Nadella: How Empathy Sparks Innovation," *Knowledge@Wharton*, 22 February 2018, knowledge .wharton.upenn.edu.

24. Rachel Lerman, "More 'Boomerang' Employees Return to Microsoft as Corporate Culture Shifts," *Seattle Times*, 3 March 2018, www.seattletimes.com.

25. Daft, *Management*, 4.

26. "Benchmarking," American Society for Quality, accessed 27 August 2018, asq.org.

27. "Balanced Scorecard Basics," Balanced Scorecard Institute, accessed 27 April 2018, www.balancedscorecard.org.

28. Robert E. Kaplan and Robert B. Kaiser, "Developing Versatile Leadership," *MIT Sloan Management Review*, Summer 2003, 19–26.

29. Roger L. Martin and Tony Golsby-Smith, "Management Is Much More Than a Science," *Harvard Business Review*, September-October 2017, 129–135.

30. Sam Schechner, "Meet Your New Boss: An Algorithm," *Wall Street Journal*, 10 December 2017, www.wsj.com; Vinay Mummigatti, "Robotic Process Automation (RPA) to Intelligent and Cognitive Automation—3 Basic Questions to Help You Navigate the Automation Conundrum," LinkedIn, 4 April 2017, www.linkedin.com; "Knowledge Management Gets Cognitive," Attivio, accessed 26 April 2018, www .attivio.com.

31. Julie Bort, "How Salesforce CEO Marc Benioff Uses Artificial Intelligence to End Internal Politics at Meetings," *Business Insider*, 18 May 2017, www.businessinsider.com.

32. See note 1.

8 Organization and Teamwork

1 Explain the major decisions needed to design an organization structure.

2 Define four major types of organization structure.

3 Explain how a team differs from a group, and describe the six most common forms of teams.

4 Highlight the advantages and disadvantages of working in teams, and list the characteristics of effective teams.

5 Review the five stages of team development, and explain why conflict can arise in team settings.

6 Explain the concept of an unstructured organization, and identify the major benefits and challenges of taking this approach.

7 Describe the use of taskbots and robotic process automation in contemporary business.

MyLab Intro to Business

Improve Your Grade!

If your instructor is using MyLab Intro to Business, visit **www.pearson.com/mylab/intro-to-business**.

BEHIND THE SCENES
Zappos: Applying a Freethinking Management Style to the Foundations of Management

dpa picture alliance/Alamy Stock Photo

Looking for a better way to organize the activities of his 1,500 employees, Zappos CEO Tony Hsieh got rid of traditional organization entirely.

www.zappos.com

Tony Hsieh's approach to business and to life in general could be described as "putting normal on trial." If the normal way of doing things works, then fine, he'll be normal. But if he sees a better way, he won't let conventional expectations stop him from pursuing it. For example, success as an investor and entrepreneur has made him wealthy, but rather than buying a mansion or two, he lives in a travel trailer in a trailer park. Why? "I just love it because there's so many random, amazing things that happen around the campfire at night. I think of it as the world's largest living room."

Granted, it's no normal trailer park but rather a quirky village that is part of an urban redevelopment project that Hsieh launched in Las Vegas. The city is also home to Zappos, the online shoe and clothing retailer in which he was an early investor and where he took over as CEO in 2004.

From its early days, Zappos has shunned the normal in pursuit of satisfied customers and happy employees. Its core values include "create fun and a little weirdness" and "be adventurous, creative, and open-minded." A television profile of the company once said it "might be the wackiest workplace in America." The page on the company website that profiles the leadership team isn't titled "Leadership Team" or "Executives," as these corporate webpages usually are, but rather "Meet Our

Monkeys." However, behind the silliness is a seriously successful business that grew from the then-revolutionary idea of selling shoes over the internet to more than $1 billion in annual sales. (Hsieh eventually sold the company to Amazon, but Zappos is run independently, and he remains at the helm as CEO.)

Always on the lookout for better ways to do things, Hsieh was one of the first company leaders to embrace a management approach called Holacracy. This "self-management practice"

invented by a software developer replaces traditional notions of hierarchy, managers, and fixed job descriptions with fluid roles and distributed authority. It's a radically different approach, and no company as large as Zappos had tried to adopt it.

Would it work for Zappos? If you were Tony Hsieh, how would you lead a successful company into this uncharted territory? Could you make the company better without losing all the things that already made it great?[1]

INTRODUCTION

Individual effort is essential to the success of any business, but professionals rarely work in complete isolation. Most employees are members of one or more departments or teams, and even solo freelancers join virtual teams for many of their projects. This chapter discusses the key issues to consider in designing an organization structure, introduces you to the most common ways companies structure themselves, and explores the important matter of teamwork. It concludes with a look at the *unstructured organization*.

Designing an Effective Organization Structure

Although they don't get the same attention as marketing campaigns or big financial deals, choices about how to organize people are some of the most important decisions any company must make. A company's **organization structure** has a profound influence on the way employees and managers make decisions, communicate, and accomplish important tasks. This structure helps the company achieve its goals by providing a framework for managers to divide responsibilities, distribute the authority to make decisions, coordinate and control the organization's work, and hold employees accountable for their work.

Organizational choices are rarely simple. If the structure is too rigid, teams can't respond quickly to customer demands or competitive threats, or their work bogs down as organizational boundaries get in the way. If the structure is too loose, goals and responsibilities can be unclear, resulting in confusion and chaos. Moreover, change is a constant for many companies these days. An organizational scheme that works today might not work next month or next year, as Zappos's Tony Hsieh (profiled in the chapter-opening Behind the Scenes) concluded when he wondered how to make the company even more responsive to customer needs.

When managers design an organization's structure, they use an **organization chart** to provide a visual representation of how employees and tasks are grouped and how the lines of communication and authority flow (see Exhibit 8.1 on the next page). An organization chart depicts the official design for accomplishing tasks that lead to achieving the organization's goals, a framework known as the *formal organization*. Every company also has an *informal organization*—the network of interactions that develop on a personal level among workers. Sometimes the interactions among people in the informal organization parallel their relationships in the formal organization, but often interactions transcend formal boundaries, such as when employees from various parts of the company participate in sports, social, or charitable activities together or use social media to reach across organizational barriers.

IDENTIFYING CORE COMPETENCIES

Before they can decide how to organize, companies need to identify which business functions they should focus on themselves and which they should *outsource* (see page 277) to other companies. For instance, many small and midsize companies outsource the payroll function because it doesn't make sense for them to invest the time needed to stay on top of frequent changes in income tax laws and related financial matters.[2]

1 LEARNING OBJECTIVE
Explain the major decisions needed to design an organization structure.

organization structure
A framework that enables managers to divide responsibilities, ensure employee accountability, and distribute decision-making authority.

organization chart
A diagram that shows how employees and tasks are grouped and where the lines of communication and authority flow.

EXHIBIT 8.1	Simplified Organization Chart

An organization chart portrays the division of activities and responsibilities across a company.

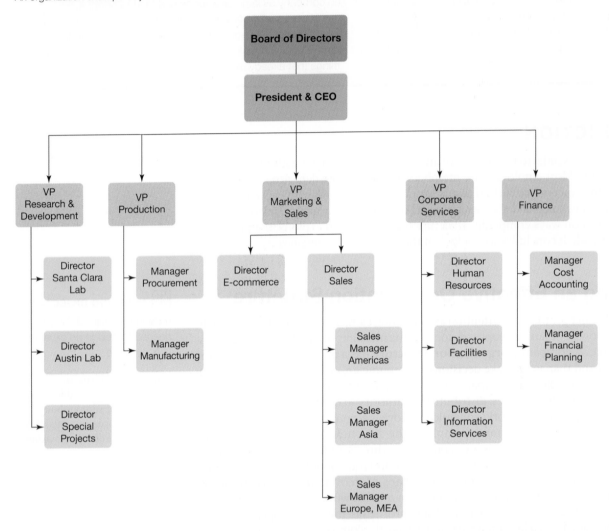

core competencies
Activities that a company considers central and vital to its business.

Core competencies are those activities at which a company excels and that give it the potential to create competitive advantages. For example, it's a virtual certainty that you've seen or used a product designed by Frog (www.frogdesign.com), a global design consultancy with talents in consumer research, design, and the commercialization phase of bringing new products to market. Frog has worked behind the scenes for many of the world's best-known companies, from Apple to Disney to Sony, but it stays focused on its core competencies in product strategy and design, rather than becoming a manufacturer itself.[3]

IDENTIFYING JOB RESPONSIBILITIES

work specialization
Specialization in or responsibility for some portion of an organization's overall work tasks; also called division of labor.

Once a company knows what it wants to focus on, it can design each job needed to deliver those competencies. A key decision here is finding the optimal level of **work specialization**, sometimes referred to as the *division of labor*—the degree to which organizational tasks are broken down into separate jobs.[4] Work specialization can improve organizational efficiency by enabling each worker to perform tasks that are well defined and that require specific skills. When employees concentrate on the same specialized tasks, they can perfect their skills and perform those tasks more quickly. In addition to aligning skills with job tasks, specialization prevents overlapping responsibilities and communication breakdowns.

However, organizations can overdo specialization. If a job is defined too narrowly, employees may become bored with performing the same limited, repetitive tasks over and over. They may also feel unchallenged and alienated. As you'll see later in the chapter, many companies are adopting a team-based approach to give employees a wider range of work experiences and responsibilities.

DEFINING THE CHAIN OF COMMAND

With the various jobs and their individual responsibilities identified, the next step is defining the **chain of command**, the lines of authority that connect the various groups and levels within the organization. The chain of command helps the organization function smoothly by making two things clear: who is responsible for each task and who has the authority to make decisions.

chain of command
A pathway for the flow of authority from one management level to the next.

All employees have a certain amount of *responsibility*—the obligation to perform the duties and achieve the goals and objectives associated with their jobs. As they work toward the organization's goals, employees must also maintain their *accountability*—their obligation to report the results of their work to supervisors or team members and to justify any outcomes that fall below expectations. Managers ensure that tasks are accomplished by exercising *authority*—the power to make decisions, issue orders, carry out actions, and allocate resources. Authority is vested in the positions that managers hold, and it flows down through the management pyramid. *Delegation* is the assignment of work and the transfer of authority, responsibility, and accountability to someone lower down the chain of command.[5]

The simplest and most common chain-of-command system is known as *line organization* because it establishes a clear line of authority flowing from the top down, as Exhibit 8.1 depicts. Everyone knows who is accountable to whom, as well as which tasks and decisions each manager is responsible for. However, line organization sometimes falls short because the technical complexity of a firm's activities may require specialized knowledge that individual managers don't have and can't easily acquire. A more elaborate system, called *line-and-staff organization,* was developed to address the need to combine specialization with management control. In such an organization, managers in the chain of command are supplemented by functional groupings of people known as *staff,* who provide advice and specialized services but who are not in the line organization's overall chain of command (see Exhibit 8.2 on the next page).

Span of Management

The number of people a manager directly supervises is called the **span of management**, or *span of control*. When a large number of people report directly to one person, that person has a wide span of management. This situation is common in *flat organizations* with relatively few levels in the management hierarchy. In contrast, *tall organizations* have many hierarchical levels, typically with fewer people reporting to each manager than is the case in a flat organization. In these organizations, the span of management is narrow.

span of management
The number of people under one manager's control; also known as span of control.

To reduce the time it takes to make decisions, many companies are now flattening their organization structures by removing layers of management and pushing responsibilities and authority to lower levels (see Exhibit 8.3 on page 247). Such moves have the additional benefit of putting senior executives in closer contact with customers and the daily action of the business.[6]

However, a flatter structure is not necessarily better in all respects. For example, it can increase the demand on individual managers and give them less time to spend with each employee. The Container Store, for instance, added a layer of management specifically to reduce the span of management so that each manager could have more time "to nurture and develop and train and counsel" his or her employees. "I think it's the best thing we ever did," cofounder Kip Tindell said, noting that even with the added costs, financial performance improved.[7]

Moreover, the deep experience base that midlevel managers have accrued, regarding both external market dynamics and internal working knowledge of the company itself, can

EXHIBIT 8.2	**Simplified Line-and-Staff Structure**

A line-and-staff organization divides employees into those who are in the direct line of command and those who provide staff (support) services to line managers at various levels. In this simplified example, the government affairs and legal departments report to the CEO but provide support to any department in the company, as needed.

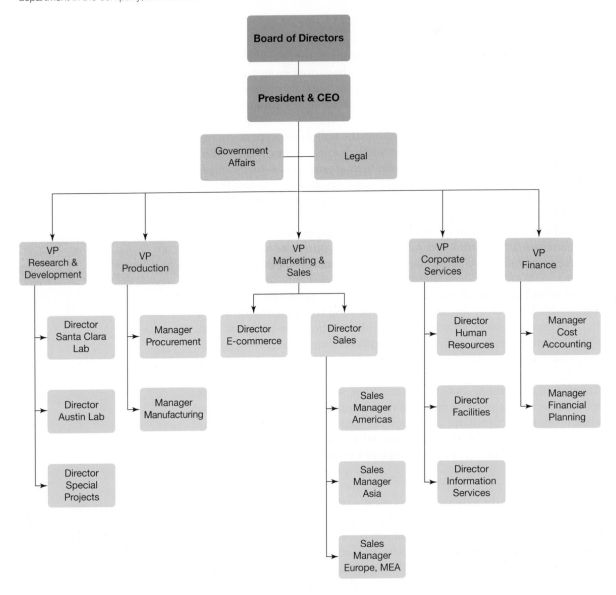

be lost when these positions are eliminated. These managers can be particularly crucial in knowledge-driven industries, where insight and creative thinking are crucial to strategic decision-making.[8]

Centralization Versus Decentralization

centralization
Concentration of decision-making authority at the top of an organization.

Organizations that focus decision-making authority in the upper tiers of the chain of command are said to be centralized. **Centralization** can benefit a company by taking advantage of top management's experience and broad view of organizational goals. In addition, it can help companies coordinate large undertakings more efficiently, simplify decisions that might otherwise get bogged down in discussions and disagreements, and reduce the number of overlapping capabilities.

decentralization
Delegation of decision-making authority to employees in lower-level positions.

In contrast, **decentralization** pushes decision-making authority down to lower organizational levels while control over essential companywide matters remains with

| EXHIBIT 8.3 | Flattening an Organization |

In this simplified example, a layer of management (the business units) was removed to flatten the organization. In theory, this move reduces costs and speeds communication and decision-making. Two obvious downsides are the increased span of management for the two group managers and the loss of knowledge and relationships that the business unit managers brought to the organization.

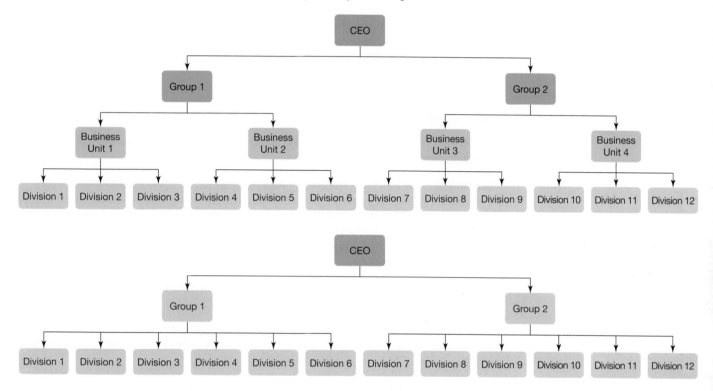

top management. Decentralization has the potential to make companies more responsive to forces and changes in the marketplace and in the workforce, pull in a more diverse range of perspectives, and give employees more input into decisions that affect their work.[9]

Although the trend in business in recent years has been toward decentralization, there is no single answer to the question of centralization versus decentralization that will work for every firm in every situation. Each company needs to decide what the right balance is for its unique strengths and challenges.[10]

RETHINKING ORGANIZATION IN THE AGE OF AGILITY

The notion of "designing" an organization structure can be a bit misleading, because it suggests that you design it and build it, and then you're finished. However, many companies are in a nearly continuous state of redesigning their structures to respond to changing market conditions. Large companies reorganize every two to three years on average, for example.[11] And in *self-organizing* models such as the one that Zappos uses, the change is constant as people move in and out of "circles," the basic organizing unit in Holacracy. Tony Hsieh says the organization chart at Zappos can change as often as 50 times a *day*.[12]

Structure can bring stability and predictability to an organization, but it can also make a company unresponsive and inflexible. As speed become paramount in business and the rate of change increases in one industry after another, many companies are looking for ways

REAL-TIME UPDATES

Learn More by Reading This Article

Rethinking organization when speed is the top priority

Organizational strategies designed to optimize control and predictability are losing their value to companies in fast-moving markets. Go to **real-timeupdates.com/bia9** and select Learn More in the Students section.

agile organization
A company whose structure, policies, and capabilities allow employees to respond quickly to customer needs and changes in the business environment.

to be more adaptable. The goal for many companies is to develop an **agile organization** that allows employees to respond quickly to customer needs and changes in the business environment and to bring the best mix of talents and resources to every challenge. The "agile" concept grew out of software developers who were looking for a faster way to create and refine programs and apps, and it is now being applied to manufacturing and management in general.

As you study the principles of organization in this chapter, be aware that many companies are rethinking the conventional ideas of organization—and, as Zappos demonstrated, more or less abandoning them in some cases. The implications are potentially profound and could change what it means to be an employee and radically alter what it means to be a leader.

 CHECKPOINT

LEARNING OBJECTIVE 1: Explain the major decisions needed to design an organization structure.

SUMMARY: The first major decision in designing an organization structure is identifying core competencies, those functions where the company excels and on which it wants to focus. From there, managers can identify job responsibilities (who does what and how much work specialization is optimum), the chain of command, the span of management for each manager, and the degree of centralization or decentralization of decision-making authority.

CRITICAL THINKING: (1) What are the risks of a poorly designed organization structure? (2) How does a flat structure change the responsibilities of individual managers?

IT'S YOUR BUSINESS: (1) What would you say are your two or three core competencies at this point in your career? (2) Would you function better in a highly centralized or a highly decentralized organization? Why?

KEY TERMS TO KNOW: organization structure, organization chart, core competencies, work specialization, chain of command, span of management, centralization, decentralization, agile organization

② **LEARNING OBJECTIVE**
Define four major types of organization structure.

departmentalization
Grouping people within an organization according to function, division, matrix, or network.

functional structure
Grouping workers according to their similar skills, resource use, and expertise.

Organizing the Workforce

The decisions regarding job responsibilities, span of management, and centralization versus decentralization provide the insights that managers need in order to choose the best organization structure. The arrangement of activities into logical groups that are then clustered into larger departments and units to form the total organization is known as **departmentalization**.[13] The choice must involve both the *vertical structure*—how many layers the chain of command is divided into from the top of the company to the bottom—and the *horizontal structure*—how the various business functions and work specialties are divided across the company.

Variations in the vertical and horizontal designs of organizations can produce an almost endless array of structures—some flat, some wide; some simple and clear, others convoluted and complex. Within this endless variety of structure possibilities, most designs fall into one of four types: functional, divisional, matrix, and network. Companies can also combine two or more of these types in *hybrid structures*.

FUNCTIONAL STRUCTURES

The **functional structure** groups employees according to their skills, resource use, and job requirements. Common functional subgroups include research and development (R&D), production or manufacturing, marketing and sales, and human resources.

The advantages of the functional structure include economies of scale, the opportunity for people to pursue an upward career path within their professional specialties, and the chance for companies to develop deep expertise in each functional area. The primary disadvantage is the *silo effect*, whereby people become isolated within the vertical "towers" of their own functional areas, which can inhibit vital communication and collaboration across functions.[14] These silos can become cultural as well as structural, with groups developing their own subcultures and an "us versus them" mentality.[15] For example, defining and developing new products usually requires close coordination among R&D, production, marketing, and accounting, and that coordination can suffer if the various functional areas don't commit to collaboration. Firms that use functional structures often try to counter this weakness by using *cross-functional teams* to coordinate efforts across functional boundaries, as you'll see later in the chapter.

DIVISIONAL STRUCTURES

The **divisional structure** establishes self-contained suborganizations that encompass all the major functional resources required to achieve their goals—such as R&D, manufacturing, finance, and marketing. In some companies, these divisions operate with great autonomy and are often called *business units*.

Many organizations use a structure based on *product divisions*—grouping around each of the company's products or family of products. In contrast, *process divisions* are based on the major steps of a production process. For example, petroleum companies such as Chevron and ExxonMobil typically divide their operations into "upstream" divisions (exploration and development of energy sources) and "downstream" divisions (refining, transportation, and retailing).[16] The third approach, *customer divisions*, concentrates activities on satisfying specific groups of customers (see Exhibit 8.4). Finally, *geographic divisions* help companies respond more easily to local customs, styles, and product preferences.

Divisional structures offer both advantages and disadvantages. First, because divisions are self-contained, they can react quickly to change, making the organization more flexible. In addition, because each division focuses on a limited number of products, processes, customers, or locations, divisions can often provide better service to customers.

However, divisional departmentalization can also increase costs through duplication (if every product division has its own human resources department, for example). Furthermore, poor coordination between divisions may cause them to focus too narrowly on divisional goals at the expense of the organization's overall goals.

divisional structure
Grouping departments according to similarities in product, process, customer, or geography.

MATRIX STRUCTURES

A **matrix structure** is an organizational design in which employees from functional departments form teams to combine their specialized skills (see Exhibit 8.5 on the next page). This structure allows the company to pool and share resources across divisions and functional groups. The matrix may be a permanent feature of the organization's design, or it may be established to complete a specific project.

The matrix structure can help big companies function like smaller ones by allowing teams to devote their attention to specific projects or customers without permanently reorganizing

matrix structure
A structure in which employees are assigned to both a functional group and a project team (thus using functional and divisional patterns simultaneously).

EXHIBIT 8.4	**Customer Division Structure**

Focusing each division on a single type of customer can help a company market its products more efficiently and serve customers more responsively.

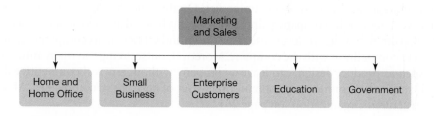

EXHIBIT 8.5	**Matrix Structure**

In a matrix structure, each employee is assigned to both a functional group (with a defined set of basic functions, such as production management) and a project team (which consists of members of various functional groups working together on a project, such as bringing out a new consumer product). Even in this simplified model, you can sense how complex matrix management can be when employees have multiple managers and managers share employees with other projects and departments.

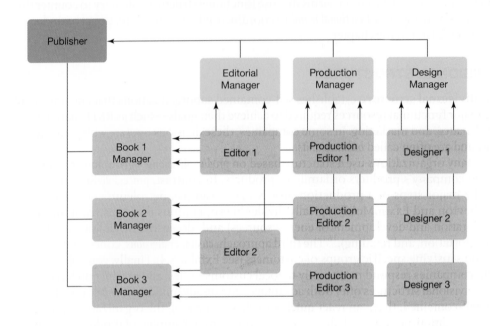

the company's structure. A matrix can also make it easier to deploy limited resources where they're needed the most and to bring a mix of skills to bear on important tasks.

On the downside, people in a matrix structure must juggle the situation of having two bosses, more communication and coordination is usually required, and struggles over resources can foster unhealthy competition between the two sides of the matrix.[17] Strong support from upper management, a culture that values collaboration, and hands-on attention from managers to make sure employees don't get lost in the matrix are essential to using this structural form successfully.[18]

NETWORK STRUCTURES

network structure
A structure that coordinates resources inside and outside the company to form a cohesive whole.

A **network structure** coordinates resources inside and outside the company to form a cohesive whole. Also called a *virtual organization*, a network organization can outsource engineering, marketing, research, accounting, production, distribution, or other functions. The design of a network structure stems from decisions about core competencies, with executives deciding which functions to focus on internally and which to outsource.

The network structure presents an intriguing blend of benefits and risks. A virtual structure can lower costs and increase flexibility, allowing a company to react more quickly to market demands. It can also boost competitiveness by taking advantage of specific skills and technologies available in other companies. On the other hand, relying too heavily on outsiders can render the company vulnerable to events beyond its control, such as a key supplier going out of business, offering the same goods and services to its competitors, or going into direct competition with the company. Moreover, outsourcing too many fundamental tasks, such as product design, can leave a company without any real competitive distinctions to speak of.[19] For more on contemporary uses of network structures, see "Managing an Unstructured Organization" on page 261.

CHECKPOINT

LEARNING OBJECTIVE 2: Define four major types of organization structure.

SUMMARY: Companies can organize in four primary ways: by function, which groups employees according to their skills, resource use, and expertise; by division, which establishes self-contained departments formed according to similarities in product, process, customer, or geography; by matrix, which assigns employees from functional departments to interdisciplinary project teams and requires them to report to both a department head and a team leader; and by network, which connects separate companies that perform selected tasks for a headquarters organization.

CRITICAL THINKING: (1) Should a retail store use the same organization structure in each of its stores around the country? Why or why not? (2) Why does a matrix structure create potential problems in the chain of command?

IT'S YOUR BUSINESS: (1) Do you think you would function well in a matrix structure, where you would need to report to two bosses simultaneously? Why or why not? (2) How well would you function as a manager in a matrix—could you share control with another manager?

KEY TERMS TO KNOW: departmentalization, functional structure, divisional structure, matrix structure, network structure

Organizing in Teams

Although the vertical chain of command is a tried-and-true method of organizing for business, it is limited by the fact that decision-making authority is often located high up the management hierarchy while real-world feedback from customers is usually located at or near the bottom. Companies that organize vertically may become slow to react to change, and high-level managers may overlook many great ideas for improvement that originate in the lower levels of the organization. In addition, many business tasks and challenges demand the expertise of people who work in many parts of the company, isolated by the formal chain of command. To combat these issues, organizations can involve employees from all levels and functions in the decision-making process, using a variety of team formats in day-to-day operations.

This section looks at the most common types of teams, and the following two sections address the challenges of improving team productivity and fostering teamwork.

WHAT IS A TEAM?

A **team** is a unit of two or more people who work toward a shared goal and, unlike other work groups, depend on one another to achieve that goal.[20] Teams differ from work groups in that work groups interact primarily to share information and to make decisions to help one another perform within each member's area of responsibility. In other words, the performance of a work group is merely the summation of all group members' individual contributions.[21] In contrast, the members of a team have a shared mission and are collectively responsible for their work.

TYPES OF TEAMS

Companies use a variety of team formats and sizes, with different degrees of structure and formality. The simplest team consists of two people assigned to collaborate on a task, with no more formality than the mandate to get the job done. This pair might not even think of themselves as team, but the potential advantages and disadvantages of teamwork apply to their work just the same. At the other extreme, a team could have a hundred or more members and a formal management structure.

---

3   LEARNING OBJECTIVE

Explain how a team differs from a group, and describe the six most common forms of teams.

team
A unit of two or more people who share a mission and collective responsibility as they work together to achieve a goal.

The type, structure, and composition of individual teams within an organization depend on the organization's strategic goals and the objective for forming the team. Six common forms of teams are problem-solving teams, self-managed teams, functional teams, cross-functional teams, virtual teams, and social networks and virtual communities. Such classifications are not exclusive, of course. A problem-solving team may also be self-managed and cross-functional.

Problem-Solving Teams

problem-solving team
A team that meets to find ways to improve quality, efficiency, and the work environment.

A **problem-solving team** is assembled to find ways to improve quality, efficiency, or other performance measures. In some cases, a team attacks a single, specific problem and disbands after presenting or implementing the solution. In other cases, the team continues to meet over time, evaluating trends and fixing new problems as they crop up.

Self-Managed Teams

self-managed team
A team in which members are responsible for an entire process or operation.

As the name implies, a **self-managed team** manages its own activities and requires little or no supervision. Self-managed teams represent a significant change for organizations and managers accustomed to rigid command-and-control structures, and they are central to the idea of an agile organization. The potential advantages include lower costs, faster decision-making, greater flexibility and innovation, and improved quality stemming from the increased pride of ownership that an independent team feels in its work. However, self-managed teams aren't necessarily more productive than manager-led teams, and their success depends on the commitment of the people involved and the nature of the work they are expected to perform.[22]

functional team
A team whose members come from a single functional department and that is based on the organization's vertical structure.

Functional Teams

A **functional team**, or *command team*, is organized along the lines of the organization's vertical structure and thus may be referred to as a *vertical team*. Such teams are composed of managers and employees within a single functional department, and the structure of a vertical team typically follows the formal chain of command. Large functional teams may include several levels of the organizational hierarchy within the same functional department.[23]

cross-functional team
A team that draws together employees from different functional areas.

Cross-Functional Teams

A **cross-functional team** includes people from more than one department or functional area across the company. Cross-functional teams are a powerful scheme for assembling talent, because they overcome the fixed organizational structure and unite people from a variety of departments who have different areas of expertise and responsibility. Cross-functional teams can be an effective way to overcome the silo effect, and these teams can also serve as a vital communication network that disperses information across the company.

task force
A team of people from several departments who are temporarily brought together to address a specific issue.

committee
A team that may become a permanent part of the organization and is designed to deal with regularly recurring tasks.

Although they are a compelling and often necessary way to organize team efforts, cross-functional teams face the particular challenge of coordinating the work of people with different priorities and workstyles and who formally report to different managers in different parts of the company. These teams are more vulnerable to internal conflict and competition than single-function teams and need strong leadership to be successful.[24]

A cross-functional team can take a number of forms. A **task force** is formed to work on a specific activity with a completion point. Several departments are usually involved so that all parties who have a stake in the outcome of the task are able to provide input. In contrast, a **committee** usually has a long life span and may become a permanent part of the organization structure. Committees typically deal with regularly recurring tasks, such as addressing employee grievances.

kantver/123RF.com

A cross-functional team brings together employees from different parts of the organization. The diversity of skills and experience can help a company address complex, interwoven problems.

Virtual Teams

A **virtual team** is one in which members work in at least two different locations and rely on technology to communicate and collaborate. Professionals in a wide variety of situations work in virtual teams, including through telecommuting (working from home or other off-site locations), collaborating with colleagues in other offices, and working as independent contractors from remote locations.

virtual team
A team that uses communication technology to bring together geographically distant employees to achieve goals.

Advantages of Virtual Teams Virtual teams can pull together the best people for a task, even if they work in different offices or different countries. Companies and employees can take advantage of the economic and personal benefits of telecommuting, and employees in geographically dispersed firms can reduce the amount of travel and the wear and tear it has on them and their families. In many cases, virtual teamwork is the only option available, such as when a company outsources its manufacturing to a firm in another country and teams made up of employees from both companies need to collaborate frequently.

Virtual teams can also yield some surprising benefits. Multiple studies show that successful virtual teams can be more effective, more engaged, and more productive than *co-located teams* (those in the same physical location).[25]

Disadvantages of Virtual Teams However, virtual teams present some challenges that must be addressed by any firm that uses them. Because virtual teams rely on technology to stay connected, any limitations in those tools hamper team performance. For instance, if a team is forced to rely on email for all communication, collaboration, and file sharing, it is likely to end up with message overload, misunderstandings, overlooked messages, lost files, and other problems.

Interpersonal communication is a constant challenge in virtual environments. Teams play an important social role in many cases, for instance, and long-distance team members can develop a sense of emotional isolation and the feeling of being "out of the loop." This can be particularly acute if most of the team members work in the same physical location and only a few members connect long distance. Distance and separation can also foster a competitive mentality between factions in a team.[26] Plus, virtual teams often miss out on the random interactions that co-located teams experience, such as members running into one another while getting coffee or crossing paths in other work settings.[27]

Agile organizations may find it difficult to use virtual teams, because agile project management relies on fast, flexible coordination and cooperation, which is easier when everyone is in the same location. IBM, for example, has begun reversing its long-standing policy of letting employees work from home because of a switch to agile management.[28]

REAL-TIME UPDATES
Learn More by Reading This Article

Overcome the limitations of virtual teamwork

These 21 tips can help any virtual team overcome the inherent limitations of long-distance collaboration. Go to **real-timeupdates .com/bia9** and select Learn More in the Students section.

Social Networks and Virtual Communities

Social networking technologies are redefining teamwork and team communication by helping to erase the constraints of geographic and organization boundaries. In addition to enabling and enhancing teamwork, social networks have numerous other business applications and benefits (see Exhibit 8.6 on the next page). Although they are not always teams in the traditional sense, social networks and *virtual communities* often function as teams, helping people coordinate their efforts in pursuit of a shared goal. In addition, social networking has become an essential tool for many teams, matrix organizations, temporary organizations, and other structures.

Some companies use social networking technologies to form virtual communities or *communities of practice* that link employees with similar professional interests throughout the company and sometimes with customers and suppliers as well. The huge advantage that social networking brings is in identifying the best people to collaborate on each problem or project, no matter where they are around the world or what their official roles are in the organization. Such communities are similar to teams in many respects, but one major difference is the responsibility for accumulating organizational knowledge over

EXHIBIT 8.6	Business Uses of Social Networking Technology

Social networking has emerged as a powerful technology for improving operations, gathering intelligence, and fostering positive business relationships.

Operations	Intelligence	Relationships
Fostering collaboration. Networks can help identify the best people to collaborate on projects and find pockets of knowledge and expertise within the organization.	**Understanding target markets**. Many companies monitor and analyze social media traffic to pick up on consumer trends, complaints, rumors, and other bits of environmental intelligence.	**Onboarding new employees**. Internal networks can help new employees navigate their way through the organization and find experts, mentors, and other important contacts.
Recruiting employees and business partners. Companies use social networks to find potential employees, short-term contractors, subject-matter experts, product and service suppliers, and business partners. A key advantage here is that these introductions are often made via trusted connections in a professional network.	**Monitoring company and brand reputations**. Tools for *sentiment analysis* and *reputation analysis* assess the reputations of companies and individuals, measure the emotional quality of online conversations, and identify outrage "hot spots" on social media.	**Integrating company workforces**. Internal social networks can help companies grow closer, including encouraging workforces to "gel" after reorganizations or mergers and overcoming structural barriers in communication channels.
Supporting customers. *Social customer service* involves using social media to give customers a more convenient way to get help from the company and to help each other.	**Identifying opinion influencers**. Social media influencers can sway public opinion, so companies try to identify opinion leaders in their markets.	**Accelerating team development**. Networks can help members get to know one another, identify individual areas of expertise, and share resources.
Extending the organization. Social networking is also fueling the growth of *networked organizations*, sometimes known as *virtual organizations*, where companies supplement the talents of their employees with services from one or more external partners, such as a design lab, a manufacturing firm, or a sales and distribution company.	**Supplementing the formal communication network**. Internal social networks can bypass the formal communication system to collect and distribute information in a more timely fashion.	**Extending professional networking**. Social media can give seminar and conference participants a way to meet before an event and to maintain relationships afterward.
Crisis communication. When companies need to communicate with broad audiences in a hurry, social media are ideal channels.	**Finding sales prospects**. Salespeople on networks such as LinkedIn can use their connections to identify potential buyers and ask for introductions through those shared connections. Sales networking can reduce *cold calling*, contacting potential customers without a prior introduction.	**Building communities**. Social networks can bring together *communities of practice*, people who engage in similar work, and *communities of interest* (sometimes called *brand communities*), people who share enthusiasm for a particular product or activity.

Sources: Based in part on Lexalytics website, accessed 7 January 2018, www.lexalytics.com; Evolve24 website, accessed 7 January 2018, www.evolve24.com; Matt Charney, "How to Use Social Media for Employee Onboarding," *Recruiting Daily*, 27 April 2015, recruitingdaily.com; Shep Hyken, "Social Customer Care Is the New Marketing," *Forbes*, 22 April 2017, www.forbes.com.

the long term. For example, the pharmaceutical company Pfizer has a number of permanent product safety communities that provide specialized advice on drug safety issues to researchers across the company.[29] Social networking can also help a company maintain a sense of community even as it grows beyond the size that normally permits a lot of daily interaction.

 CHECKPOINT

LEARNING OBJECTIVE 3: Explain how a team differs from a group, and describe the six most common forms of teams.

SUMMARY: The primary difference between a team and a work group is that the members of a team work toward a shared goal, whereas members of a work group strive toward individual goals. The six most common forms of teams are (1) problem-solving teams, which seek ways to improve a situation and then submit their recommendations; (2) self-managed teams, which manage their own activities and seldom require supervision; (3) functional teams, which are composed of employees within a single functional department; (4) cross-functional teams, which draw together employees from various departments and areas of expertise into a number of forms such as task forces and committees; (5) virtual teams, which bring together employees from distant locations; and (6) social networks and virtual communities, which are typically less structured than teams but nonetheless share many aspects of teamwork and promote shared goals.

CRITICAL THINKING: (1) How might the work of a task force or committee disrupt the normal chain of command in an organization? (2) Should new hires with no business experience be assigned to virtual teams? Why or why not?

IT'S YOUR BUSINESS: (1) Would you function well in a virtual team setting that offered little or no chance for face-to-face contact with your colleagues? Why or why not? (2) If you had two similar job offers, one with a company that stresses teamwork and another with a company that stresses independent accomplishment, which would you choose? Why?

KEY TERMS TO KNOW: team, problem-solving team, self-managed team, functional team, cross-functional team, task force, committee, virtual team

Ensuring Team Productivity

Even though teams can play a vital role in helping an organization reach its goals, they are not appropriate for every situation, nor do they automatically ensure higher performance. Understanding the advantages and disadvantages of working in teams and recognizing the characteristics of effective teams are essential steps in ensuring productive teamwork.

⊞ **4** **LEARNING OBJECTIVE**
Highlight the advantages and disadvantages of working in teams, and list the characteristics of effective teams.

ADVANTAGES AND DISADVANTAGES OF WORKING IN TEAMS

Managers must weigh the pros and cons of teams when deciding whether and how to use them. A well-run team can provide a number of advantages:[30]

- **More information and knowledge.** By pooling the experience of several individuals, a team has access to more information in the decision-making process.
- **Learning opportunities.** Teams that bring together people with various work specialties give people the chance to learn from each other.
- **Boldness.** People who might hesitate to take calculated risks on their own can be more willing to make bold moves as part of the team.
- **Accountability.** Most people want to avoid letting others down, and participating in teams creates a built-in sense of accountability to others.
- **Trust building.** Working closely in teams lets people develop trust in their colleagues, which can be beneficial outside the confines of the team activities as well.
- **A broader range of viewpoints.** Diverse teams can bring a variety of perspectives that improve decision-making.
- **Buy-in for solutions the team creates.** Those who participate in making a decision are more likely to support it and encourage others to accept it.
- **Improved performance.** Effective teams can be better than top-performing individuals at solving complex problems.
- **A sense of community in good times and bad.** Being on a team helps individuals share in the celebration of successes and provides emotional support during challenging periods.

Although the advantages of teamwork help explain the widespread popularity of teams in today's business environment, teams also present some potential disadvantages, particularly if they are poorly structured or poorly managed:

- **Groupthink.** Like other social structures, business teams can generate tremendous pressures to conform. **Groupthink** occurs when peer pressures cause individual team members to withhold contrary opinions and to go along with decisions they don't really believe in. The consequences of groupthink can range from bland, unimaginative work to outright disasters. A particularly insidious aspect of groupthink is that a team suffering from it can appear to be highly functional, given the lack of disagreement, when in fact the team could be failing spectacularly.[31]

groupthink
Uniformity of thought that occurs when peer pressures cause individual team members to withhold contrary or unpopular opinions.

hidden agenda
Private, counterproductive motives in a team setting, such as a desire to take control of the group, to undermine someone else on the team, or to pursue an incompatible goal.

- **Hidden agendas.** Some team members may have a **hidden agenda**—private, counterproductive motives, such as a desire to take control of the group, to undermine someone else on the team, or to pursue an incompatible goal.
- **Cost and inefficiency.** Aligning schedules, arranging meetings, and coordinating individual parts of a project can eat up a lot of time and money. And even successful teams need to be on constant watch for inefficiency—spending more time than necessary on their decisions and activities or simply losing sight of the team's goals.
- **Overload.** Some companies have embraced collaborative work approaches to such an extent that they're overloading employees with team assignments.[32]

CHARACTERISTICS OF EFFECTIVE TEAMS

A wide variety of factors can account for team success:[33]

- A shared sense of purpose and compatible values
- A clear and challenging goal
- A belief in the value of the team's efforts
- A well-balanced mix of people who can provide the insights and skills needed to achieve the goal
- A size that aligns well with the team's responsibilities
- Positive behavioral norms that promote *psychological safety*, encouraging people to share information, propose unproven ideas, and express vulnerability without fear of repercussion
- A willingness to put the team's needs ahead of individual needs
- Open and honest communication

Exhibit 8.7 lists the characteristics of effective teams.

The types of individuals on a team are also a vital consideration. People who assume the *task-specialist role* focus on helping the team reach its goals. In contrast, members who take on the *socioemotional role* focus on supporting the team's emotional needs and strengthening the team's social unity.[34] Some team members assume dual roles, contributing to the task and still meeting members' emotional needs. These members often make effective team leaders. At the other end of the spectrum are members who are *nonparticipators*, contributing little to reaching the team's goals or to meeting members' socioemotional needs. Obviously, a team staffed with too many inactive members isn't going to accomplish much of anything. Exhibit 8.8 on page 258 outlines the behavior patterns associated with each of these roles.

REAL-TIME UPDATES
Learn More by Reading This Article

Too much of a good thing?

The potential benefits of team-based collaboration are undeniable, but some experts worry that companies are going overboard and overloading the employees they need the most. Go to **real-timeupdates .com/bia9** and select Learn More in the Students section.

 CHECKPOINT

LEARNING OBJECTIVE 4: Highlight the advantages and disadvantages of working in teams, and list the characteristics of effective teams.

SUMMARY: The potential advantages of teamwork include pooling more information and knowledge, providing learning opportunities, fostering boldness, providing accountability, building trust, accessing a broader range of viewpoints, getting buy-in for solutions a team creates, improving performance, and building a sense of community. The potential disadvantages include groupthink, hidden agendas, costs and inefficiency, and excessive workloads. Effective teams have a clear sense of purpose, a clear and challenging goal, a belief in the value of the team's efforts, a well-balanced mix of people, a size that aligns well with the team's responsibilities, positive behavioral norms that promote psychological safety, a willingness to put the team's needs ahead of individual needs, and open and honest communication.

EXHIBIT 8.7	**Characteristics of Effective Teams**

Effective teams practice these good habits.

Make Effective Teamwork a Top Management Priority
- Recognize and reward group performance where appropriate
- Provide ample training opportunities for employees to develop team skills

Select Team Members Wisely
- Involve key stakeholders and decision makers
- Limit team size to the minimum number of people needed to achieve team goals
- Select members with a diversity of views
- Select creative thinkers

Build A Sense of Fairness in Decision-Making
- Encourage debate and disagreement without fear of reprisal
- Allow members to communicate openly and honestly
- Consider all proposals
- Build consensus by allowing team members to examine, compare, and reconcile differences— but don't let a desire for 100 percent consensus bog down the team
- Avoid quick votes
- Keep everyone informed
- Present all relevant facts

Manage Conflict Constructively
- Share leadership
- Encourage equal participation
- Discuss disagreements openly and calmly
- Focus on the issues, not the people
- Don't let minor disagreements boil over into major conflicts

Stay on Track
- Make sure everyone understands the team's purpose
- Communicate what is expected of team members
- Stay focused on the core assignment
- Develop and adhere to a schedule
- Develop rules and follow norms

CRITICAL THINKING: (1) Is groupthink similar to peer pressure? Why or why not? (2) Is supporting a group decision you don't completely agree with always a case of groupthink? Explain your answer.

IT'S YOUR BUSINESS: (1) How would you characterize the experience you've had working in teams throughout your high school and college years? (2) How can you apply experience gained on athletic teams and other collaborative activities to the business world?

KEY TERMS TO KNOW: groupthink, hidden agenda

Fostering Teamwork

Because teams are composed of unique individuals with different perspectives, the interpersonal relationships among team members require careful consideration. Two particularly important issues are team development and team conflict.

TEAM DEVELOPMENT

Teams typically evolve through several phases on their way to becoming productive. A popular model of team development proposed by Dr. Bruce Tuckman identifies five phases a new team goes through as it evolves:[35]

5 **LEARNING OBJECTIVE**

Review the five stages of team development, and explain why conflict can arise in team settings.

| EXHIBIT 8.8 | Team Member Roles |

Team members assume one of these four roles. Members who assume a dual role—emphasizing both task progress and people needs—often make the most effective team leaders.

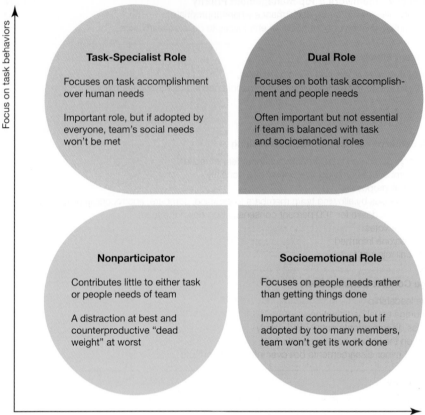

Forming. In this initial phase, the group comes together through online or virtual meetings, and various members begin to establish themselves in specific roles. In some cases, one person is given the formal role of team leader, but in others an informal leader may emerge as the members establish their roles. If the group's goal hasn't already been defined, the team leader or the team members themselves will establish it.

Storming. As team members begin to discuss their positions and become more assertive in establishing their roles, disagreements and uncertainties are natural in this phase. Much of the conflict may be constructive as team members share ideas for meeting the team's goals. However, if conflict threatens to get destructive, active conflict resolution might be necessary. Everyone has responsibility for helping the team get through this turbulent phase as quickly as possible. Positive steps include appreciating the benefit of having diverse viewpoints, assuming that people are there to do good work, and giving everyone the opportunity to be heard.[36]

Norming. As conflicts resolve themselves (or are resolved through intervention), the team begins to take on a cohesive personality with clear behavioral **norms**. For example, the team leader or those taking assertive roles might establish expectations that meetings start and end on schedule and that all members are ready to present or otherwise contribute as expected. If this sort of dependability becomes the norm, everyone will feel the group expectation to perform at this level. Norms define acceptable behavior by setting limits, identifying values, and clarifying expectations. By encouraging consistent behavior, norms boost efficiency and help ensure the group's survival. Individuals who deviate from these norms can find themselves ridiculed, isolated, or even removed from the group entirely. (This fear is a leading cause of groupthink, by the way.)

norms
Informal standards of conduct that guide team behavior.

- **Performing.** With a cohesive, distinct personality and norms to guide behavior, the group is ready to perform its task. The nature of the teamwork varies widely based on the type of work and the type of team. In some cases, members will work on individual assignments and periodically reconvene to share updates. In others, members may work side by side on shared tasks. It's not uncommon for issues to emerge as the work progresses, and the team may spend some time storming and re-norming again.

- **Adjourning.** When temporary teams accomplish their goal, the fifth and final step is to adjourn, or disband, the team. This stage may involve some post-project analysis in which members assess how well the team performed and compile advice for future teams.

REAL-TIME UPDATES
Learn More by Exploring This Interactive Website

Give your team an eight-point health checkup

Any work team can run these checkups to find out how healthy it is and get remedies for problem areas. Go to **real-timeupdates .com/bia9** and select Learn More in the Students section.

TEAM CONFLICT

As teams mature and go about their work, conflicts can arise. Although the term *conflict* sounds negative, conflict isn't necessarily bad. It can be *constructive* if it brings important issues into the open, increases the involvement of team members, and generates creative ideas for solving a problem. Sometimes two mediocre ideas can collide and produce one really great idea that no one had considered. Even teams that have some interpersonal friction can excel with effective leadership and team players committed to shared goals. As teamwork experts Andy Boynton and Bill Fischer put it, "Virtuoso teams are not about getting polite results."[37]

In contrast, conflict is *destructive* if it saps productivity, damages morale, or threatens to spread to other people in the organization. Destructive conflict can lead to *win-lose* or *lose-lose* outcomes, in which one or both sides lose, to the detriment of the entire team. If you approach conflict with the idea that both sides can satisfy their goals to at least some extent (a *win-win strategy*), you can minimize losses for everyone. For a win-win strategy to work, everybody must believe that (1) it's possible to find a solution that both parties can accept, (2) cooperation is better for the organization than competition, (3) the other party can be trusted, and (4) greater power or status doesn't entitle one party to impose a solution.

Conflict within teams is common as people bring different ideas and expectations to the table. Constructive conflict can help a team generate fresh ideas and devise new solutions, but destructive conflict can divide a team and slow or destroy its progress.

Sources of Team Conflict

Conflicts within a team and within the workplace in general can arise from a variety of causes (see Exhibit 8.9 on the next page).[38] Some conflicts are *structural*, meaning they are more or less permanent aspects of being in business. For example, every company has a finite amount of money to spend on operations every year, and every department is competing for a share of those funds. A second category involves *situational* conflicts, which arise from temporary forces within an industry or a company. The people assigned to a project team, for instance, may not agree on what the team's goals and priorities should be. A third category, *interpersonal* conflicts, stem from the choices, behaviors, and personality traits of the people within a team, department, or other work group.

As you can see from the examples in Exhibit 8.9, some conflicts are "blameless," in that they stem from natural forces in the business environment. Other conflicts have a more personal origin, and they may well be the fault of some of the people involved. In addition, structural and situational conflicts can magnify interpersonal conflicts, and vice versa. For instance, when business is booming and people are getting raises and promotional opportunities, occasional personality clashes might not be terribly disruptive because life in general is good for everybody. However, when times are tough, such as when sales are dropping or a team project is failing, this stress can amplify interpersonal conflicts as people's tolerances drop and they become more sensitive to perceived injustices and personal insults.

EXHIBIT 8.9	Sources of Team and Workplace Conflict

Conflict can come from a wide variety of sources.

Type	Examples
Structural: a permanent aspect of doing business	Competition for opportunities, such as promotions into management positions
	Competition for resources, such as project budgets, equipment, or staff
	Disagreements over fundamental values, such as the company's responsibilities to society or its workers
Situational: based on temporary forces	Disagreements over project goals
	Conflict between individual goals and team goals
	Workload and work–life imbalances
	Resistance to change
Interpersonal: stemming from personal choices, behaviors, and personality differences	Poor communication
	Personality clashes
	Unprofessional behavior
	Cultural differences

Solutions to Team Conflict

As with any other human relationship, the way a team approaches conflict depends to a large degree on how well the team was functioning in the first place. A strong, healthy team is more likely to view a conflict as simply another challenge to overcome—and it can emerge from the conflict even stronger than before. In contrast, a generally dysfunctional team can disintegrate even further when faced with a new source of conflict.

The following seven measures can help team members successfully resolve conflict:

- **Proactive attention.** Deal with minor conflict before it becomes major conflict.
- **Communication.** Get those directly involved in a conflict to participate in resolving it.
- **Openness.** Get feelings out in the open before dealing with the main issues.
- **Research.** Seek factual reasons for a problem before seeking solutions.
- **Flexibility.** Don't let anyone lock into a position before considering other solutions.
- **Fair play.** Insist on fair outcomes and don't let anyone avoid a fair solution by hiding behind the rules.
- **Alliance.** Get opponents to fight together against an "outside force" instead of against each other.

Team members and team leaders can also take several steps to prevent conflicts. First, by establishing clear goals that require the efforts of every member, the team reduces the chance that members will battle over their objectives or roles. Second, by developing well-defined tasks for each member, the team leader ensures that all parties are aware of their responsibilities and the limits of their authority. Finally, by facilitating open communication, the team leader can ensure that all members understand their own tasks and objectives as well as those of their teammates. Communication builds respect and tolerance, and it provides a forum for bringing misunderstandings into the open before they turn into full-blown conflicts.

 CHECKPOINT

LEARNING OBJECTIVE 5: Review the five stages of team development, and explain why conflict can arise in team settings.

SUMMARY: Several models have been proposed to describe the stages of team development; the well-known model defined by researcher Bruce Tuckman identifies the stages as forming, storming, norming, performing, and adjourning. In the forming stage, team members become acquainted with each other and with the group's purpose. In the storming stage, team members begin to discuss their positions and become more assertive in establishing their roles, and disagreements and uncertainties are natural in this phase. In the norming stage, conflicts are resolved, group norms are established, and harmony develops. In the performing stage, members focus on achieving the team's goals. In the adjourning stage, the team dissolves on completion of its task. This stage may involve some post-project analysis in which members assess how well the team performed and compile advice for future teams. Causes of conflicts can be *structural* (tensions that are essentially permanent aspects of being in business), *situational* (arising from temporary forces such as disagreement on a team's goals and priorities), or *interpersonal* (stemming from choices, behaviors, and personality traits of the people within a team).

CRITICAL THINKING: (1) How can a team leader know when to step in when conflict arises and when to step back and let the issue work itself out? (2) What are the risks of not giving new teams the time and opportunity to "storm" and "norm" before tackling the work they've been assigned?

IT'S YOUR BUSINESS: (1) Have you ever had to be teammates (in any activity) with someone you simply didn't like on a personal level? If so, how did this situation affect your performance as a team member? (2) Have you ever had to adapt your personality in order to succeed on a particular team? Was this a positive or negative experience?

KEY TERM TO KNOW: norms

Managing an Unstructured Organization

 LEARNING OBJECTIVE

Explain the concept of an unstructured organization, and identify the major benefits and challenges of taking this approach.

Companies such as Zappos have found themselves asking if they really need a traditional organization structure. That line of inquiry can be pushed even further to ask: Do we even need a company at all in the usual sense of the term? Some entrepreneurs and leaders are pushing the concepts of network structures and virtual teams to the extreme to create **unstructured organizations** that have little or no permanent structure, at least in terms of the traditional forms. These companies use digital technologies—and global socioeconomic changes enabled by these technologies—to rapidly form and re-form work patterns that bear almost no resemblance to the classic structures.

unstructured organization
An organization that doesn't have a conventional structure but instead assembles talent as needed from the open market; the virtual and networked organizational concepts taken to the extreme.

Innovators are experimenting with various combinations of virtual organizations, networked organizations, crowdsourcing, and outsourcing.[39] The new "formless forms" are enabled by cloud computing, mobile communication, online collaboration platforms, robotic process automation (see page 266), and social networking. All these elements have been in use for some time, but the mashup of new thinking and new technology is unleashing them in revolutionary ways. In a sense, by binding together a temporary organization, these technologies take the place of the lines and boxes that define a traditional organization chart.

Just about any category and skill level of work—particularly those that can be conducted digitally—is a possible candidate for these new approaches. Professions and functions already being affected include management consulting, software development, product design, visual design, scientific research, legal research, business writing, clerical work, and customer support.[40]

For example, a solo entrepreneur can now quickly assemble a product development team to conceptualize and design a product, then immediately disassemble that team and build a manufacturing team to make the product, and then assemble a sales and customer support team to get the product on the market—all without hiring a single employee. Moreover, this entrepreneur could tap into some of the best technical talent in the world, with top scientists, engineers, and software developers competing to see who can do the best job

REAL-TIME UPDATES
Learn More by Visiting This Website

Interested in exploring the freelance alternative?

Freelancers Union supports independent workers with resources, services, and community events. Go to **real-timeupdates.com/bia9** and select Learn More in the Students section.

on the new product. And rather than taking months to establish a company by recruiting employees, leasing office space, hiring supervisors, buying computers, setting up a payroll system, training staffers, and doing all the many other tasks involved in running a conventional company, this entrepreneur could sit at home in his or her pajamas and, in a matter of days, create an essentially formless company that successfully competes in the global marketplace.

The talent marketplace Topcoder (**www.topcoder.com**) offers a great illustration of the potential of this new way of working. Topcoder boasts a membership of more than a million design and technology specialists (including many who are still in college), representing virtually every country in the world. Clients such as our pajama-clad entrepreneur present Topcoder with one or more design challenges, and the members then compete to come up with the best solution.[41] Instead of auditioning several regular vendors and hoping to make the right choice or hiring a small staff of generalists and hoping they'll be able to handle the many specialized tasks involved in developing the software for a new product, our entrepreneur can have the best of the best work on each part of the design. When the design work is completed, the various Topcoder members move on to compete for other client projects, and the entrepreneur moves on to assembling other teams to create a virtual company.

On the talent marketplace Upwork (**www.upwork.com**), our entrepreneur could find someone to handle just about every business function imaginable, including basic administration tasks, customer service, accounting, legal matters, marketing, and sales. If manufacturing is required, *contract manufacturers* all over the world can handle every conceivable type of product. It's no exaggeration to say that our pajama-clad entrepreneur could build a fully functioning virtual company without ever getting off the sofa.

Just where these changes are taking the business enterprise is difficult to guess because the revolution is still under way. Some firms may adopt these structureless approaches extensively, whereas others may use them for specific projects. Even if you spend your career in a conventionally structured company, these changes are likely to affect you because they are accelerating the pace of business, influencing the worldwide talent market, and even changing the nature of work itself in some cases (such as by introducing project-by-project talent competition).

The following sections look at the potential benefits and points of concern that are emerging in relation to these new approaches to organization (see Exhibit 8.10 for a summary).

POTENTIAL BENEFITS OF UNSTRUCTURED ORGANIZATIONS

The unstructured organization concept has several potential benefits for firms of all sizes, from entrepreneurs who apply the concept to their entire operations to larger firms that use it for specific parts of the company or individual projects:[42]

- **Increased agility.** In many instances, virtual organizations can be assembled, reconfigured as needed, and disassembled much faster than a conventional employee-based organization can be created, changed, or dismantled. This agility makes it easier to jump on emerging market trends and then change course when the market changes again.
- **Lower fixed costs and more flexible capacity management.** Hiring employees to build organizational capacity increases a company's *fixed costs*—those that are incurred regardless of production or sales volumes. With the unstructured approach, companies have much more flexibility in adjusting their expense levels to match revenue levels.
- **Access to otherwise unreachable talent.** Talent marketplaces such as Topcoder give many more companies access to highly developed and often hyperspecialized talents. Companies that might never be able to attract or afford top experts in a field can essentially rent them on a project-by-project basis instead.
- **Benefits of competition.** Whereas most employees are motivated to do good work most of the time, independent contractors working through Topcoder, Upwork, Guru

EXHIBIT 8.10	Benefits and Challenges of Unstructured Organizations

The unstructured organization is an extreme version of the virtual and networked models, in which a company assembles freelance talent as needed from the open market rather than hiring and organizing employees in a conventional organizational structure.

Potential Benefits		Potential Challenges	
For Companies	**For Workers**	**For Companies**	**For Workers**
• **Increased agility**: Companies can respond to or create opportunities faster and then reorganize and move on when needed. • **Lower fixed costs**: Fewer employees means fewer bills to pay every month. • **More flexible capacity management**: Firms can ramp capacity up and down more quickly and with less trauma. • **Access to star talent**: Managers can "rent" top talent that is too expensive to hire full time or unwilling to work full time. • **Benefiting from competition**: Firms can stage competitions in talent markets to see who can devise the best solutions to problems.	• **Performance-based evaluation**: The only thing that matters is getting the job done. • **Freedom and flexibility**: Workers have more leeway in choosing which projects they want and how much they want to work. • **Access to more interesting and more fulfilling work**: Workers can connect with opportunities that might be unreachable otherwise.	• **Complexity and control issues**: Workers often have competing demands on their time and attention, and managers lack many of the organizational control and incentive "levers" that a regular company has. • **Uncertainty**: Without staff at the ready, companies won't always know if they'll be able to get the talent they need. • **Diminished loyalty**: Managers must deal with a workforce that doesn't have the same sense of loyalty to the organization that many full-time employees do. • **Management succession**: Companies with fewer employees will find it harder to groom replacement managers and executives. • **Accountability and liability**: Unstructured organizations lack the built-in accountability of conventional structures, and the distribution of work among multiple independent parties could create liability concerns.	• **Uncertainty**: Workers can't be sure they'll have work from one project to the next. • **Loss of meaning and connection**: Independent workers don't get the same sense of working together for a larger, shared purpose that employees get. • **Diminished loyalty**: Workers don't have the same sense employees often do that an organization is looking out for them and will reward sacrifices and effort above and beyond contractual obligations. • **Career development**: Without full-time employers to guide, support, and train them, workers are left to fend for themselves and to keep their skills current at their own expense.

Sources: "How It Works," Upwork, accessed 3 May 2018, www.upwork.com; Robert J. Thomas, *Leading the Digital Enterprise* (Accenture Institute for High Performance, 2016); Darren Dahl, "Want a Job? Let the Bidding Begin," *Inc.*, March 2011, 93–96; Thomas W. Malone, Robert J. Laubacher, and Tammy Johns, "The Age of Hyperspecialization," *Harvard Business Review*, July–August 2011, 56–65; Jennifer Wang, "The Solution to the Innovator's Dilemma," *Entrepreneur*, August 2011, 24–32; Marjorie Derven, "Managing the Matrix in the New Normal," *T+D*, July 2010, 42–47.

(www.guru.com), InnoCentive (www.innocentive.com), and other marketplaces must do their best on every single project—and compete with other independents in what is essentially a global marketplace—or risk not getting more assignments. Companies that engage contract talent clearly benefit from this competition. In addition, talent marketplaces such as Topcoder and InnoCentive structure projects as competitions, in which potential solution providers compete to offer the best ideas and work products.

For workers, the unstructured model also offers several potential benefits:[43]

- **Performance-based evaluation.** Workers tend to be evaluated almost entirely on measurable performance, project by project—on what they can do for a client, not on who they know in the executive suite, where they went to college, or what they did last year.
- **Freedom and flexibility.** The flip side of agility for companies is extreme flexibility for workers, particularly after they establish themselves in a field. Within the limits of financial need and project availability, of course, independent contractors can often pick and choose the clients and projects that interest them most and decide how much or how little they want to work.

- **Access to jobs that might be otherwise unattainable.** For people geographically removed from major employment centers, finding decent employment can be a serious challenge. The distributed, virtual approach gives people in rural areas and small towns greater access to job opportunities.

POTENTIAL CHALLENGES OF UNSTRUCTURED ORGANIZATIONS

For all its benefits, the unstructured approach presents several potential drawbacks, some of them considerable. These challenges will discourage many companies and workers from taking this route, and they make it more difficult for those who do:[44]

- **Complexity and control issues.** Unstructured organizations can be even more complex than matrix organizations because workers not only have multiple bosses but also report to multiple bosses in multiple companies. In addition, even though companies can in effect hire and fire independent contractors more easily, they have less control over this talent than they have over permanent employees.
- **Uncertainty.** Without full-time staff at the ready, companies won't always know if they can get the talent they need for upcoming projects. Conversely, workers won't always know if they'll have a job from one project to the next.
- **Loss of meaning and connection.** Being a full-time employee of an organization means more than just employment to many people. Companies also provide a social structure that is as close as family for some employees. Moreover, the opportunity to help an organization succeed over the long haul, to work with others for a greater purpose, is an important motivator and provides a sense of pride for many employees. Independent contractors who move from project to project don't have the chance to form such bonds.
- **Diminished loyalty.** The bond that develops between employers and employees over time creates a sense of loyalty that can carry both parties through hard times. Employers often make accommodations for employees who are going through tough personal circumstances, for instance. And many employees are willing to make or at least accept short-term sacrifices that benefit their companies in the long term (such as helping colleagues in addition to doing their own work or accepting pay reductions during periods of slow sales). However, this sense of "all for one and one for all" is not likely to factor heavily in most unstructured scenarios, where workers are more like competing vendors than members of a family.
- **Career development.** Conventional organizations do much more than just put resources in place to tackle one project after another. They invest in employees over months or years, giving them time and opportunities to develop deep knowledge and skills, with the idea that the investment will pay off in the long term. However, independent contractors are responsible for developing themselves while they're busy making a living, so keeping up with developments in their professions presents a greater burden than it does for typical employees.
- **Management succession.** As companies develop their employees, they also groom future managers and executives who understand both the company internally and its multiple external environments. Without these development channels in place, companies could be hard pressed to replace upper managers when the time comes.
- **Accountability and liability.** Conventional structures tend to have clear lines of accountability up and down the chain of command (meaning it's clear who is responsible if things go awry) and clear assignments of legal or financial liability in the event of major foul-ups. However, the situation might not be quite so clear in an unstructured organization that relies on a temporary assemblage of independent companies and contractors.

Although these challenges should not be taken lightly by companies or workers, they are likely to be manageable in enough different scenarios that the unstructured approach will catch on in more and more industries. Exactly where unstructured organizations will take the world of business will be interesting to see.

CHECKPOINT

LEARNING OBJECTIVE 6: Explain the concept of an unstructured organization, and identify the major benefits and challenges of taking this approach.

SUMMARY: An unstructured organization doesn't rely on conventional organizational structures to assemble the resources needed to pursue business goals. Instead, it assembles independent contractors or companies, as needed, for specific tasks or functions, relying on electronic communications to replace much of the structural linkages in a conventional company. The potential benefits for companies are increased agility, lower fixed costs and more flexible capacity management, access to otherwise unreachable talent, and the benefits of competition among workers or service providers. For workers, the benefits include performance-based evaluation of their efforts, more freedom and flexibility to choose which projects to work on and how much to work, and access to jobs that might be otherwise unattainable. The potential disadvantages of the unstructured approach include complexity and control issues for managers, greater uncertainty for companies and workers, the loss of meaning and connection to a greater purpose for employees, diminished loyalty for both employers and employees, uncertainties in career development and management succession, and concerns over accountability and liability.

CRITICAL THINKING: (1) "Unstructured organization" is something of a contradiction in terms; are such companies still "organized" if they have no permanent structure? Why or why not? (2) How can workers develop marketable skills if they work as independent contractors?

IT'S YOUR BUSINESS: (1) Where do you think you would be most comfortable: as a regular employee in a conventionally structured firm or as an independent contractor, moving from project to project? Why? (2) Assume that you went to work for a conventional employer and then left to work as an independent contractor as soon as you developed enough of a skill set to make it on your own. (Assume, as well, that you were not violating any sort of employment contract and were free to leave.) Would you have any ethical concerns about leaving an employer who had invested in your professional development? Why or why not?

KEY TERM TO KNOW: unstructured organization

Thriving in the Digital Enterprise: Taskbots and Robotic Process Automation

 LEARNING OBJECTIVE

Describe the use of taskbots and robotic procession automation in contemporary business.

Humans aren't the only participants who need to be organized in today's business environment. An increasing amount of routine office work is being done by software agents, working side-by-side with their human teammates.

TASKBOTS

If the thought of living in some sci-fi future where you work with robot colleagues makes you uneasy, you might as well relax—you're already doing it. The internet and mobile phone apps are teeming with *bots,* pieces of software that perform a wide variety of tasks. They may not have mechanical arms and cute or creepy humanoid faces, but they are robots just the same.

The distinctions can be a little vague, but bots can be divided into two general categories: *chatbots* and *taskbots.* As their names suggest, the former primarily engage in conversation and the latter handle chores, although many bots can do both. Chatbots such as Apple's Siri and Amazon's Alexa use voice interaction, whereas many online chatbots and taskbots use text input and output.

A **taskbot** (not to be confused with a particular product called TaskBot) is a software agent that can be programmed to handle a variety of routine tasks. Taskbots can assist

taskbot
A software agent that can be assigned to complete a variety of tasks within an app or business system.

EXHIBIT 8.11   **Taskbots**

Bots such as TaskOnBot (shown here) are now a common feature on collaboration platforms such as Slack. They function as virtual team members and can be assigned a variety of tasks and assign tasks to their human teammates.

teams with scheduling, data collection, document distribution, routine communication, and other tasks to give teams more time to focus on higher-level work. Some bots can guide online discussions and project update meetings. Work group messaging systems such as Slack (**www.slack.com**) treat them as team members; bots can be assigned tasks and can assign tasks to their human teammates (see Exhibit 8.11).[45]

ROBOTIC PROCESS AUTOMATION

robotic process automation (RPA)

A software capability that does for knowledge work what mechanical robots do for manufacturing and other physical processes.

Taskbots are a key feature in **robotic process automation (RPA)**, a software capability that does for knowledge work what robots do for manufacturing and other physical processes (see Exhibit 8.12). RPA targets the high-volume "paperwork" aspects of business, such as entering and retrieving records, creating database reports, and processing customer orders.

In contrast to cognitive automation(see page 235), which involves sophisticated artificial intelligence (AI) capabilities, RPA is a rules-based method of automation. RPA is best suited to high-volume transactional situations with predictable inputs, well-structured data, and clear rules. For instance, insurance companies can use RPA to process incoming claims, entering the client information into the system, checking it against rules for granting or denying claims, and then taking the appropriate action. RPA applications are often human-bot hybrids, with bots handling routine tasks until they encounter something they can't solve, at which point they transfer the problem to a human staffer.[46]

RPA is a well-established technology at this point and can deliver a significant return on investment in terms of increasing efficiency, reducing errors, and freeing people to do more creative and complex work. Despite recurring worries about robots and AI destroying jobs, employees generally welcome RPA because it takes on the tedious and repetitive work that most people dislike.[47]

REAL-TIME UPDATES

Learn More by Visiting This Website

Explore the latest advances in RPA

The Institute for Robotic Process Automation & Artificial Intelligence covers the latest developments in RPA. Go to **real-timeupdates .com/bia9** and select Learn More in the Students section.

EXHIBIT 8.12	**Robotic Process Automation**

Robotic process automation capabilities such as WorkFusion's automate repetitive business tasks in order to free employees for more creatively demanding work.

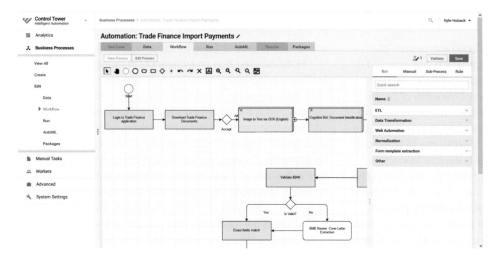

 CHECKPOINT

LEARNING OBJECTIVE 7: Describe the use of taskbots and robotic procession automation in contemporary business.

SUMMARY: Taskbots are software agents that can be programmed to handle a variety of routine tasks. They play a key role in robotic process automation (RPA), a software capability that does for knowledge work what robots do for manufacturing and other physical processes. RPA targets the high-volume "paperwork" aspects of business, such as entering and retrieving records, creating database reports, and processing customer orders. Businesses are adopting RPA to improve efficiency and process accuracy.

CRITICAL THINKING: (1) Should a company apply any RPA solution without critically examining its processes first? Why or why not? (2) If taskbots, RPA, and related technologies eventually take over so much work that they affect employment opportunities, how should society respond?

IT'S YOUR BUSINESS: (1) Would you rather work alongside a human teammate who occasionally makes mistakes that cost you time and energy or an AI-enabled taskbot that performs flawlessly? Explain your answer. (2) Would you be comfortable getting a medical diagnosis from a bot? Why or why not?

KEY TERMS TO KNOW: taskbot, robotic process automation (RPA)

 **BEHIND THE SCENES**

Smashing the Hierarchy at Zappos

When Tony Hsieh decided to abolish the conventional management hierarchy at Zappos, it was not a small-scale whim conducted at some fringe start-up that had nothing to lose. Zappos was a 15-year-old company with 1,500 employees and more than $1 billion in annual revenue. Moreover, it was and is owned by a $200 billion corporation (Amazon) with an obsession for efficiency. *Business Insider* called it "one of the biggest experiments in management history."

However, Hsieh has never shied away from taking bold leaps down unconventional paths. He began to worry that as it grew, Zappos could morph into a stodgy, unresponsive, and very conventional corporation where people settled into functional silos and bureaucracy ruled. He was determined to find a different way to run a company—or for a company to run itself, to be more precise.

The solution he settled on is a manager-less system of distributed authority known as Holacracy, which was invented by software entrepreneur Brian Robertson. Holacracy replaces the idea of managers and the conventional hierarchy of people in specific organizational positions with *roles*, which correspond to a function or activity. People usually fill more than one role at a time. One person might have the roles of social media marketing and customer training, for instance. The tasks that managers traditionally do, from planning to decision-making, are distributed among the various roles. Although the idea of getting rid of managers and a hierarchy based on managerial authority conjures the image of an uncontrolled free-for-all with no rules, Holacracy is in fact guided by precise rules, clear accountability, and a hierarchy of roles (rather than a hierarchy of people or positions).

Holacracy's rather intricate system of roles and rules is beyond the scope of this discussion, but Hsieh's decision to adopt it is a fascinating case study in challenging the conventional thinking about management and organizational design.

Hsieh acknowledges that the manager-less approach is not for everyone. People who need a lot of direction or don't want to be responsible for directing their own work aren't likely to be comfortable with it, nor are people who like the power and prestige that comes with being a manager. He and Robertson are also open about the fact that a transition as profound as getting rid of management is likely to be tumultuous, and a company could take from several months to several years to settle into the new way of thinking and working. Author Frederic Laloux, who left the prestigious management consulting firm McKinsey & Company to evangelize the concept of self-management, was intrigued by the possibility of a company as large as Zappos making this transition. His assessment was blunt: "I expect quite a bit of confusion and chaos."

It's not surprising, then, that Zappos experienced some resistance and confusion after Hsieh began rolling out the new system across the company. Some managers were reluctant to surrender authority, some employees were no longer sure how to get things done, and anger and fear occasionally boiled over during meetings about the new scheme.

Over time, more and more employees gradually bought into it, but the slow pace of the transition frustrated Hsieh, and he eventually issued an ultimatum: Either get on board with the new system or find a new opportunity outside of Zappos. True to the company's considerate treatment of employees, though, he offered anyone who wanted to leave a generous severance package.

Roughly 18 percent of the company's workers and managers took him up on the offer. A loss of that many employees would be cause for concern under usual circumstances, but Hsieh's take is that whatever number of employees quit was the right number, because that left Zappos with a workforce fully committed to the new model. (Of course, this doesn't account for employees who didn't take the buyout because they were unwilling or unable to leave for other reasons.)

Holacracy remains an experiment in progress at Zappos, and the coming years will continue to provide more evidence of its success or failure. One intriguing and, so far, disappointing measure is the company's fall in *Fortune* magazine's 100 Best Companies to Work For ranking, which is based on employee surveys and "culture audits" by an outside firm. Before the transition, Zappos had ranked as high as 6th, rubbing shoulders with some of the most elite companies in the United States. However, its ranking plummeted after the change, dropping to 38th in 2014 (the year of Hsieh's ultimatum), then 86th in 2015. In 2016 it fell off the list entirely and was still off the list as of 2018.

A nonscientific perusal of insider rankings on Glassdoor and Indeed suggests a clear split between employees who love or at least like the new manager-less approach and those who strongly don't. The average scores are reasonably high, though, so the fans outnumber the naysayers. Hsieh remains committed to Holacracy and backs up his enthusiasm with internal surveys of employee happiness and other measures. (Amazon doesn't report Zappos's annual revenue, so it's unclear what financial impact the transformation has had on the company.)

Aside from whatever verdict Hsieh's experiment might eventually deliver on Holacracy specifically, the more intriguing general question is how well a fairly large company can get by without managers or a formal organization structure.[48] Companies will be struggling with questions of authority and organization for as long as companies exist, so the results of the Zappos experiment should be interesting for years to come.

Critical Thinking Questions

8-1. A wealthy individual such as Hsieh and a Zappos employee just getting by on his or her hourly wage are likely to have profoundly different views about work and the meaning of a job. Does someone in Hsieh's position have an ethical responsibility to protect his employees' livelihoods even if they don't agree with his management philosophy—particularly if that philosophy changed after some people uprooted their families to join the company? Why or why not?

8-2. What effect would a culture of self-management be likely to have on any company's recruiting efforts? How would it influence the type and quality of candidates who apply?

8-3. How important is a public ranking such as *Fortune*'s 100 Best Companies to Work For? Explain your answer.

Learn More Online

Visit **www.zappos.com/about** and explore the sections "Beyond the Box" and "Zappos Insights"; then visit the careers section at **jobs.jobvite.com/zappos**. What impression do you get of the company's work culture? Do you find any mention of Holacracy or self-management? Would the culture appeal to you as an employee? Why or why not?

End of Chapter

KEY TERMS

agile organization (248)
centralization (246)
chain of command (245)
committee (252)
core competencies (244)
cross-functional team (252)
decentralization (246)
departmentalization (248)
divisional structure (249)
functional structure (248)
functional team (252)
groupthink (255)
hidden agenda (256)
matrix structure (249)

network structure (250)
norms (258)
organization chart (243)
organization structure (243)
problem-solving team (252)
robotic process automation (RPA) (266)
self-managed team (252)
span of management (245)
task force (252)
taskbot (265)
team (251)
unstructured organization (261)
virtual team (253)
work specialization (244)

TEST YOUR KNOWLEDGE

Questions for Review

8-4. What is a core competency?

8-5. What are the four types of organization structure?

8-6. What are the differences between a group and a team?

8-7. How do you distinguish between a formal and an informal organization?

8-8. What are the advantages and disadvantages of divisional organizational structures?

8-9. What is meant by the term behavioral norm in the context of teams?

8-10. What are the potential benefits and potential disadvantages of the unstructured organization model?

8-11. What is robotic process automation?

Questions for Analysis

8-12. Why is it important for companies to decide on their core competencies before choosing an organization structure?

8-13. How can a virtual organization reduce costs?

8-14. Describe the stages of team development. Where might the conflicts arise?

8-15. What are the major characteristics of an effective team?

8-16. How might a team leader use conflict in a positive way?

8-17. Why are self-managed teams becoming more popular in business?

8-18. Why are many companies now rethinking or abandoning classical concepts of organization structure?

8-19. **Ethical Considerations.** A company executive accidentally emailed you a confidential spreadsheet with the salaries of all employees in the company. You took only a quick peek before deleting it, but you looked at it long enough to discover that other managers at your level are earning anywhere from 10 to 40 percent more than you are, even though you've been at the company longer than any of them. Based on this discovery, you believe you deserve consideration for a raise. How will you handle the situation?

Questions for Application

8-20. Bruce Tuckman published his forming, storming, norming, and performing model in 1965. He added a fifth stage, adjourning, in the 1970s. Why do you think Tuckman felt it necessary to add the fifth stage? Why is this stage important?

8-21. You work for a midsized global business that has small offices in twelve capital cities around the world. Organizational coordination is good, with excellent, compatible IT support; a culture of remote team-working; and a shared view of the organizational mission and values across the offices and employees. Virtual teamwork is successful, but some employees strongly believe that there are insurmountable challenges in this type of teamwork. What problems are likely to be highlighted?

8-22. **Concept Integration.** One of your competitors has approached you with a merger proposal. The economies of scale would be terrific. So are the growth possibilities. There's just one issue to be resolved. Your competitor is organized under a flat structure and uses many cross-functional teams. Your company is organized under a traditional tall structure that is departmentalized by function. Using your knowledge of culture clash (see page 180), what are the likely issues you will encounter if these two organizations are merged?

8-23. **Concept Integration.** Chapter 7 discussed several styles of leadership: autocratic, democratic, and laissez-faire. Using your knowledge of the differences in these leadership styles, which style would you expect to find under the following organization structures: (a) tall organization with departmentalization by function, (b) tall organization with departmentalization by matrix, (c) flat organization, and (d) self-directed teams?

EXPAND YOUR KNOWLEDGE

Discovering Career Opportunities

Management jobs require a range of skills and experience, and, not surprisingly, the demands increase with the scope and scale of the opportunity. Use a website such as Indeed or Simply Hired to find three supervisor or management jobs in different companies or industries. Study the listed qualifications, then choose which of the three jobs is most appealing to you. Compare the requirements of this job with your current qualifications, and outline a plan (additional education or stepping-stone positions) you could pursue to develop the skills and experience needed to land your chosen job.

Intelligent Communication Technology: Robotic Process Automation

Research a current robotic process automation system or a system that includes this capability. In a brief report, summarize the function of the system and its potential benefits to businesses.

PRACTICE YOUR SKILLS

Resolving Ethical Dilemmas

In the past, you have been encouraged by your employer to communicate with colleagues using social media, chatrooms and groups, and video-calls within and outside normal working hours. In recent weeks, however, there have been two occasions when confidential information has leaked into the public domain as a result of conversations between employees over insecure networks and platforms. Your employer has now banned the use of social media as a means of communicating with colleagues inside and outside the workplace.

The final decision about implementing this new rule has not yet been made. You have sufficient time to try to put together a compelling case as to why it is important for the company to retain social media as a vital communication tool among colleagues. What are the benefits of social media? What is your own experience of confidentiality while using social media to communicate with colleagues? What lessons have you learned as a result?

Growing as a Professional

Many situations in your personal, professional, and academic spheres offer the opportunity to develop your capability and capacity as a teammate. The next time you're involved with a collaborative effort or simply helping a friend or family member, think about how you can contribute to a positive outcome by engaging in both a task-specialist role and a socioemotional role. You probably perform both roles instinctively to some degree already, but look for ways to make stronger and more deliberate contributions by applying what you've learned in this chapter.

Sharpening Your Communication Skills

In group meetings, some of your colleagues have a habit of interrupting and arguing with the speaker, taking credit for ideas that aren't theirs, and shooting down ideas they don't agree with. You're the newest person in the group and not sure if this is accepted behavior in this company, but it concerns you both personally and professionally. Should you go with the flow and adopt your colleagues' behavior or stick with your own communication style, even though you might get lost in the noise? In two paragraphs, explain the pros and cons of both approaches.

Building Your Team Skills

What's the most effective organization structure for your college or university? With your team, obtain a copy of your school's organization chart. If this chart is not readily available, gather information by talking with people in administration, and then draw your own chart of the organization structure.

Analyze the chart in terms of span of management. Is your school a flat or a tall organization? Is this organization structure appropriate for your school? Does decision-making tend to be centralized or decentralized in your school? Do you agree with this approach to decision-making?

Finally, investigate the use of formal and informal teams in your school. Are there any problem-solving teams, task forces, or committees at work in your school? Are any teams self-directed or virtual? How much authority do these teams have to make decisions? What is the purpose of teamwork in your school? What kinds of goals do these teams have?

Share your team's findings during a brief classroom presentation and then compare the findings of all teams. Is there agreement on the appropriate organization structure for your school?

Developing Your Research Skills

Although teamwork can benefit many organizations, introducing and managing team structures can be a real challenge. Search past issues of business journals or newspapers to locate articles about how an organization has overcome problems with teams.

8-24. Why did the organization originally introduce teams? What types of teams are being used?

8-25. What problems did each organization encounter in trying to implement teams? How did the organization deal with these problems?

8-26. Have the teams been successful from management's perspective? From the employees' perspective? What effect has teamwork had on the company, its customers, and its products?

Writing Assignments

8-27. What are some possible benefits and risks of having teams compete against each other, such as having the sales teams from various regions compete to add the most new customers?

8-28. Review the "Loss of meaning and connection" bullet point on page 264 in the discussion of the potential challenges of unstructured organizations. If you were planning to launch an unstructured organization, what steps could you take to help ensure that any independent contractors you hire on a project-by-project basis will have the same pride in their work that a dedicated, full-time employee would have?

ENDNOTES

1. Zappos, accessed 2 May 2018, www.zappos.com; "Holacracy and Self-Organization," Zappos Insights, accessed 2 May 2018, www.zapposinsights.com; Emmie Martin, "Why Multi-Millionaire Zappos CEO Tony Hsieh Chooses to Live in a Trailer Park," *CNBC*, 8 May 2017, www.cnbc.com; "100 Best Companies to Work For (2015–2018)," *Fortune*, fortune.com/best-companies; Zappos reviews, Indeed, accessed 2 May 2018, www.indeed.com; Richard Feloni, "Inside Zappos CEO Tony Hsieh's Radical Management Experiment That Prompted 14% of Employees to Quit," *Business Insider*, 16 May 2015, www.businessinsider.com; Richard Feloni, "Zappos CEO Tony Hsieh Explains Why 18% of Employees Quit During the Company's Radical Management Experiment," *Business Insider*, 14 May 2016, www.businessinsider.com; Richard Feloni, "Here's How the 'Self-Management' System That Zappos Is Using Actually Works," *Business Insider*, 3 June 2015, www.businessinsider.com; Bourree Lam, "Why Are So Many Zappos Employees Leaving?" *Atlantic*, 15 January 2016, www.theatlantic.com; "How It Works," Holacracy, accessed 2 May 2018, www.holacracy.org.
2. Sujan Patel, "The Benefits of Outsourcing Your Payroll," *Inc.*, 7 July 2016, www.inc.com.
3. Frog Design website, accessed 28 April 2018, www.frogdesign.com.
4. Stephen P. Robbins, Mary Coulter, and David A. DeCenzo, *Fundamentals of Management*, 4th ed. (New York: Pearson, 2017), 163.
5. Richard L. Daft, *Management*, 13th ed. (Boston: Cengage, 2018), 307
6. Caroline Ellis, "The Flattening Corporation," *MIT Sloan Management Review*, Summer 2003, 5.
7. "Container Store's Hiring Secret," *Fortune* video, accessed 23 August 2011, money.cnn.com.
8. "Why Middle Managers May Be the Most Important People in Your Company," *Knowledge@Wharton*, 25 May 2011, knowledge.wharton.upenn.edu.
9. Stephen P. Robbins and Timothy A. Judge, *Essentials of Organizational Behavior*, 14th ed. (New York: Pearson, 2018), 250.
10. Daft, *Management*, 310–312.
11. Aaron De Smet and Chris Gagnon, "Organizing for the Age of Urgency," *McKinsey Quarterly*, January 2018, www.mckinsey.com.
12. "Safe Enough to Try: An Interview with Zappos CEO Tony Hsieh," *McKinsey Quarterly*, October 2017, www.mckinsey.com.
13. Daft, *Management*, 312.
14. Robbins and Judge, *Essentials of Organizational Behavior*, 253; Daft, *Management*, 314.
15. Julie Goran, Laura LaBerge, and Ramesh Srinivasan, "Culture for a Digital Age," *McKinsey Quarterly*, July 2017, www.mckinsey.com.
16. "Business Divisions," ExxonMobil, accessed 28 April 2018, corporate.exxonmobile.com; "Operations," Chevron, accessed 28 April 2018, www.chevron.com.
17. Robbins and Judge, *Essentials of Organizational Behavior*, 254; Daft, *Management*, 318–319.

18. Marjorie Derven, "Managing the Matrix in the New Normal," *TD*, June 2010.

19. Pete Engardio and Bruce Einhorn, "Outsourcing Innovation," *BusinessWeek*, 21 March 2005, 84–94.

20. Leigh L. Thompson, *Making the Team: A Guide for Managers*, 6th ed. (New York: Pearson, 2018), 4.

21. Robbins and Judge, *Essentials of Organizational Behavior*, 155.

22. Thompson, *Making the Team: A Guide for Managers*, 13–15; Daft, *Management*, 609; Robbins, Coulter, and DeCenzo, *Fundamentals of Management*, 310.

23. Daft, *Management*, 607.

24. Behnam Tabrizi, "75% of Cross-Functional Teams Are Dysfunctional," *Harvard Business Review*, 23 June 2015, hbr.org.

25. Gregory Ciotti, "How Remote Teams Are Becoming the Future of Work," HelpScout, 23 April 2016, www.helpscout.com.

26. Mark Mortensen, "A First-Time Manager's Guide to Leading Virtual Teams," *Harvard Business Review*, 25 September 2017, hbr.org.

27. Rob Rawson, "21 Tips to Help You Manage a High-Performing Virtual Team," Time Doctor, accessed 1 March 2018, biz30 .timedoctor.com.

28. "Is IBM's Rethinking of Its Remote Work Policy a Bellwether?" *Knowledge@Wharton*, 22 June 2017, knowledge.wharton. upenn.edu.

29. Richard McDermott and Douglas Archibald, "Harnessing Your Staff's Informal Networks," *Harvard Business Review*, March 2010, 82–89.

30. "Advantages and Disadvantages of Team Decision-Making," *Human Capital Review*, accessed 23 February 2017, www.humancapitalreview.com; Dave Mattson, "6 Benefits of Teamwork in the Workplace," Sandler Training, 19 February 2015, www.sandler.com; Edmund Lau, "Why and Where Is Teamwork Important?" *Forbes*, 23 January 2013, www.forbes .com; "Five Case Studies on Successful Teams," *HR Focus*, April 2002, 18; Max Landsberg and Madeline Pfau, "Developing Diversity: Lessons from Top Teams," *Strategy + Business*, Winter 2005, 10–12; "Groups Best at Complex Problems," *Industrial Engineer*, June 2006, 14.

31. Liane Davey, "Toxic Teams," *Leadership Excellence*, 2 November 2012, 3.

32. Rob Cross, Reb Rebele, and Adam Grant, "Collaborative Overload," *Harvard Business Review*, January–February 2016, 74–79.

33. Thompson, *Making the Team: A Guide for Managers*, 34; Heidi K. Gardner, "Getting Your Stars to Collaborate," *Harvard Business Review*, January–February 2017, 100–108; Dave Winsborough and Tomas Chamorro-Premuzic, "Great Teams Are About Personalities, Not Just Skills," *Harvard Business Review*, 25 January 2017, www.hbr.org; Charles Duhigg, "What Google Learned from Its Quest to Build the Perfect Team," *New York Times Magazine*, 25 February 2016, www.nytimes.com; Martine Haas and Mark Mortensen, "The Secrets of Great Teamwork," *Harvard Business Review*, June 2016, 71–76.

34. Daft, *Management*, 618.

35. Stephen P. Robbins and Mary Coulter, *Management*, 14th ed. (New York: Prentice Hall, 2018), 418–419; Denise Bonebright, "40 Years of Storming: A Historical Review of Tuckman's Model of Small Group Development," *Human Resource Development International* 13, no. 1 (February 2010): 111–120.

36. "Tuckman: Forming, Storming, Norming, Performing," *Consultant's Mind*, accessed 28 February 2018, www.consultantsmind.com.

37. Andy Boynton and Bill Fischer, *Virtuoso Teams: Lessons from Teams That Changed Their Worlds* (Harrow, UK: FT Prentice Hall, 2005), 10.

38. Stephen P. Robbins and Timothy A. Judge, *Essentials of Organizational Behavior*, 14th ed. (New York: Pearson, 2018), 226–227.

39. Robert J. Thomas, *Leading the Digital Enterprise* (Accenture Institute for High Performance, 2016); Darren Dahl, "Want a Job? Let the Bidding Begin," *Inc.*, March 2011, 93–96; Thomas W. Malone, Robert J. Laubacher, and Tammy Johns, "The Age of Hyperspecialization," *Harvard Business Review*, July–August 2011, 56–65.

40. PWC Talent Exchange, accessed 3 May 2018, talentexchange. pwc.com; Malone, Laubacher, and Johns, "The Age of Hyperspecialization."

41. Topcoder website, accessed 3 May 2018, www.topcoder.com.

42. Based in part on Dahl, "Want a Job? Let the Bidding Begin"; Malone, Laubacher, and Johns, "The Age of Hyperspecialization"; Jennifer Wang, "The Solution to the Innovator's Dilemma," *Entrepreneur*, August 2011, 24–32; Derven, "Managing the Matrix in the New Normal."

43. "How It Works," Upwork, accessed 3 May 2018, www.upwork.com; Thomas, *Leading the Digital Enterprise*; "LiveOps and Vision Perry Create New Work Opportunities for Rural Tennessee," LiveOps press release, 18 July 2011, www.liveops.com; Malone, Laubacher, and Johns, "The Age of Hyperspecialization."

44. Based in part on Dahl, "Want a Job? Let the Bidding Begin"; Malone, Laubacher, and Johns, "The Age of Hyperspecialization"; Wang, "The Solution to the Innovator's Dilemma"; Derven, "Managing the Matrix in the New Normal."

45. Bot My Work, accessed 1 March 2018, botmywork.com.

46. Clint Boulton, "What Is RPA? A Revolution in Business Process Automation," *CIO*, 13 November 2017, www.cio.com; "What Is Robotic Process Automation?" Institute for Robotic Process Automation & Artificial Intelligence, accessed 3 May 2018, irpaai.com.

47. Xavier Lhuer, "The Next Acronym You Need to Know About: RPA (Robotic Process Automation)," McKinsey, December 2016, www.mckinsey.com.

48. See note 1.

9 Production Systems

LEARNING OBJECTIVES   After studying this chapter, you will be able to

1 Explain the systems perspective, and identify seven principles of systems thinking that can improve your skills as a manager.

2 Describe the value chain and value web concepts, and discuss the controversy over offshoring.

3 Define *supply chain management*, and explain its strategic importance.

4 Identify the major planning decisions in production and operations management.

5 Explain the unique challenges of service delivery.

6 Define *quality*, explain the challenge of quality and product complexity, and identify four major tools and strategies for ensuring product quality.

7 Explain the concept of *Industry 4.0* and the smart factory.

MyLab Intro to Business
Improve Your Grade!

If your instructor is using MyLab Intro to Business, visit **www.pearson.com/mylab/intro-to-business**.

BEHIND THE SCENES   **Voodoo Manufacturing: Building the Factory of the Future**

Oliver Ortlieb, Jonathan Schwartz, Patrick Deem, and Max Friefeld launched Voodoo Manufacturing to offer on-demand 3D printing.

Courtesy of Voodoo Manufacturing

www.voodoomfg.com

Chances are you've seen and perhaps used a 3D printer in a school project or at Maker Faire or another "maker" event. With low-cost 3D printing now widely available, students, hobbyists, and DIY designers have access to a universe of manufacturing capability that previously was beyond the reach of most people. Anyone with a computer can now make toys, jewelry, and just about any kind of small gadget they can dream up and visualize as a digital model.

3D printing is a boon for people who love to create things in the physical realm, but can it be a viable manufacturing business? Four entrepreneurs from Brooklyn—Max Friefeld, Jonathan Schwartz, Oliver Ortlieb, and Patrick Deem—were determined to find out. Although selling 3D printers is a well-established business model at this point, they wanted to offer 3D printing as a service—and not as a small-time operation, but as a major, "factory-level" enterprise.

If you were Max Friefeld, who serves as Voodoo's CEO, how would you approach this opportunity? Could you create the equivalent of cloud computing with "cloud manufacturing," offering on-demand manufacturing to anyone with a printable idea? How could you scale up the idea of using individual printers to produce hundreds or thousands of pieces at high speed? What kind of customers could you attract to your digital factory?[1]

INTRODUCTION

Voodoo Manufacturing (profiled in the chapter-opening Behind the Scenes) represents the leading-edge capabilities that today's digitally disrupted manufacturing has made possible. This chapter explores the world of goods and services production, starting with a look at the systems concept, followed by value chains and value webs, supply chain management, production and operations management, services delivery, and product and process quality.

The Systems View of Business

One of the most important skills you can develop as a leader is the ability to view business from a systems perspective. A **system** is an interconnected and coordinated set of *elements* and *processes* that convert *inputs* into desired *outputs*. A company is made up of numerous individual systems in the various functional areas, not only in manufacturing or operations but also in engineering, marketing, accounting, and other areas that together constitute the overall system that is the company itself. Each of these individual systems can also be thought of as a *subsystem* of the overall business.

THINKING IN SYSTEMS

To grasp the power of systems thinking, consider a point, a line, and a circle (see Exhibit 9.1). If you poked your head into a nearby office building, what would this snapshot tell you? You would be able to see only one part of the entire operation—and only at this one moment in time. You might see people in the advertising department working on plans for a new ad campaign or people in the accounting department juggling numbers in spreadsheets, but neither view would tell you much about what it takes to complete these tasks or how this department interacts with the rest of the company.

If you observed the operation for several days, though, you could start to get a sense of how people do their jobs in a department. In the advertising department, for instance, you could watch as the staff transforms ideas, information, and goals into a plan that leads to the creation of a new online advertising campaign. Your "point" view would thereby extend into a "line" view, with multiple points connected in sequence.

However, you still wouldn't have a complete picture of the entire process in action. Was the campaign successful? What did the advertising department learn from the campaign that could help it do even better next time? To see the process operate over and over, you need to connect the end of the line (the completion of this ad campaign) back to the beginning of the line (the start of the next ad campaign) to create a circle. Now you're beginning to form a *systems view* of what this department does and how its performance can be improved.

This circular view helps you understand the advertising system better, but it still isn't complete, because it doesn't show you how the advertising system affects the rest of the company and vice versa. For instance, did the finance department provide enough money to run the ad campaign? Was the information technology group prepared to handle the surge in website traffic? Was the manufacturing department ready with enough materials to build the product after customers started placing orders? Were the sales and customer service departments ready to handle the increase in their workloads? All of these subsystems connect to form the overall business system. Only by looking at the interconnected business system can you judge whether the ad campaign was a success for the company as a whole.

MANAGING SYSTEMS FOR PEAK PERFORMANCE

Much of the art and science of management involves understanding systems or creating new systems and figuring out ways to make them work more efficiently (using fewer resources) and more effectively (meeting goals more successfully). In some situations, *systems analysts* can run computer simulations to experiment with changes before making any resource decisions. However, even without these formal techniques and tools, you can benefit from systems thinking by keeping these principles in mind:[2]

EXHIBIT 9.1 **From Point to Line to Circle: The Systems View**

The systems view considers all steps in a process and "closes the loop" by providing feedback from the output of one cycle back to the input of the next cycle.

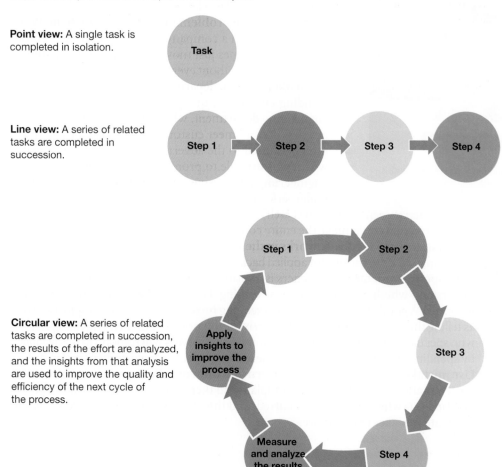

Point view: A single task is completed in isolation.

Task

Line view: A series of related tasks are completed in succession.

Step 1 → Step 2 → Step 3 → Step 4

Circular view: A series of related tasks are completed in succession, the results of the effort are analyzed, and the insights from that analysis are used to improve the quality and efficiency of the next cycle of the process.

Step 1 → Step 2 → Step 3 → Step 4 → Measure and analyze the results → Apply insights to improve the process

- **Help everyone see the big picture.** It's not uncommon for individual employees and departments to focus on their own goals and lose sight of what the company as a whole is trying to accomplish. Showing people how they contribute to the overall goal—and rewarding them for doing so—helps ensure that the entire system works efficiently.
- **Understand how individual systems really work and how they interact.** Managers need to avoid the temptation to jump in and try to fix systems without understanding how each one works and how they interact with one another. For instance, as a wholesaling distribution manager, you might notice that delivery drivers are spending more time at retail sites than deliveries should take, so you instruct drivers to reduce the amount of time they spend at each site. However, it might be that drivers are spending that time gathering market intelligence that they then turn over to the sales staff. If you're not careful, you could improve the distribution system but damage the sales system.
- **Understand problems before you try to fix them.** The most obvious answer is not always the right answer, and poorly conceived solutions often end up causing more harm than good. When you analyze systems behavior and malfunctions, make sure you focus on things that are *meaningful*, not merely things that are *measurable*. For instance, it's easy to measure how many reports employees write every month, but that might not be the most meaningful gauge of how well a process is working.
- **Understand the potential impact of solutions before you implement them.** Let's say you manage the customer support department, and to encourage high productivity, you run a weekly contest to see who can handle the most phone calls. Trouble is, you're

A vital aspect of systems thinking is understanding problems and fixing them at the point of maximum leverage.

essentially rewarding people based on how quickly they can get the customer off the phone, not on how quickly they actually solve customer problems. Customers who aren't happy keep calling back—which adds to the department's workload and *decreases* overall productivity.

- **Don't just move problems around—solve them.** When one subsystem in a company is malfunctioning, its problems are sometimes just moved around from one subsystem to the next, without ever getting solved. For example, if the market research department does a poor job of understanding customers, this problem will be shifted to the engineering department, which is likely to design a product that doesn't meet customer needs. The problem will then be shifted to the advertising and sales departments, which will struggle to promote and sell the product. The engineering, advertising, and sales departments will all underperform, but the real problem is back in the market research department. Market research in this case is a *leverage point*, where a relatively small correction could make the entire company perform better.

- **Understand how feedback works in the system.** Systems respond to *feedback*, which is information from the output applied back to the input. In the case of an ad campaign, the response from target customers is a form of feedback that helps the department understand whether the campaign is working. Feedback can work in unanticipated ways, too. A good example is managers sending mixed signals to their employees, such as telling them that customer satisfaction is the top priority but then criticizing anyone who spends too much time helping customers. Employees will respond to this feedback by spending less time with customers, leading to a decline in customer satisfaction.

- **Use mistakes as opportunities to learn and improve.** When mistakes occur, resist the temptation to just criticize or complain and then move on. Pull the team together and find out why the mistake occurred, and then identify ways to fix the system to eliminate mistakes in the future.

✔ CHECKPOINT

LEARNING OBJECTIVE 1: Explain the systems perspective, and identify seven principles of systems thinking that can improve your skills as a manager.

SUMMARY: The systems perspective involves looking at business as a series of interconnected and interdependent systems rather than as many individual activities and events. Seven principles of systems thinking that can help every manager are (1) helping everyone see the big picture, (2) understanding how individual systems really work and how they interact, (3) understanding problems before you try to fix them, (4) understanding the potential impact of solutions before you implement them, (5) avoiding the temptation to just move problems from one subsystem to the next without fixing them, (6) understanding how feedback works in a system so that you can improve each process by learning from experience, and (7) using mistakes as opportunities to learn and improve a system.

CRITICAL THINKING: (1) Why are leverage points in a system so critical to understand? (2) Why should a manager in marketing care about systems in the finance or manufacturing departments?

IT'S YOUR BUSINESS: (1) How could a systems approach to thinking help you get up to speed quickly in your first job after graduation? (2) Think back to your experience of registering for this class. How might you improve that system?

KEY TERM TO KNOW: system

Value Chains and Value Webs

As Chapter 1 explains, the essential purpose of a business is adding value—transforming lower-value inputs into higher-value outputs. The details vary widely from industry to industry, but all businesses focus on some kind of transformation (see Exhibit 9.2). The **value chain** is a helpful way to consider all the elements and processes that add value as input materials are transformed into the final products made available to the ultimate customer.[3] Each industry has a value chain, and each company has its own value chain as well. (Exhibit 1.1 on page 50 is a simplified example of the value chain in the bread industry.)

EXTENDING ORGANIZATIONS WITH VALUE WEBS

As Chapter 8 notes, many companies have come to realize that doing everything themselves is not always the most efficient or most successful way to run a business. Many now opt to focus on their core competencies and let other companies handle the remaining business functions—a strategy known as **outsourcing**. Hiring other firms to handle some tasks is not a new concept, to be sure; advertising, public relations, and transportation are among the services that have a long history of being handled by outside firms. The term *outsourcing* is usually applied when a firm decides to move a significant function that was previously done in-house, such as information technology or manufacturing, to an outside vendor.

The combination of extensive globalization in many industries and the development of electronic networking has made it easy for companies to connect with partners around the world. Instead of the linear value chain, some businesses now think in terms of **value webs**, multidimensional networks of suppliers and outsourcing partners.[4] A value web can connect an entire *ecosystem* of partners and suppliers, and in some industries, these ecosystems compete against one another as much as companies do.[5] For example, Google created an online shopping ecosystem, Google Express, to compete with the Amazon ecosystem.

The outsourced, value web approach has several key advantages, including speed, flexibility, and the opportunity to access a wide range of talents and technologies that might be expensive or impossible to acquire otherwise. Established companies can narrow their focus to excel at their core competencies; entrepreneurs with product ideas can quickly assemble a team of designers, manufacturing plants, and distributors in far less time than it would take to build an entire company from scratch.

> **2 LEARNING OBJECTIVE**
>
> Describe the value chain and value web concepts, and discuss the controversy over offshoring.
>
> **value chain**
> All the elements and processes that add value as raw materials are transformed into the final products made available to the ultimate customer.
>
> **outsourcing**
> Contracting out certain business functions or operations to other companies.
>
> **value webs**
> Multidimensional networks of suppliers and outsourcing partners.

EXHIBIT 9.2	Business Transformation Systems

All businesses engage in a transformation process of some kind, converting one type of value (inputs) to another type (outputs).

	Representative Inputs	Transformation Components	Transformation Functions	Representative Outputs
Restaurant	Hungry customers, food ingredients	Chef, wait staff, physical environment	Prepare and serve food	Satisfied diners
Automaker	Sheet metal, engines, electrical components	Tools, equipment, robots, engineers, assemblers	Fabricate parts, assemble cars	Safe, dependable cars and trucks
Retailer	Shoppers, stocks of goods	Displays, physical location, salesclerks	Attract shoppers, promote products	Sales to satisfied customers
Research Service	Company reports, interviews, research services	Researchers, writers, web producers, website servers	Research, analyze, write content, produce webpages	Insightful online reports

SantiPhotoSS/Shutterstock

Long-distance transportation is just one of the risks involved with offshoring.

offshoring
Transferring a part or all of a business function to a facility (a different part of the company or another company entirely) in another country.

For all its potential advantages, outsourcing does carry some risks, particularly in terms of control. For example, to get its new 787 Dreamliner to market as quickly as possible, Boeing outsourced the manufacturing of many parts of the new plane to other manufacturers. Boeing managers initially decided not to impose the "Boeing way" on these suppliers, so it took a hands-off approach. However, the lack of control eventually came to haunt the company. Many suppliers missed target dates and quality standards, throwing the Dreamliner off schedule by at least three years and costing Boeing billions of dollars in extra work, canceled sales, and delivery penalties.[6]

THE OFFSHORING CONTROVERSY

When companies outsource any function in the value chain, they may eliminate many of the jobs associated with that function as well. In many cases, those jobs don't go across the street to another local company but rather around the world in pursuit of lower labor costs, a variation on outsourcing known as **offshoring**. (Offshoring can shift jobs to another company or to an overseas division of the same company.)

Offshoring has been going on for decades, but it began to be a major issue for U.S. manufacturing in the 1980s and then for information technology in the 1990s. Today, offshoring is affecting jobs in science, engineering, law, finance, banking, and other professional areas.[7] The offshoring debate is a great example of conflicting priorities in the stakeholder model, because offshoring can help some stakeholders (investors and customers) and harm others (employees and local communities).

Measuring the impact of offshoring on the U.S. economy is difficult because isolating the effect of a single variable in such a complex system is not easy. For example, economists often struggle to identify the specific reasons one country gains jobs or another loses them. The emergence of new technology (particularly automation and artificial intelligence), phasing out of old technology, shifts in consumer tastes, changes in business strategies, and other factors can all create and destroy jobs. In addition, jobs don't always go to another company simply because of lower costs; in some instances, companies move work to other countries because they can't find enough of the right kind of talent at home.[8]

Even with its potential benefits, offshoring is not a simple decision for any company. Managers must consider such issues as time zone differences, transportation costs and delays, quality assurance, responsiveness, and the loss of direct control. The complexities and rising costs of long-distance manufacturing have prompted some companies to move their production back to home soil, a phenomenon known as *onshoring* or *reshoring*. Other companies in North America and Europe may decide to move production to nearby countries rather than to traditional low-cost areas in Asia, a strategy known as *nearshoring*.[9]

With all its complexities and controversies, globalized manufacturing is here to stay, so it's in everyone's best interest to make it work as well as possible for as many stakeholders as possible. For example, how should U.S. companies be taxed when they have operations all over the world? Also, should unions and regulatory agencies make it more difficult for companies to move jobs overseas, or would it be more beneficial in the long run to let companies compete as vigorously as possible and focus on retraining U.S. workers for new jobs here? These issues are not simple, and you can expect this debate to continue.

 CHECKPOINT

LEARNING OBJECTIVE 2: Describe the value chain and value web concepts, and discuss the controversy over offshoring.

SUMMARY: The value chain includes all the elements and processes that add value as input materials are transformed into the final products made available to the ultimate customer. The value web concept expands this linear model to a multidimensional network of suppliers and outsourcing partners. In the complex argument over offshoring—the transfer of business functions to entities in other countries in pursuit of lower costs—proponents claim that (a) companies have a responsibility to shareholder interests to pursue the lowest cost of production, (b) offshoring benefits U.S. consumers through lower prices, (c) many companies don't have a choice once their competitors move offshore, (d) some companies need to offshore in order to support customers around the world, and (e) offshoring helps U.S. companies be more competitive. Those who question the value or wisdom of offshoring raise points about (a) the future of good jobs in the United States, (b) hidden costs and risks, (c) diminished responsiveness, (d) knowledge transfer and theft issues, (e) product safety issues, and (f) national security and public health concerns.

CRITICAL THINKING: (1) Do U.S. companies have an obligation to keep jobs in the United States? Why or why not? (2) Will global labor markets eventually balance out, with workers in comparable positions all over the world making roughly the same wages? Explain your answer.

IT'S YOUR BUSINESS: (1) How vulnerable are your target professions to offshoring? (2) Should such concerns affect your career planning?

KEY TERMS TO KNOW: value chain, outsourcing, value webs, offshoring

Supply Chain Management

Regardless of how and where it is structured, the lifeblood of every production operation is the **supply chain**, a set of connected systems that coordinate the flow of goods and materials from suppliers all the way through to final customers. **Supply chain management (SCM)** combines business procedures and policies with information systems that integrate the various elements of the supply chain into a cohesive system.

THE STRATEGIC ROLE OF SUPPLY CHAIN MANAGEMENT

SCM goes far beyond supplying materials and can have a profound strategic impact on companies and the broader economy, in several important ways:

- **Managing risks.** SCM can help companies manage the complex risks involved in a supply chain, risks that include everything from cost and availability to health, safety, and national security.[10]
- **Responding to customer needs.** Today's customers expect high quality products, timely delivery of goods, and flawless execution of services, all of which require expertly managed supply chains.
- **Managing business relationships.** SCM can coordinate the numerous relationships in the supply chain and help managers focus their attention on the most important company-to-company relationships. For example, many companies now emphasize low inventory levels as a way to control costs, which means they have less slack and flexibility when it comes to managing incoming materials and outgoing products. Close coordination with supply chain partners is therefore essential.[11]
- **Promoting sustainability.** As the part of business that moves raw materials and finished goods around the world, supply chains have an enormous effect on resource usage, waste, and environmental impact. A major effort is under way in the field of SCM to develop greener supply chains. A key player in this initiative is the giant retailer Walmart, which buys products from more than 100,000 suppliers and has tremendous influence on global supply chains. Its efforts include supporting transparency throughout the supply chain, protecting

 LEARNING OBJECTIVE
Define supply chain management, and explain its strategic importance.

supply chain
A set of connected systems that coordinate the flow of goods and materials from suppliers all the way through to final customers.

supply chain management (SCM)
The business procedures, policies, and computer systems that integrate the various elements of the supply chain into a cohesive system.

 REAL-TIME UPDATES
Learn More by Visiting This Website

Improving sustainability across the supply chain

The Sustainability Consortium offers tools and techniques for companies to improve the sustainability of their supply chain operations. Go to **real-timeupdates.com/bia9** and select Learn More in the Students section.

Wollertz/Shutterstock

Promoting sustainability is one of the most important aspects of contemporary supply chain management.

workers, promoting sustainable agriculture and manufacturing, and reducing emissions through a massive effort called Project Gigaton that aims to reduces the emissions across its supply chain by a billion metric tons by 2030.[12]

SUPPLY CHAIN SYSTEMS AND METHODS

The focus of supply chain management is getting the right goods and materials at the right price in the right place at the right time for successful production. Unfortunately, you can't just pile up huge quantities of everything you might eventually need, because **inventory**, the goods and materials kept in stock for production or sale, costs money to purchase and to store. On the other hand, not having an adequate supply of inventory can result in expensive delays and lost market opportunities. This balancing act is the job of **inventory control**, which tries to determine the right quantities of supplies and products to have on hand and then tracks where those items are.

Procurement, or *purchasing*, is the acquisition of the raw materials, parts, components, supplies, and finished products required to produce goods and services. The goal of purchasing is to make sure that the company has all the materials it needs, when it needs them, at the lowest possible cost. A company must always have enough supplies on hand to cover a product's *lead time*—the period that elapses between placing the supply order and receiving materials.

Today's supply chains are among the most technologically advanced aspects of business. Here are some of the most significant and emerging systems:

inventory
Goods and materials kept in stock for production or sale.

inventory control
Determining the right quantities of supplies and products to have on hand and tracking where those items are.

procurement
The acquisition of the raw materials, parts, components, supplies, and finished products required to produce goods and services.

materials requirements planning (MRP)
A planning system that works backward from a company's sales forecasts to make sure it has enough of everything required to build those goods or perform those services in a timely manner.

enterprise resource planning (ERP)
A planning system that addresses the needs of the entire organization, from manufacturing to sales to human resources.

- **Planning systems.** Every company needs an effective and efficient way to acquire the materials it needs in order to conduct business. Creating goods and delivering services can require thousands or millions of individual parts, supplies, and components of raw material, and figuring out when to order these items and in what quantities is the task of **materials requirements planning (MRP)**. MRP systems work backward from a company's sales forecasts to make sure it has enough of everything required to build those goods or perform those services in a timely manner, taking into account the firm's inventory levels and production capacity.[13] The MRP concept is often expanded to embrace all the financial and administrative activities that support production, in an approach called *manufacturing resource planning (MRP II)*. The most comprehensive approach is **enterprise resource planning (ERP)**, which addresses the needs of the entire organization, from manufacturing to sales to human resources.[14]

- **Tracking methods.** Accurate resource management requires the ability to identify and track where everything is in the system at any point in time. Several technologies are now in use to track products, people, and vehicles. *Radio frequency identification (RFID)* uses small antenna tags attached to products or shipping containers; special sensors detect the presence of the tags and can track the flow of goods through the supply chain. The GPS function in mobile devices can track the location of personnel and vehicles in a delivery fleet. And Internet of Things (IoT) sensors connected through wired or wireless networks can send continuously updated information from machinery or shipments.

- **Blockchain.** Today's supply chains are immensely complex; a single company's supply chain can involve hundreds or thousands of companies spread around the globe. With so many companies involved, transparency and traceability can be difficult to achieve, raising concerns over counterfeit goods, unethically or illegally sourced materials, and product safety. The "distributed ledger" technology known as *blockchain* (see page 467) can connect all the participants in a supply chain in a

REAL-TIME UPDATES
Learn More by Visiting This Website

Interested in a career in supply chain management?

The Council of Supply Chain Management Professionals offers advice on how to launch a career in this important field. Visit **real-timeupdates.com/bia9** and select Learn More in the Students section.

single, secure database that verifies and records every transaction. Blockchain is now being used by major consumer goods companies such as Unilever and Nestlé, retailers such as Walmart, and a wide variety of companies in manufacturing, mining, and other sectors.[15]

✔ CHECKPOINT

LEARNING OBJECTIVE 3: Define *supply chain management*, **and explain its strategic importance.**

SUMMARY: Supply chain management (SCM) combines business procedures and policies with information systems that integrate the various elements of the supply chain into a cohesive system. SCM helps companies manage risks, respond to customer needs, manage business relationships, and promote sustainability throughout their supply chains.

CRITICAL THINKING: (1) Why can't companies just stockpile huge inventories of all the parts and materials they need rather than carefully manage supply from one day to the next? (2) Why would a company invest time and money in helping its suppliers improve their business practices? Why not just dump underperformers and get better suppliers?

IT'S YOUR BUSINESS: (1) In any current or previous job, what steps have supervisors taken to help you understand your role in the supply chain? (2) How might a manufacturer or retailer use the transparency and traceability afforded by blockchain to promote closer relationships with its customers?

KEY TERMS TO KNOW: supply chain, supply chain management (SCM), inventory, inventory control, procurement, materials requirements planning (MRP), enterprise resource planning (ERP)

Production and Operations Management

The term *production* suggests factories, machines, and assembly lines making automobiles, computers, furniture, motorcycles, or other tangible goods. With the growth in the number of service-based businesses and their increasing importance to the economy, however, the term *production* is now used to describe the transformation of resources into both goods and services. The broader term **production and operations management**, or simply *operations management*, refers to overseeing all the activities involved in producing goods and services. Operations managers are involved in a wide range of strategic and tactical decisions, from high-level design of the production system to forecasting and scheduling. This section explores key concepts and methods in operations management.

LEAN SYSTEMS

Throughout all the activities in the production process, operations managers pay close attention to **productivity**, or the efficiency with which they can convert inputs to outputs. (Put another way, productivity is equal to the value of the outputs divided by the value of the inputs.) Productivity is one of the most vital responsibilities in operations management because it is a key factor in determining the company's competitiveness and profitability. Companies that can produce similar goods or services with fewer resources have a distinct advantage over their competitors. Moreover, high productivity in the fullest sense also requires low waste, whether it's leftover

4 **LEARNING OBJECTIVE**
Identify the major planning decisions in production and operations management.

production and operations management
Overseeing all the activities involved in producing goods and services.

productivity
The efficiency with which an organization can convert inputs to outputs.

REAL-TIME UPDATES
Learn More by Visiting These Websites

Join the production and operations management professionals

Explore five major professional organizations that focus on production, operations, and quality assurance. Go to **real-timeupdates .com/bia9** and select Learn More in the Students section.

lean systems
Systems (in manufacturing and other functional areas) that maximize productivity by reducing waste and delays.

materials, shoddy products that must be scrapped, or excess energy usage. Consequently, productivity improvements and sustainability improvements often complement each other.

Lean systems, which maximize productivity by reducing waste and delays, are at the heart of many productivity improvement efforts. Many lean systems borrow techniques developed and refined by the Japanese automaker Toyota; the *Toyota Production System* is world renowned for its ability to continually improve both productivity and quality.[16] Central to the notion of lean systems is **just-in-time (JIT)** inventory management, in which goods and materials are delivered throughout the production process right before they are needed rather than being stockpiled in inventories. Reducing stocks to immediate needs decreases waste and forces factories to keep production flowing smoothly.

The potential benefits of the lean philosophy extend well beyond productivity and quality. The lean approach can also help a company refine its core mission because it is based on customer needs, it can encourage employees to be more engaged at work because their inputs and concerns are respected and acted upon, and it can help a company clarify its competitive strategy.[17] However, because this approach places a lot of responsibility on front-line employees and lower-level managers, top managers need to make sure that appropriate goals, incentives, and support systems are in place to ensure smart and ethical decision-making.[18]

MASS PRODUCTION, CUSTOMIZED PRODUCTION, AND MASS CUSTOMIZATION

just-in-time (JIT)
Inventory management in which goods and materials are delivered throughout the production process right before they are needed.

mass production
The creation of identical goods or services, usually in large quantities.

customized production
The creation of a unique good or service for each customer.

Goods and services can be created through *mass production, customized production*, or *mass customization*. In **mass production**, identical goods or services are created, usually in large quantities, such as when Apple churns out millions of identical iPhones. Although not normally associated with services, mass production is also what American Airlines is doing when it offers hundreds of opportunities for passengers to fly from, say, Dallas to Chicago every day: Every customer on these flights gets the same service at the same time.

At the other extreme is **customized production**, sometimes called *batch-of-one production* in manufacturing, in which the producer creates a unique good or service for each customer. If you order a piece of furniture from a local craftsperson, for instance, you can specify everything from the size and shape to the types of wood and fabric used. Or you can hire a charter pilot to fly you wherever you want, whenever you want. Both products are customized to your unique requirements.

Mass production has the advantage of economies of scale, but it can't deliver many of the unique or personalized goods and services that today's customers demand. On the other hand, fully customized production can offer uniqueness but usually at a much higher price. An attractive compromise in many cases is **mass customization**, in which part of the product is mass produced and then the remaining features are customized for each buyer. With design and production technologies getting ever more flexible, the opportunities for customization continue to grow. To succeed at mass customization, companies can employ *agile manufacturing*, which relies on the principles of an agile organization discussed in Chapter 8 to empower manufacturing teams to quickly build products that meet specific customer needs.[19]

mass customization
A manufacturing approach in which part of the product is mass produced and the remaining features are customized for each buyer.

FACILITIES LOCATION AND DESIGN

Choosing the location of production facilities is a complex decision that must consider such factors as land, construction, availability of talent, taxes, energy, living standards, transportation, and proximity to customers and business partners. Support from local communities and governments often plays a key role in location decisions as well. To provide jobs and expand their income and sales tax bases, local, state, and national governments often compete to attract companies by offering generous financial incentives such as tax reductions.

After a site has been selected, managers turn their attention to *facility layout*, the arrangement of production work centers and other elements (such as materials, equipment, and support departments) needed to process goods and services. Layout planning includes such decisions as how many steps are needed in the process, the amount and type of equipment and workers needed for each step, the best way for materials and work in progress to flow from stage to stage, how each step should be configured, and where the steps should be located relative to one another. Layout is an essential design consideration for lean manufacturing to ensure high efficiency and minimal waste.[20]

Well-designed facilities help companies operate more productively by reducing wasted time and wasted materials, but that is far from the only benefit. Smart layouts support close communication and collaboration among employees and help ensure their safety, both of which are important for employee satisfaction and motivation. In the delivery of services, facility layout can be a major influence on customer satisfaction because it affects the overall service experience.[21]

Well-designed facility layouts minimize wasted effort and promote collaboration.

FORECASTING AND CAPACITY PLANNING

Using customer feedback, sales orders, market research, past sales figures, industry analyses, and educated guesses about the future behavior of customers and competitors, operations managers prepare *production forecasts*—estimates of future demand for the company's products. After product demand has been estimated, management must balance that with the company's capacity to produce the goods or services. The term *capacity* refers to the volume of manufacturing or service capability that an organization can handle. **Capacity planning** is the collection of long-term strategic decisions that establish the overall level of resources needed to meet customer demand. When managers at Boeing plan for the production of an airliner, they have to consider not only the staffing of thousands of people but also massive factory spaces, material flows from hundreds of suppliers around the world, internal deliveries, cash flow, tools and equipment, and dozens of other factors. Because of the potential impact on finances, customers, and employees—and the difficulty of reversing major decisions—capacity choices are among the most important decisions that top-level managers make.[22]

capacity planning
Establishing the overall level of resources needed to meet customer demand.

SCHEDULING

In any production process, managers must do *scheduling*—determining how long each operation takes and deciding which tasks are done in which order. Manufacturing facilities often use a *master production schedule (MPS)* to coordinate production of all the goods the company makes.[23] Service businesses use a variety of scheduling techniques as well, from simple appointment calendars for a small business to the comprehensive online systems that airlines and other large service providers use.

To plan and track projects of all kinds, managers throughout a company can use a *Gantt chart*, a special type of bar chart that shows the progress of all the tasks needed to complete a project (see Exhibit 9.3 on the next page). For more complex projects, the *program evaluation and review technique (PERT)* is useful. PERT helps managers identify the optimal sequencing of activities, the expected time for project completion, and the best use of resources. To use PERT, managers map out all the activities in a network diagram (see Exhibit 9.4 on the next page). The longest path through the network is known as the **critical path** because it determines how soon the project can be completed.[24] In other words, the project can't be completed any faster than the critical path. Tasks in the critical path usually receive special attention because they have the most impact on when the project can be completed. (If anyone ever says *you* are in the critical path, make sure you stay on schedule!)

critical path
In a PERT network diagram, the sequence of operations that requires the longest time to complete; the project can't be completed any faster than the critical path.

EXHIBIT 9.3	Gantt Chart

A Gantt chart is a handy tool in project and production management because it shows the order in which tasks must be completed and which tasks are dependent on other tasks. For the new-product launch shown here, for example, the analysis task is dependent on all three tasks before it, which means those tasks must be completed before analysis can begin. With periodic updates, it's also easy to show a team exactly where the project stands at any particular moment.

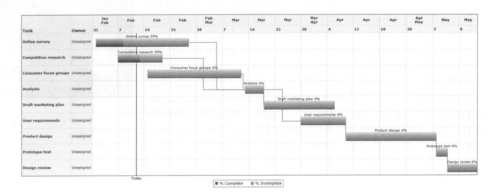

EXHIBIT 9.4	Simplified PERT Diagram for a Store Opening

This PERT diagram shows a subset of the many tasks involved in opening a new retail store. The tasks involved in staffing are on the critical path because they take the longest time to complete (51 days), whereas the promotion tasks can be completed in 38 days and the merchandise tasks can be completed in 39 days. In other words, some delay can be tolerated in the promotion or merchandise tasks, but any delay in any of the staffing tasks will delay the store's opening day.

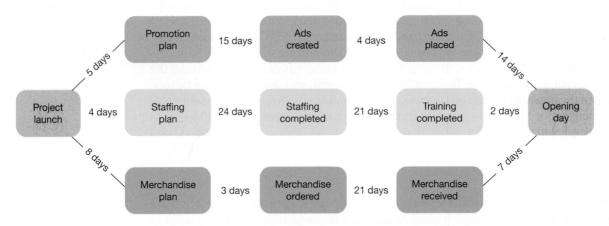

 CHECKPOINT

LEARNING OBJECTIVE 4: Identify the major planning decisions in production and operations management.

SUMMARY: The major decisions in operations management include (1) facilities location and design; (2) forecasting and capacity planning to match resources with demand; (3) scheduling; (4) lean system design to reduce waste and delays; and (5) the choice of mass production, customized production, or mass customization.

CRITICAL THINKING: (1) Why is it essential to identify tasks in the critical path of a project? (2) How does mass customization help a company balance productivity and customer satisfaction?

The Unique Challenges of Service Delivery

With most workers in the United States now involved in the service sector, managers in thousands of companies need to pay close attention to the unique challenges of delivering services: perishability, location constraints, scalability challenges, performance variability and perceptions of quality, and customer involvement and service provider interaction.

5 **LEARNING OBJECTIVE**
Explain the unique challenges of service delivery.

PERISHABILITY

Most services are *perishable*, meaning that they are consumed at the same time they are produced and cannot exist before or after that time. For example, if a 200-seat airliner takes off half-empty, those 100 sales opportunities are lost forever. The airline can't create these products ahead of time and store them in inventory until somebody is ready to buy. Similarly, restaurants can seat only so many people every night, so empty tables represent revenue lost forever. This perishability can have a profound impact on the way service businesses are managed, from staffing (making sure enough people are on hand to help with peak demands) to pricing (using discounts to encourage people to buy services when they are available).

LOCATION CONSTRAINTS

Perishability also means that for many services, customers and providers need to be in the same place at the same time. The equipment and food ingredients used in a restaurant can be produced just about anywhere, but the restaurant itself needs to be located close to customers. One of the most significant commercial advantages of the internet is the way it has enabled many service businesses to get around this constraint. Online retailers, information providers, and other e-businesses can locate virtually anywhere on the planet.

SCALABILITY CHALLENGES AND OPPORTUNITIES

Any business that wants to grow must consider the issue of **scalability**, the potential to increase production by expanding or replicating its initial production capacity. Scaling up always creates some challenges, but service businesses that depend on the skills of specific professionals can be particularly difficult to scale. Examples range from chefs and interior designers to business consultants and graphic designers, particularly when the business is built around the reputation of a single person. Of course, many goods businesses also rely on highly skilled production workers, but the potential to mechanize goods production can make it easier to scale up manufacturing.

scalability
The potential to increase production by expanding or replicating its initial production capacity.

PERFORMANCE VARIABILITY AND PERCEPTIONS OF QUALITY

For many types of services, the quality of performance can vary from one instance to the next—and that quality is in the eye of the beholder and often can't be judged until after the service has been performed. If you manufacture scissors, you can specify a certain grade of steel from your suppliers and use automated machinery to produce thousands of identical pairs of scissors of identical quality. Many key attributes such as the size and

The quality of the experience is an important element of the delivery of many services.

strength of the scissors are *objective* and measurable, and customers can experience the *subjective* variables such as the feel and cutting action before they buy. In other words, there is little mystery and little room for surprise in the purchase. Plus, if a customer isn't satisfied with the purchase, it's a tangible good and therefore it can be returned for a refund.

However, if you create a haircut using a pair of those scissors, perceptions of quality become almost entirely subjective *and* impossible to judge until after the service is complete. Hair styling is also a good example of a service in which *quality of experience* is an important part of customer perceptions as well, which is why, for instance, most salons pay a lot of attention to architecture, interior design, lighting, music, robes, refreshments, and other amenities that have nothing to do with the actual haircut itself.

CUSTOMER INVOLVEMENT AND SERVICE PROVIDER INTERACTION

Finally, one of the biggest differences between goods and services production is the fact that customers are often involved in—and thereby can affect the quality of—the service delivery. For instance, personal trainers can instruct clients in the proper way to exercise, but if the clients don't follow directions, the result will be unsatisfactory. Similarly, a business consultant relies on accurate information from managers in a client organization; lacking that, he or she will be unable to craft the most effective advice.

When customers and service providers interact, the quality of the interpersonal experience also affects customer perceptions of quality. In this sense, service delivery is something of a performance that needs to instill confidence in the client. Weak communication skills or poor etiquette can create dissatisfaction with a service that is satisfactory or even exceptional in all other respects.

 CHECKPOINT

LEARNING OBJECTIVE 5: Explain the unique challenges of service delivery.

SUMMARY: The delivery of services presents a number of unique challenges, including (1) perishability, which means that services are consumed at the same time they are produced; (2) location constraints, which often require that customers and service providers be in the same place at the same time; (3) scalability challenges, which can make some types of service businesses more difficult to expand; (4) performance variability and perceptions of quality, which heighten the challenge of delivering consistent quality and increase the subjectivity of the customer experience; and (5) customer involvement and service provider interaction, which can put some of the responsibility for service quality on the customer's shoulders and increase the importance of good interpersonal skills.

CRITICAL THINKING: (1) How can technology help some service businesses address the challenge of scalability? (2) If customers are paying for a service, why should they ever have to share in the responsibility of ensuring quality results?

IT'S YOUR BUSINESS: (1) Do you think you have a natural personality for working in a service business? Why or why not? (2) If you're not a "natural," what steps could you take to succeed in a service job anyway?

KEY TERM TO KNOW: scalability

[6] **LEARNING OBJECTIVE**

Define *quality*, explain the challenge of quality and product complexity, and identify four major tools and strategies for ensuring product quality.

Product and Process Quality

The term *quality* is often used in a vague sense of "goodness" or "excellence," but to be meaningful from a managerial standpoint, it needs to be defined in context. Hyundai and Aston Martin both make quality automobiles, but quality means dramatically different things to the makers and buyers of these two car brands. People who spend $15,000 or $20,000 on a Hyundai are likely to be satisfied with the quality they receive in return, but people who spend 10 times that much on an Aston Martin have vastly different expectations, even if the two cars are equally reliable. Accordingly, **quality** is best defined as the degree to which a product or process meets reasonable or agreed-on expectations. Within the framework of this general definition, a specific set of parameters can be identified that defines quality in each situation. These dimensions of quality can include performance, capability, reliability, conformance to specifications, and aesthetics.[25]

Defining those expectations of quality and then organizing the resources and systems needed to achieve that level are vital responsibilities in today's competitive, resource-constrained environment. With numerous choices available in most product categories, consumers and business buyers alike tend to avoid or abandon products and companies that can't meet their expectations. Moreover, poor quality wastes time and money, squanders resources, frustrates customers and employees, erodes confidence in companies and their products, and can even put people in danger.

Expectations of quality vary widely; buyers of luxury automobiles have different expectations than people who buy economy cars, for instance.

pluut/Shutterstock

quality
The degree to which a product or process meets reasonable or agreed-on expectations.

QUALITY AND COMPLEXITY

As many products become increasingly complex, defining and maintaining quality becomes an ever-greater challenge. For example, even identical, mass-produced computers immediately become unique when their new owners start adding software, downloading files, and connecting them to printers and other devices, each of which is a complex hardware/software system in its own right. All these changes and connections increase the chances that something will go wrong and thereby lower the functional quality of the product. In other words, even though the company verified the quality of the products before they left the factory, it could have thousands of quality issues on its hands over time.

STRATEGIES FOR ENSURING PRODUCT QUALITY

Companies use two related management processes for ensuring quality: *quality control* and *quality assurance*. You can think of **quality control** as the tactical aspect of quality—measuring goods and services to see whether they meet their established quality specifications and fine-tuning production methods as needed to improve the results. **Quality assurance** is a more strategic function that focuses on the policies, practices, and procedures that influence product quality, with the goal of increasing the level of confidence that quality outcomes will be achieved.[26] Many firms organize their quality-oriented activities under a companywide commitment to **total quality management (TQM)**, in which every aspect of company operations pushes toward excellence in goods and services delivery.[27]

Product quality starts long before the production stage by designing products that meet customer needs and that are designed for manufacturability and service. At the production stage, companies can use a variety of tools and strategies to help ensure quality; four of the most significant are continuous improvement, statistical process control, Six Sigma, and ISO 9000.

quality control
Measuring quality against established standards after the good or service has been produced and weeding out any defective products.

quality assurance
A more comprehensive approach of companywide policies, practices, and procedures to ensure that every product meets quality standards.

total quality management (TQM)
An approach to quality assurance that encompasses every aspect of a company's operations.

Continuous Improvement

Delivering quality goods and services is as much a mindset as it is a technical challenge. Companies that excel tend to empower their employees to continuously improve the quality of goods production or service delivery, a strategy often expressed through the Japanese word *kaizen*. By making quality everyone's responsibility, the kaizen approach encourages all employees to look for ways to implement quality improvements in their own work functions.[28]

Statistical Process Control

Any quality control or improvement effort depends on reliable feedback that tells workers and managers how well products and processes are performing. Quality assurance often includes the use of **statistical process control (SPC)**, which involves taking samples from the process periodically and analyzing these data points to look for trends and anomalies. One of the most important SPC tools is the *control chart*, which plots measured data over time and helps identify performance that is outside the normal range of operating conditions and therefore in need of investigation.[29]

Six Sigma

Whereas *kaizen* is more of a general mindset and SPC is a set of analytical tools, **Six Sigma** is a comprehensive approach that encompasses a philosophy of striving toward perfection, a rigorous methodology for measuring and improving quality, and specific tools such as SPC to track progress.[30] (The term *six sigma* is used in statistics to indicate 3.4 defects per 1 million opportunities—near perfection, in other words.) Six Sigma is a highly disciplined, systematic approach to reducing the deviation from desired goals in virtually any business process, whether it's eliminating defects in the creation of a product or improving a company's cash flow.[31] Six Sigma efforts typically follow a five-step approach, known as DMAIC for short (see Exhibit 9.5).[32]

Many companies now marry the concepts of lean production and Six Sigma, seeking to reduce waste and defects simultaneously. And moving beyond operations, this hybrid approach of *Lean Six Sigma* is also being applied at a strategic level to help identify opportunities in the marketplace and align the resources needed to pursue them.[33]

ISO 9000

Buyers and business partners often want reassurance that the companies they do business with take quality seriously and have practices and policies in place to ensure quality outputs. **ISO 9000** is a globally recognized family of standards for quality management systems, administered by the International Organization for Standardization (ISO). ISO 9000 is based on eight quality management principles, including customer focus, a systems approach to management, and fact-based decision-making.[34]

EXHIBIT 9.5	**The DMAIC Process in Six Sigma Quality Management**

The five-step process of *define, measure, analyze, improve,* and *control* (DMAIC) is at the heart of Six Sigma quality management efforts. Notice how this is a specific implementation of the control cycle described on page 231.

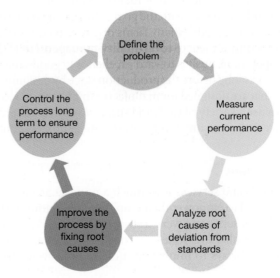

Source: Based on Kelly D. Sloan, "The Path to a Sustainable Playbook," *Industrial Engineer*, April 2011, 41–46.

Over a million organizations around the world have implemented ISO standards, making it a universally recognized indicator of compliance. Achieving ISO certification sends a reassuring signal to other companies that a firm's internal processes meet these widely accepted standards, and many organizations now require that their suppliers meet ISO standards.[35]

For more insights on production systems, visit real-timeupdates.com/bia9 and select Chapter 9.

REAL-TIME UPDATES
Learn More by Visiting This Website

The vital importance of quality standards

See why quality standards are one of the most significant advances in modern business. Go to **real-timeupdates.com/bia9** and select Learn More in the Students section.

 CHECKPOINT

LEARNING OBJECTIVE 6: Define *quality*, explain the challenge of quality and product complexity, and identify four major tools and strategies for ensuring product quality.

SUMMARY: Quality is the degree to which a product or process meets reasonable or agreed-on expectations. As products become more complex, the challenges of defining what quality means, ensuring quality production or service performance, and ensuring quality once the product is out in the field all increase. Four major tools and strategies for ensuring product quality are (1) continuous process improvement, enabling employees to search for and correct quality problems; (2) statistical process control (SPC), the use of random sampling and tools such as control charts to monitor the production process; (3) Six Sigma, a rigorous quality management program that strives to eliminate deviations between the actual and desired performance of a business system; and (4) ISO 9000, a globally recognized family of standards for quality management systems.

CRITICAL THINKING: (1) How significant is the role of software in product quality today? (2) How can process simplicity contribute to quality?

IT'S YOUR BUSINESS: (1) Are the grades you get in your various classes an example of quality control or of quality assurance? Explain your answer. (2) Have you ever tried anything like the Six Sigma DMAIC process in your own life, even partially or informally? If so, did it improve whatever process you were trying to change?

KEY TERMS TO KNOW: quality, quality control, quality assurance, total quality management (TQM), statistical process control (SPC), Six Sigma, ISO 9000

Thriving in the Digital Enterprise: Industry 4.0 and the Smart Factory

 LEARNING OBJECTIVE

Explain the concept of *Industry 4.0* and the smart factory.

Many of the disruptive technologies you're reading about in this book come together in what has been called a fourth industrial revolution after (1) the original Industrial Revolution of the late 18th and early 19th centuries with factories powered by steam and water, (2) the mass production and assembly lines of the late 19th and early 20th centuries, and then (3) computerization and automation in the second half of the 20th century and early 21st century. In its broadest sense, **Industry 4.0** refers to the digital transformation of manufacturing, moving from automated factories to *smart factories*. (As with most revolutions, Industry 4.0 is not a distinct break with the past or a rigid boundary around a specific set of things, but rather a label for the gathering consensus that a new way of doing things has emerged.)[36]

The Industry 4.0 concept encompasses a variety of technologies, but one of the most fundamental are *cyber-physical systems* in which the digital realm and the physical realm are seamlessly integrated. Three prominent examples of cyber-physical systems are industrial

Industry 4.0
The digital transformation of manufacturing, moving from automated factories to smart factories that emphasize the use of cyber-physical systems.

Olga Serdyuk/123RF

The smart factories of Industry 4.0 promise greater agility and adaptability in addition to improvements in efficiency and productivity.

robots (which perform actions in response to digital commands), *additive manufacturing* or 3D printing (which creates physical items from digital models), and the Internet of Things (which connects computer networks to the physical world through sensors and actuators). The smart factory idea can also embrace big data and analytics, machine vision, AI, new forms of human-machine interaction such as augmented reality, and simulations that let production engineers test processes virtually before implementing them on the factory floor.[37]

As with the previous industrial revolutions, Industry 4.0 promises improvements in speed and efficiency while reducing the need for tedious or dangerous manual work. However, it also promises a significant benefit that earlier modes were mostly unable to deliver on, which is greater agility and adaptability. Picture a networked team of robots and other cyber-physical systems that can reconfigure themselves on the fly in response to a unique customer order, or a production line that corrects itself automatically when an AI "observer" with machine vision detects product-quality problems.

Industry 4.0 does raise two significant concerns that companies and society need to address. First, the reliance on networking makes smart factories more vulnerable to hacking and other malicious attacks. Just as companies need to *harden* their other computer networks to prevent intrusion, they also need to make sure factory networks are secure.[38]

Second, as on the business side of digital disruption, Industry 4.0 is likely to displace some workers in the manufacturing sector and redefine the nature of work for many others. It will create new jobs in the design, manufacture, programming, and maintenance of cyber-physical systems and other smart-factory elements, but there will be a period of disruption as workforces get reskilled for different types of work. Organizations such as the Smart Manufacturing Leadership Coalition (**smartmanufacturingcoalition.org**) are coordinating efforts across industry, government, and academia to help current and future workers prepare for careers in this new world of manufacturing.

REAL-TIME UPDATES

Learn More by Visiting This Website

Get the latest on Industry 4.0

This collection of articles, videos, and other materials will help you get up to speed on the smart factory and its role in contemporary business. Go to **real-timeupdates.com/bia9** and select Learn More in the Students section.

✓ CHECKPOINT

LEARNING OBJECTIVE 7: Explain the concept of *Industry 4.0* and the smart factory.

SUMMARY: Industry 4.0 refers to the digital transformation of manufacturing, moving from automated factories to smart factories. The Industry 4.0 concept encompasses a variety of technologies, notably *cyber-physical systems* such as industrial robots, additive manufacturing, and the Internet of Things. Other major technologies include big data and analytics, machine vision, AI, augmented reality, and simulations. Smart factories promise to improve not only efficiency but also agility and adaptability.

CRITICAL THINKING: (1) Would you characterize Industry 4.0 as a revolution or more of an evolution? Why? (2) Why might various companies have an interest in promoting Industry 4.0 as a conceptual "brand"?

IT'S YOUR BUSINESS: Business students don't always consider the manufacturing sector as a career; do the innovations of Industry 4.0 make manufacturing more appealing to you? Why or why not?

KEY TERM TO KNOW: Industry 4.0

BEHIND THE SCENES

Printing the Impossible at Voodoo Manufacturing

It's a safe bet that Brooklyn's Voodoo Manufacturing is the only company in the world that has manufactured custom mannequins, prosthetic hands, action figures from video games, trophies for VH1's Hip Hop Honors show, architectural models, brain-sensor helmets, and dog goggles. These are only a few of the products the company has made for its growing list of more than 2,000 customers.

Max Friefeld, Jonathan Schwartz, Oliver Ortlieb, and Patrick Deem hatched the idea of offering 3D printing as a service while working for one of the leading makers of 3D printers. Many people are aware of 3D printing from a hobbyist's perspective, but the three colleagues and roommates saw the potential for a fresh take on the idea of contract manufacturing. Their mission is both simple and bold: "We're giving everyone on Earth the power to manufacture."

Voodoo's business model is based on on-demand 3D printing, in which clients upload digital models of whatever they would like to have made, then Voodoo's battalion of printers (more than 200 already, with more to come) go to work creating them. The process doesn't require the expensive molds or tooling that traditional manufacturing needs, and the turnaround time is usually a matter of days rather than the months that ramping up traditional manufacturing can involve.

With no start-up costs, no minimum volume requirements, and rapid turnaround, this mode of manufacturing opens up powerful possibilities for Voodoo's clients. Advertising agencies and other marketing firms use the service to create small batches of promotional items, for instance. Other companies use the service for rapid and iterative *prototyping*, in which they quickly test a physical product for design errors or functional issues, tweak their digital model, get another physical item to test, and repeat the cycle until the design is optimized. This is also a great way to test-market products by putting them in the hands of potential customers to get their reactions.

To support a wide range of customers, Voodoo expanded its business model both upstream and downstream from the manufacturing stage. If customers don't have the design or technical skills to create digital models of the products they would like to make, Voodoo offers custom design services to take clients from the idea stage through manufacturing. And on the downstream side, it offers *fulfillment* services from its Brooklyn factory, in which it can ship finished products directly to a client's customers. In other words, if you had an idea for a

product but no clue how to design it or make it and no company in place to ship products to customers, Voodoo could handle the entire process for you.

The 3D printing that Voodoo uses is a form of *additive manufacturing* (the terms are sometimes used interchangeably), in which digital models are reproduced in plastic, metal, or other substances by applying or "printing" successive layers of material. Voodoo currently offers its clients two types of plastic: a biodegradable corn-based plastic and a plastic with the elasticity and flexibility of rubber. Other types of additive manufacturing include metal powders that are melted into solids using lasers and machines that can print houses using fast-drying concrete. Additive manufacturing is used for a vast range of products today, including movie props, custom-fit hearing aids, machinery components, car parts, shoes, and even rocket parts.

Voodoo has received several rounds of investment funding, and Friefeld and his colleagues are upbeat about the company's prospects. Their next move is continuing to automate the manufacturing process using robotic arms that extract finished goods from those hundreds of printers so that production can continue virtually without pause 24 hours a day.

The next time you get an idea for a great product that no one has ever made, don't dismiss it as an idle daydream. Voodoo can help you make that dream a reality.[39]

Critical Thinking Questions

9-1. How does a service such as Voodoo support the concepts of virtual and unstructured organizations discussed in Chapter 8?

9-2. What advantages does iterative prototyping offer companies that are introducing new types of products to the market?

9-3. How does Voodoo represent the concepts of cyber-physical systems and the smart factory?

Learn More Online

Visit **voodoomfg.com** and explore the examples section to see what the company has been manufacturing for its customers. Read about the printing, design, and fulfillment services to get a better idea of how the company can support a wide range of customers. What materials and printing services does Voodoo currently offer? How does it present those capabilities to potential customers?

End of Chapter

KEY TERMS

capacity planning (283)
critical path (283)
customized production (282)
enterprise resource planning (ERP) (280)
Industry 4.0 (289)
inventory (280)
inventory control (280)
ISO 9000 (288)
just-in-time (JIT) (282)
lean systems (282)
mass customization (282)
mass production (282)
materials requirements planning (MRP) (280)
offshoring (278)
outsourcing (277)

procurement (280)
production and operations management (281)
productivity (281)
quality (287)
quality assurance (287)
quality control (287)
scalability (285)
Six Sigma (288)
statistical process control (SPC) (288)
supply chain (279)
supply chain management (SCM) (279)
system (274)
total quality management (TQM) (287)
value chain (277)
value webs (277)

TEST YOUR KNOWLEDGE

Questions for Review

9-4. What role does feedback play in a system?

9-5. How does a value web differ from a value chain?

9-6. Why is offshoring controversial?

9-7. What is meant by lead time?

9-8. What is a lean system?

9-9. What is supply chain management?

9-10. What aspects of a restaurant's business could be considered perishable?

9-11. What is Industry 4.0?

9-12. What is additive manufacturing?

Questions for Analysis

9-13. When analyzing systems behavior and malfunctions, why is it important to focus on things that are meaningful in addition to things that are measurable?

9-14. Why do some firms now think in terms of value webs instead of value chains?

9-15. How can supply chain management (SCM) help a company establish a competitive advantage?

9-16. How does the lean approach to manufacturing put more responsibility in the hands of front-line workers?

9-17. Why is a rigorous quality management program important for businesses?

9-18. How does complexity affect product quality?

9-19. **Ethical Considerations.** How does society's concern for the environment affect a company's decisions about facility location and layout?

Questions for Application

9-20. Business is booming. Sales last month were 50 percent higher than the month before, and so far, this month is looking even better than last month. Should you hire more people to accommodate the increase? Explain your answer.

9-21. You manage a multiplex theater. Each screen has 100 seats. Seat occupancy is at 40 percent. This means that you are losing 60 percent of potential sales each day. Are there any location constraints? What steps would you suggest to identify and analyze the problems?

9-22. You've developed a reputation as an outstanding math tutor, and you want to turn your talent into a full-time business after graduation. How will you address the challenge of scalability in your new venture?

9-23. **Concept Integration.** How might supply chain management issues influence your decision on how to expand your vitamin and nutritional supplements company internationally?

EXPAND YOUR KNOWLEDGE

Discovering Career Opportunities

Visit **www.careers-in-business.com/om.htm** for information on careers in operations management.

9-24. What factors would you consider in deciding whether to apply or, alternatively, not apply for an internship position at an international manufacturing company in your country?

9-25. What are the career prospects in the production and operations management profession in your country? Research newspaper articles (print or online editions) to explore the trends in local and global production and operations management businesses in your domestic environment.

9-26. Read the article "The Two Questions That Help You to Produce Both Cheaper and Better" by Freek Vermeulen at www.forbes.com. Based on what you have read, what additional skills would you consider acquiring before working in a production-related job?

Intelligent Business Technology

Research the latest offerings from several industrial robot makers, such as ABB, Fanuc, and Kawasaki. What innovations are these companies promoting? How do they position their robots within the Industry 4.0 and smart factory concepts? Summarize your findings in a brief report.

PRACTICE YOUR SKILLS

Resolving Ethical Dilemmas

Your business has a reputation for using quality ingredients in its food products. In fact, when the business was founded, the advertising tagline was "Quality first, last, and always." Continued growth has put this ethos under strain and, as a result, some shortcuts and compromises have had to be made. Around 60 percent of all the food ingredients are now sourced via third-party suppliers, making the provenance of the ingredients difficult to establish. Your business has asked you to brief an advertising agency on a new marketing campaign, and it is keen to reuse the old tagline despite the changes. Explain why retaining this tagline would or would not be ethical.

Growing as Professional

Analyze the quality of three goods or services that you use regularly. Start by identifying the criteria that are important to you, then evaluate each product on its ability to deliver on each criterion. What would you change about each product to improve its quality, relative to your expectations? How much more would you be willing to pay to receive that level of quality? Practice this analysis with the products you own and use, and you'll find that it gives you important insights when you move into the business arena and play a role in creating or delivering products for your company's customers.

Sharpening Your Communication Skills

Communication is vital throughout a supply chain. Without clear communication, key targets or objectives would not be met. With this in mind, imagine you are working for a small firm that regularly supplies a large manufacturing company. In recent months, order levels from your customers have been erratic, resulting in employees working overtime significantly to fulfill orders. You feel that the problem lies in poor communication along the supply chain. In a brief, one-page report to your line manager, outline the potential areas for poor communication and give suggestions for improving communication along the supply chain.

Building Your Team Skills

In small teams, research the supply chain for a product of your choice. You should consider and discuss any areas where issues might occur. Make sure you also consider particular areas of strength along with scope for future development. In undertaking this task, ensure that you link your discussions as a group specifically to the product you have chosen. Prepare a short presentation for the benefit of the other teams, allowing time for questions and debate in the class.

Developing Your Research Skills

Research a company that has updated its production operations with a new generation of technology, and try to find answers to as many of these questions as you can.

9-27. What problems or opportunities led the company to rethink its operations? What kind of technology did it choose to address these problems or opportunities? What goals did the company set for applying technology in this way?

9-28. Before adding the new technology, what did the company do to analyze its existing operations? What changes, if any, were made as a result of this analysis?

9-29. How did technology-enhanced operations help the company achieve its goals for financial performance? For customer service? For growth or expansion?

Writing Assignments

9-30. How does the offshoring controversy reflect the larger question of balancing the competing demands of stakeholder groups?

9-31. Why might a service business be more selective than a goods-producing business regarding the customers it pursues or accepts?

ENDNOTES

1. Voodoo Manufacturing, accessed 10 May 2018, voodoomfg .com; John Biggs, "Voodoo Manufacturing Raises $1.4 Million to Make a Factory Full of 3D Printers," *TechCrunch*, 24 January 2017, techcrunch.com; Dyllan Furness, "Meet Project Skywalker: a Fully-Automated 3D Printing Factory Operated by a Robotic Arm," Digital Trends, 16 March 2017, www .digitaltrends.com; Laura Cox, "5 Companies Pushing the Boundaries of 3D Printing," *Disruption*, 25 October 2017,

disruptionhub.com; "What Is 3D Printing?" 3D Hubs, accessed 10 May 2018, www.3dhubs.com; Lora Kolodny, "This Start-Up Is Using Robots and 3-D Printers to Staff a Factory with Almost No Humans," *CNBC*, 23 June 2017, www.cnbc.com.

2. Based in part on Russell L. Ackoff, "Why Few Organizations Adopt Systems Thinking," Ackoff Center Weblog, 7 March 2007, ackoffcenter.blogs.com; Daniel Aronson, "Introduction to Systems Thinking," The Thinking Page, accessed 21 June 2007, www.thinking.net; "What Is Systems Thinking?" The Systems Thinker, accessed 21 June 2007, www.thesystemsthinker.com; Peter Senge, *The Fifth Discipline: The Art and Practice of the Learning Organization* (New York: Doubleday, 1994), 57–67.

3. Stephen P. Robbins, Mary Coulter, and David A. DeCenzo, *Fundamentals of Management*, 10th ed. (New York: Pearson, 2017), 457.

4. Peter Fingar and Ronald Aronica, "Value Chain Optimization: The New Way of Competing," *Supply Chain Management Review*, September–October 2001, 82–85.

5. Eamonn Kelly and Kelly Marchese, "Supply Chains and Value Webs," *Deloitte Insights*, 15 April 2015, www.deloitte.com.

6. John Gillie, "Boeing Says Dreamliner Testing on Schedule for Third Quarter Delivery," *News Tribune* (Tacoma, Wash.), 25 February 2011, www.thenewstribune.com; Jeffrey Rothfeder, "Bumpy Ride," *Portfolio*, May 2009, www.portfolio.com.

7. Toni Waterman, "Big Name US Firms 'Reshoring' from China," *Channel NewsAsia*, 2 November 2013, www.channelnewsasia .com; Alan S. Brown, "A Shift in Engineering Offshore," *Mechanical Engineering*, March 2009, 24–29.

8. "DowDuPont's Andrew Liveris: How America Can Bring Back Manufacturing," *Knowledge@Wharton*, 12 October 2017, knowledge.wharton.upenn.edu.

9. Sarah Shannon, "Is 'Nearshoring the New Offshoring'," *Business of Fashion*, 29 May 2017, www.businessoffashion.com.

10. Jay Heizer, Barry Render, and Chuck Munson, *Operations Management: Sustainability and Supply Chain Management*, 12th ed. (New York: Pearson, 2017), 449.

11. Lee J. Krajewski, Manoj K. Malhotra, and Larry P. Ritzman, *Operations Management: Processes and Supply Chains*, 11th ed. (New York: Pearson, 2016), 211.

12. "Sustainability in Our Value Chains," Walmart, accessed 5 May 2018, corporate.walmart.com.

13. Heizer, Render, and Munson, *Operations Management: Sustainability and Supply Chain Management*, 566.

14. Krajewski, Malhotra, and Ritzman, *Operations Management: Processes and Supply Chains*, 456; "What Is ERP?" Oracle, accessed 9 May 2018, www.oracle.com.

15. Bernard Marr, "How Blockchain Will Transform the Supply Chain and Logistics Industry," *Forbes*, 23 March 2018, www.forbes.com.

16. Paul A. Myerson, *Lean and Technology* (New York: Pearson, 2017), 27.

17. Eli Boufis and Mark L. Frigo, "The Unseen Advantages of Adopting Lean Manufacturing Principles," *IndustryWeek*, 2 February 2018.

18. Alastair Gale and Sean McLain, "Companies Everywhere Copied Japanese Manufacturing. Now the Model Is Cracking; Concepts Celebrated in Business Publications World-Wide Have Been Tarnished by a String of Scandals," *Wall Street Journal*, 4 February 2018.

19. "What Is the Difference Between Lean and Agile Manufacturing?" Team Quality Services, accessed 9 May 2018, teamqualityservices.com.

20. Heizer, Render, and Munson, *Operations Management: Sustainability and Supply Chain Management*, 370–371; Krajewski, Malhotra, and Ritzman, *Operations Management: Processes and Supply Chains*, 218.

21. Heizer, Render, and Munson, *Operations Management: Sustainability and Supply Chain Management*, 372–374.

22. Krajewski, Malhotra, and Ritzman, *Operations Management: Processes and Supply Chains*, 137.

23. Krajewski, Malhotra, and Ritzman, *Operations Management: Processes and Supply Chains*, 441.

24. Heizer, Render, and Munson, *Operations Management: Sustainability and Supply Chain Management*, 67.

25. S. Thomas Foster, *Managing Quality: Integrating the Supply Chain*, 6th ed. (New York: Pearson, 2017), 4.

26. J.P. Russell, "What Are Quality Assurance and Quality Control?" ASQ, accessed 7 May 2018, asq.org; Foster, *Managing Quality: Integrating the Supply Chain*, 17.

27. Heizer, Render, and Munson, *Operations Management: Sustainability and Supply Chain Management*, 219.

28. Richard L. Daft, *Management*, 13th ed. (Boston: Cengage, 2018), 653.

29. Foster, *Managing Quality: Integrating the Supply Chain*, 283.

30. Donald W. Benbow and T. M. Kubiak, "Six Sigma," ASQ, accessed 27 August 2011, asq.org.

31. Steven Minter, "Six Sigma's Growing Pains," *IndustryWeek*, May 2009, 34–36; Tom McCarty, "Six Sigma at Motorola," *European CEO*, September–October 2004, www.motorola.com.

32. McCarty, "Six Sigma at Motorola"; General Electric, "What Is Six Sigma?" GE website, accessed 21 March 2005, www.ge.com.

33. George Byrne, Dave Lubowe, and Amy Blitz, "Driving Operational Innovation Using Lean Six Sigma," IBM, accessed 27 August 2011, www.ibm.com.

34. *Quality Management Principles*, International Organization for Standardization, 2015, www.iso.org.

35. "ISO 9000 Family—Quality Management," International Organization for Standardization, www.iso.org.

36. Mike Moore, "What Is Industry 4.0? Everything You Need to Know," TechRadar, 23 April 2018, www.techradar.com; Bernard Marr, "What Everyone Must Know About Industry 4.0," *Forbes*, 20 June 2016, www.forbes.com.

37. Cornelius Baur and Dominik Wee, "Manufacturing's Next Act," McKinsey, June 2015, www.mckinsey.com; Olivier Scalabre, "Embracing Industry 4.0—and Rediscovering Growth," Boston Consulting Group, accessed 9 May 2018, www.bcg.com; Tom Simonite, "The Researcher Who Wants to Bring AI to Factories," *Wired*, 14 December 2017, www.wired.com.

38. Tom Kennedy, "This Year's Big Cyber Target Could Be the Factory Floor," LinkedIn, 3 January 2018, www.linkedin.com.

39. See note 1.

Despite all the dizzying advances in digital systems, people remain the heart and soul of every business organization. This part looks at two essential people topics: how to keep employees motivated and how to manage the employment life cycle from recruiting through retirement.

Andrey Popov/Shutterstock

10 Employee Motivation

LEARNING OBJECTIVES   After studying this chapter, you will be able to

1 Define motivation, and identify the classical motivation theories.

2 Explain why many consider expectancy theory to be the best current explanation of employee motivation.

3 Identify the strengths and weaknesses of goal-setting theory.

4 Describe the job characteristics model, and explain how it helps predict motivation and performance.

5 Define reinforcement theory, and differentiate between positive and negative reinforcement.

6 List five managerial strategies that are vital to maintaining a motivated workforce.

7 Discuss the potential strengths and weaknesses of performance management systems.

MyLab Intro to Business
Improve Your Grade!

If your instructor is using MyLab Intro to Business, visit **www.pearson.com/mylab/intro-to-business**.

BEHIND THE SCENES   **Blizzard Entertainment: Keeping the Creative Wizards Happy and Productive**

Blizzard Entertainment's Mike Morhaime oversees the company's strategic direction and its workplace culture.

www.blizzard.com

If you've followed the development of video games over the past few years, you've no doubt become impressed by the quality of today's games. With deep storylines, stunning visuals, and immersive playing experiences, the leading games are bona fide works of art.

Given the richness of these digital products, it probably comes as no surprise that they require large teams of visual artists, animators, sound designers, engineers, and other highly skilled specialists. With such popular game franchises as Warcraft, Diablo, StarCraft, and Overwatch, Blizzard Entertainment employs nearly 5,000 people in a wide range of artistic, technical, and business disciplines.

This creative community is united in pursuit of the company's bold mission statement: "We're on a quest: bring our dreams to life and craft the most epic entertainment experiences, ever." While Blizzard has an enviable advantage of being in the business of fun, it is indeed a business. The pressure to delight and amaze the company's millions of enthusiastic customers with each new release is relentless, and the company's own quality expectations are exacting.

If you were Michael Morhaime, president of Blizzard and one of its three founders, how would you keep the company's high-octane talent satisfied and engaged with their work? What steps could you take to help people avoid creative burnout? How could you make sure that people can continue to put their creative gifts to work while contributing to the company's goals? Can you apply the same methods for creative, technical, and business professionals?[1]

INTRODUCTION

Michael Morhaime (profiled in the chapter-opening Behind the Scenes) knows that a one-size-fits-all approach to managing and motivating employees has never been entirely satisfactory, and it is growing less effective every year as the workplace and the workforce continue to change. Motivation is an intriguing business challenge, because no single theory or model can explain every situation. The forces that affect motivation can vary widely from person to person and from situation to situation. The various theories and models discussed in this chapter each provide some insight into the complicated question of employee motivation, and taken as a whole, they offer an overall picture of the challenges and rewards of motivating employees to higher performance.

REAL-TIME UPDATES
Learn More by Visiting This Website

Considering a career in the video game industry?

Blizzard Entertainment can help you explore the possibilities with internships and student competitions. Go to **real-timeupdates .com/bia9** and select Learn More in the Students section.

What Motivates Employees to Peak Performance?

Motivating employees is one of the most important challenges every manager faces. No matter how skillful employees may be and how supportive the work environment is, without the motivation to excel, they won't perform at a high level. Engaged and motivated employees are more effective at their jobs and more careful and attentive in the workplace. Unfortunately, surveys suggest that a vast cross-section of the workforce is not engaged and not motivated to perform at peak potential.[2] This section digs into the meaning of motivation and then explores some of the early attempts to provide practical models for motivating employees.

1 LEARNING OBJECTIVE
Define motivation, and identify the classical motivation theories.

WHAT IS MOTIVATION?

Motivation is a complex subject that defies easy explanation, and some of the brightest minds in the field of management have been working for decades to understand this mysterious force. For one example, things that motivate you might have no effect on other people—or may even *demotivate* them. For another, some of the factors that motivate your behavior stem from deep within your subconscious mind, which means you might be driven by forces that you don't understand and can't even identify.

Starting with a basic definition, **motivation** is the combination of forces that drive individuals to take certain actions and avoid others in pursuit of individual objectives.[3] Pay close attention to *drive* and *actions* in this definition; they are key to understanding motivation.

In a workplace setting, motivation can be assessed by measuring four indicators: *engagement, satisfaction, commitment,* and *rootedness* (see Exhibit 10.1 on the next page).[4] First, **engagement** reflects the degree of energy, enthusiasm, and effort each employee brings to his or her work. If you're "just not into it," chances are you won't perform at your best. Second, *satisfaction* indicates how happy employees are with the experience of work and the way they are treated. Third, *commitment* suggests the degree to which employees support the company and its mission. Fourth, *rootedness* (or its opposite, the intention to quit) predicts the likelihood that employees will stay or leave their jobs. An employee who is engaged, satisfied, and committed and who has no intention of quitting can be safely said to be *motivated*.

These four indicators can identify who is motivated and who isn't, but they don't explain why. For that, it's necessary to dig deeper, looking into what drives people to choose certain actions and avoid others. Contemporary research suggests that motivation stems from four fundamental drives:[5]

motivation
The combination of forces that drive individuals to take certain actions and avoid other actions.

engagement
An employee's rational and emotional commitment to his or her work.

- **The drive to acquire.** This includes fulfilling the need not only for physical goods such as food and clothing but also for enjoyable experiences and "psychological goods" such as prestige. Note that this drive is relative: Individuals want to know how well they're doing compared to others around them.

EXHIBIT 10.1	**Four Indicators of Motivation**

Employees can be said to be fully motivated when they are *engaged, satisfied, committed*, and *rooted* (meaning they have little or no intention to leave).

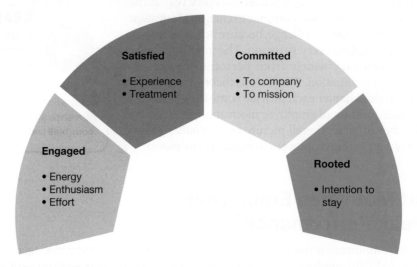

Source: Based on Nitin Nohria, Boris Groysberg, and Linda-Eling Lee, "Employee Motivation: A Powerful New Model," *Harvard Business Review*, July–August 2008, 78–84.

- **The drive to bond.** Humans are social creatures, and the need to feel a part of something larger is a vital aspect of employee motivation. This drive can be helpful, such as when it inspires employees to contribute to common goals, but it can also be harmful, such as when it pits groups of employees against one another in an "us-versus-them" mentality.
- **The drive to comprehend.** Learning, growing, meeting tough challenges, making sense of things—these are satisfying outcomes based on the drive to understand the world around us.
- **The drive to defend.** An instinct to protect and a sense of justice can lead human beings to vigorously defend the people, ideas, and organizations they hold dear. This drive is beneficial when it motivates people to fight for what is right, but it can be harmful as well, such as when it motivates people to resist change.

According to Harvard Business School's Nitin Nohria and his colleagues, who helped identify and explain these four drives, satisfying all four is essential to being motivated. When a need goes unsatisfied—or even worse, is betrayed, such as when employees believe an organization they've supported and defended no longer cares about them—poor motivation is the result.[6]

REAL-TIME UPDATES
Learn More by Watching This Presentation

Satisfying the four fundamental drives of employee behavior

Identify techniques that help satisfy the four fundamental drives in any workplace. Go to **real-timeupdates.com/bia9** and select Learn More in the Students section.

CLASSICAL THEORIES OF MOTIVATION

The quest to understand employee motivation has occupied researchers for more than a century. This section offers a brief overview of some of the important early theories that helped shape ideas about motivation. Although subsequent research has identified shortcomings in all these theories, each contributed to our current understanding of motivation, and each continues to influence managerial practice.

Taylor's Scientific Management

scientific management
A management approach designed to improve employees' efficiency by scientifically studying their work.

One of the earliest motivational researchers, Frederick W. Taylor, a machinist and engineer from Philadelphia, studied employee efficiency and motivation in the late 19th and early 20th centuries. He is credited with developing **scientific management**, an approach that sought to improve employee efficiency through the scientific study of work. In addition to analyzing work and business processes in order to develop better methods, Taylor popularized financial incentives for good performance. His work truly revolutionized business and had a direct influence on the rise of the United States as a global industrial power in the first half of the 20th century.[7]

Although money proved to be a significant motivator for workers under scientific management, this approach didn't consider other motivational elements, such as opportunities for personal satisfaction. For instance, scientific management can't explain why a successful executive will take a hefty pay cut to serve in government or a not-for-profit organization. Therefore, other researchers have looked beyond money to discover what else motivates people.

The Hawthorne Studies and the "Hawthorne Effect"

Between 1924 and 1932, a series of pioneering studies in employee motivation and productivity were conducted at the Hawthorne Works of the Western Electric Company in Chicago. The Hawthorne studies are intriguing both for what they uncovered and as an example of how management ideas can become oversimplified and misunderstood over time. The research began as an experiment in scientific management: testing the effect of various levels of electric lighting on worker productivity. The researchers varied the lighting level for one group of workers (the experimental group) and kept it the same for a second group (the control group). Both groups were engaged in the tedious and exacting task of wrapping wire to make telephone coils, so lighting presumably played a key role in eye strain and other factors influencing productivity.[8]

Whatever the researchers expected to find, they surely didn't expect to see productivity increase in *both* groups as the lighting level was increased for the experimental group—and productivity kept increasing in both groups even when the lighting level was then lowered for the experimental group. In other words, no correlation between the level of lighting and the level of productivity was observed, and productivity increased among the control group workers even though their environment hadn't changed at all. This perplexing outcome was followed by a range of tests on other variables in the work environment and in employee rewards. The research team eventually concluded that group norms (see page 258) affected individual performance more than any other factor and that to understand employee performance one needed to understand an employee's total emotional and cultural makeup, on and off the job.[9]

By themselves, these conclusions are important, and the Hawthorne studies helped launch the entire field of industrial psychology and began to enlighten the practice of management in general.[10] Then, a couple of decades later, a researcher not connected with the studies suggested the phenomenon of the **Hawthorne effect**, in which the behavior of the Western Electric workers changed because they were being observed and given special treatment as research subjects. In the years that followed, the concept of the Hawthorne effect took on a life of its own and became widely assumed across many fields of research, from management to medicine, even though the original research never reached this conclusion. Moreover, the phenomenon has come to be defined in so many ways that the use of the term could obscure more than it explains. The outcome of the Hawthorne studies has too often been reduced to this oversimplified and uncertain conclusion about the behavior of research subjects; the real and lasting contribution of the studies was to open many eyes to the benefits of understanding human behavior in organizational settings.[11]

Hawthorne effect
A supposed effect of organizational research, in which employees change their behavior because they are being studied and given special treatment; the validity of the effect is uncertain, and the Hawthorne studies were richer and more influential than this simple outcome would suggest.

Maslow's Hierarchy of Needs

In 1943, psychologist Abraham Maslow hypothesized that behavior is determined by a variety of needs, which he organized into categories arranged in a hierarchy. As Exhibit 10.2 on the next page shows, the most basic needs are at the bottom of this hierarchy, and the more advanced needs are toward the top. In **Maslow's hierarchy**, all the requirements for basic survival—food, clothing, shelter, and the like—fall into the category of *physiological needs*. These basic needs must be satisfied before the person can consider higher-level needs such as *safety needs, social needs* (the need to give and receive love and to feel a sense of belonging), and *esteem needs* (the need for a sense of self-worth and integrity).[12]

At the top of Maslow's hierarchy is *self-actualization*—the need to become everything one can be. This need is also the most difficult to fulfill—and even to identify in many cases.

Maslow's hierarchy
A model in which human needs are arranged in a hierarchy, with the most basic needs at the bottom and the more advanced needs toward the top.

EXHIBIT 10.2 | **Maslow's Hierarchy of Needs**

Abraham Maslow suggested that needs on the lower levels of the hierarchy must be satisfied before higher-level needs can be addressed (examples are shown to the right). This model offers a convenient way to categorize needs, but it lacks empirical validation.

Source: Based on Andrew J. DuBrin, *Human Relation for Career and Personal Success*, 11th ed. (New York: Pearson, 2017), 62–64.

REAL-TIME UPDATES

Learn More by Watching This Presentation

The power of intrinsic motivation

Explore the differences between intrinsic and extrinsic motivation, and see why intrinsic motivators are so powerful. Go to **real-time updates.com/bia9** and select Learn More in the Students section.

Employees who reach this point work not just because they want to make money or impress others but because they feel their work is worthwhile and satisfying in itself.

Maslow's hierarchy is a convenient and logical tool for classifying human needs, and many people continue to use it to explain behavior. However, other researchers have not been able to verify that this is how motivation actually works.[13]

Theory X and Theory Y

Theory X
A managerial assumption that employees are irresponsible, are unambitious, and dislike work and that managers must use force, control, or threats to motivate them.

Theory Y
A managerial assumption that employees enjoy meaningful work, are naturally committed to certain goals, are capable of creativity, and seek out responsibility under the right conditions.

Herzberg's two-factor theory
A model that divides motivational forces into satisfiers ("motivators") and dissatisfiers ("hygiene factors").

In the 1960s, psychologist Douglas McGregor proposed two radically different sets of assumptions that underlie most management thinking, which he classified as *Theory X* and *Theory Y*. According to McGregor, **Theory X**–oriented managers believe that employees dislike work and can be motivated only by the fear of losing their jobs or by *extrinsic rewards*—those given by other people, such as money and promotions. In contrast, **Theory Y**–oriented managers believe that employees like to work and can be motivated by working for goals that promote creativity or for causes they believe in. Consequently, Theory Y–oriented managers seek to motivate employees through *intrinsic rewards*—which employees essentially give to themselves. As with Maslow's hierarchy, Theory X and Theory Y seem to have a permanent place in the management vocabulary, but they suffer from the same lack of empirical evidence.[14] However, the distinction between intrinsic and extrinsic rewards remains a valid and essential aspect of many theories of motivation.

Herzberg's Two Factors

Also in the 1960s, Frederick Herzberg and his associates explored the aspects of jobs that make employees feel satisfied or dissatisfied. The researchers found that two entirely different sets of factors were associated with dissatisfying and satisfying work experiences. In **Herzberg's two-factor theory** (see Exhibit 10.3), so-called *hygiene factors* are associated with dissatisfying experiences, and *motivators* are associated with satisfying experiences. Hygiene factors are mostly extrinsic and include working conditions, company policies, pay, and job security. Motivators tend to be intrinsic and include achievement, recognition, responsibility, and other personally rewarding factors.[15]

EXHIBIT 10.3	Herzberg's Two-Factor Theory

According to Herzberg, *hygiene factors* such as working conditions and company policies can influence employee dissatisfaction. On the other hand, *motivators* such as opportunities for achievement and recognition can influence employee satisfaction.

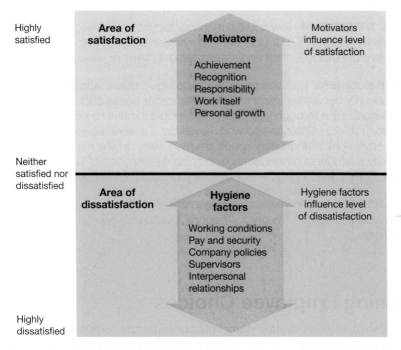

According to Herzberg's model, managers need to remove dissatisfying elements *and* add satisfying elements—doing one or the other is not enough.[16]

Like Maslow's hierarchy and Theory X/Theory Y, the two-factor theory seems logical and helps explain part of the motivation puzzle. However, it has been criticized because of the methodology used in the original research and the inability of subsequent research to validate the model. Also, although there is a strong causal link between customer satisfaction and profitability, it is far less clear whether satisfied *employees* automatically lead to satisfied *customers*.[17]

McClelland's Three Needs

The last of the classical theories to consider is the **three-needs theory** developed by David McClelland. McClelland's model highlights three acquired needs: the *need for power* (having—and demonstrating—control over others), the *need for affiliation* (being accepted by others and having opportunities for social interaction), and the *need for achievement* (attaining personally meaningful goals). Someone with a high need for achievement, for example, may make a successful entrepreneur but a less successful manager, because the need for personal achievement is stronger than the need for power or affiliation. Unlike with the other classical theories, there is a lot of research to validate McClelland's ideas and to explain particular outcomes in the workplace.[18]

three-needs theory
David McClelland's model of motivation that highlights the needs for power, affiliation, and achievement.

 CHECKPOINT

LEARNING OBJECTIVE 1: Define motivation, and identify the classical motivation theories.

SUMMARY: Motivation is the combination of forces that prompt individuals to take certain actions and avoid others in pursuit of individual objectives. Research suggests that four drives underlie all motivation: the drive to acquire tangible and intangible rewards, the drive to bond with others, the drive to comprehend, and the drive to defend. The classical motivation theories and research that helped shape today's thinking include Taylor's scientific management, the Hawthorne studies, Maslow's hierarchy of needs, McGregor's Theory X and Theory Y, Herzberg's two factors, and McClelland's three needs.

CRITICAL THINKING: (1) How could a manager tap into the drive to defend as a way to help rally employees? (2) Could Herzberg's hygiene factors help explain the significant problem of employee theft and embezzlement? Why or why not?

IT'S YOUR BUSINESS: (1) If you are a typical college student who doesn't have much financial security but is also trying to fulfill higher-order needs such as social interaction and self-actualization through your education, would it make more sense, according to Maslow, to drop out of college and work seven days a week so you could help ensure that your physiological and safety needs are met? Why or why not? (2) Do you think today's college students more closely match the descriptions of Theory X employees or Theory Y employees? What evidence can you provide to support your conclusion?

KEY TERMS TO KNOW: motivation, engagement, scientific management, Hawthorne effect, Maslow's hierarchy, Theory X, Theory Y, Herzberg's two-factor theory, three-needs theory

---

[2] **LEARNING OBJECTIVE**

Explain why many consider expectancy theory to be the best current explanation of employee motivation.

Explaining Employee Choices

The classical theories of motivation contributed in important ways to both managerial practices and the ongoing research into employee motivation, but each has been found wanting in some way or another. Starting with more contemporary theories, two models, known as expectancy theory and equity theory, help explain the choices that employees make.

EXPECTANCY THEORY

expectancy theory
The idea that the effort employees put into their work depends on expectations about their own ability to perform, expectations about likely rewards, and the attractiveness of those rewards.

Expectancy theory, considered by some experts to offer the best available explanation of employee motivation, connects an employee's efforts to the outcome he or she expects from those efforts. Expectancy theory focuses less on the specific forces that motivate employees and more on the process they follow to seek satisfaction in their jobs. As shown in Exhibit 10.4, the effort employees will put forth depends on (1) their expectations regarding the level of performance they will be able to achieve, (2) their beliefs regarding the rewards that the organization will give in response to that performance, and (3) the attractiveness of those rewards relative to their individual goals.[19]

Exploring these connections from both an employee's and a manager's perspective will give you an idea of how the expectancy model can explain employee behavior and prescribe managerial tactics to help motivate employees. First, as an employee, if you don't believe that the amount of effort you are willing or able to apply to a task will result in an acceptable level of performance, a natural response will be to say, "Well, why bother?" This uncertainty could come from many sources, such as doubts about your skills, confusion about the task, or a belief that "the system" is so broken that no matter how hard you try you can't succeed. Belief in your ability to complete a task is known as *self-efficacy,* and it can be increased by gaining experience, mimicking successful role models, getting encouragement from others, and sometimes even "psyching yourself up."[20] As a manager, your challenges would be to ensure that employees have the skills and confidence they need, that tasks are clearly defined, and that company policies and processes are functional.

Your second concern as an employee is whether the organization will recognize and reward your performance. Knowing you've done great work is its own reward,

EXHIBIT 10.4	Expectancy Theory

Expectancy theory suggests that employees base their efforts on expectations of their own performance, expectations of rewards for that performance, and the value of those rewards.

The quality of the effort an employee puts forth depends on . . .

(1) expectations of → Individual performance → (2) and expectations of → Organizational rewards → (3) and the attractiveness of those rewards relative to → Individual goals

Source: Based on Stephen P. Robbins, Mary Coulter, and David A. DeCenzo, *Fundamentals of Management*, 10th ed. (New York: Pearson, 2017), 341.

of course, but for many employees, this isn't enough. As a manager, your challenges include establishing reward systems and expectations to minimize employee uncertainty and taking time from the daily chaos to acknowledge the efforts your employees make.

Finally, if you're confident in your performance and the organization's response, your third concern is whether the promised reward is something you value. What if you are offered a raise but what you really want is for your boss to acknowledge how important your contributions have been to the company? As a manager, aligning rewards with employee priorities is an ongoing challenge; see "Reinforcing High-Performance Behavior" on page 309.

EQUITY THEORY

If you work side by side with someone, doing the same job and giving the same amount of effort, only to learn that your colleague earns more money, will you be satisfied in your work and motivated to continue working hard? Chances are, you will perceive a state of *inequity*, and you probably won't be happy with the situation. **Equity theory** suggests that employee satisfaction depends on the perceived ratio of inputs to outputs. To remedy a perception of inequity, you might ask for a raise, decide not to work as hard, try to change perceptions of your efforts or their outcomes, or simply quit and find a new job. Any one of these steps has the potential to bring your perceived input-to-output ratio back into balance.[21] Some of the choices employees can make to address perceived inequity are obviously not desirable from an employer's point of view, so it's important to understand why employees might feel they aren't getting a fair shake.

Equity issues can show up in a number of areas, such as in complaints about gender pay fairness and executive compensation (see page 338) and in many unionizing efforts, whenever employees feel they aren't getting a fair share of corporate profits or are being asked to shoulder more than their fair share of hardships.

Research into equity theory has led to thinking about the broader concept of *organizational justice*, or perceptions of fairness in the workplace. These perceptions relate to outcomes, the processes used to generate those outcomes, and the way employees are treated during the process.[22] No reasonable employee expects to make as much as the CEO, for example, but as long as the process seems fair (both the employee's and the CEO's pay are related to performance, for example), most employees will be satisfied, and the disparity won't affect their motivation. In fact, perceptions of fairness can have as much impact on overall employee satisfaction as satisfaction with pay itself.[23]

equity theory
The idea that employees base their level of satisfaction on the ratio of their inputs to the job and the outputs or rewards they receive from it.

CHECKPOINT

LEARNING OBJECTIVE 2: Explain why many consider expectancy theory to be the best current explanation of employee motivation.

SUMMARY: Expectancy theory suggests that the effort employees put into their work depends on expectations about their own ability to perform, expectations about the rewards the organization will give in response to that performance, and the attractiveness of those rewards relative to their individual goals. This theory is thought to be a good model because it considers the links between effort and outcome. For instance, if employees think a link is "broken," such as having doubts that their efforts will yield acceptable performance or worries that they will perform well but no one will notice, they're likely to put less effort into their work.

CRITICAL THINKING: (1) What steps could managers take to alleviate the self-doubt employees often feel when they join a company or move into a new position? (2) If you were a human resources manager in a large corporation, how might you respond to employees who complain that the CEO makes 200 or 300 times more than they make?

IT'S YOUR BUSINESS: (1) Have you ever given less than your best effort in a college course because you didn't believe you were capable of excelling in the course? (2) If so, was the outcome satisfying? Would you handle a similar situation the same way in the future?

KEY TERMS TO KNOW: expectancy theory, equity theory

---

3 LEARNING OBJECTIVE

Identify the strengths and weaknesses of goal-setting theory.

goal-setting theory
A motivational theory suggesting that setting goals can be an effective way to motivate employees.

Motivating with Challenging Goals

With the expectancy and equity theories offering some insight into why employees make the choices they do, the next step in understanding motivation is to explore specific leadership strategies that motivate employees. **Goal-setting theory**, the idea that carefully designed goals can motivate employees to higher performance, is one of the most important contemporary theories of motivation. It is both widely used and strongly supported by experimental research.[24] (However, as "Risks and Limitations of Goal-Setting Theory" on page 305 explains, some researchers assert that the benefits of goal setting have been overstated and the risks have been understated, partly because some research studies fail to measure the full consequences of goal-driven behaviors.)

For goals to function as effective motivators, a number of criteria must be met. These criteria include[25]

- Goals that are specific enough to give employees clarity and focus
- Goals that are difficult enough to inspire energetic and committed effort
- Clear "ownership" of goals so that accountability can be established
- Timely feedback that lets people know if they're progressing toward their goals and, if not, how to change course
- Individuals' belief in their ability to meet their goals
- Cultural support for the individual achievement and independence needed to reach the goals

Goals that are both bold and personally meaningful to employees can be powerful motivators. For example, one of the leading developers of technology for self-driving cars, Aurora Innovation, sets goals that it labels "outrageous" and believes in these goals because "they require us to focus and make sacrifices." The company also believes that in striving to make travel safer on a global scale, it is "solving one of the most challenging problems of our generation." An Aurora engineer described the effect that this goal has on her work: "The first time I watched an Aurora vehicle drive itself, I felt thrilled—we are going to

EXHIBIT 10.5   **Management by Objectives (MBO)**

The four steps of the MBO cycle are refined and repeated as managers and employees at all levels work toward establishing goals and objectives, thereby accomplishing the organization's strategic goals.

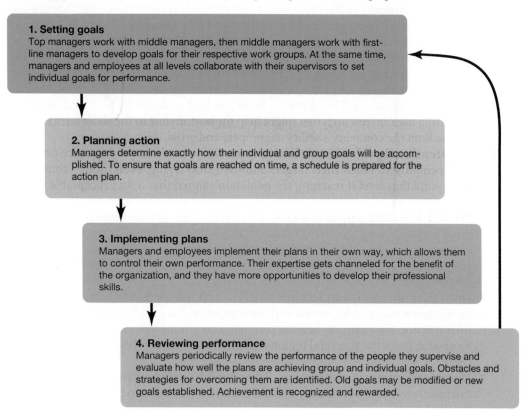

1. Setting goals
Top managers work with middle managers, then middle managers work with first-line managers to develop goals for their respective work groups. At the same time, managers and employees at all levels collaborate with their supervisors to set individual goals for performance.

2. Planning action
Managers determine exactly how their individual and group goals will be accomplished. To ensure that goals are reached on time, a schedule is prepared for the action plan.

3. Implementing plans
Managers and employees implement their plans in their own way, which allows them to control their own performance. Their expertise gets channeled for the benefit of the organization, and they have more opportunities to develop their professional skills.

4. Reviewing performance
Managers periodically review the performance of the people they supervise and evaluate how well the plans are achieving group and individual goals. Obstacles and strategies for overcoming them are identified. Old goals may be modified or new goals established. Achievement is recognized and rewarded.

change people's lives! Aurora is an adventure, and the weeks fly by as we advance in solving one of the biggest challenges in robotics and transportation."[26]

MANAGEMENT BY OBJECTIVES

Goal-setting theory is frequently implemented through a technique known as **management by objectives (MBO)**, a companywide process that empowers employees and involves them in goal setting and decision-making. This process consists of four steps: setting goals, planning actions to meet those goals, implementing the plans, and reviewing performance (see Exhibit 10.5). Because employees at all levels are involved in all four steps, they learn more about company objectives and feel that they are an important part of the companywide team. Furthermore, they understand how their individual job functions contribute to the organization's long-term success.

One of the key elements of MBO is the collaborative goal-setting process. Together, a manager and an employee define the employee's goals, the responsibilities for achieving those goals, and the means of evaluating individual and group performance so that the employee's activities are directly linked to achieving the organization's long-term goals. Jointly setting clear and challenging but achievable goals can encourage employees to reach higher levels of performance, although participation alone is no guarantee of higher performance.[27]

RISKS AND LIMITATIONS OF GOAL-SETTING THEORY

As powerful as goal setting can be, it can misfire in a variety of ways, with results ranging from employee frustration to systematic underperformance to serious ethical and legal problems:[28]

management by objectives (MBO)
A motivational approach in which managers and employees work together to structure personal goals and objectives for every individual, department, and project to mesh with the organization's goals.

- **Overly narrow goals.** When goals are too narrow, people can miss or intentionally ignore vital aspects of the bigger picture. Salespeople trying to meet their quotas, for example, might be tempted to offer huge discounts or extend credit to customers who can't make the payments.
- **Overly challenging goals.** Lofty goals can inspire great performance, but they can also lead to risky behavior, belligerent negotiating tactics, and ethical lapses as employees cut corners or commit ethical lapses to reach targets.
- **Inappropriate time horizons.** Too much emphasis on short-term performance can degrade long-term performance. A good example is the unhealthy focus that a publicly traded company can place on quarterly performance in order to meet the stock market's expectations. This distorted focus can lead to decisions such as downsizing or cutting back on research that might help the bottom line in the short term but ultimately limit the company's ability to compete and grow.
- **Unintentional performance limitations.** Goals can limit performance potential when employees reach their targets and then stop trying, even though they could go beyond that level if reaching the goal didn't signal that it was acceptable to stop there.
- **Missed learning opportunities.** Employees can get so focused on meeting deadlines and other goals that they overlook opportunities to learn, whether to improve their own skills, fix process problems, or adapt to changes in the business environment—all of which could benefit the company more than meeting the original goal.[29]
- **Unhealthy internal competition.** Goals can pit groups within a company against each other, which can be beneficial if the competition is healthy but ultimately harmful if it is not. For example, healthy competitions among sales regions can be a great motivator, but what if several regions refuse to cooperate to help land a big national client?
- **Decreased intrinsic motivation.** Relying too heavily on exterior goals and their extrinsic rewards can eventually dull the intrinsic motivation to do well for the sake of the work itself—one of the most powerful and sustainable motivators.

As you ponder these limitations of goal-setting theory, you can start to sense how important it is to set goals carefully and only after considering the potential consequences.

 CHECKPOINT

LEARNING OBJECTIVE 3: Identify the strengths and weaknesses of goal-setting theory.

SUMMARY: Setting challenging goals has proven to be a dependable way to inspire employees to high levels of performance; goal setting is the foundation of a popular management system known as management by objectives (MBO). In addition to being widely used, goal-setting theory is strongly supported by experimental research. The weaknesses of goal setting generally lie in the ways that the pursuit of goals can distort behavior. Potential problems include overly narrow or overly challenging goals, inappropriate time horizons, unintentional performance limitations, missed learning opportunities, unhealthy internal competition, and decreased intrinsic motivation.

CRITICAL THINKING: (1) Why is collaboration between employee and manager essential to goal setting in MBO? (2) How can overly narrow goals and overly challenging goals contribute to ethical lapses?

IT'S YOUR BUSINESS: (1) Do goals motivate you? Why or why not? (2) Does the motivation depend on whether the goals are your own or imposed by someone else?

KEY TERMS TO KNOW: goal-setting theory, management by objectives (MBO)

Redesigning Jobs to Stimulate Performance

Along with setting challenging goals, many companies are exploring ways to redesign the work itself to improve employee satisfaction and motivation.

4 **LEARNING OBJECTIVE**

Describe the job characteristics model, and explain how it helps predict motivation and performance.

THE JOB CHARACTERISTICS MODEL

Using the **job characteristics model** proposed by Richard Hackman and Greg Oldman has proven to be a reliable way to predict the effects of five *core job dimensions* on employee motivation and other positive outcomes:[30]

- **Skill variety**—the range of skills and talents needed to accomplish the responsibilities associated with the job. The broader the range of skills required, the more meaningful the work is likely to be to the employee.
- **Task identity**—the degree to which the employee has responsibility for completing an entire task. Greater task identity contributes to the sense of meaning in work.
- **Task significance**—the employee's perception of the impact the job has on the lives of other people.
- **Autonomy**—the degree of independence the employee has in carrying out the job.
- **Feedback**—timely information that tells employees how well they're doing in their jobs.

job characteristics model
A model suggesting that five core job dimensions influence three critical psychological states that determine motivation, performance, and other outcomes.

You can see that some of these dimensions relate to the nature of the work itself and others relate more to management decisions and leadership styles. All of them contribute in one way or another to three *critical psychological states*:[31]

- **Experienced meaningfulness of the work**—a measure of how much employees care about the jobs they are doing
- **Experienced responsibility for results**—the sense each employee has that his or her efforts contribute to the outcome
- **Knowledge of actual results**—employees' awareness of the real-life results of their efforts

As these psychological states increase in intensity, they lead to improvements in motivation, performance, job satisfaction, absenteeism (the amount of time employees miss work), and turnover (the rate at which employees leave their jobs). In other words, if employees believe their work is meaningful, believe their individual efforts are responsible at least in large part for the outcome of that work, and can see evidence of the results of their efforts, they are likely to be more motivated than they would otherwise. It's not hard to see that the reverse is also true. Employees who believe their work is meaningless, who don't feel much responsibility for the outcome, or who never get to see the results of their efforts aren't likely to be terribly motivated or satisfied.

One final aspect of job characteristics research explores is how various types of employees respond to changes in the core job dimensions. Employees with strong *growth needs*, meaning they feel a strong need to increase self-esteem and self-actualization, respond more dramatically to improvements in job dimensions—and improvements in the critical psychological states will lead to greater increases in their motivation and the other positive outcomes.[32] Conversely, employees who feel little intrinsic need to grow can be among the most difficult to motivate, no matter what steps managers take.

The job characteristics model continues to offer helpful guidance as companies grapple with the challenges in today's work environment. For instance, as more companies increasingly rely on temporary workers to control costs or acquire skills that are needed only for specific projects, managers need to think carefully about the ways they supervise permanent versus

REAL-TIME UPDATES
Learn More by Watching This Video

Two fundamental secrets to employee motivation

Opportunities to grow and to do meaningful work are essential to employee motivation. Go to **real-timeupdates.com/bia9** and select Learn More in the Students section.

Companies can boost performance by designing jobs so that employees feel the meaning in their work and a sense of responsibility for results.

Antonio Guillem Fernández/Alamy Stock Photo

job enrichment
Making jobs more challenging and interesting by expanding the range of skills required.

cross-training
Training workers to perform multiple jobs and rotating them through these various jobs to combat boredom or burnout.

temporary employees. As two examples, temporary workers may need to be assigned more discrete tasks that have enough task identity and autonomy to provide a sense of ownership and control, and managers need to make sure they don't take permanent employees for granted and fail to give them adequate feedback about their efforts.[33]

APPROACHES TO MODIFYING CORE JOB DIMENSIONS

The job characteristics model identifies the generic aspects of a job that can be adjusted to improve motivation, but it's up to individual companies and departments to identify and make the specific changes that are relevant to each job in the organization. Three popular approaches are job enrichment, job enlargement, and cross-training:

ESB Professional/Shutterstock

Cross-training employees to perform multiple jobs can help companies minimize boredom and burnout.

- **Job enrichment.** The strategy behind **job enrichment** is to make jobs more challenging and interesting by expanding the range of skills required—typically by expanding upward, giving employees some of the responsibilities previously held by their managers.[34] For example, an employee who had been preparing presentations for his or her boss to give to customers could be asked to give the presentations as well. Job enrichment needs to be approached carefully, however. Some employees respond well, but for others, the increased responsibility is more a source of stress than of inspiration.[35]
- **Job enlargement.** Whereas job enrichment expands vertically, *job enlargement* is more of a horizontal expansion, adding tasks that aren't necessarily any more challenging. If it simply gives workers more to do, job enlargement won't do much to motivate and will more likely demotivate. However, if jobs are enlarged in ways that increase worker knowledge, expansion can improve job satisfaction.[36]
- **Cross-training.** Job enrichment and job enlargement expand the scope of an individual job, whereas **cross-training**, or *job rotation*, involves training workers to perform multiple jobs and rotating them through these various jobs to combat boredom or burnout.

Companies can also work to improve motivation though changes in management attitudes and practices, such as giving employees more control over their work and providing timely feedback. The best solution is usually a combination of changes that accommodate the nature of the work and the abilities and interests of individual employees and managers.

✔ **CHECKPOINT**

LEARNING OBJECTIVE 4 : Describe the job characteristics model, and explain how it helps predict motivation and performance.

SUMMARY: The job characteristics model identifies five core job dimensions (skill variety, task identity, task significance, autonomy, and feedback) that create three critical psychological states (experienced meaningfulness of the work, experienced responsibility for results, and knowledge of actual results). Achieving these three states leads to improvements in motivation, job satisfaction, performance, absenteeism, and turnover.

CRITICAL THINKING: (1) Can the job characteristics model be used to motivate employees in such positions as janitors or security guards in a factory? How? (2) Is modifying the five core job dimensions likely to motivate employees who have low growth needs? Why or why not?

IT'S YOUR BUSINESS: (1) Has the requirement of working in teams ever lowered your motivation or satisfaction on a school project? If so, how does the job characteristics model explain this? (2) How does taking elective courses improve your experience of meaningfulness in your college "work"?

KEY TERMS TO KNOW: job characteristics model, job enrichment, cross-training

Reinforcing High-Performance Behavior

Challenging goals and creative job designs can motivate employees to higher levels of performance, but managers also need to make sure that performance can be sustained over time. Employees in the workplace, like people in all other aspects of life, tend to repeat behaviors that create positive outcomes for themselves and to avoid or abandon behaviors that result in negative outcomes. **Reinforcement theory** suggests that managers can motivate employees by shaping their actions through *behavior modification*.[37] Using reinforcement theory, managers try to systematically encourage those actions considered beneficial to the company. Reinforcement is a valuable motivational tool, but it has broad application whenever managers want to shape employee behavior.

TYPES OF REINFORCEMENT

Reinforcement can be either *positive* or *negative*. In casual speech, the two terms are usually equated with praise for desirable behavior and criticism or punishment for undesirable behavior, respectively, but they have different and specific meanings in psychological terminology (see Exhibit 10.6). Both positive and negative reinforcement encourage behaviors to be repeated; the difference is in how they do it.

Positive reinforcement offers pleasant consequences for particular actions or behaviors, increasing the likelihood that the behaviors will be repeated. For example, even a simple but sincere "thank you" provides emotional reward and encourages employees to repeat whatever behavior elicited the praise.[38] Positive reinforcement can also have a multiplier effect, in which employees who receive positive reinforcement for one type of behavior are motivated to perform well in other areas, a process known as *chaining*.[39] Many companies use some form of **incentives**, either monetary payments or other rewards of value, as positive reinforcement to motivate employees to achieve specific performance targets.

The terminology of reinforcement theory can be confusing because the terms are used differently in everyday speech than in psychology. Three points will help you keep the terms straight in your mind. First, both positive and negative reinforcement encourage a behavior to be repeated—they *reinforce* it, in order words. The difference is in how they work. Second, punishment (not negative reinforcement) is the opposite of positive reinforcement. Third, positive reinforcement can encourage undesirable behaviors, so it isn't necessarily a good thing, despite the "positive" label.

Negative reinforcement also encourages a particular behavior to be repeated, but it does so through the reduction, removal, or absence of an unpleasant outcome. For example, if you initially received some complaints about publicly humiliating your employees after taking over as department manager, but those complaints dwindled over time as people gave up and accepted your poor behavior, their silence would encourage you to continue

---

EXHIBIT 10.6	**Reinforcement and Punishment**

The terminology of reinforcement theory can be confusing because the terms are used differently in everyday speech than in psychology. Three points will help you keep the terms straight in your mind. First, both positive and negative reinforcement encourage a behavior to be repeated—they *reinforce* it, in order words. The difference is in how they work. Second, punishment (not negative reinforcement) is the opposite of positive reinforcement. Third, positive reinforcement can encourage undesirable behaviors, so it isn't necessarily a good thing, despite the "positive" label.

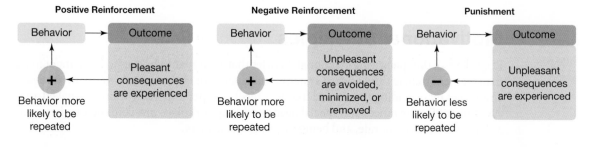

being a bully. Many people mistakenly use the term *negative reinforcement* when they are actually talking about *punishment*, which refers to actions used to diminish the repetition of unwanted behaviors by adding unpleasant outcomes.[40]

UNINTENDED CONSEQUENCES OF REINFORCEMENT

Reinforcement sounds like a simple enough concept, but the mechanisms of reinforcement can be subtle and the effects unexpected. Managers must be on constant alert for unintended consequences of incentives and other reinforcement efforts. For example, because they often focus on a single variable, incentive programs can distort performance by encouraging employees to focus on that variable to the detriment of other responsibilities.[41] If your salespeople get a bonus every time they land a new client but receive no penalties whenever an unhappy client leaves for a competitor, sales staffers will naturally tend to focus more on acquiring new clients than on making sure existing clients are satisfied.

Reinforcement doesn't have to involve explicit monetary incentives to distort behavior, either. For instance, imagine that a manager offers enthusiastic praise whenever employees suggest new ideas during meetings but never follows up to see whether those employees actually do any work to implement their great ideas. He or she can be encouraging empty "happy talk" through both positive reinforcement (there are pleasant consequences for spouting out ideas during meetings) *and* negative reinforcement (there are no unpleasant consequences for not doing any of the work, so employees will continue to not do it).

 CHECKPOINT

LEARNING OBJECTIVE 5 : Define reinforcement theory, and differentiate between positive and negative reinforcement.

SUMMARY: Reinforcement theory suggests that managers can motivate employees by systematically encouraging actions that are beneficial to the company. Positive and negative reinforcement both tend to increase the specific behavior in question, but positive reinforcement does so by providing pleasant consequences for engaging in the behavior, whereas negative reinforcement does so by removing unpleasant consequences. The term *negative reinforcement* is sometimes used in casual speech when people are really talking about punishment, which involves discouraging a particular behavior by offering unpleasant consequences for it.

CRITICAL THINKING: (1) Is demoting an employee for failing to finish a project an attempt at negative reinforcement or punishment? Why? (2) In what ways is reinforcement theory similar to goal-setting theory?

IT'S YOUR BUSINESS: (1) How does your instructor in this course use reinforcement to motivate students to higher levels of performance? (2) If you study diligently to avoid being embarrassed when a professor calls on you in class, is this behavior positive or negative reinforcement in action? Why?

KEY TERMS TO KNOW: reinforcement theory, positive reinforcement, incentives, negative reinforcement

[6] **LEARNING OBJECTIVE**

List five managerial strategies that are vital to maintaining a motivated workforce.

Motivational Strategies

Regardless of the specific motivational theories that a company chooses to implement in its management policies and reward systems, managers can improve their ability to motivate employees by providing timely and frequent feedback, personalizing motivational efforts, adapting to circumstances and special needs, tackling workplace problems before they have a chance to destroy morale, and being inspirational leaders.

PROVIDING TIMELY AND FREQUENT FEEDBACK

Imagine how you'd feel if you worked for weeks on a complex project for one of your classes, turned it in on time, and then heard . . . nothing. As days passed with no feedback, doubts would begin to creep in. Was your work so good that your professor is passing it around to other faculty members in sheer astonishment? Was it so bad that your professor is still searching for the words to describe it? Was your project simply lost in the shuffle, and no one knows it is missing yet?

No matter which theory of motivation an organization or a manager subscribes to, providing timely and frequent feedback is essential. From the perspective of reinforcement theory, for example, feedback is the mechanism that shapes employee behavior. Without it, opportunities for reinforcement will be missed, and the effort put forth by employees will eventually wane because they'll see little reason to continue.

Feedback "closes the loop" in two important ways: It gives employees the information they need in order to assess their own performance and make improvements if necessary, and it serves the emotional purpose of reassuring employees that their work is meaningful and valued.[42] Even if the feedback is constructive criticism, it lets employees know that what they do is important enough to be done correctly.

Providing timely feedback helps employees adjust their performance if needed and can send a strong signal that their work is appreciated and important to the company.

MAKING IT PERSONAL

A recurring theme in just about every attempt to explain motivation is that motivation is a deeply personal phenomenon. Rewards and feedback that stimulate one employee to higher achievement can have no effect on a second employee and may demotivate a third.

In an ideal world, managers would be able to personalize motivational efforts completely, giving each employee the rewards and feedback that spur him or her to peak achievement. However, the need for fairness and the demands on a manager's time place practical limits on the degree to which motivational efforts can be individualized. The situation calls for a three-pronged approach (see Exhibit 10.7 on the next page). First, establish systems and policies that are as equitable and as automatic as possible, and explain to employees why they are fair. Second, build in as much flexibility as you can, such as offering employees the cash equivalent of paid time off if they prefer money over time. Third, get to know employees as individuals in order to understand what is important to each person. For example, research suggests that younger employees are more likely to be demotivated by uninteresting work than their older counterparts. Offering training opportunities or the chance to participate in decision-making can motivate people when the core work responsibilities might not.[43]

Of course, managers need to give everyone an equal shot at opportunities, but as much as possible, they should let employees choose which opportunities and rewards they want to pursue. Employees understand that their managers can't always change "the system," but they do expect their managers to exercise some individual control over how policies are implemented and rewards are given.[44]

GAMIFYING FOR HEALTHY COMPETITION

One of the newest motivational strategies is **gamification**, applying game principles to various business processes. Importantly, gamification isn't about "playing games" in a business context, but rather about applying the motivational power of scorekeeping,

REAL-TIME UPDATES
Learn More by Visiting This Website

Practical advice to motivate yourself and others

Put these tips and techniques to use in every facet of life. Go to **real-timeupdates.com/bia9** and select Learn More in the Students section.

gamification
Applying game principles such as scorekeeping to various business processes.

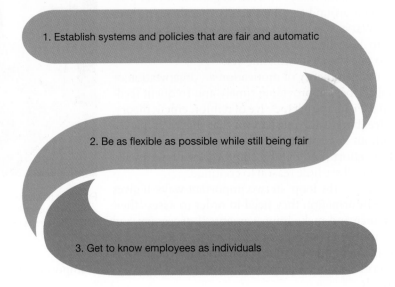

| EXHIBIT 10.7 | **Personalizing Motivation** |

Gearing motivational efforts to the individual makes them more effective, but this approach must be conducted in a way that is fair for everyone. Achieving a balance is not always easy, because various employees are motivated by different things.

1. Establish systems and policies that are fair and automatic

2. Be as flexible as possible while still being fair

3. Get to know employees as individuals

competition, and other game-playing mechanics to existing business activities.[45] Companies are now gamifying processes ranging from sales and customer service to employee recruiting, training, and health and fitness. Encouraging participation in and contribution to social networks and other communities is a good example of how gamification can motivate employees and other stakeholders. Depending on the system, members can earn points, badges, and other rewards.[46]

ADDRESSING WORKPLACE NEGATIVITY

No workplace is immune to problems and conflicts, but negativity is an emotional "virus" that can infect an entire organization. Just as with physical health, in the workplace managers must address problems and conflicts quickly, before they multiply and erode employee morale. Left to fester long enough, these problems can destroy the sense of community in a company and leave employees feeling hopeless about the future.[47]

Jumping on a problem quickly can have a double positive impact: It solves the problem, and it demonstrates to everyone that managers care about the emotional health of the workforce.

Thoughtful hiring is a critical aspect of ensuring a positive workplace, because a single negative employee can damage the emotional health of everyone around. Aurora Innovation, for instance, has an explicit "No jerks" policy when it comes to hiring: "We debate and solve hard technical problems. We don't waste time battling over personalities and egos, and we have no tolerance for time-wasters and nonsense."[48]

BEING AN INSPIRING LEADER

Theories and systems aside, inspired motivation in a business enterprise requires inspired leadership. To a large degree, good employees come to work already motivated—that's part of what makes them good employees. One of your jobs as a manager is to make sure you don't *demotivate* them. For example, when supervisors engage in **micromanaging**—overseeing

micromanaging
Overseeing every small detail of employees' work and refusing to give them freedom or autonomy.

every small detail of employees' work and refusing to give them freedom or autonomy—they can destroy morale.[49] Managers with low emotional intelligence can create toxic work environments that demotivate even the most driven employees, so it is essential for managers to understand the effect that their behaviors and attitudes have on employees.

MOTIVATING YOURSELF

This chapter has focused on systems that organizations can put in place and various steps that managers can take to motivate employees. However, this emphasis shouldn't obscure the role and responsibility of employees themselves. Every employee has an ethical obligation to find the motivation to accomplish the tasks for which he or she is getting paid. Managers can foster motivation (and they can certainly diminish it through clumsy leadership), but the motivation must originate from within each employee.

For more insights into employee motivation, visit **real-timeupdates.com/bia9** and select Chapter 10.

 CHECKPOINT

LEARNING OBJECTIVE 6 : List five managerial strategies that are vital to maintaining a motivated workforce.

SUMMARY: No matter which motivational theories a company chooses to implement in its management policies and reward systems, managers can motivate employees more effectively by (1) providing timely and frequent feedback, (2) personalizing motivational efforts as much as possible while still being fair to all employees, (3) gamifying for healthy competition, (4) addressing workplace negativity before it has a chance to destroy morale, and (5) being inspirational leaders.

CRITICAL THINKING: (1) Referring to the job characteristics model, how does micromanaging destroy motivation? (2) Annual performance reviews are common in many companies; how might they fail to motivate employees?

IT'S YOUR BUSINESS: (1) If you are motivated more by the love of learning than the promised rewards of a grade, how can you motivate yourself when grades play a key role in your success as others perceive it? (2) At work or in academic situations, how do you prevent someone else's negative attitude and behavior from dragging down your own performance?

KEY TERMS TO KNOW: gamification, micromanaging

Thriving in the Digital Enterprise: Performance Management Systems

 LEARNING OBJECTIVE

Discuss the potential strengths and weaknesses of performance management systems.

If you surveyed which aspects of business are loathed by employees and managers with equal intensity, the annual performance review would probably top the list. Employees often find these reviews unfair or irrelevant, and managers often find them to be a time-consuming burden that doesn't improve performance.[50] Not many people are happy with the conventional ways of assessing performance, but most would agree that measurement and feedback mechanisms are important. Employees want to know how they're doing, and managers want to know what they can do to help their staffs perform to their full potential.

Companies are trying a variety of approaches in search of a more satisfying solution to the puzzle. The biggest overall change in many cases involves moving away from annual reviews to *real-time* monitoring and feedback. With this approach, managers can see how their employees are performing as the work is being done, and they can provide immediate

performance management systems
Systems that help companies establish goals for employees and track performance relative to those goals.

feedback—both praise and advice for improvement. In addition, because progress toward goals is tracked in real time rather than checked at long intervals such as once a year, employees and managers can make course corrections before things get too far off track.

A variety of **performance management systems** are now available to help companies set goals, monitor performance, provide feedback, and adjust plans in real time. Employees and their managers first agree on goals, which are then entered into the system. As work progresses toward each goal, the progress is updated so everyone stays on the same page. Managers (and in some systems, anyone on the system) can provide feedback and "pats on the back" along the way. Some systems also have artificial intelligence (AI)–enhanced team and cross-functional capability so that managers can get a sense of how often and how well their employees collaborate with colleagues across the company.[51]

By capturing goals and logging measured performance as work progresses, these systems also have the potential to avoid the human biases and errors that can plague traditional performance evaluation. With the system transparently evaluating how well each employee is doing, this approach is less susceptible to race, gender, or "likeability" biases and to cognitive errors such as *recency bias*, in which a manager overemphasizes the most recent work an employee has done because that is what he or she remembers most vividly.[52]

While these systems show promise at overcoming the weaknesses of traditional approaches, they still must address the fundamental questions of *what* to measure and *how* to measure it. Many of these systems continuously gather data on employees' use of the various apps and systems available on their computers and mobile devices, such as how much time they spend using spreadsheets, social networking, and email. While it's easy to count how many emails an employee sends per day, for example, it's much more difficult to assess how well a person is truly communicating with colleagues and customers. In any system, whether it's entirely manual or fully automated and AI enhanced, there is the never-ending challenge of measuring what is meaningful, not just what is easy to measure.

Iakov Filimonov/123RF

Employee performance monitoring and management systems raise important questions about privacy and the difficulty of measuring what really matters regarding employee contributions.

✓ CHECKPOINT

LEARNING OBJECTIVE 7 : Discuss the potential strengths and weaknesses of performance management systems.

SUMMARY: Performance management systems help managers and employees set goals, monitor performance, provide feedback, and adjust plans in real time. Their biggest strengths are transparency (everything is in view) and objectivity (the systems mathematically assess performance toward goals). The biggest potential weaknesses of these systems—and other methods of performance evaluation—are figuring out what to measure and how to measure it. Data points such as app usage or message volume are easy to measure, but they may not reflect true performance.

CRITICAL THINKING: (1) How could a performance management system help managers avoid recency bias in employee evaluations? (2) Can a performance management system completely eradicate biases from performance evaluations? Explain your answer.

IT'S YOUR BUSINESS: (1) Would you take a job at a company knowing that it will use workplace analytics to monitor how you use your computer and mobile devices? Why or why not? (2) Would you welcome or resist the use of a goal-setting and tracking system? Why?

KEY TERMS TO KNOW: performance management systems

BEHIND THE SCENES

Motivating the Minds Behind Some of the World's Most Popular Video Games

When your firm has job titles like *dungeon designer* and *lore-master* and the statue in front of company headquarters is a 12-foot-tall, 2-ton Orc riding a wolf, you know you don't work in an everyday sort of company. Welcome to life at Irvine, California–based Blizzard Entertainment, developers of Warcraft and other video game franchises with hundreds of millions of enthusiastic fans all over the world. If you haven't played a Blizzard game, chances are you've played one produced by one of its corporate siblings in the Activision Blizzard empire—titles that include Call of Duty, Guitar Hero, and the Candy Crush Saga series.

As one of the three recent college graduates who founded Blizzard in 1991, company president Michael Morhaime guides strategic direction and watches over a workforce that has been cranking out hits for three decades. Although Blizzard shares some key attributes with other technology-driven companies, one thing stands out, particularly in contrast to many tech firms further up the coast in Silicon Valley: the longevity of that workforce. In an industry where job-hopping is considered normal, Blizzard employees clearly like the company enough to spend years of their working lives there.

Many companies acknowledge longevity with awards at major intervals such as 5 or 10 years, but few do it with the panache of Blizzard. Where else are you given a richly decorated sword after 5 years, a shield after 10 years, or an ornate helm (similar to a helmet) at 20 years—all inspired by the games you've been contributing to throughout your career? These service awards are presented in celebrations that acknowledge the contributions employees have made in their years at the company. (You can see at the rewards employees receive at **eu.blizzard.com/en-gb/company/about/service-awards .html.**)

Respect for longevity is a sign of an organizational culture that values employees and maintains an atmosphere in which people want to stay. In fact, respect for employees is one of several key aspects of Blizzard's culture that can motivate people to perform their best work and remain committed to the company's vision year after year. As Morhaime puts it, "Honestly, one of the things I'm most proud of about Blizzard is that disagreeing is okay. A really good culture actually encourages healthy debate." Another company manager explains that, "You are here because you are great, and you're expected to do great things and be an active voice in what we're building."

Another important factor is the emphasis on doing quality work. Professionals who are committed to doing their best can't abide doing substandard work, and being forced to compromise because of deadlines, budgets, or an organizational tolerance for shoddiness can be a major demotivator. In contrast to the usual corporate practice of setting product release deadlines and then compromising on quality or capability if necessary to meet the date, Blizzard employees are allowed to keep iterating and improving products until they get them right.

A strong sense of community is another important "stickiness" factor when it comes to keeping employees engaged. One employee offered the following comment in an anonymous online review of the company: "Blizzard is such a relationship-driven company. It's refreshing to see a company that prides itself on that first." That strong sense of connection helps employees celebrate the highs and survive the lows—and keeps them working together.

The opportunity to grow, both professionally and personally, is yet another strong motivator. The company rewards talent and dedication foremost, and it isn't too concerned about where or how an employee got started. Many of the top creative professionals started in administrative positions or elsewhere in the company but proved themselves capable of contributing on a broader scale and were given the opportunity to do so. In fact, one of the company's eight core values is "Every voice matters." All employees are encouraged to contribute new ideas, to challenge existing ideas, and to embrace criticism as a vital way to learn.

Growth is also encouraged with a full slate of learning opportunities. Many companies offer training courses to employees, but at Blizzard, employees can take courses in sword fighting, martial arts, modeling, screenwriting, weight lifting—and the list goes on. Some of these courses relate to current or future work responsibilities, but others simply provide an opportunity to grow on a personal level.

The firm's culture and support for employees is clearly paying off. The company maintains very high ratings on anonymous employee surveys such as Glassdoor, with almost unanimous approval of Morhaime's work as president, and makes regular appearances on "best places to work" lists. The business of fun is serious business, and Blizzard's concern for employees is likely to keep its workforce engaged and motivated for years to come.[53]

Critical Thinking Questions

10-1. Would someone who isn't interested in video games find it motivating to work at Blizzard? Why or why not?

10-2. Would Blizzard need to use different motivational strategies for people who work on the creative side and the business side of the company? Why or why not?

10-3. How might a company that isn't in a "fun" industry use the motivational techniques that Blizzard uses?

Learn More Online

Visit Blizzard's careers website, **careers.blizzard.com/en-us**, and its mission statement and values at **us.blizzard.com/en-us/ company/about/mission.html.** What impression do you get about the company from reading this material? Would you find it inspiring to work for such a company? How does it compare to other companies you have explored as you consider your next career move?

End of Chapter

KEY TERMS

cross-training (308)
engagement (297)
equity theory (303)
expectancy theory (302)
gamification (311)
goal-setting theory (304)
Hawthorne effect (299)
Herzberg's two-factor theory (300)
incentives (309)
job characteristics model (307)
job enrichment (308)
management by objectives (MBO) (305)

Maslow's hierarchy (299)
micromanaging (312)
motivation (297)
negative reinforcement (309)
performance management systems (314)
positive reinforcement (309)
reinforcement theory (309)
scientific management (298)
Theory X (300)
Theory Y (300)
three-needs theory (301)

TEST YOUR KNOWLEDGE

Questions for Review

10-4. What is motivation?

10-5. What is scientific management?

10-6. What is management by objectives?

10-7. What are the four fundamental drives that influence motivation?

10-8. What are the risks of goal-setting theory?

10-9. What is the Hawthorne effect?

Questions for Analysis

10-10. Should managers apply theories of motivation that lack strong empirical proof? Why or why not?

10-11. Are there any similarities between the classical theories of motivation? Explain your answer by comparing any two theories.

10-12. How might a deadline that is too easy to meet cause someone to work more slowly than he or she might otherwise?

10-13. Is positive reinforcement a good thing? Explain your answer.

10-14. What is cross-training, and how can it be used to combat boredom and burnout in the workplace?

10-15. Why do managers often find it difficult to motivate employees who remain after downsizing? Explain your answer in terms of one or more motivational theories discussed in the chapter.

10-16. How can gamification improve employee motivation and performance?

10-17. **Ethical Considerations.** Motivational strategies that reward employees for meeting specific performance targets can encourage them to work hard—sometimes too hard. Overwork can contribute to mental and physical health problems as well as interfere with other aspects of employees' lives. As a manager, how do you determine how much work is too much for your employees?

10-18. Who ultimately has responsibility for motivation, the employee or his or her manager? Why?

Questions for Application

10-19. You manage a busy office that deals with customer complaints for two major global electronics companies. Employee turnover is high in your office, which suggests boredom and lack of motivation. Despite increases in pay and the introduction of "fast resolution" bonus payments, employees call in sick very often. Each complaint team is focused on one electronics category and specializes in that area alone. Efficiency rates are, however, dropping. How would you modify the core job dimensions to improve employee satisfaction and performance?

10-20. How do you motivate yourself when faced with school assignments or projects that are difficult or tedious? Do you ever try to relate these tasks to your overall career goals? Are you more motivated by doing your personal best or by outperforming other students?

10-21. As a manager, you're intrigued by the job characteristics model and are looking at ways to expand and enrich jobs to make work more meaningful for your employees. Some employees hear about your investigation and start to circulate complaints about being asked to do more for the same pay. How should you respond?

10-22. Imagine you are in your first job. After a period of training, you feel confident enough to tackle most tasks that are thrown at you each day. However, your manager does not feel the same. She insists on supervising virtually everything you do. It's no different for your colleagues who have been in the same role for over a year. What is your manager doing, and what are the consequences of her actions?

10-23. **Concept Integration.** Chapter 7 discusses several styles of leadership, including autocratic, democratic, and laissez-faire. How do each of these styles relate to Theory X and Theory Y assumptions about workers?

EXPAND YOUR KNOWLEDGE

Discovering Career Opportunities

Feeling valued and motivated at work can have a huge impact on your satisfaction and productivity. However, what motivates one person may be very different from what motivates another. Make a list outlining the factors that motivate you to work. Explain each item on the list and then try to look for a job description that meets as many of your motivators as possible. Would you be interested in this role? Why?

Intelligent Business Technology: Performance Management Systems

Research one of the employee performance management solutions currently on the market. What benefits does the company promote for this system? Do any of them relate to motivation? Do you see any aspects of using the system that have the potential to demotivate employees? How does the system handle privacy and data security?

PRACTICE YOUR SKILLS

Resolving Ethical Dilemmas

You're on a cross-functional team responsible for launching your company's latest product. As is usually the case with product launches, it's a stressful affair with immovable deadlines, more work than the team seems capable of handling, and dozens of "fires" that need to be put out. Fortunately, the team leader is a master at motivation, and so far the team is accomplishing the impossible. As the weeks (and late nights and weekends) roll on, though, you get the uncomfortable feeling that the leader's motivational techniques have crossed the line from inspirational to manipulative. The "let's do this for the team" ethos has taken on a "you're either with us, or you're against us" vibe, with subtle jabs at people whose family commitments prevent them from working 60 or 70 hours a week. How should you respond?

Growing as a Professional

Daily life in college offers multiple opportunities to develop a vital professional skill, which is motivating yourself to perform at your best. Each time you face a deadline, a difficult situation with teammates or family, or any activity or project that is more work than fun, take a moment to reflect on your motivational state. If you're less than completely fired up, what can you use from this chapter to increase your motivation?

Can you use goal-setting theory, for instance? If the activity itself doesn't present a compelling reward, see if you can shift your focus to a different goal, such as the emotional relief of getting the activity off your to-do list. Visualize what it will feel like to be on the other side of the finish line, and use that to motivate you. Perhaps you could gamify the activity, such as by seeing how many words you can write in a 10-minute flurry of creativity. Can you find a different sort of meaning in the activity, such as learning to be patient when you know a lab partner or family member is going to test your

peace of mind? Or think of the job characteristics model, and focus on how you're cross-training yourself by developing a new skill.

Sharpening Your Communication Skills

What motivates you to attend your college or university and drives you to complete your graduation? Write a blog post explaining your motivations and how they link to some of the theories discussed in this chapter—expectancy, goal-setting, job characteristics, and reinforcement theory.

Building Your Team Skills

With teammates assigned by your instructor, explore the careers sections of the websites of six companies in different industries. Look for descriptions of the work environment, incentive plans, career paths, and other information about how the company develops, motivates, and supports its employees. After you've compiled notes about each company, vote on which company would be most appealing to work for. Next, review the notes for this company, and identify all the theories of motivation described in this chapter that the company appears to be using, based on the information on its website.

Developing Your Research Skills

Various periodicals and websites feature "best companies to work for" lists. Locate one of these lists and find a company that does a great job of attracting and motivating high performers. Learn as much as you can about the company's management philosophies. Which of the motivation theories does the company appear to be using? Summarize your findings in a brief email message to your instructor.

Writing Assignments

10-24. If a manager does nothing in response to a particular type of employee behavior that the company wants to encourage, is this an instance of reinforcement? Why or why not?

10-25. Do you have an ethical responsibility to motivate yourself at work, no matter the circumstances? Why or why not?

ENDNOTES

1. Blizzard Careers, accessed 7 May 2018, careers.blizzard.com; "Activision Blizzard," *Fortune*, accessed 7 May 2018, fortune.com; Andrew Nusca, "Inside the Zany, Enormous, Amazing World of Activision Blizzard," *Fortune*, 15 February 2018, fortune.com; "Blizzard Entertainment," *Glassdoor*, accessed 7 May 2018, www.glassdoor.com; Activision Blizzard, accessed 7 May 2018, www.activisionblizzard.com.

2. Katy Kiely, "Productivity: Getting the Most from Your Most Expensive Asset," *Disruption*, 5 April 2018, disruptionhub.com.

3. Scott O. Lilienfeld, Steven Jay Lynn, and Laura L. Namy, *Psychology: From Inquiry to Understanding*, 4th ed. (New York: Pearson, 2018), 430.

4. Nitin Nohria, Boris Groysberg, and Linda-Eling Lee, "Employee Motivation: A Powerful New Model," *Harvard Business Review*, July–August 2008, 78–84.

5. Nohria, Groysberg, and Lee, "Employee Motivation."

6. Nohria, Groysberg, and Lee, "Employee Motivation."

7. Stephen P. Robbins, Mary Coulter, and David A. DeCenzo, *Fundamentals of Management*, 10th ed. (New York: Pearson, 2017), 7.

8. Augustine Brannigan and William Zwerman, "The Real 'Hawthorne Effect,'" *Society*, January/February 2001, 55–60; Stephen P. Robbins and Mary Coulter, *Management*, 14th ed. (Upper Saddle River, N.J.: Pearson Prentice Hall, 2018), 36.

9. Brannigan and Zwerman, "The Real 'Hawthorne Effect'"; Robbins and Coulter, *Management*, 36.

10. Frank Merrett, "Reflections on the Hawthorne Effect," *Educational Psychology*, February 2006, 143–146; Brannigan and Zwerman, "The Real 'Hawthorne Effect.'"

11. Mecca Chiesa and Sandy Hobbs, "Making Sense of Social Research: How Useful Is the Hawthorne Effect?" *European Journal of Social Psychology* 38 (2008): 67–74; Brannigan and Zwerman, "The Real 'Hawthorne Effect'"; Robbins and Coulter, *Management*, 36.

12. Andrew J. DuBrin, *Human Relation for Career and Personal Success*, 11th ed. (New York: Pearson, 2017), 62–64.

13. Robbins and Coulter, *Management*, 521.

14. Richard L. Daft, *Management*, 13th ed. (Boston: Cengage, 2018), 52; Robbins, Coulter, and DeCenzo, *Fundamentals of Management*, 333.

15. Daft, *Management*, 540–541.

16. Stephen P. Robbins and Timothy A. Judge, *Essentials of Organizational Behavior*, 14th ed., (New York: Pearson, 2018), 102.

17. Rosa Chun and Gary Davies, "Employee Happiness Isn't Enough to Satisfy Customers," *Harvard Business Review*, April 2009, 19; Robbins and Judge, *Essentials of Organizational Behavior*, 102.

18. Robbins and Judge, *Essentials of Organizational Behavior*, 102–103.

19. Robbins, Coulter, and DeCenzo, *Fundamentals of Management*, 341.

20. Robbins and Judge, *Essentials of Organizational Behavior*, 108.

21. Daft, *Management*, 545–557.

22. Robbins and Judge, *Essentials of Organizational Behavior*, 111–112.

23. Deborah Archambeault, Christopher M. Burgess, and Stan Davis, "Is Something Missing from Your Company's Satisfaction Package?" *CMA Management*, May 2009, 20–23.

24. Robbins and Coulter, *Management*, 524–526.

25. Bill Lycette and John Herniman, "New Goal-Setting Theory," *Industrial Management*, September 2008, 25–30; Robbins and Coulter, *Management*, 524–525.

26. Aurora Innovation, accessed 5 May 2018, aurora.tech.

27. Robbins and Coulter, *Management*, 524.

28. Lisa Ordóñez, Maurice Schweitzer, Adam Galinsky, and Max Bazerman, "Goals Gone Wild: The Systematic Side Effects of Overprescribing Goal Setting," *Academy of Management Perspectives*, February 2009, 6–16.

29. Robert D. Ramsey, "Why Deadlines and Quotas Don't Always Work," *Supervision*, October 2008, 3–5.

30. Richard J. Hackman and Greg R. Oldman, "Motivation Through the Design of Work: Test of a Theory," *Organizational Behavior & Human Performance*, August 1976, 250–279; Robbins and Judge, *Essentials of Organizational Behavior*, 121; Jed DeVaro, Robert Li, and Dana Brookshire, "Analysing the Job Characteristics Model: New Support from a Cross-Section of Establishments," *International Journal of Human Resource Management*, June 2007, 986–1003.

31. Robbins and Judge, *Essentials of Organizational Behavior*, 122.

32. Daft, *Management*, 554.

33. Stuart D. Galup, Gary Klein, and James J. Jiang, "The Impacts of Job Characteristics on IS Employee Satisfaction: A Comparison Between Permanent and Temporary Employees," *Journal of Computer Information Systems*, Summer 2008, 58–68.

34. Robbins and Coulter, *Management*, 348.

35. Scott Lazenby, "How to Motivate Employees: What Research Is Telling Us," *Public Management*, September 2008, 22–25.

36. Robbins and Coulter, *Management*, 527.

37. Daft, *Management*, 549.

38. Debi O'Donovan, "Motivation Is Key in a Crisis and Words Can Be the Best Reward," *Employee Benefits*, April 2009, 5.

39. Timothy R. Hinkin and Chester A. Schriesheim, "Performance Incentives for Tough Times," *Harvard Business Review*, March 2009, 26.

40. Lilienfeld, Lynn, and Namy, *Psychology: From Inquiry to Understanding*, 214.

41. Dan Heath and Chip Heath, "The Curse of Incentives," *Fast Company*, February 2009, 48–49.

42. Paul McDonald, "Employee Loyalty Not for Sale," *Workforce*, 15 January 2018, www.workforce.com.

43. Chris Petersen, "BankThink: Millennial Workers Can Help Community Banks Compete," *American Banker*, 22 March 2018, 1; "Tailor Motivation Techniques to the Worker," *Teller Vision*, March 2009, 5–6.

44. Nohria, Groysberg, and Lee, "Employee Motivation."

45. "What Is Gamification?" Bunchball, accessed 5 April 2018, www.bunchball.com.

46. Robert Stanley, "Top 25 Best Examples of Gamification in Business," Clickipedia, 24 March 2014, blogs.clicksoftware.com; Brian Burke, "The Gamification of Business," *Forbes*, 21 January 2013, www.forbes.com.

47. Betty MacLaughlin Frandsen, "Overcoming Workplace Negativity," *Long-Term Living: For the Continuing Care Professional*, March 2009, 26–27.

48. Aurora Innovation, accessed 5 May 2018, aurora.tech.

49. Sean Hannah and Kathryn Stewart, "The Bedrock of Effective Leadership," *TD*, May 2018, 62–63.

50. Bryan Hancock, Elizabeth Hioe, and Bill Schaninger, "The Fairness Factor in Performance Management," *McKinsey Quarterly*, April 2018, www.mckinsey.com.

51. "Product Overview," BetterWorks, accessed 6 May 2018, www.betterworks.com.

52. Bernard Marr, "The Future of Performance Management: How AI and Big Data Combat Workplace Bias," *Forbes*, 17 January 2017, www.forbes.com.

53. See note 1.

Human Resources Management

11

LEARNING OBJECTIVES After studying this chapter, you will be able to

1   Identify four contemporary human resources (HR) challenges, and discuss the evolving role of HR.

2   Discuss the challenges and advantages of a diverse workforce, and identify five major dimensions of workforce diversity.

3   Describe the three phases involved in managing the employment life cycle.

4   Explain the steps used to develop and evaluate employees.

5   Describe the major elements of employee compensation, benefits, and support services.

6   Characterize the role of labor unions in today's business world.

7   Describe the use of workforce analytics in HR management.

MyLab Intro to Business
Improve Your Grade!
If your instructor is using MyLab Intro to Business, visit **www.pearson.com/ mylab/intro-to-business**.

BEHIND THE SCENES

Kaiser Permanente: Delivering Quality Services to a Hundred Unique Cultures

Kaiser Permanente CEO Bernard J. Tyson believes a culturally competent workforce is essential to the health provider's aim of serving the diverse U.S. population.

Mario Anzuoni/Thomson Reuters (Markets) LLC

healthy.kaiserpermanente.org

No business is more personal and intimate than health care. Nurses, doctors, and other care providers interact with patients at the most vulnerable, painful, occasionally joyful, and sometimes tragic moments of their lives. The work can require penetrating the veils of privacy in ways that no other line of business does.

The closer that caregivers get to patients, the more significant each patient's personal inclinations and cultural influences become. In the course of a single day, a caregiver might deal with people from a dozen or more unique cultures— different languages, different religious beliefs, different family structures, and so on. These factors can influence each patient's comfort level, willingness to participate in care, and satisfaction with medical services, and ultimately the quality of care.

Bernard Tyson is CEO of Oakland-based Kaiser Permanente, the largest not-for-profit health-care system in the United States. Kaiser Permanente's client base includes more than 10 million members from over 100 distinct cultures. If you were in Tyson's position, how would you ensure that Kaiser Permanente develops a workforce that can serve such a diverse population? What programs and policies would you put in place to attract, hire, and support the thousands of employees required—and to help them flourish as unique individuals as well?[1]

INTRODUCTION

Kaiser Permanente's Bernard Tyson (profiled in the chapter-opening Behind the Scenes) knows that hiring the right people to help a company reach its goals and then overseeing their training and development, motivation, evaluation, and compensation are critical to a company's success. This chapter explores the many steps companies take to build productive, engaged, and healthy workforces.

1 **LEARNING OBJECTIVE**

Identify four contemporary human resources (HR) challenges, and discuss the evolving role of HR.

human resources (HR) management
The specialized function of planning how to obtain employees, oversee their training, evaluate them, and compensate them.

Guiding the Human Side of Business

The field of **human resources (HR) management** encompasses all the tasks involved in attracting, developing, and supporting an organization's staff, as well as maintaining a safe and fair working environment that meets legal requirements and ethical expectations.[2] With all the disruptions taking place in business these days, the HR function has never been more complex or more important. This section explores the key challenges in contemporary HR management and looks at HR's evolving strategic role.

CONTEMPORARY HR CHALLENGES

All the disruptions and transformations you've been studying in this course have one thing in common: They affect the people who work in business and are therefore a concern for HR managers. Here are four key challenges that today's HR leaders face.

Aligning the Workforce with Business Requirements

Matching the right employees to the right jobs at the right time is a constant challenge. Externally, changes in market needs, competitive moves, advances in technology, and new regulations can all affect the ideal size and composition of the workforce. Internally, shifts in strategy, process changes, and growing or declining revenue can force managers to realign their workforces.

Keeping workforces in alignment with business needs is no easy task. HR managers must focus in three areas simultaneously: retaining the firm's existing talent, *reskilling* current employees whose skill sets no longer align with job requirements, and attracting a continuing stream of new talent to fill newly created positions or to replace employees who leave.

Moreover, the disruptions brought about by automation, artificial intelligence (AI), and other technological developments are going to be major challenges for HR departments in the coming years, as potentially millions of employees will need to develop new skill sets to align with different job requirements. For example, in 2013, the telecommunications giant AT&T analyzed the work being done by its 230,000 employees and determined that 100,000 of those jobs would probably disappear by 2023—nearly half its workforce. The company embarked on a billion-dollar training initiative to help those employees develop the skills needed for a new generation of jobs.[3]

Across industries, many of the new jobs in the coming years will be in the middle of a continuum between purely "human work" at one extreme and purely "machine work" at the other. In this middle zone, humans and smart machines will work in complementary roles, often side by side. For instance, humans will be involved in training smart robots, self-driving cars, and other cyber-physical systems, and cognitive automation systems will give humans new "superpowers" through AI-assisted decision-making.[4]

Creating Safe Workplaces

Every company has a responsibility to create safe workplaces for its employees, and that includes physical as well as psychological safety. In addition, all employees share the responsibility to conduct themselves in ways that don't compromise the physical or psychological safety of their colleagues.

Unfortunately, toxic workplaces continue to be a problem, particularly with regard to **sexual harassment**, defined as either unwelcome requests for sexual favors with an implicit reward or punishment related to work or the creation of an environment in which

sexual harassment
Unwelcome sexual advances, requests for sexual favors, or other verbal or physical conduct of a sexual nature within the workplace.

employees are made to feel uncomfortable by lewd jokes, remarks, or gestures.[5] Even though male employees may also be targets of sexual harassment and both male and female employees may experience same-sex harassment, sexual harassment of female employees by male colleagues or superiors makes up the majority of reported cases.[6] Sexual harassment by customers against staff can be a concern in service industries as well. Two-thirds of all flight attendants in the United States report being sexually harassed by passengers, for instance.[7]

Harassment of any kind is a serious workplace issue. It is unethical and can be illegal, it damages the mental health of those who are victims, it lowers productivity, it can limit employees' career growth because harassment is often a precursor to employment discrimination, and it opens up companies to significant legal and reputational risks.

Managers have the responsibility to educate their employees on the definition and consequences of sexual harassment.

However, HR departments in some companies are still struggling to get upper management to take the problem seriously, and many are grappling with how to prevent harassment and how to respond when accusations come to light. In one broad-reaching survey, only 55 percent of men and 34 percent of women say their employers "often or always" respond quickly to disrespectful behavior toward women.[8] In some recent high-profile cases such as Uber and Nike, companies reacted only after women reported harassment via social media or presented upper management with results of internal surveys they had conducted themselves.[9]

Social and technological shifts could be leading more companies toward positive change. The #MeToo movement on social media, in which many women and some men have volunteered reports of harassment and assault, has highlighted the extent of the problem and the growing unwillingness of many to dismiss it as harmless. And with more evidence now available, thanks to the ubiquitous use of digital communication and camera-equipped mobile devices, experts say harassment cases are often more clear-cut than they used to be. The threat of legal and reputational risks could be pushing more executives and corporate boards to put no-tolerance policies in place and to back them up with managerial attention and swift action.[10]

Ensuring Fair Treatment and Equal Opportunity

In addition to providing a safe work environment, companies must also ensure that employees are treated fairly and given equal opportunities. Some specific aspects of fairness are dictated by employment laws, but treating employees fairly is always the decent and ethical approach, and it is smart business, too. Five important areas where HR departments and company leadership should focus are fairness in recruiting, transparent and inclusive networking opportunities, fairness in project assignments and promotion opportunities, and fairness in compensation.

Fairness in Recruiting   Fairness and opportunity start with candidate screening, interviewing, and hiring, making sure that all qualified applicants are given the opportunity to present themselves and their qualifications to potential employers. Methods such as blind auditions (see page 348) can help remove implicit and explicit bias from the screening stage.

Fairness in Employee Development   Once employees are hired, they should be given equal opportunities to improve their skills and gain important experience. Of course, employees vary in their ability and motivation to develop, but all should be given the opportunity.

Transparent and Inclusive Networking Opportunities   Informal connections among people at various levels in the company hierarchy and interactions that take place outside the regular course of business can unfairly advantage some employees and disadvantage others. For instance, if a few managers and employees regularly socialize after work, such

Comstock/Getty Images

Women make up nearly half the entry-level professional workforce, but the ratio declines steadily as one looks up the corporate ladder.

glass ceiling
An invisible barrier attributable to subtle discrimination that keeps women and minorities out of the top positions in business.

as by playing ping pong or other games in the company lounge, employees who have family commitments after the workday ends will not be able to participate in these networking opportunities. This lack of "face time" with the managers could affect these employees' career development.

Fairness in Project Assignments and Promotion Opportunities In addition to making sure all employees have the chance to improve their qualifications, HR leaders must ensure that all qualified employees have the chance to be considered for desirable project assignments and promotion opportunities. Even though gender equality has been identified as a top priority by most U.S. companies, imbalances remain.[11] For example, women hold nearly half of all entry-level professional positions, but that ratio shrinks considerably the higher you look in an organization. Among the 500 corporations that make up the S&P 500 stock market index, fewer than 5 percent have women as CEOs.[12] A lack of opportunities to advance into the top ranks is often referred to as the **glass ceiling**, which implies that one can see the top but can't get there.

A great deal of attention is focused on the "pipeline" leading from lower-level positions to higher-level positions. One response to the criticism for the lack of women and nonwhite managers in higher positions is that not enough of them are coming up through the ranks to compete for higher positions. The suggested solution is to wait until more women and people of color move up as their careers advance, after which the problem will eventually sort itself out. However, this issue has been visible for at least an entire generation of corporate management, which means that if the pipeline still isn't supplying enough qualified candidates, it's a fundamental problem that management has failed to address.

Research indicates that the problems start at the very beginning of the pipeline. Although more women than men now earn college degrees, fewer women are hired into professional positions. When they are hired, their first step up the corporate ladder takes longer, and they are promoted at lower rates than men.[13]

Several factors appear to be contributing to this situation:

- Women report getting less coaching and mentoring than men do, and women are less likely to have contact with influential senior executives.[14] (The issue of noninclusive networking mentioned in the last section could be having an effect here.)
- Many people tend to associate with and look favorably upon people who are like them, so a white, male executive might be more inclined to offer coaching to a white male coming up the ranks or assume that he is ready for a promotion but someone else isn't.
- People are less likely to see problems that don't affect them (or perhaps to acknowledge problems whose solutions could negatively affect them). Men are less likely to support diversity programs or to say that women are underrepresented in corporate leadership, even though the gender imbalance is stark.[15]
- The work environment in the typical U.S. company is less family-friendly than in many other countries. For instance, only 15 percent of employees in the United States can take advantage of paid family leave to care for children, and U.S. employees work more hours per week than employees in many European countries. Consequently, it is often more difficult for U.S. employees to balance work and family responsibilities, and when this happens, the careers of women can suffer disproportionately.[16]

Fairness in Compensation The issue of fairness continues with compensation. The *gender pay gap* is one of the most discussed questions of equity in today's workplace. Women in the United States earn, on average, a little over 80 percent of what men earn, and this disparity has been fairly consistent for more than a decade.[17] While this appears on the surface to be a blatant case of simple discrimination, a closer look at the data reveals a more nuanced picture that requires a lot of digging to figure out how much of that 20 percent gap is a result of discriminatory practices on the part of employers and how much is attributable to the choices made by individual employees or other factors.

For example, a higher percentage of men choose careers in the lucrative fields of engineering and computer science, whereas a higher percentage of women choose careers in teaching, which pays considerably less. Tellingly, men dominate the 10 most lucrative careers, and women dominate the 10 least lucrative careers.[18]

These numbers help explain the pay gap, but they don't tell the whole story. Within the same profession, men often earn more than women—even in professions such as nursing and teaching, where women outnumber men.[19] Researchers have found several other factors that found add nuance to the picture. On average, men work more hours per week, take less time off to raise children, and are more likely to try to negotiate pay raises. According to an in-depth statistical analysis released by the U.S. Department of Labor, when adjusted for individual choices, the average pay gap is roughly 5 to 7 percent.[20]

However, even a rigorous statistical investigation doesn't provide all the insights needed to right the imbalance, whatever that figure might be. Important issues that need to be considered include whether girls and young women are being subtly steered away from computer science and other lucrative fields, why pay varies so much across different professions, the degree to which the glass ceiling is keeping women out of higher-paying positions, whether women have access to equal work opportunities even when they have the same job titles as men, and how companies should accommodate employees who want or need to step away from work to care for children or elderly parents.[21]

In response to pressure from employees and from activist shareholders in some cases, a number of companies have begun publishing their gender wage gap data and committing to closing the gap. Such disclosure is voluntary in the United States, but the United Kingdom now requires any company with more than 250 UK employees to disclose its gender wage gap.[22]

Promoting Employee Well-Being

As companies try to outrace competitors and keep workforce costs to a minimum, managers need to be on guard for *employee burnout*, a state of physical and emotional exhaustion that can result from constant exposure to stress over a long period of time. In addition to the toll that burnout and other emotional difficulties exact on employees and their families, they can cause serious problems with absenteeism and turnover.[23]

The concern over workloads is one of the factors behind the growing interest in **work–life balance**, the idea that employees, managers, and entrepreneurs need to balance the competing demands of their professional and personal lives. Many companies are trying to make it easier for employees to juggle multiple responsibilities with on-site daycare facilities, flexible work schedules, and other options designed to improve **quality of work life (QWL)**.

work–life balance
Efforts to help employees balance the competing demands of their personal and professional lives.

quality of work life (QWL)
An overall environment that results from job and work conditions.

THE EVOLVING ROLE OF HR

HR holds an intriguing and often conflicted position in the business hierarchy. Some people view it as a tactical administrative function tasked with getting all the paperwork in place and making sure no employment laws are violated. At the same time, many companies now recognize that talent is a vital competitive need, and HR should in theory be leading the efforts to acquire and support this important resource and to help develop the next generation of leaders.[24]

HR departments also need to balance competing interests in two important ways. First, HR sometimes gets caught in a battle of loyalties between employees and management. While many HR departments have employee representatives who can assist workers with both routine matters and special circumstances such as harassment complaints, HR ultimately works

Deadlines and other pressures can put employees in danger of burnout and other emotional problems.

KieferPix/Shutterstock

for the company, not for the employees. If an employee is being harassed by an executive or owner, the employee may wonder whose side HR is on—helping workers or protecting the company? In case after case in recent years, employees have reported being disappointed when they asked HR for help.[25]

Second, while supporting employees and contributing to an enjoyable work experience, HR also has a wide range of important legal responsibilities that cannot be compromised. Some HR departments have rebranded themselves with employee-friendly titles such as People Operations or Employee Success, but this doesn't change the reality that HR is still responsible for legal compliance, performance evaluations, and even surveillance tasks such as monitoring employee communications.[26]

With all the forces pushing and pulling on HR, the HR department of the future could end up looking quite different from the old *personnel department* of days gone by. In many companies, the tactical work of benefits administration and recruiting process management is gradually being taken over by robotic process automation and bot-enabled "self-serve" systems that let employees manage their own insurance and other benefits. Such moves could improve the operational efficiency of HR and free up resources to focus on value-added, strategic activities such as talent acquisition and leadership development.[27]

 CHECKPOINT

LEARNING OBJECTIVE 1: Identify four contemporary human resources (HR) challenges, and discuss the evolving role of HR.

SUMMARY: Four challenges that every HR department faces are aligning the workforce with changing job requirements, creating safe workplaces, ensuring fair treatment and equal opportunities, and promoting employee well-being. The role of HR in today's companies is often one of conflicted expectations and divided loyalties. HR has many tactical responsibilities but is also expected to help develop the company's most important resource, its people. HR can also experience divided loyalties between helping employees but ultimately being responsible to the company and between making the workplace enjoyable while still fulfilling its responsibilities regarding legal compliance, surveillance, and other serious matters.

CRITICAL THINKING: (1) How can alternative work arrangements help companies reduce costs and their impact on the environment? (2) How can digital communication and mobile connectivity contribute to employee burnout?

IT'S YOUR BUSINESS: (1) Have you ever had the need to approach HR for help in a work situation? If so, how satisfied were you with the outcome? (2) Given the importance of engaged talent and enlightened leadership in business today, does working in HR appeal to you? Why or why not?

KEY TERMS TO KNOW: human resources (HR) management, sexual harassment, glass ceiling, work–life balance, quality of work life (QWL)

---

[2] **LEARNING OBJECTIVE**

Discuss the challenges and advantages of a diverse workforce, and identify five major dimensions of workforce diversity.

Managing a Diverse Workforce

The companies that are most successful at managing and motivating their employees take great care to understand the diversity of their workforces and establish inclusive programs and policies that embrace that diversity and take full advantage of diversity's benefits. While there is a simple motivation of justice in providing equal opportunity and fair treatment to all employees, and removing barriers that impede the progress of any particular groups, it is also smart business strategy.

Over the past few decades, many innovative companies have changed the way they approach diversity, from seeing it as a legal requirement (providing equal opportunities for all) to seeing it as a strategic opportunity. Smart business leaders recognize the competitive advantages of a diverse workforce that offers a broader spectrum of viewpoints and ideas, helps businesses understand and identify with diverse markets, and enables companies to benefit from a wider range of employee talents.[28] Numerous studies show a positive correlation between company performance and workforce diversity.[29] In a comprehensive study of more than 1,000 firms in a dozen countries, the top-performing companies had markedly greater gender and ethnic diversity in the executive ranks compared to the worst-performing companies.[30]

Smart companies recognize that diversity is strongly correlated with financial performance.

DIMENSIONS OF WORKFORCE DIVERSITY

Although the concept is often framed in terms of race or gender, a broader and more useful definition of **diversity** includes "all the characteristics and experiences that define each of us as individuals."[31] The pharmaceutical company Merck, for instance, recognizes 20 separate dimensions of diversity.[32] Some aspects of diversity, such as race and age, are inherent. Others, such as work history, language, religion, cultural immersion, military training, and education, are acquired through life experience.[33] Together, these characteristics and experiences can have a profound effect on the way businesspeople interact.

> **diversity**
> All the characteristics and experiences that define each person as an individual.

Differences enrich the workplace but can create managerial challenges. A diverse workforce brings with it a wide range of skills, traditions, backgrounds, experiences, outlooks, and attitudes toward work—all of which can affect employee behavior on the job. Supervisors face the challenge of communicating with these diverse employees, motivating them, and fostering cooperation and harmony among them. Teams face the challenge of working together closely, and companies are challenged to coexist peacefully with business partners and with the community as a whole. Some of the most important diversity issues today include age, gender, race and ethnicity, religion, and ability.

REAL-TIME UPDATES
Learn More by Reading This Article

The business case for diversity and inclusion

Explore the correlation between diversity and financial performance. Go to **real-timeupdates.com/bia9** and select Learn More in the Students section.

Age

Today's workplaces can have three, four, or even five generations working side by side. Each has been shaped by dramatically different world events, social trends, and technological advances, so it is not surprising that they often have different values, expectations, and behaviors. Exhibit 11.1 on the next page lists the commonly designated generations in the U.S. population.

Be aware, however, that there are no official labels or year ranges for these generations. Over time, these labels have come into general use by population researchers and the news media. The only one of these used by the U.S. Census Bureau, for instance, is Baby Boomers. The labels and birth years shown in Exhibit 11.1 are those used by the Pew Research Center, a leading independent research organization. (Pew is waiting for a consensus to emerge regarding a label for the "Post-Millennial" generation.)[34]

When you hear statements about the beliefs and behaviors of a particular generation, always bear in mind that these are broad generalities. More than 70 million people in the United States alone fall in the Millennial designation, for instance, and any group that large is bound to have a wide range of beliefs and behaviors. In addition, the age ranges are not hard-and-fast boundaries in terms of human behavior. The first "Gen Xer" (born on January 1, 1965) doesn't automatically think and behave differently than the last Baby Boomer (born one day earlier on December 31, 1964).

REAL-TIME UPDATES
Learn More by Visiting This Website

Looking for jobs at diversity-minded companies?

These sites connect job searchers with companies that recognize the value of diverse workforces. Go to **real-timeupdates.com/bia9** and select Learn More in the Students section.

EXHIBIT 11.1	Generations in the Workplace

Lumping people into generations is an imprecise science at best, but it helps to know the labels commonly applied to various age groups in the workplace. (Note that these labels are not official, and there is no general agreement on when some generations start and end.)

Label	Birth Years
Greatest Generation	1901–1927
Silent Generation	1928–1945
Baby Boomers	1946–1964
Generation X	1965–1980
Millennials	1981–1996
"Post-Millennials"	1997–

Source: Michael Dimock, "Defining Generations: Where Millennials End and Post-Millennials Begin," Pew Research Center, 1 March 2018, www.pewresearch.org.

Federal law protects workers aged 40 and older from employment discrimination.

fizkes/Shutterstock

In your workplace interactions, approach age as you would any other dimension of diversity: Resist the urge to make assumptions about an individual from another age group, and don't assume that your own group's approach is automatically superior.

Age is a protected demographic factor, so companies must take care to avoid discriminatory practices throughout the employment life cycle. Federal law prohibits age discrimination against anyone 40 or older, and some states protect workers younger than 40.[35] The ability of digital advertising to target narrow demographic groups is creating some controversy in this regard. Several companies have been sued for using Facebook ads that targeted people within specific age ranges, for example.[36]

Gender

Perceptions, roles, and treatment of men and women in the workplace have been complex and at times contentious issues. The Equal Pay Act of 1963 mandated equal pay for comparable

sexism
Discrimination based on gender.

work, and the Civil Rights Act of 1964 made it illegal for employers to practice **sexism**, or discrimination based on gender. The United States has made important strides toward gender equity since then, but significant issues remain. For example, the U.S. Equal Employment Opportunity Commission (EEOC) fields 25,000 to 30,000 complaints a year regarding gender discrimination.[37]

Outdated concepts of gender and sexual orientation also continue to be a source of confusion, controversy, and discrimination. Many people do not fit or wish to be fit into a simplistic heterosexual, male/female categorization scheme, but discriminatory company policies and the behaviors and attitudes of supervisors and coworkers can deprive these individuals of a fair and satisfying work experience. In response, many companies have taken steps to ensure equal opportunities and fair treatment for lesbian, gay, bisexual, and transgender (LGBT) job applicants and employees. Companies can also take steps to make sure their nondiscrimination policies protect employees' right to gender expression based on personal gender identity.[38]

REAL-TIME UPDATES

Learn More by Visiting This Website

Removing barriers in the workplace

With the support of more than 800 companies, Catalyst endeavors to "build workplaces that work for women." Go to **real-timeupdates .com/bia9** and select Learn More in the Students section.

Race and Ethnicity

In many respects, the element of race and ethnicity in the diversity picture involves the same concerns as gender: equal pay for equal work, access to promotion opportunities, and ways to break through the glass ceiling. However, whereas the ratio of men and women in the workforce remains fairly stable year to year, the ethnic composition of the United States has been on a long-term trend of greater and greater diversity.

Grasping this changing situation can be complicated by confusion about the terms *race*, *ethnicity*, and *minority*. Ethnicity is a broader concept than race, incorporating both the genetic background of race and cultural issues such as language and national origin. Neither term is absolute or precise; millions of people have mixed racial heritage, and ethnicity doesn't always have fixed boundaries that clearly distinguish one group from another. *Minority* is a term often used to designate any race or ethnic segment other than white Americans of European descent. Aside from the negative connotations of *minority*, the term makes less and less numerical sense every year, because in a growing number of U.S. cities and counties, "minorities" constitute the majority of the population.[39]

Labels aside, race remains an important issue in the workforce. The EEOC receives even more complaints about racial discrimination than about gender discrimination.[40] And as with average wages between women and men, disparity still exists along racial lines.[41] But as with gender, these aggregate figures need to be viewed in the context of individual decisions and opportunities for advancement.

REAL-TIME UPDATES

Learn More by Visiting This Website

The changing face of contemporary society

The Pew Research Center explores a wide range of social and demographic trends. Go to **real-timeupdates.com/bia9** and select Learn More in the Students section.

Religion

The effort to accommodate employees' life interests on a broader scale has led a number of companies to address the issue of religion in the workplace. As one of the most personal aspects of life, religion brings potential for controversy in a work setting. On the one hand, some employees feel they should be able to express their beliefs in the workplace and not be forced to "check their faith at the door" when they come to work. On the other hand, companies want to avoid situations in which openly expressed religious differences might cause friction between employees or distract employees from their responsibilities.

Beyond accommodating individual beliefs to a reasonable degree, as required by U.S. law, companies occasionally need to resolve situations that pit one group of employees against another or against the company's business needs.[42] As more companies work to establish inclusive workplaces, and as more employees seek to integrate religious convictions into their daily work, you can expect to see this issue being discussed at many companies in the coming years.

Ability

People whose hearing, vision, cognitive ability, or physical ability to operate digital devices or machinery is impaired can be at a significant disadvantage in today's workplace. As with other elements of diversity, success starts with respect for individuals and sensitivity to differences.

Employers can also invest in a variety of assistive technologies that help people with disabilities perform activities that might otherwise be difficult or impossible. These technologies include devices and systems that help workers communicate, interact with computers and other equipment, and enjoy greater mobility in the workplace. AI and robotics are enabling an exciting new generation of assistive technologies (see Exhibit 11.2 on the next page). See the Real-Time Update on the right for links to companies in this field.

REAL-TIME UPDATES

Learn More by Visiting This Website

Consider a career in assistive technologies

Use these links to explore the many companies applying AI, robotics, and other innovations in the field of assistive technologies. Go to **real-timeupdates.com/bia9** and select Learn More in the Students section.

DIVERSITY AND INCLUSION INITIATIVES

To respond to the many challenges—and to capitalize on the business opportunities offered by diverse marketplaces and diverse workforces—companies across the country are finding that embracing diversity in the richest sense is simply good business. In response, thousands of U.S. companies have established **diversity and inclusion initiatives**, which can include

diversity and inclusion initiatives
Programs and policies that help companies support diverse workforces and markets.

Assistive technologies can help employees with cognitive, sensory, or physical impairments function to their full potential in the workplace. This Seeing AI app from Microsoft, for example, can identify objects and describe what it sees in an audio feed so that people with impaired vision can navigate through the office or down the street.

a desk with a computer monitor

Share

such steps as contracting with more diverse suppliers, targeting a more diverse customer base, and supporting the needs and interests of a diverse workforce.

For these initiatives to have meaningful impact, they must be integrated in a company's strategic planning, decision-making, and employee development efforts. In particular, the idea of inclusion needs to be *active*—whether that is helping military veterans make the transition to civilian work or recruiting employees from a broader range of socioeconomic segments. In addition to taking positive steps, companies may also need to identify and overcome destructive attitudes and behaviors and resistance to equal opportunity and fair treatment. And holding managers and executives accountable with diversity-related performance metrics helps ensure that company values will be practiced and not just preached.[43]

REAL-TIME UPDATES
Learn More by Visiting This Website

Advancing diversity and inclusion in the workplace

More than 400 CEOs of some of the world's leading companies are behind CEO Action for Diversity & Inclusion. Go to **real-timeupdates.com/bia9** and select Learn More in the Students section.

Beyond formal policies and programs, companies need to consider all the choices that might exclude some employees from full participation. For example, organized social events and activities can be important career-building opportunities because they often give employees the chance to interact with executives or other influential people they may not encounter in the course of their regular work. Adventure sports can exclude people incapable of or unwilling to participate, for instance, and pub crawls and other activities that emphasize alcohol consumption will not appeal to everyone in a company. If executives participate in these events, they should be sure to organize a sufficient variety of activities so that everyone will have the opportunity to join in at some point.

✓ CHECKPOINT

LEARNING OBJECTIVE 2: Discuss the challenges and advantages of a diverse workforce, and identify five major dimensions of workforce diversity.

SUMMARY: Differences in everything from religion to ethnic heritage to military experience enrich the workplace and give employers a competitive advantage by offering better insights into a diverse marketplace. A diverse workforce brings with it a wide range of skills, traditions, backgrounds, experiences, outlooks, and attitudes toward work—all of which can affect employee behaviors, relationships, and communication habits. Five major dimensions of workforce diversity addressed in this chapter are age, gender, race and ethnicity, religion, and ability.

CRITICAL THINKING: (1) How could a company benefit by investing in assistive technologies for its workers? (2) How might socioeconomic diversity in a company's workforce create both challenges and opportunities for the company?

IT'S YOUR BUSINESS: (1) What general opinions do you have of the generation that is older than you and the generation that is younger than you? What experiences and observations shaped these opinions? (2) Do you believe that any aspect of your background or heritage has held you back in any way in college or at work? If so, why?

KEY TERMS TO KNOW: diversity, sexism, diversity and inclusion initiatives

Managing the Employment Life Cycle

HR managers oversee employment-related activities ranging from evaluating staffing needs to recruiting new employees to managing the final phases of employment in retirement or termination.

3 LEARNING OBJECTIVE

Describe the three phases involved in managing the employment life cycle.

PLANNING FOR A COMPANY'S STAFFING NEEDS

Planning for staffing needs is a delicate balancing act. Hire too few employees, and you can't keep pace with the competition or satisfy customers. Hire too many, and you raise fixed costs above a level that revenues can sustain. To avoid either problem, HR managers work carefully to evaluate the requirements of every job in the company and to forecast the supply and demand for all types of talent (see Exhibit 11.3). Many companies now rely on *workforce analytics*, a computer-based approach to analyzing and planning for workforce needs (see page 344).

Evaluating Job Requirements

Through the process of *job analysis*, employers try to identify the nature and demands of each position within the firm as well as the optimal employee profile to fill each position.[44] Once job analysis has been completed, the HR staff develops a **job description**, a formal statement summarizing the tasks involved in the job and the conditions under which the employee will work. In most cases, the staff will also develop a **job specification**, which identifies the type of personnel a job requires, including the skills, education, experience, and personal attributes that candidates need to possess[45] (see Exhibit 11.4 on the next page).

Forecasting Supply and Demand

To forecast demand for the numbers and types of employees who will be needed at various times, HR managers weigh (1) forecasted sales revenues; (2) the expected **turnover rate**, the percentage of the workforce that leaves every year; (3) the current workforce's skill level relative to the company's future needs; (4) impending strategic decisions; (5) changes in technology or other business factors that could affect the number and type of workers needed; and (6) the company's current and projected financial status.[46]

In addition to overall workforce levels, every company has a number of employees and managers who are considered so critical to the company's ongoing operations that HR managers work with top executives to identify potential replacements in the event of the loss of any of these people, a process known as **succession planning**.[47] Workforce analytics can play a key role here. The system used by General Electric, for instance, can find likely candidates for every position in the company. Because such systems use measured results and talents, rather than personal connections, they can help identify overlooked talent and create fairer paths for people to move up in a company.[48]

With some idea of future workforce demands, the HR staff then tries to estimate the *supply* of available employees. To ensure a steady supply of experienced employees for new opportunities and to maintain existing operations, successful companies focus heavily on

job description
A statement of the tasks involved in a given job and the conditions under which the holder of a job will work.

job specification
A statement describing the kind of person who would be best for a given job—including the skills, education, and previous experience that the job requires.

turnover rate
The percentage of the workforce that leaves every year.

succession planning
Workforce planning efforts that identify possible replacements for specific employees, usually senior executives.

EXHIBIT 11.3	**Steps in Human Resources Planning**

Careful attention to each phase of this sequence helps ensure that a company will have the right mix of talent and experience to meets its business goals.

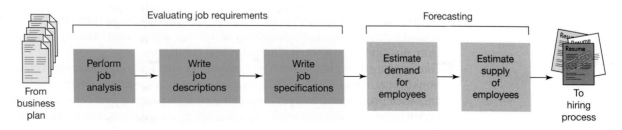

EXHIBIT 11.4	Job Description and Specification

A well-written job description and specification tells potential applicants what to expect from the job and what employers will expect from them.

Job Title
Director of E-Marketing

Location
Denver, CO

Reports to
Vice President of Marketing

Job Detail
Soccer Scope is a leading retailer of soccer equipment, apparel, and accessories based in Denver, Colorado, with retail locations in 23 states. We seek to expand our online presence under the guidance of a director of e-marketing, a new managerial position to be based in our Denver headquarters. The candidate who fills this position will be responsible for all nonstore aspects of our retailing efforts, including Soccer Scope's primary U.S. website and our country and region websites around the world, search-related advertising strategies, search engine optimization strategies, social media strategy and campaigns, email marketing campaigns, clicks-and-bricks integration strategy, affiliate marketing campaigns, customer retention efforts, and all aspects of online marketing research. The director of e-marketing will also work closely with the director of information technology to ensure the successful deployment of e-marketing platforms and with the director of retail operations to ensure a smooth clicks-and-bricks integration of offline and online retailing operations.

In addition to developing e-marketing strategies and directing e-marketing operations, the director is also responsible for leading a team of marketing and technical specialists who will implement and manage various programs.

Responsibilities
- Develop e-marketing strategies and plans consistent with Soccer Scope's overall business strategy and brand imperatives
- Integrate all outbound and inbound media streams to ensure seamless customer contact
- Establish and achieve aggressive customer acquisition and retention goals
- Coordinate efforts with technology and retailing counterparts to ensure successfully integrated online and offline marketing operations
- Assemble, lead, and develop an effective team of e-marketing professionals

Skills and Experience
- BA or BS in business, advertising, marketing, or related discipline required; MBA preferred
- Minimum 8 years of marketing experience, with at least 3 years in e-commerce and social media
- Current and thorough understanding of e-marketing strategies
- Demonstrated proficiency in developing and executing marketing strategies
- Excellent communication skills in all media

---

employee retention
Efforts to keep current employees.

contingent employees
Nonpermanent employees, including temporary workers, independent contractors, and full-time employees hired on a probationary basis.

employee retention. If existing employees cannot be tapped for new positions, the HR team looks outside the company for people to join as either permanent employees or **contingent employees** who fulfill many of the responsibilities of regular employees but on a temporary basis.

Alternative Work Arrangements

To meet today's staffing and demographic challenges, many companies are adopting alternative work arrangements to better accommodate the needs of employees—and to reduce costs in many cases. Four of the most popular arrangements are flextime, telecommuting, job sharing, and flexible career paths:

- *Flextime* is a scheduling system that allows employees to choose their own hours, within certain limits. Of course, the feasibility of flextime differs from industry to industry and from position to position within individual companies.
- *Telecommuting*—working from home or another location using electronic communications to stay in touch with colleagues, suppliers, and customers—helps employees balance their professional and personal commitments because they can spend less time in transit between home and work. Telecommuting also plays an important role in efforts

to reduce energy use, traffic, and mass transit overload. However, telecommuting isn't appropriate for every job, and some notable companies such as Apple and Google never embraced it, while others reduced its use after trying it. At IBM, for instance, some 40 percent of the company's employees used to work from home. As Chapter 8 mentions, though, an evolution toward agile management with its need for frequent face time prompted the company to call thousands of employees back to the office.[49]

- *Job sharing*, which lets two employees share a single full-time job and split the salary and benefits, can be an attractive alternative for people who want part-time hours in situations normally reserved for full-time employees.

- Perhaps the most challenging of all alternative work arrangements are situations in which employees want to limit their work time or leave the workforce entirely for an extended period to raise children, attend school, volunteer, or pursue other personal interests.

HIRING EMPLOYEES

The employment life cycle starts with **recruiting**, the process of attracting suitable candidates for an organization's jobs. The recruiting function is often judged by a metric known as *quality of hire*, which can include such factors as employees' performance level after a year on the job, the length of time they stay with the company, and how quickly they are promoted.[50] Exhibit 11.5 illustrates the general process that companies go through to hire new employees.

To find attractive candidates, recruiters use a variety of resources, including internal searches, online *job boards* (websites such as Monster), posted openings on their own websites, referrals from current employees, campus recruiting visits, high school and college internships, job fairs, networking events, recruiting agencies (outside agencies that specialize in finding and placing employees, informally referred to as *headhunters*), LinkedIn, and social networking platforms such as Twitter.[51] *Social recruiting* has become an important method for many companies (see Exhibit 11.6 on the next page).

recruiting
The process of attracting appropriate applicants for an organization's jobs.

EXHIBIT 11.5   **The Recruiting Process**

This general model of the recruiting process shows the steps most companies go through to select the best employee for each position.

Step 1: Assemble candidate pool	Step 2: Screen candidates	Step 3: Interview candidates	Step 4: Compare candidates	Step 5: Investigate candidates	Step 6: Make an offer
• Recruiters select a small number of qualified candidates from all the internal and external applicants. • Many organizations now use computer-based applicant tracking systems to manage the hiring process.	• Recruiters then screen candidates, typically through phone interviews, online tests, or on-campus interviews. • Interviews at this stage are usually fairly structured, with applicants asked the same questions so that recruiters can easily compare responses.	• Candidates who make it through screening are invited to visit the company for another round of interviews. • This stage usually involves several interviews with a mix of colleagues, HR specialists, and managers.	• The interview team compares notes and assesses the remaining candidates. • Team members sometimes lobby for or against individual candidates based on what they've seen and heard during interviews.	• Recruiters talk to references, conduct background checks, scan social media postings, and in many cases subject applicants to preemployment tests. • Given the financial and legal risks associated with bad hiring decisions, smart employers research candidates carefully and thoroughly.	• With all this information in hand, the hiring manager selects the most suitable person for the job and makes a job offer.

EXHIBIT 11.6	**Social Recruiting**

Social media have become essential tools for finding and establishing relationships with potential employees.

Federal and state laws and regulations govern many aspects of the hiring process. (See Exhibit 11.7 for a list of some of the most important employment-related laws.) In particular, employers must respect the privacy of applicants and avoid discrimination. For instance, any form or test that can be construed as a preemployment medical examination is prohibited by the Americans with Disabilities Act.[52]

Screening job candidates and selecting which applicants to offer jobs to is one of HR's most important responsibilities. To help manage the process and make better hiring decisions, many companies now use *workforce analytics* (see page 344) and *applicant tracking systems*.

MANAGING EMPLOYEE RETIREMENT

At the other end of the employment life cycle, HR departments must handle the process of employee retirement. In the past, mandatory retirement policies forced people to quit working as soon as they turned a certain age. However, the Age Discrimination in Employment Act outlaws mandatory retirement based on age alone, unless an employer can demonstrate that age is a valid qualification for "normal operation of the particular business."[53]

A company's strategy at this stage depends on its talent needs and financial circumstances. A firm that needs to cut its workforce for economic reasons may try to persuade employees to depart ahead of their planned retirement by offering early retirement with financial incentives known as *severance packages* or *buyouts*. This can be a mixed blessing for a company, because its most experienced workers are often its highest paid. While such a move can reduce costs, it can also deprive a firm of years of institutional knowledge, industry connections, and advanced skills.[54]

EXHIBIT 11.7	Major Employment Legislation	

Here are some of the most significant sets of laws that affect employer-employee relations in the United States.

Category	Legislation	Highlights
Labor and Unionization	National Labor Relations Act, also known as the Wagner Act	Establishes the right of employees to form, join, and assist unions and the right to strike; prohibits employers from interfering in union activities
	Labor-Management Relations Act, also known as the Taft-Hartley Act	Expands union member rights; gives employers free speech rights to oppose unions; restricts union's strike options; gives the president the authority to impose injunctions against strikes
	Labor-Management Reporting and Disclosure Act, also known as the Landrum-Griffin Act	Gives union members the right to nominate and vote for union leadership candidates; combats financial fraud within unions
	State right-to-work laws	Give individual employees the right to choose not to join a union
	Fair Labor Standards Act	Establishes minimum wage and overtime pay for nonexempt workers; sets strict guidelines for child labor
	Immigration Reform and Control Act	Prohibits employers from hiring illegal immigrants
Workplace Safety	State workers' compensation acts	Require employers (in most states) to carry either private or government-sponsored insurance that provides income to injured workers
	Occupational Health and Safety Act	Empowers the Occupational Safety and Health Administration (OSHA) to establish, monitor, and enforce standards for workplace safety
Compensation and Benefits	Employee Retirement Income Security Act	Governs the establishment and operation of private pension programs
	Consolidated Omnibus Budget Reconciliation Act (usually known by the acronym COBRA)	Requires employers to let employees or their beneficiaries buy continued health insurance coverage after employment ends
	Federal Unemployment Tax Act and similar state laws	Require employers to fund programs that provide income for qualified unemployed persons
	Social Security Act	Provides a level of retirement, disability, and medical coverage for employees and their dependents; jointly funded by employers and employees
	Lilly Ledbetter Fair Pay Act	Amends and modifies several pieces of earlier legislation to make it easier for employees to file lawsuits over pay and benefit discrimination
	Patient Protection and Affordable Care Act	Requires companies with more than 50 full-time employees to offer health insurance coverage for employees

Sources: Henry J. Kaiser Family Foundation, *Focus on Health Reform: Summary of the Affordable Care Act*, 23 April 2013; U.S. Department of Labor website, accessed 15 May 2018, www.dol.gov; Henry R. Cheeseman, *Contemporary Business and E-Commerce Law*, 7th ed. (Upper Saddle River, N.J.: Pearson Prentice Hall, 2010), 487–495; "The Lilly Ledbetter Fair Pay Act of 2009," U.S. White House, accessed 23 June 2009, www.whitehouse.gov.

Conversely, a firm facing a talent shortage can find itself in the situation of wanting to encourage older employees to stay on past the ages at which they had planned to retire. Companies can take a variety of steps to retain older employees, including offering part-time schedules and bringing retired workers back as contract workers or consultants.[55]

Retirement policies and practices are going to be an important issue for business and society in the coming years. As life expectancy continues to rise and people are healthy and able to contribute well past the traditional retirement age of 65, more employees will want or need to keep working. Keeping older employees in the workforce can reduce the burden on retirement programs, but it also sets up the potential for increased generational competition for jobs.

TERMINATING EMPLOYMENT

HR managers have the unpleasant responsibility of **termination**—permanently laying off employees because of cutbacks or firing employees for poor performance or other reasons. **Layoffs** are terminations for economic or business reasons unrelated to employee

termination
The process of getting rid of an employee through layoff or firing.

layoffs
Termination of employees for economic or business reasons.

performance. To help ease the pain of layoffs, many companies provide laid-off employees with job-hunting assistance and other *outplacement services*.

Terminating employment by firing is a complex legal subject. For the most part, employment in the United States is considered *at will*, meaning that in situations that are not explicitly covered by contracts (either individual employment contracts or *collective bargaining agreements* in the case of unionized employees), employers and employees are free to end the arrangement at any time for any reason. However, over the years, many federal and state laws have put restrictions on termination decisions, so employers must proceed carefully if they intend to remove an employee. For example, employers are legally prohibited from discriminating when terminating an employee, such as releasing someone because of his or her age or race. Fired employees who believe that any laws have been violated can file *wrongful termination* lawsuits against their employers, although wrongful termination can be difficult to prove in court.[56]

 CHECKPOINT

LEARNING OBJECTIVE 3: Describe the three phases involved in managing the employment life cycle.

SUMMARY: The three phases of managing the employment life cycle are hiring, retirement, and termination. The hiring phase typically involves six steps: selecting a small number of qualified candidates from all of the applications received, screening those candidates to identify the most attractive prospects, interviewing those prospects in depth to learn more about them and their potential to contribute to the company, evaluating and comparing interview results, conducting background checks and pre-employment tests, and then selecting the best candidate for each position and making job offers. Retirement offers a variety of challenges depending on the industry and the company's situation; overstaffed companies may induce some employees to retire early through buyouts, whereas others that face talent shortages may try to persuade retirement-age employees to delay retirement. Termination can involve firing employees for poor performance or other reasons or laying off employees for financial reasons.

CRITICAL THINKING: (1) Why would a company spend money on outplacement counseling and other services for laid-off employees? (2) Why would a company spend money to induce retirement-age employees to stay on board for a while, rather than simply hiring younger employees to take their place?

IT'S YOUR BUSINESS: (1) What impression would a potential employer get from studying your current online presence? (2) Many companies now use online and AI-assisted interviewing tools to screen and evaluation employees. How do you feel about presenting yourself and your qualifications to potential employers through this sort of digital intermediation?

KEY TERMS TO KNOW: job description, job specification, turnover rate, succession planning, employee retention, contingent employees, recruiting, termination, layoffs

---

[4] **LEARNING OBJECTIVE**

Explain the steps used to develop and evaluate employees.

Developing and Evaluating Employees

Another major contribution that HR makes is helping managers throughout the company align employee skill sets with the evolving requirements of each position. This effort includes appraising employee performance, managing training and development programs, and promoting and reassigning employees.

APPRAISING EMPLOYEE PERFORMANCE

performance reviews
Periodic evaluations of employees' work according to specific criteria.

Performance reviews, also known as *performance appraisals*, are periodic evaluations of employee performance designed to clarify job requirements, give employees feedback on their performance, and establish personal action plans. The traditional annual performance review combines a written assessment with a one-on-one conversation in which the manager shares the review with the employee and discusses the evaluation (see Exhibit 11.8). Reviews often include a scoring system that can be used to rank employees and establish target pay levels.

EXHIBIT 11.8	Sample Performance Appraisal Form

This sample form suggests the range of performance variables on which companies typically evaluate their employees.

Name_____ Title_____ Service Date_____ Date_____

Location_____ Division_____ Department_____

Length of Time in Present Position Period of Review   Appraised by _____

_____ From: _____ To: _____ Title of Appraisor_____

Area of Performance	Comment	Rating
Job Knowledge and Skill Understands responsibilities and uses background for job. Adapts to new methods/techniques. Plans and organizes work. Recognizes errors and problems.		5 4 3 2 1
Volume of Work Amount of work output. Adherence to standards and schedules. Effective use of time.		5 4 3 2 1
Quality of Work Degree of accuracy—lack of errors. Thoroughness of work. Ability to exercise good judgment.		5 4 3 2 1
Initiative and Creativity Self-motivation in seeking responsibility and work that needs to be done. Ability to apply original ideas and concepts.		5 4 3 2 1
Communication Ability to exchange thoughts or information in a clear, concise manner. Ability to deal with different organizational levels of clientele.		5 4 3 2 1
Dependability Ability to follow instructions and directions correctly. Performs under pressure. Reliable work habits.		5 4 3 2 1
Leadership Ability/Potential Ability to guide others to the successful accomplishment of a given task. Potential for developing subordinate employees.		5 4 3 2 1

5. Outstanding   Employee who consistently exceeds established standards and expectations of the job.

4. Above Average   Employee who consistently meets established standards and expectations of the job. Often exceeds and rarely falls short of desired results.

3. Satisfactory   Generally qualified employee who meets job standards and expectations. Sometimes exceeds and may occasionally fall short of desired expectations. Performs duties in a normally expected manner.

2. Improvement Needed Not quite meeting standards and expectations. An employee at this level of performance is not quite meeting all the standard job requirements.

1. Unsatisfactory   Employee who fails to meet the minimum standards and expectations of the job.

I have had the opportunity to read this performance appraisal.   How long has this employee been under your supervision?

_____

Signature   Date   Signature of Supervisor   Date

_____

Although this approach has been widely used for years, it has some potential weaknesses: Writing these reports consumes a lot of management's time, the long gaps between evaluations can result in employees drifting far off course before getting corrective input, and ranked evaluations can foster an unhealthy atmosphere of competition in the workplace.[57]

In response to these issues, some companies have abandoned the traditional annual review in favor of shorter and more frequent forms of feedback. Some have dropped written reviews altogether in favor of ongoing coaching and feedback sessions between managers and employees, simpler survey methods, and the use of feedback apps.[58] Salesforce.com, for example, replaced performance reviews with its custom Feedback App, which enables all employees to give and receive feedback in real time. The benefits include recognizing contributions when they occur and addressing performance issues quickly.[59]

360-degree review

A multidimensional review in which a person is given feedback from subordinates, peers, superiors, and possibly outside stakeholders such as customers and business partners.

To give a more complete picture of employee performance and contribution to organizational success, some companies now solicit the input of several people who interact with an employee, such as a supervisor and several coworkers. This practice further promotes fairness by correcting for possible biases. The ultimate in multidimensional reviews is the **360-degree review**, in which a person is given feedback from subordinates (if the employee has supervisory responsibility), peers, superiors, and possibly customers or outside business partners. In some cases, employees review themselves as part of the process as well.[60] The multiple viewpoints can uncover weaknesses that employees and even their direct managers might not be aware of, as well as contributions and achievements that might have been overlooked in normal reviews.

Performance appraisal might be best described as a work in progress, and companies continue to search for fairer and more effective methods. The performance management systems discussed in Chapter 10 (see page 314) incorporate data analytics and sometimes AI in an attempt to improve the process.

TRAINING AND DEVELOPING EMPLOYEES

new-employee orientation

Sessions or procedures for acclimating new employees to the organization.

onboarding

Programs to help new employees get comfortable and productive in their assigned roles.

skills inventory

A list of the skills a company needs from its workforce, along with the specific skills that individual employees currently possess.

With the fast pace of change in everything from government regulations to consumer tastes to technology, employee knowledge and skills need to be updated constantly. Consequently, most successful companies place heavy emphasis on employee training and development efforts, for everyone from entry-level workers to the CEO.

Training usually begins with **new-employee orientation**, one or more meetings designed to ease the new hire's transition into the company and to impart important knowledge about the organization and its rules, procedures, and expectations. Many companies also have more comprehensive **onboarding** programs, which may extend for several months and help new employees get up to speed in their specific roles, establish important relationships, and get comfortable with the organizational culture.[61]

Training and other forms of employee development continue throughout the employee's career in most cases. Many HR departments maintain a **skills inventory**, often as an element of workforce analytics, which identifies both the current skill levels of all the employees and the skills the company needs in order to succeed. (If your employer doesn't maintain one for you, be sure to maintain your own skills inventory so you can stay on top of developments and expectations in your field.)

fizkes/Shutterstock

Onboarding programs help new employees get comfortable and productive.

PROMOTING AND REASSIGNING EMPLOYEES

Many companies prefer to look within the organization to fill job vacancies. In part, this promote-from-within policy allows a company to benefit from the training and experience of its own workforce. This policy also rewards employees who have worked hard and demonstrated the ability to handle more challenging tasks. In addition, morale is usually better when a company promotes from within because other employees see the possibility of advancement. For example, Enterprise Holdings (the parent company of Enterprise Rent-A-Car, Alamo, and National Car Rental) highlights its promote-from-within philosophy and the opportunity to move into managerial responsibilities.[62]

However, a possible pitfall of internal promotion is that a person may be given a job beyond his or her competence or comfort level. The best sales representative in the company is not necessarily the best candidate for sales manager, because managing requires a different set of skills. If the promotion is a mistake, the company not only loses its sales leader but also risks demoralizing the sales staff. Companies can reduce such risks through careful promotion policies and by providing support and training to help newly promoted employees fulfill their new responsibilities.

 CHECKPOINT

LEARNING OBJECTIVE 4: Explain the steps used to develop and evaluate employees.

SUMMARY: The effort to develop and evaluate employees includes providing performance appraisals, managing training and development programs, and promoting and reassigning employees. Managers use performance appraisals to give employees feedback and develop plans to improve performance shortcomings. In a 360-degree review, an employee is evaluated by subordinates (if applicable), peers, and superiors. Training and development efforts begin with orientation for new hires and continue throughout a person's career in many cases. When employees have reached sufficient skill levels to take on new challenges, they may be considered for promotion into positions of more responsibility.

CRITICAL THINKING: (1) How can employers balance the need to provide objective appraisals that can be compared across the company's entire workforce with the desire to evaluate each employee on an individual basis? (2) Beyond increasing their skill and knowledge levels, how can training improve employees' motivation and job satisfaction? (Review Chapter 10 if you need to.)

IT'S YOUR BUSINESS: (1) Have you ever had a performance appraisal that you felt was inaccurate or unfair? If so, how would you change the process? (2) Do the methods your college or university uses to evaluate your performance as a student accurately reflect your progress? What changes would you make to the evaluation process?

KEY TERMS TO KNOW: performance reviews, 360-degree review, new-employee orientation, onboarding, skills inventory

Compensating and Supporting Employees

Pay and benefits are of vital interest to all employees, of course, and these subjects also consume considerable time and attention in HR departments. For many companies, payroll is the single biggest expense, and the cost of benefits, particularly health care, continues to climb. Consequently, **compensation**, the combination of direct payments such as wages or salary and indirect payments through employee benefits, is one of the HR manager's most significant responsibilities. The full package of monetary and nonmonetary compensation is sometimes referred to as *total rewards*.

SALARIES AND WAGES

Most employees receive the bulk of their compensation in the form of a **salary**, if they receive a fixed amount per year, or **wages**, if they are paid by the unit of time (hourly, daily, or weekly) or by the unit of output (often called "getting paid by the piece" or "piecework").

 5 LEARNING OBJECTIVE

Describe the major elements of employee compensation, benefits, and support services.

compensation
Money, benefits, and services paid to employees for their work.

salary
Fixed cash compensation for work, usually by a yearly amount; independent of the number of hours worked.

wages
Cash payment based on the number of hours an employee has worked or the number of units an employee has produced.

The Fair Labor Standards Act, introduced in 1938 and amended many times since then, sets specific guidelines that employers must follow when administering salaries and wages, including setting a minimum wage and paying overtime for time worked beyond 40 hours a week. However, most professional and managerial employees are considered exempt from these regulations, meaning, for instance, that their employers don't have to pay them for overtime. The distinction between *exempt employees* and *nonexempt employees* is based on job responsibilities and pay level. In general, salaried employees are exempt, although there are many exceptions.[63]

Defining compensation levels for employees up and down the organization chart is a complex challenge. Companies need to manage compensation in a way that allows them to simultaneously earn a profit, create appealing goods and services, and compete with other companies for the same employees. A firm could attract most of the talent it needs by paying huge salaries, but that probably wouldn't be profitable. Conversely, it could keep salaries low to hold down costs, but then it couldn't attract the talent it needs to be competitive, so it might not generate enough revenue to turn a profit anyway.

In the broadest terms, compensation is dictated by prevailing conditions in the job market and the value each employee brings to the organization. Such variables as geography (locations with higher living expenses tend to have higher salaries), industry, and company size (larger companies tend to pay more) can also factor into the equation. Although it seems like going around in circles to base compensation on prevailing market rates when all the other companies in the market are doing the same thing, the market is the best quasi-independent arbiter available. As executive compensation consultant Russell Miller puts it, "If we don't look to the market to determine if we're paying competitively, where else should we look?"[64]

Judging an employee's worth to an organization is no simple matter, either. Few jobs—sales is a notable exception—have an immediate and measurable impact on revenue, which makes it difficult to say how much most employees are worth to the company. For most positions, companies tend to establish a salary range for each position, trying to balance what it can afford to pay with prevailing market rates. Each employee's salary is then set within that range based on performance evaluations, with higher-performing employees deemed more valuable to the company and therefore deserving of higher pay.

REAL-TIME UPDATES
Learn More by Exploring This Interactive Website

How much are you worth?

Find real-life salary ranges for a wide range of jobs. Go to **real-timeupdates.com/bia9** and select Learn More in the Students section.

Not surprisingly, people expect to get paid what they believe they are worth—particularly relative to what other people are making. Recall from the discussion of equity theory (page 303) that most employees don't expect to make as much as the CEO, but they do expect the ratio of value provided to rewards gained to be at least reasonable. In the 1950s, CEOs made roughly 20 times more than the median employee salary in their companies, and the ratio has been steadily climbing. (The median employee salary is the midpoint of all salaries; half make more than that and half make less.) Depending on the survey methodology, average CEO pay in public corporations has been calculated as anywhere from 140 to more than 300 times the median employee salary.[65] Although it's impossible to identify exactly how much more valuable a CEO is than an average employee, it is reasonable to ask if today's CEOs are 10 or 15 times more valuable than CEOs were in years past.

INCENTIVE PROGRAMS

As Chapter 10 mentions, many companies provide managers and employees with *incentives* to encourage productivity, innovation, and commitment to work. Incentives are typically cash payments linked to specific goals for individual, group, or companywide performance. In other words, achievements, not just activities, are made the basis for payment. The success of these programs often depends on how closely incentives are linked to actions within the employee's control:

bonus
A cash payment, in addition to regular wage or salary, that serves as a reward for achievement.

- A **bonus** is a single payment in addition to the regular wage or salary. Bonuses might be individual rewards or companywide rewards, and they are sometimes paid quarterly or annually based on the company's financial performance.

- **Commissions** are a form of compensation that pays employees in sales positions based on the level of sales they make within a given time frame. Many sales professionals get a *base salary* plus commissions; some are paid entirely on commissions.
- Employees may be rewarded for staying with a company and encouraged to perform at higher levels with **profit sharing**, a system in which employees receive a portion of the company's profits.
- Similar to profit sharing, *gain sharing* ties rewards to profits (or cost savings) achieved by meeting specific goals such as quality and productivity improvement.[66]
- A variation of gain sharing, *pay for performance* requires employees to accept a lower base pay but rewards them with bonuses, commissions, or stock options if they reach agreed-on goals.
- Another approach to compensation being explored by some companies is *knowledge-based pay*, also known as *competency-based pay* or *skill-based pay*, which is tied to employees' knowledge and abilities rather than to their job per se.

Sales professionals usually earn at least part of their income through commissions; the more they sell, the more they earn.

EMPLOYEE BENEFITS

Companies also attract and award employees with **employee benefits**—elements of compensation other than wages, salaries, and incentives. The benefits most commonly provided by employers are insurance, retirement benefits, employee stock-ownership plans, stock options, and family benefits.

Insurance

Employers can offer a range of insurance plans to their employees, including life, health, dental, vision, disability, and long-term care insurance. Perhaps no other issue illustrates the challenging economics of business today better than health-care costs in general and health insurance in particular. Health-care costs are on an unsustainable upward spiral in the United States, and because millions of people rely on their employers for health insurance, it is a major concern for employers. In addition, millions of people lack health insurance, including many who own or work for small businesses, which presents the risk of financial calamity in the event of serious injuries or illnesses.

The United States arguably spends enough to provide adequate care for everyone, but the health-care sector is plagued by waste, inefficiency, and imbalance. As the only advanced economy in the world without some form of universal health care, the United States spends more per capita on health care than any other country—twice as much as many European countries—but gets less in return. According to a number of key measures, health-care outcomes are lower in the United States than in many other countries.[67]

The Affordable Care Act (ACA) of 2010, often referred to informally as *Obamacare,* sought to fix a number of problems within U.S. health care, including millions of people without health insurance and the ability of insurers to reject people with *preexisting conditions.* Among other elements in this complex and controversial piece of legislation, the ACA requires that companies with more than 50 workers provide health insurance benefits, and that people who don't get insurance through work buy individual policies or pay a penalty. The ACA helped millions of people get health insurance and prevents insurers from denying insurance based on preexisting conditions, but it also led to price increases for some people who had been buying their own policies, and the legislation continues to be a point of political contention.[68]

Retirement Benefits

Many employers offer **retirement plans**, which are designed to provide continuing income after an employee retires. Company-sponsored retirement plans can be categorized as either *defined-benefit plans,* in which companies specify how much they will pay employees on retirement, or *defined-contribution plans,* in which companies specify how much they will put into the

commissions
Employee compensation based on a percentage of sales made.

profit sharing
The distribution of a portion of the company's profits to employees.

employee benefits
Compensation other than wages, salaries, and incentive programs.

retirement plans
Company-sponsored programs for providing retirees with income.

Karramba Production/Shutterstock

pension plans
Generally refers to traditional, defined-benefit retirement plans.

retirement fund (by matching employee contributions, for instance), without guaranteeing specific payout levels during retirement. Although both types are technically **pension plans**, when most people speak of pension plans, they are referring to traditional defined-benefit plans, which are far less common than they were in years past.[69]

Defined-contribution plans are similar to savings plans; they provide a future benefit based on annual employer contributions, voluntary employee matching contributions, and accumulated investment earnings. Employers can choose from several types of defined-contribution plans, the most common being the **401(k) plan**. The details of 401(k) plans vary, but in general, employees can invest a portion of their salary, and this amount is deducted from their taxable income; employers often match all or a portion of the employee's contribution. The tax deduction and the employer matching can make 401(k) plans a great investment option for employees, but they have few choices and less control than with other investment vehicles.[70]

401(k) plan
A defined-contribution retirement plan in which employers often match the amount employees invest.

employee stock-ownership plan (ESOP)
A program that enables employees to become partial owners of a company.

More than 10 million U.S. employees are now enrolled in an **employee stock-ownership plan (ESOP)**, in which a company places some or all of its stock in trust, with each eligible employee entitled to a certain portion. (Most ESOPs are in closely held corporations whose stock isn't available for sale to the public.) Many companies report that ESOPs help boost employee productivity because workers perceive a direct correlation between their efforts and the value of the company stock price.[71]

Stock Options

stock options
A contract that allows the holder to purchase or sell a certain number of shares of a particular stock at a given price by a certain date.

Compensation packages for executives and in-demand professionals can include **stock options**, which are the right to purchase a certain number of shares of the employer's stock at a predetermined price (usually but not always below the current market price). Options typically *vest* over a number of years, meaning that employees can purchase a prorated portion of the shares every year until the vesting period is over, at which time they can purchase all the shares they are entitled to. The major attractions of stock options from an employer's point of view are that they provide a means of compensation that doesn't require any cash outlay, they can motivate employees to work hard to make sure the stock price increases, and they can keep valuable employees in the company at least until their options are fully vested.[72]

Other Employee Benefits

Employers offer a variety of other benefits in addition to those just discussed. Some of them are mandated by government regulation and some are offered voluntarily to attract and support employees. Here are some of the most common benefits:

- **Paid vacations and sick leave.** Some companies offer separate vacation and sick days; others combine the paid time off in a single "bucket" and let employees choose how to use the time.
- **Family and medical leave.** The Family Medical Leave Act (FMLA) of 1993 requires employers with 50 or more workers to provide up to 12 weeks of unpaid leave per year for childbirth, adoption, or the care of oneself, a child, a spouse, or a parent with a serious illness.[73]
- **Child-care assistance.** Many companies offer child-care assistance, such as discounted rates at nearby child-care centers or on-site daycare centers.
- **Elder-care assistance.** Many employers offer some form of elder-care assistance to help employees with the responsibility of caring for aging parents.
- **Tuition loans and reimbursements.** Many companies offer to help employees who want to continue their educations.
- **Employee assistance programs.** To help employees deal with personal issues that could affect their work, a company can choose to establish an **employee assistance program (EAP)**. Such programs offer private and confidential counseling for issues related to substance abuse, domestic violence, finances, stress, family issues, and other personal matters.[74]

employee assistance program (EAP)
A company-sponsored counseling or referral plan for employees with personal problems.

For more information on employee benefits and other human resources topics, visit **real-timeupdates.com/bia9** and select Chapter 11.

 **CHECKPOINT**

LEARNING OBJECTIVE 5: Describe the major elements of employee compensation, benefits, and support services.

SUMMARY: For most employees, the bulk of their compensation comes in the form of a salary, if they receive a fixed amount per year, or wages, if they are paid by the unit of time or the unit of output. In addition to their base salary or wages, some employees are eligible for a variety of incentive programs, including bonuses, commissions, profit sharing, and gain sharing. In some cases, employers offer pay-for-performance plans that have a lower base salary but allow employees to earn more by hitting specific performance goals. Some companies are also exploring knowledge-based pay, which rewards employees for acquiring information or developing skills related to their jobs. Nonsalary rewards include insurance, retirement benefits, stock options, vacation and sick leave, child- and elder-care assistance, tuition assistance, and employee assistance (counseling) programs.

CRITICAL THINKING: (1) What are some potential risks or limitations of performance-based pay systems? (2) How does equity theory (see Chapter 10) explain the anger some employees feel about the compensation packages their company CEOs receive?

IT'S YOUR BUSINESS: (1) If you worked for a large corporation, would a profit-sharing plan motivate you? Why or why not? (2) What questions would you ask before you accepted a sales position in which most of your compensation would be based on commissions, rather than base salary?

KEY TERMS TO KNOW: compensation, salary, wages, bonus, commissions, profit sharing, employee benefits, retirement plans, pension plans, 401(k) plan, employee stock-ownership plan (ESOP), stock options, employee assistance program (EAP)

Understanding the Role of Labor Unions in Today's Business World

 LEARNING OBJECTIVE

Characterize the role of labor unions in today's business world.

labor relations
The relationship between organized labor and management (in its role as the representative of company ownership).

labor unions
Organizations that represent employees in negotiations with management.

Perhaps nothing represents the potential for stress in the stakeholder model more than **labor relations**, the relationship between organized labor and business owners. Although they work toward common goals in most cases, managers and employees face an inherent conflict over resources: Company owners and managers want to minimize the costs of operating the business, whereas employees want to maximize salaries and ensure good benefits and safe, pleasant working conditions.

If employees believe they are not being treated fairly and can't get their needs met by negotiating individually with management, they may have the option of joining **labor unions**, organizations that seek to protect employee interests by negotiating with employers for better wages and benefits, improved working conditions, and increased job security. As Exhibit 11.9 on the next page shows, the role of unions varies widely by industry, dominating workforce matters in some industries but having little impact in others. (A note on terminology: *Labor* can refer to either unions specifically or the workforce as a whole; you can tell by the context which definition is meant. *Organized labor* always refers to unions. And *management* in a discussion of union issues refers to managers in their role as representatives of company ownership.)

UNIONIZATION: THE EMPLOYEE'S PERSPECTIVE

The most fundamental appeal of unionization is strength in numbers, giving workers the opportunity to negotiate on a more equal footing with management. With this negotiating power, union members and supporters point to a number of ways workers benefit from union membership:[75]

EXHIBIT 11.9	Union Membership in Selected Industries

Union membership varies widely by industry, as you can see from this selection of 24 industry sectors.

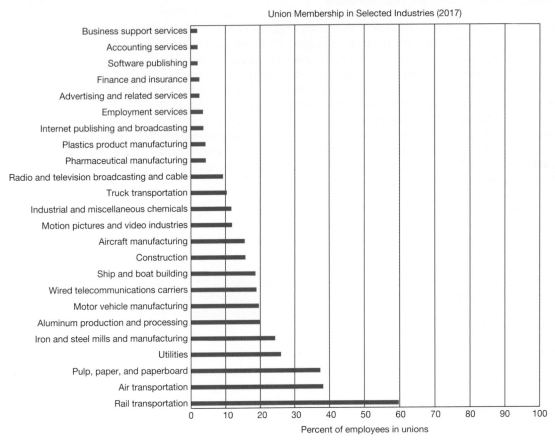

Source: Data from "Union Membership and Coverage Database from the CPS," Unionstats.com, 15 May 2018, www.unionstats.com.

seniority
The length of time someone has worked for his or her current employer, relative to other employees.

- **Higher compensation.** According to the U.S. Bureau of Labor Statistics, private-sector union members currently earn about 25 percent more than nonunion workers, taken as an average across the entire workforce.[76] (This is based on averages of all workers in all types of jobs, not on a comparison of union and nonunion employees in the same types of jobs.)
- **Greater benefits.** As with compensation, on average, union members receive better nonwage benefits such as health-care insurance, and a greater percentage of union employees receive these benefits, than nonunion employees.[77]
- **Influence over hiring, promotions, and layoffs.** Union contracts usually have specific provisions about hiring, promotions, and layoffs, particularly with regard to **seniority**, the length of time someone has worked for his or her current employer. For example, when a company is laying off employees, union contracts often specify that those with lowest seniority are let go first, and when employees are rehired, those with the most seniority are hired first.
- **Working conditions and workplace safety.** Many unionization efforts focus on issues of workplace safety, work breaks, training, and other aspects of life on the job.
- **Formal processes for employee grievances, discipline, and other matters.** Union contracts typically spell out formal procedures for such matters as disciplining employees. According to Mariah DeForest, a management consultant who specializes in manufacturing employment, "Unfair supervisory behavior is the most important reason that employees seek out a union."[78]

- **Solidarity and recognition.** Aside from tangible and measurable benefits, union membership can appeal to workers who feel unappreciated, humiliated, or let down by management.

Given the apparent advantages of belonging to a union, why don't all workers want to join? One possible explanation comes from the success of union efforts that led to such legislative victories as creating the standard 40-hour workweek, setting the minimum wage, abolishing child labor, mandating equal pay for equal work, and prohibiting job discrimination. With these improvements already in place, many workers don't feel the need to join a union.[79] Other reasons employees might not want to join include being forced to pay union dues, being forced to help fund (through those monthly dues) political activities they may not support, being held back in their careers by union seniority rules, and being forced to accept the union as the sole intermediary with management rather than negotiating raises, job assignments, and other matters on their own.

Union membership is down considerably from its peak in the 1950s, but organized labor remains a strong force in some industries.

UNIONIZATION: MANAGEMENT'S PERSPECTIVE

Either as business owners themselves or as the representatives of owners, managers obviously have an interest in minimizing costs to maximize profits. Although union sympathizers sometimes portray this attitude as simple greed, in general, management's top priority is making sure their firms can remain competitive. For example, by containing the ongoing costs of providing compensation and benefits, a firm is better able to invest in facilities, equipment, and new-product development.[80]

In addition to direct costs, other management concerns regarding unions include flexibility and productivity. Union contracts often include **work rules**, or *job rules*, that specify such things as the tasks certain employees are required to do or are forbidden to do. For instance, management might be prevented from having employees cross-trained on a variety of tasks and machines to allow production supervisors more flexibility in responding to changes in product demand without increasing headcount. In the auto industry, for example, an analysis that compared Chrysler, Ford, and GM with Toyota concluded that union work rules forced the U.S. carmakers to create 8,200 more jobs than they would have created otherwise.[81]

The effect of unionization has been studied extensively over the years. In a review of 73 of these studies, professors Christos Doucouliagos and Patrice Laroche found 45 that showed a positive effect of unions on productivity and 28 that showed a negative effect. Their analysis of this research suggests that unions have had a net negative effect on productivity in the United Kingdom and Japan but a net positive effect on productivity in the United States. However, those productivity gains are offset by the higher average wages that unionized workers receive. "When the productivity and wage effects are combined, we can conclude that unions have a negative impact on profitability."[82]

Whether this outcome is negative or positive depends on your perspective. It is clearly a negative outcome for shareholders and proprietors, but the higher wages are obviously a positive outcome for workers and, by extension, the communities in which those workers live—including the various businesses they patronize with their paychecks.

work rules
A common element of labor contracts that specifies such things as the tasks certain employees are required to do or are forbidden to do.

THE FUTURE OF ORGANIZED LABOR

Labor relations remains a classic case of stakeholder conflict, with one side pursuing lower costs and more operational flexibility and the other side pursuing higher wages, better benefits, and more stability. Union membership numbers don't tell the whole story of this conflict, because the influence of the labor movement stretches beyond just those workplaces that are unionized. However, one can't avoid looking at membership numbers either, and by that score, unions have been on the losing side of this contest for several decades. From a peak of more than one-third of the U.S. private-sector workforce in the 1950s, only 6.5 percent of private-sector workers now belong to unions.[83]

Unions have had one notable success in recent years: working to raise the minimum wage in several large cities to $15 per hour, twice the federal minimum wage. However, it remains to be seen how widely that progress will spread or whether the initiative might be extended to higher-wage jobs. Union leaders are exploring new models and methods of organizing to promote workers' rights, but it's unlikely that union membership in the private sector will ever return to its former levels.[84]

 CHECKPOINT

LEARNING OBJECTIVE 6: Characterize the role of labor unions in today's business world.

SUMMARY: *Labor unions* are organizations that seek to protect employee interests by negotiating with employers for better wages and benefits, improved working conditions, and increased job security. The foundation of unionization is strength in numbers, giving workers the opportunity to negotiate on a more equal footing with company management. From an employee's perspective, unions offer the tangible benefits of greater compensation and benefits and the intangible benefits of solidarity and recognition. From an employer's perspective, unions can present challenges in terms of costs and flexibility, ultimately creating concerns about a firm's ability to compete against companies that have lower costs and greater agility. Union membership in the private sector peaked many years ago and isn't likely to recover anytime soon.

CRITICAL THINKING: (1) Why is it so difficult to come up with a single conclusive answer about the effects of unionization on business productivity? (2) How do labor relations demonstrate the stresses inherent in the stakeholder model?

IT'S YOUR BUSINESS: (1) Union supporters often talk about the need for greater democracy in the workplace. Explain why you agree or disagree with this sentiment. (2) Would you rather be promoted on the basis of seniority or of merit? Why?

KEY TERMS TO KNOW: labor relations, labor unions, seniority, work rules

---

7 | **LEARNING OBJECTIVE**

Describe the use of workforce analytics in HR management.

workforce analytics
The application of big data and analytics to workforce management.

Thriving in the Digital Enterprise: Workforce Analytics

Improving the tactical efficiency and strategic value of HR management requires accurate data and the ability to extract useful insights from that data. **Workforce analytics**, also called *people analytics*, applies the tools of big data and analytics across the full scope of HR management, from recruiting and hiring to training and development to compensation and employee benefits.[85] These systems are designed to give HR leaders the answers to such as questions as[86]

- Are we attracting the kind of talent we need in order to meet our business objectives?
- Are we bringing that talent on board in a fast and cost-effective way? Where are the biggest bottlenecks in our hiring process? Are we losing out on top candidates, and if so, why?
- What are our most productive channels for finding new employees?
- Which candidates are most likely to respond to our recruiting efforts (see Exhibit 11.10)?
- Are we at risk of losing our existing talent? Which employees are most likely to leave? What steps can we take to keep our top performers?

EXHIBIT 11.10   **Workforce Analytics**

Workforce analytics can be used throughout the employee life cycle, beginning with recruiting. This system from Engage Talent helps recruiters predict target candidates that are most likely to respond to a recruiting effort.

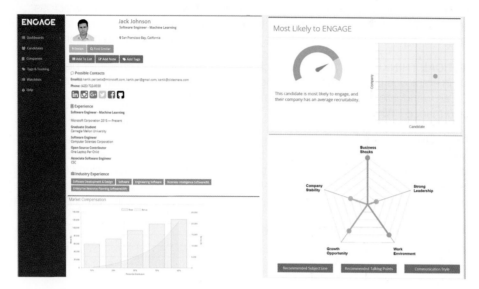

- Which employees have the potential to move into leadership positions?
- Are we evaluating incoming candidates and current employees fairly and objectively?
- Are we compensating employees fairly and objectively?
- Are we making smart investments with our compensation and benefit programs?
- How do our employees contribute to the business?
- How well does our current talent pool align with future business needs? What new skills do we need to develop or hire for?

As you can see, these insights are a combination of performance measurements and *predictive analytics* that help managers make better decisions. By emphasizing objective, data-driven decision-making, workforce analytics can also help companies overcome instances of explicit and implicit bias in hiring, compensation, and promotion opportunities.[87]

Workforce analytics can also be a valuable tool whenever major shifts occur in the workforce. For example, if two companies or two divisions within a company are preparing to merge, managers can compile and compare the skills inventories of both workforces to find areas of overlap.[88]

Moving to data-driven HR also gives companies the opportunity to conduct controlled experiments with clearly measurable results. Google, for instance, has long been an innovator in workforce analytics. The company was once notorious for its lengthy and convoluted interviewing process, which could drag out for as long as nine months and involve numerous interviews. After conducting some experiments and analyzing the data, the company discovered that with only four interviews it could predict with 86 percent confidence whether a candidate was a good choice. As a result, the average *time to hire* dropped from 6 months to 45 days.[89]

Google's data analytics also uncovered some interesting connections between education and employee performance. After learning that employees from a wide range of colleges and universities could excel at the company, it broadened its recruiting focus beyond the prestigious private universities where it had originally focused. And it discovered that grades and test scores were not terribly useful in predicting performance. The ability to learn on the job turned out to be a more important predictor of success than past performance on standardized tests.[90]

✓ CHECKPOINT

LEARNING OBJECTIVE 7: Describe the use of workforce analytics in HR management.

SUMMARY: Workforce analytics applies the tools of big data and analytics across the full scope of HR management with the goal of making more objective, fact-based decisions regarding hiring, promotions, compensation, and other HR matters.

CRITICAL THINKING: (1) Attributes such as grit, creativity, and character play a big role in employee performance. How might companies measure such attributes? (2) Can workforce analytics tools give managers a full picture of employee performance? Why or why not?

IT'S YOUR BUSINESS: (1) If you are interviewing at a company that places a lot of weight on grades and where you went to college, but you don't meet those criteria particularly well, what steps could you take to make a positive impression? (2) If you don't fit the "template" that a particular company has a reputation of using to select employees, would you bother applying for work there? Why or why not?

KEY TERM TO KNOW: workforce analytics

BEHIND THE SCENES

Aligning a Workforce with a Diverse Customer Base

Delivering quality health care is difficult enough, given the complexities of technology, government regulations, evolving scientific and medical understanding, and the variability of human performance. It becomes even more daunting when you add the challenges of communication among medical staff and between patients and their caregivers, which often takes place under stressful circumstances. Those communication efforts are challenging in an environment where everyone speaks the same language and feels at home in a single cultural context—and they're infinitely more complex in the United States, whose residents identify with dozens of different cultures and speak several hundred languages.

The Oakland-based health-care system Kaiser Permanente has been embracing the challenges and opportunities of diversity since its founding in 1945. It made a strong statement with its very first hospital when it refused to follow the then-common practice of segregating patients by race. Now, as the largest not-for-profit health system in the United States, Kaiser Permanente's client base includes more than 10 million members from over 100 distinct cultures.

At the core of Kaiser Permanente's approach is *culturally competent care*, which it defines as "health care that acknowledges cultural diversity in the clinical setting, respects members' beliefs and practices, and ensures that cultural needs are considered and respected at every point of contact." These priorities are woven into the company's organizational culture, structure, and business practices.

Delivering this standard of care requires a mix of skills and knowledge that range from an awareness of medical issues of concern to specific cultures to language fluency (and translation skills in more than 100 languages) to the awareness needed to handle cultural traditions and values in a sensitive manner. Kaiser Permanente's Centers of Excellence in Culturally Competent Care at facilities around the country are a good example of the effort the company makes to serve its diverse clientele. Each center focuses on one or more cultures prominent in a given locale, with a particular emphasis on improving care outcomes for population segments that have historically been underserved.

The company believes that effectively serving a diverse client base requires an equally diverse staff. As Bernard Tyson explains, "The rich diversity of our organization reflects the diversity of the people we serve each and every day." Nearly half the executive team are women, for example, and people of color make up nearly 60 percent of the company's workforce.

The company's success at attracting and supporting a top-flight workforce is reflected in the many employment-related awards it has won. In addition to being acknowledged by numerous diversity-related organizations, Kaiser Permanente has been recognized for being a military-friendly employer, as one of the best places for information-technology professionals, and as a top employer for healthy employee lifestyles.

In addition to helping the company communicate more effectively with its customers, the strategic emphasis on diversity and inclusion is good for business. Its target market segments also happen to be among the country's fastest-growing demographic groups, and Kaiser Permanente's ability to connect with these audiences gives it an important competitive advantage.[91]

Critical Thinking Questions

11-1. In addition to its employment-related awards, Kaiser Permanente has also received dozens of awards for the quality of the health care it provides to clients. What are the implications of such recognition on the quality of work life at the company?

11-2. Would health-care professionals require a different level or different type of support from their employers than professionals in other industries? Why or why not?

11-3. What is the significance of Kaiser Permanente being recognized for having one of the best employee wellness programs in the nation?

Learn More Online

Visit **www.kaiserpermanentejobs.org** and read about working at Kaiser Permanente. What impression do you get of the company? In what ways does the company support its employees? How does Kaiser Permanente compare to other employers that you might be considering?

End of Chapter

KEY TERMS

bonus (338)
commissions (339)
compensation (337)
contingent employees (330)
diversity (325)
diversity and inclusion initiatives (327)
employee assistance program (EAP) (340)
employee benefits (339)
employee retention (330)
employee stock-ownership plan (ESOP) (340)
401(k) plan (340)
glass ceiling (322)
human resources (HR) management (320)
job description (329)
job specification (329)
labor relations (341)
labor unions (341)
layoffs (333)
new-employee orientation (336)
onboarding (336)

pension plans (340)
performance reviews (334)
profit sharing (339)
quality of work life (QWL) (323)
recruiting (331)
retirement plans (339)
salary (337)
seniority (342)
sexism (326)
sexual harassment (320)
skills inventory (336)
stock options (340)
succession planning (329)
termination (333)
360-degree review (336)
turnover rate (329)
wages (338)
work rules (343)
workforce analytics (344)
work–life balance (323)

TEST YOUR KNOWLEDGE

Questions for Review

11-4. What are some common employee benefits?

11-5. What are the differences between a job description and a job specification?

11-6. Why is succession planning an essential HR function?

11-7. How do bonuses differ from commissions?

11-8. What is the glass ceiling?

11-9. What is the purpose and duration of an onboarding program?

11-10. How does big data assist workforce management?

Questions for Analysis

11-11. What does it mean to align a workforce with a company's business objectives?

11-12. Why is it important that all employees have access to the same networking opportunities with senior management?

11-13. How would employees achieving work-life balance benefit businesses?

11-14. Why do some employers offer comprehensive benefits even though the costs of doing so have risen significantly in recent years?

11-15. Are clear diversity and inclusion policies sufficient to ensure a supportive and inclusive workplace? Explain your answer.

11-16. Why would a company spend money on an employee assistance program?

11-17. Why would HR managers be concerned with employee retention?

11-18. Why is it in a company's best interests to break down the glass ceiling?

11-19. **Ethical Considerations.** Corporate headhunters have been known to raid other companies of their top talent to fill vacant or new positions for their clients. Is it ethical to contact the CEO of one company in an attempt to lure him or her to join the management team of another company?

Questions for Application

11-20. Assume that you are the manager of human resources at a manufacturing company that employs about 500 people. A recent cyclical downturn in your industry has led to financial losses, and top management is talking about laying off workers. Several supervisors have come to you with creative ways of keeping employees on the payroll, such as sharing workers with other local companies. Why might you want to consider this option? What other options exist besides layoffs?

11-21. When you begin interviewing as you approach graduation, you will need to analyze job offers that include a number of financial and nonfinancial elements. Which of these aspects of employment are your top three priorities: a good base wage, bonus or commission opportunities, profit-sharing potential, rapid advancement opportunities, flexible work arrangements, good health-care insurance coverage, or a strong retirement program? Which of these elements would you be willing to forgo in order to get your top three?

11-22. What steps could you take as the owner of a small software company to foster "temporary loyalty" from the independent programmers you frequently hire for short durations (one to six months)?

11-23. **Concept Integration.** Of the five levels in Maslow's hierarchy of needs, which is satisfied by offering salary? By offering health-care benefits? By offering training opportunities? By offering flexible work arrangements?

EXPAND YOUR KNOWLEDGE

Discovering Career Opportunities

If you pursue a career in human resources, you'll be deeply involved in helping organizations find, select, train, evaluate, and retain employees. You have to like people and be a good communicator to succeed in HR. Is this field for you? Find job postings for positions in the field of human resources, and then answer the following questions.

11-24. What educational qualifications, technical knowledge, or specialized skills are applicants for these jobs expected to have? How do these requirements fit with your background and educational plans?

11-25. Next, look at the responsibilities and duties described for each job. What do you think you would be doing on an average day in these jobs? Does the work in each job sound interesting and challenging?

11-26. Now think about how you might fit in one of these positions, based on what you can surmise about the daily challenges and long-term prospects. Considering your answers to these questions, which of the HR jobs seems to be the closest match for your personal style?

Intelligent Business Technology: Blind Auditions

To minimize the potential for biased decision-making early in the recruiting process, some companies now use *blind auditions* or *blind assessments*, in which they evaluate candidates' basic skill sets before knowing anything about their age, gender, education, or personal history. Research one of the systems or methods now in use, and write a brief summary of its capabilities, benefits, and limitations.

PRACTICE YOUR SKILLS

Resolving Ethical Dilemmas

Traditionally, your business has favored candidates who have attended certain schools within 10 miles of the main site of its operations, and hired such candidates as its regular employees. For managerial positions, the business has recruited from just five universities in the country—universities that have connections with the business and place students in it for a year's work experience. This "safe recruitment" policy has worked well over the past couple of decades, but the HR department is acutely aware that many promising applicants have been rejected purely because they came from some other school or university. How would you go about changing the recruitment system? What are the drawbacks of the current system being used by the business?

Growing as a Professional

Much of what you learn in business courses focuses on how to be a good manager and a good leader. However, it's equally important to learn how to be a good employee and a good follower, particularly in your early years on the job. Being a good follower isn't demeaning but rather an indication of your ability and willingness to contribute to a larger cause. Key skills include understanding and following instructions, meeting commitments, seeking guidance when you need it, managing yourself well so that you're not a "high-maintenance" member of the team, keeping your ego in check, and doing your part to help a team or department succeed even if you don't completely agree with its goals or methods. Consider all the situations in which you now participate as someone who is expected to follow a leader. This could be at work, in athletics, in team projects for your classes, or as a member of your family, for instance. Think about your role in these situations and identify how to be the best "employee" you can be.

Sharpening Your Communication Skills

As the HR director of a business based in the United Kingdom, you are concerned about how your organization can make the best use of its senior talent. A quarter of your senior management is over 65. It is not uncommon for senior managers to work into their early seventies. At some point, you will have to assist them in their transition into retirement. So, you need to establish a succession planning. This is vital to the organization's continuing success and for the older employees' health and happiness. Draft a short memo outlining your concerns and suggesting how you might begin to organize succession planning (make up any details you need). Suggest a timeframe for monitoring the activities mentioned in the succession planning.

Building Your Team Skills

Appraisals or performance monitoring is an important part of employment. In teams assigned by your instructor, each member should conduct an appraisal of the other member's performance so far at college or university. As part of the process, take turns to talk about each other's efforts and build a personal development plan based on the findings from your appraisal session.

Developing Your Research Skills

Read the article "The Best Places to Work in 2019" at www.forbes.com, or visit the page "Best Places to Work" at www.glassdoor.com. Various policies implemented in these companies resulted in high engagement and satisfaction among different generations in the workplace. These companies are actively pursuing workforce diversity initiatives as a strategic opportunity. Management of these companies retain talented employees by implementing equal gender opportunities in recruitment and promotion, and higher representation of women at the board.

11-27. Select the top five companies from 2019 and compare their rankings to 2018. What workforce initiatives were implemented that enabled these companies to emerge as the best companies in 2019? Were there any significant changes in the workforce diversity initiatives? How do the initiatives differ?

11-28. What would be the main constraint(s) of small- and medium-size (SME) companies to achieve high engagement of workforce diversity? How important are these initiatives to SMEs as opposed to global companies?

11-29. Research newspapers (print or online editions) to identify the top five companies in your country. In what ways does workforce diversity differ among them? Do you think the leaders of these companies will promote or discourage workforce diversity at the workplace? Why?

Writing Assignments

11-30. How is management likely to change as companies increasingly use contingent workers instead of full-time employees?

11-31. What are some ways that pay-for-performance schemes could backfire if a company doesn't set them up carefully or effectively manage the factors that affect employee performance?

ENDNOTES

1. "Local and National Diversity Programs," Kaiser Permanente, accessed 11 May 2018, kp.org; Bernard J. Tyson, "Diversity and Inclusion Are in Kaiser Permanente's DNA," Kaiser Permanente, accessed 11 March 2016, kp.org; Marianne Aiello, "Diversity No Gimmick in Kaiser Permanente Ad Campaign," *HealthLeaders Media*, 25 November 2015, www.healthleadersmedia.com; "Top Reasons to Join Kaiser Permanente as a Woman in Tech," Kaiser Permanente, accessed 11 May 2018, kp.org; "Kaiser Permanente—Achieving Our Mission and Growing the Business Through the National Diversity Agenda," Catalyst, 25 January 2011, www.catalyst.org; "DiversityInc Top 50" and "Diversity Leadership: Dr. Ronald Copeland, Kaiser Permanente," DiversityInc, accessed 11 March 2016, www.diversityinc.com; "Census Bureau Reports at Least 350 Languages Spoken in U.S. Homes," U.S. Census Bureau, 3 November 2015, www.census.gov.

2. Gary Dessler, *Human Resource Management*, 15th ed. (New York: Pearson, 2017), 3.

3. Aaron Pressman, "Can AT&T Retrain 100,000 People?" *Fortune*, 15 March 2017, fortune.com.

4. Paul R. Daugherty and H. James Wilson, *Human + Machine: Reimagining Work in the Age of AI* (Boston: Harvard Business Review Press, 2018), Kindle locations 1500–1608.

5. "Sexual Harassment at Work," FindLaw, accessed 12 May 2018, employment.findlaw.com.

6. Michael Alison Chandler, "Men Account for Nearly 1 in 5 Complaints of Workplace Sexual Harassment with the EEOC," *Washington Post*, 8 April 2018, www.washingtonpost.com.

7. Leslie Josephs, "68 Percent of Flight Attendants Say They Have Experienced Sexual Harassment on the Job," *CNBC*, 10 May 2018, www.cnbc.com.

8. Alexis Krivkovich, Kelsey Robinson, Irina Starikova, Rachel Valentino, and Lareina Yee, "Women in the Workplace 2017," *McKinsey Quarterly*, October 2017, www.mckinsey.com.

9. Julie Creswell and Kevin Draper, "5 More Nike Executives Are Out amid Inquiry into Harassment Allegations," *New York Times*, 8 May 2018, www.nytimes.com; Jena McGregor, "As Sexual-Harassment Allegations Multiply, H.R. Departments Seek a New Playbook," *Seattle Times*, 1 December 2017, www.seattletimes.com.

10. Elizabeth C. Tippett, "Nike's #MeToo Moment Shows a Better Approach to Tackling Sexual Harassment," MarketWatch, 4 May 2018, www.marketwatch.com; McGregor, "As Sexual-Harassment Allegations Multiply, H.R. Departments Seek a New Playbook."

11. Dominic Barton and Lareina Yee, "How Companies Can Guard Against Gender Fatigue," *McKinsey Quarterly*, February 2018, www.mckinsey.com; Dominic Barton and Lareina Yee, "Time for a New Gender-Equality Playbook," *McKinsey Quarterly*, February 2017, www.mckinsey.com.

12. "Women CEOs of the S&P 500," Catalyst, 13 May 2018, www.catalyst.org.

13. Krivkovich, Robinson, Starikova, Valentino, and Yee, "Women in the Workplace 2017."

14. Krivkovich, Robinson, Starikova, Valentino, and Yee, "Women in the Workplace 2017"; "Women in the Workplace 2016," *McKinsey Quarterly*, September 2017, www.mckinsey.com.

15. Krivkovich, Robinson, Starikova, Valentino, and Yee, "Women in the Workplace 2017."

16. Melinda Gates, "We're Sending Our Daughters into a Workplace Designed for Our Dads," LinkedIn, 26 September 2017, www.linkedin.com.

17. "Highlights of Women's Earnings in 2016," U.S. Bureau of Labor Statistics, August 2017, www.bls.gov.

18. Christina Hoff Sommers, "No, Women Don't Make Less Money Than Men," *The Daily Beast*, 1 February 2014, www.thedailybeast.com.

19. Lydia Dishman, "The Other Wage Gap: Why Men in Female-Dominated Industries Still Earn More," *Fast Company*, 8 April 2015, www.fastcompany.com.

20. *An Analysis of Reasons for the Disparity in Wages Between Men and Women*, U.S. Department of Labor Employment Standards Administration, 12 January 2009, 1.

21. Danielle Paquette, "The Gender Wage Gap Just Shrank for the First Time in a Decade," *Washington Post*, 15 September 2017, www.washingtonpost.com; Hanna Rosin, "The Gender Wage Gap Lie," *Slate*, 30 August 2013, www.slate.com.

22. Laura Colby and Hugh Son, "JPMorgan Joins U.S. Banks Showing Pay Gap for Women of Only 1%," *Bloomberg*, 23 February 2018, www.bloomberg.com.

23. Dessler, *Human Resource Management*, 438.

24. David Mendlewicz, "People Don't Take HR Seriously; Here's Why That's Dangerous," *Workforce*, 20 July 2017, www.workforce.com.

25. Erika Fry and Claire Zillman, "HR Is Not Your Friend," *Fortune*, 1 March 2018, fortune.com.

26. Fry and Zillman, "HR Is Not Your Friend."

27. Frank Bafaro, Diana Ellsworth, and Neel Gandhi, "The CEO's Guide to Competing Through HR," *McKinsey Quarterly*, July 2017, www.mckinsey.com.

28. Richard D. Bucher, *Diversity Consciousness: Opening Our Minds to People, Cultures, and Opportunities*, 4th ed. (New York: Pearson, 2015), 50; Nancy R. Lockwood, "Workplace Diversity: Leveraging the Power of Difference for Competitive Advantage," *HR Magazine*, June 2005, special section, 1–10.

29. Marjorie Derven, "Diversity & Inclusion Are Essential to a Global Virtual Team's Success," *TD*, July 2016, 54–59; David Rock, Heidi Grant, and Jacqui Grey, "Diverse Teams Feel Less Comfortable—and That's Why They Perform Better," *Harvard Business Review*, 22 September 2016, hbr.org.

30. Vivian Hunt, Lareina Yee, Sara Prince, and Sundiatu Dixon-Fyle, "Delivering Through Diversity," *McKinsey*, January 2018, www.mckinsey.com.

31. Michael R. Carrell, Everett E. Mann, and Tracey Honeycutt-Sigler, "Defining Workforce Diversity Programs and Practices in Organizations: A Longitudinal Study," *Labor Law Journal*, Spring 2006, 5–12.

32. "How We Operate: Diversity," Merck, accessed 15 May 2018, www.merck.com.

33. Rock, Grant, and Grey, "Diverse Teams Feel Less Comfortable—and That's Why They Perform Better."

34. Richard Fry, "Millennials Projected to Overtake Baby Boomers as America's Largest Generation," Pew Research Center, 1 March 2018, www.pewresearch.org; Michael Dimock, "Defining Generations: Where Millennials End and Post-Millennials Begin," Pew Research Center, 1 March 2018, www.pewresearch.org.

35. "Age Discrimination," U.S. Equal Employment Opportunity Commission, accessed 14 May 2018, www.eeoc.gov.

36. Elizabeth Dwoskin, "T-Mobile, Amazon, and Other Companies Are Accused of Using Facebook Ads to Exclude Older Americans from Jobs," *Washington Post*, 20 December 2017, www.washingtonpost.com.

37. "Sex-Based Charges: FY 1997–FY 2017," U.S. Equal Employment Opportunity Commission, accessed 14 May 2018, www.eeoc.gov.

38. "First Step: Gender Identity in the Workplace," Catalyst, June 2015, www.catalyst.org.

39. Paul Taylor, "The Next America," Pew Research Center, 10 April 2014, www.pewressarch.com; "More Than 300 Counties Now 'Majority–Minority'," press release, U.S. Census Bureau, 9 August 2007, www.census.gov; Robert Kreitner, *Management*, 9th ed. (Boston: Houghton Mifflin, 2004), 84.

40. "Race-Based Charges: FY 1997–FY 2017," U.S. Equal Employment Opportunity Commission, accessed 14 May 2018, www.eeoc.gov.

41. "Table 3. Median Usual Weekly Earnings of Full-Time Wage and Salary Workers by Age, Race, Hispanic or Latino Ethnicity, and Sex, First Quarter 2018 Averages, Not Seasonally Adjusted," U.S. Bureau of Labor Statistics, 14 May 2018, www.bls.gov.

42. Kabrina Krebel Chang, "What Companies Can Do When Work and Religion Conflict," *Harvard Business Review*, 15 March 2016, hbr.org; Vadim Liberman, "What Happens When an Employee's Freedom of Religion Crosses Paths with a Company's Interests?" *Conference Board Review*, September/October 2007, 42–48.

43. Susana Rinderle, "5 Proven Strategies to Guarantee Your Diversity Initiative Produces Results," *Workforce*, 13 December 2017.

44. Dessler, *Human Resource Management*, 98.

45. Dessler, *Human Resource Management*, 98.

46. Dessler, *Human Resource Management*, 130–134.

47. Shari Randall, "Succession Planning Is More Than a Game of Chance," *Workforce Management*, accessed 1 May 2004, www.workforce.com.

48. Steven Prokesch, "Reinventing Talent Management: How GE Uses Analytics to Guide a More Digital, Far-Flung Workforce," *Harvard Business Review*, September–October 2017, 54–55.

49. Carol Kinsey Gorman, "Why IBM Brought Remote Workers Back to the Office—and Why Your Company Might Be Next," *Forbes*, 12 October 2017, www.forbes.com.

50. Ian Cook, "Measure Quality of Hire with These Three Critical Factors," Visier, 17 November

51. Rachel Gray, "7 Ways Recruiters Can Make Sourcing Candidates a Breeze," Top Echelon, 3 May 2017, www.topechelon.com; James Hu, "5 Ways Recruiters Find Candidates," Jobscan, 30 June 2017, www.jobscan.co; Alexia Elejalde-Ruiz, "Employers Reach Out to the Next Generation of Workers: Gen Z," *Seattle Times*, 15 April 2017, www.seattletimes.com.

52. "The ADA: Your Employment Rights as an Individual with a Disability," U.S. Equal Employment Opportunities Commission, accessed 13 May 2018, www.eeoc.gov.

53. "The Age Discrimination in Employment Act of 1967," U.S. Equal Employment Opportunity Commission, accessed 13 May 2018, www.eeoc.gov.

54. Jessica A. Lee, "Beyond Millennials: Valuing Older Adults' Participation in Innovation Districts," Brookings, 22 March 2017, www.brookings.edu.

55. Dessler, *Human Resource Management*, 323.

56. Mark Feffer, "'Employment at Will' Isn't a Blank Check to Terminate Employees You Don't Like," Society for Human Resource Management, 7 November 2017, www.shrm.org; Dessler, *Human Resource Management*, 325; "Age Discrimination," U.S. Equal Employment Opportunities Commission, accessed 13 May 2018, www.eeoc.gov; Elizabeth Olson, "Shown the Door, Older Workers Find Bias Hard to Prove," *New York Times*, 7 August 2017, www.nytimes.com.

57. Lori Goler, Janelle Gale, and Adam Grant, "Let's Not Kill Performance Evaluations Yet," *Harvard Business Review*, November 2016, 91–94; Aliah D. Wright, "SAP Ditches Annual Reviews," *HR Magazine*, October 2016, 16.

58. Jon Wolper, "A New Look for Performance Reviews," *TD*, May 2016, 12; Jeff Kauflin, "Hate Performance Reviews? Good News: They're Getting Shorter and Simpler," *Forbes*, 9 March 2017, www.forbes.com; Lori Goler, "Why Facebook Is Keeping Performance Reviews: Interaction," *Harvard Business Review*, January/February 2017, 18.

59. "Salesforce: Perks and Programs," Great Place to Work, accessed 28 March 2018, reviews.greatplacetowork.com.

60. Richard L. Daft, *Management*, 13th ed. (New York: Pearson, 2018), 403.

61. Gloria Sims, "Employee Onboarding vs. Orientation: Why You Need Both," Insperity, accessed 15 May 2018, www.insperity.com.

62. "Moving up with Enterprise: Our Promote-from-Within Philosophy," Enterprise Holdings, accessed 14 May 2018, go.enterpriseholdings.com.

63. Dessler, *Human Resource Management*, 349.

64. Vadim Liberman, "What About the Rest of Us?" *Conference Board Review*, Summer 2011, 40–47.

65. "Executive Paywatch," AFL-CIO, accessed 15 May 2018, www.aflcio.org; "Survey Results Show a Median CEO Pay Ratio of 140:1," Equilar, 1 February 2018, www.equilar.com.

66. Dessler, *Human Resource Management*, 404.

67. Susan Brink, "What Country Spends the Most (and Least) on Health Care per Person?" *NPR*, 20 April 2017; Melissa Etehad and Kyle Kim, "The U.S. Spends More on Healthcare Than Any Other Country—But Not with Better Health Outcome," *Los Angeles Times*, 18 July 2017, www.latimes.com.

68. Tami Luhby, "How Obamacare Affects Everyone," *CNN Money*, 27 March 2017, money.cnn.com; Dessler, *Human Resource Management*, 426.

69. "Choosing a Retirement Plan: Defined Benefit Plan," U.S. Internal Revenue Service, 3 August 2017, www.irs.gov; "Ultimate Guide to Retirement," *CNN Money*, accessed 15 May 2018, money.cnn.com.

70. Jeff Madura, *Personal Finance*, 6th ed. (New York: Pearson, 2017), 540; Dessler, *Human Resource Management*, 432.

71. "ESOP Statistics," ESOP Association, accessed 19 April 2015, www.esopassociation.org; Dessler, *Human Resource Management*, 406.

72. Tim Stobierski, "Your Quick Guide to Understanding Everything About Your Employee Stock Options," *Forbes*, 17 March 2017, www.forbes.com.

73. "FMLA (Family & Medical Leave)," U.S. Department of Labor, accessed 15 May 2018, www.dol.gov.

74. Tess Taylor, "About Employee Assistance Programs (EAP)," *The Balance Careers*, 30 December 2017, www.thebalancecareers.com.

75. Based in part on Michael R. Carrell and Christina Heavrin, *Labor Relations and Collective Bargaining: Cases, Practice, and Law*, 9th ed. (Upper Saddle River, N.J.: Pearson Prentice Hall, 2010), 76–81.

76. "Union Members Summary," U.S. Bureau of Labor Statistics, 19 January 2018, www.bls.gov.

77. "The Union Advantage: Facts and Figures," Service Employees International Union, accessed 15 November 2013, www.seiu.org.

78. Mariah DeForest, "Will Your Employees Go Union?" *Foundry Management & Technology*, September 2008, 36–39.

79. Carrell and Heavrin, *Labor Relations and Collective Bargaining*, 79.

80. Carrell and Heavrin, *Labor Relations and Collective Bargaining*, 316–317.

81. Michelle Krebs, "Study: Union Work Rules Cost Big Three," *Edmunds AutoObserver*, 20 June 2007, www.autoobserver.com.

82. Christos Doucouliagos and Patrice Laroche, "What Do Unions Do to Productivity: A Meta-analysis," *Industrial Relations*, October 2003, 650–691.

83. Jon Talton, "Heyday for Unions in the Rearview Mirror," *Seattle Times*, 3 September 2011, www.seattletimes.com; "Union Members Summary," U.S. Bureau of Labor Statistics, 19 January 2018, www.bls.gov.

84. David Rolf, "The Labor Movement as We Know It Is Dying. Here's How It Can Survive." *PBS*, 5 September 2016, www.pbs.org.

85. "Workforce Analytics," Gartner, accessed 15 May 2018, www.gartner.com.

86. Ian Cook, "Workforce Analytics 101," Visier, 16 November 2016, www.visier.com.

87. Richard Stolz, "Driving Employee Diversity with Workforce Analytics," *Employee Benefit News*, 11 April 2018, www.benefitnews.com.

88. Ian Cook, "HR Intelligence," *Retail Merchandiser*, July/August 2017, 86–87.

89. "Open Sourcing Google's HR Secrets," *Knowledge@Wharton*, 26 February 2016, knowledge.wharton.upenn.edu.

90. "Open Sourcing Google's HR Secrets."

91. See note 1.

Previous chapters have explored how companies organize and create products; now it's time to see how they attract and satisfy customers. Chapter 12 introduces the marketing concept and the key decisions companies make regarding overall marketing strategy. Chapter 13 looks at the decisions involved in defining products and setting prices, and Chapter 14 addresses customer communication and the wholesaling and retailing elements of product distribution.

12

The Art and Science of Marketing

LEARNING OBJECTIVES After studying this chapter, you will be able to

1 Define *marketing*, and explain its role in society.

2 Identify five trends that help define contemporary marketing.

3 Differentiate between consumer buying behavior and organizational buying behavior.

4 Define *strategic marketing planning*, and identify the four basic options for pursuing new marketing opportunities.

5 Identify the four steps in crafting a marketing strategy.

6 Describe the four main components of the marketing mix.

7 Define *marketing analytics*, and characterize its use in contemporary marketing.

MyLab Intro to Business
Improve Your Grade!
If your instructor is using MyLab Intro to Business, visit **www.pearson.com/mylab/intro-to-business**.

BEHIND THE SCENES

Lego: Creating the World's Top Toy Brand One Brick at a Time

Lego's chief marketing officer, Julia Goldin, oversees the company's multifaceted marketing efforts.

CARTA image/Alamy Stock Photo

www.lego.com

Creative kids and grownups in a mood to build things have a wide variety of construction sets, blocks, and other put-it-together toys to choose from. All around the world, though, the set that more people reach for is Lego. In the mood to build a pizza van? A farm? A beauty salon? The *Millennium Falcon* from *Star Wars*? A functional robot or an unnamable contraption from your own imagination? Lego has you covered.

How did a small company from Denmark launch what both *Fortune* magazine and the British Association of Toy Retailers proclaimed the toy of the century? (That would be the 20th century, and the company is going even stronger in the 21st century.) It's difficult to decide which is more impressive—how the company created this smash hit of a product, or how it continues to change with the times, decade after decade, without ever fundamentally changing.

If you were Julia Goldin, chief marketing officer at Lego, how would you help the company continue its amazing run, more than six decades after introducing its iconic bricks, even as kids and grownups alike are tempted by an ever-growing array of video games, apps, and other digital entertainment? How would you guide the product development effort to feed customers' insatiable appetite for new sets and designs? What decisions would you make regarding pricing and distribution? And how would you use the wide array of media options available to foster close relationships with Lego's millions of fans?[1]

INTRODUCTION

Lego (profiled in the chapter-opening Behind the Scenes) illustrates the complex challenge of fashioning an appealing blend of products, prices, distribution methods, and customer communication efforts—the essential elements of marketing. This chapter introduces the basic concepts of marketing; products and pricing are addressed in Chapter 13, and customer communication and product distribution are covered in Chapter 14.

Marketing in a Changing World

Marketing requires a wide range of skills, including research and analysis, strategic planning, and persuasive communication. On the job and in the media, you will encounter many uses of the term *marketing*, from the broad and strategic to the narrow and tactical. However, noted marketing professors Philip Kotler and Gary Armstrong offer a definition that does a great job of highlighting the contemporary flavor of customer-focused marketing: **Marketing** is "the process by which companies create value for customers and build strong customer relationships in order to capture value from customers in return."[2] The ideas of *value*, the *exchange* of value, and lasting *relationships* are essential elements of successful marketing.

In addition to goods and services, marketing applies to people, places, causes, and not-for-profit organizations. Politicians and celebrities constantly market themselves. So do places that want to attract residents, tourists, and business investments. *Place marketing* describes efforts to market geographic areas ranging from neighborhoods to entire countries. *Cause-related marketing* promotes a cause or a social issue—such as physical fitness, cancer awareness, or environmental sustainability—while also promoting a company and its products.

THE ROLE OF MARKETING IN SOCIETY

Marketing plays an important role in society by helping people satisfy their needs and wants and by helping organizations determine what to produce.

Needs and Wants

Individuals and organizations have a wide variety of needs, from food and water necessary for survival to transaction-processing systems that make sure a retail store gets paid for all the credit card purchases it records. As a consumer, you experience needs any time there are differences or gaps between your actual state and your ideal state. You're hungry and you don't want to be hungry: You need to eat. **Needs** create the motivation to buy products and therefore are at the core of any discussion of marketing. For instance, Lego responds to the innate need to create that many people have.

Your **wants** are based on your needs but are more specific. Producers do not create needs, but they do try to shape your wants by exposing you to attractive choices. For instance, when you *need* some food, you may *want* a Snickers bar, an orange, or a seven-course dinner at the swankiest restaurant in town. If you have the means, or *buying power*, to purchase the product you want, you create *demand* for that product.[3]

Exchanges and Transactions

When you participate in the **exchange process**, you trade something of value (usually money) for something else of value. When you make a purchase, you encourage the producer of that item to create or supply more of it. In this way, supply and demand tend toward balance, and society obtains the goods and services that are most satisfying. When the exchange actually occurs, it takes the form of a **transaction**. Party A gives Party B $1.29 and gets a medium Coke in return. A trade of values takes place.

---

1 LEARNING OBJECTIVE
Define *marketing*, and explain its role in society.

marketing
The process of creating value for customers and building relationships with those customers in order to capture value back from them.

REAL-TIME UPDATES
Learn More by Visiting This Website

Marketing advice from specialists in marketing, sales, and service

HubSpot publishes a blog packed with useful advice for marketing professionals. Go to **real-timeupdates.com/bia9** and select Learn More in the Students section.

needs
Differences between a person's actual state and his or her ideal state; they provide the basic motivation to make a purchase.

wants
Specific goods, services, experiences, or other entities that are desirable in light of a person's experiences, culture, and personality.

exchange process
The act of obtaining a desired object or service from another party by offering something of value in return.

transaction
An exchange of value between parties.

Although most transactions in today's society involve money, money is not necessarily required. Bartering or trading, which predates the use of cash, is making a big comeback thanks to the internet. Hundreds of online barter exchanges are now in operation in the United States alone. Intermediaries such as BizX (www.bizx.com) facilitate cashless trading among multiple members through a system of credits and debits. For instance, an advertising agency might trade services to a dairy farm, which then trades products to a catering company, which then trades services to the advertising agency. By eliminating the need for trading partners to have exactly complementary needs at exactly the same time, these exchanges make it easy for companies to put excess capacity to productive use and to buy and sell without using cash.[4] Some countries also barter for goods and services when they lack the ready cash or credit to pay.[5]

The Four Utilities

utility
The power of a good or service to satisfy a human need.

To encourage the exchange process, marketers enhance the appeal of their goods and services by adding **utility**, which is any attribute that increases the value that customers place on the product. When companies change raw materials into finished goods, they are creating *form utility* desired by consumers. When supermarkets provide fresh, ready-to-eat dishes as an alternative to food ingredients, they are creating form utility. In other cases, marketers try to make their products available when and where customers want to buy them, creating *time utility* and *place utility*. Couriers such as FedEx and UPS create time utility, whereas espresso stands in office buildings and ATMs in shopping malls create place utility. Services such as Apple's iTunes create both time and place utility: You can purchase music any time and from just about anywhere. The final form of utility is *possession utility*—the satisfaction that buyers get when they actually possess a product, both legally and physically. Mortgage companies, for example, create possession utility by offering loans that allow people to buy homes they could otherwise not afford.

THE MARKETING CONCEPT

Business's view of the marketing function has evolved dramatically over the decades. In years past, many companies pursued what was known as the *product concept*, which was essentially to focus on the production of goods and then count on customers to figure out which products they needed and take the steps to find and purchase them. In other words, the product concept views the primary purpose of a business as making things, not satisfying customers. As markets evolved and competition heated up, the *selling concept*, which emphasizes building a business by generating as many sales transactions as possible, began to take over. The customer features more prominently in the selling concept, but only as a target to be sold to, not as a partner in a mutually satisfying relationship.

marketing concept
An approach to business management that stresses customer needs and wants, seeks long-term profitability, and integrates marketing with other functional units within the organization.

In contrast, today's most successful companies tend to embrace the **marketing concept**, the idea that companies should respond to customers' needs and wants while seeking long-term profitability and coordinating their own marketing efforts to achieve the company's long-term goals (see Exhibit 12.1). The term **relationship marketing** is often applied to these efforts to distinguish them from efforts that emphasize production or sales transactions.

relationship marketing
A focus on developing and maintaining long-term relationships with customers, suppliers, and distribution partners for mutual benefit.

Relationship marketing looks beyond individual transactions with a view toward *customer lifetime value*—the predicted cumulative profit that a customer represents over the expected span of the business relationship.[6] Looking at lifetime value, rather than trying to maximize the profit from isolated transactions, is smart business: Keeping existing customers is usually much cheaper and easier than finding new customers, and satisfied customers are the best promotion a company can hope for, particularly given the power of social media and social commerce.

customer loyalty
The degree to which customers continue to buy from a particular retailer or buy the products of a particular manufacturer or service provider.

One of the most significant goals of relationship marketing is **customer loyalty**, the degree to which customers continue to buy from a particular retailer or buy the products offered by a particular manufacturer. However, this notion of loyalty is even more important in the opposite direction: Customers will continue to buy from a company only if the company is loyal to them, year in and year out, by meeting their needs and treating them with fairness and respect.

EXHIBIT 12.1	The Selling Concept Versus the Marketing Concept

Firms that practice the selling concept sell what they make rather than making what the market wants. In contrast, firms that practice the marketing concept determine the needs and wants of a market and deliver the desired product or service more effectively and efficiently than competitors do.

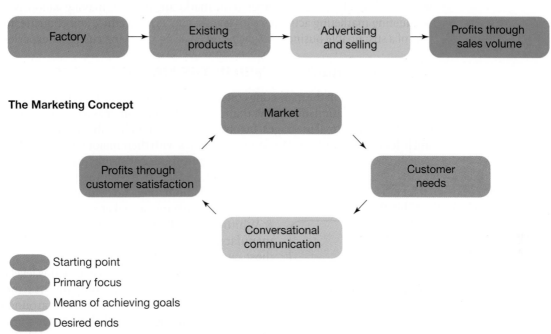

Source: Based in part on Philip Kotler and Gary Armstrong, *Principles of Marketing*, 17th ed. (New York: Pearson, 2018), 12.

 CHECKPOINT

LEARNING OBJECTIVE 1: Define marketing, and explain its role in society.

SUMMARY: Marketing can be defined as "the process by which companies create value for customers and build strong customer relationships in order to capture value from customers in return." The marketing function guides a company in selecting which products to offer, how much to charge for them, how to distribute them to customers, and how to promote them to potential buyers. Marketing plays an important role in society by helping people satisfy their needs and wants and by helping organizations determine what to produce.

CRITICAL THINKING: (1) Should every company see long-term relationships with customers as vitally important? Why or why not? (2) Would a company that already dominates its markets ever care about the marketing concept? Why or why not?

IT'S YOUR BUSINESS: (1) What is your reaction when you feel as though you're being "sold to" by a company that is clearly more interested in selling products than in meeting your needs as an individual consumer? (2) Do you want to have a "relationship" with any of the companies that you currently patronize as a customer? Why or why not?

KEY TERMS TO KNOW: marketing, needs, wants, exchange process, transaction, utility, marketing concept, relationship marketing, customer loyalty

2 **LEARNING OBJECTIVE**
Identify five trends that help define contemporary marketing.

Challenges in Contemporary Marketing

As business has progressed from the product concept to the selling concept to the marketing concept—with the critical emergence of social commerce—the role of marketing has become increasingly complicated. You'll read about some specific challenges in this and the next two chapters, but here are five general issues that many marketing organizations are wrestling with today: involving the customer in the marketing process, making data-driven decisions, conducting marketing activities with greater concern for ethics and etiquette, marketing as part of a sustainable business strategy, and creating satisfying customer experiences.

INVOLVING THE CUSTOMER IN THE MARKETING PROCESS

A central element in the marketing concept is involving the customer as a partner in a mutually beneficial relationship, rather than treating the customer as a passive recipient of products and promotional messages. Involving the customer has always been relatively easy for small, local companies and for large companies with their major customers. For instance, a neighborhood bistro or coffee shop can prepare foods and drinks just the way its regular customers want, and satisfied customers are happy to tell friends and relatives about their favorite places to eat and drink. At the other extreme, a maker of jet engines such as Pratt & Whitney or Rolls-Royce works closely with its airplane manufacturing customers to create exactly the products those customers want.

The challenge has been to replicate this level of intimacy on a broader scale, when a company has thousands of customers spread across the country or around the world. Two sets of technologies have helped foster communication and collaboration between companies and their customers.

REAL-TIME UPDATES
Learn More by Visiting This Website

See what's on the minds of today's marketing leaders

CMO, published for chief marketing officers, explores key marketing challenges. Go to **real-timeupdates.com/bia9** and select Learn More in the Students section.

customer relationship management (CRM)
A type of information system that captures, organizes, and capitalizes on all the interactions that a company has with its customers.

social commerce
The creation and sharing of product-related information among customers and potential customers.

voice of the customer (VoC)
Everything that current and potential customers are saying and writing about a company and its products; also refers to efforts to capture all this feedback.

The first is **customer relationship management (CRM)** systems, which capture, organize, and capitalize on all the interactions that a company has with its customers, from marketing surveys and advertising through sales orders and customer support. A CRM system functions like an institutional memory for a company, allowing it to record and act on the information that is pertinent to each customer relationship.

CRM can be a powerful means to foster relationships, but to a certain degree, conventional CRM simply computerizes an existing way of doing business. Companies can also support and enable **social commerce** using social networks, *user-generated content* such as online reviews and videos, Twitter updates, and other social media. These tools let customers communicate with companies, with each other, and with other influencers in the marketplace such as prominent bloggers and journalists. As Chapter 14 explains, advertisers are learning to enable and participate in these online conversations, rather than blasting out messages to passive audiences as they did in the past. Both CRM and social media are important elements of *marketing analytics* (see page 374).

CRM, social media, and other "listening" efforts aim to capture the **voice of the customer (VoC)**—everything that current and potential customers are saying and writing about a company and its products (or would like to say about them if given the chance). Companies with comprehensive and systematic VoC programs enjoy significantly higher financial results than companies that fail to integrate customer input.[7] As you'll read at the end of the chapter, much of Lego's success stems from a complete turnaround in its willingness to listen to customers and involve them in product planning.

MAKING DATA-DRIVEN MARKETING DECISIONS

Learning more about customers is one aspect of the larger challenge of collecting, analyzing, and using data to make marketing decisions. Marketers in every industry would like to have better insights for making decisions and better ways of measuring the results of every marketing initiative. Pioneering retailer John Wannamaker said 100 years ago that "half the money I spend on advertising is wasted. The trouble is, I don't know which half."[8] Companies have been wrestling with this conundrum ever since.

EXHIBIT 12.2	**AI-Enhanced Marketing Research**

Innovative research techniques such as Affectiva's *Emotion AI* give marketers new insights into consumer attitudes and behaviors.

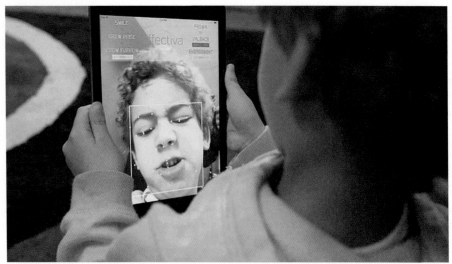

Affectiva

The challenge of measuring the effectiveness of marketing efforts focuses largely on the matter of **attribution**—how much does each marketing activity contribute to sales and other marketing metrics? In some instances, attribution can be fairly straightforward, such as when you send digital coupons via a shopping app and measure how many customers redeem the coupons at purchase. However, the full scope of a company's marketing activities is often so broad and multidimensional that attributing impact to each element can be quite difficult. This is one of the key challenges being taken up by marketing analytics.

The process of gathering and analyzing *market intelligence* about customers, competitors, and related marketing issues through any combination of methods is known as **marketing research**. Research techniques range from the basic to the exotic, from simple surveys to advanced statistical techniques to artificial intelligence (AI) methods such as Affectiva's Emotion AI that you read about in Chapter 1 (see Exhibit 12.2). Exhibit 12.3 on the next page lists the common categories of marketing research methods.

attribution
The contribution a given marketing activity makes to sales and other marketing goals.

marketing research
The collection and analysis of information for making marketing decisions.

MARKETING WITH GREATER CONCERN FOR ETHICS AND ETIQUETTE

Under pressure to reach and persuade buyers in a business environment that gets more fragmented and noisy all the time, marketers occasionally step over the line and engage in practices that are rude, manipulative, or even downright deceptive. The result is an increasing degree of mistrust of and hostility toward advertising and other marketing activities.[9]

To avoid intensifying the vicious circle in which marketers keep doing the same old things, only louder and longer—leading customers to get angrier and more defensive—smart marketers are looking for a better way. Social commerce shows a lot of promise for redefining marketing communication from one-way promotion to two-way conversation. Another hopeful sign is **permission-based marketing**, in which marketers invite potential or current customers to receive information in areas that genuinely interest them. Many websites and email newsletters now take this approach, letting visitors sign up for specific content streams with the promise that they won't be bombarded with information they don't care about. In the European Union, permission for email marketing is no longer voluntary; the General Data Protection Regulation prohibits commercial email without the recipient's explicit consent.[10]

REAL-TIME UPDATES
Learn More by Visiting This Website

See how Google is trying to solve the attribution puzzle

Google Attribution attempts to measure marketing success across the entire digital marketplace. Go to **real-timeupdates.com/bia9** and select Learn More in the Students section.

permission-based marketing
A marketing approach in which firms first ask permission to deliver messages to an audience and then promise to restrict their communication efforts to those subject areas in which audience members have expressed interest.

EXHIBIT 12.3	Marketing Research Techniques

Marketers can use a wide variety of techniques to learn more about customers, competitors, and threats and opportunities in the marketplace.

Technique	Examples
Observation	Any in-person, mechanical, or electronic technique that monitors and records behavior, including website usage tracking, television viewing monitoring, and social media monitoring.
Ethnographic research	A branch of anthropology that studies people in their daily lives to learn about their needs, wants, and behaviors in real-life settings.
Surveys	Data collection efforts that measure responses from a representative subset of a larger group of people; can be conducted in person (when people with clipboards stop you in a mall, that's called a *mall intercept*), over the phone, by mail or email, or online. Designing and conducting a meaningful survey requires thorough knowledge of statistical techniques such as *sampling* to ensure valid results that truly represent the larger group. For this reason, many of the simple surveys that you see online these days do not produce statistically valid results.
Interviews and focus groups	One-on-one or group discussions that try to probe deeper into issues than a survey typically does. *Focus groups* involve a small number of people guided by a facilitator while being observed or recorded by researchers. Unlike surveys, interviews and focus groups are not designed to collect statistics that represent a larger group; their real value is in uncovering issues that might require further study.
Process data collection	Any method of collecting data during the course of other business activities, including warranty registrations, sales transactions, gift and loyalty program usage, and customer service interactions.
Experiments	Controlled scenarios in which researchers adjust one or more variables to measure the effect these changes have on customer behavior. *Test marketing*, the launch of a product under real-world conditions but on a limited scale (such as in a single city), is a form of experimental research.
Neuromarketing studies	Research that measures brain activity and other biological responses while customers are viewing or interacting with products, websites, or other elements; can help explain the subconscious decisions that people have difficulty describing in surveys, interviews, and focus groups.
Emotion AI	AI-based techniques that identify emotional states based on facial expressions and voice inflections.
Reverse engineering	Disassembling competitive products to see how they are designed and manufactured.

Sources: Philip Kotler and Gary Armstrong, *Principles of Marketing*, 17th ed. (New York: Pearson, 2018), 108–114; Raphaelle March, "Why Market Research Is Flawed, and What You Can Do About It," *Disruption*, 12 April 2018, www.disruptionhub.com; Michael R. Solomon, Greg W. Marshall, and Elnora W. Stuart, *Marketing: Real People, Real Choices*, 9th ed. (New York: Pearson, 2018), 96–110.

The widespread adoption of social media has also increased the attention given to transparency, which in this context refers to a sense of openness, of giving all participants in a conversation access to the information they need in order to accurately process the messages they are receiving. Two important concerns in this regard are *native advertising* and *stealth marketing*. Native advertising, also known as *sponsored content*, is advertising material that is designed to look like regular news stories, articles, or social media posts. The U.S. Federal Trade Commission requires companies to label such material as sponsored content if it is likely to mislead consumers into thinking it is "anything other than an ad."[11] Industry groups such as the Word of Mouth Marketing Association and the Interactive Advertising Bureau give their members specific guidelines to help prevent consumer confusion.[12]

MARKETING AS PART OF A SUSTAINABLE BUSINESS STRATEGY

Chapter 4 points out that sustainable development is a core value for a growing number of companies and a strong purchase consideration for many customers, too.[13] Marketing plays a key role in educating customers about a company's sustainable business practices, including the qualities of individual products.

Of course, there is an inherent conflict regarding sustainability and marketing because an important way for everyone to live more sustainably is to use less of everything. However, effectively marketing the products of a sustainable business can be an ethical and environmental "win" if it encourages consumers and business to use more sustainable alternatives. Moreover, the marketing process itself can be managed more sustainably, such as by limiting the energy (electricity and fossil fuels) and physical resources used in advertising, sales activities, and promotional events.

CREATING SATISFYING CUSTOMER EXPERIENCES

Today's consumers expect the goods and services they buy to be satisfying, of course, but increasingly they also expect the experience of acquiring those products to be satisfying as well. Companies are responding to this expectation by evaluating the **customer experience** at every **touchpoint**, which is any point of interaction—online, on the phone, or in person—between a company and its current and potential customers.[14] The customer experience (which you'll often see referred to as *CX*) begins the moment a buyer starts to consider a purchase and extends through the entire time the customer owns the good or experiences the service. Particularly in markets in which products are fairly similar, customer experience can be an important competitive differentiator.

All customers want a buying experience that is fast, simple, and *seamless*, meaning they can smoothly transition from each step to the next. Poorly designed and managed processes can detract from the experience in many ways, such as if customers are forced to fill out lengthy forms, click through page after page on a website, explain their needs to more than one person, dig through confusing information about products, wait in long lines, or wait for salespeople or customer support staff to respond to messages.

The quality of interpersonal communication is important as well. Rude or inattentive salespeople can turn customers off instantly, and the company may lose their business permanently. Buyers also expect salespeople to be experts in the products they sell, particularly in business-to-business marketing.[15] In addition, customers differ in how they would like to interact; some prefer to talk with a sales specialist in person or on the phone, some are fine with online chat, and others prefer to do everyone online with no human interaction—and an increasing number of those customers want to shop through a conversational voice interface on their mobile devices rather than by typing on a website.[16]

Customers of particular goods and services expect a certain type of shopping and buying experience as well. For instance, shoppers don't expect a discount retail store to be a luxurious environment with expensive carpeting, soft lighting, and soothing music, but they do expect that in high-end department stores and specialty retailers.

Managing the customer experience is not an easy task, because customers judge the total experience of moving through all the touchpoints. Even if a company performs well at every stage through the purchase decision, a missed delivery date or a rude support technician can sour the whole experience. It's the entire *customer journey* that counts.[17]

Customers want a buying experience that is fast, simple, and seamless.

Jim West/Alamy Stock Photo

customer experience
The cumulative effect of the customer journey from presales exploration through purchase through product use and ownership.

touchpoint
Any point of interaction—online, on the phone, or in person—between a company and its current and potential customers.

REAL-TIME UPDATES
Learn More by Watching This Presentation

Map the customer journey

Get step-by-step advice for mapping the customer journey from touchpoint to touchpoint. Go to **real-timeupdates.com/bia9** and select Learn More in the Students section.

 CHECKPOINT

LEARNING OBJECTIVE 2: Identify five trends that help define contemporary marketing.

SUMMARY: First, today's companies are working to involve customers in the marketing process, because giving customers greater involvement is essential to relationship marketing and the marketing concept. Increasingly, this involvement is enabled by social commerce—customers using social media to converse with companies and each other. Second, marketers are trying to reduce the guesswork and gut feel in marketing and make it more data driven. Third, public opinion of business in general and marketing in particular is at a low point these days, prompting many professionals to take a closer look at their business practices and relationships with customers to make sure they are marketing with a sense of etiquette and ethics. Fourth, marketing plays an important role in business's increasing emphasis on sustainability. Fifth, companies are paying closer attention to the customer experience as a way to differentiate their offerings.

CRITICAL THINKING: (1) How can technology help companies replicate the community feel of a small neighborhood business on a global scale? (2) Why do its critics consider stealth marketing to be unethical?

IT'S YOUR BUSINESS: (1) Are you so loyal to any brands or companies that you refuse to accept substitutes—so much so that if you can't have your favorite product, you'll do without? If so, what is it about these products that earns your continued loyalty? (2) Have you ever been a target of stealth marketing? If so, how did you feel about the company after you learned you had been marketed to without your knowledge?

KEY TERMS TO KNOW: customer relationship management (CRM), social commerce, voice of the customer (VoC), attribution, marketing research, permission-based marketing, customer experience, touchpoint

---

[3] **LEARNING OBJECTIVE**

Differentiate between consumer buying behavior and organizational buying behavior.

consumer market
Individuals or households that buy goods and services for personal use.

organizational market
Companies, government agencies, and other organizations that buy goods and services either to resell or to use in the creation of their own goods and services.

Understanding Today's Customers

Today's customers, both individual consumers and organizational buyers, are a diverse and demanding group, with little patience for marketers who do not understand them or will not adapt business practices to meet their needs. The first step toward understanding customers is recognizing the purchase and ownership habits of the **consumer market**, made up of individuals and families who buy for personal or household use, and the **organizational market**, composed of companies and a variety of noncommercial institutions, from local school districts to the federal government.

Exhibit 12.4 models two decision-making paths that buyers can take when they perceive the need to make a purchase, one for routine purchases and one for new, unusual, or highly significant purchases. Consumers and organizations can follow either path, depending on a specific purchase. Broadly speaking, however, organizational buyers tend to approach purchasing in a more rational, data-driven fashion, because organizational choices are nearly always about functional and financial value.

THE CONSUMER DECISION PROCESS

Consumers can use three distinct approaches to making purchase decisions, depending on the situation:[18]

- **Cognitive decision-making.** This is the rational, data-driven approach shown in Exhibit 12.4. When you compare labels in the grocery store to see which item is healthier or read the technical specifications for a smartphone, you are engaged in cognitive decision-making. This approach takes time and energy, so we tend to reserve it for purchases that have significant impacts on our lives, or when a situation makes it easy to do so (as with standardized nutrition labeling on food products). Note that cognitive decision-making isn't necessarily *logical*. People can attempt to make rational, data-driven decisions but commit a variety of logical errors while doing so. For instance, research into the influence of online reviews indicates that when confronted

EXHIBIT 12.4	**Buyer Decision-Making**

The steps buyers go through on the way to making a purchase vary widely, based on the magnitude of the purchase and the significance of the outcome. In general, businesses and other organizations use a more formal and more rational process than consumers, and nonroutine decisions in either sector require more time and energy than routine decisions. Defining *routine* is not a simple matter, however; a company might make huge resupply purchases automatically, whereas a consumer might spend days agonizing over a pair of jeans.

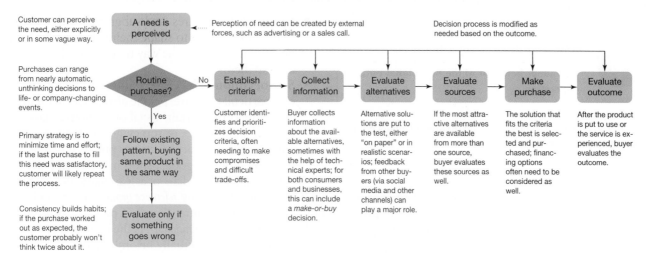

with the choice between Product A with a lot of reviews but only a middling ranking and Product B with high ratings but fewer reviews, they lean toward Product A—the more popular but lower-rated product.[19]

- **Habitual decision-making.** In many instances, consumers simply buy the same model or brand they bought last time, without going through the process of choosing. Sometimes this is more or less automatic. If a product performed satisfactorily for you last week, it probably will this week, so you buy it again without much thought. For some other purchases, habitual choice is a conscious matter of brand loyalty—when only one particular brand will do.[20]
- **Affective decision-making.** Affective choices are those driven primarily by moods and emotions.[21] You can get a good idea of the power of affective choice by studying all the advertising you are exposed to: Marketers know that fear, hope, pride, joy, love, sadness, disgust, envy, embarrassment, and other emotions are powerful forces.

Consumers can use more than one approach for a given purchase, and the approaches can yield conflicting answers. If you have ever thoughtfully compared the functional and financial benefits of two products and then purchased the less logical one because it made you feel better about yourself, you understand this phenomenon.

Even in situations in which consumers gather plenty of information and appear to be going through the cognitive decision-making process, they are sometimes using the cognitive model to justify an affective decision they have already made. For instance, you might see some jaw-dropping sports car glide past you on the street, and in that split second—before you even start "thinking" about it—you've already decided to buy one just like it. Sure, you'll gather brochures, research online, test-drive other models, and so on, but chances are you're not really evaluating alternatives. Instead, your rational mind is just looking for evidence to support the decision that your emotional mind has already made.

Moreover, consumers make all kinds of decisions that are hard to explain by rational means. We might spend two weeks gathering and carefully analyzing data on $50 video game controllers but choose a college with a $20,000 annual tuition because a best friend is going there. As a result, at one time

When you compare labels or otherwise do research before a purchase, you are engaging in cognitive decision-making.

d13/Shutterstock

cognitive dissonance
Tension that exists when a person's beliefs don't match his or her behaviors; a common example is *buyer's remorse*, when someone regrets a purchase immediately after making it.

or another, all consumers suffer from **cognitive dissonance**, which occurs when one's beliefs and behaviors don't match. A common form of this situation is *buyer's remorse*, in which one makes a purchase and then regrets doing so—sometimes immediately after the purchase.

You can start to understand why so many decisions seem mysterious from a rational point of view if you consider all the influences that affect purchases:

REAL-TIME UPDATES

Learn More by Listening to This Podcast

Consumer behavior of the first digital-native generation

The buying habits of the Millennial generation were shaped by growing up with digital technology. Go to **real-timeupdates.com/bia9** and select Learn More in the Students section.

- **Culture.** The cultures (and subgroups within cultures) that people belong to shape their values, attitudes, and beliefs and influence the way they respond to the world around them.
- **Socioeconomic level.** In addition to being members of a particular culture, people also perceive themselves as members of a certain social or economic class—be it upper, middle, lower, or somewhere in between. In general, members of various classes pursue different activities, buy different goods, shop in different places, and react to different media—or at least like to believe they do.
- **Reference groups.** Individuals are influenced by *reference groups* that provide information about product choices and establish values that they perceive as important. Reference groups can be either *membership* or *aspirational*. As the name suggests, membership groups are those to which consumers actually belong, such as families, networks of friends, clubs, and work groups. In contrast, consumers are not members of aspirational reference groups but use them as role models for style, speech, opinions, and various other behaviors.[22] For instance, millions of consumers buy products that help them identify with popular musicians or professional athletes—and avoid buying products they associate with socially undesirable groups.
- **Situational factors.** These factors include events or circumstances in people's lives that are more circumstantial but that can influence buying patterns. Such factors can range from having a coupon to celebrating a holiday to being in a bad mood. If you've ever indulged in "retail therapy" to cheer yourself up, you know all about situational factors—and the buyer's remorse that often comes with it.
- **Self-image.** Many consumers tend to believe that "you are what you buy," so they make or avoid choices that support their desired self-images. Marketers capitalize on people's need to express their identity through their purchases by emphasizing the image value of goods and services.

THE ORGANIZATIONAL CUSTOMER DECISION PROCESS

Marginon/Alamy Stock Photo

Organizational purchases often involve teams of decision-makers and an extensive evaluation process.

The purchasing behavior of organizations is easier to understand than the purchasing behavior of consumers because it's more clearly driven by economics and influenced less by subconscious and emotional factors. Here are some of the significant ways in which organizational purchasing differs from consumer purchasing:[23]

- **An emphasis on economic payback and other rational factors.** Much more so than with consumer purchases, organizational purchases are carefully evaluated for financial impact, reliability, and other objective factors. Organizations don't always make the best decisions, of course, but their choices are usually based on a more rational analysis of needs and alternatives. This isn't to say that emotions play little or no role in the purchase decision, however; organizations don't make decisions, people do. Fear of change, fear of failure, excitement about new technologies, and the pride of being associated with world-class suppliers are just a few of the emotional factors that can influence organizational purchases.

- **A formal buying process.** From office supplies to new factories, most organizational purchases follow a formal buying process, particularly in mid- to large-size companies.
- **Greater complexity in product usage.** Even for the same types of products, organizational buyers have to worry about factors that consumers may never consider, such as user training, compatibility with existing systems and procedures, established purchasing agreements, and compliance with government regulations. Also, organizations sometimes continue to use products long after better substitutes become available if the costs and complexity of updating outweigh the advantages of the newer solutions. With all these other considerations in play, organizations don't always buy the product with the highest performance or the most capability but rather look for the overall best fit with their needs.
- **The participation and influence of multiple people.** Except in the very smallest of businesses, the purchase process usually involves a group of people. This team can include end users, technical experts, the manager with ultimate purchasing authority, and a professional purchasing agent whose job includes researching suppliers, negotiating prices, and evaluating supplier performance. Multiple family members play a part in many consumer purchases, of course, but not with the formality apparent in organizational markets.
- **Close relationships between buyers and sellers.** Close relationships between buyers and sellers are common in organizational purchasing. In some cases, employees of the seller even have offices inside the buyer's facility to promote close interaction.

 CHECKPOINT

LEARNING OBJECTIVE 3: Differentiate between consumer buying behavior and organizational buying behavior.

SUMMARY: Classical economic theory suggests that consumers follow a largely rational process of recognizing a need, searching for information, evaluating alternatives, making a purchase, and evaluating the product after use or consumption. However, consumers can engage in three separate types of decision-making, often at the same time: cognitive, habitual, and affective. Much of this decision-making happens subconsciously and is driven to a large degree by emotion, culture, and situational factors. Organizational buying behavior comes much closer to the rational model of classical economics because purchases are usually judged by their economic value to the organization. The most significant ways in which organizational purchasing differs from consumer purchasing are an emphasis on economic payback, a formal buying process, greater complexity in product usage, purchasing groups, and close relationships between buyers and sellers.

CRITICAL THINKING: (1) Can business-to-business marketers take advantage of new insights into consumer buying behavior? Why or why not? (2) How could families and individual consumers benefit from adopting some elements of organizational buying behavior?

IT'S YOUR BUSINESS: (1) Do you read product reviews online before making important purchases? Why or why not? Have you ever contributed to social commerce by posting your own reviews or product advice? (2) Why did you buy the clothes you are wearing at this very moment?

KEY TERMS TO KNOW: consumer market, organizational market, cognitive dissonance

strategic marketing planning
The process of examining an organization's current marketing situation, assessing opportunities and setting objectives, and then developing a marketing strategy to reach those objectives.

Identifying Market Opportunities

With insights into your customers' needs and behaviors, you're ready to begin planning your marketing strategies. **Strategic marketing planning** is a process that involves three steps: (1) examining the current marketing situation, (2) assessing opportunities and setting objectives, and (3) crafting a marketing strategy to reach those objectives (see Exhibit 12.5). Companies often document their planning efforts in a formal *marketing plan*.

EXAMINING THE CURRENT MARKETING SITUATION

Examining the current marketing situation includes reviewing past performance (how well each product is doing in each market where it is sold), evaluating the competition, examining a firm's internal strengths and weaknesses, and analyzing the external environment.

Reviewing Performance

Unless you're starting a new business, your company has a history of marketing performance. Maybe sales have slowed in the past year, maybe you've had to cut prices so much that you're barely earning a profit, or maybe sales have been strong and you have money to invest in new marketing activities. Reviewing where you are and how you got there is critical, because you want to learn from your mistakes and repeat your successes—without getting trapped in mindsets and practices that need to change for the future, even if they were successful in the past.

Evaluating Competition

In addition to reviewing past performance, you must evaluate your competition. If you own a Burger King franchise, for example, you need to watch what McDonald's and Wendy's are doing. You also have to keep an eye on Taco Bell, KFC, Pizza Hut, and other restaurants, as well as pay attention to any number of other ways your customers might satisfy their hunger—including fixing a sandwich at home. Furthermore, you need to watch for trends that could

EXHIBIT 12.5	**The Strategic Marketing Planning Process**

Strategic marketing planning can involve a range of major decisions that fall into three general steps: (1) examining the current marketing situation, (2) assessing opportunities and setting objectives, and (3) developing a marketing strategy. The nature of these steps depends on the products and markets involved; for example, emerging markets and mature markets have very different sets of customer and competitor dynamics.

1. Examine current marketing situation
- Review past performance
- Evaluate competition
- Examine strengths and weaknesses
- Analyze the business environment

2. Assess opportunities and set objectives
- Explore product and market opportunities
- Set sales targets that are invigorating while being realistic

3. Develop marketing strategy
- Divide market into strategically productive segments
- Choose best-fit segments
- Identify ideal position in minds of target customers
- Develop marketing mix

affect your business, such as consumer interest in organic foods or in locally produced ingredients.

Examining Internal Strengths and Weaknesses

Successful marketers try to identify sources of competitive advantage and areas that need improvement. They look at such factors as financial resources, production capabilities, distribution networks, brand awareness, business partnerships, managerial expertise, and promotional capabilities. (Recall the discussion of SWOT analysis on page 220.) On the basis of your internal analysis, you will be able to decide whether your business should (1) limit itself to those opportunities for which it possesses the required strengths or (2) challenge itself to reach higher goals by acquiring and developing new strengths.

Analyzing the External Environment

Marketers must also analyze trends and conditions in the business environment when planning their marketing strategies. For example, customer decisions are greatly affected by interest rates, inflation, unemployment, personal income, and savings rates. When consumers are confident about their financial prospects, they are more likely to buy luxury items and take out loans to purchase homes or cars. Conversely, when consumer confidence wanes, buyers are more likely to pull back and perhaps indulge only in "affordable luxuries" such as their favorite coffee drink.

ASSESSING OPPORTUNITIES AND SETTING OBJECTIVES

After you've examined the current marketing situation, you're ready to assess your marketing opportunities and set your objectives. Successful companies are always on the lookout for new marketing opportunities, which can be classified into four options (see Exhibit 12.6).[24] **Market penetration** involves selling more of your existing products into the markets you already serve. A **product development** strategy involves creating new products for those current markets, and **market development** is selling your existing products to new markets. Finally, **diversification** involves creating new products for new markets.

Generally speaking, these four options are listed in order of increasing risk. Market penetration can be the least risky, because your products already exist and the market has already demonstrated some level of demand for them. At the other extreme, creating new products for new markets is usually the riskiest choice of all because you encounter

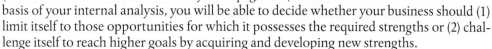

REAL-TIME UPDATES
Learn More by Reading This Article

Looking for opportunities in customer dissatisfaction

Find out why a big competitor's unhappy customers can be a small company's best sales prospects. Go to **real-timeupdates.com/bia9** and select Learn More in the Students section.

market penetration
Selling more of a firm's existing products in the markets it already serves.

product development
Creating new products for a firm's current markets.

market development
Selling existing products to new markets.

diversification
Creating new products for new markets.

EXHIBIT 12.6	**Pursuing Market Opportunities**

Every company has four basic options when it comes to pursuing market opportunities. The arrows show the increasing level of risk, from the lowest to the highest.

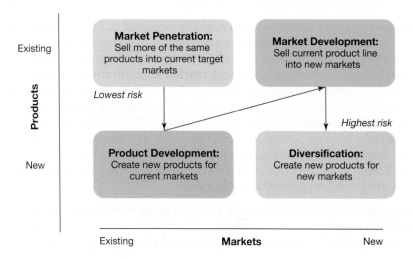

uncertainties in both dimensions (you may fail to create the product you need, and the market might not be interested in it).

After you've framed the opportunity you want to pursue, you are ready to set your marketing objectives. A common marketing objective is to achieve a certain level of **market share**, which is a firm's portion of the total sales within a market (market share can be defined either by number of units sold or by sales revenue).

market share
A firm's portion of the total sales in a market.

 CHECKPOINT

LEARNING OBJECTIVE 4: Define *strategic marketing planning,* and identify the four basic options for pursuing new marketing opportunities.

SUMMARY: Strategic marketing planning involves three steps: (1) examining the current marketing situation (including past performance, competition, internal strengths and weaknesses, and the external environment); (2) assessing market opportunities and setting marketing objectives; and (3) developing a marketing strategy to reach those objectives. The four basic options for pursuing market opportunities are market penetration (selling more of existing products in current markets), product development (creating new products for current markets), market development (selling existing products to new markets), and diversification (creating new products for new markets).

CRITICAL THINKING: (1) Why is it important to analyze past performance before assessing market opportunities and setting objectives? (2) Why is diversification considered riskier than market penetration, product development, and market development strategies?

IT'S YOUR BUSINESS: (1) Do you see yourself as a trendsetter in any aspect of your life? (2) How could the four options for pursuing market opportunities be applied to your career planning at various stages in your career? (Think of your skills as the products you have to offer.)

KEY TERMS TO KNOW: strategic marketing planning, market penetration, product development, market development, diversification, market share

---

5 **LEARNING OBJECTIVE**

Identify the four steps in crafting a marketing strategy.

marketing strategy
An overall plan for marketing a product; includes the identification of target market segments, a positioning strategy, and a marketing mix.

market
A group of customers who need or want a particular product and have the money to buy it.

market segmentation
The division of a diverse market into smaller, relatively homogeneous groups with similar needs, wants, and purchase behaviors.

demographics
The study of the statistical characteristics of a population.

Crafting a Marketing Strategy

Using the current marketing situation and your objectives as your guide, you're ready to develop a **marketing strategy**, which consists of dividing your market into *segments,* choosing your *target markets* and the *position* you'd like to establish in those markets, and then developing a *marketing mix* to help you get there.

DIVIDING MARKETS INTO SEGMENTS

A **market** contains all the customers who might be interested in a product and can pay for it. However, most markets contain subgroups of potential customers with different interests, values, and behaviors. To maximize their effectiveness in reaching these subgroups, many companies subdivide the total market through **market segmentation**, grouping customers with similar characteristics, behaviors, and needs. Each of these market segments can then be approached by offering products that are priced, distributed, and promoted in a unique way that is most likely to appeal to that segment. The overall goal of market segmentation is to understand why and how certain customers buy what they buy so that a firm's resources can be used to create and market products in the most efficient manner possible.[25]

Four fundamental factors that marketers use to identify market segments are demographics, psychographics, geography, and behavior:

- **Demographics.** When you segment a market using **demographics**, the statistical analysis of a population, you subdivide your customers according to characteristics such as age, gender, income, race, occupation, and ethnic group.

- **Psychographics.** Whereas demographic segmentation is the study of people from the outside, **psychographics** is the analysis of people from the inside, focusing on their psychological makeup, including attitudes, interests, opinions, and lifestyles. Psychographic analysis focuses on why people behave the way they do by examining such issues as brand preferences, media preferences, values, self-concept, and behavior.

- **Geography.** When differences in buying behavior are influenced by where people live, it makes sense to use **geographic segmentation**. Segmenting the market into geographic units such as regions, cities, counties, or neighborhoods allows companies to customize and sell products that meet the needs of specific markets and to organize their operations as needed.

- **Behavior. Behavioral segmentation** groups customers according to their relationship with products or response to product characteristics. To identify behavioral segments, marketers study such factors as the occasions that prompt people to buy certain products, the particular benefits they seek from a product, their habits and frequency of product usage, and the degree of loyalty they show toward a brand.[26]

> **psychographics**
> Classification of customers on the basis of their psychological makeup, interests, and lifestyles.

> **geographic segmentation**
> Categorization of customers according to their geographical location.

> **behavioral segmentation**
> Categorization of customers according to their relationship with products or response to product characteristics.

Starting with these variables, researchers can also combine types of data to identify target segments with even greater precision, such as merging geographic, demographic, and behavioral data to define specific types of consumer neighborhoods.

CHOOSING YOUR TARGET MARKETS

After you have segmented your market, the next step is to find appropriate target segments, or **target markets**, on which to focus your efforts. Marketers use a variety of criteria to narrow their focus to a few suitable market segments, including the magnitude of potential sales within each segment, the cost of reaching those customers, the fit with a firm's core competencies, and any risks in the business environment.

> **target markets**
> Specific customer groups or segments to whom a company wants to sell a particular product.

Exhibit 12.7 diagrams four strategies for reaching target markets. Companies that practice *undifferentiated marketing* (also known as *mass marketing*) ignore differences among buyers and offer only one product or product line and present it with the same communication, pricing, and distribution strategies to all potential buyers. Undifferentiated marketing has the advantages of simplicity and economies of scale, but it can be less effective at reaching some portions of the market.

EXHIBIT 12.7	**Market-Coverage Strategies**

Four alternative market-coverage strategies are undifferentiated marketing, differentiated marketing, concentrated marketing, and micromarketing.

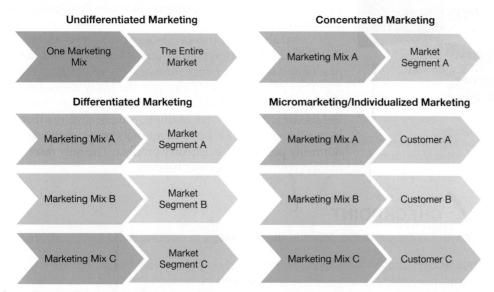

Source: Based on Philip Kotler and Gary Armstrong, *Principles of Marketing*, 17th ed. (New York: Pearson, 2018), 198–200.

By contrast, companies that manufacture or sell a variety of products to several target customer groups practice *differentiated marketing*. This is Toyota's approach, for example, aiming the Toyota brand at a mainstream audience and its Lexus brand at those wanting luxury cars. Differentiated marketing is a popular strategy, but it requires substantial resources because the company has to tailor products, prices, promotional efforts, and distribution arrangements for each customer group. The differentiation should be based on meaningful differences that don't alienate any audiences.

Concentrated marketing focuses on only a single market segment. With this approach, you acknowledge that various other market segments may exist, but you choose to target just one. The biggest advantage of concentrated marketing is that it allows you to focus all your time and resources on a single type of customer (which is why this approach is usually the best option for start-up companies, by the way). The strategy can be risky, however, because you've staked your fortunes on just one segment.

Micromarketing, or *individualized marketing*, is the narrowest strategy of all, in which firms target a single location or even a single customer.[27] This approach can range from producing customizable products to creating *major accounts* sales teams that craft entire marketing programs for each of their largest customers.

Achieving success in any market segment can take time and significant investment, so embracing market segments for the long term is essential. In addition, to avoid spreading its resources too thinly, a company may need to keep its focus narrow in the beginning, then gradually move into additional segments as it builds up its production and support capacity.

STAKING OUT A POSITION IN YOUR TARGET MARKETS

positioning
Managing a business in a way designed to occupy a particular place in the minds of target customers.

After you have decided which segments of the market to enter, your next step is to decide what *position* you want to occupy in those segments. **Positioning** is the process of designing a company's offerings, messages, and operating policies so that both the company and its products occupy distinct and desirable competitive positions in your target customers' minds. For instance, for every product category that you care about as a consumer, you have some ranking of desirability in your mind—you believe that certain colleges are more prestigious than others, that certain brands of shoes are more fashionable than others, that one video game system is better than the others, and so on. Successful marketers are careful to choose the position they'd like to occupy in buyers' minds.

In their attempts to secure favorable positions, marketers can emphasize such variables as product attributes, customer service, brand image (such as reliability or sophistication), price (such as low cost or premium), or category leadership (such as the leading online bookseller). For example, BMW and Porsche work to associate their products with performance, Mercedes Benz with luxury, and Volvo with safety.

A vital and sometimes overlooked aspect of positioning is that although marketers take all kinds of steps to position their products, it is *customers* who ultimately decide on the positioning: They're the ones who interpret the many messages they encounter in the marketplace and decide what they think and feel about each product. For example, you can advertise that you have a luxury product, but if consumers aren't convinced, it's not really positioned as a luxury product. The only result that matters is what the customer believes.

bankerwin/Shutterstock

Marketers try to position their products relative to the competition in customers' minds, but it is customers who ultimately decide how products are positioned.

✓ CHECKPOINT

LEARNING OBJECTIVE 5: Identify the four steps in crafting a marketing strategy.

SUMMARY: Crafting a marketing strategy involves dividing your market into segments, choosing your target markets, identifying the position you hope to achieve, and developing the marketing mix needed to get you there. Segmentation (using demographics, psychographics, geography, and behavior) allows a company to select parts of the market most likely to respond to specific marketing programs. Companies can use one of four approaches to selecting target markets: undifferentiated (mass) marketing, differentiated marketing (with a different marketing mix for each segment), concentrated marketing (focusing on a single market segment), and micromarketing or individualized marketing. A position refers to the position a company or brand occupies in the mind of the target market segments.

CRITICAL THINKING: (1) Would two companies interested in the same group of customers automatically use the same target market approach (such as differentiated or concentrated)? Why or why not? (2) Why aren't marketers ultimately in control of the positions their products achieve in the marketplace?

IT'S YOUR BUSINESS: (1) Think of three car brands or specific models. How are these products positioned in your mind? What terms do you use to describe them? (2) Given your transportation needs in the near future (assuming you will need a car), which model is the most desirable? The least desirable?

KEY TERMS TO KNOW: marketing strategy, market, market segmentation, demographics, psychographics, geographic segmentation, behavioral segmentation, target markets, positioning

The Marketing Mix

After you've segmented your market, selected your target market, and taken steps to position your product, your next task is to develop a marketing mix. A firm's **marketing mix** consists of product, price, distribution, and customer communication (see Exhibit 12.8). (You might also hear references to "the four Ps" of the marketing mix, which is short for products, pricing, place or physical distribution, and promotion. However, with the advent of digital goods and services, distribution is no longer exclusively a physical concern. And many companies now view customer communication as a broader and more interactive activity than the functions implied by *promotion*.)

6 **LEARNING OBJECTIVE**

Describe the four main components of the marketing mix.

marketing mix
The four key elements of marketing strategy: product, price, distribution, and customer communication.

EXHIBIT 12.8 **The Marketing Mix**

The marketing mix consists of four key elements: the products a company offers to potential buyers, the price it asks in return, its methods of distributing those products to customers, and the various efforts it makes to communicate with customers before and after the sale.

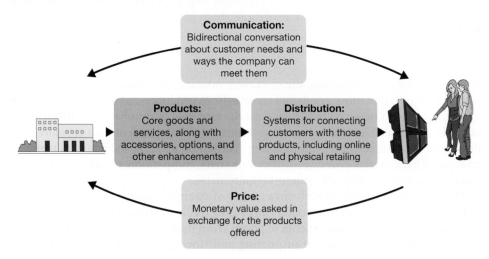

Communication: Bidirectional conversation about customer needs and ways the company can meet them

Products: Core goods and services, along with accessories, options, and other enhancements

Distribution: Systems for connecting customers with those products, including online and physical retailing

Price: Monetary value asked in exchange for the products offered

PRODUCTS

product
A bundle of value that satisfies a customer need or want.

In common usage, *product* usually refers to a tangible good, whereas *service* refers to an intangible performance. However, for the purposes of studying marketing, it is helpful to define **product** as the bundle of value offered for the purpose of satisfying a want or a need in a marketing exchange. In this expanded definition, both tangible goods and intangible services are considered products. The reason for taking this broader view of *product* is that it encourages a more holistic look at the entire offering, which can include the brand name, design, packaging, support services, warranty, ownership experience, and other attributes.

For example, if you buy a pair of $900 Dolce & Gabbana sunglasses with the brand name emblazoned along the side, you are buying much more than a device that holds a couple of protective lenses in front of your eyes. You are buying a shopping and ownership experience that is distinctly different from the experience of buying and owning a pair of $5 sunglasses from a discount drugstore. You are buying the opportunity to feel a particular way about yourself and to present a particular image to the world around you. You are buying the right to brand yourself with the Dolce & Gabbana brand and everything that brand means to you. All these elements constitute the Dolce & Gabbana product. You'll explore products in more detail in Chapter 13.

Chris Leachman/
Alamy Stock Photo

What bundles of benefits are you looking for with the products you buy?

PRICING

price
The amount of money charged for a product or service.

Price, the amount of money customers pay for the product (including any discounts), is the second major component of a firm's marketing mix. Looking back at Kotler and Armstrong's definition of marketing, price is the *value captured* from customers in exchange for the value offered in the product. Setting and managing a product's price is one of the most critical decisions a company must make, because price is the only element in a company's marketing mix that produces revenue; all other elements represent costs. Moreover, setting a product's price not only determines income but also can differentiate a product from the competition. Determining the right price is not an easy task, and marketers constantly worry about whether they've turned away profitable customers by charging too much or "left money on the table" by charging too little.

A number of factors influence pricing decisions, including marketing objectives, government regulations, production costs, customer perceptions, competition, and customer demand. A company's costs establish the minimum amount it can charge, and various external forces establish the maximum. Somewhere in between those two extremes lies an optimum price point. Products also exhibit different levels of *price elasticity*, which is a measure of how sensitive customers are to changes in price. If you've had your eye on virtual reality headsets and see that their prices have dropped by 25 percent, you might be tempted to buy one. In contrast, if the price of broccoli drops by 25 percent, chances are you won't eat more veggies as a result. You can read more about pricing in Chapter 13.

DISTRIBUTION

distribution channels
Systems for moving goods and services from producers to customers; also known as marketing channels.

Distribution is the third element in the marketing mix. It covers the organized networks of firms and systems that move goods and services from producers to final customers. These networks are also known as *marketing channels, marketing intermediaries,* or **distribution channels**. As you can imagine, channel decisions are interdependent with virtually everything else in the marketing mix. Key factors in distribution planning include customer needs and expectations, market coverage, distribution costs, competition, positioning, customer support requirements, and sales support requirements.

Marketing intermediaries perform a variety of essential marketing functions, including providing information to customers, providing feedback to manufacturers, providing sales support, gathering assortments of goods from multiple producers to make shopping easier for customers, and transporting and storing goods. These intermediaries fall into two general categories: *wholesalers* and *retailers*. The basic distinction between them is that wholesalers sell to other companies, whereas retailers sell to individual consumers. Across industries, you can find tremendous variety in the types of wholesalers and retailers, from independent representatives who sell products from several manufacturers to huge distribution companies with national or international scope to purely digital retailers such as Apple's iTunes service. You can read more about distribution in Chapter 14.

CUSTOMER COMMUNICATION

In traditional marketing thought, the fourth element of the marketing mix is **promotion**, all the activities a firm undertakes to promote its products to target customers. The goals of promotion include *informing, persuading,* and *reminding.* Among these activities are advertising in various media, personal selling, public relations, and sales promotion. Promotion may take the form of direct, face-to-face communication or indirect communication through such media as television, radio, magazines, newspapers, direct mail, billboards, transit ads, social media, and other channels.

However, as "Involving the Customer in the Marketing Process" on page 358 points out, forward-thinking companies have moved beyond the unidirectional approach of promotion to interactive customer communication. By talking *with* their customers instead of *at* their customers, marketers get immediate feedback on everything from customer service problems to new product ideas.

Promotion is still a vital part of customer communication, but by encouraging two-way conversations, whether it's two people talking across a desk or via an online network spread across the globe, marketers can also learn while they are informing, persuading, and reminding. Moreover, by replacing "sales pitches" with conversations and giving customers some control over the dialogue, marketers can also help break down some of the walls and filters that audiences have erected after years of conventional marketing promotion.[28] Chapter 14 offers a closer look at customer communication.

For the latest information on marketing principles, visit **real-timeupdates.com/bia9** and select Chapter 12.

promotion
A wide variety of persuasive techniques used by companies to communicate with their target markets and the general public.

CHECKPOINT

LEARNING OBJECTIVE 6: Describe the four main components of the marketing mix.

SUMMARY: The four elements of the marketing mix are product, price, distribution, and customer communication. Products are goods, services, persons, places, ideas, organizations, or anything else offered for the purpose of satisfying a want or need in a marketing exchange. Price is the amount of money customers pay for the product. Distribution is the organized network of firms that move the goods and services from the producer to the customer. Customer communication involves the activities used to communicate with and promote products to target markets.

CRITICAL THINKING: (1) Why is price sometimes referred to as captured value? (2) Why do companies that embrace relationship marketing focus on "customer communication" rather than "promotion"?

IT'S YOUR BUSINESS: (1) If you could buy a product from a website or from a store right down the street and the prices were the same, where would you make your purchase? Why? (2) When buying products, do you tend to seek out products with visible logos (such as the Nike swoosh or the Dolce & Gabbana initials), or do you shun such products? Or do you not care one way or the other? Why?

KEY TERMS TO KNOW: marketing mix, product, price, distribution channels, promotion

7 **LEARNING OBJECTIVE**

Define *marketing analytics*, and characterize its use in contemporary marketing.

marketing analytics
A range of analytical tools and techniques that help marketers plan and evaluate marketing activities.

Thriving in the Digital Enterprise: Marketing Analytics

Marketing analytics refers to a range of tools and techniques that help marketers plan and evaluate marketing activities. (You will also see references to *martech*, short for *marketing technology*.) A key emphasis with marketing analytics is pulling together the multiple tools and data streams that companies often collect over time so that they can get a cohesive, integrated view of their marketing performance.[29]

MAJOR GOALS OF MARKETING ANALYTICS

The primary goals of marketing analytics are to increase revenue and profits while improving the cost effectiveness of the entire marketing effort.[30] Behind all the computer power and mathematical techniques, it's really still about solving the attribution problem that John Wannamaker described more than a century ago. Today's marketers have measurement solutions that Wannamaker could only dream about, but the problem keeps getting more complex as more digital communication channels enter the picture.

As companies work to measure and optimize the marketing effort, they focus on a variety of supporting goals, including these:

- **Tracking the customer journey.** To evaluate marketing effectiveness, companies need to know where customers come from and how they make the journey toward a purchase.[31] For example, one customer might have heard about a product on Twitter, looked at some photos of it on Pinterest, done some more research via Google, been exposed to some targeted ads on Facebook and various websites, chatted with a salesperson or chatbot on the company's website, and eventually clicked through to make a purchase on Amazon. Ideally, a company would like to follow the customer across all these touchpoints.
- **Measuring effectiveness.** The overall effectiveness of the marketing effort is the sum of all the individual components of that effort, from broadcast advertising to digital marketing to personal sales. Exhibit 12.9 defines some of the key *marketing metrics* that companies try to measure. A company's most important metrics are often referred to as *key performance indicators (KPIs)*.
- **Testing and tuning promotional messaging.** With an ability to measure the response to advertising efforts, companies can test and adjust their promotional messaging.[32] This can be done through *A/B tests*, in which one audience segment receives the "A" version of the message and a second segment receives the "B" version.
- **Optimizing the timing and placement of ads.** Just as with messaging, marketing analytics can measure the effectiveness of ad buying and help companies optimize their "ad spend."
- **Prioritizing customers.** Analytics can tell companies which customers are the most valuable in terms of current and potential profitability. A company might then assign the top level of support resources to its highest-priority customers or reward its most loyal customers differently, such as how airline and hotel reward programs work in tiers.[33]
- **Measuring share of customer.** Given how expensive it usually is to acquire new customers, companies try to get as much business as possible from their existing customers. The percentage of a given customer's spending in a particular product category that a company captures is known as *share of customer* or *share of wallet*. Share of customer can be a particularly telling metric because it can reflect the customer's overall journey or experience and involve product quality, support policies, and other elements that aren't always under the marketing department's direct control. A low share of customer can be a warning sign that you're not satisfying customers as well as you need to be, or perhaps they view you as a risk and don't want to rely on you too heavily. It can also signal an opportunity—that customers like what you do but you don't offer enough goods or services to meet their needs.

EXHIBIT 12.9	Marketing Metrics

Here are some of the key marketing metrics that companies use to measure the effectiveness and efficiency of their market efforts. Note that companies and industries may use different labels or calculations for some metrics.

Metric and Meaning	How It Is Calculated
Customer acquisition cost Average cost to acquire a new customer	$$\frac{\text{Total marketing costs during a given period}}{\text{Number of new customers}}$$
Cost per order Average cost of getting individual orders; usually takes a narrower view than customer acquisition cost	$$\frac{\text{Relevant marketing costs during a given period}}{\text{Number of new orders}}$$
Conversion rate General term signifying percentage of audience members who take a targeted action, such as viewing a video or placing an order	$$\frac{\text{Number of times desired customer action is performed}}{\text{Number of opportunities for it to be performed}}$$
Churn rate Percentage of customers lost during a given time period; most commonly used for recurring contracts and subscriptions, such as mobile phone service	$$\frac{\text{Customers at start of period} - \text{customers at end of period}}{\text{Customers at start of period}}$$
Customer lifetime value Total expected revenue or profit from a customer over the expected life span of the business relationship	*Can be calculated in a variety of ways, with varying degrees of mathematical sophistication; here is one simple way to do it:* Average order value $\times$ average orders per year $\times$ expected life span of relationship
Click-through rate The percentage of website visitors or email recipients who click on an ad or link	$$\frac{\text{Number of clickthroughs}}{\text{Number of impressions (instances of an ad or link presented to readers)}}$$
Margin on sales Difference between the price a product is sold at and its cost to the seller; can be expressed as a dollar amount or a percentage	*In dollars:* Revenue $-$ cost of the product $-$ marketing costs *As percentage:* $$\frac{\text{Revenue}}{\text{Costs of the product} + \text{marketing costs}}$$
Redemption rate Rate at which customers redeem coupons or points in a loyalty program	$$\frac{\text{Coupons (or points) redeemed during time period}}{\text{Coupons (or points) issued during time period}}$$
Net promoter score A customer's willingness to recommend a company to a friend, relative, or colleague	*Can be measured on various scales, such as 0 to 10 or −100 to +100.*

Sources: Alex McEachern, "The Easy Way to Calculate Customer Lifetime Value," Smile.io, 2 August 2017, blog.smile.io; Michael R. Solomon, Greg W. Marshall, and Elnora W. Stuart, *Marketing: Real People, Real Choices*, 9th ed. (New York: Pearson, 2018), 128–130, 150–152; Kirsten Burkard, "11 Key Retention Metrics You Need to Know," Smile.io, 10 January 2017, blog.smile.io; Shep Hyken, "How Effective Is Net Promoter Score (NPS)?" *Forbes*, 3 December 2016, www.forbes.com.

- **Measuring competitors' marketing activities.** Marketing analytics can also be used to measure your competitors' marketing activities.[34] You won't be able to analyze these activities to the same depth that you can your own, as you don't have the insider information that you have on your own activities. However, it's vital to know where your competitors are advertising, what messages they are sharing with customers, and what they're saying about your company and its products.

DATA SOURCES FOR MARKETING ANALYTICS

The promises and capabilities of marketing analytics are enticing for every company, but the mountains of data involved in analytics are a constant challenge. That challenge starts with collecting the data. Ideally, a company would get all the relevant data from every stage along the customer journey. That can be much easier said than done, given the number and variety of touchpoints that a company can have with customers—call centers, social media, retail locations, onsite visits to customer locations, email newsletters, website visits, chatbots, and so on. In addition, there are all the *influencer* situations in which a customer is involved but the company isn't, such as when a potential customer reads a product review from an independent blogger.

Merely collecting the data is only the first step, of course. As with all big data applications, marketing data often need to be *cleaned* or *cleansed,* which can involve deleting duplicates, standardizing information into consistent formats, repairing faulty records, and other tasks. Data can be either *structured* or *unstructured* as well. Structured data fit a preset pattern, such as all the entry fields in a customer address form on a website. Unstructured data can range from video clips and recorded phone calls to tweets and email messages. As you can imagine, unstructured data can be much more challenging to process and interpret.

Even when data sources can be cleaned and processed, companies still need to put all the data to use. Being able to tie it all together and use data productively remains a challenge for many companies.[35] An important goal for every marketing analytics effort is to establish a *unified data layer* across the entire enterprise, so that all the various data collection "pipes" can feed into a centralized and well-organized repository and all the decision-making applications work from the same set of data.[36]

 CHECKPOINT

LEARNING OBJECTIVE 7: Define *marketing analytics,* and characterize its use in contemporary marketing.

SUMMARY: Marketing analytics refers to a range of tools and techniques that help marketers plan and evaluate marketing activities. The primary goals of marketing analytics are to increase revenue and profits while improving the cost effectiveness of the entire marketing effort. Specific goals and uses include tracking the customer journey, measuring the effectiveness of specific marketing initiatives and channels, testing and tuning promotional messaging, optimizing the timing and placement of ads, prioritizing customers, measuring share of customer, and measuring competitors' marketing activities.

CRITICAL THINKING: (1) Does the power of marketing analytics replace the need for creative decision-making in marketing? Why or why not? (2) How might customers' risk management strategies account for a supplier's low share of customer?

IT'S YOUR BUSINESS: (1) As a consumer yourself, does the convenience of online shopping outweigh the loss of privacy that marketing analytics can create? Why or why not? (2) If the creative side of marketing appeals to you, how do you feel about the data-heavy nature of marketing analytics?

KEY TERM TO KNOW: marketing analytics

 **BEHIND THE SCENES**

Lego Stacks Billions of Bricks to Become the World's Most Valuable Toy Brand

The name Lego combines the Danish words for *play* (leg) and *well* (godt). It might just as easily combine the words for *market* and *well*, given how impressively the company has conquered the toy world through effective marketing. By the time you read this, at the company's current rate of sales, an enthusiastic builder somewhere in the world will have purchased the *one-trillionth* Lego brick.

The Lego brand is now worth nearly $8 billion, roughly twice the value of the next 10 toy brands combined, and much of that staggering growth in financial value has happened since

2015. The six core values that Lego established for its brand—imagination, creativity, fun, learning, caring, and quality—help explain why the brand is so valuable and why it connects so well with millions of children and adults. Julia Goldin, Lego's chief marketing officer, says that "everybody she meets has a personal story to tell" about their experience of giving, receiving, or building with Lego.

A trillion plastic bricks would have been difficult to imagine at Lego's founding in 1932, when it was a small carpentry shop dedicated to making wooden toys—toys that didn't sell well in a world wracked with economic depression followed by global war. The company's fortunes began to change when founder Ole Kirk Christiansen purchased an injection molding machine and began creating cheaper plastic toys. He introduced the forerunner of the now-iconic plastic brick in 1949, but it didn't take off until his son Godtfred came up with the idea of marketing the bricks as a "system for creative play" that encouraged children to experiment and invent.

With that emphasis on stirring the imagination, the company's marketing efforts moved into full swing. The first Legoland Park opened in the company's hometown of Billund in 1968, and this was followed by a magazine, a series of books, and more parks around the world. Growth continued on a solid but not spectacular trajectory until 1999, when the company made two fateful decisions. The first was to begin making products with branded themes licensed from popular movies and other entertainment products, starting with a series of *Star Wars*–themed products. *Star Wars* Legos have been a big seller ever since, with a variety of standard sets and limited special editions, such as a *Millennium Falcon* model nearly 3 feet long made of 7,500 parts.

The second decision was a 180-degree reversal in its attitude toward involving customers in marketing and product design. Even though it had become a global success story and run its entire business on the principles of being good for customers, it had gradually closed itself off from customer contact out of fear of litigation. Children would frequently send the company ideas for new sets, and if Lego introduced anything remotely like a child's suggestion, parents would sometimes threaten to sue for a piece of the sales revenue.

This reluctance to accept outside ideas eventually led to a company culture that was closed off from the outside world. The company got a rude awakening right before the Christmas shopping season in 1999, when its three largest retailers said Lego was so out of touch it no longer understood he market—including the major shift that adults had become a significant portion of their sales, with some spending thousands of dollars a year on Lego. In addition, the firm was basically ignoring the vast community of Lego fans online. In those early days of the internet and social media, the idea of customers communicating with one another on their own unnerved many companies, because they couldn't control the conversations and weren't sure what to do with all the information flying around online.

This wake-up call "kind of freaked the CEO out," as a former employee put it, and prompted immediate action. To connect with its adult customers, the company established the Lego Ambassador Network, which unites some 300 online communities of Lego user and fan groups. The company now stays in constant contact with these product enthusiasts, sharing advice and ideas. And it continues to expand the range of products aimed at grown-up tastes, including a range of sophisticated architectural sets based on real-life cities and buildings. To provide a safe place for kids to share their love of Lego, the company created the social network Lego Life. For a company once described as living inside a silo, it is now engaged and customer-centric in every way imaginable.

Creative marketing efforts continued, highlighted by *The Lego Movie* in 2014, a box office smash that triggered a flood of social media commentary and reinforced the company's core brand values. Dozens of other movies and TV shows followed. Lego has a huge presence on Facebook, Twitter, and YouTube; it's the most popular branded channel on YouTube, in fact. And fans continue to carry the Lego message across every form of media. A TV show in the UK that featured a contest to find the country's best Lego builder attracted more than 2 million viewers per episode and drove an increase in sales as people were inspired by what they saw.

Even the best-managed companies can stumble from time to time, of course, and after nearly two decades of torrid, marketing-driven growth, Lego hit a rough patch in 2017. Following several years of not producing enough product to meet demand, it overproduced and got stuck with more inventory than it could sell. Offering discounts to clear out this inventory dampened its financial results, but as of 2018, the company said it had addressed the problem and expected to grow in line with the global toy market.

Whether the company can continue to capture the fancy of new generations of children and adults will depend to a large degree on the imaginations of its 250 designers and whatever opportunities for hot licensing deals might appear. Julia Goldin explains that new products are essential to the company's growth because kids and adults are always on the lookout for something new. Lego faces tough competition in an entertainment world going increasingly digital, but its focus on imagination and creativity are likely to keep millions of active minds and hands coming back for more.[37]

Critical Thinking Questions

12-1. Lego products are designed to last for generations. How might this level of quality affect Lego's ongoing sales, both positively and negatively?

12-2. Currently available recycled and recyclable plastics are not strong enough for Lego's needs, but the company is working on a plant-based alternative and aims to manufacture its products from sustainable sources by 2030. How should its marketing efforts address the issue of sustainability in the interim?

12-3. How do you imagine that the meaning of the Lego brand differs between adults and children?

Learn More Online

Explore the Lego website at **www.lego.com**. How are the various elements of the marketing mix represented? How does the style of communication help Lego connect with customers? What sort of practical information is provided to help customers select and order products?

End of Chapter

KEY TERMS

attribution (359)
behavioral segmentation (369)
cognitive dissonance (364)
consumer market (362)
customer experience (361)
customer loyalty (356)
customer relationship management (CRM) (358)
demographics (368)
distribution channels (372)
diversification (367)
exchange process (355)
geographic segmentation (369)
market (368)
market development (367)
market penetration (367)
market segmentation (368)
market share (368)
marketing (355)
marketing analytics (374)
marketing concept (356)

marketing mix (371)
marketing research (359)
marketing strategy (368)
needs (355)
organizational market (362)
permission-based marketing (359)
positioning (370)
price (372)
product (372)
product development (367)
promotion (373)
psychographics (369)
relationship marketing (356)
social commerce (358)
strategic marketing planning (366)
target markets (369)
touchpoint (361)
transaction (355)
utility (356)
voice of the customer (VoC) (358)
wants (355)

TEST YOUR KNOWLEDGE

Questions for Review

12-4. What is relationship marketing?

12-5. What is *voice of the customer*?

12-6. What value does user-generated content hold for a business?

12-7. Why is permission-based marketing such a breakthrough in marketing?

12-8. How does the organizational market differ from the consumer market?

12-9. What is strategic marketing planning, and what is its purpose?

12-10. Who decides how products are positioned in the minds of customers?

12-11. What are the four basic components of the marketing mix?

12-12. Why would a company want to measure *share of customer*?

Questions for Analysis

12-13. Why is relationship marketing fundamental to the marketing concept?

12-14. How do customer service, warranty policies, and other post-sales elements affect the customer experience?

12-15. Why would consumers knowingly buy counterfeit luxury brands?

12-16. Should companies open themselves up to criticism by being active on social media? Why or why not?

12-17. Despite various debates and discussions surrounding the lack of nutrition labeling on fast-food products, why do consumers continue to buy them?

12-18. Why do companies segment markets?

12-19. Could a company effectively apply any aspect of marketing analytics if it can't track the customer journey? Why or why not?

12-20. **Ethical Considerations.** Is it ethical to observe shoppers for the purposes of marketing research without their knowledge and permission? Why or why not?

Questions for Application

12-21. How might a retailer use relationship marketing to improve customer loyalty?

12-22. Suppose you are the marketing manager of the credit-card department of a financial institution. Your objective is to support the company's growth through a market-penetration strategy. How would you apply this strategy to increase the profitability of your company's credit cards based on current market conditions?

12-23. **Concept Integration.** How might the key economic indicators discussed in Chapter 2, including consumer price index, inflation, and unemployment, affect a company's marketing decisions?

EXPAND YOUR KNOWLEDGE

Discovering Career Opportunities

Make an appointment with someone who is in a marketing position that interests you, such as a brand or product manager, customer relationship manager, or a marketing research manager. Conduct a 15-minute informational interview with him or her on a career in marketing.

12-24. Make a list of the five most important attributes and skills required by candidates applying for a marketing job at the end of the informational interview. Reflect on your personal strengths and weaknesses. Do you think your strengths fit the requirements, duties, and responsibilities of this job?

12-25. Find out how you would go about closing the gap in terms of job attributes and skill deficiencies. What further academic qualifications or training would you seek to improve your career prospects? Would you accept a lower wage to improve your chances of securing a job?

12-26. Competing with hundreds of applicants for an interview to secure a marketing job can be stressful and frustrating. How would you personally cope with and overcome rejection and the prospect of being unemployed?

Intelligent Business Technology: Marketing Analytics

Find a company that offers marketing analytics software and explore its products. How many of the measurement goals identified in the chapter does this software appear to address? What evidence does the company offer that its software can perform these functions?

PRACTICE YOUR SKILLS

Resolving Ethical Dilemmas

Imagine you're a sales manager at a major kitchen-appliances manufacturing business. Your business makes dependable, mid to higher priced products. There has always been a concern to make the business more profitable. It is unlikely that any real savings can be made at the manufacturing end of the operations; it is already lean and highly efficient. Profits need to come from other parts of the overall operations. Understandably, the pressure has now fallen on you to deliver a higher profit margin. From the beginning of the new financial year, the CEO has decided that prices payable on the product line by global distributors and stockists will increase by 15 percent. However, as sales manager, you are adamant that prices to consumers will remain the same; that is, at competitive levels. Your CEO thinks that distributors are reliant on your products and that they will comply and accept lower profits. The CEO is putting the needs of the business above long-term relationship and partnership with distributors. Do you think this is an ethical way to deal with long-term distributors and stockists?

Growing as a Professional

Getting inside the heads of other people, particularly people with different life experiences and values, is an essential skill for marketing professionals. Pick a product that you couldn't imagine yourself ever buying under any circumstances, even if money were no object. If you've ever muttered to yourself, "I can't believe anybody would buy this," that's the product you should choose for this exercise. Now figure out why anybody *would* buy it. Make a sincere effort to get inside the heads of the people this product appeals to. What does this tell you about their needs and wants and how they view the world and their place in it? Practice this skill every time you see a product that you can't believe anyone would buy. It will help you be a more effective businessperson and might give you a different perspective on other people and their lives and values.

Sharpening Your Communication Skills

Emotion-based purchase decisions do not rely on consumers having a need for a product or service. The purchase decision is created by an external source, like a social media influencer. The stimuli that trigger affective decision-making are often highly personal. Do you think marketers take advantage of the power of affective choice? Choose a brand that is popular in your country that uses this type of approach to encourage purchases. Summarize your reflections in a brief email to your instructor.

Building Your Team Skills

In a team assigned by your instructor, choose a product or a brand that interests one of you. Make a careful assessment of the product or the brand, and identify how the business has pursued market opportunities with it. Has the brand been developed to reflect some or all of the options in Exhibit 12.6? How might it be developed in the future? Share your team's findings during a brief classroom presentation and then compare the findings of all teams.

Developing Your Research Skills

Consumer decision-making can be cognitive, habitual, or affective. More than one approach can be used for a given purchase. Research business journals for articles on the influence of cultural factors on the consumer decision-making process.

12-27. How are cultural values being transmitted today? How do values influence consumer decision-making during the purchase of products and services?

12-28. How do marketers influence the purchasing behavior of family members?

12-29. What would you consider as your core values, and how do they influence your purchase decisions?

Writing Assignments

12-30. If you have a product that appeals to the majority of consumers in a given market, would there be any value in segmenting the market before launching the product? Why or why not?

12-31. Is there still any need for traditional marketing techniques in a world of social commerce? Why or why not?

ENDNOTES

1. Lego, accessed 16 May 2018, www.lego.com; Lindsay Kolowich, "Building a Creative Brand Strategy, Brick by Brick: The History of Lego Marketing," HubSpot, 2 May 2018, blog.hubspot. com; Lucy Handley, "How Marketing Built Lego into the World's Favorite Toy Brand," CNBC, 27 April 2018, www.cnbc.com; Haniya Rae, "Lego's Aggressive Brick-by-Brick Marketing," Digiday, 12 February 2014, digiday.com; Patrick Morgan, "How the LEGO Marketing Team Built Their Beloved Brand," Conductor, 31 May 2017, www.conductor.com; "Lego Fun Facts," Brick-Recycler, accessed 19 May 2018, www.brickrecycler.com; Tom Espiner, "Why Is Lego Not Clicking with Customers," BBC News, 6 March 2018, www.bbc.com; "Lego Admits It's Made Too Many Bricks," BBC News, 6 March 2018, www.bbc.com; "Most Popular YouTube Brand Channels as of October 2017, Ranked by Total Number of Video Views (in Billions)," Statista, www.statista.com.
2. Philip Kotler and Gary Armstrong, *Principles of Marketing*, 17th ed. (New York: Pearson, 2018), 5.
3. Kotler and Armstrong, *Principles of Marketing*, 6.
4. BizX, accessed 14 May 2018, www.bizx.com.
5. Kotler and Armstrong, *Principles of Marketing*, 551.
6. Michael R. Solomon, Greg W. Marshall, and Elnora W. Stuart, *Marketing: Real People, Real Choices*, 9th ed. (New York: Pearson, 2018), 16.
7. Michael Hinshaw, "The Real Value in Voice of the Customer: The Customer Experience," CMO, 29 March 2016, www.cmo.com.
8. "Sorry, John," Adweek, 22 June 2009, 9.
9. Kimberlee Morrison, "Consumers Don't Like and Don't Trust Digital Advertising," Adweek, 5 May 2017, www.adweek.com; Jeff Pundyk, "We've Come Undone," CMO, 17 January 2017, www.cmo.com.
10. Bettina Specht, "5 Things You Must Know About Email Consent Under GDPR," Litmus, 22 January 2018, litmus.com.
11. "Native Advertising: A Guide for Businesses," U.S. Federal Trade Commission, accessed 18 February 2017, www.ftc.gov.
12. "Don't Be Naïve About Native," white paper, Word of Mouth Marketing Association, November 2014, womma.org.
13. Peter Roesler, "New Research Shows That Marketing Sustainability Can Sway Customers Worldwide," Inc., 9 January 2017, www.inc.com.
14. Michael R. Solomon, *Consumer Behavior*, 12th ed. (New York: Pearson, 2017), 126.
15. Tim Howell, "Marketing Transformation Is a Movement, Not a Trend," CMO, 17 February 2017, www.cmo.com.
16. Erik Wander, "Infographic: Here's How Much Consumers Will Use Voice Technology in the Near Future," AdWeek, 29 October 2017, www.adweek.com.
17. "The CEO Guide to Customer Experience," McKinsey Quarterly, August 2016, www.mckinsey.com
18. Solomon, *Consumer Behavior*, 313.
19. Katherine Schwab, "Online Reviews Influence What We Buy—But Not in the Way You'd Think," Co.Design, 23 August 2017, www.fastcodesign.com.
20. Solomon, *Consumer Behavior*, 330–331.
21. Solomon, *Consumer Behavior*, 158.
22. Solomon, *Consumer Behavior*, 158, 395–396.
23. Based in part on Kotler and Armstrong, *Principles of Marketing*, 166–172; Solomon, Marshall, and Stuart, *Marketing: Real People, Real Choices*, 186–192.
24. Kotler and Armstrong, *Principles of Marketing*, 43–46.
25. Gordon A. Wyner, "Pulling the Right Levers," *Marketing Management*, July/August 2004, 8–9.
26. Kotler and Armstrong, *Principles of Marketing*, 191.
27. Kotler and Armstrong, *Principles of Marketing*, 200.
28. Paul Gillin, *The New Influencers: A Marketer's Guide to the New Social Media* (Sanger, Calif.: Quill Driver Books, 2007), xi.
29. "Marketing Analytics," SAS, accessed 17 May 2018, www.sas.com.
30. Casey Carey, "Dealing with Data: Today's Marketing Analytics Challenges and Opportunities," *Think with Google*, March 2017, www.thinkwithgoogle.com.
31. "Marketing Analytics," SAS, accessed 17 May 2018, www.sas.com.
32. Solomon, Marshall, and Stuart, *Marketing: Real People, Real Choices*, 144.
33. Solomon, Marshall, and Stuart, *Marketing: Real People, Real Choices*, 130.
34. "Marketing Analytics," SAS.
35. Carey, "Dealing with Data: Today's Marketing Analytics Challenges and Opportunities."
36. Giselle Abramovich, "Companies with Mature Data Practices Perform Better," CMO, 10 May 2018, www.cmo.com.
37. See note 1.

13 Product Management and Pricing Strategies

LEARNING OBJECTIVES After studying this chapter, you will be able to

1. Identify the main types of consumer and organizational products, and describe the four stages in the life cycle of a product.

2. Describe six stages in the product development process.

3. Define *brand*, and explain the concepts of brand equity and brand loyalty.

4. Identify four ways of expanding a product line, and discuss two risks that product-line extensions pose.

5. List the factors that influence pricing decisions, and explain break-even analysis.

6. Compare the three foundational pricing methods, and list six situational pricing methods.

7. Describe how companies are using virtual and augmented reality to create new products and new customer experiences.

MyLab Intro to Business

Improve Your Grade!

If your instructor is using MyLab Intro to Business, visit **www.pearson.com/ mylab/intro-to-business**.

BEHIND THE SCENES   **OXO: Launching a Design Revolution with the Humble Vegetable Peeler**

Something as seemingly simple as a new design for a vegetable peeler improved the lives of millions of consumers and helped launch a revolution in product design.

Veja/Shutterstock!

www.oxo.com

"Can't you make something that doesn't hurt my hands?"

With all the attention and investment money that high-technology start-ups get, it's easy to overlook the fact that many successful companies address basic, unglamorous customer needs. Take the vegetable peeler—it's hard to imagine a humbler product. For decades, peelers used a simple, inexpensive design with a thin band of metal bent in the approximate shape of a handle and attached to a cutting blade. The design was inexpensive to manufacture and therefore inexpensive to sell, and it met the basic requirement of removing the peel from potatoes, apples, and other produce.

For most people, the basic peeler did the job, albeit in a slightly uncomfortable way. For people with arthritis and other manual limitations, however, that metal band masquerading as a handle could be difficult, painful, and sometimes dangerous to use.

Sam Farber was a successful housewares magnate who had sold his company and retired. He and his wife, Betsey, were living in France when she got fed up with the peeler she was trying to use and turned to him in exasperation and asked if he couldn't come up with something for people like her with arthritis. Farber jumped on the challenge and in the process helped launch and evangelize the discipline of *universal design*—designing products that can be used by as many people as possible.

Working with experts in a New York design studio, Farber was able to solve the ergonomics challenge, but could his design be the foundation for a new business? That old design with the metal band lasted for decades because it did the job and was cheap. How much would people pay for a more comfortable peeler, and how many people beyond Betsey Farber would even care about it? If you were Sam Farber, how would you go about building a business on the foundation of universal design?[1]

INTRODUCTION

This chapter explores two of the four elements in the marketing mix: product and price. Even for products as relatively simple as OXO's vegetable peeler (profiled in the chapter-opening Behind the Scenes), product management and pricing strategy can involve complex decisions. Careful product management and pricing can make the difference between success and failure for every business.

1 **LEARNING OBJECTIVE**

Identify the main types of consumer and organizational products, and describe the four stages in the life cycle of a product.

Characteristics of Products

As the central element in every company's exchanges with its customers, products naturally command a lot of attention from managers who are planning new offerings and coordinating the marketing mixes for existing offerings. To understand the nature of these decisions, it's important to recognize the various types of products and the stages that products go through during their "lifetime" in the marketplace.

TYPES OF PRODUCTS

Think about Doritos tortilla chips, Intel semiconductors, and your favorite musical artist. You wouldn't market these products in the same way, because buyer behavior, product characteristics, market expectations, competition, and other elements of the equation are entirely different.

Classifying products on the basis of tangibility and application can provide useful insights into the best ways to market them. Some products are predominantly tangible; others are mostly intangible. Most products, however, fall somewhere between those two extremes. The *product continuum* indicates the relative amounts of tangible and intangible components in a product (see Exhibit 13.1).

EXHIBIT 13.1	**The Product Continuum**

Products contain both tangible and intangible components; predominantly tangible products are categorized as goods, whereas predominantly intangible products are categorized as services.

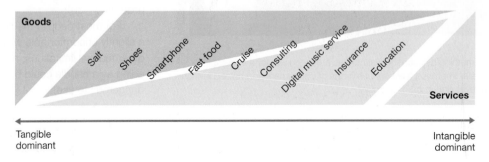

EXHIBIT 13.2	**Augmenting the Basic Product**

Product decisions also involve how much or how little to augment the core product with additional goods and services.

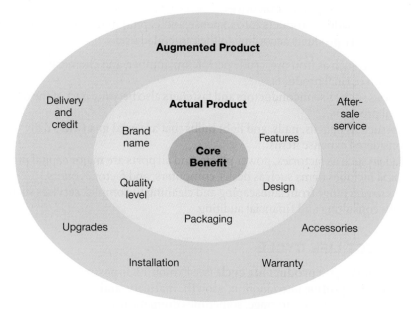

Source: Philip Kotler and Gary Armstrong, *Principles of Marketing,* 17th ed. (New York: Pearson, 2018), 221.

Every product can also be viewed as a bundle of attributes, starting from a core customer value or benefit and the actual product itself (see Exhibit 13.2). Companies often *augment* that product with accessories, services, and other elements.[2] When the actual products are fairly similar in a market, competitors can try to differentiate themselves with unique augmentations, such as a 100,000-mile warranty when others offer only 50,000 miles.

REAL-TIME UPDATES
Learn More by Reading This Article

The power of design

Design choices, from visual aesthetics to the human-machine interface to the customer experience, are increasingly important in today's competitive markets. Go to **real-timeupdates.com/bia9** and select Learn More in the Students section.

Consumer Products

Organizations and consumers use many of the same products, but they can use them for different reasons and in different ways. Products that are primarily sold to individuals for personal consumption are known as *consumer products*. They can be classified into four subgroups, depending on how people shop for them:[3]

- Everyday goods and services that people buy frequently, usually without much conscious planning, are known as **convenience products**.
- **Shopping products** are more important goods and services that people buy less frequently, such as smartphones and college educations. Because the stakes are higher and the decisions more complex, such products require more thought and comparison shopping.
- **Specialty products** are particular brands that the buyer especially wants and will seek out, often regardless of location or price, such as single-origin coffees, high-end audio gear, and luxury cars.
- When it comes to some products, such as life insurance, cemetery plots, and items that are new to the marketplace, consumers aren't looking for them. The marketing challenges for these *unsought products* include making consumers aware of their existence and convincing people to consider them.

Industrial and Commercial Products

Organizational products, or *industrial and commercial products,* are generally purchased by organizations (including companies, not-for-profit organizations, and governments) in large quantities and used to create other products or to operate the organization. **Expense items**

convenience products
Everyday goods and services that people buy frequently, usually without much conscious planning.

shopping products
Fairly important goods and services that people buy less frequently with more planning and comparison.

specialty products
Particular brands that the buyer especially wants and will seek out, regardless of location or price.

expense items
Inexpensive products that organizations generally use within a year of purchase.

capital items
More expensive organizational products with a longer useful life, ranging from office and plant equipment to entire factories.

are relatively inexpensive goods that are generally used within a year of purchase, such as printer cartridges and paper. **Capital items** are more expensive products with a longer useful life. Examples include computers, vehicles, production machinery, and even entire factories. Businesses and other organizations also buy a wide variety of services, from facilities maintenance to temporary executives.

Aside from dividing products into expense and capital items, industrial buyers and sellers often classify products according to their intended use:

- *Raw materials* such as iron ore, crude petroleum, lumber, and chemicals are used in the production of final products.
- *Components* such as semiconductors and fasteners also become part of the manufacturers' final products.
- *Supplies* such as pencils, nails, and light bulbs that are used in a firm's daily operations are considered expense items.
- *Installations* such as factories, power plants, and airports are major capital projects.
- *Equipment* includes items such as desks, computers, and factory robots.
- *Business services* range from landscaping and cleaning to complex services such as management consulting and financial auditing.

THE PRODUCT LIFE CYCLE

product life cycle
Four stages through which a product progresses: introduction, growth, maturity, and decline.

Most products undergo a **product life cycle** (see Exhibit 13.3), passing through four distinct stages in sales and profits: introduction, growth, maturity, and decline.[4] The marketing challenge changes from stage to stage, sometimes dramatically.

The product life cycle can apply to a product class (gasoline-powered automobiles), a product form (sport utility vehicles), or a brand or model (Ford Explorer). Product classes and forms tend to have the longest life cycles, specific brands somewhat shorter life cycles, and individual products even shorter cycles. The amount of time that a product remains in any

EXHIBIT 13.3	The Product Life Cycle

Most products and product categories move through a life cycle similar to the one represented by the curve in this diagram, with new innovations pushing existing products along the time axis. However, the duration of each stage varies widely from product to product. Automobiles have been in the maturity stage for decades, but faxing services barely made it into the introduction stage before being knocked out of the market by low-cost fax machines that every business and home office could afford—which were themselves pushed along the curve by digital document formats.

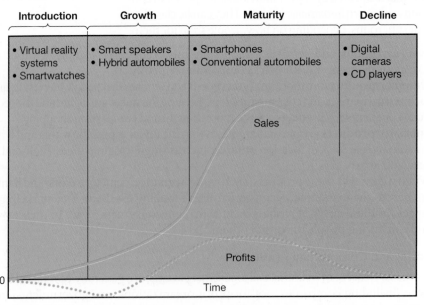

Source: Adapted from Philip Kotler and Gary Armstrong, *Principles of Marketing*, 17th ed. (New York: Pearson, 2018), 265.

one stage depends on customer needs and preferences, economic conditions, the nature of the product, and the marketer's strategy and overall business competence. A few well-known brands and products have been around for more than a century, but some categories and products appear and disappear quickly. The Lego brick has been around for more than 60 years, but the Pet Rock lasted only a few months.

Introduction

The first stage in the product life cycle is the *introductory stage*, which extends from the research-and-development (R&D) phase through the product's first commercial availability. The introductory stage is a crucial phase that requires careful planning and often considerable investment. For new types of products, companies may need to educate potential customers and *influencers* (such as widely read bloggers) on the uses and benefits of the product.

Speed can be a major concern as well. Some markets offer the luxury of building demand over time if the introduction isn't a blockbuster, but in others a slow introduction can doom a product. The opening weekend for a movie, for instance, often determines its success or failure—a tremendously stressful scenario for people who have invested months or years and many millions of dollars making the film.

Growth

After the introductory stage comes the *growth stage*, marked by a rapid jump in sales—if the product is successful—and, usually, an increase in the number of competitors and distribution outlets. As competition increases, so does the struggle for market share. This situation creates pressure to maintain large promotional budgets and competitive prices. With enough growth, however, a firm may be able to reach economies of scale that allow it to create and deliver its products less expensively than in the introduction phase. The growth stage can reap handsome profits for those products that survive.

Maturity

During the *maturity stage*, usually the longest in the product life cycle, sales begin to level off. Markets tend to get saturated with all the supply that buyers demand, so the only way a firm can expand its sales in this phase is to win sales away from other suppliers. Because the costs of introduction and growth have diminished at this point, most companies try to keep mature products alive so they can use the resulting profits to fund the development of the next generation of new products (often referred to as "milking a cash cow").

Decline

Although maturity can be extended for many years, most products eventually enter the *decline stage*, when sales and profits slip and may eventually fade away. Declines occur for several reasons: changing demographics, shifts in popular taste, overwhelming competition, and advances in technology. For instance, feature-rich smartphones pushed a bunch of other product categories toward or into decline, including personal digital assistants (PDAs), handheld global positioning system (GPS) navigation devices, voice recorders, music players, digital cameras, calculators, and portable gaming devices—not to mention landline phones.[5]

When a product begins to decline, the company must decide whether to reduce the product's costs to compensate for declining sales or to discontinue it altogether and focus on developing newer products. Of course, companies can try to make their products more compelling and competitive at any stage. From subtle refinements to complete makeovers, product improvements can sometimes be a way to maintain competitiveness and maximize the returns on the money and effort invested in a product.

Products can stay in the maturity stage for decades if they continue to meet customer needs.

CHECKPOINT

LEARNING OBJECTIVE 1: Identify the main types of consumer and organizational products, and describe the four stages in the life cycle of a product.

SUMMARY: Consumer products can be identified as convenience, shopping, specialty, or unsought, distinguished primarily by the amount of thought and effort that goes into buying them. Organizational products are divided into expense items, less expensive goods used in production or operations; capital items, more expensive goods and facilities with useful lives longer than a year; and business services. The product life cycle consists of (1) the introductory stage, during which marketers focus on stimulating demand for the new product; (2) the growth stage, when marketers focus on increasing the product's market share; (3) the maturity stage, during which marketers try to extend the life of the product by highlighting improvements or by repackaging the product in different sizes; and (4) the decline stage, when firms must decide whether to reduce the product's costs to compensate for declining sales or to discontinue it.

CRITICAL THINKING: (1) Do manufacturers have a responsibility to create safe products even if customers don't care and don't want to pay for safety features? Why or why not? (2) Do automobiles ever enter the decline stage of the product life cycle? Explain your answer.

IT'S YOUR BUSINESS: (1) Have you ever had the urge to be "the first one on the block" to buy a new product, try a new fashion, or discover a new musical artist? If so, were you pleased or displeased when "the masses" began to imitate your choice? What does your reaction say about you as a consumer? (2) Have you ever replaced a product (such as a computer or smartphone) that was still functional, just because a newer version had hit the market? What influenced your decision?

KEY TERMS TO KNOW: convenience products, shopping products, specialty products, expense items, capital items, product life cycle

---

2 **LEARNING OBJECTIVE**

Describe six stages in the product development process.

product development process
A formal process of generating, selecting, developing, and commercializing product ideas.

The New-Product Development Process

Mad scientists and basement inventors still create new products, but many of today's products appear on the market as a result of a rigorous, formal **product development process**—a method of generating, selecting, developing, and commercializing product ideas (see Exhibit 13.4).

IDEA GENERATION

The ideas for new products can come from a variety of sources. In many instances, an individual is dissatisfied with the available solutions to a common problem and starts looking for a better way, as with Sam Farber and his ergonomic kitchen tools. In others, a company with an existing product line looks for opportunities to expand by adding products that might appeal to buyers. Many companies have set up innovation centers, idea labs, social networks, employee or customer contests, or idea-pitching events for the express purpose of generating or collecting new product ideas.[6] In some cases, customers or retailers may approach the companies they already do business with and suggest ideas. Sometimes ideas are lucky accidents that appear while an individual or a company is working on something else. And many "new" product ideas are simply improvements to or variations on existing products, but even those slight alterations can generate big revenues.

IDEA SCREENING

When entrepreneurs or companies have more than one product idea, they need ways to evaluate which ideas are most worthwhile to develop. The purpose of *idea screening* is to identify which concepts have the most promise and which should be abandoned. Ideas need

EXHIBIT 13.4	**The Product Development Process**

The product development process aims to identify the product ideas most likely to succeed in the marketplace. The process varies widely by company, of course; entrepreneurs and start-ups sometimes begin with a single product idea and take it all the way through to commercialization.

Idea Generation	Idea Screening	Business Analysis	Prototyping	Test Marketing	Commercialization
Brainstorm product concepts that could satisfy unmet market needs or enhance the company's product portfolio	Subject those ideas to *feasibility* or *concept testing* to identify those with the best chance of turning into successful products	Subject those ideas to a *business-case analysis* based on estimates of production costs, sales volumes, and selling price	Develop functioning "pre-release" versions that can be used by target customers to check for design flaws, market appeal, and so on	Release a finished or nearly finished *(beta)* version to selected customers or market segments and measure customer reaction	Fine-tune the product design and the rest of the marketing mix and then officially launch the product and push sales in all target markets

to be screened to minimize the chances of discovering later that they can't be built, can't deliver the envisioned benefits, or will cost more than the market is willing to pay for them. Of course, companies can't predict viability with 100 percent accuracy, and sometimes the only way to find out if an idea will work is to build the thing.

BUSINESS ANALYSIS

A product idea that survives the screening stage is subjected to a business analysis. During this stage, the company reviews the sales, costs, and profit projections to determine whether they meet the company's objectives. In addition, it estimates the costs associated with various levels of production. Given these projections, analysts calculate the potential profit that will be achieved if the product is introduced. If the product meets the company's objectives, it can then move to the prototype development stage.

PROTOTYPE DEVELOPMENT

prototypes
Preproduction samples of products used for testing and evaluation.

At this stage, the firm may develop a concept into a functioning "prerelease" product. The firm creates and tests working samples, or **prototypes**, of the product. These units are rigorously analyzed for usability, durability, manufacturability, customer appeal, and other vital criteria, depending on the type of product. In addition, the company begins to plan for large-scale manufacturing (for tangible goods) or *scalability* (for digital services, for example), then identifies the resources required to bring the product to market.

Given the time and expense required to fully develop products, many companies now try to get feedback from potential buyers as soon as possible. With *rapid prototyping* such as the kind offered by three-dimensional (3D) printing services such as Voodoo Manufacturing (see page 273), companies can get working models in the hands of product evaluators to confirm the viability of the concept and improve its design. Companies can also release products early to get feedback from potential customers before finalizing features and functions. Software developers often do so through *beta* versions.

Creating prototypes is a critical step in most product development efforts because it lets companies verify performance and function, get user input, and fine-tune designs.

SeventyFour/Shutterstock

TEST MARKETING

test marketing
A product development stage in which a product is sold on a limited basis to gauge its market appeal.

During **test marketing**, the firm introduces the product in selected markets and monitors consumer reactions. Test marketing gives the company experience with marketing the product before going to the expense of a full introduction. In a variation on crowdsourcing, a company can let customers vote directly on which products it should bring to market. When Amazon began producing television shows through its Amazon Studios division, it released pilot episodes of several potential series and asked viewers of its Prime service to vote on which ones should move into full series production.[7]

Test marketing can be expensive and time-consuming, however, so not all companies choose to take this step with every new product. An alternative that is growing in popularity with the rise of crowdfunding sites such as Kickstarter is to offer a product for sale on the condition that a specified number of customers preorder it first. This approach helps validate market demand before a company moves into the production phase, and it provides vital funding during the start-up phase.

COMMERCIALIZATION

commercialization
Large-scale production and distribution of a product.

The final stage of development is **commercialization**, the large-scale production and distribution of products that have survived the testing process. This phase (also referred to as a *product launch*) requires the coordination of many activities—manufacturing, packaging, distribution, pricing, media relations, and customer communication.

Even after following a rigorous process to reduce risk, companies have no guarantee that products will take off when they hit the commercialization phase. Self-inflicted wounds, such as poor advertising, buggy software, or supply shortages, can doom even promising products. And in the external environment, an unexpected new competitor, shifts in consumer tastes, or faltering economic conditions can cause a new product to stall in the marketplace.

 CHECKPOINT

LEARNING OBJECTIVE 2: Describe six stages in the product development process.

SUMMARY: The first two stages of product development involve generating and screening ideas to isolate those with the most potential. In the third stage, promising ideas are analyzed to determine their likely profitability. Those that appear worthwhile enter the fourth stage, the prototype development stage, in which limited numbers of the products are created. In the fifth stage, the product is test marketed to determine buyer response. Products that survive the testing process are then commercialized, the final stage.

CRITICAL THINKING: (1) Apple claims to never do any marketing research for new product ideas but instead creates products that Apple employees themselves would be excited to have. What are the risks of this approach? Would it work for all consumer and organizational markets? (2) Consumers and government regulators sometimes complain about identical products being sold at different prices to different customers as part of test marketing efforts. Are such tests ethical? Why or why not?

IT'S YOUR BUSINESS: (1) What currently unavailable service can you think of that could be offered on mobile phones? (2) In addition to the mobile phone itself, what other product elements (such as a website or phone accessories) would be required to launch such a service?

KEY TERMS TO KNOW: product development process, prototypes, test marketing, commercialization

Product Identities

Creating an identity for products is one of the most important decisions marketers make. That identity is encompassed in the **brand**, which can have meaning at three levels: (1) a unique name, symbol, or design that sets the product apart from those offered by competitors; (2) the legal protections afforded by a trademark and any relevant intellectual property; and (3) the overall company or organizational brand.[8] For instance, the Nike "swoosh" symbol is a unique identifier on every Nike product, a legally protected piece of intellectual property, and a symbol that represents the entire company.

Branding helps a product in many ways. It gives customers the means to recognize and specify a particular product so that they can choose it again or recommend it to others. It provides consumers with information about the product. It facilitates the marketing of the product. And it creates value for the product. This notion of the value of a brand is also called **brand equity**. In fact, a brand name can be an organization's most valuable asset, and the value of major brands is in the billions of dollars. The Apple and Google brands are valued at more than $100 billion, and those of Amazon and Facebook will cross that threshold soon.[9] Strong brands simplify marketing efforts because the target audience tends to associate positive qualities with any product that carries a respected brand name—and vice versa.

Customers who buy the same brand again and again are evidence of the strength of **brand loyalty**, or commitment to a particular brand. Some brands, such as Harley-Davidson motorcycles and American Girl dolls, can acquire such a deep level of meaning to loyal consumers that the brands become intertwined with the narratives of the consumers' life stories.[10]

3 **LEARNING OBJECTIVE**

Define brand, and explain the concepts of brand equity and brand loyalty.

brand
A name, term, sign, symbol, design, or combination of those used to identify the products of a firm and to differentiate them from competing products.

brand equity
The value that a company has built up in a brand.

brand loyalty
The degree to which customers continue to purchase a specific brand.

REAL-TIME UPDATES
Learn More by Listening to These Podcasts

Advice from some of today's top brand builders

The On Brand podcast features insightful discussions with successful brand managers. Go to **real-timeupdates.com/bia9** and select Learn More in the Students section.

BRAND NAME SELECTION

Jeep, OXO, and iPod are **brand names**, the portion of a brand that can be spoken, including letters, words, or numbers. In contrast, the McDonald's golden arches and the Nike "swoosh" symbol are **brand marks**, the portion of a brand that cannot be expressed verbally. The term **logo** (from *logotype*) once referred to the typesetting treatment of a brand name but is now used more variably to refer to the nonverbal brand mark, the visual treatment of the brand name, or a combination of the two.

The choice of a brand name and any associated brand marks can be a critical success factor. Imagine if Nike had chosen a cute fuzzy duckling or a balanced, static shape of some kind rather than the dynamic and "athletic" swoosh shape—not to mention naming the brand after the Greek goddess of victory.

In the United States, brand names and brand symbols may be registered with the U.S. Patent and Trademark Office as **trademarks**, brands that have been given legal protection so that their owners have exclusive rights to their use. (Similar protections exist in other countries.) The Lanham Trademark Act prohibits the unauthorized use of a trademark on goods or services when the use would likely confuse consumers as to the origin of those goods and services.[11] Companies zealously protect their brand names because if a name becomes too widely used in a general sense, it no longer qualifies for protection under trademark laws. Cellophane, kerosene, linoleum, escalator, zipper, and shredded wheat are just a few of the many brand names that have since lost trademark protection and can now be used by anyone.[12]

BRAND OWNERSHIP

Brand names may be associated with a manufacturer, a retailer, a wholesaler, or a combination of business types. Brands offered and promoted by a national manufacturer, such as Procter & Gamble's Tide detergent and Pampers disposable diapers, are called **national brands**. **Private brands** are not owned by a manufacturer but rather by

brand names
The portion of brands that can be spoken, including letters, words, or numbers.

brand marks
The portion of brands that cannot be expressed verbally.

logo
A graphical and/or textual representation of a brand.

trademarks
Brands that have been given legal protection so that their owners have exclusive rights to their use.

private brands
Brands that carry the label of a retailer or a wholesaler rather than a manufacturer.

national brands
Brands owned by manufacturers and distributed nationally.

A trusted and instantly recognizable brand mark is a valuable business asset.

co-branding
A partnership between two or more companies to closely link their brand names together for a single product.

brand licensing
Agreement in which one company pays to use another company's brand on its products.

a wholesaler or a retailer. For example, Kirkland is a private brand sold by Costco, Private Selection is a private brand sold in Kroger supermarkets, and Amazon now produces dozens of its own brands. These *store brands*, as they are also called, have become a major force in food, fashion, and other product categories.[13]

As an alternative to branded products, retailers can also offer *generic products*, which are packaged in plain containers that bear only the name of the product. Note that *"generics"* is also a term used in the pharmaceutical industry to describe products that are copies of an original drug (other companies are allowed to make these copies after the patent on the original drug expires).

Co-branding occurs when two or more companies team up to closely link their names in a single product, usually to leverage the brand associations and awareness of one product onto the other. Companies can also use **brand licensing**, in which one company pays to use another company's brand on its products. Mainstream movies, for example, often hit the market with an array of licensing deals with fast-food chains and other consumer products companies. As you read in Chapter 12, brand licensing has been a major marketing success for Lego, for example. Companies need to choose such deals carefully, however, to minimize the impact of negative associations in the mind of potential customers to avoid diluting a brand so much that it loses its core meaning to buyers.

PACKAGING

Most tangible products need some form of packaging to protect them from damage or tampering, but packaging can also play an important role in a product's marketing strategy. Packaging makes products easier to display, facilitates the sale of smaller products, serves as a means of product differentiation, and enhances the product's overall appeal and convenience. Packaging can significantly influence buyer perceptions, too, sometimes in surprising ways. For instance, packages with simple geometric lines (such as cylinders or rectangles) are perceived as being larger than geometrically complex packages of the same volume. Package designers can use these perceptual effects to create particular images for their products.[14]

Packaging can also involve decisions about which items to include as the product offering and in what quantities. For example, Costco and other warehouse-style retailers offer many of the same products available through regular grocery stores but in packages of larger quantities. At the other extreme, many food brands offer individual serving-size packages, such as 100-calorie snacks designed to help people limit their calorie intake.

In addition to its functional purpose, packaging often plays an important role in communicating with customers.

Packaging can be a complex tug-of-war between competing priorities. Consumers are often frustrated by how difficult it can be to open packages—and thousands are injured every year trying to open packages using knives, scissors, hammers, and other tools.[15] Plastic "clamshell" packages can be particularly frustrating and even dangerous to open. Manufacturers and sellers don't set out to antagonize buyers, naturally, but they adopt various packaging methods in order to protect products, reduce shoplifting, and enhance merchandizing efforts. Packaging is also a major environmental concern, in both the resources used and the waste generated. However, intelligent packaging can also reduce environmental impact, such as by reducing food spoilage. Food production and distribution have considerable environment consequences, and reducing the amount of food that has to be thrown out because of spoilage decreases that environmental impact.[16]

In an effort to balance the competing interests of all parties, a number of companies are working to change their packaging strategies. For example, many manufacturers now participate in Amazon's "Frustration-Free Packaging" program, in which products sold through the online giant use packaging formats that are easier to open, consume fewer materials, and are 100 percent recyclable.[17] Amazon's e-commerce structure is a key element in this effort, because the packages don't need to meet the same anti-shoplifting and display considerations as products sold through physical retail channels.

REAL-TIME UPDATES
Learn More by Visiting This Website

Explore membership in the American Marketing Association

The AMA offers student membership and the chance to join one of more than 370 student chapters. Go to **real-timeupdates.com/ bia9** and select Learn More in the Students section.

LABELING

Labeling is an integral part of packaging. Whether the label is a separate element attached to the package or a printed part of the container, it serves to identify a brand and communicate multiple types of information, from promotional messages to legally required safety or nutritional data. The labeling of foods, drugs, cosmetics, and many health products is regulated under various federal laws, which often require disclosures about potential dangers, benefits, and other issues consumers need to consider when making a buying decision.

 CHECKPOINT

LEARNING OBJECTIVE 3: Define brand, and explain the concepts of brand equity and brand loyalty.

SUMMARY: Brand encompasses the various elements of product identity and meaning. Brand equity reflects the value of a brand name based on its strength and appeal in the marketplace and its power as a communication vehicle. Brand loyalty is the strength of buyers' commitment to a particular company or product.

CRITICAL THINKING: (1) Can a brand with a bad reputation be rescued? Would a company be wiser to just drop a "bad brand" and start fresh with something new? (2) Is staying with the same product only a case of brand "loyalty"? Could other factors be in play that lead consumers or organizations not to switch brands? Explain your answer.

IT'S YOUR BUSINESS: (1) How many visible brand marks are you currently wearing? Are these common brands? (2) What do you think these brands say about you?

KEY TERMS TO KNOW: brand, brand equity, brand loyalty, brand names, brand marks, logo, trademarks, national brands, private brands, co-branding, brand licensing

Product-Line and Product-Mix Strategies

In addition to developing product identities, a company must continually evaluate what kinds of products it will offer. To stay competitive, most companies continually add and drop products to ensure that declining items will be replaced by growth products. Companies that offer more than one product also need to pay close attention to how those products are positioned in the marketplace relative to one another. The responsibility for managing individual products, product lines, and product mixes is usually assigned to one or more managers in the marketing department. In a smaller company, the *marketing manager* tackles this effort; in larger companies with more products to manage, individual products or groups of products are usually assigned to **brand managers**, known in some companies as *product managers* or *product-line managers*.

 4 LEARNING OBJECTIVE

Identify four ways of expanding a product line, and discuss two risks that product-line extensions pose.

brand managers
Managers who develop and implement the marketing strategies and programs for one or more of a company's products or brands.

PRODUCT LINES

product line
A series of related products offered by a firm.

A **product line** is a group of products from a single manufacturer that are similar in terms of use or characteristics. The General Mills (**www.generalmills.com**) snack-food product line, for example, includes Bugles, Cascadian Farm organic snacks, and Nature Valley Granola Bars. Within each product line, a company confronts decisions about the number of goods and services to offer. On the one hand, offering additional products can help a manufacturer to boost revenues and increase its visibility in retail stores. On the other hand, creating too many products and product variations can be expensive for everyone in the supply chain and can be confusing to buyers.

PRODUCT MIX

product mix
The complete portfolio of products that a company offers for sale.

An organization with several product lines has a **product mix**—a collection of diverse goods or services offered for sale. The General Mills product mix includes cereals, baking products, desserts, snack foods, and entrees (see Exhibit 13.5). Three important dimensions of a product mix are *width, length,* and *depth,* and each dimension presents its own set of challenges and opportunities. A product mix is *wide* if it has several product lines. A product mix is *long* if it carries several items in its product lines. For instance, General Mills produces multiple cereal brands within the ready-to-eat cereal line. A product mix is *deep* if it has a number of versions of *each* product in a product line. The Cheerios brand, for example, has nearly 20 varieties.[18]

REAL-TIME UPDATES
Learn More by Reading This Article

Designing products for a circular economy

Sustainability advocates are pushing companies to consider the entire life cycle of products, including what happens to them and the materials they are made of when customers no longer want them. Go to **real-timeupdates.com/bia9** and select Learn More in the Students section.

When deciding on the dimensions of a product mix, a company must weigh the risks and rewards associated with various approaches. Some companies limit the number of product offerings and focus on selling a few items in higher quantities. Doing so can keep production and marketing costs lower through economies of scale. However, counting too heavily on a narrow set of products leaves a company vulnerable to competitive threats and market shifts. Other companies diversify their product offerings as a protection against shifts in consumer tastes, economic conditions, and technology, or as a way to build marketing synergy by offering complementary products.[19]

A company's choice of distribution channels can also affect decisions regarding product mix. Shelf space in physical stores is limited, and manufacturers often must pay to get on store shelves. In general, the more revenue a manufacturer represents, the better chance it has of getting all-important shelf space. Consequently, retail store aisles tend to be dominated by a few large brands, and manufacturers look for ways to build portfolios of best sellers that can command attention at the retail level.

Online retailing presents better opportunities for large numbers of specialized and low-volume products. Without the physical limitations of a bricks-and-mortar facility, online retailers can offer a much greater variety of products. Although some of these products may individually sell at lower volumes, collectively they represent a substantial business opportunity that has been termed the *long tail* (referring to a sales volume graph in which a vast number of low-volume products stretches out toward infinity).[20]

REAL-TIME UPDATES
Learn More by Reading This Article

The scourge of counterfeit products

Counterfeit products are a global threat to legitimate business—and often a safety threat to customers. Go to **real-timeupdates.com/bia9** and select Learn More in the Students section.

PRODUCT EXPANSION STRATEGIES

As Exhibit 13.6 on page 394 shows, you can expand your product line and product mix in a number of ways. One approach is to introduce additional items—such as new flavors, forms, colors, ingredients, or package sizes—in a given product category under the same brand name. Another approach is to expand a product line to add new and similar products with the same product name—a strategy known as **family branding**.

family branding
Using a brand name on a variety of related products.

EXHIBIT 13.5	The Product Mix at General Mills (Selected Products)

These selected products from General Mills illustrate the various dimensions of its product mix. The mix is *wide* because it contains multiple product lines (cereals, fruit snacks, pasta, soup, yogurt, and more). The cereal product line is *long* because it contains many individual brands (only four of which are shown here). And these four cereal brands show different depths. The Lucky Charms and Trix brands are *shallow* product lines, whereas the Cheerios brand is *deep*.

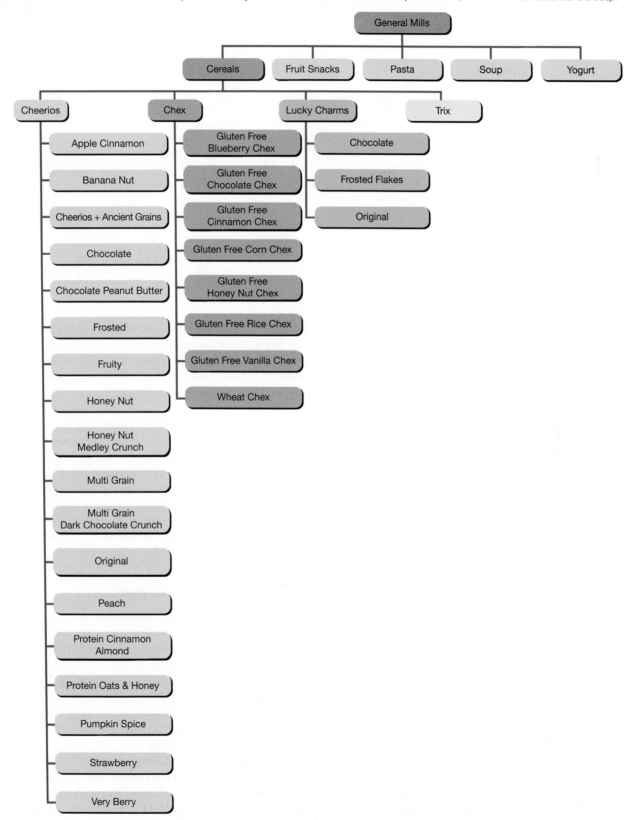

Source: Data from Cheerios, Chex, and Lucky Charms websites, accessed 21 May 2018, www.cheerios.com, www.chex.com, www.luckycharms.com.

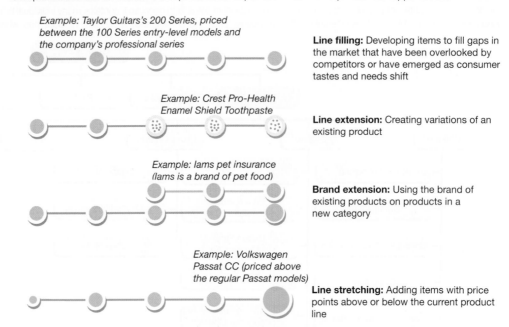

EXHIBIT 13.6   **Expanding a Product Line**

Companies use one or more of these product-line expansion methods to pursue new opportunities.

Example: Taylor Guitars's 200 Series, priced between the 100 Series entry-level models and the company's professional series

Line filling: Developing items to fill gaps in the market that have been overlooked by competitors or have emerged as consumer tastes and needs shift

Example: Crest Pro-Health Enamel Shield Toothpaste

Line extension: Creating variations of an existing product

Example: Iams pet insurance (Iams is a brand of pet food)

Brand extension: Using the brand of existing products on products in a new category

Example: Volkswagen Passat CC (priced above the regular Passat models)

Line stretching: Adding items with price points above or below the current product line

brand extension
Applying a successful brand name to a new product category.

Conversely, in a **brand extension**, a company applies a successful brand name to a new product category in the hopes that the recognition and reputation of the brand will give it a head start in the new category. Building on the name recognition of an existing brand can reduce the costs and risks of introducing new products. As you'll read at the end of the chapter, OXO has extended its original Good Grips brand into four other related product categories.

However, product-line extensions present two important risks that marketers need to consider carefully. First, stretching a brand to cover too many categories or types of products can dilute the brand's meaning in the minds of target customers. For instance, if the sports broadcaster ESPN were to branch out into business and financial news, its original sports audience might wonder whether the company is still committed to being a leader in sports journalism, and the business news audience might wonder what value a sports media company could bring to financial news. Second, additional products do not automatically guarantee increased sales revenue. Marketers need to make sure that new products don't simply *cannibalize*, or take sales away from, their existing products.

PRODUCT STRATEGIES FOR INTERNATIONAL MARKETS

As Chapter 3 notes, product adaptation is one of the key changes that companies need to consider when moving into other countries. First, managers must decide which products and services to introduce in which countries. When selecting a country, they must take into account the type of government, market-entry requirements, tariffs and other trade barriers, cultural and language differences, consumer preferences, foreign-exchange rates, and differing business customs. Then, they must decide whether to standardize the product, selling it everywhere, or to customize the product to accommodate the lifestyles and habits of local target markets. A company might change only the product's name or packaging, or it can modify the product's components, size, and functions.

For example, French consumers have been eating at McDonald's (**www.mcdonalds.fr**) since the company first arrived in 1972, but the burger giant has a unique look in that country—which happens to be its second-largest market outside of the United States. To accommodate a culture known for its cuisine and dining experience, many McDonald's outlets in France have upgraded their decor to a level that would make them almost unrecognizable in the United

States. Menus include such variations as McBaguette and Le Croque McDo, a McDonald's take on the traditional French *croque monsieur* grilled ham-and-cheese sandwich.[21]

For fresh insights on product and branding strategies, visit **real-timeupdates.com/ bia9** and select Chapter 13.

 CHECKPOINT

LEARNING OBJECTIVE 4: Identify four ways of expanding a product line, and discuss two risks that product-line extensions pose.

SUMMARY: A product line can be expanded by filling gaps in the market, extending the line to include new varieties of existing products, extending the brand to new product categories, and stretching the line to include lower- or higher-priced items. Two of the biggest risks with product-line extensions are losing brand identity and coherence (weakening of the brand's meaning) and cannibalizing sales of other products in the product line.

CRITICAL THINKING: (1) If McDonald's had been relatively unknown to French diners when the company entered that market in 1972, would it have made more sense to use a different and more "French-sounding" brand name? Why or why not? (2) Would a consumer products manufacturer ever want to create more product extensions and variations than it could explain in terms of pure market appeal? Why or why not?

IT'S YOUR BUSINESS: (1) Citing specific examples, how has branding helped you as a consumer? Think about the assurance you have in buying a known and trusted brand, for example. (2) Think about some of the consumer products you buy frequently, such as cereal, painkillers, or snack foods. Do you appreciate the range of choices available to you when you shop for these items, or do you wish that companies would narrow the options to a handful in each category? Why?

KEY TERMS TO KNOW: brand managers, product line, product mix, family branding, brand extension

---

Pricing Strategies

The second key element in the marketing mix is pricing. Recall from the definition in Chapter 12 that pricing involves *capturing value* back from the customer in exchange for the value provided in the product. Setting and managing prices is a combination of strategic considerations and careful financial analysis.

STRATEGIC CONSIDERATIONS IN PRICING

Managers must consider a variety of internal and external factors when establishing prices:

- **Marketing objectives.** The first step in setting a price is to match it to the objectives set in the strategic marketing plan. Is the goal to increase market share, increase sales, improve profits, project a particular image, or combat competition? Price is a flexible tool that can help a firm achieve a wide variety of marketing objectives.
- **Government regulations.** To protect consumers and encourage fair competition, governments around the world have enacted various price-related laws over the years. These regulations are particularly important in three areas of prohibited behavior: (1) *price discrimination*, unfairly offering attractive discounts to some customers but not to others; (2) *deceptive pricing*, pricing schemes that are considered misleading; and (3) *price fixing*, an agreement among two or more companies supplying the same type of products as to the prices they will charge or other financial decisions that affect buyers.[22]
- **Customer perceptions.** Another consideration in setting price is the perception of quality and value that a price elicits from customers. An unexpectedly low price can trigger fears of low quality, but a high price can connote quality and even exclusivity. Specific

5 **LEARNING OBJECTIVE**

List the factors that influence pricing decisions, and explain break-even analysis.

Marketers often select the digits in a price to trigger specific cognitive and emotional responses.

price elasticity
A measure of the sensitivity of demand to changes in price.

numbers can have a perceptual effect as well. You have no doubt noticed that many prices end in 9, such as $5.99 or $499. Two theories have been advanced to explain this common practice. First, buyers tend to rely on the leftmost digit in the price, so that the 4 in $499 factors heavily in perception, even though $499 is only 0.2 percent cheaper than $500. Second, when the rightmost digit is a 9, buyers are more likely to perceive the price as a good deal. Conversely, rounded figures such as $500 instead of $499 can foster the perception of luxury or exclusivity.[23]

- **Market demand.** The discussion of supply and demand in Chapter 2 points out that market demand usually fluctuates as prices fluctuate. However, some goods and services are relatively *insensitive* to changes in price; others are highly *sensitive*. Buyers can also exhibit individual levels of price sensitivity. For instance, brand-loyal customers tend to be less sensitive to price, meaning they will stick with a brand even as the price increases, whereas other buyers will begin switching to cheaper alternatives.[24] Marketers refer to this sensitivity as **price elasticity**—how responsive demand will be to a change in price.

- **Competition.** Competitive prices are obviously a major consideration whenever a firm is establishing or changing its prices. Technology has profoundly shifted the balance of power in this respect from sellers to buyers in recent years, as social commerce websites and mobile apps make it easy to find the lowest prices for a wide variety of goods and services. The easier it is for buyers to compare prices, for instance, the more important competitive prices become—particularly when buyers don't perceive much difference among the available products. Changes in the retail sector, growing consumer interest in specialty and alternative brands, and the spread of private labels have also restricted the pricing flexibility that some manufacturers once had. Consumer goods giants such as General Mills and Campbell Soup, for example, no longer have the pricing maneuverability they once enjoyed as they find themselves facing new competitors and more pressure from retailers to keep prices low.[25]

COST STRUCTURE AND BREAK-EVEN ANALYSIS

fixed costs
Business costs that remain constant regardless of the number of units produced or number of customers served.

variable costs
Business costs that increase with the number of units produced or customers served.

break-even analysis
A method of calculating the minimum volume of sales needed at a given price to cover all costs.

break-even point
Sales volume at a given price that will cover all of a company's costs.

Every company has a particular *cost structure* that determines how much it must spend to create and market its products. Some costs remain the same regardless of production and sales volume. Such **fixed costs** include rent or mortgage payments, insurance premiums, real estate taxes, and salaries. These are costs incurred just to "keep the doors open," without creating or selling anything. In contrast, **variable costs**, including raw materials, supplies consumed during production, shipping, and sales commissions, vary with changes in production and sales volume. Obviously, the more a company can lower its cost structure, the more flexibility it has in setting prices and ensuring desirable levels of profit.

The cost to create and sell each product is a combination of fixed and variable costs. A critical calculation in setting prices is **break-even analysis**, determining the number of units a firm must sell at a given price to recoup both fixed and variable costs—to "break even," in other words. The **break-even point** is the minimum sales volume the company must achieve to avoid losing money. Sales volume beyond the break-even point will generate profits; sales volume below the break-even amount will result in losses.

You can determine the break-even point in number of units with this simple calculation:

$$\text{Break-even point} = \frac{\text{Fixed costs}}{\text{Selling price} - \text{Variable costs per unit}}$$

For example, if you wanted to price haircuts at $20 and you had fixed costs of $60,000 and variable costs per haircut of $5, you would need to sell 4,000 haircuts to break even:

$$\text{Break-even point} = \frac{60{,}000}{\$20 - \$5}$$

Naturally, $20 isn't your only pricing option. Why not charge $30 instead? At that price, you need to sell only 2,400 haircuts to break even (see Exhibit 13.7). Of course, you would have to convince 2,400 people to pay the higher price, and depending on market dynamics and your cost structure, you might make more money selling at the lower price.

Note that break-even analysis doesn't dictate what price you *should* charge; rather, it provides some insight into the price you *can* charge and begin to generate profit. With the

EXHIBIT 13.7	**Break-Even Analysis**

The break-even point is the point at which revenues just cover costs. After fixed and variable costs have been met, any additional income represents profit. The graphs show that at $20 per haircut, the break-even point is 4,000 haircuts; charging $30 yields a break-even point at only 2,400 haircuts.

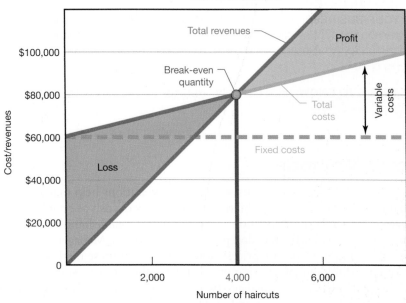

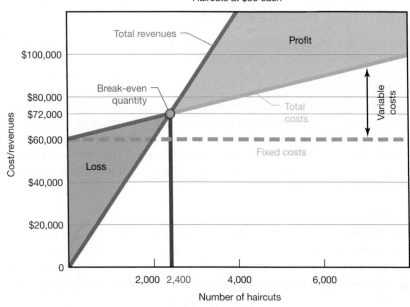

break-even point in hand, you can then factor in the various strategic considerations to determine price using one of the methods discussed in the next section.

 CHECKPOINT

LEARNING OBJECTIVE 5: List the factors that influence pricing decisions, and explain break-even analysis.

SUMMARY: Strategic considerations in pricing include marketing objectives, government regulations, customer perceptions, market demand, and competition. Break-even analysis is a way to determine how many units (the break-even point) a firm needs to produce in order to begin turning a profit by covering its fixed and variable costs. The break-even point is calculated by dividing fixed costs by the difference between the selling price and the variable costs per unit.

CRITICAL THINKING: (1) Why wouldn't a firm just drop any product that isn't selling in high enough volume to reach its break-even point? (2) Is "9"-style pricing ethical? Why or why not?

IT'S YOUR BUSINESS: (1) Do you factor in the value of your time when you price-comparison shop? Why or why not? (2) As a consumer taking charge of your own financial future, what lessons could you take from the business concepts of fixed and variable costs?

KEY TERMS TO KNOW: price elasticity, fixed costs, variable costs, break-even analysis, break-even point

---

6 **LEARNING OBJECTIVE**

Compare the three foundational pricing methods, and list six situational pricing methods.

Pricing Methods

Break-even analysis and the various strategic considerations help managers establish an overall framework of pricing possibilities. You can think of costs as establishing the pricing "floor," whereas demand, competition, and other factors establish the "ceiling." Somewhere between those two limits lies the ideal price for each product. Managers can apply a variety of methods to pinpoint specific prices. Note that some of these methods aren't mutually exclusive; companies can use two or more methods, either in succession or at the same time.

Pricing methods can be divided into two categories: *foundational* methods that define the overall approach to setting prices and *situational* methods that can be applied temporarily or in special situations.

FOUNDATIONAL PRICING METHODS

Marketers can use one of three fundamental drivers as the primary factor in establishing prices: cost, perceived value, or competition.

Cost-Based Pricing

cost-based pricing
A method of setting prices based on production and marketing costs, rather than conditions in the marketplace.

With **cost-based pricing**, also known as *cost-plus pricing*, a company starts with the cost of producing a good or a service and then adds a *markup* to arrive at the selling price. Cost-based pricing is simple, but it suffers from a major weakness: It doesn't consider external factors such as customer demand or competitive prices. The price could be too high for market conditions, leaving the company uncompetitive, or it could be too low, generating less profit than it could otherwise.

Value-Based Pricing

value-based pricing
A method of setting prices based on customer perceptions of value.

In contrast to cost-based pricing, **value-based pricing** establishes a price based on a product's perceived value in the marketplace. In other words, rather than starting with cost and then working upward to identify the price, this method starts with a target price and works downward to identify a cost structure that will yield acceptable profit margins. This method can improve profits and competitiveness, but it is more difficult because it requires measuring or estimating customer perceptions of value.

Companies can promote value pricing in one of two ways: They can emphasize how low the price is or how much customers get for the price. In other words, despite the word *value*, value-based pricing isn't just about low prices. Even extremely expensive products can be priced and promoted on their value.[26]

Competition-Based Pricing

Prices can also be established and promoted relative to similar products or suppliers with **competition-based pricing**. Companies that promise to match competitors' prices or that promote themselves as the lowest-priced supplier are taking this approach. When customers believe that there is little difference among the goods and services in a given market, they are usually reluctant to pay more than the prevailing price. If the companies providing these goods and services can't distinguish their offerings in a meaningful way, they often have little choice but to match whatever the competition is charging. Whenever you shop for airline tickets, for example, you will probably see multiple flights to your destination at exactly or very nearly the same price. (Note that it's legal for competitors to *match* each other's prices—they just can't *agree* to sell at the same prices.)

Competition-based pricing in parity markets can be destructive for all suppliers if it triggers *price wars* between competitors. If one supplier drops its prices below the prevailing level, other suppliers will feel compelled to match it or lose business. If the cycle of dropping and matching continues, everyone can find themselves losing money on every sale.

If a company *is* able to distinguish its products from the competition, it can use competition-based pricing in a way that reflects the additional perceived value. For instance, a manufacturer might show that while its product is 10 percent more expensive than the competition, it offers 20 percent more value.

competition-based pricing
A method of setting prices based on what suppliers of similar products are charging.

If a company can't find any other way to distinguish its products, competing on price might be its only option. However, competing on price alone can be a tough business model to sustain.

SITUATIONAL PRICING METHODS

In addition to deciding on the foundation of its pricing structure, a company can apply a variety of other methods to optimize and adjust prices. These often combine one or more elements of cost, value, and competitive pricing strategies.

Algorithmic Pricing

Algorithmic pricing refers to a variety of computational methods used to set price, either in more nuanced ways than simple cost- or competition-based pricing or in dynamic ways that respond in real time to fluctuations in demand and other market conditions. These methods go by a variety of names, including *optimal pricing, dynamic pricing, yield management,* and *surge pricing*. Thousands of companies also use artificial intelligence (AI) to enhance their price-setting decisions.[27]

In general, all these methods try to apply as much information as is currently available in an attempt to capture the maximum amount of value from the customer in each transaction. Here are four examples:

algorithmic pricing
A variety of computational methods used to set price, either in more nuanced ways than simple cost- or competition-based pricing or in dynamic ways that respond in real time to fluctuations in demand and other market conditions.

- Uber's surge pricing raises fares during periods of peak demand, such as can occur during daily rush hours and special events. The Uber app alerts riders when surge pricing is in effect, and they can choose to pay the premium or wait until prices go back down.[28]
- AirBnB's Smart Pricing feature helps property owners set prices based on the probability of getting bookings. The tool uses machine learning to build neighborhood-level models that predict the likelihood that each property will attract visitors at various price points.[29]
- Like Uber and AirBnB, airlines wrestle with the challenge of perishability: Every time a seat leaves the ground empty, it represents a lost revenue opportunity that can never

be recaptured. In response, the airlines were pioneers in the concept of algorithmic pricing with *yield management systems.* Yield management is based on the realization that travelers have different levels of price sensitivity and are willing to pay varying amounts for tickets based on when they book and how many alternatives are available. These systems can both lower fares if the airline needs to fill seats and raise fares as the date of a flight approaches and only relatively price-insensitive customers such as business travelers are likely to book. Yield management (or *revenue management,* as it is sometimes called) has been a boon for the airline and hotel industries, sometimes boosting a company's revenue by hundreds of millions of dollars a year.[30]

- Gas stations have been prone to price wars for years, given the similarity of their products and the willingness of many drivers to search around for the lowest price. AI-based systems are now helping station owners improve profit margins by adapting prices in real time without resorting to the brute-force method of simply undercutting the competition. The systems can even make counterintuitive decisions such as raising prices when a nearby competitor lowers its prices, because those low prices are likely to create long lines that prompt some drivers to find an alternative.[31]

Life-Cycle Pricing

skim pricing
Charging a high price for a new product during the introductory stage and lowering the price later.

penetration pricing
Introducing a new product at a low price in hopes of building sales volume quickly.

Companies can adjust their pricing strategies as products move throughout the life cycle. During the introductory phase of the product life cycle, for instance, a company may opt to take advantage of strong demand before competitors can enter the market and exert downward pressure on prices. To achieve this goal, the company can charge a high initial price—a practice known as **skim pricing**—with the intention of dropping the price later. *Early adopters* are often willing to pay a premium to get their hands on new products as soon as possible. In consumer markets, some people simply want to have the latest and greatest before anyone else; in organizational markets, new types of equipment can give companies a short-term competitive advantage.

When early adopters and enthusiasts are excited about the release of a new product, a company has the option of using skim pricing to maximize profits before the market matures.

The opposite of skim pricing is **penetration pricing**, in which a company tries to build sales volume and secure market share by charging a low initial price. This approach has the added advantage of discouraging competition, because the low price—which competitors would be pressured to match—limits the profit potential for everyone. (If the intent of penetration is to drive competitors out of business, though, companies open themselves up to charges of illegal *predatory pricing.*)

However, penetration pricing doesn't work if the company can't sustain the low price levels profitably, if prices for a particular product are inelastic, or if customers weigh other factors more heavily than price. Moreover, prices that are far below the market's expectations can raise concerns about quality, reliability, and safety. Everyone would like to pay less for medical care, but many people would be unwilling to go to cut-rate clinics if they thought their health might be jeopardized.

Loss-Leader Pricing

loss-leader pricing
Selling one product at a loss as a way to entice customers to consider other products.

As part of a larger marketing plan, some companies occasionally resort to **loss-leader pricing**, setting a price on one product so low that they lose money on every sale but recoup that loss by enticing customers to try a new product or buy other products. For instance, grocery stores can use milk and other staples as loss leaders to encourage shoppers to visit. (And there's a reason these products are often all the way at the back of the store—you have to walk past hundreds of higher-margin products that you might suddenly decide you can't live without.)

Auctions and Participative Pricing

In an *auction,* the seller doesn't set a firm price but allows buyers to competitively bid on the products being sold. Auctions used to be confined to a few market sectors such as fine art, agricultural products, and government bonds, but that all changed when eBay turned selling and buying via auctions into a new national pastime. Many companies now use eBay and other auction sites to sell everything from modular buildings to tractors to industrial equipment.

An unusual way of letting customers decide what to pay is participative pricing, sometimes known as "pay what you want." Customers literally get to pay as much as they think a product or service is worth. Although it might sound like a strategy for financial disaster—and it occasionally is—buyers sometimes pay more than the company would normally charge. In addition to the financial risk, pay-what-you-want pricing can drive potential customers away because they don't want to take on the stress of deciding what is fair.[32]

With auction pricing, whether in a in-person auction or any online auction such as eBay, customers establish the value of each item by bidding against each other.

Mark Richardson/Alamy Stock Photo

Free and Freemium Pricing

Even more radical than participative pricing is no price at all. However, giving away goods and services can make a lot of sense in the right situation, such as when a new company is trying to make a name for itself in the marketplace.[33] Another use of free pricing is when some customers are charged enough to provide free goods and services for other customers, a tactic known as **freemium pricing** (*free + premium*). For example, a number of software products, online services, and mobile apps offer a free version with fewer capabilities and one or more paid versions of the full product. The hope behind freemium pricing is that by allowing a large enough base of people to use the free version, you'll attract enough paying customers to support the business.[34] Giving away some products while maintaining full prices for others (the common approach of "buy one, get one free") is also a way to effectively offer discounted pricing without the risk of creating expectations of lower prices.[35]

freemium pricing
A hybrid pricing strategy of offering some products for free while charging for others, or offering a product for free to some customers while charging others for it.

Subscription Pricing

With **subscription pricing**, customers are charged a recurring fee for the right to continue using a product. Magazines and newspapers have used this model for hundreds of years, and many other products such as mobile phone service are sold as contracts with recurring payments. In a growing number of product categories, companies are moving away from a single product sale to the subscription model. Many apps and other software products, for example, have shifted to the subscription model and charge users a monthly or annual fee, rather than selling the product at a single, one-time price. In enterprise software, this is known as *software as a service (SaaS)* and is now common for business software. Rather than buying, installing, and maintaining software, SaaS customers subscribe to a cloud-based service in which the supplier takes care of all the maintenance choices.

subscription pricing
A pricing model in which customers are charged a recurring fee for the right to continuing using a product.

The appeal of recurring revenue streams has caught the attention of manufacturers of tangible goods as well, creating a new class of products known as *device as a service (DaaS)*. (You'll also see DaaS used to refer to *desktop* as a service and *data* as a service, as well as a variety of other "x-as-a-service" business models.) DaaS contracts differ from simple equipment rental in that the supplier typically takes care of everything from installation to maintenance, repair, tech support, and upgrades. This model is now being used to market products as diverse as smartphones, cars, and trucking fleets. In addition to the revenue stability that DaaS offers suppliers, customers often find it appealing because it can eliminate a host of tech support tasks, assure them of having the latest releases of hardware and software, and eliminate the risk of getting stuck with obsolete machinery and equipment. DaaS can also help customers deal with fluctuating needs more easily than buying or selling equipment as their needs change.[36]

REAL-TIME UPDATES
Learn More by Watching This Presentation

The rise of the subscription economy

See why so many companies are shifting their business models toward subscription pricing. Go to **real-timeupdates.com/bia9** and select Learn More in the Students section.

PRICE ADJUSTMENT TACTICS

After they've established initial price points, companies need to stay on the lookout for potential advantages that can be gained by adjusting prices up or down over time. They can offer a variety of **discounts**, such as temporary price reductions to stimulate sales, reductions for paying early or paying in cash, or *volume discounts* for buying in bulk.

discounts
Temporary price reductions to stimulate sales or lower prices to encourage certain behaviors such as paying with cash.

bundling
Offering several products for a single price that is presumably lower than the total of the products' individual prices.

Sometimes sellers combine several of their products and sell them at one reduced price. This practice, called **bundling**, can also promote sales of products that consumers might not otherwise buy—especially when the combined price is low enough to entice them to purchase the bundle. Examples of bundled products are season tickets, vacation packages, computer software with hardware, and wrapped packages of shampoo and conditioner. In contrast, a company can also *unbundle* elements of a product and charge separately for the individual elements. Many airlines have done this recently, instituting separate fees for checked baggage and meals, for example.

For more information on pricing strategies and tactics, visit **real-timeupdates.com/bia9** and select Chapter 13.

 CHECKPOINT

LEARNING OBJECTIVE 6: Compare the three foundational pricing methods, and list six situational pricing methods.

SUMMARY: The three foundational pricing methods are *cost-based*, which takes the cost of producing and marketing a product and adds a markup to arrive at the selling price; *value-based*, which tries to establish the perceived value of the product in the eyes of target customers and sets a price based on that; and *competition-based*, which sets prices based on what suppliers of similar products are charging. Six situational methods that can be used to implement and fine-tune the three foundational methods are algorithmic pricing, life-cycle pricing (including skim pricing and penetration pricing), loss-leader pricing, auctions and participative pricing, free and freemium pricing, and subscription pricing.

CRITICAL THINKING: (1) What steps could a company take to determine the perceived value of its products in its target markets? (2) How can patterns of temporary price discounts "train" consumers to stop buying at full price?

IT'S YOUR BUSINESS: (1) Have you ever bid on anything on eBay, another online auction site, or an in-person auction? If so, how did you decide how much to bid? Did you set a maximum price you'd allow yourself to spend? Did you get caught up in the competitive emotions of bidding against someone else? (2) Have you ever purchased a hot new product as soon as it hit the market, only to see the price drop a few months later? If so, did you resolve never to buy so quickly again?

KEY TERMS TO KNOW: cost-based pricing, value-based pricing, competition-based pricing, algorithmic pricing, skim pricing, penetration pricing, loss-leader pricing, freemium pricing, subscription pricing, discounts, bundling

 LEARNING OBJECTIVE

Describe how companies are using virtual and augmented reality to create new products and new customer experiences.

Thriving in the Digital Enterprise: Virtual and Augmented Reality

Virtual reality and augmented reality are finding a wide variety of applications in business, both as product experiences themselves and as ways to enhance and improve business functions. Here is a quick look at how both technologies are being used in business today.

VIRTUAL REALITY

virtual reality (VR)
Computer-generated simulations that create the sensation of being in a real environment.

Virtual reality (VR) systems create a simulation in which the person experiences the sensation of being in an environment, even though that environment is entirely computer generated. If it is difficult, expensive, or dangerous to put people in a real-life situation, a VR simulation can let people experience the sensation of being there and doing whatever tasks are required. Here are some of the current business applications of VR:

- **Product design and evaluation.** VR can help people experience a product or structure before it is built. Ford uses VR to let engineers "see" design ideas before building anything (see Exhibit 13.8) and to get feedback from drivers by letting them sit in and experience prototype designs before the cars are manufactured.[37] Safety testing is another key application of *virtual prototyping*, such as subjecting virtual models to crash test procedures.[38]
- **Virtual walk-throughs.** Architects and interior designers are using VR to let clients experience living and working in buildings before they are built or decorated. The systems are so realistic that clients can see where sunlight will stream through windows throughout the day or check sight lines from various places within buildings to minimize personal security risks.[39] Similarly, manufacturing engineers can create virtual factories to verify process flows and other vital parameters.[40]
- **Retailing and business-to-business sales.** VR can let buyers check out a variety of products without leaving home, such as walking through a virtual showroom, examining and placing various pieces of furniture and accessories in the space, and then ordering whatever catches their fancy.[41] VR is also being used to demonstrate industrial equipment that is too big to display in physical showrooms.[42]
- **Advertising.** Just as YouTube quickly became a major channel for "advertainment" videos, as more consumers acquire VR headsets it's likely that VR experiences will become a widespread advertising medium as well.
- **Virtual fittings.** If the thought of trying on clothes in a retailer's fitting rooms doesn't appeal to you, keep an eye out for new VR fitting systems. They create a 3D map of your body and then let you try on clothes in the privacy of your own virtual reality.[43]
- **Training.** Company trainers can use simulated on-the-job scenarios to let employees practice skills before moving into real situations. For example, Walmart uses VR to immerse employees in situations such as holiday crowds so they can practice dealing with multiple customers in a high-pressure situation. VR training is particularly valuable when it's dangerous or expensive to put trainees in real-life situations, such as on oil rigs or in operating rooms.[44]
- **Remote meetings, conferences, and interviews.** Moving one step beyond teleconferencing, VR meetings and interviews let participants interact without leaving their homes or offices.[45] Lloyds Banking Group uses VR to see how well candidates for its leadership training program can solve problems.[46]

EXHIBIT 13.8   **Virtual Reality**

At Ford, designers use virtual reality to envision design ideas before building physical cars.

Pending Warren Crone/Ford

| EXHIBIT 13.9 | Augmented Reality |

By simply pointing a mobile device equipped with Panasonic's augmented reality maintenance software at a machine, technicians can get detailed information needed for maintenance and repair by tapping the text labels that pop up on screen.

Photo courtesy of Panasonic

AUGMENTED REALITY

augmented reality (AR)
Systems that superimpose visual or textual information on live images of real scenes.

Unlike VR's ability to simulate reality, **augmented reality (AR)** starts with reality and enhances the user experience by superimposing visual or textual information on it. These additional layers of information, which are displayed in headsets or on mobile device screens, are relevant to the user's immediate surroundings, allowing them to interact with reality in more productive ways. Here are some of the current AR applications in business:

- **Manufacturing.** AR can help workers perform complex procedures in fabrication and assembly by superimposing images of parts, such as showing how the next piece in an engine needs to be positioned and attached.[47] These systems are sometimes referred to as *augmented virtuality* systems when they combine elements of real and virtual worlds.
- **Training.** Similar to the manufacturing applications, AR in training situations can guide trainees step by step, combining virtual and real parts and systems. And rather than forcing trainees to look away to consult training manuals, AR systems can project instructions into the air directly in front of users or onto work surfaces.[48]
- **Maintenance and repair.** Technicians who face the daunting task of troubleshooting and maintaining complex equipment often need massive service manuals to navigate the inner workings of the machinery in front of them. AR applications such as the Panasonic system shown in Exhibit 13.9 display information whenever a technician aims the camera of a mobile device at a machine. Some field AR systems can also be equipped with two-way communication so that techs in the field can get real-time guidance from experts in a central control center.[49]

CHECKPOINT

LEARNING OBJECTIVE 7: Describe how companies are using virtual and augmented reality to create new products and new customer experiences.

SUMMARY: Virtual reality (VR) systems create a simulation in which the person experiences the sensation of being in an environment, even though that environment is entirely computer generated. Current business applications of VR include product design and evaluation, virtual walk-throughs, retailing and business-to-business sales, advertising, virtual fittings, training, and remote meetings, conferences, and interviews. Augmented reality (AR) starts with reality and enhances the user experience by superimposing visual or textual information on it. Current applications include manufacturing, training, and maintenance and repair.

CRITICAL THINKING: How might the growth of VR gaming affect the application of VR in business?

IT'S YOUR BUSINESS: Have you used a VR headset for gaming? If so, did you experience any drawbacks that business users should be aware of?

KEY TERMS TO KNOW: virtual reality (VR), augmented reality (AR)

BEHIND THE SCENES

OXO Gets a Handle on Universal Design

When Sam Farber set his mind to creating a more comfortable vegetable peeler, his immediate concern was relieving the discomfort that the conventional design caused in his wife's arthritic hands. He solved that problem—and helped launch both a revolution in universal design and a highly regarded company that is still going strong 30 years later.

Ever the entrepreneur, Farber also saw an opportunity that reached far beyond a single kitchen utensil. Why couldn't every tool and utensil used around the house work better? He came out of retirement to launch a new company based on this premise. He named it OXO (he chose the name because of its symmetry—it can be read in any direction and orientation) and gave a New York design studio called Smart Design the task of designing a new generation of kitchen implements under the brand name OXO Good Grips.

The vegetable peeler is a simple enough product, but getting the ergonomics and the cutting function just right was no simple task. Refining the first 15 OXO Good Grips utensils required "hundreds of models and dozens of design iterations," according to the company. That exploration led to the soft plastic handle (made from a material called Santoprene) that made the utensils easier to use and that is now as integral to the brand as any logo. And the long effort paid off in terms of business success. OXO products are now used in millions of homes, and the designs are so well crafted that some of the company's products are on display in museums around the world.

For crafting products that meet the needs of people with arthritis and other physical challenges, OXO and Smart Design are credited with helping to launch a wave of universal, inclusive design. The appeal isn't limited to those with arthritis and similar problems, however. The designs are more comfortable for anyone to use, and the attention paid to functionality means they often work better than traditional designs, too. During their three-decade strategic partnership, OXO and Smart Design have amassed detailed insights into how people use household tools and utensils by interviewing thousands of consumers and visiting hundreds of homes.

Thoughtful design extends to packaging as well. Walk into most any store that sells utensils, and you can quickly spot the selection of OXO products on the display. The bold and clear black, white, and red packaging for the Good Grips line is almost as iconic as the products themselves.

With more components and more material than sparse traditional design, that first peeler and its companion products cost more to produce and therefore hit the market with higher prices. However, Ferber was confident that people would pay more for tools that worked better. He was correct, and the strategy of value-based pricing has served the company well ever since.

The company's product mix has expanded rather dramatically since those first 15 products. It currently numbers more than 1,000 products, including just about every imaginable sort of kitchen utensil and dozens of products designed to improve everyday life elsewhere around the house.

Brand extensions have played an important part as well. The original OXO Good Grips brand is now joined by four others: OXO SteeL (stainless steel tools and utensils), OXO On (electrical appliances), OXO Strive (products for sports, exercise, and outdoor activities), and OXO Tot (products for small children). These brands are a great example of smart brand extensions: They expand the reach of the brand without diluting it in any way, they let the company apply the "halo" of the original OXO Good Grips to new product lines, and they make sense to the millions of customers who have had good experiences with OXO. Davin Stowell, the founder of Smart Design, sums up the wisdom of the OXO brand extensions nicely:

> The degree of clarity to the OXO brand is quite rare. Most companies struggle to expand without losing what made them great in the first place. Not OXO. This notion of "making everyday life easier" has become the driving force behind everything OXO does, and it's allowed them to expand into adjacent categories very successfully.

With more than 1,000 products for the home, OXO shows no signs of slowing down, and its long-time partner Smart Design is still working on new ways to bring universal design to the tasks of everyday life.[50]

Critical Thinking Questions

13-1. How far could OXO take its brand extensions and the promise of making everyday tasks easier? Should it consider an OXO-branded smartphone, for instance? Smartphones are everyday tools, after all—would an expansion into this product category make sense? Why or why not?

13-2. What other products are you aware of that could benefit from more inclusive design?

13-3. The bent-metal style of vegetable peeler is still widely available. Why do you suppose this is, given how much more comfortable the ergonomically designed alternatives like OXO are?

Learn More Online

Explore the company's product offerings at **www.oxo.com**. What do you notice in terms of commonality across the entire product mix? Read the Our Philosophy and Our Team pages in the About Us section. Would you enjoy the experience of working at OXO?

End of Chapter

KEY TERMS

algorithmic pricing (399)
augmented reality (AR) (404)
brand (389)
brand equity (389)
brand extension (394)
brand licensing (390)
brand loyalty (389)
brand managers (391)
brand marks (389)
brand names (389)
break-even analysis (396)
break-even point (396)
bundling (402)
capital items (384)
co-branding (390)
commercialization (388)
competition-based pricing (399)
convenience products (383)
cost-based pricing (398)
discounts (401)
expense items (383)
family branding (392)

fixed costs (396)
freemium pricing (401)
logo (389)
loss-leader pricing (400)
national brands (389)
penetration pricing (400)
price elasticity (396)
private brands (389)
product development process (386)
product life cycle (384)
product line (392)
product mix (392)
prototypes (387)
shopping products (383)
skim pricing (400)
specialty products (383)
subscription pricing (401)
test marketing (388)
trademarks (389)
value-based pricing (398)
variable costs (396)
virtual reality (VR) (402)

TEST YOUR KNOWLEDGE

Questions for Review

13-4. What are the four stages of the product life cycle?

13-5. Why is idea screening an essential part of the product development process?

13-6. What is a product mix?

13-7. What is the purpose of co-branding?

13-8. What are the functions of labeling?

13-9. How many books will a publisher have to sell to break even if fixed costs are $100,000, the selling price per book is $60, and the variable costs per book are $40?

13-10. How does cost-based pricing differ from value-based pricing?

13-11. What is algorithmic pricing?

13-12. How does virtual reality differ from augmented reality?

Questions for Analysis

13-13. How does branding help consumers?

13-14. What factors may have led to the popularity of private brands among shoppers?

13-15. Given the weaknesses of cost-based pricing, why would any company use this method?

13-16. Why is it important to review the objectives of a strategic marketing plan before setting a product's price?

13-17. **Ethical Considerations.** If your college neighborhood is typical, many companies in the area adorn themselves in your school colors and otherwise seek to identify their names with your school name and thereby encourage business from students.

Some of these firms probably have brand licensing agreements with your college or are involved in sponsoring various groups on campus. However, chances are some of them are using school colors and other branding elements without having any formal arrangement with the college. In other words, they may be getting commercial benefit from the association without paying for it.[51] Is this ethical? Why or why not?

13-18. Is subscription pricing likely to be as popular with customers as it is becoming with many product suppliers? Why or why not?

Questions for Application

13-19. In what ways might Mattel modify its pricing strategies during the life cycle of a toy product?

13-20. Why would a company ever want to sell its goods or services for less than they cost to produce?

13-21. Based on your personal experience, do you think loss-leader pricing strategy can be impactful and persuasive? Have you made additional purchases as a result?

13-22. Concept Integration. Review the theory of supply and demand in Chapter 2 (see pages 85–89). How do skimming and penetration pricing strategies influence a product's supply and demand?

13-23. Concept Integration. Review the discussion of cultural differences in international business in Chapter 3 (see pages 120–121). Which cultural differences do you think Disney had to consider when planning its product strategies for Disneyland Paris? Originally the company offered a standardized product but was later forced to customize many of the park's operations. What might have been some of the cultural challenges Disney experienced under a standardized product strategy?

EXPAND YOUR KNOWLEDGE

Discovering Career Opportunities

Being an international marketing manager entails huge responsibilities. Collect information from local or national chambers of commerce websites regarding codes and rules, products and services, and find more resources related to the nature of work, qualifications, and job expectations of a marketing manager. You may access the International Chamber of Commerce's page on products and services at **www.iccwbo.org/products-andservices**, the U.S. government's (export) page on sales and marketing at **www.export.gov/salesandmarketing**, or the American Marketing Association's site at **www.ama.org**.

13-24. What attributes should an international marketing manager acquire?

13-25. Is the job of a local marketing manager any different from that of an international marketing manager?

13-26. What factors influence a marketing manager's decision to work overseas?

Intelligent Business Technologies: Subscription Pricing

Research one of the newer forms of subscription services, such as meal boxes, men's razors, or beauty products. Why is this subscription model so effective? In what ways does it ensure that businesses have a more predictable revenue stream? How does this subscription pricing model suit the modern-day demands of consumers?

PRACTICE YOUR SKILLS

Resolving Ethical Dilemmas

You work in the marketing department of a domestic airline. In the past, the airline sold a bundled product consisting of a flight ticket, refreshments, and on-board entertainment. To be more competitive, the airline has decided to unbundle its services and charge individually for each service. The headline price of the flight ticket has dropped, but the overall price of all the unbundled services added together has slightly increased. Is it ethical to advertise a lower headline price to customers and then levy additional charges at the end of the purchase process? How do you think the airline should market the new pricing structure to be competitive and remain fair to its customers? Explain your answer.

Growing as a Professional

Many of the goods and services you use are satisfying largely because of the augmented elements that make up the whole product. Without apps, for example, a smartphone would just be an expensive, albeit convenient, way to make phone calls. When you use products in your daily life, think about what it is that makes them satisfying—or not. For example, what aspects of a car make it more satisfying than simply being a means to move you from point A to point B? Get in the habit of evaluating products in this way, and it'll help you create and market products more effectively on the job.

Sharpening Your Communication Skills

Now's your chance to play the role of a marketing specialist trying to convince a group of customers that your product concept is better than the competition's. You're going to wade into the industry battle over digital photo printing. Choose a side: either the photo printer manufacturers (such as Brother, Epson, or HP) who want consumers to buy printers to print their own digital photos, or the service providers (such as Walmart or Costco) who want consumers to use their services instead. Prepare a short presentation on why the approach you've chosen is better for consumers. Feel free to segment the consumer market and choose a particular target segment if that bolsters your argument.

Building Your Team Skills

Select a high-profile product with which you and your teammates are familiar. Do some online research to learn more about that brand. Then answer these questions and prepare a short group presentation to your classmates summarizing your findings:

- Is the product a consumer product, an organizational product, or both?
- At what stage in its life cycle is this product?
- Is the product a national brand or a private brand?
- How do the product's packaging and labeling help boost consumer appeal?
- How is this product promoted?
- Is the product mix to which this product belongs wide? Long? Deep?
- Is the product sold in international markets? If so, does the company use a standardized or a customized strategy?
- How is the product priced in relation to competing products?

Developing Your Research Skills

Scan recent business journals and newspapers (print or online editions) and read more about intelligent cars, such as Google's electric two-seater self-driving car and Apple's CarPlay. Select any article and answer the following:

13-27. Which other automobile companies are building their own intelligent cars? What is their outlook on the future of existing gas- and diesel-powered cars?

13-28. If you were the owner of an intelligent car that drives by itself using mobile apps, what concerns would you have? What do you consider as the main selling point of such vehicles?

13-29. How do newspaper articles cover the environmental impact of intelligent cars as compared to the gas-powered version? Based on your research, would you consider investing in an intelligent vehicle?

Writing Assignments

13-30. What sort of customers should a company target for the introductory phase of a product's life cycle?

13-31. Is it ethical for companies to *split-test* price points by offering different prices to different groups of customers? Why or why not?

ENDNOTES

1. OXO, accessed 22 May 2018, www.oxo.com; Smart Design, accessed 22 May 2018, smartdesignworldwide.com; "Freedom Machines: The Principles of Universal Design," *PBS*, 14 September 2004, www.pbs.org; Margalit Fox, "Sam Farber, Creator of Oxo Utensils, Dies at 88," *New York Times*, 21 June 2013, www.nytimes.com; "Samuel Farber, Developer of Kitchen Utensils, Dies at 88," *UPI*, 22 June 2013, www.upi.com; Dan Formosa, "OXO Good Grips," Dan Formosa, accessed 22 May 2018, danformosa.com.

2. Philip Kotler and Gary Armstrong, *Principles of Marketing*, 17th ed. (New York: Pearson, 2018), 221.

3. Kotler and Armstrong, *Principles of Marketing*, 222.

4. Kotler and Armstrong, *Principles of Marketing*, 265.

5. Christoper Mims, "A Surprisingly Long List of Everything Smartphones Replaced," *Technology Review*, 23 July 2012, www.technologyreview.com; Jenna Wortham, "Sending GPS Devices the Way of the Tape Deck?" *New York Times*, 7 July 2009, www.nytimes.com.

6. Kotler and Armstrong, *Principles of Marketing*, 257.

7. Hilary Lewis, "Amazon Orders 5 New Series Including 'Man in the High Castle,'" *Hollywood Reporter*, 18 February 2015, www.hollywoodreporter.com.

8. David Haigh and Jonathan Knowles, "How to Define Your Brand and Determine Its Value," *Marketing Management*, May/June 2004, 22–28.

9. "The World's Most Valuable Brands: 2017," *Fortune*, fortune.com.

10. Robert Klara, "How American Girl's Storied Dolls Became Such a Surprising Success," *Adweek*, 18 April 2016, www.adweek.com; Nina Diamond, John F. Sherry, Albert M. Muñiz, Mary Ann McGrath, Robert V. Kozinets, and Stefania Borghini, "American Girl and the Brand Gestalt: Closing the Loop on Sociocultural Branding Research," *Journal of Marketing*, May 2009, 118–134.

11. Janell M. Kurtz and Cynthia Mehoves, "Whose Name Is It Anyway?" *Marketing Management*, January/February 2002, 31–33.

12. Dictionary.com, accessed 21 May 2018, www.dictionary.com.

13. Jason Dely Rey, "Surprise! Amazon Now Sells More than 70 of Its Own Private-Label Brands," *Recode*, 7 April 2018, www.recode.net; Stephanie Strom, "Store-Label Brands Cleaning Up in Supermarket Aisle," *Seattle Times*, 2 October 2013, www.seattletimes.com.

14. Lawrence L. Garber, Jr., Eva M. Hyatt, and Ünal Ö. Boya, "The Effect of Package Shape on Apparent Volume: An Exploratory Study with Implications for Package Design," *Journal of Marketing Theory & Practice*, Summer 2009, 215–234.

15. Sean Poulter, "The Perils of Opening Impossible Packaging: Four in Ten of Us Have Suffered an Injury While Opening Everyday Goods," *Daily Mail*, 20 August 2013, www.dailymail.co.uk.

16. Kristin Heist, "How Packaging Protects the Environment," *Harvard Business Review*, 14 June 2012, www.hbr.org.

17. "Amazon Certified Frustration-Free Packaging," Amazon, accessed 21 May 2018, www.amazon.com.

18. Cheerios website, accessed 21 May 2018, www.cheerios.com.

19. Betsy Morris and Joan L. Levinstein, "What Makes Apple Golden," *Fortune*, 17 March 2008, 68–74; Bharat N. Anand, "The Value of a Broader Product Portfolio," *Harvard Business Review*, January 2008, 20–22.

20. Robin Lewis, "The Long Tail Theory Can Be Reality for Traditional Megabrands," *Forbes*, 31 May 2016, www.forbes.com; Chris Anderson, "The Long Tail," *Wired*, October 2004, www.wired.com.

21. McDonald's France, accessed 21 May 2018, www.mcdonalds.fr; Eleanor Beardsley, "Why McDonald's in France Doesn't Feel Like Fast Food," *NPR*, 24 January 2012, www.npr.org.

22. "Pricing Fixing," U.S. Federal Trade Commission, accessed 21 May 2018, www.ftc.gov.

23. Bouree Lam, "The Psychological Difference Between $12.00 and $11.67," *Atlantic*, 30 January 2015, www.theatlantic.com.

24. Edward Ramirez and Ronald E. Goldsmith, "Some Antecedents of Price Sensitivity," *Journal of Marketing Theory & Practice*, Summer 2009, 199–213.

25. Nathaniel Meyersohn, "Trouble in Big Food: America's Cereal, Soda and Soup Companies Are in Turmoil," *CNN Money*, 21 May 2018, money.cnn.com.

26. Kotler and Armstrong, *Principles of Marketing*, 285–288.

27. Sam Schechner, "Why Do Gas Station Prices Constantly Change?" *Wall Street Journal*, 8 May 2017, www.wsj.com.

28. "How Surge Pricing Works," Uber, accessed 21 May 2018, www.uber.com.

29. Janna Bray, "The Price Is Right," AirBnB, accessed 21 May 2018, airbnb.design; Hector Yee and Bar Ifrach, "Aerosolve: Machine Learning for Humans," *Medium*, 4 June 2015, medium.com.

30. "Yield Management in the Airline Industry," Travel & Technology Solutions, accessed 21 May 2018, www.tts.com.

31. Schechner, "Why Do Gas Station Prices Constantly Change?"

32. Utpal Dholakia, "When Does Pay What You Want Pricing Work?" *Psychology Today*, 5 March 2017, www.psychologytoday.com; Ju-Young Kim, Martin Natter, and Martin Spann, "Pay What You Want: A New Participative Pricing Mechanism," *Journal of Marketing*, January 2009, 44–58.

33. Don Moyer, "That's Going to Cost You," *Harvard Business Review*, May 2009, 132.

34. Drew Beechler, "8 Types of Freemium Pricing," *Medium*, 30 May 2017, www.medium.com.

35. "How About Free? The Price Point That Is Turning Industries on Their Heads," *Knowledge@Wharton*, 4 March 2009, knowledge.wharton.upenn.edu.

36. Christoph Schell, "Device-as-a-Service Makes Device Ownership and Management a Thing of the Past," *CIO*, 11 May 2017, www.cio.com; Laura Cox, "The Evolution of the Subscription Business Model," *Disruption*, 9 May 2018, disruptionhub.com.

37. "Make Way for Holograms: New Mixed Reality Technology Meets Car Design as Ford Tests Microsoft Hololens Globally," Ford, 21 September 2017, media.ford.com.

38. Hannah Williams, "What Industries Are Using Virtual Reality?" *Computerworld UK*, 17 November 2017, www.computerworlduk.com.

39. Jackie Crobsy, "Virtual Reality Brings Architect's Blueprints to Life," *Star Tribune*, 25 January 2016, www.startribune.com.

40. James Anderton, "Could Virtual Reality Be the Future of Factory Floor Planning?" *Engineering.com*, 2 November 2016, www.engineering.com.

41. Chris Morris, "10 Industries Rushing to Embrace Virtual Reality," *CNBC*, 1 December 2016, www.cnbc.com.

42. Anderton, "Could Virtual Reality Be the Future of Factory Floor Planning?"

43. "Beyond Gaming: 13 Industries AR/VR Is Poised to Transform," CB Insights, 23 June 2017, www.cbinsights.com.

44. Richard Feloni, "Walmart Is Using Virtual Reality to Train Its Employees," *Business Insider*, 1 June 2017, www.businessinsider.com.

45. Rose Leadem, "12 Amazing Uses of Virtual Reality," *Entrepreneur*, 2 June 2017, www.entrepreneur.com.

46. "Beyond Gaming: 13 Industries AR/VR Is Poised to Transform."

47. "Beyond Gaming: 13 Industries AR/VR Is Poised to Transform."

48. "Beyond Gaming: 13 Industries AR/VR Is Poised to Transform."

49. *Mixed Reality for Professionals*, Fujitsu, accessed 21 May 2018, www.fujitsu.com.

50. See note 1.

51. Aubrey Kent and Richard M. Campbell, Jr., "An Introduction to Freeloading: Campus-Area Ambush Marketing," *Sport Marketing Quarterly* 16, no. 2 (2007): 118–122.

14

Customer Communication and Product Distribution

LEARNING OBJECTIVES After studying this chapter, you will be able to

1 Describe the three major tasks in crafting a communication strategy, and identify six important legal aspects of marketing communication.

2 Identify the most common advertising appeals and the most important media used in advertising and direct response marketing.

3 Describe consultative selling, and explain the personal selling process.

4 Define sales promotion, and characterize the differences between consumer and trade promotions.

5 Explain the uses of social media in customer communication and the role of public relations.

6 Discuss the importance of marketing intermediaries, and contrast the roles of wholesalers and retailers.

7 Describe how companies are using augmented and automated writing to communicate with customers.

MyLab Intro to Business
Improve Your Grade!
If your instructor is using MyLab Intro to Business, visit **www.pearson.com/ mylab/intro-to-business**.

BEHIND THE SCENES **Tata Harper: Pursuing a More Natural Way to Care for Skin**

Charley Gallay/Stringer

When she launched her line of luxury skin care products, entrepreneur Tata Harper faced two key marketing questions: how to promote her new products to potential customers and which distribution channels to use.

www.tataharperskincare.com

Skin care has been an important part of Tata Harper's life for about as long as she can remember. As a girl in her native Colombia, she would spend Saturdays as "spa days" with her aunts and cousins at her grandmother's house, trying out products they had purchased from beauty shops and preparing her grandmother's homemade beauty recipes.

Later, while living in Miami, she assisted her stepfather through cancer treatment and recovery, which is when she had the eye-opening and life-changing realization about how many chemicals she and her family were exposed to every day. Her stepfather's doctors advised that he limit his exposure to chemicals, and Harper took the advice to heart herself.

She cleaned out her home from top to bottom and went looking for all-natural alternatives for everything from food to shampoo to household products. However, when she searched for skin care products, a category close to her heart from childhood, she was disappointed by what she found. In her usual shopping haunts, she could find brands that boasted a natural ingredient or two, but when she checked the ingredient lists, she saw long lists of chemicals. Some all-natural products were available in health-food stores, but she wasn't always impressed with their quality or effectiveness. And these products didn't fulfill her aesthetic need for a luxury skin care experience.

Figuring she couldn't be the only person looking for high-quality, all-natural products with luxury feel and performance, she set out to make them herself. After spending nearly five years working with a team of eight chemists, she formulated her initial line of products.

Transforming a great idea into a thriving company is a major step, of course. If you were Tata Harper, how would you present your products to consumers? Would you focus on the natural aspect, the performance aspect, the luxury aspect, or some combination of all three? How would you distinguish them from the high-end but chemical-laden products on the one hand and the natural but less satisfying products on the other? And how would you get your products into the hands of consumers? Would you take the health-food-store route and get on the shelves next to other natural products, or would you take the luxury route and distribute them through Sephora and other high-end retailers?[1]

INTRODUCTION

Tata Harper (profiled in the chapter-opening Behind the Scenes) faced several key questions that every new company and every company with new products must answer: What do we want people to think about our products, how can we use advertising and other communication tools to reach them, and how can we make our products available to potential buyers? This chapter explains how marketers set communication goals, define messages, use the ever-growing array of media options to reach target audiences, and choose distribution channels to get their products into customers' hands.

Customer Communication: Challenges, Strategies, and Issues

Not long ago, marketing communication was largely about companies broadcasting carefully scripted messages to a mass audience that often had few, if any, ways to respond. Moreover, customers and other interested parties had few ways to connect with one another to ask questions about products, influence company decisions, or offer each other support.

However, various technologies have enabled and inspired a new approach to customer communication. In contrast to the "we talk, you listen" mindset of the past, the **social communication model** is *interactive* and *conversational*. As you know from your own experience with social media, today's audiences are no longer content to be passive recipients of messages; instead, they expect to be active participants in a meaningful conversation. On the surface, this approach might look like it has just added a few new digital media tools to the traditional arsenal of television, radio, newspapers, and magazines. However, as Exhibit 14.1 on the next page shows, the changes are much deeper and more profound. "Social Media in the Marketing Process" on page 427 discusses this new model in more detail.

The desire to participate in conversations regarding companies and brands is not the only profound change, either. Today's consumers are more demanding, more distracted, and less patient than ever before, and the entire advertising industry is still trying to adapt.[2] In this new world of interactive communication, it's more vital than ever to have a strategy that (1) establishes *clear communication goals*, (2) defines *compelling messages* to help achieve those goals, and (3) outlines a *cost-effective media mix* to engage target audiences.

ESTABLISHING COMMUNICATION GOALS

Communication activities can help companies meet a wide range of marketing objectives, but only if these activities are crafted with clear and specific goals based on where the target audience is in the purchasing cycle.[3] Marketers take the following steps to move potential customers toward purchases:

- **Generating awareness.** People obviously can't buy things they don't know about, so creating awareness is essential for new companies and new products.

1 **LEARNING OBJECTIVE**

Describe the three major tasks in crafting a communication strategy, and identify six important legal aspects of marketing communication.

social communication model
An approach to communication based on interactive social media and conversational communication styles.

EXHIBIT 14.1	The Social Model of Customer Communication

The social model of customer communication differs from the conventional promotion model in a number of significant ways.

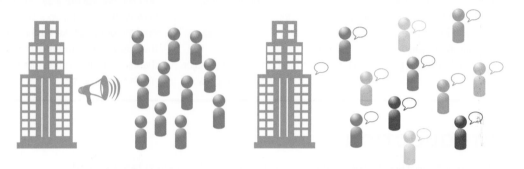

Conventional Promotion: "We Talk, You Listen"	The Social Model: "Let's Have a Conversation"
Tendencies	**Tendencies**
Publication, broadcast	Conversation
Lecture	Discussion
Intrusion	Permission
Undirectional	Bidirectional, multidirectional
One to many; mass audience	One to one; many to many
Control	Influence
Low message frequency	High message frequency
Few channels	Many channels
Information hoarding	Information sharing
Static	Dynamic
Hierarchical	Egalitarian
Structured	Amorphous
Isolated	Collaborative
Planned	Reactive
Resistive	Responsive

- **Providing information and creating positive emotional connections.** The next step is to build logical and emotional acceptance for the company and its products. As you'll read at the end of the chapter, Tata Harper uses a combination of logical and emotional appeals to generate interest in her products. Note that social media can work for or against companies in a significant way at this stage. If customers are pleased with a product, they'll help spread the message through the virtual word-of-mouth communication of social media. However, they'll also spread the word if a product does not meet their expectations.
- **Building preference.** If buyers accept a product as a potential solution to their needs, the next step is to encourage them to prefer it over all other products they may be considering.
- **Stimulating action.** Now comes the most critical step: convincing a consumer or an organization to act on that product preference to make a purchase, using a compelling *call to action*.
- **Reminding past customers.** Past customers are often the best prospects for future sales, so *reminder advertising* tells these buyers that a product is still available or that a company is ready to serve their needs.

One of the classic approaches to promotional communication is the *AIDA model*, which presents this process in the four steps of getting **A**ttention, building **I**nterest, increasing **D**esire, and prompting **A**ction (see Exhibit 14.2). Study the ads and commercials you encounter every day, and you'll be able to spot the AIDA model in action.

DEFINING CUSTOMER MESSAGES

core message
The single most important idea an advertiser hopes to convey to the target audience about its products or the company.

After establishing communication goals, the marketer's next step is to define the **core message**. This is the single most important idea the company hopes to convey to the target audience about a product. Advertisers often try to craft a *unique selling proposition (USP)*, an

EXHIBIT 14.2   **The AIDA Model of Persuasive Communication**

With the AIDA model, marketers craft one or more messages to move recipients through the four stages of attention, interest, desire, and action.

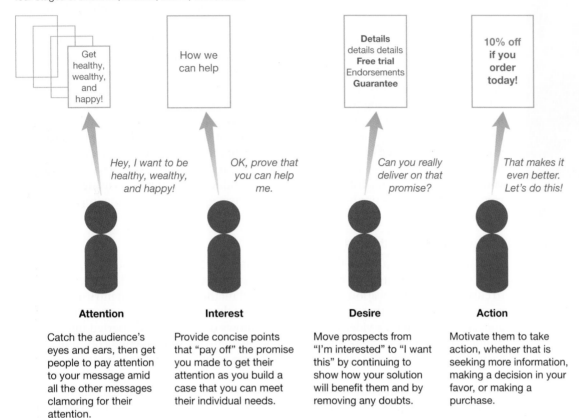

Attention	**Interest**	**Desire**	**Action**
Catch the audience's eyes and ears, then get people to pay attention to your message amid all the other messages clamoring for their attention.	Provide concise points that "pay off" the promise you made to get their attention as you build a case that you can meet their individual needs.	Move prospects from "I'm interested" to "I want this" by continuing to show how your solution will benefit them and by removing any doubts.	Motivate them to take action, whether that is seeking more information, making a decision in your favor, or making a purchase.

objective claim of competitive uniqueness. This core message is the foundation on which the marketing team can build successive layers of detail and explanation, with each communication effort expanding on the core message. For instance, advertisements try to communicate a few key points quickly, without going into great detail. A sales presentation can then go into more detail, and a technical brochure, an online video, or a website can provide extensive information.

As Exhibit 14.1 notes, one of the most significant changes that the social communication model has brought to marketing is that companies now have far less control of their messages. After a message is released into the wild, so to speak, bloggers, reporters, industry analysts, and other parties will begin to repeat it, enhance it, change it, and even refute it. Starting with a clear and compelling core message increases the chances that it will reach its target audience intact. If the core message is not clear or credible, it will surely be altered or refuted as it passes from one outside commentator to the next.

ASSEMBLING THE COMMUNICATION MIX

With clear goals and a compelling message, the next step is to share that message using a **communication mix** of advertising, digital marketing, direct marketing, personal selling, sales promotion, social media, and public relations. Some companies refer to this as a *media mix* or *promotional mix*.

To assemble the most effective mix, companies have to consider a range of factors involving the product, the market, and the distribution channel. Product factors include the type of product, its price range, and its stage in the product life cycle. For example, an innovative technical product may require intensive educational efforts in the introduction and growth stages to help customers understand and appreciate its value.

communication mix
A blend of communication vehicles—advertising, direct response marketing, personal selling, sales promotion, social media, and public relations—that a company uses to reach current and potential customers.

Splash News/Alamy Stock Photo

Celebrities can have significant influence on the purchasing habits of consumers.

Market factors include the type of intended customers (consumers versus organizations), the nature of the competition, and the size and geographic spread of the target market. In addition to knowing their target customers, firms need to identify forces in the market that influence customer behavior. For instance, celebrities and social media users with large groups of followers can influence sales of clothes, food, music, movies, and other products.

Channel factors include the need for intermediaries, the type of intermediaries available, and the ability of those companies to help with communication. If a company relies on retailers or other intermediaries, it must decide whether to focus its communication efforts on the intermediaries or on final customers. With a *push strategy*, a producer focuses on intermediaries, trying to persuade wholesalers or retailers to carry its products and promote those products to *their* customers. Conversely, with a *pull strategy*, the producer appeals directly to end customers. Customers learn of the product through these communication efforts and request it from retailers (in the case of consumers) or wholesalers (in the case of business customers). For example, if a television commercial encourages you to "ask your pharmacist" about a specific product, the company is using a pull strategy. Many companies use both push and pull strategies to increase the impact of their promotional efforts.

Inbound Versus Outbound Marketing

With the digital disruption in the media landscape over the past few years and the shift to a more conversational and interactive style, many companies are rethinking their approach to customer communication. Many promotional methods are based on intrusion or interrupting people when they are engaged in some other activity, such as commercials that appear before YouTube videos or during TV shows or ads that are inserted into print or online articles. This is essentially the traditional approach to marketing communication, even though it is also used extensively in contemporary digital media in addition to television, radio, and print media.

Unless the commercial interruptions are entertaining (Super Bowl commercials have become something of an annual cultural event, for instance), consumers resent these intrusions and take steps to avoid or block them—including changing the channel, muting commercials, and installing ad blockers on their web browsers. As marketing expert Annalea Krebs puts it, "You can't hijack consumer attention anymore."[4]

inbound marketing
Strategy that attracts customers by offering value-added information related to the subjects they are already engaged in and the products that already interest them.

Rather than interrupting people while they are pursuing something else, the strategy of **inbound marketing** *attracts* customers by offering value-added information related to the subjects they are already engaged in and the products that already interest them. Today's shoppers rely heavily on social media and search engines to gather information on products and companies, and the basic strategy of inbound marketing is to be "findable" wherever and whenever target customers are searching for information. A company using inbound marketing can engage with potential buyers on social media, use *search engine optimization (SEO)* to make its content online more visible in searches, and provide useful content that builds relationships with potential buyers.[5] In contrast to many traditional outbound marketing efforts, consumers *want* to see inbound marketing information that is relevant to their needs.

For example, a company that sells products that improve Wi-Fi performance in homes and apartments could write a *Free Guide to Better Wi-Fi Performance* and use SEO to make sure it shows up when people Google such phrases as "better Wi-Fi performance." People who are frustrated with slow connections or dead spots in their homes would be likely to read this guide and think positively of the company that provided the information. The tactic of offering helpful, value-added content to potential customers is known as **content marketing**.

REAL-TIME UPDATES
Learn More by Visiting This Website

The ins and outs of inbound marketing

HubSpot, a marketing company that popularized inbound marketing, shows how it's done. Go to **real-timeupdates.com/bia9** and select Learn More in the Students section.

content marketing
The tactic of offering helpful, value-added content to potential customers.

Integrated Marketing Communications

With the number of communication vehicles continuing to expand, the need for companies to "speak with one voice" becomes even greater. **Integrated marketing**

EXHIBIT 14.3   **Message Integration in Customer Communication**

To maximize efficiency and consistency, companies need to integrate their customer communication efforts. However, customers also integrate messages on the receiving end—including messages that might contradict messages from the company.

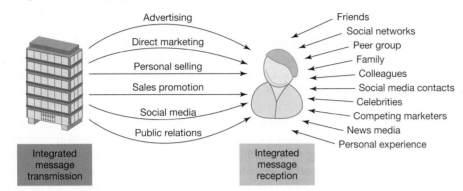

communications (IMC) is a strategy of coordinating and integrating "all marketing communications tools, avenues, and sources in a company into a seamless program designed to maximize the impact on customers and other stakeholders."[6] However, companies obviously can't control all the messages their target audiences receive, particularly now that customers are empowered through social media. While the company is working to integrate its outgoing communication efforts, the customer is also integrating all the incoming messages he or she is receiving (see Exhibit 14.3).

integrated marketing communications (IMC)
A strategy of coordinating and integrating communication and promotion efforts with customers to ensure greater efficiency and effectiveness.

COMMUNICATION LAWS AND ETHICS

As marketing and selling grow increasingly complex, so do the legal ramifications of marketing communication. In the United States, the Federal Trade Commission (FTC) has the authority to impose penalties against advertisers that violate federal standards for truthful advertising. Other federal agencies have authority over advertising in specific industries, such as transportation and financial services. Individual states have additional laws that apply. The legal aspects of promotional communication can be quite complex, and they vary from state to state and from country to country. For all marketing and sales efforts, pay close attention to the following legal considerations:[7]

- **Advertising and sales messages must be truthful and nondeceptive.** The FTC considers messages to be deceptive if they include statements that are likely to mislead reasonable customers and are an important part of the purchasing decision. The FTC distinguishes between *subjective* claims (commonly known as *puffery*), which cannot be proven true or false, and *objective* claims, which can be proven or disproven.[8] Puffery is legally allowable, but deception is not. For example, "Tastiest Coffee in Tennessee" is puffery because it is neither provable nor disprovable. However, claiming that a coffee is organic when it was grown with chemical fertilizers is deceptive.
- **Objective claims must be backed up with evidence.** According to the FTC, offering a money-back guarantee or providing letters from satisfied customers is not enough. Companies must still be able to support claims for their products with objective evidence such as surveys or scientific studies.
- **"Bait-and-switch" advertising is illegal.** Trying to attract buyers by advertising a product that you don't intend to sell—and then trying to sell them another (and usually more expensive) product—is illegal.
- **Marketing messages, websites, and mobile apps aimed at children are subject to special rules.** For example, online marketers must obtain consent from parents before collecting personal information about children under age 13.
- **In many instances, promotional relationships with people outside the company must be disclosed.** For example, celebrities and other social media influencers must

disclose when they are compensated endorsing products. (The FTC suggests that celebrities use the hashtag #ad when posting photos or tweets that endorse products.) Similarly, when companies give products to online reviewers in exchange for reviews, this must be disclosed. In addition, companies that coordinate with product enthusiasts and social media influencers have a degree of responsibility for what those people say to the public. Marketers are expected to train these people in responsible communication and monitor what these outside parties write and say about their products.

- **Marketers must follow laws governing customer privacy and data security.** For example, the European Union's General Data Protection Regulation (GDPR), which went into effect in 2018, is causing sweeping changes in how companies can use digital marketing techniques. The GDPR requires companies to get *opt-in* permission from consumers before using their personal data in advertising activities, for instance. This requirement could dramatically reduce the use of *behavioral targeting*, which tracks the online behavior of website visitors and serves up ads based on what they appear to be interested in, and *remarketing* or *retargeting*, in which behaviorally targeted ads follow users even as they move to other websites. (Even though GDPR is an EU regulation, it affects any company that collects or processes data on EU citizens, which includes many U.S. companies.)[9]

Regarding privacy and other aspects of communication, responsible companies recognize the vital importance of ethical standards. Professional associations such as the American Association of Advertising Agencies (www.aaaa.org), the Data & Marketing Association (www.the-dma.org), and the American Marketing Association (www.ama.org) devote considerable time and energy to ethical issues in marketing, including ongoing education for practitioners and self-regulation efforts aimed at avoiding or correcting ethical lapses. Several national advertising organizations also coordinate their efforts via the Advertising Self-Regulatory Council (www.asrcreviews.org).[10]

 CHECKPOINT

LEARNING OBJECTIVE 1: Describe the three major tasks in crafting a communication strategy, and identify six important legal aspects of marketing communication.

SUMMARY: The three major tasks in developing a communication strategy are establishing clear communication goals, defining compelling messages to help achieve those goals, and outlining a cost-effective media mix to engage target audiences. Six important legal aspects of marketing communications are (1) advertising and sales messages must be truthful and nondeceptive; (2) objective claims must be backed up with evidence; (3) "bait-and-switch" advertising is illegal; (4) marketing messages, websites, and mobile apps aimed at children are subject to special rules; (5) in many instances, promotional relationships with people outside the company must be disclosed; and (6) marketers must follow laws governing customer privacy and data security.

CRITICAL THINKING: (1) Why do credit card companies target students even though most of them have little or no income? (2) Would it be wise for a manufacturer that is new to a particular industry (and unknown within it) to invest most of its promotional resources in a pull strategy? Why or why not?

IT'S YOUR BUSINESS: (1) What is your "core message" as a future business professional? How would you summarize, in one sentence, what you can offer a company? (2) Would you consent to allowing companies to track your online behavior in order to present more personalized advertising to you? Why or why not?

KEY TERMS TO KNOW: social communication model, core message, communication mix, inbound marketing, content marketing, integrated marketing communications (IMC)

Advertising and Direct Response Marketing

Today's companies can connect with customers in a dizzying variety of ways. This section looks at advertising and direct response marketing, then the next three sections look at personal selling, sales promotion, and social media and public relations.

ADVERTISING

Advertising is the paid placement of promotional messages in various forms of media, which can range from television and radio to highway billboards to mobile apps. (One exception to this definition is when companies can run their own ads on their own websites and within their mobile apps.)

Companies use advertising for a variety of purposes. *Product advertising* promotes the features and benefits of specific products. *Institutional advertising* is designed to create goodwill and build a desired image for a company rather than to promote specific products. For example, a firm might promote its commitment to sustainable business practices or workforce diversity. Institutional ads that address public issues are called *advocacy advertising*. Companies with a financial stake in the outcome of public policy decisions can use advocacy ads to persuade voters or legislators to consider a particular point of view.

Advertising Appeals

A key decision in planning a promotional campaign is choosing the **advertising appeal**, a creative tactic designed to capture the audience's attention and promote preference for the product or company being advertised. Marketers can use a variety of appeals (note that these appeals are not limited to advertising; they are used in other types of persuasive communication as well):[11]

- **Logic.** The basic approach with a logical appeal is to make a claim based on a rational argument supported by solid evidence. Not surprisingly, business-to-business advertising relies heavily on logical appeals because businesses have logical concerns—profitability, process improvements, quality, and other financial and technical concerns. However, marketers should not ignore the emotional aspects of business purchasing. Managers put their reputations and sometimes their careers on the line when they make major purchase decisions, so advertisers need to consider these emotional elements. Logical appeals are also used in consumer advertising whenever the purchase decision has a rational component and logic might help persuade buyers to consider or prefer a particular product (see Exhibit 14.4 on the next page).
- **Emotion.** An emotional appeal calls on audience feelings and sympathies rather than on facts, figures, and rational arguments. Emotional appeals range from sentimental to terrifying. On the lighter side, flowers, greeting cards, and gifts are among the products usually sold with a positive emotional appeal. At the other end of the spectrum are appeals to a broad range of fears: personal and family safety, financial security, social acceptance, and business success or failure. To be effective, appeals to fear must be managed carefully. Laying it on too thick can anger the audience or even cause them to block out the message entirely. Exhibit 14.5 on page 419 shows an advertising message that combines a logical appeal with an adventuresome emotional appeal.
- **Humor.** Humor is one of the most common tactics for overcoming consumer resistance to advertising. Using humor can be tricky, however; sometimes it can offend audiences, tainting the brand, or the humor can be so memorable that audiences recall the joke but not the product being advertised.
- **Celebrity.** The thinking behind celebrity involvement in advertising is that people will be more inclined to use products endorsed by a celebrity because they will identify with and want to be like this person (no matter how far-fetched such aspirations might be at a purely logical level).

2 **LEARNING OBJECTIVE**

Identify the most common advertising appeals and the most important media used in advertising and direct response marketing.

advertising
The delivery of announcements and promotional messages via time or space purchased in various media.

REAL-TIME UPDATES
Learn More by Visiting This Website

AI on the leading edge of advertising
See all the ways that IBM applies its Watson artificial intelligence (AI) capacity to advertising. Go to **real-timeupdates.com/bia9** and select Learn More in the Students section.

advertising appeal
A creative tactic designed to capture the audience's attention and promote preference for the product or company being advertised.

| EXHIBIT 14.4 | **Emotional and Logical Appeals** |

Depending on the product and the target audience, marketers can emphasize logic or emotions in the advertising appeal by "dialing up" one or the other through specific choices of words, images, and sounds. Even an identical product marketed to consumers and businesses could have dramatically different messages, as these two headlines for an electronic security system suggest.

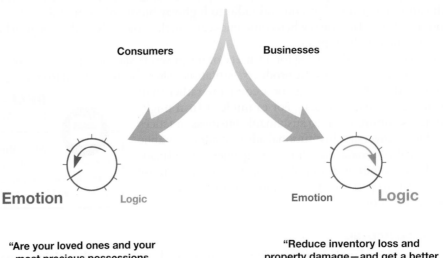

Balancing Emotion and Logic
Example: promoting an electronic security system

Consumers

Businesses

Emotion · Logic

Emotion · Logic

"Are your loved ones and your most precious possessions safe from intruders?"

"Reduce inventory loss and property damage—and get a better deal on your facilities insurance"

- **Sex.** Sex-oriented appeals are the most controversial type of advertising, in terms of both social reaction and promotional effectiveness. Although the phrase "sex sells" is often repeated, it isn't always true. Sexual appeals can definitely be effective, but the degree of effectiveness varies by product, audience, and the role of the sexual imagery or narrative in the advertising. For example, sexual appeals have been shown to be more effective with audiences who have a low level of emotional or intellectual engagement with the purchase than with audiences who are more involved.[12]
- **Music.** With its ability to create emotional bonds and "embed" itself in listeners' memories, music can be a powerful aspect of advertising. Marketers can take several approaches to integrating music into radio, television, or online advertising, including composing *jingles* specifically for ads, licensing popular songs for use in commercials (although these fees can run into the millions of dollars for hit songs), or working with emerging artists to write songs specifically with advertising use in mind.[13]
- **Scarcity.** If a product is in limited supply or available for only a limited time, advertisers can use this scarcity to encourage consumer responses.

Note that these appeals are not mutually exclusive. For example, ads can use humor to catch an audience's attention and then use an emotional appeal to strengthen the bond with the brand or logic to show the superiority of a product.

Advertising Media

advertising media
Communication channels that companies use to reach target audiences.

Advertising media are the communication channels companies use to reach target audiences. Media choices continue to evolve as advertisers invent new ways to be found wherever consumers and business buyers are, and the lines between media types continue to blur. For instance, many newspapers and magazines offer both print and digital (online) versions. As a high-level categorization, though, most media choices fall into these five groups (see Exhibit 14.6 on page 420):

- Television (over the air, cable, and satellite)
- Radio (over the air and satellite)

- Print (magazines and newspapers)
- Out-of-home, also called outdoor (billboards, vehicle wraps, taxi placards, bench ads, stadium signs—essentially, any print or digital signage)
- Digital (all forms of website and mobile-device advertising)

EXHIBIT 14.5	**Combining Advertising Appeals**

This promotional message from Filson combines logical and emotional appeals. "Carry everything through anything" conveys the practical advantage of the product's versatility and ruggedness, and the photo evokes an outdoorsy feeling of adventure.

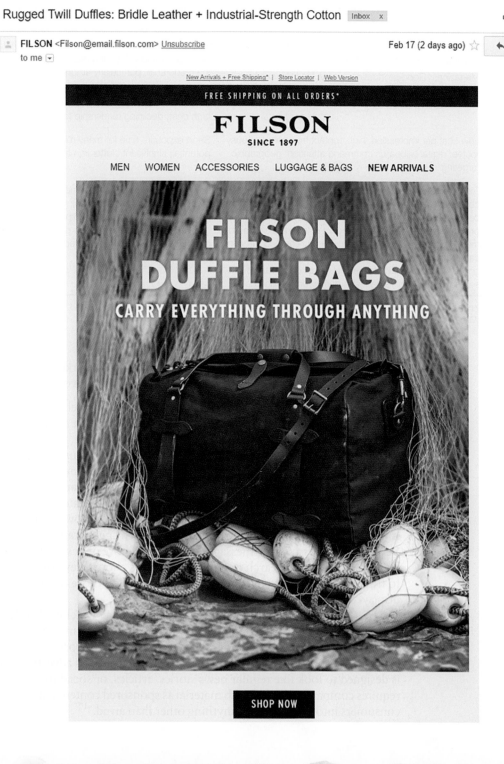

EXHIBIT 14.6	Advantages and Disadvantages of Major Advertising Media

Each medium has strengths and weaknesses; companies often combine two or more media in an advertising campaign to maximize their promotional effectiveness.

Medium	Advantages	Disadvantages
Television	Great impact; broad reach; appeals to senses of sight, sound, and motion; creative opportunities for demonstration; high attention; entertainment carryover; low cost per contact	High cost for production and air time; less audience selectivity; long preparation time; commercial clutter; short life for message; vulnerable to being skipped or muted; losing ground to new media options
Radio	Low cost; high frequency; immediacy; highly portable; high geographic and demographic selectivity; creative potential with sound and music	No visual possibilities; short life for message; commercial clutter; lower attention and narrower reach than television; declining audience share; low level of engagement
Print (magazines and newspapers)	Newspapers: Extensive market coverage; low cost; short lead time for placing ads; good local market coverage; geographic selectivity; credibility Magazines: Good production quality; long life; selective market selectivity; authority and credibility; multiple readers extend reach of each issue; close bond with readers	Newspapers: Poor graphic quality; short life span; cluttered pages; visual competition from other ads; printed newspapers have rapidly declining readership in many cities; declining readership, particularly among younger consumers Magazines: Limited demonstration possibilities; long lead time between placing and publishing ads; a lot of ad clutter; high cost; declining readership for many titles
Out-of-home	Low cost per impression; high contact frequency on busy routes; digital billboards command attention; geographic targeting	Short exposure time for many messages; limited content potential; significant clutter in many environments
Digital	Rich media options and interactivity can make ads more compelling and more effective; changes and additions can be made quickly and easily in most cases; webpages can provide an almost unlimited amount of information; can be measured and personalized through tracking and targeting capabilities; instant links to online retailing and influence on store-based retail sales; social media connections can spread marketing messages through word of mouth	Low click-through rates; extreme degree of audience fragmentation (millions of websites); increasing clutter; not as portable as magazines or newspapers (except for mobile use); ad-blocking software can prevent ads from being displayed; risk of being displayed next to inappropriate content

Sources: Based in part on Kenneth E. Clow and Donald Baack, *Integrated Advertising, Promotion, and* Marketing Communication, 8th ed. (New York: Pearson, 2018), 198, 204, 208, 210; Philip Kotler and Gary Armstrong, *Principles of Marketing*, 17th ed. (New York: Pearson, 2018), 493.

The digital category is diverse and constantly evolving as marketers look for fresh ways to engage online and mobile audiences. Here are the major types of digital advertising:

- **Display.** *Display ads* are square or rectangular spaces on websites that contain some combination of text, visuals, animation, or video. They can appear as banners at the top of webpages, run as sidebars next to the page content, or be embedded within articles. Display ads can also be presented momentarily as users click from one page to the next (these are called *interstitials*), as semi-transparent *overlays* that appear on top of page content, or as *pop-ups*—separate windows that appear when users are viewing other content. These latter types tend to be particularly resented by users, and they can be the worst type of intrusive advertising. Most browsers now block pop-ups, and the misuse of these ad types can hurt a website's search engine ranking.[14]
- **Search.** *Search ads* are brief messages that display above or beside the results generated by Google and other search engines. Advertisers choose keywords that are relevant to their products, and whenever people search using those terms, those ads can be displayed next to the search results.[15]
- **Video.** Collectively, people spend a billion hours a day watching YouTube videos, so naturally YouTube has become a major advertising platform. Advertisers can target their ads using a variety of demographic and behavioral factors.[16]
- **Native.** *Native advertising*, also known as *sponsored content*, is advertising material that is designed to look like regular news stories, articles, or social media posts. The FTC requires companies to label such material as sponsored content if it is likely to mislead consumers into thinking it is "anything other than an ad."[17]

- **Video games.** In-game advertising is now a multibillion-dollar business. Ads can appear in a variety of formats. With **product placement**, which is also a popular tactic in television and movies, advertisers pay to have their brands and products displayed during games.[18] (That "Drink Coca-Cola" billboard you just drove past wasn't put there randomly.) Another approach is *rewarded video*, where players can choose to watch a promotional video during a game and get rewarded with coins or other game tokens.[19]
- **Mobile.** All these types of digital advertising can also be optimized for mobile devices, plus ads can be served up within mobile apps. Given how much time people now spend with their mobile devices, it's not surprising that mobile is the fastest-growing category of advertising.[20]

Product placements in video games have become a significant advertising method.

A *media plan* outlines the advertising budget, the schedule of when and where ads will appear, and a discussion of the media mix—the combination of print, broadcast, online, and other media to be used in the campaign. To create the media mix, advertising experts factor in the characteristics of the target audience, the types of media that will reach the largest audience in the most cost-effective way, and the strengths and weaknesses of the various media as they relate to the product and its marketing message.

Much of today's digital media buying is *programmatic*, meaning ad space or time is purchased automatically by algorithms that try to optimize cost and audience response. In some cases, the ad space is sold in an auction format in real time as people browse the web or use a mobile app. Advertisers place bids to have their ads shown whenever users who fit a particular profile land on a specific web or app page. When a user gets to that location, whichever company bid the most for that space gets its ad displayed.[21]

product placement
The paid display or use of products in television shows, movies, and video games.

DIRECT RESPONSE MARKETING

Direct response marketing, also known as *direct marketing*, is personalized marketing communication that doesn't rely on a third-party communication channel. Although it is similar to advertising in many respects, direct response marketing has two unique characteristics. First, it can often be *personalized*, such as when an online retailer sends you emails after a purchase suggesting other products you might like. Second, as its name suggests, direct response marketing aims to inspire a purchase decision right now.

Direct marketing has evolved dramatically from its early days, when pioneering promotional efforts such as the Sears catalog in the late 1800s helped establish *mail order* on a massive scale.[22] Direct marketing is now a data-driven multimedia effort that includes print mail, email, text messaging, telephone, personalized website messages, and mobile media. The heart of any direct marketing effort is a customer database such as a customer relationship management (CRM) system that contains contact histories, purchase records, and profiles of each buyer or potential buyer. (Direct marketing is sometimes referred to as *database marketing*.)

The catalogs that helped launch direct marketing more than a hundred years ago are still a force today, as a peek inside any mailbox in the country will confirm. Direct mail, email, and telemarketing are the other most common forms of direct marketing.[23]

The interactive, adaptable nature of websites and mobile apps allows them to go far beyond static advertising media to become direct marketing channels as well. For example, Sweetwater Sound, a retailer of musical instruments and sound equipment, delivers a variety of personalized website and email messages based on customers' purchase histories and interests. A customer who orders an amplifier for live music production might see messages about cables, speakers, and other equipment that will complement the amplifier purchase. By reaching out to the customer right at the moment of the original purchase decision, Sweetwater can prompt the buyer to consider additional products tailored to his or her individual needs.

direct response marketing
Direct communication with potential customers other than personal sales contacts designed to stimulate a measurable response; also known as direct marketing.

amirraizat/Shutterstock

✓ CHECKPOINT

LEARNING OBJECTIVE 2: Identify the most common advertising appeals and the most important media used in advertising and direct response marketing.

SUMMARY: The most common advertising appeals are logic, emotion, humor, celebrity, sex, music, and scarcity. The five major media choices for advertising are television, radio, print (magazines and newspaper), out-of-home, and digital. Digital can be subdivided into display ads, search advertising, video ads, native advertising, video game advertising, and mobile advertising. Catalogs, direct mail, email, and tele-marketing are the most common forms of direct response marketing.

CRITICAL THINKING: (1) Do fragmented media make it easier or harder for market-ers to engage in segmented or concentrated marketing? Explain your answer. (2) Why would a company such as McDonald's, which is already well known to virtually all consumers in the United States, continue to spend heavily on advertising?

IT'S YOUR BUSINESS: (1) Have you ever believed that you could create better adver-tising for a product than the company behind the product created? If so, explain the type of appeal you would've used and why. (2) Do you find that you tend to watch and listen to most television commercials, or do you mute or channel-surf during commer-cials? If you pay attention to commercials, what captures your interest?

KEY TERMS TO KNOW: advertising, advertising appeal, advertising media, product placement, direct response marketing

---

3 **LEARNING OBJECTIVE**

Describe consultative selling, and explain the personal selling process.

personal selling
One-on-one interaction between a salesperson and a prospective buyer.

Personal Selling

Even with the rapid advance of e-commerce and other marketing technologies, **personal selling**, the one-on-one interaction between a salesperson and a prospective buyer, remains a fundamentally important part of the promotional mix in many consumer and organiza-tional markets. You are probably most familiar with the sales staff positions in retail stores, but salespeople work in many areas of professional services, advertising and media, finance, real estate, wholesaling, and a wide variety of scientific and technical industries. In addition to those people whose primary function is sales, many other professionals are expected to engage in selling activities as part of their jobs. For example, management consultants and creative directors in advertising agencies are often tasked with bringing in new clients and managing relationships through personal selling.

Although a sales force can't reach thousands or millions of customers at once like a website or a direct marketing program can, today's highly trained sales professionals are able to build relationships and solve problems in ways that even the most highly targeted digital media can't match. Many companies now combine the wide reach and cost efficiencies of online promo-tion with the individualized touch of personal sales. You've probably seen this in action when you're shopping online and a window pops up with an offer from a sales associate or a chat-bot to answer any questions you might have. Chatbots can be programmed to handle basic questions and then connect shop-pers with human agents for more specific queries.

Some companies closely integrate e-commerce with per-sonal selling to provide the efficiency and selection of online retailing with the individualized attention of personal sales. At Sweetwater Music, for instance, each customer is assigned a sales engineer. For routine purchases, customers can order through the company's website without sales interaction, but

Highly trained professional salespeople are an important element of the marketing mix for many companies.

Grzegorz Czapski/Shutterstock

when customers need advice on product selection or usage, they have a person to call or email. The sales engineers have musical backgrounds, either as performing musicians or as "gear heads" who enjoy working with musical technology, so they can offer a level of advice that customers can't get on typical e-commerce sites.

CONTEMPORARY PERSONAL SELLING

As with other elements of the communication mix, personal selling has evolved over the years to support the contemporary idea of the customer-oriented marketing concept. One of the most important shifts in the sales profession is the advent of **consultative selling**, in which the salesperson acts as a consultant and adviser who helps current and potential customers find the best solutions to their personal or business needs. Consultative selling is as much a matter of strategizing and problem solving with the customer as it is about persuasion and promotion.[24] At Sweetwater Music, for instance, the company views each sales engineer as his or her own "store" with its own set of customers, and sales engineers are expected to develop long-term relationships so they can respond to each customer's needs.[25]

consultative selling
An approach in which a salesperson acts as a consultant and adviser to help customers find the best solutions to their personal or business needs.

THE PERSONAL SELLING PROCESS

Personal selling varies widely from industry to industry, with some sales being completed in a matter of minutes and others taking weeks or months. Time is the salesperson's most valuable asset, so it must be spent wisely and focus on the most valuable prospects who are most likely to purchase. The following steps can be adapted to almost any sales situation (see Exhibit 14.7):

1. **Prospecting.** The process of finding and qualifying potential customers is known as **prospecting**. In some industries, it is referred to as *account development* or *business development*.[26] This step usually involves three activities: (1) *generating sales leads*—names of individuals and organizations that are likely to be interested in the company's products; (2) *identifying prospects*—potential customers who indicate a need or a desire for the seller's products; and (3) *qualifying prospects*—the process of figuring out which prospects have the authority, the budget, and the motivation to buy. On a per-customer basis, personal selling is the most expensive form of marketing there is, so it's vital to focus attention on the most viable prospects. Today's CRM systems help sales teams collect and analyze information to help with prospecting, and AI-enhanced tools such as Salesforce.com's Einstein use predictive analytics to pinpoint the best prospects.[27]

2. **Preparing.** With a qualified prospect in mind, the next step is to refine the information already known from prospecting in order to prepare for the first *sales call*, which might be a phone call, an online presentation, or an in-person meeting. Salespeople usually have very little time during the initial meeting, and in business-to-business selling they may need to go through one or more gatekeepers before getting the chance to present to

prospecting
The process of finding and qualifying potential customers.

EXHIBIT 14.7	**The Personal Selling Process**

The personal selling process can involve up to seven steps, starting with prospecting for sales leads and ending with following up after the sale has been closed. This diagram gives you a general idea of how salespeople approach major sales opportunities.

1. Prospecting	2. Preparing	3. Approaching the Prospect	4. Aligning with Customer Needs	5. Handling Objections	6. Closing	7. Following Up
Finding and qualifying potential customers; usually involves generating sales leads, indentifying prospects, and qualifying prospects	Getting ready for the sales call; researching the customer in more depth, establishing objectives, and preparing a presentation	Taking steps to make a good first impression; crafting the right appearance, maintaining professional behavior, and preparing an engaging introduction	Listening to the prospect describe what is needed and proposing a solution to meet those needs	Addressing any concerns the prospect might raise; exploring the deeper reasons that might be behind the expressed objections	Asking the prospect to choose the solution being offered	Checking in with the customer after the sale to make sure the solution is working out as expected and to keep building a long-term relaionship

the key decision-makers. It is therefore essential to be fully prepared for initial contact and to have a clear plan in place for moving the conversation forward. Two important steps here are establishing clear objectives and preparing the sales presentation.[28]

3. **Approaching the prospect.** First impressions can make or break a sale, so knowledgeable salespeople take care to (1) craft the appropriate appearance for themselves and for everything that represents them; (2) maintain behaviors and attitudes that are professional, courteous, and confident without being arrogant; and (3) prepare opening lines that include a brief greeting and introduction, followed by a few carefully chosen words that establish a good rapport with the potential customer. Building rapport is essential to developing credibility and earning the customer's trust.[29]

4. **Aligning with customer needs.** After the conversation has been initiated, the next step is understanding the customer's specific needs. The biggest mistake a salesperson can make at this stage is talking instead of listening. The most extreme form of this error is the *canned sales pitch*, in which the salesperson recites or even reads a stock message, with no regard for the customer's unique circumstances. In contrast, today's enlightened sales professionals focus on questioning and listening before offering a solution that meets each prospect's unique needs. Of course, with careful prospecting and preparing, the salesperson should have a good general idea of what the customer needs and be ready to discuss a range of options (if relevant) that could fill those needs.

5. **Handling objections.** Potential customers can express a variety of objections to the products they are considering, and salespeople need to be ready with answers and alternatives. The process sometimes evolves into a negotiation at this step as well, particularly in business-to-business selling where buyers are often training in negotiation techniques.[30]

closing
The point at which a sale is completed.

6. **Closing.** Bringing the sales process to a successful conclusion by asking for and receiving an affirmative purchase decision is known as **closing**. In keeping with the consultative selling philosophy, professional and ethical salespeople don't view closing as a triumph over the customer but rather as helping customers finalize the process of finding the right solution to their needs.[31]

7. **Following up.** Most companies depend on repeat sales and referrals from satisfied customers, so it's important that salespeople follow up after the sale to make sure customers are satisfied with their purchases. Staying in touch gives a company the opportunity to answer questions, address areas of confusion or dissatisfaction with a purchase, and show customers it is a reliable partner for the long haul.

 CHECKPOINT

LEARNING OBJECTIVE 3: Describe consultative selling, and explain the personal selling process.

SUMMARY: Consultative selling is a combination of persuasion and advice, in which the salesperson acts as a consultant and adviser who helps current and potential customers find the best solutions to their personal or business needs. The seven general steps in personal selling are (1) prospecting—finding prospects and qualifying them; (2) preparing—creating a prospect profile, setting objectives for the call, and preparing a presentation; (3) approaching the prospect, with the goal of making a positive first impression; (4) uncovering the customer's needs and presenting appropriate solutions; (5) handling objections and negotiating a mutually acceptable solution; (6) closing—focusing on completing the sale; and (7) following up after the sale to make sure the buyer is satisfied.

CRITICAL THINKING: (1) Why is the canned approach inadequate for many selling situations? (2) Why should a salesperson take the time to qualify sales leads?

IT'S YOUR BUSINESS: (1) Would you be comfortable in a personal selling role? Why or why not? (2) What can you learn from professional selling methods to help you in a job interview?

KEY TERMS TO KNOW: personal selling, consultative selling, prospecting, closing

Sales Promotion

Sales promotion involves short-term incentives to build the reputation of a brand, encourage the purchase of a product, or simply enhance relationships with current and potential customers. Sales promotion tactics consists of two basic categories: consumer promotion and trade promotion.

CONSUMER PROMOTIONS

Sales promotions are an important tactic for consumer marketers. Consumer packaged-goods companies, in particular, devote an average of 60 percent of their marketing budgets to sales promotions.[32] Companies use a variety of consumer promotional tools and incentives to stimulate repeat purchases and to entice new users:

- **Contests and other forms of audience participation.** Giving consumers the opportunity to participate in contests, games, sweepstakes, surveys, and other activities is a great way to build energy around a brand.
- **Experiential marketing.** Companies can engage consumers even more deeply with **experiential marketing**, special events that emphasize fun, discovery, or community involvement. To introduce a new flavor, for example, M&Ms used augmented reality to turn New York City's Times Square into a giant immersive video game that people could play on their phones.[33]
- **Coupons and promotional codes.** *Coupons* are printed or digital certificates that entitle consumers to discounts; *promotion codes* are "on-demand" coupons that customers can use while shopping online. Most U.S. households redeem coupons occasionally, but the overall redemption rate is quite low—less than 1 percent for printed coupons and typically about 15 percent for digital coupons. The value of coupons as a promotional tool is sometimes debated. For example, most shoppers who use coupons have a strong brand preference, which raises the question of whether they would buy the same products anyway at full price.[34] Marketers are trying to target coupons more precisely, such as by offering them to consumers who use a competitor's product to entice them to switch.[35]
- **Rebates.** With **rebates**, companies offer partial reimbursement of the price as a purchase incentive. Rebates can be an effective tool for boosting sales, but they obviously cut into per-unit profits—and the effect can be long-lasting if frequent rebates in an industry encourage buyers to delay purchases until a rebate program is available.
- **Point-of-purchase.** A **point-of-purchase (POP) display** is an in-store presentation designed to stimulate immediate sales and can include *endcaps* at the ends of aisles, sample stands where shoppers can taste products, and racks in checkout lines. POP displays are a vital element in the marketing effort for many products sold at retail stores, because they can stimulate and capture *impulse purchases*—unplanned purchases that can make up a significant portion of sales in mass merchandise stores and supermarkets.[36]
- **Samples and trial-use versions.** Distributing samples can be an effective way to introduce a new product, encourage nonusers to try an existing product, encourage current buyers to use the product in a new way, or expand distribution into new areas. Many software products are also offered as trial versions to let customers try before buying.
- **Sponsorships.** Sponsoring special events, cultural attractions, and sports teams is now a major promotional category. Worldwide, companies spend $60 billion on sponsorships, with 70 percent of that going to sports. Sponsorship can bring a company visibility and help it share in the positive emotions that participants experience while at an event.[37]

More companies are trying to engage consumers with experiential marketing events and environments.

Terry Mathews/Alamy Stock Photo

Sports sponsorship gives companies visibility and the chance to capture some of the positive emotions associated with sporting events.

trade promotions
Sales promotion efforts aimed at inducing distributors or retailers to push a producer's products.

trade allowances
Discounts or other financial considerations offered by producers to wholesalers and retailers.

• **Other promotions.** Other popular consumer sales promotion techniques include in-store demonstrations, loyalty and frequency programs such as frequent-flyer programs, and *premiums*, which are free or bargain-priced items offered to encourage the consumer to buy a product. *Specialty advertising* (on pens, calendars, T-shirts, mouse pads, and other items) helps keep a company's name in front of customers for a long period of time.

TRADE PROMOTIONS

In contrast to consumer promotions, **trade promotions** are aimed at members of "the trade," which refers to intermediaries in a distribution chain.[38] For instance, a manufacturer might entice industrial distributors to sell more of its products by staging a sales contest, or a wholesaler might entice retailers to sell more of a particular product by offering it to them at a discount or contributing to their advertising budgets. Trade promotions are often the largest item in a manufacturer's marketing budget.[39]

Some of the most widely used trade promotions are **trade allowances**, which involve discounts on product prices, free merchandise, or other financial considerations. The intermediary can either pocket the savings to increase profits or pass the savings on to the consumer to generate additional sales. Other popular trade promotions are dealer contests and bonus programs designed to motivate distributors or retailers to push particular merchandise. Product samples are also common in many business marketing efforts. For instance, semiconductor manufacturers provide samples of electronic components to engineers who are designing new products, knowing that if the prototype is successful, it could lead to full-scale production—and orders for thousands or millions of components.

One major difference between consumer and trade promotions is that some trade promotions are not voluntary. With limited display space, the need to maximize profit from every foot of shelf space, and the knowledge that the majority of new products fail to catch on with consumers, retailers are naturally cautious about taking on unproven new products. To boost profits and protect against potential loss, many retail chains charge manufacturers *slotting fees* to add products to their shelves and *pay-to-stay fees* to continue stocking products. These fees can range from a few thousand dollars up to $100,000 or more. In one recent year, one-third of the grocery chain Safeway's annual profits came from slotting fees. Critics of the practice say it can stymie innovation, limit consumer choice, and leave small manufacturers at a disadvantage.[40] With retail chains fending off Amazon and other threats to their profitability and even survival, however, it's unlikely that they will voluntarily curtail the practice.

REAL-TIME UPDATES
Learn More by Reading This Article

The arguments for and against slotting fees

Hear both sides of the controversy over these trade allowances. Go to **real-timeupdates.com/bia9** and select Learn More in the Students section.

✓ CHECKPOINT

LEARNING OBJECTIVE 4: Define sales promotion, and characterize the differences between consumer and trade promotions.

SUMMARY: Consumer promotions are intended to motivate consumers to try new products or continue buying favorite brands. Examples include contests, experiential marketing, coupons and promotional codes, rebates, point-of-purchase (POP) displays, samples, special-event sponsorship, premiums, and specialty advertising. Trade promotions are aimed at members of "the trade," which refers to intermediaries in a distribution chain. Common trade promotions include trade allowances, dealer contests, bonus programs, and samples. A key distinction between consumer and trade promotions is that some trade promotions are not voluntary; many retailers demand slotting fees or other financial considerations in order to add or continue to carry a manufacturer's products.

CRITICAL THINKING: (1) If most coupons are never used, why do companies keep distributing so many? (2) If wholesalers and retailers can make money selling a manufacturer's product, why would the manufacturer need to offer incentives such as sales contests?

IT'S YOUR BUSINESS: (1) Do you use coupons? If not, what stops you from doing so, given that they can save you money on many of the goods and services you buy? (2) Do you think it is ethical for a retailer to steer you toward a particular brand because of trade promotions offered by that brand's manufacturer, without telling you so? Why or why not?

KEY TERMS TO KNOW: sales promotion, experiential marketing, rebates, point-of-purchase (POP) display, trade promotions, trade allowances

Social Media and Public Relations

⑤ **LEARNING OBJECTIVE**
Explain the uses of social media in customer communication and the role of public relations.

All the communication methods discussed so far in this chapter involve activities by companies to transmit carefully crafted and controlled messages to target audiences. The final two methods, social media and public relations, differ from those traditional methods in two key respects: They rely, at least in part, on other parties to forward or create promotional messages, and they don't provide anywhere near the level of control over those messages that conventional marketing methods offer.

SOCIAL MEDIA IN THE MARKETING PROCESS

Social media play an important role in contemporary marketing, and companies use virtually all of the same platforms that consumers use, from Facebook and Twitter to Pinterest, Instagram, and more. Social media activities combine the newest communication technologies with the oldest form of marketing communication in the world, **word of mouth**—when customers and other parties transmit information about companies and products through personal conversations.

word of mouth
Communication among customers and other parties, transmitting information about companies and products through online or offline personal conversations.

Word-of-mouth marketing is sometimes called *viral marketing*, in reference to the transmission of messages in much the same way that biological viruses are transmitted from person to person. However, viral marketing is not really an accurate metaphor. A real virus spreads from host to host on its own, whereas word-of-mouth marketing spreads *voluntarily* from person to person. The distinction is critical, because marketers need to give people a good reason—good content, in other words—to pass along their messages.

REAL-TIME UPDATES
Learn More by Visiting This Website

Ethical guidelines for word-of-mouth marketing

The Word of Mouth Marketing Association advises its members on how to use social media marketing ethically. Go to **real-timeupdates.com/bia9** and select Learn More in the Students section.

Marketing Communication Strategies for Social Media

Business use of social media is a good example of companies moving away from the sales concept to the marketing concept and working to foster positive, long-term relationships with customers. Audiences in the social media environment are not willing to be passive recipients in a structured, one-way information delivery process—or to rely solely on promotional messages from marketers. This notion of interactive participation is the driving force behind **conversation marketing**, in which companies *initiate* and *facilitate* conversations in a networked community of customers, journalists, bloggers, Twitter users, and other interested parties. Social media can be an effective communication channel, but companies should follow these guidelines in order to meet audience expectations:

conversation marketing
An approach to customer communication in which companies initiate and facilitate conversations in a networked community of potential buyers and other interested parties.

- **Listen as much as you talk.** One of the most powerful business benefits of social media is the opportunity to hear what is on people's minds and incorporate those voice-of-the-customer insights into marketing plans. Companies can use a variety of *social listening* tools to hear what is being said about them, their products, and their competitors. Social

| **EXHIBIT 14.8** | **Using Social Media to Deliver Value-Added Content** |

Farms.com, which publishes news for agricultural customers, uses Twitter to announce new articles.

listening can also uncover "pain points," aspects of work or life that people are frustrated about and that may represent opportunities for new or improved products.[41]

- **Develop relationships with market influencers.** Influencers can be anyone who shapes customer perceptions, from YouTubers to bloggers to journalists. *Influencer marketing* involves identifying these influential voices, supporting their efforts to communicate with their audiences, and in some cases featuring them in promotional campaigns.[42]
- **Remember that it's a conversation, not a sales pitch.** One of the great appeals of social media is the feeling of conversation, of people talking *with* one another instead of one person talking *at* everyone else. Many companies use social media to announce new products and share other promotional messages, but to maintain the interest of its followers, such posts should be balanced with information that is helpful, inspiring, or entertaining.
- **Offer valuable content to members of your online communities.** People don't join social networks to be sales targets. They join looking for connections, information, and entertainment. Social media are an excellent way to share value-added material as part of a content marketing strategy (see Exhibit 14.8).
- **Identify and support champions.** *Champions*, sometimes referred to as *advocates*, are enthusiastic fans of a company and its products—so enthusiastic that they help spread the company's message, defend it against detractors, and help other customers use its products. Companies can also set up formal programs to recruit and support *brand ambassadors*, and some firms employ their own brand ambassadors to promote products at in-store events, trade shows, and other venues.
- **Facilitate community building.** Make sure customers and other audiences can connect with the company and with each other. If appropriate, encourage user-generated content, in which customers and enthusiasts share videos and other material.
- **Be real.** Social media audiences respond positively to companies that are open and conversational about themselves, their products, and subjects of shared interest. In contrast, if a company is serving its stakeholders poorly with shoddy products, bad customer service, or unethical behavior, an attempt to improve its reputation by adopting social media without fixing the underlying problems is likely to fail as soon as audiences see through the superficial attempt to "be social."

REAL-TIME UPDATES
Learn More by Reading This Article

Building audience relationships with content marketing

Offering potential customers information of value is a popular marketing technique; read these tips to do it successfully. Go to **real-time updates.com/bia9** and select Learn Mçore in the Students section.

brand communities
Formal or informal groups of people united by their interest in and ownership of particular products.

Brand Communities

Another major impact of social media has been the rapid spread of **brand communities**, people united by their interest in and ownership of particular products. These communities range from loose-knit groups of people who hang out on the same social media platform to formal, company-sponsored membership organizations. For example, the Texas company Synthesizers.com, a maker of modular music synthesizers, hosts an informal discussion group on Facebook for owners and enthusiasts of the brand. There is no formal organization or membership; anyone who is a fan of the brand can join. At the other extreme is Harley Owners Group (H.O.G.), which is sponsored and managed by the motorcycle manufacturer and now boasts more than a million members. (*Hog* is an affectionate nickname for a Harley).[43]

Social media are natural communication vehicles for brand communities because these tools let people bond and share information on their own terms. And because a majority of consumers now trust their peers more than any other source of product information—including conventional advertising techniques—formal and informal brand communities are becoming an essential information source in consumer buying behavior.[44]

Social Customer Care

Companies that have adopted the marketing concept and that value customer relationships know that communication after the sale is every bit as important as communication before the sale. Social media have emerged as a powerful tool for postsales communication and support. With **social customer care**, companies use Twitter, Facebook, YouTube, and other social media platforms to listen for complaints or frustrations, to respond to customers who ask for help, and to share useful information with their brand communities. Responsive customer service is one of the best forms of marketing any company can engage in, and social customer care can be an essential part of the total customer experience.

PUBLIC RELATIONS

Public relations (PR) encompasses a wide variety of nonsales communications that businesses have with their many stakeholders, including communities, investors, industry analysts, government agencies, and activists. Companies rely on PR to build a favorable corporate image and foster positive relations with all these groups.

PR professionals often work through outside, independent communication channels to reach their target audiences. Historically, these efforts focused on the news media, including newspapers, magazines, radio, and TV. PR staffers "pitch" story ideas to journalists in the hope that these journalists will find the ideas compelling enough to their readers or listeners to warrant a print article or broadcast segment. To reach a wide number of journalists at once, a company can issue a **press release**, or *news release*, a brief written summary of company news and events such as a factory opening or a new-product launch (see Exhibit 14.9 on the next page). When a business has significant news to announce, it can arrange a **press conference**, at which reporters can listen to company representatives and ask questions.

With the rise of social media, the scope of PR has expanded to include influential bloggers, Twitter users, and others outside the boundaries of traditional journalism. In fact, many companies now view the press release as a general-purpose tool for communicating directly with customers and other audiences, creating *direct-to-consumer news releases*.[45] Many of these releases also include social networking links, "Tweetables" (Twitter-ready statements that can be shared on Twitter at the click of a button), online video links, and other sharable content.

For the latest information on customer communication strategies, techniques, and tools, visit **real-timeupdates.com/bia9** and select Chapter 14.

social customer care
The use of social media to listen for complaints or frustrations, to respond to customers who ask for help, and to share useful information with their brand communities.

public relations (PR)
Nonsales communication that businesses have with their various audiences (including both communication with the general public and press relations).

press release
A brief statement or video program released to the press announcing new products, management changes, sales performance, and other potential news items; also called a *news release*.

press conference
An in-person or online gathering of media representatives at which companies announce new information; also called a *news conference*.

 CHECKPOINT

LEARNING OBJECTIVE 5: Explain the uses of social media in customer communication and the role of public relations.

SUMMARY: Social media play an important role in contemporary marketing, and companies use virtually all of the same platforms that consumers use. Business uses of social media include fostering word-of-mouth marketing, initiating and facilitating conversations, offering valuable content to customers and enthusiasts, promoting the growth of brand communities, and engaging in social customer care.

Public relations (PR) encompasses a wide variety of nonsales communications that businesses have with their many stakeholders, including communities, investors, industry analysts, government agencies, and activists. Companies rely on PR to build a favorable corporate image and foster positive relations with all these groups. The two most important communication tools for PR are press releases and press conferences.

CRITICAL THINKING: (1) If marketers are advised against blatantly promoting their products in social media, why should they bother using these media at all? (2) How should companies respond to unfair criticism leveled at them through social media?

IT'S YOUR BUSINESS: (1) Have you ever used social media to ask questions about a product or to criticize or compliment a company? Did anyone from the company respond? (2) Do you consider yourself a member of any brand communities (formal or informal)? If so, what effect do these groups have on your purchasing behavior?

KEY TERMS TO KNOW: word of mouth, conversation marketing, brand communities, social customer care, public relations (PR), press release, press conference

EXHIBIT 14.9	**Media Relations**

Companies use press releases, also known as news releases, to share information with the news media.

Product Distribution and Marketing Intermediaries

Think of all the products you buy: food, cosmetics, clothing, sports equipment, train tickets, gasoline, stationery, appliances, music, books, and all the rest. How many of these products do you buy directly from the producer? For most people, the answer is not many. Most companies that create products do not sell these goods directly to the final users. Instead, producers in many industries work with **marketing intermediaries** to bring their products to market. And, of course, wholesalers and retailers are business entities themselves, with their own strategic questions and operating challenges. A **distribution channel** is an organized network of intermediaries that work together to move goods from producer to customer or to facilitate the delivery of services.

THE ROLE OF MARKETING INTERMEDIARIES

Intermediaries can be grouped into two general types: wholesalers and retailers. **Wholesalers** sell to organizational customers, including other wholesalers, companies, government agencies, and educational institutions. In turn, the customers of wholesalers either resell the products or use them to make products of their own.

Unlike wholesalers, **retailers** sell products to consumers for personal use. Terminology in the distribution field can get a bit confusing, starting with the multiple uses of the term *wholesale*. For instance, even though Costco and other warehouse-type stores often use the "wholesale" label to describe themselves, they function as both wholesalers (when they sell to other businesses) and retailers (when they sell to consumers).

Wholesalers and retailers are instrumental in creating three of the four forms of utility mentioned in Chapter 12: They provide the items customers need in a convenient location (place utility), they save customers the time of having to contact each manufacturer to purchase a good (time utility), and they provide an efficient process for transferring products from the producer to the customer (possession utility). In addition to creating utility, wholesalers and retailers perform a variety of important business functions:

- **Matching buyers and sellers.** By making sellers' products available to multiple buyers, intermediaries reduce the number of transactions between producers and customers. In the business-to-business market, the industrial distributor Grainger (**www.grainger.com**) is a good example of the enormous scale that can be achieved in bringing buyers and sellers together. With a portfolio of nearly 2 million products, Grainger connects more than 5,000 suppliers with 3 million organizational customers.[46] These customers are saved the time and trouble of working with multiple suppliers, and the product suppliers get access to more customers than all but the very largest of them could ever hope to reach on their own. Although "cutting out the middleman" is sometimes used as a promotional slogan to suggest lower costs, intermediaries such as Grainger can make commerce more efficient by reducing the number of connections that need to be made between buyers and sellers (see Exhibit 14.10 on the next page).
- **Providing market information.** Retail intermediaries, such as Amazon and Macy's, collect valuable data about customer purchases, which they can then share with producers to optimize product mixes and promotional efforts.
- **Providing promotional and sales support.** Many intermediaries assist with advertising, in-store displays, and other promotional efforts for some or all of the products they sell. Some also employ sales representatives who can perform a number of selling and customer relationship functions.
- **Gathering assortments of goods.** Many intermediaries receive bulk shipments from producers and break them into more convenient units (known as *breaking bulk*) by sorting, standardizing, and dividing bulk quantities into smaller packages.
- **Transporting and storing products.** Intermediaries often maintain inventories of merchandise that they acquire from producers so they can quickly fill customers' orders. In many cases, retailers purchase this merchandise from wholesalers who,

6 LEARNING OBJECTIVE

Discuss the importance of marketing intermediaries, and contrast the roles of wholesalers and retailers.

marketing intermediaries
Businesspeople and organizations that assist in moving and marketing goods and services between producers and consumers.

distribution channel
An organized network of intermediaries that work together to move goods from producer to customer or to facilitate the delivery of services.

wholesalers
Intermediaries that sell products to other intermediaries for resale or to organizations for internal use.

retailers
Intermediaries that sell goods and services to individuals for their own personal use.

EXHIBIT 14.10	How Intermediaries Simplify Commerce

Intermediaries actually lower the price customers pay for many goods and services, because they reduce the number of contacts between producers and consumers that would otherwise be necessary. They also create place, time, and possession utility.

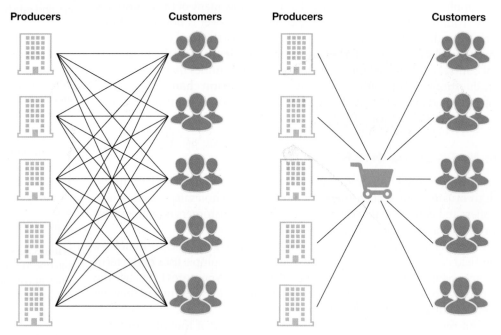

Source: Philip Kotler and Gary Armstrong, *Principles of Marketing*, 17th ed. (New York: Pearson, 2018), 336.

in addition to breaking bulk, may also transport the goods from the producer to the retail outlets.

- **Assuming risks.** When intermediaries accept goods from manufacturers, they usually take on the risks associated with damage, theft, product perishability (in the sense of tangible goods that are vulnerable to rotting, for instance), and obsolescence.
- **Providing financing.** Large intermediaries sometimes provide loans to smaller producers.
- **Completing product solutions.** In the information technology sector, manufacturers often rely on a class of intermediaries called *value-added resellers (VARs)* or *system integrators* to complete or customize solutions for customers. These channel partners can bring specialized technical expertise or provide geographic reach into smaller markets.

WHOLESALING AND INDUSTRIAL DISTRIBUTION

Although largely unseen by consumers, wholesaling is a huge presence in the economy. Approximately 6 million people work in wholesaling in the United States, and the sector generates roughly $7 trillion in sales every year.[47] By connecting producers with retailers and organizational customers, wholesalers play a vital role in nearly every industry in the world.

merchant wholesalers
Independent wholesalers that take legal title to goods they distribute.

Most wholesalers are independent companies that can be classified as *merchant wholesalers, agents,* or *brokers.* The majority of wholesalers are **merchant wholesalers**, independently owned businesses that buy from producers, take legal title to the goods, and then resell them to retailers or to organizational buyers. Merchant wholesalers are usually grouped into the two subcategories of *wholesalers,* which sell products to retailers, and *distributors,* which sell products to manufacturers and other companies for their own use.

Agents and brokers, in contrast, arrange transactions between buyers and sellers but don't take legal title to the products themselves. Specific titles vary by industry, and *agent* and *broker* are sometimes used interchangeably. One common type of agent is the *manufacturers' representative*, someone who sells lines of noncompeting products from multiple manufacturers to organizational customers. Various types of agents and brokers also work at the retailing level, such as in real estate, insurance, and investments.

RETAILING

The retailing sector ranges from tiny neighborhood shops to some of the world's largest companies, including Walmart and Amazon. Many manufacturers also engage in retailing when they sell products directly to consumers.

Retailing's Role in the Buying Process

In addition to providing convenient access to products and performing the various intermediary functions listed on page 431, retailers play a major role in the buying process. Many consumer buying decisions are made in the retail setting (both in-store and online), so retailing frequently involves a blend of the distribution and customer communication elements of the marketing mix. The term *shopper marketing*, or *in-store marketing*, refers to communication efforts directed at consumers while they are in the retail setting.

Take a look around the next time you are in a grocery store, and notice how many promotional signs, sample displays, and special displays there are. Chances are you'll see big displays in high-visibility locations, such as endcaps that feature the brands of a single manufacturer. Many of these promotional activities are done in coordination with manufacturers and are often designed to continue an advertising "conversation" that might have started in a television commercial, an online ad, or a coupon notification in a shopping app.

The Challenging Economics of Retailing

Retailing can be a tough business. Manufacturers can build competitive advantages with new features, new flavors, higher performance, appealing designs, and other factors. Retailers, however, don't have the option of competing through product design, because they are in the business of selling things that other companies make. Most of the factors they can compete on are relatively easy to emulate, such as price, selection, service, and convenience. If you want a box of Cheerios, you can probably buy it from several retailers within walking or driving distance, and if you don't feel like leaving home, Amazon is happy to deliver it. The product is the same wherever you buy it, so retailers have to find other ways to compete to get your business.

Because competitive differentiation is difficult to achieve and maintain, most retailers run on razor-thin profit margins. Compare Walmart, the world's largest retailer, with Apple, one of the world's largest manufacturers. Both are successful, extremely well-run companies. In a good year, Walmart manages to eke out an after-tax profit of about 3 percent, whereas Apple routinely generates profits of 20 percent.[48]

> **REAL-TIME UPDATES**
> **Learn More by Visiting This Website**
>
> **Love the retail experience?**
>
> Why not make a career of it? Check out the National Retail Foundation's career center. Go to **real-timeupdates.com/bia9** and select Learn More in the Students section.

Given the challenging economics of retailing, it's easy to see why slotting fees and other trade promotions play such a key role in the relationship between manufacturers and retailers. Financial pressure is also why successful retailers such as Walmart and Amazon put so much effort into continually improving internal operations. Both are renowned for the efficiency of their physical distribution networks, both rely heavily on big data and analytics, and Amazon values automation so much that it has its own robotics company.[49]

The Outlook for Retailing: Innovation, Disruption, and the Great Divide

Like all areas of business, retailing has been going through waves of disruption as new technologies, new competitive models, and new customer expectations shake up the sector. Here are some key issues that will continue to affect retailing in the next few years:

- **Online versus in-store retailing.** In spite of the occasional cry that Amazon is destroying the brick-and-mortar retail sector, after more than 20 years, online retailing still accounts for less than 10 percent of all retail sales. However, online retailing is growing much faster than offline retailing, so it will continue to take market share and challenge offline retailers to come up with innovative ways to capture and keep customers.[50] Of course, e-commerce retailers will continue to innovate as well. For instance, traditional retailers now find themselves competing against smart speakers, of all things. Voice shopping—using gadgets such as Amazon's Echo devices, powered by the company's Alexa voice-recognition technology—makes it practically effortless for customers to order food and household products.[51]

- **Omnichannel retailing.** Today's consumers increasingly hop across channels as they move through the buying process, such as researching products online and then making the purchase in a physical store, or checking out a product in a retail store and then making the purchase online (a practice known in the trade as "showrooming")—sometimes while standing in the store using their mobile phones. In response to this behavior, some retailers are adopting an **omnichannel retailing** strategy. With this approach, a company builds an integrated online and offline presence so that consumers have a seamless experience throughout the buying process, even if they move from mobile to desktop web to in-store shopping.[52]

- **Retail theater and experiential merchandising.** Increasingly, retail stores aren't just places to buy things; they're becoming places to research new technologies, learn about cooking, socialize, or simply be entertained for a few minutes while going through the routine of picking out the week's groceries. These forms of **retail theater** seek to engage consumers in ways that foster store loyalty, keep shoppers in stores longer, and encourage repeat business. *Experiential merchandising* creates interactive shopping experiences, such as using virtual reality headsets to let clothes shoppers experience being at a fashion show.[53]

- **Mobile commerce.** Within the growing online sector, mobile shopping is growing much faster than computer-based shopping and will soon represent half of all e-commerce sales.[54] In response to this shift in consumer behavior, retailers are responding with mobile-friendly websites, customized shopping apps, and digital coupons. Mobile is particularly influential in retailing because more than any other technology or communication medium, mobile is the one shoppers have on hand in the store. They can do price comparisons, research products, read reviews from other consumers—and, of course, order from an online retailer while standing in another company's retail store.

- **Subscription shopping.** Many household essentials are now available via subscription services on Amazon and other retailers, which simplifies the shopping experience by automating the repurchase of these "low-thought" items. Amazon also offers discounts when shoppers buy multiple items via subscription, which encourages additional purchases and lowers Amazon's shipping costs by consolidating more items into a single shipment.

- **Data-driven personalization.** Big data and AI can help retailers personalize the shopping experience by suggesting items consumers are most likely to be interested in. Both Amazon and the Chinese e-commerce giant Alibaba use AI to personalize their online storefronts for each shopper, for example.[55]

- **The retail apocalypse—and what many headlines miss.** You don't have to look far in many places across the country to see stores, shopping centers, and entire malls that have closed in recent years. So many have closed that the term *retail apocalypse* is now commonly used to describe the devastation.

omnichannel retailing
Strategy in which a company builds an integrated online and offline presence so that consumers have a seamless experience throughout the buying process.

retail theater
Tactics designed to engage retail consumers in ways that foster store loyalty, keep shoppers in stores longer, and encourage repeat business.

REAL-TIME UPDATES
Learn More by Reading This Article

Retail theater or better data?

Which could help struggling retailers more: jazzier in-store experiences or deeper data on their customers? Go to **real-timeupdates.com/bia9** and select Learn More in the Students section.

Mobile commerce is the fastest-growing segment of retailing.

Syda Productions/Shutterstock

In some retailing categories, there are simply too many stores to support current levels of business activity, and the United States has *five times* as much retail floor space per capita than other advanced economies.[56] Major malls, in particular, have been hit hard recently, thanks to years of overbuilding followed by the shock wave of e-commerce and changes in consumer habits. However, a more nuanced look at the situation shows that it is not a universal calamity wiping out all brick-and-mortar stores. To the contrary, retailers at the low end (those that compete on price) and the high end (those that cater to high-income shoppers) have actually been growing at a healthy clip. The devastation is happening in the middle, among "balanced" stores that try to compete on a combination of price and other factors, such as quality and selection, but don't stand out in any unique way. Some of these stores and malls are responding by adopting retail theater tactics or becoming mixed-use venues with entertainment options, upscale dining, or even apartments or office space. However, the future could be bleak for those that can't find something unique to offer today's consumers.[57]

Thousands of retail locations have closed in recent years, but the news is more positive at the low and high ends of the retail spectrum.

MANUFACTURERS' DISTRIBUTION DECISIONS

Manufacturers and other producers face some critical decisions when selecting marketing channels for their products. Should they sell directly to end users, rely on intermediaries, or do both? Which intermediaries, and how many should they choose? Should they use more than one channel? Whether you're selling digital music files or scrap iron stripped out of old ships, your **distribution strategy**, or overall plan for moving products to buyers, will play a major role in your success.

The ideal *distribution mix*, the number and type of intermediaries, varies widely from industry to industry and even from company to company within the same industry. Exhibit 14.11 on the next page shows the most common distribution models that manufacturers can choose. Producers consider several factors when designing their distribution mixes:

- **Customer needs and expectations.** The primary function of distribution channels is delivering value to customers, so channel strategy decisions should start with customer needs and expectations.[58] For instance, how do customers want and expect to purchase the product? If it is a food product, for example, are customers willing to drive to specialty stores to buy it, or does it need to be available in their regular grocery stores? Do customers expect to sample or try on products before they buy? Do they need help from trained product experts? What other products do customers expect to be able to purchase at the same time or from the same outlet?

- **Positioning objectives and brand compatibility.** Intermediaries present manufacturers' products to the world, so manufacturers want channel partners who can help them achieve their desired market positions and who will reflect well on their brands. As you'll read at the end of the chapter, for example, Tata Harper distributes her luxury skin care products through a select number of high-end department stores and day spas, rather than through health-oriented stores.

- **Established industry patterns and requirements.** Over the years, all industries develop certain patterns of distribution. If you try to "buck the system," you might uncover a

distribution strategy
A firm's overall plan for moving products through intermediaries and on to final customers.

Manufacturers of luxury products choose retailers carefully to make sure these outlets align with their positioning goals and brand image.

EXHIBIT 14.11	Common Distribution Channel Models

Producers can choose from a variety of distribution channel configurations. Channels in consumer markets tend to be longer (with more participants) than channels in organizational markets.

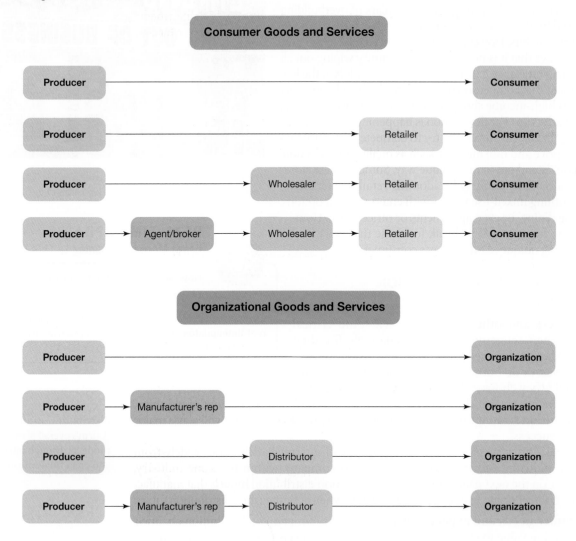

profitable new opportunity—or you might fail to reach your target customers entirely. Specific industries have other considerations as well, such as the need to get perishable food items to retail locations quickly or government regulations that dictate how and where certain products (hazardous chemicals and pharmaceuticals, for example) can be sold.

intensive distribution
A market coverage strategy that tries to place a product in as many outlets as possible.

exclusive distribution
A market coverage strategy that gives intermediaries exclusive rights to sell a product in a specific geographic area.

selective distribution
A market coverage strategy that uses a limited number of carefully chosen outlets to distribute products.

- **Market coverage.** The appropriate market coverage—the number of wholesalers or retailers that will carry a product—depends on several factors in the marketing strategy. With **intensive distribution**, producers try to get their products into as many outlets as possible. Producers expect to have a lot of competition in these retail settings and little or no marketing assistance from the retailer. At the other extreme, with **exclusive distribution**, producers may designate only one outlet in a given geographic area, and they expect a high level of marketing support and little or no competition from other products. **Selective distribution** falls between these two extremes; competing retail outlets can carry the products, and producers accept that their products will be sold alongside competitors, but they may expect some level of marketing and customer support.[59]
- **Distribution costs.** Performing all the functions that are handled by intermediaries requires time and resources, so cost plays a major role in determining channel selection. Many firms cannot afford the cost of building and maintaining their own distribution

channels, so they rely on intermediaries to promote and distribute their products. Even though they must sell their products to these intermediaries at a discount (or pay sales commissions), this cost is usually lower than trying to build a distribution network from the ground up.

Of course, manufacturers don't get to automatically pick and choose which intermediaries will carry their products. Wholesalers and retailers have their own selection criteria as well, and manufacturers often need to persuade intermediaries to take them on.

 CHECKPOINT

LEARNING OBJECTIVE 6: Discuss the importance of marketing intermediaries, and contrast the roles of wholesalers and retailers.

SUMMARY: Intermediaries can be responsible for any and all aspects of distribution, one of the key elements in any firm's marketing mix. Marketing intermediaries bring products to market and help ensure that the goods and services are available at the right time, in the right place, and in the right amount. Depending on their position in the channel, intermediaries can perform the key functions of matching buyers and sellers, providing market information, providing promotional and sales support, gathering assortments of goods, transporting and storing products, assuming risks, providing financing, and completing product solutions. The two major categories are *wholesalers*, which buy from producers and sell to retailers, to other wholesalers, and to organizational customers such as businesses, government agencies, and institutions; and *retailers*, which buy from producers or wholesalers and sell to the final consumers.

CRITICAL THINKING: (1) Why would a manufacturer such as Apple choose to establish its own retail chain? (2) Why are "balanced" retail stores struggling in today's environment?

IT'S YOUR BUSINESS: (1) When you have the choice between buying a product in a local retail store or buying it online, which do you normally choose? Why? (2) Have you ever had to work with more than one retailer to get a complete product solution (such as getting car parts or home improvement supplies from multiple stores)? If so, was the experience satisfactory?

KEY TERMS TO KNOW: marketing intermediaries, distribution channel, wholesalers, retailers, merchant wholesalers, omnichannel retailing, retail theater, distribution strategy, intensive distribution, exclusive distribution, selective distribution

---

Thriving in the Digital Enterprise: Augmented and Automated Writing

7 LEARNING OBJECTIVE
Describe how companies are using augmented and automated writing to communicate with customers.

Even in this visual age, the written word remains an essential element of customer communication. As companies try to personalize communication with current and potential customers, the amount of writing required can increase dramatically. To help marketers write more effectively and to reduce the time needed to generate routine promotional messages, some companies are exploring tools for *augmented writing* and *automated writing*.

AUGMENTED WRITING

Anyone who crafts written messages wonders at times if he or she has expressed important thoughts in the most effective way possible. For anything beyond the simplest messages, writers can never be entirely sure that they've found the most powerful words or crafted the most effective phrases. They must send their messages out into the marketplace and hope they've done their best.

Digital tools have been assisting writers for decades, as far back as spell checkers that predate the PC era, but most haven't done much beyond applying simple rules. However, advances in

augmented writing
Systems that provide real-time advice about the effectiveness of written language.

natural language processing show potential to fill this feedback void with **augmented writing** systems that provide real-time advice about the effectiveness of written language.

For example, Textio's augmented writing platform suggests words and phrases that it has determined to be more effective in a particular context (see Exhibit 14.12). It does so by measuring the success of similar writing efforts and analyzing language choices that proved to be more effective or less effective.

Textio's initial focus was on helping companies write job postings that can attract more of the most desirable candidates. By analyzing hundreds of millions of postings and comparing the candidate pools that they attracted, the system can figure out the most compelling way to describe a variety of job opportunities.

Organizations ranging from Twitter to Apple to the National Basketball Association are now using the system to improve their job postings. Human resources departments enter their job descriptions into Textio's *predictive engine*, which analyzes the text and suggests specific wording changes to attract target candidates. It also provides overall assessment points when it analyzes a posting, such as "Uses corporate clichés," "Sentences are too short," and "Contains too many questions," all based on how other job descriptions have performed.

Textio's clients are reporting success in terms of the number and quality of candidates they attract and how much faster they can fill job openings as a result. Plus, the system can help writers avoid biased or exclusionary language by showing how various demographic groups respond to different word choices.

EXHIBIT 14.12   **Augmented Writing**

Augmented writing tools can help companies craft compelling customer messages by analyzing word and phrase choices to suggest more effective ways to convey ideas. This system from Textio helps companies write more-persuasive job descriptions, and it is now being adapted to sales messages.

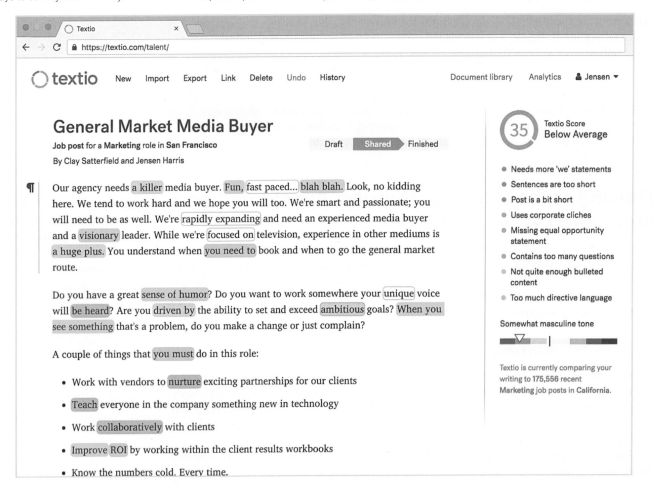

Of course, a system like this relies on a large set of similar messages and the ability to measure the success of those messages, so it's not yet a general-purpose solution that one can apply to every kind of business writing. However, Textio and its clients are now applying the system to sales emails and other types of recurring messages, and it has the potential to help writers with a variety of marketing communication tasks.

AUTOMATED WRITING

Automated writing goes beyond augmented writing to produce finished or near-finished writing. Chances are you've already read product descriptions and other content on e-commerce websites that was written by an AI system, rather than by a human copywriter.[60] Automated writing technologies are a great way to maintain relationships with large customer bases, too. For instance, Yahoo! Sports uses AI to generate millions of personalized draft reports and game recaps for members of its fantasy football leagues (see Exhibit 14.13).

automated writing
The use of AI to to produce finished or near-finished writing.

EXHIBIT 14.13	**Automated Writing**

Automated writing goes beyond augmented writing to produce finished or near-finished writing. Yahoo! Sports uses this AI built by Automated Insights to generate millions of personalized draft reports and game recaps for members of its fantasy football leagues, and other systems use AI to personalize a variety of customer messages.

Coca-Cola is experimenting with ways to use AI to write social media posts and narratives for advertising. Given the company's huge advertising presence, if it shows significant progress in applying AI to advertising writing, other companies are likely to follow.[61]

✔ **CHECKPOINT**

LEARNING OBJECTIVE 7: Describe how companies are using augmented and automated writing to communicate with customers.

SUMMARY: Augmented writing systems provide real-time advice about the effectiveness of written language so that writers can adjust their phrasing and word choices to maximize the chances of success. Companies are beginning to use this technology to fine-tune marketing messages. Automated writing goes a step further to have AI systems generate text, such as the product descriptions on websites and routine customer communication.

CRITICAL THINKING: Could a company endanger its brand image by using AI to generate messages that consumers think are written by humans? Why or why not?

IT'S YOUR BUSINESS: Would you respond differently to advertising messages if you knew they were written by AI rather than by a human? Why or why not?

KEY TERMS TO KNOW: augmented writing, automated writing

BEHIND THE SCENES

Staking Out a New Position in the Skin Care Market

One gets the distinct impression that Tata Harper doesn't do anything by half measure. When she wanted to create a line of high-end, all-natural skin care products, she spent nearly five years collaborating with a team of eight chemists to test the safety and efficacy of hundreds of flowers, roots, seeds, and other botanical ingredients from all over the world. In addition, her approach to product design is "more is more." Unlike the one or two natural ingredients that some brands add to a synthetic chemical base, her products start from an all-natural base and pack in as many natural ingredients as it takes— sometimes dozens—to create an effective, satisfying product.

This product strategy establishes a definite direction for her communication and distribution strategies. These are not mass-market products that can be promoted on low price or distributed through discount retailers.

If you can picture a positioning matrix of *synthetic* to *natural* up the vertical axis and *low performance* to *high performance* along the horizontal axis, Harper wants to position Tata Harper Skincare in the upper right corner: the most fully natural and highest-performance products on the market. The opening statement on her company's website makes that intention clear:

Made for uncompromising women who want the best skincare in the world, without a single drop of artificial chemicals. You shouldn't have to choose between natural and high performance.

At first glance, these two sentences might sound like the advertising copy you see on most websites, but on closer examination, they highlight four important marketing lessons.

First, although this message is clearly about the products, it is framed around the consumer and her needs. It's not "We're the best" but rather "You deserve the best." Companies with breakthrough products sometimes fall into the temptation of talking about themselves and how great they and their products are, and Harper's messaging deftly avoids this.

Second, although there is a strong suggestion of a competitive comparison, that is also subordinated to the consumer and her needs. This is a great example of effective promotional copywriting, keeping it about the customer while conveying messaging points in a subtle way.

Third, the phrase "made for uncompromising women who want the best skin care in the world" is an example of *segmenting through the appeal*. The very first sentence of the website makes it clear that these are high-end products intended for consumers who are willing to spend to get the best. The phrase identifies the company's target market segment and sends the message to those people that "This is your place." Conversely, budget-conscious shoppers can read the phrase and conclude that their needs will be better met somewhere else.

Fourth, the message makes an interesting statement about the skin care market. By saying "You shouldn't have to choose between natural and high performance," the message indicates that the Tata Harper line aims to take a previously unoccupied position in the market. Until Harper arrived, that upper-right corner of positioning matrix was empty, in other words. Truly innovative products face this situation whenever they hit the market, and it can mean one of several things:

1. Consumers want something like this product but haven't been able to get it. Such a scenario of pent-up demand is a marketer's dream—people are already waiting for the product you're bringing to market.

2. Consumers don't know they want it because they've never heard of something like this before. You've probably experienced this as a consumer yourself, when you discover a product that you didn't know you needed until you saw it. This scenario is still good news for a marketer, because latent demand is there, but it might take some time and educational efforts to help consumers understand how they can benefit.

3. Consumers don't have a need for something like this; there is no demand. This scenario is a marketer's nightmare—spending time and money to create a new product that no one wants. Sometimes there are holes in a market simply because no one wants that particular combination of features.

Judging from the success Tata Harper has enjoyed since launching her line of products, the market was obviously in some combination of the first and second situations. Some customers had been looking for high-end natural products but couldn't find them, and others had been using luxury products but didn't realize these products contained so many synthetic chemicals. Harper says that when she launched her first products, many people didn't believe that high-performance, all-natural skin care was possible, but now she says, "there isn't much convincing we need to do."

To support the top-level message of natural and high performance, Harper's communication strategy emphasizes authenticity and transparency. The company operates from her family's 1,200-acre farm in Vermont, where all the company's research, formulation, and production takes place. The postcard-perfect farm features prominently on the company's website in sumptuous photos and videos that suggest natural goodness and freedom from synthetic chemicals. Equally appealing photos of various natural ingredients echo the message. The messaging manages to evoke the purity of nature without the "health-food store" vibe that many people associate with natural beauty products. It's natural, but luxuriously natural.

Harper appears in many of these visuals as well, reinforcing the message that these products are not produced in an industrial plant by some faceless corporate manufacturing entity, but rather by this woman and her team on this very farm. The imagery is so appealing that one beauty editor theorized that one of the reasons the Tata Harper line has been so successful is that so many women aspirationally identify with Harper and the idyllic life she appears to live.

The transparency extends to the product descriptions, with each offering a complete ingredient list, even to the point of identifying which ingredients were grown with organic farming methods. Unlike the long list of complicated chemical names that appears on many skin care and cosmetic products, the Tata Harper line list the names of flowers, tree barks, and other natural elements. Every product bottle is also stamped with a production code, and consumers can enter that code on the company's website to see when "their" batch was made. This performs the useful function of letting customers know how fresh the product is, and it gives the products an air of personalization ("Ah, *my* batch was made on January 15.")

To reach target customers while maintaining the brand image and ensuring a positive customer experience, Harper follows a highly selective distribution strategy. Products are available in a limited number of department stores and day spas, all of which cater to customers seeking the best in skin care products. The company sends its own trainers to educate these retailers on product selection and application, and Harper herself makes in-store appearances to demonstrate products. The exclusive distribution applies to online sales as well, with the products available only through a small number of online retailers that align with Tata Harper's positioning objectives. The products are available on Amazon, but only through the Tata Harper Skincare storefront on the site, and no other sellers are authorized to sell them.

Tata Harper's success is proof that even in today's hypercrowded consumer markets, there is still room for innovative products that satisfy unmet and possibly unknown needs. Marrying those products with effective communication and distribution strategies ensures that the products reach the right consumers and express the points that make these breakthrough products so compelling. She has no intentions of slowing down, either. "We really want to focus on making the best skin care products in the world. One hundred years from now that's what we want our line to still represent."[62]

Critical Thinking Questions

14-1. How does Tata Harper's messaging incorporate both logical and emotional appeals?

14-2. Should Harper consider expanding sales by putting her name on a lower-priced line of skin care products that are a hybrid of natural ingredients and a synthetic chemical base? Why or why not?

14-3. Assume Harper wants to engage in a cooperative advertising campaign with another luxury brand, outside the skin care market. Identify a brand that would make a good complementary fit and explain your choice.

Learn More Online

Visit **www.tataharperskincare.com** and study the current presentation of the natural + high performance message. Has the messaging changed? Do Harper and her farm still feature prominently? In how many retail stores are the products now available?

End of Chapter

KEY TERMS

advertising (417)
advertising appeal (417)
advertising media (418)
augmented writing (438)
automated writing (439)
brand communities (428)
closing (424)
communication mix (413)
consultative selling (423)
content marketing (414)
conversation marketing (427)
core message (412)
direct response marketing (421)
distribution channel (431)
distribution strategy (435)
exclusive distribution (436)
experiential marketing (425)
inbound marketing (414)
integrated marketing communications (IMC) (415)
intensive distribution (436)
marketing intermediaries (431)

merchant wholesalers (432)
omnichannel retailing (434)
personal selling (422)
point-of-purchase (POP) display (425)
press conference (429)
press release (429)
product placement (421)
prospecting (423)
public relations (PR) (429)
rebates (425)
retail theater (434)
retailers (431)
sales promotion (425)
selective distribution (436)
social communication model (411)
social customer care (429)
trade allowances (426)
trade promotions (426)
wholesalers (431)
word of mouth (427)

TEST YOUR KNOWLEDGE

Questions for Review

14-4. What is the first necessary step that marketers take to move a potential customer towards making a purchase?

14-5. What is the AIDA model, and how is it used?

14-6. What is a communication mix?

14-7. What are the advantages of personal selling over other forms of customer communication?

14-8. How do display ads differ from search ads?

14-9. What is integrated marketing communications (IMC)?

14-10. What are some common types of consumer promotion?

Questions for Analysis

14-11. Why is social customer care an essential part of marketing?

14-12. How does inbound marketing demonstrate the marketing concept?

14-13. Why is it important for sales professionals to qualify prospects?

14-14. Is native advertising ethical? Why or why not?

14-15. What are the potential disadvantages of using celebrity appeals in advertising?

14-16. Why do some companies avoid email marketing, particularly to noncustomers?

14-17. What would experiential marketing need to accomplish in order to be a useful promotional technique?

14-18. Do marketers have any control over social media? Why or why not?

14-19. **Ethical Considerations.** Is your privacy being violated when a website you visit displays ads that are personalized in any way, even if it's just geographically targeted to the local area (based on your computer's internet address)? Why or why not?

Questions for Application

14-20. You run a business that needs to buy highly technical and specialized equipment. Ideally, what type of salesperson would be able to guide you through the options and help you meet the long-term needs of your business?

14-21. Choose a television commercial sponsored by a not-for-profit organization on a matter of social or ethical concern in your country. Good examples would be homelessness, poverty, or health-related concerns. What kind of advertising appeal do you think the campaign is utilizing to capture the audience's attention? Suggest other types of advertising appeals that you think could be more effective in achieving its advertising objectives.

14-22. To what extent could an organization rely on word-of-mouth communication via social media to launch a product and maintain the marketing effort for it?

14-23. **Concept Integration.** Should companies involve their marketing channels in the design of their customer communication programs? What are the advantages and disadvantages of doing so?

EXPAND YOUR KNOWLEDGE

Discovering Career Opportunities

Scan websites, newspapers, and company directories to find advertisements for sales and marketing positions. Marketing graduates usually begin their career as sales or marketing executives for numerous types of industries. Assume that, as a sales manager, you have been invited by the local chamber of commerce to address a group of marketing graduates on the various aspects of sales and marketing and the challenges faced by a salesperson.

14-24. What are the activities that salespersons engage in during a typical working day? What are some of the job responsibilities of a salesperson? What are the most important characteristics a salesperson should possess?

14-25. What are the common challenges faced by new sales recruits? What advice would you give newcomers to overcome the challenges faced by a salesperson?

14-26. What are the benefits of being a professional salesperson? What are the differences between the traditional selling approach and the contemporary selling approach?

Intelligent Communication Technology: Individualized Advertising

Online advertisers continue to experiment with a variety of technologies that allow them to pinpoint individual audience members with targeted ads or customized messages. One interesting result is that some advertising media or retailing formats are starting to look more like direct marketing media. Amazon.com, for example, personalizes a storefront for every one of its customers. Google's behavioral targeting technology, which it refers to as "interest-based advertising," displays ads based on your web-surfing patterns. With the specific technique of *dynamic retargeting*, you might see an ad related to a website you just left, designed to nudge you into returning for another look.[63]

Identify one form of individualized advertising now in use (you can search for "individualized advertising," "personalized advertising," "behavioral targeting," or "interest-based advertising"). In a brief email message to your instructor, describe the technology, explain how it helps businesses reach customers more effectively, and identify any privacy concerns involved with the medium (including restrictions resulting from the EU's GDPR).

PRACTICE YOUR SKILLS

Resolving Ethical Dilemmas

Imagine you're the marketing manager for a company that uses a celebrity as the "face and voice" of its brand. The relationship between the company and the product endorser has been long and mutually rewarding, but the celebrity is now being implicated in a major financial fraud scandal. What should you do?

Growing as a Professional

Developing the core message to promote a product is a useful skill to practice. Pick three products that you own or use frequently and identify the most significant benefits they offer users. For each product, summarize those benefits in a brief message, preferably one sentence. Whenever you are impressed with a product that you encounter, practice this skill of generating a core message. It will help you develop a customer-focused perspective on business and fine-tune your communication skills.

Sharpening Your Communication Skills

The good news: The current events blog you started as a hobby has become quite popular. The bad news: The blog now takes up so much of your time that you've had to quit a part-time job you were using to supplement your regular income. After some discussions with other bloggers, you decide to join Google's AdSense program (www.google.com/adsense) to help pay for the costs of operating your blog. With this program, small ads triggered by keywords in the content you publish will appear on your site. However, you're worried that your audience will think you've "sold out" because you're now generating revenue from your blog. Write a short message that could be posted on your blog explaining why you consider it necessary to run ads and assuring your readers of your continued objectivity, even if that means criticizing organizations whose ads might appear on your blog.

Building Your Team Skills

In small groups, discuss three or four recent ads or consumer promotions (in any media) that you think were particularly effective. Using the knowledge you've gained from this chapter, try to agree on which attributes contributed to the success of each ad or promotion. For instance: Was it persuasive? Informative? Competitive? Creative? Did it have logical or emotional appeal? Did it stimulate you to buy the product? Why or why not? Compare your results with those of other teams. Did you mention the same ads? Did you list the same attributes?

Developing Your Research Skills

Choose an article from a recent issue of a business journal or newspaper (print or online editions) that features an advertisement promoting the launch of an upmarket retirement village.

14-27. What is the core message? How persuasive is the advertisement?

14-28. Would you consider the advertisement to be institutional advertising or advocacy advertising?

14-29. What role does social media marketing play in the promotional campaign for the retirement village? Did the advertisement target senior citizens or the youth?

Writing Assignments

14-30. What is likely to happen to a company's promotional efforts if it fails to define the core message for a new product before launching it?

14-31. Other than image, what factors might prompt manufacturers of high-end technical or luxury products to decide not to sell their products through Costco?

ENDNOTES

1. Tata Harper, accessed 30 May 2018, www.tataharperskincare.com; Vivienne Decker, "Organic Skincare Mogul Tata Harper Pioneers Green Beauty," *Forbes*, 13 February 2017, www.forbes.com; Ilan Mochari, "Is This Strategy More Effective Than a Killer Startup Story?" *Inc.*, 20 May 2015, www.inc.com; Tata Harper product listings, Sephora, accessed 25 May 2018, www.sephora.com; Michelle Villett, "Tata Harper on Starting a Natural Skincare Line, Her Favourite Products and Best Skin Tips," *Beautyeditor*, 18 January 2017, beautyeditor.ca; Robin L. Flanigan, "With Tata Harper, Queen of Green Skincare, Told Rochester," *Democrat & Chronicle*, 27 December 2017, www.democratandchronicle.com; Jean Godfrey-June, "Tata Harper: The Natural Skin-Care Queen from Vermont by Way of Colombia," *Vanity Fair*, 8 September 2015, www.vanityfair.com.

2. Sara Fischer, "Impatient, Distracted Consumers Upend the Media Landscape," *Axios*, 22 May 2018, www.axios.com.

3. Philip Kotler and Gary Armstrong, *Principles of Marketing*, 17th ed. (New York: Pearson, 2018), 408.

4. Annalea Krebs, "5 Reasons Why Demographic Targeting Is Out and Behavioral Targeting Is In for 2018," *Adweek*, 14 February 2018, www.adweek.com.

5. "What Is Inbound Marketing?" HubSpot, accessed 1 June 2018, www.hubspot.com.

6. Kenneth E. Clow and Donald Baack, *Integrated Advertising, Promotion, and Marketing Communication*, 8th ed. (New York: Pearson, 2018), 55.

7. "The FTC's Endorsement Guides: What People Are Asking," U.S. Federal Trade Commission, accessed 16 April 2017, www.ftc.gov; "Advertising FAQ's: A Guide for Small Business," U.S. Federal Trade Commission, accessed 16 April 2017, www.ftc.gov; Cassidy Mantor, "FTC Cracks Down on Social Media Influencers," *Fashion Network*, 19 December 2017, us.fashionnetwork.com.

8. Michael R. Solomon, Greg W. Marshall, and Elnora W. Stuart, *Marketing: Real People, Real Choices*, 9th ed. (New York: Pearson, 2018), 482.

9. Barry Levine, "'Consent Is Unworkable' for Programmatic Ads in the Era of GDPR," *Martech Today*, 11 January 2018, martechtoday.com; Lara O'Reilly, "Snapchat Is About to Introduce Something Advertisers Have Been Wanting for Ages: Behavioral Targeting," *Business Insider*, 26 August 2016, www.businessinsider.com; Robert Brady, "The Dark Side of Remarketing," *Clix*, 21 January 2014, www.clixmarketing.com.

10. Advertising Self-Regulatory Council website, accessed 1 June 2018, www.asrcreviews.org.

11. Based in part on Clow and Baack, *Integrated Advertising, Promotion, and Marketing Communications*, 153–167.

12. Sanjay Putrevu, "Consumer Responses Toward Sexual and Nonsexual Appeals," *Journal of Advertising*, Summer 2008, 57–69.

13. Clow and Baack, *Integrated Advertising, Promotion, and Marketing Communications*, 162–164.

14. Rand Fishkin, "Pop-Ups, Overlays, Modals, Interstitials, and How They Interact with SEO—Whiteboard Friday," *Moz*, 28 April 2017, moz.com; Lily Hay Newman, "Pop-Up Mobile Ads Surge as Sites Scramble to Stop Them," *Wired*, 8 January 2018, www.wired.com.

15. "Google AdWords," Google, accessed 2 June 2018, adwords.google.com.

16. "YouTube in Numbers," YouTube, accessed 2 June 2018, www.youtube.com.

17. "Native Advertising: A Guide for Businesses," U.S. Federal Trade Commission, accessed 18 February 2017, www.ftc.gov.

18. Clow and Baack, *Integrated Advertising, Promotion, and Marketing Communications*, 292.

19. John Koestsier, "Mobile Advertising Will Drive 75% of All Digital Ad Spend in 2018: Here's What's Changing," *Forbes*, 23 February 2018.

20. Koestsier, "Mobile Advertising Will Drive 75% of All Digital Ad Spend in 2018: Here's What's Changing."

21. Bruce Rogers, "The Trade Desk Reaps Rewards of Growing Programmatic Advertising Market It Helped Create," *Forbes*, 7 February 2018, www.forbes.com; Charlotte Rogers, "What Is Programmatic Advertising? A Beginner's Guide," *Marketing Week*, 27 March 2017, www.marketingweek.com; "Display Advertising/Display Marketing vs. Real-Time Advertising (RTA)," 1&1, 19 October 2016, www.1and1.com.

22. "History of the Sears Catalog," Sears Archives, accessed 15 August 2009, www.searsarchives.com.

23. Clow and Baack, *Integrated Advertising, Promotion, and Marketing Communications*, 323.

24. Gerald Manning, Michael Ahearne, and Barry L. Reece, *Selling Today: Partnering to Create Value* (New York: Pearson, 2018), 35–36.

25. Sales engineer job description, Sweetwater Music, accessed 27 May 2018, www.sweetwater.com.

26. Manning, Ahearne, and Reece, *Selling Today: Partnering to Create Value*, 175.

27. Salesforce.com, accessed 27 May 2018, www.salesforce.com.

28. Manning, Ahearne, and Reece, *Selling Today: Partnering to Create Value*, 202.

29. Manning, Ahearne, and Reece, *Selling Today: Partnering to Create Value*, 211.

30. Manning, Ahearne, and Reece, *Selling Today: Partnering to Create Value*, 286.

31. Manning, Ahearne, and Reece, *Selling Today: Partnering to Create Value*, 294.

32. Kotler and Armstrong, *Principles of Marketing*, 472.

33. Kristina Monllos, "Brands Are Doing More Experiential Marketing. Here's How They're Measuring Whether It's Working," *Adweek*, 1 October 2017, www.adweek.com.

34. Clow and Baack, *Integrated Advertising, Promotion, and Marketing Communications*, 342.

35. Kotler and Armstrong, *Principles of Marketing*, 474.

36. Kali Hawlk, "Point of Purchase Marketing: How Retailers Can Optimize POP Areas for Higher Sales," Shopify, 23 February 2017, www.shopify.com; Clow and Baack, *Integrated Advertising, Promotion, and Marketing Communications*, 296–297.

37. Clow and Baack, *Integrated Advertising, Promotion, and Marketing Communications*, 380.

38. Solomon, Marshall, and Stuart, *Marketing: Real People, Real Choices*, 448.

39. Clow and Baack, *Integrated Advertising, Promotion, and Marketing Communications*, 353.

40. "Know Your Slotting Fees," Observa, 29 January 2018, www.observanow.com; Chase Purdy, "Inside the Secret, Backroom Deals Big Brands Make to Vie for Control over Grocery Stores," *Quartz*, 13 October 2016, qz.com.

41. Christina Newberry, "Social Listening: What It Is, Why You Should Care, and How to Do It Well," Hootsuite, 13 June 2017, blog.hootsuite.com.

42. Deborah Weinswig, "Influencers Are the New Brands," *Forbes*, 5 October 2016, www.forbes.com.

43. "Harley Davidson—The Grandaddy of All Communities," *Community Building Blog*, 27 May 2016, communitybuildingblog.wordpress.com.

44. Jason Kornwitz, "When It Comes to Social Media, Consumers Trust Each Other, Not Big Brands," *News@Northeastern*, 18 September 2017, news.northeastern.edu.

45. David Meerman Scott, *The New Rules of Marketing and PR*, 5th ed. (Hoboken, N.J.: Wiley, 2015), Kindle location 7497.

46. "Company Snapshot," Grainger, 31 December 2017, www.grainger.com.

47. "Manufacturing & Trade Inventories & Sales," U.S. Census Bureau, accessed 28 May 2018, www.census.gov; "Wholesale Trade," U.S. Bureau of Labor Statistics, accessed 28 May 2018, www.bls.gov.

48. Walmart and Apple financial statements from MarketWatch, accessed 3 June 2018, www.martketwatch.com.

49. Amazon Robotics, accessed 3 June 2018, www.amazonrobotics.com; "5 Ways Walmart Uses Big Data to Help Customers," Walmart Today, 7 August 2017, www.blog.walmart.com.

50. Stephanie Pandolph, "The Future of Retail 2018," *Business Insider*, 5 December 2017, www.businessinsider.com.

51. Nathaniel Meyersohn, "Amazon's Alexa Is the Biggest Challenge for Brands Since the Internet," *CNN Money*, 10 May 2018, money.cnn.com.

52. Barry Berman, Joel R. Evans, and Patrali Chatterjee, *Retail Management: A Strategic Approach*, 13th ed. (New York: Pearson, 2018), 156.

53. Berman, Evans, and Chatterjee, *Retail Management: A Strategic Approach*, 456.

54. Pandolph, "The Future of Retail 2018."

55. Laura Cox, "Disrupted Retail Fighting Back with Tech," *Disruption*, 21 February 2018, disruptionhub.com.

56. "Who Will Survive the Retail Reckoning of 2017?" *Knowledge@Wharton*, 2 June 2017, knowledge.wharton.upenn.edu.

57. Kasey M. Lobaugh, Christina Bieniek, Bobby Stephens, and Preeti Pincha, "The Great Retail Bifurcation," Deloitte Insights, 14 March 2018, www.deloitte.com; "Who Will Survive the Great Mall Shake-Out?" *Knowledge@Wharton*, 31 March 2015, knowledge.wharton.unpenn.edu; Nelson D. Schwartz, "The Economics (and Nostalgia) of Dead Malls," *New York Times*, 3 January 2015, www.nytimes.com; Benjamin Romano, "Retail Turmoil Triggers New Visions for Shopping Malls Like Northgate in Seattle," *Seattle Times*, 19 March 2018, www.seattletimes.com.

58. Kotler and Armstrong, *Principles of Marketing*, 345.

59. Berman, Evans, and Chatterjee, *Retail Management: A Strategic Approach*, 8.

60. "Wordsmith for Ecommerce," Automated Insights, accessed 4 June 2018, automatedinsights.com.

61. Mike Kaput, "Coca-Cola Exploring Artificial Intelligence for Content Creation, Media Buying, and More," Marketing Artificial Intelligence Institute, 7 March 2017, www.marketingaiinstitute.com.

62. See note 1.

63. Google AdSense Help, accessed 4 June 2018, www.google.com; Anja Lambrecht and Catherine Tucker, "When Personalized Ads Really Work," *Harvard Business Review*, 13 June 2013, hbr.org.

Managing the Money: Accounting and Financial Resources

Now it's time to look at the money side of business: how companies acquire funding, track spending, and analyze how well they're doing. Chapters 15 and 16 offer a brief introduction to accounting and finance—essential information if you ever plan to start a business, manage a business, or invest in a business.

CHAPTER **15** **Financial Information and Accounting Concepts**

CHAPTER **16** **Financial Management and Financial Markets**

Simon Belcher/Alamy Stock Photo

15 Financial Information and Accounting Concepts

LEARNING OBJECTIVES After studying this chapter, you will be able to

1 Define accounting, and describe the roles of private and public accountants.

2 Explain the impact of accounting standards such as GAAP and the Sarbanes-Oxley Act on corporate accounting.

3 Describe the accounting equation, and explain the purpose of double-entry bookkeeping and the matching principle.

4 Identify the major financial statements, and explain how to read a balance sheet.

5 Explain the purpose of the income statement and the statement of cash flows.

6 Explain the purpose of ratio analysis, and list the four main categories of financial ratios.

7 Explain why businesses would be interested in blockchain and other distributed ledger technologies.

MyLab Intro to Business
Improve Your Grade!
If your instructor is using MyLab Intro to Business, visit **www.pearson.com/mylab/intro-to-business**.

BEHIND THE SCENES   General Electric: Under Pressure to Simplify Its Accounting

Christopher Millette/Erie Times-News/AP Images

As GE's chief financial officer, Jamie Miller oversees the company's accounting and financial management activities, including communicating with investors.

www.ge.com

If you enjoy solving puzzles, here's one for you: Try to figure out how much money General Electric (GE) makes. The company's quarterly reports have at times listed as many as four different amounts for the closely watched figure of earnings per share (EPS). EPS is a critical variable for investors because it heavily influences stock price. EPS seems like a simple fraction of net income (revenue minus costs) over the number of shares held by stockholders. However, the numbers that go into this simple fraction can be adjusted—or manipulated, depending on one's perspective—in an endless variety of ways.

Reporting more than one EPS value by including or excluding various financial components is not uncommon, but reporting four is definitely unusual. And that's just the beginning of the problem. As the Bloomberg financial reporting service put it, "GE stands out for the sheer head-scratching complexity of its quarterly reports."

After announcing a plan in 2015 to slim down its vast conglomerate structure by selling off struggling business units, one of the adjusted EPS calculations that GE used excluded the financial performance of businesses it had put up for sale. The company defended the practice by explaining that unique metrics like this help it to "set operational targets and incentivize our leaders through our compensation plans." While this version of EPS may well serve those purposes, critics argue it doesn't reflect the firm's true performance as long as those business units are still part of the company and still weighing down its financial results.

The company has had a history of financial reporting practices that frustrate investors and occasionally catch the eye of regulators in the U.S. Securities and Exchange Commission, which oversees the financial reporting of public corporations. As GE's stock price plummeted throughout 2017, a year when the vast majority of companies saw vigorous growth in their stock prices, investors lost patience and demanded changes. Noted investor Warren Buffett, who sold his holdings in GE in 2017, was blunt: "The accounting at GE has not been a model at all in recent years."

As the once-mighty and still important company tries to work its way out of financial trouble, investors are clamoring for it to clarify its accounting and improve the *quality* of its earnings—meaning they want the company to demonstrate that its profits come from financially sustainable business operations and not from one-time events or artful accounting. As that same Bloomberg article put it in a headline, "Everyone's Fed Up with GE's Confusing Accounting."

If you were GE's chief financial offer, Jamie Miller, how would you respond to the demands for greater financial clarity? And what steps would you take to help stabilize the business?[1]

INTRODUCTION

GE's Jamie Miller (see the chapter-opening Behind the Scenes) has her hands full trying to satisfy the information demands of investors and company management, and she'll be applying the principles you will read about in this chapter. After describing what accountants do and the rules they are expected to follow, the chapter explains the fundamental concepts of the accounting equation and double-entry bookkeeping. It then explores the primary "report cards" used in accounting: the balance sheet, income statement, and statement of cash flows. The chapter continues with a look at trend analysis and ratio analysis, the tools that managers, lenders, and investors use to predict a company's ongoing health, and then it wraps up with a look at the distributed ledger technology known as blockchain.

Understanding Accounting

Accounting is the process of capturing, identifying, measuring, and reporting a company's financial transactions.[2] Accurate and timely financial information is important to businesses such as GE for two reasons: First, it helps managers and owners plan and control a company's operations and make informed business decisions. Second, it helps outsiders evaluate a business. Suppliers, banks, and other parties want to know whether a business is creditworthy; shareholders and other investors are concerned with its profit potential; and government agencies are interested in its tax accounting.

Because outsiders and insiders use accounting information for different purposes, accounting has two distinct facets. **Financial accounting** is concerned with preparing financial statements and other information for outsiders such as stockholders and *creditors* (people or organizations that have lent a company money or have extended its credit); **management accounting** is concerned with preparing cost analyses, profitability reports, budgets, and other information for insiders such as management and other company decision-makers. Note that internal decision-makers can also make use of the information generated by financial accounting.[3] To be useful, all accounting information must be accurate, objective, consistent over time, and comparable to information supplied by other companies—one of the key issues that investors have with the use of nonstandard metrics such as GE's adjusted EPS values.

WHAT ACCOUNTANTS DO

The work accountants do is sometimes confused with **bookkeeping**, which is the clerical function of recording the economic activities of a business. Although some accountants do perform bookkeeping functions, their work goes well beyond the scope of this activity. Accountants prepare financial statements, analyze and interpret financial information,

REAL-TIME UPDATES
Learn More by Visiting This Website

Considering a career in accounting?

This comprehensive directory can help you explore the profession and find potential employers. Go to **real-timeupdates.com/bia9** and select Learn More in the Students section.

prepare financial forecasts and budgets, and prepare tax returns. Some accountants specialize in certain areas of accounting, such as *cost accounting* (computing and analyzing production and operating costs), *tax accounting* (preparing tax returns and interpreting tax law), *financial analysis* (evaluating a company's performance and the financial implications of strategic decisions such as product pricing, employee benefits, and business acquisitions), or *forensic accounting* (combining accounting and investigating skills to assist in legal and criminal matters).

In addition to traditional accounting work, accountants may also help clients improve business processes, develop business plans, evaluate product performance, analyze profitability, design new information systems, and provide a variety of other management consulting services. Performing these functions requires a strong business background and a variety of skills beyond accounting.

PRIVATE ACCOUNTANTS

private accountants
In-house accountants employed by organizations and businesses other than a public accounting firm; also called *corporate accountants*.

controller
The highest-ranking accountant in a company, responsible for overseeing all accounting functions.

certified public accountants (CPAs)
Professionally licensed accountants who meet certain requirements for education and experience and who pass a comprehensive examination.

Private accountants work for corporations, government agencies, and not-for-profit organizations. Their titles vary by function and include *corporate accountant, managerial accountant,* and *cost accountant.*[4] Private accountants generally work together as a team under the supervision of the organization's **controller**, who reports to the vice president of finance or the chief financial officer (CFO), such as GE's Jamie Miller. Exhibit 15.1 shows the typical finance department of a large company. In smaller organizations, the controller may be in charge of the company's entire finance operation and report directly to the president.

Although certification is not required of private accountants, many are licensed **certified public accountants (CPAs)**. Specific requirements vary by state, but to receive a CPA license, an individual must complete a certain number of hours of college-level course work, have a minimum number of years of work experience in the accounting field,

---

EXHIBIT 15.1   **Typical Finance Department**

Here is a typical finance department of a large company. In smaller companies, the controller may be the highest-ranking accountant and report directly to the president. The top executive in charge of finance is often called the chief financial officer (CFO).

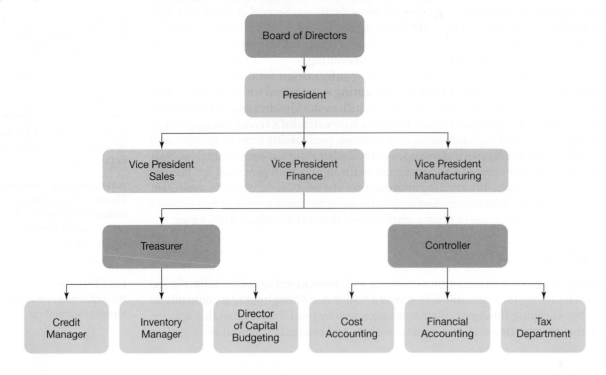

and pass the Uniform CPA Exam.[5] Many private accountants also become *certified management accountants (CMAs)* by passing an exam sponsored by the Institute of Management Accountants.[6]

PUBLIC ACCOUNTANTS

In contrast to private accountants, **public accountants** are independent of the businesses, organizations, and individuals they serve. Most public accountants are employed by public accounting firms that provide a variety of accounting and consulting services to their clients. The largest of these, four international networks known as the "Big Four," are Deloitte Touche Tohmatsu (simply "Deloitte" in the United States, www.deloitte.com); EY, formerly known as Ernst & Young (www.ey.com); KPMG (www.kpmg.com); and PwC, formerly known as PricewaterhouseCoopers (www.pwc.com). The Big Four are indeed big—together, they employ nearly a million people.[7] Many thousands of other accountants work for midsize regional firms and smaller local firms.

Whether they belong to one of these giant networks or to a smaller independent firm, public accountants generally are CPAs. Accountants must obtain CPA and state licensing certifications before they are eligible to conduct an **audit**—a formal evaluation of a company's accounting records and processes to ensure the integrity and reliability of a company's financial statements.

public accountants
Professionals who provide accounting services to other businesses and individuals for a fee.

audit
Formal evaluation of the fairness and reliability of a client's financial statements.

 CHECKPOINT

LEARNING OBJECTIVE 1: Define accounting, and describe the roles of private and public accountants.

SUMMARY: Accounting is the system a business uses to identify, measure, and communicate financial information to others, inside and outside the organization. Accountants perform a wide variety of tasks, including preparing financial statements, analyzing and interpreting financial information, preparing financial forecasts and budgets, preparing tax returns, interpreting tax law, computing and analyzing production costs, evaluating a company's performance, and analyzing the financial implications of business decisions. Private accountants work for corporations, government agencies, and not-for-profit organizations, performing various accounting functions for their employers. Public accountants, in contrast, sell their services to individuals and organizations. One of the most important functions of public accountants is performing audits, a formal evaluation of a company's accounting records and processes.

CRITICAL THINKING: (1) Why would a private accountant bother with becoming a CPA? (2) What effect can unreliable or uncertain accounting have on the economy?

IT'S YOUR BUSINESS: (1) How rigorous are your personal bookkeeping and accounting efforts? Do you keep accurate records, analyze spending, and set budgets? (2) If you don't really account for your personal finances, how might doing so help you, now and in the future?

KEY TERMS TO KNOW: accounting, financial accounting, management accounting, bookkeeping, private accountants, controller, certified public accountants (CPAs), public accountants, audit

Major Accounting Rules

To make informed decisions, investors, bankers, suppliers, and other parties need a way to verify the quality of the financial information that companies release to the public. They also need some way to compare information from one company to the next. To accommodate these needs, financial accountants are expected to follow a number of rules, some of which are voluntary and some of which are required by law.

 LEARNING OBJECTIVE

Explain the impact of accounting standards such as GAAP and the Sarbanes-Oxley Act on corporate accounting.

GENERALLY ACCEPTED ACCOUNTING PRINCIPLES (GAAP)

Accounting is based on numbers, so it might seem like a straightforward task to tally up a company's revenues and costs to determine its net profits. However, as GE's financials demonstrate, accounting is often anything but simple. For instance, *revenue recognition*, which involves how and when a company records incoming revenue, is a particularly complex topic.[8] Should a company record revenue (a) when it ships products or performs services, (b) when it bills customers, (c) when customers actually pay, or (d) after everyone has paid and any products that are going to be returned for refunds have been returned (because refunds reduce revenue)? If customers are in financial trouble and taking a long time to pay or are not paying at all, or if a poorly designed product is generating a lot of returns, the differences can be substantial.

From booking revenues and expenses to placing a value on assets and liabilities, these decisions affect just about every aspect of a company's stated financial picture. That picture in turn affects how much tax the company must pay, how attractive it is as an investment opportunity, how creditworthy it is from a lender's point of view, and other significant outcomes.

generally accepted accounting principles (GAAP)
Standards and practices used by publicly held corporations in the United States and a few other countries in the preparation of financial statements.

external auditors
Independent accounting firms that provide auditing services for public companies.

To help ensure consistent financial reporting so that all stakeholders understand what they're looking at, over the years regulators, auditors, and company representatives have agreed on a series of accounting standards and procedures. U.S. public corporations are required to report financial results using the **generally accepted accounting principles (GAAP)**, overseen by the Financial Accounting Standards Board (FASB). The FASB is an independent, not-for-profit organization recognized by the U.S. government as the authority on accounting standards for U.S. public companies. GAAP aims to give a fair and true picture of a company's financial position and to enable outsiders to make confident analyses and comparisons.[9]

Companies whose stock is publicly traded in the United States are required to file audited financial statements with the Securities and Exchange Commission (SEC). During an audit, CPAs who work for an independent accounting firm, also known as **external auditors**, review a client's financial statements to determine whether they have been prepared in accordance with GAAP. The auditors then summarize their findings in a report attached to the client's published financial statements.

Sometimes these reports disclose information that might affect the client's financial position, such as the bankruptcy of a major supplier, a large obsolete inventory, costly environmental problems, or questionable accounting practices. An *unqualified* or "clean" audit report means that to the best of the auditor's knowledge a company's financial statements are accurate and conform to GAAP practices. Auditors issue *qualified* reports when they are unable to verify all relevant information or to call attention to nonstandard elements within the report. If the departures from normal practices are significant and unfairly represent the company's finances, the auditor issues an *adverse* opinion.[10]

To assist with the auditing process, many large organizations use *internal auditors*—employees who investigate and evaluate the organization's internal operations and data to determine whether they are accurate and whether they comply with GAAP, federal laws, and industry regulations. Although this self-checking process is vital to an organization's financial health, an internal audit is not a substitute for having an independent auditor.

Non-GAAP Metrics

U.S. public companies are required to report financial results that meet GAAP standards, but they can also publish "non-GAAP" results (also called *pro forma* results) that don't conform to the standards. The *adjusted EPS* figures released by GE and many other companies are a good example. Companies may opt to report non-GAAP metrics when executives believe the GAAP calculations don't provide a complete or compelling picture of the company's performance and prospects.

Public companies are required to use the services of an external auditor to verify that their financial reports have been prepared in accordance with GAAP.

NicoElNino/Shutterstock

However, the practice is controversial, and some accountants and investors are wary that companies really use non-GAAP metrics to obscure poor performance rather than to highlight areas of good performance. Moreover, because the definitions of these measurements are not standardized, companies can change them over time, potentially to make performance look better.[11] In any event, companies must label these figures as non-GAAP data in their financial reports, and securities regulators can ask companies to remove or modify the presentation of non-GAAP data if these figures might mislead investors.[12]

Global Reporting Standards

GAAP has helped standardize accounting and financial reporting for companies in the United States, but the situation is more complex at the international level because GAAP standards are not used in other countries. The lack of a global standard creates extra work and complicates cross-border transactions, mergers, and investments because companies don't have a single set of tools to compute assets, liabilities, and other vital quantities.

Most other countries use **international financial reporting standards (IFRS)** maintained by the London-based International Accounting Standards Board. After a decade-long effort to harmonize the GAAP and IFRS, the two systems are closer in some respects but still different in some significant ways. In fact, there was a lot of momentum over the years to converge the two systems into a single, global set of standards, but that convergence effort now appears to be stalled.[13]

international financial reporting standards (IFRS)
Accounting standards and practices used in many countries outside the United States.

SARBANES-OXLEY

The need for and complexity of financial reporting standards is highlighted in the story of **Sarbanes-Oxley**, the informal name of the Public Company Accounting Reform and Investor Protection Act. (You'll hear it referred to as "Sox" or "Sarbox" as well.) Passed in 2002 in the wake of several cases of massive accounting fraud, most notably involving the energy company Enron and the telecom company WorldCom, Sarbanes-Oxley changed public company accounting in the United States in a number of important ways. Its major provisions include[14]

Sarbanes-Oxley
The informal name of comprehensive legislation designed to improve the integrity and accountability of financial information.

- Creating the Public Company Accounting Oversight Board (PCAOB) to oversee external auditors, rather than letting the industry regulate itself
- Outlawing most loans by corporations to their own directors and executives
- Requiring corporate lawyers to report evidence of financial wrongdoing
- Requiring that audit committees on the board of directors have at least one financial expert and that the majority of board members be independent (not employed by the company in an executive position)
- Requiring CEOs and CFOs to sign statements attesting to the accuracy of their financial statements
- Requiring companies to document and test their internal financial controls and processes

Sarbox generated many complaints initially, particularly regarding the amount of work involved in documenting internal financial controls. However, after a lot of initial criticism about the costs of compliance and a shift in the PCAOB's stance to let companies focus on monitoring the riskiest financial decisions instead of every mundane transaction, complaints about Sarbox leveled off.[15] Although opinions vary on whether some aspects went too far or didn't go far enough, the consensus now seems to be that, by and large, the law has improved the quality of financial reporting, increased protections for shareholders, and increased the emphasis on legal compliance and ethical decision-making.[16]

CHECKPOINT

LEARNING OBJECTIVE 2: Explain the impact of accounting standards such as GAAP and the Sarbanes-Oxley Act on corporate accounting.

SUMMARY: Accounting standards such as GAAP help ensure consistent financial reporting, which is essential for regulators and investors to make informed decisions. Sarbanes-Oxley introduced a number of rules covering the way publicly traded companies manage and report their finances, including restricting loans to directors and executives, creating a new board to oversee public auditors, requiring corporate lawyers to report financial wrongdoing, requiring CEOs and CFOs to sign financial statements under oath, and requiring companies to document their financial systems.

CRITICAL THINKING: (1) Should U.S. public companies with no significant overseas business activity be forced to follow international accounting standards? Why or why not? (2) How does requiring CEOs to personally attest to the accuracy of financial statements eliminate errors and misrepresentations?

IT'S YOUR BUSINESS: (1) If you were considering buying stock in a company, would you support rigorous (and potentially expensive) financial accountability such as that called for by Sarbanes-Oxley? Why or why not? (2) Would you consider investing in a privately held company whose financial records had not been reviewed by an external auditor? Why or why not?

KEY TERMS TO KNOW: generally accepted accounting principles (GAAP), external auditors, international financial reporting standards (IFRS), Sarbanes-Oxley

---

3 **LEARNING OBJECTIVE**

Describe the accounting equation, and explain the purpose of double-entry bookkeeping and the matching principle.

assets
Any things of value owned or leased by a business.

liabilities
Claims against a firm's assets by creditors.

owners' equity
The portion of a company's assets that belongs to the owners after obligations to all creditors have been met.

accounting equation
The equation stating that assets equal liabilities plus owners' equity.

Fundamental Accounting Concepts

In their work with financial data, accountants are guided by three basic concepts: the *fundamental accounting equation, double-entry bookkeeping*, and the *matching principle*. Here is a closer look at each of these essential ideas.

THE ACCOUNTING EQUATION

Assets are valuable items companies own or lease, such as equipment, cash, land, buildings, inventory, and investments. Claims against those assets are **liabilities**, or what the business owes to its creditors—such as lenders and suppliers. For example, when a company borrows money to purchase a building, the lender has a claim against the company's assets. What remains after liabilities have been deducted from assets is **owners' equity**:

$$\text{Owners' equity} = \text{Assets} - \text{Liabilities}$$

As a simple example, if your company has $1,000,000 in assets and $800,000 in liabilities, your equity is $200,000:

$$\$200,000 = \$1,000,000 - 800,000$$

This equation can be restated in a variety of formats. The most common is the **accounting equation**, which serves as the framework for the entire accounting process:[17]

$$\text{Assets} = \text{Liabilities} + \text{Owners' equity}$$
$$\$1,000,000 = \$800,000 + 200,000$$

This equation suggests that either creditors or owners provide all the assets in a corporation. Think of it this way: If you were starting a new business, you could contribute cash to the company to buy the equipment, supplies, and facilities you needed to run the business, or you could borrow money from a bank (the creditor), or you could do both. The company's liabilities are placed before owners' equity in the accounting equation because creditors get paid first. After liabilities have been paid, anything left over belongs to the owners. As a business engages in economic activity, the value and composition of its assets, liabilities, and owners' equity change. However, the equation must always be in balance; in other words, one side of the equation must always equal the other side.

REAL-TIME UPDATES
Learn More by Reading This Article

Introduction to the accounting equation

Get a better feel for the accounting equation with these practical examples. Go to **real-timeupdates.com/bia9** and select Learn More in the Students section.

DOUBLE-ENTRY BOOKKEEPING AND THE MATCHING PRINCIPLE

To keep the accounting equation in balance, most companies use a **double-entry bookkeeping** system that records every transaction affecting assets, liabilities, or owners' equity. Each transaction is entered twice, once as a *debit* and once as a *credit*, and these entries must offset each other to keep the accounting equation in balance. The double-entry method predates computers by hundreds of years and was originally created to minimize errors caused by entering and adding figures by hand and to give business owners a more immediate view of how they were doing. Accounting software now handles all this behind the scenes.

The **matching principle** requires that expenses incurred in producing revenues be deducted from (matched to, in other words) the revenue they generated during the same accounting period.[18] This matching of expenses and revenue is necessary for the company's financial statements to present an accurate picture of profitability. Accountants match revenue to expenses by adopting the **accrual basis** of accounting, which states that revenue is recognized when a company makes the sale, not when it gets paid. Similarly, expenses are recorded when a company receives the benefit of a service or when it uses an asset to produce revenue—not when it pays the bill.

Accrual-based accounting focuses on the economic substance of an event rather than on the movement of cash. It's a way of recognizing that revenue can be earned either before or after cash is received and that expenses can be incurred when a company receives a benefit (such as a shipment of supplies) either before or after the benefit is paid for.

If a business runs on a **cash basis**, the company records revenue only when money from a sale is actually received or when a bill is actually paid. Your bank account is a simple cash-based accounting system: You record deposits at the time of receipt (not when you earned the money), and you record expenses such as debit card charges and cash transfers made via mobile apps at the time of purchase. Cash-based accounting is simple, but it can be misleading. It's easy to inflate the appearance of income, for example, by delaying the payment of bills. For that reason, public companies are required to keep their books on an accrual basis.

The matching principle can get a bit complicated when major, long-term assets are involved. For instance, a company might spend $10 million on a new factory this year but generate revenue from it for the next 10 or 20 years. To more accurately match revenues and expenses, accounts use a calculation called **depreciation**, which spreads the cost of a tangible long-term asset over a period of time. (For intangible assets, this allocation over time is known as *amortization*.) When GE buys a piece of real estate, instead of deducting the entire cost of the item at the time of purchase, the company *depreciates* it, or spreads the cost over a certain number of years as specified by tax regulations, because the asset will likely generate income for many years. If the company were instead to *expense* long-term assets at the time of purchase, meaning it records the entire expense at one time, its apparent financial performance would be distorted negatively in the year of purchase and positively in all future years when these assets generate revenue.

double-entry bookkeeping
A method of recording financial transactions that requires a debit entry and credit entry for each transaction to ensure that the accounting equation is always kept in balance.

matching principle
The fundamental principle requiring that expenses incurred in producing revenue be deducted from the revenues they generate during an accounting period.

accrual basis
An accounting method in which revenue is recorded when a sale is made and an expense is recorded when it is incurred.

cash basis
An accounting method in which revenue is recorded when payment is received and an expense is recorded when cash is paid.

depreciation
An accounting procedure for systematically spreading the cost of a tangible asset over its estimated useful life.

CHECKPOINT

LEARNING OBJECTIVE 3: Describe the accounting equation, and explain the purpose of double-entry bookkeeping and the matching principle.

SUMMARY: The basic accounting equation is Assets = Liabilities + Owners' equity. Double-entry bookkeeping is a system of recording every financial transaction as two counterbalancing entries in order to keep the accounting equation in balance. The matching principle makes sure that expenses incurred in producing revenues are deducted from the revenue they generated during the same accounting period.

CRITICAL THINKING: (1) How does double-entry bookkeeping help eliminate errors? (2) Why is accrual-based accounting considered more fraud-proof than cash-based accounting?

IT'S YOUR BUSINESS: (1) Does looking at the accounting equation make you reconsider your personal spending habits? (Think about taking on liabilities that don't create any long-term assets, for example.) Why or why not? (2) How would accrual-based accounting give you better insights into your personal finances?

KEY TERMS TO KNOW: assets, liabilities, owners' equity, accounting equation, double-entry bookkeeping, matching principle, accrual basis, cash basis, depreciation

---

| 4 | **LEARNING OBJECTIVE** |

Identify the major financial statements, and explain how to read a balance sheet.

closing the books
Transferring net revenue and expense account balances to retained earnings for the period.

Using Financial Statements: The Balance Sheet

As a company conducts business day after day, it records sales, purchases, and other transactions and classifies them into individual accounts. After these transactions are recorded and then summarized, accountants must review the resulting summaries and adjust or correct any errors or discrepancies before **closing the books**, or transferring net revenue and expense items to *retained earnings*. Exhibit 15.2 illustrates the *accounting cycle* that companies go through during a given accounting period, such as a month.

In a way, this is what you do every month when you get your bank statement. You might think you have $50 left in your account but then see your statement and realize with delight that you forgot to record the $100 check your grandmother sent you, and your true balance is $150. Or you might realize with dismay that you forgot to record the $300 ATM withdrawal you made on spring break, and your true balance is –$250. Before you know how much money you'll have available to spend next month—your retained earnings—you have to accurately close the books on this month.

UNDERSTANDING FINANCIAL STATEMENTS

Financial statements consist of three separate but interrelated reports: the *balance sheet*, the *income statement*, and the *statement of cash flows*. These statements are required by law for all publicly traded companies, but they are vital management tools for every company, no matter how large or small. Together, these statements provide information about an organization's financial strength and ability to meet current obligations, the effectiveness of its sales and collection efforts, and its effectiveness in managing its assets. Organizations and individuals use financial statements to spot opportunities and problems, to make business decisions, and to evaluate a company's past performance, present condition, and future prospects.

The following sections examine the financial statements of the hypothetical company Computer Central Services.

BALANCE SHEET

balance sheet
A statement of a firm's financial position on a particular date; also known as a *statement of financial position*.

The **balance sheet**, also known as the *statement of financial position*, is a snapshot of a company's financial position on a particular date (see Exhibit 15.3 on page 458). In effect, it freezes all business actions and provides a baseline from which a company can measure

EXHIBIT 15.2 **The Accounting Cycle**

Here are the general steps in the accounting process, or *accounting cycle*, from recording transactions to making sure the books are in balance to closing the books for a particular accounting period (usually a month). Steps 1 through 3 are done as transactions occur; steps 4 through 8 are usually performed at the end of the accounting period.

1. Perform *transactions*
A transaction is any relevant accounting event, including making a sale, making a purchase, or making a debt payment.

2. Analyze and record transactions in a *journal*
Journalizing means analyzing the *source document* (e.g., a sales receipt or a customer invoice) for each transaction, then separating the transaction, into its debit and credit components and recording these chronologically in a journal.

3. *Post* journal entries to the *ledger*
Entries from the chronological journals are moved to the account-based ledger. Over the course of the month or other accounting period, each account (e.g., sales revenue or expenses) in the ledger fills up with the various transaction records posted from the journals. These accounts are considered temporary because they are closed out at the end of the accounting period (see step 8).

4. Prepare a *trial balance*
At the end of the accounting period, the debits and credits in the ledger are totaled, and then the two amounts are compared. If they aren't equal, one or more errors have crept in somewhere in the previous three steps and need to be found and corrected.

5. Make *adjusting entries*, as needed
Not all relevant changes are generated by transaction records during the accounting period, so accountants enter items such as asset depreciation or transactions whose revenues or expenses occur before or after the accounting period.

6. Prepare an adjusted trial balance
This is the same procedure as in step 4 but includes the adjusting entries made in step 5. Again, if the debits total and the credits total don't match, the error needs to be investigated and corrected.

7. Prepare *financial statements*
With the accounts adjusted and in balance for the accounting period, various managerial and government compliance reports can now be generated.

8. *Close the books* for the accounting period
Transfer the balances from temporary ledger accounts to the permanent balance sheet and income statement. Record *reversing entries* as needed to start fresh temporary accounts at the beginning of the next period.

Sources: Tracie Miller-Nobles, Brenda Mattison, and Ella Mae Matsumura, *Horngren's Financial & Managerial Accounting*, 6th ed. (New York: Pearson, 2018), 201; Robert Kemp and Jeffrey Waybright, *Financial Accounting*, 4th ed. (New York: Pearson, 2017), 72, 119–121.

change from that point forward. This statement is called a balance sheet because it includes all elements in the accounting equation and shows the balance between assets on one side of the equation and liabilities and owners' equity on the other side.

Every company prepares a balance sheet at least once a year, most often at the end of the **calendar year**, covering January 1 to December 31. However, many business and

calendar year
A 12-month accounting period that begins on January 1 and ends on December 31.

EXHIBIT 15.3   **Balance Sheet for Computer Central Services**

The categories used on the year-end balance sheet for Computer Central Services are typical.

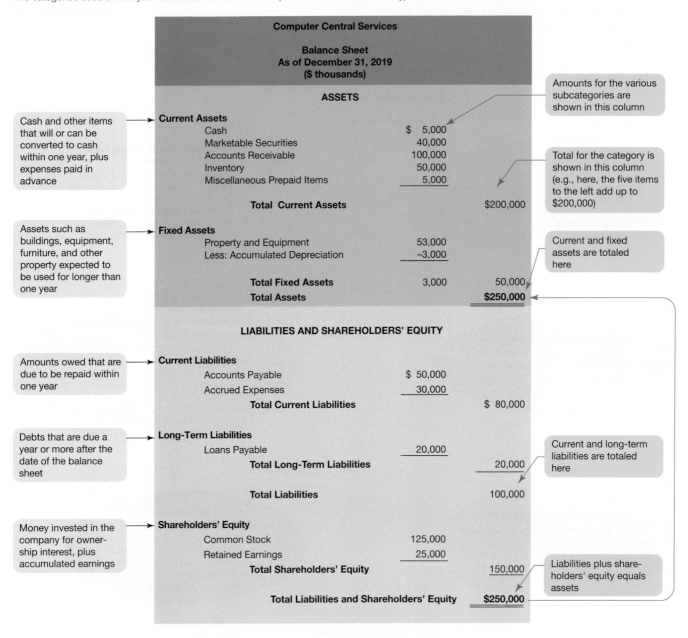

Cash and other items that will or can be converted to cash within one year, plus expenses paid in advance

Assets such as buildings, equipment, furniture, and other property expected to be used for longer than one year

Amounts owed that are due to be repaid within one year

Debts that are due a year or more after the date of the balance sheet

Money invested in the company for ownership interest, plus accumulated earnings

Amounts for the various subcategories are shown in this column

Total for the category is shown in this column (e.g., here, the five items to the left add up to $200,000)

Current and fixed assets are totaled here

Current and long-term liabilities are totaled here

Liabilities plus shareholders' equity equals assets

Computer Central Services

Balance Sheet
As of December 31, 2019
($ thousands)

ASSETS

Current Assets		
Cash	$ 5,000	
Marketable Securities	40,000	
Accounts Receivable	100,000	
Inventory	50,000	
Miscellaneous Prepaid Items	5,000	
Total Current Assets		$200,000
Fixed Assets		
Property and Equipment	53,000	
Less: Accumulated Depreciation	–3,000	
Total Fixed Assets	3,000	50,000
Total Assets		**$250,000**

LIABILITIES AND SHAREHOLDERS' EQUITY

Current Liabilities		
Accounts Payable	$ 50,000	
Accrued Expenses	30,000	
Total Current Liabilities		$ 80,000
Long-Term Liabilities		
Loans Payable	20,000	
Total Long-Term Liabilities		20,000
Total Liabilities		100,000
Shareholders' Equity		
Common Stock	125,000	
Retained Earnings	25,000	
Total Shareholders' Equity		150,000
Total Liabilities and Shareholders' Equity		**$250,000**

fiscal year
Any 12 consecutive months used as an accounting period.

government bodies use a **fiscal year**, which may be any 12 consecutive months. Every balance sheet is dated to show the exact date when the financial snapshot was taken.

By reading a company's balance sheet, you should be able to determine the size of the company, the major assets owned, any asset changes that occurred in recent periods, how the company's assets are financed, and any major changes that have occurred in the company's debt and equity in recent periods.

Assets

As discussed previously in the chapter, an asset is something owned by a company with the intent to generate income. Assets can be *tangible* or *intangible*. Tangible assets include land, buildings, and equipment. Intangible assets include intellectual property (such as patents and business methods), goodwill (any amount a company pays above market value when it acquires another company), brand awareness and recognition, workforce skills, management talent, and even customer relationships.[19] However, only those intangible assets with an identifiable value resulting from an acquisition can be included in a GAAP balance sheet.[20]

As you might expect, assigning value to intangible assets is not an easy task, but these assets make up an increasingly important part of the value of many contemporary companies.[21] For instance, much of the real value of a company such as Google is not in its tangible assets but in its search engine algorithms, brand awareness, and customer relationships. Some accounting experts now say that the asset valuation methods that companies are expected to use fail to accurately measure the assets of many modern companies—overvaluing some and undervaluing others. In fact, some professional investors have already developed their own asset valuation models to get what they believe is a more accurate view of how much these companies are worth.[22]

Every company has a variety of assets. Current assets are cash and assets that can be quickly converted to cash; fixed assets are long-term investments in buildings, equipment, furniture and fixtures, transportation equipment, land, and other tangible property.

The asset section of the balance sheet is usually divided into *current assets* and *fixed assets*. **Current assets** include cash and other items that will or can become cash within the following year, such as short-term investments like money-market funds and *accounts receivable* (amounts due from customers). **Fixed assets** (sometimes referred to as *property, plant, and equipment*) are long-term investments in buildings, equipment, furniture and fixtures, transportation equipment, land, and other tangible property used in running the business. Fixed assets have a useful life of more than one year.

Assets are listed in order by *liquidity*, or the ease with which they can be converted into cash, from the most liquid to the least liquid. The balance sheet gives a subtotal for each type of asset and then a grand total for all assets.

current assets
Cash and items that can be turned into cash within one year.

fixed assets
Assets retained for long-term use, such as land, buildings, machinery, and equipment; also referred to as *property, plant, and equipment*.

Liabilities

Liabilities may be current or long term as well, and they are listed in the order in which they will come due. The balance sheet gives subtotals for **current liabilities** (obligations that will have to be met within one year of the date of the balance sheet) and **long-term liabilities** (obligations that are due one year or more after the date of the balance sheet), and then it gives a grand total for all liabilities.

Current liabilities include accounts payable, short-term financing (which you'll read more about in Chapter 16), and accrued expenses. *Accounts payable* include the money the company owes its suppliers and service providers. *Accrued expenses* are expenses that have been incurred but for which the company has not yet received bills or paid for. For example, because salespeople at Computer Central Services earn commissions, the company has a liability to those employees after the sale is made. If such expenses and their associated liabilities were not recorded, the company's financial statements would be misleading and would violate the matching principle, because the commission expenses earned at the time of sale would not be matched to the revenue generated from the sale.

Long-term liabilities include loans, leases, and bonds. A borrower makes principal and interest payments to the lender over the term of the loan, and its obligation is limited to these payments (see the section "Debt Financing Versus Equity Financing" in Chapter 16). Rather than borrowing money to make purchases, a firm may enter into a *lease*, under which the owner of an item allows another party to use it in exchange for regular payments. Bonds, also covered in Chapter 16, are certificates that obligate the company to repay a certain sum, plus interest, to the bondholder on a specific date.

current liabilities
Obligations that must be met within a year.

long-term liabilities
Obligations that fall due more than a year from the date of the balance sheet.

Owners' Equity

The owners' investment in a business is listed on the balance sheet under owners' equity (or *shareholders' equity* or *stockholders' equity* for corporations). In a corporation, the shareholders' total investment value is the sum of two amounts: the total value of all the shares currently

retained earnings
The portion of shareholders' equity earned by the company but not distributed to its owners in the form of dividends.

held, plus **retained earnings**—cash that is kept by the company rather than distributed to shareholders in the form of dividends. As Exhibit 15.3 shows, Computer Central Services has retained earnings of $25 million. The company doesn't pay dividends—many small and growing corporations don't—but rather builds its cash reserves to fund expansion in the future. (Shareholders' equity can be slightly more complicated than this, depending on how the company's shares were first created, but this summary gives you the basic idea of how the assets portion of the balance sheet works.)

 CHECKPOINT

LEARNING OBJECTIVE 4: Identify the major financial statements, and explain how to read a balance sheet.

SUMMARY: The three major financial statements are the balance sheet, the income statement, and the statement of cash flows. The balance sheet provides a snapshot of the business at a particular point in time. It shows the size of the company, the major assets owned, the ways the assets are financed, and the amount of owners' investment in the business. Its three main sections are assets, liabilities, and owners' equity.

CRITICAL THINKING: (1) Why do analysts need to consider different factors when evaluating a company's ability to repay short-term versus long-term debt? (2) Would the current amount of the owners' equity be a reasonable price to pay for a company? Why or why not?

IT'S YOUR BUSINESS: (1) What are your current and long-term financial liabilities? Are these liabilities restricting your flexibility as a student or consumer? (2) As a potential employee, what intangible assets can you offer a company?

KEY TERMS TO KNOW: closing the books, balance sheet, calendar year, fiscal year, current assets, fixed assets, current liabilities, long-term liabilities, retained earnings

---

5 LEARNING OBJECTIVE

Explain the purpose of the income statement and the statement of cash flows.

Using Financial Statements: Income and Cash Flow Statements

In addition to the balance sheet, the two other fundamentally important financial statements are the income statement and the statement of cash flows.

INCOME STATEMENT

income statement
A financial record of a company's revenues, expenses, and profits over a given period of time; also known as a *profit-and-loss statement*.

If the balance sheet is a snapshot, the income statement is a movie. The **income statement**, or *profit-and-loss statement* or simply "P&L," shows an organization's profit performance over a period of time, typically one year. It summarizes revenue from all sources and all **expenses**, the costs that have arisen in generating revenues. Expenses and income taxes are then subtracted from revenues to show the actual profit or loss of a company, a figure known as **net income**—also called *profit* or, informally, the *bottom line*. By briefly reviewing a company's income statements, you should have a general sense of the company's size, its trend in sales, its major expenses, and the resulting net income or loss. Owners, creditors, and investors can evaluate the company's past performance and future prospects by comparing net income for one year with net income for previous years. Exhibit 15.4 shows the income statement for Computer Central Services.

expenses
Costs created in the process of generating revenues.

Expenses include both the direct costs associated with creating or purchasing products for sale and the indirect costs associated with operating the business. If a company manufactures or purchases inventory, the cost of storing the product for sale (such as heating the warehouse, paying the rent, and buying insurance on the storage facility) is added to the

net income
Profit (or loss) incurred by a firm, determined by subtracting expenses from revenues; casually referred to as the *bottom line*.

EXHIBIT 15.4	**Income Statement for Computer Central Services**

An income statement summarizes the company's financial operations over a particular accounting period, usually a year.

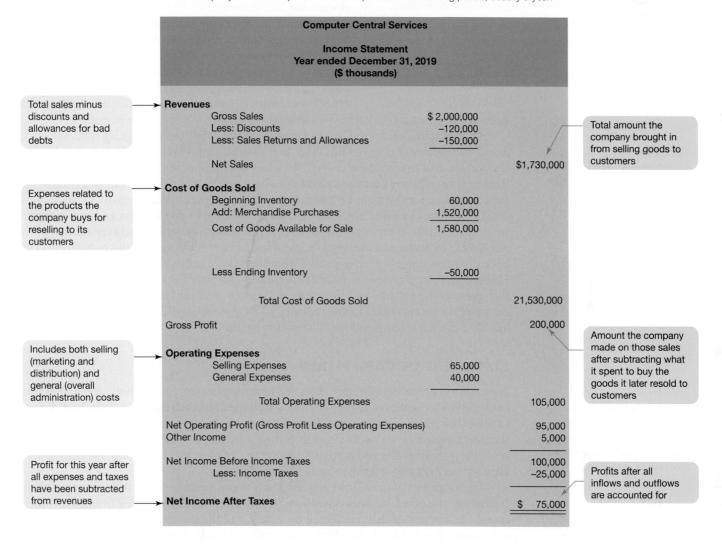

Computer Central Services

Income Statement
Year ended December 31, 2019
($ thousands)

Total sales minus discounts and allowances for bad debts →	**Revenues**		
	Gross Sales	$ 2,000,000	
	Less: Discounts	–120,000	Total amount the company brought in from selling goods to customers
	Less: Sales Returns and Allowances	–150,000	
	Net Sales		$1,730,000
Expenses related to the products the company buys for reselling to its customers →	**Cost of Goods Sold**		
	Beginning Inventory	60,000	
	Add: Merchandise Purchases	1,520,000	
	Cost of Goods Available for Sale	1,580,000	
	Less Ending Inventory	–50,000	
	Total Cost of Goods Sold		21,530,000
	Gross Profit		200,000
Includes both selling (marketing and distribution) and general (overall administration) costs →	**Operating Expenses**		Amount the company made on those sales after subtracting what it spent to buy the goods it later resold to customers
	Selling Expenses	65,000	
	General Expenses	40,000	
	Total Operating Expenses		105,000
	Net Operating Profit (Gross Profit Less Operating Expenses)		95,000
	Other Income		5,000
Profit for this year after all expenses and taxes have been subtracted from revenues →	Net Income Before Income Taxes		100,000
	Less: Income Taxes		–25,000
	Net Income After Taxes		$ 75,000

Profits after all inflows and outflows are accounted for

difference between the cost of the beginning inventory and the cost of the ending inventory in order to compute the actual cost of items that were sold during a period—or the **cost of goods sold**. The computation can be summarized as follows:

$$\text{Cost of goods sold} = \text{Beginning inventory} + \text{Net purchases} - \text{Ending inventory}$$

As shown in Exhibit 15.4, cost of goods sold is deducted from sales to obtain a company's **gross profit**—a key figure used in financial statement analysis. In addition to the costs directly associated with producing goods, companies deduct **operating expenses**, which include both *selling expenses* and *general expenses*, to compute a firm's *net operating income*. Net operating income is often a better indicator of financial health because it gives an idea of how much cash the company is able to generate. For instance, a company with a sizable gross profit level can actually be losing money if its operating expenses are out of control—and if it doesn't have enough cash on hand to cover the shortfall, it could soon find itself bankrupt.[23]

Selling expenses are operating expenses incurred through marketing and distributing the product (such as wages or salaries of salespeople, advertising, supplies, insurance for the sales operation, depreciation for the store and sales equipment, and other sales department expenses such as telephone charges). *General expenses* are operating expenses incurred in

cost of goods sold
The cost of producing or acquiring a company's products for sale during a given period.

gross profit
The amount remaining when the cost of goods sold is deducted from net sales; also known as *gross margin*.

operating expenses
All costs of operation that are not included under cost of goods sold.

REAL-TIME UPDATES

Learn More by Watching This Video

Essential points on the income statement

See what investors look for in a company's income statement. Go to **real-timeupdates.com/bia9** and select Learn More in the Students section.

the overall administration of a business. These include professional services (such as accounting and legal fees), office salaries, depreciation of office equipment, insurance for office operations, and supplies.

A firm's net operating income is then adjusted by the amount of any nonoperating income or expense items such as the gain or loss on the sale of a building. The result is the *net income before income taxes* (losses are shown in parentheses), a key figure used in budgeting, cash flow analysis, and a variety of other financial computations. Finally, income taxes are deducted to compute the company's *after-tax net income* (or loss) for the period.

An alternative (and non-GAAP) measure of profitability is *earnings before interest, taxes, depreciation, and amortization,* or **EBITDA**. (Recall from page 455 that depreciation and amortization are used to spread the cost of an asset over a number of years, rather than charging it against the company's earnings all at once.) Because EBITDA doesn't include various items such as the interest payments on loans or the effects of depreciating expensive capital equipment, it is viewed by some investors as a "purer" measure of profitability and an easier way to compare financial performance across companies or industries. And even though it is a non-GAAP indicator and must be labeled as such, many public companies publish EBITDA because it can suggest greater profitability than the standard operating profit number. However, for those same reasons, EBITDA is also criticized because it doesn't reflect costs that every company has and therefore could mask serious financial concerns. As one example, in a year in which Twitter reported EBITDA earnings of $301 million, the company lost $578 million by conventional accounting measures.[24]

EBITDA
Earnings before interest, taxes, depreciation, and amortization.

STATEMENT OF CASH FLOWS

statement of cash flows
A statement of a firm's cash receipts and cash payments that presents information on its sources and uses of cash.

In addition to preparing a balance sheet and an income statement, all public companies and many privately owned companies prepare a **statement of cash flows**, or *cash flow statement*, to show how much cash the company generated and where it went (see Exhibit 15.5). The statement of cash flows tracks the cash coming into and flowing out of a company's bank accounts. It reveals the increase or decrease in the company's cash for the period and summarizes (by category) the sources of that change.

The statement of cash flows should give you a general sense of the amount of cash created or consumed by daily operations, the amount of cash invested in fixed or other assets, the amount of debt borrowed or repaid, and the proceeds from the sale of stock or payments for dividends. In addition, an analysis of cash flows provides a good idea of a company's ability to pay its short-term obligations.

 CHECKPOINT

LEARNING OBJECTIVE 5: Explain the purpose of the income statement and the statement of cash flows.

SUMMARY: The income statement, also known as the profit-and-loss statement, reflects the results of operations over a period of time. It gives a general sense of a company's size and performance. The statement of cash flows shows how a company's cash was received and spent in three areas: operations, investments, and financing. It gives a general sense of the amount of cash created or consumed by daily operations, fixed assets, investments, and debt over a period of time.

CRITICAL THINKING: (1) How could two companies with similar gross profit figures end up with dramatically different net operating income? (2) How might a statement of cash flows help a turnaround expert decide how to rescue a struggling company?

EXHIBIT 15.5 | **Statement of Cash Flows for Computer Central Services**

A statement of cash flows shows a firm's cash receipts and cash payments as a result of three main activities—operating, investing, and financing—for an identified period of time (such as the year indicated here).

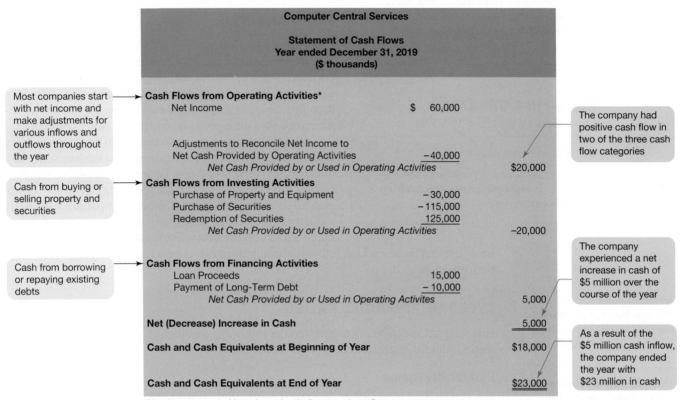

Most companies start with net income and make adjustments for various inflows and outflows throughout the year

Cash from buying or selling property and securities

Cash from borrowing or repaying existing debts

The company had positive cash flow in two of the three cash flow categories

The company experienced a net increase in cash of $5 million over the course of the year

As a result of the $5 million cash inflow, the company ended the year with $23 million in cash

Computer Central Services

Statement of Cash Flows
Year ended December 31, 2019
($ thousands)

Cash Flows from Operating Activities*

Net Income		$ 60,000
Adjustments to Reconcile Net Income to		
Net Cash Provided by Operating Activities	−40,000	
Net Cash Provided by or Used in Operating Activities		$20,000

Cash Flows from Investing Activities

Purchase of Property and Equipment	− 30,000	
Purchase of Securities	− 115,000	
Redemption of Securities	125,000	
Net Cash Provided by or Used in Operating Activities		−20,000

Cash Flows from Financing Activities

Loan Proceeds	15,000	
Payment of Long-Term Debt	− 10,000	
Net Cash Provided by or Used in Operating Activites		5,000

Net (Decrease) Increase in Cash		5,000
Cash and Cash Equivalents at Beginning of Year		$18,000
Cash and Cash Equivalents at End of Year		$23,000

*Numbers preceded by minus sign indicate cash outflows.

IT'S YOUR BUSINESS: (1) What would your personal income statement look like today? Are you operating "at a profit" or "at a loss"? (2) What steps could you take to reduce your "operating expenses"?

KEY TERMS TO KNOW: income statement, expenses, net income, cost of goods sold, gross profit, operating expenses, EBITDA, statement of cash flows

Analyzing Financial Statements

After financial statements have been prepared, managers, investors, and lenders use them to evaluate the financial health of the organization, make business decisions, and spot opportunities for improvements by looking at the company's current performance in relation to its past performance, the economy as a whole, and the performance of competitors.

TREND ANALYSIS

The process of comparing financial data from year to year is known as *trend analysis*. You can use trend analysis to uncover shifts in the nature of a business over time. Of course, when you are comparing one period with another, it's important to consider the effects of extraordinary or unusual items such as the sale of major assets, the purchase of a new line of products from another company, weather, or economic conditions that may have

6 **LEARNING OBJECTIVE**

Explain the purpose of ratio analysis, and list the four main categories of financial ratios.

REAL-TIME UPDATES
Learn More by Reading This Article

The complicated reality of a simple fraction

Companies can adjust earnings per share in an endless variety of ways—some that will bring down the wrath of the SEC. Go to **real-timeupdates.com/bia9** and select Learn More in the Students section.

REAL-TIME UPDATES
Learn More by Watching This Video

Can this company pay its bills?

Use the quick ratio to see how healthy an investment target—or potential employer—is. Go to **real-timeupdates.com/bia9** and select Learn More in the Students section.

return on sales
The ratio between net income after taxes and net sales; also known as the *profit margin*.

return on equity
The ratio between net income after taxes and total owners' equity.

earnings per share
A measure of a firm's profitability for each share of outstanding stock, calculated by dividing net income after taxes by the average number of shares of common stock outstanding.

working capital
Current assets minus current liabilities.

current ratio
A measure of a firm's short-term liquidity, calculated by dividing current assets by current liabilities.

quick ratio
A measure of a firm's short-term liquidity, calculated by adding cash, marketable securities, and receivables, then dividing that sum by current liabilities; also known as the *acid-test ratio*.

affected the company in one period but not the next. These extraordinary items are usually disclosed in the text portion of a company's annual report or in the notes to the financial statements.

RATIO ANALYSIS

Unlike trend analysis, which tracks *absolute* numbers from one year to the next, ratio analysis creates *relative* numbers by comparing sets of figures within a single time window, such as a month or a year. By using ratios rather than absolute amounts, analysts can more easily assess a company's performance over time and compare it with other companies.

A variety of commonly used ratios help companies understand their current operations and answer some key questions: Is inventory too large? Are credit customers paying too slowly? Can the company pay its bills? Ratios also allow comparison with other companies within an industry, which helps gauge how well a company is doing relative to its competitors. Every industry tends to have its own "normal" ratios, which individual companies use as benchmarks to gauge their own performance.

TYPES OF FINANCIAL RATIOS

Financial ratios can be organized into the following groups, as Exhibit 15.6 shows: profitability, liquidity, activity, and leverage (or debt).

Profitability Ratios

You can analyze how well a company is conducting its ongoing operations by computing *profitability ratios*, which show how well the company can generate profit. Three of the most common profitability ratios are **return on sales**, or *profit margin* (the net income a business makes per unit of sales); **return on equity** (net income divided by owners' equity); and **earnings per share** (the profit earned for each share of stock). Exhibit 15.6 shows how to compute these profitability ratios by using the financial information from Computer Central Services.

Liquidity Ratios

Liquidity ratios measure a firm's ability to pay its short-term obligations. As you might expect, lenders and creditors are keenly interested in liquidity measures. A company's **working capital** (current assets minus current liabilities) is an indicator of liquidity because it represents current assets remaining after the payment of all current liabilities.

A different picture of the company's liquidity is provided by the **current ratio**—current assets divided by current liabilities. This figure compares the current debt owed with the current assets available to pay that debt. The **quick ratio**, also called the *acid-test ratio*, is computed by subtracting inventory from current assets and then dividing the result by current liabilities. This ratio is often a better indicator of a firm's ability to pay creditors than the current ratio because the quick ratio leaves out inventories, which can take a long time to convert to cash. A quick ratio below 1.0 (meaning current liabilities exceed current assets) is a sign that the company could struggle to meet its near-time financial obligations and therefore might not be a safe credit risk, a good investment, or possibly a smart place to accept a job. However, quick ratios can vary widely by industry, so they should always be viewed in that context.[25] Exhibit 15.6 shows that both the current and the quick ratios of Computer Central Services are well above industry averages.

EXHIBIT 15.6	How Well Does This Company Stack Up?

Financial ratios offer a quick and convenient way to evaluate how well a company is performing in relation to prior performance, the economy as a whole, and the company's competitors.

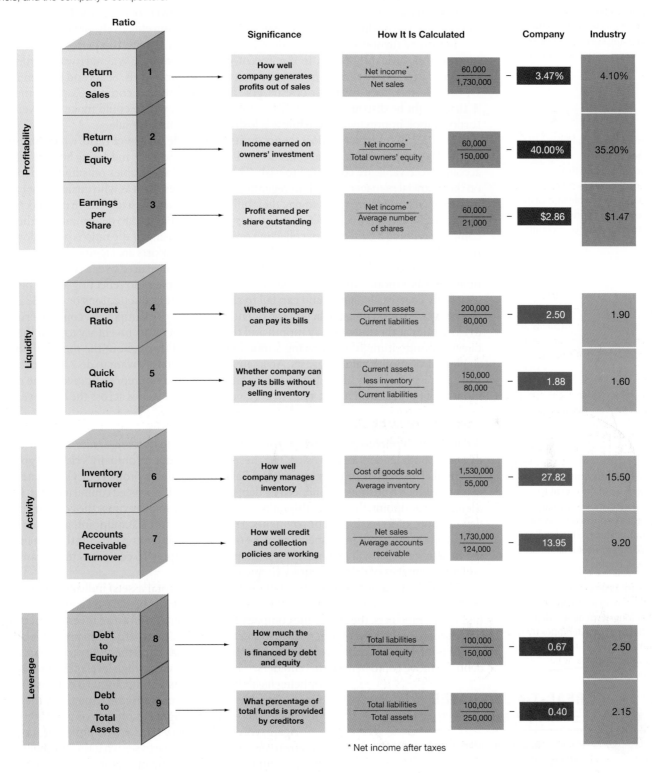

* Net income after taxes

Activity Ratios

inventory turnover ratio
A measure of the time a company takes to turn its inventory into sales, calculated by dividing cost of goods sold by the average value of inventory for a period.

Activity ratios analyze how well a company is managing and making use of its assets. For companies that maintain inventories, the most common activity ratio is the **inventory turnover ratio**, which measures how fast a company's inventory is turned into sales. A company that struggles to move inventory has more capital tied up in inventory, and the low ratio could indicate that it is having trouble forecasting accurately, selling effectively, or both.

Inventory turnover can vary widely within an industry, with top performers moving inventory significantly faster. In one recent year, for instance, Walmart was turning its inventory over two to three times faster than two struggling rivals, Sears and J.C. Penney.[26] Of course, inventory turnover doesn't give a full picture of a company's performance. A firm might be discounting heavily to move inventory, which could make its inventory turnover look impressive even while it is losing money on every sale.

accounts receivable turnover ratio
A measure of the time a company takes to turn its accounts receivable into cash, calculated by dividing sales by the average value of accounts receivable for a period.

Another useful activity ratio is the **accounts receivable turnover ratio**, which measures how well a company's credit and collection policies are working by indicating how frequently accounts receivable are converted to cash. The volume of receivables outstanding depends on the financial manager's decisions regarding several issues, such as who qualifies for credit, how long customers are given to pay their bills, and how aggressively the firm collects late payments. Be careful here as well. If the ratio is going up, you need to determine whether the company is doing a better job of collecting or if sales are rising. If the ratio is going down, it may be because sales are decreasing or because collection efforts are lagging.

With any kind of activity ratio, keep in mind that it is measured over a certain period of time, such as a month, quarter, or year. Because it's a simple ratio reflecting a time period, it's a fairly coarse calculation and can fail to show important fluctuations or trends, and it can be skewed by an unusual beginning or ending value. For example, if a company rushes to close sales at the end of every month and thereby depletes its inventory toward the end of each month, it might be carrying a much higher level throughout the month than the single end-of-month value suggests. An analyst might therefore want to do a more detailed daily average. Similarly, if the beginning or ending value is not representative of the other months of the year, you might want to average month-end values across the entire year.

Leverage, or Debt, Ratios

debt-to-equity ratio
A measure of the extent to which a business is financed by debt as opposed to invested capital, calculated by dividing the company's total liabilities by owners' equity.

A company's ability to pay its long-term debts is reflected in its *leverage ratios*, also known as *debt ratios*. Both lenders and investors use these ratios to judge a company's risk and growth potential. The **debt-to-equity ratio** (total liabilities divided by total equity) indicates the extent to which a business is financed by debt as opposed to invested capital (equity). From a lender's standpoint, the higher this ratio is, the riskier the loan, because the company must devote more of its cash to debt payments. From an investor's standpoint, a higher ratio indicates that the company is spending more of its cash on interest payments than on investing in activities that will help raise the stock price.[27] Chapter 16 compares the advantages and disadvantages of debt and equity financing.

debt-to-assets ratio
A measure of a firm's ability to carry long-term debt, calculated by dividing total liabilities by total assets.

The **debt-to-assets ratio** (total liabilities divided by total assets) indicates how much of the company's assets are financed by creditors. As with the debt-to-equity ratio, the higher this ratio gets, the riskier the company looks to a lender. From an investor's perspective, though, a high level of debt relative to assets might indicate that a company is leveraging its assets in ways that could create more revenue. As long as it has the ability to pay back the debt, the move could benefit shareholders.[28] However, having a high level of debt to assets, or being *highly leveraged*, puts a company at risk. Those assets may not be able to generate enough cash to pay back the debt, or lenders and suppliers might cut off the company's credit.

Again, you can use every ratio as a helpful indicator, but be sure to dig below the surface to see what the number really means, and use more than one indicator to judge a company's performance.

For the latest information on accounting practices and financial reporting, visit **real-timeupdates.com/bia9** and select Chapter 15.

REAL-TIME UPDATES

Learn More by Listening to This Podcast

How customer retention affects company valuation

New research highlights how important customer retention can be in determining the valuation of a corporation. Go to **real-timeupdates.com/bia9** and select Learn More in the Students section.

CHECKPOINT

LEARNING OBJECTIVE 6: Explain the purpose of ratio analysis, and list the four main categories of financial ratios.

SUMMARY: Financial ratios provide information for analyzing the health and future prospects of a business. Ratios facilitate financial comparisons among different-size companies and between a company and industry averages. Most of the important ratios fall into one of four categories: profitability ratios, which show how well the company generates profits; liquidity ratios, which measure the company's ability to pay its short-term obligations; activity ratios, which analyze how well a company is managing its assets; and debt ratios, which measure a company's ability to pay its long-term debt.

CRITICAL THINKING: (1) Why is it so important to be aware of extraordinary items when analyzing a company's finances? (2) Why is the quick ratio frequently a better indicator than the current ratio of a firm's ability to pay its bills?

IT'S YOUR BUSINESS: (1) Assume that you are about to make a significant consumer purchase and that the product is available at two local stores, one with high inventory turnover and one with low inventory turnover. Which store would you choose based on this information? Why? (2) If you were applying for a home mortgage loan today, would a lender view your debt-to-assets ratio favorably? Why or why not?

KEY TERMS TO KNOW: return on sales, return on equity, earnings per share, working capital, current ratio, quick ratio, inventory turnover ratio, accounts receivable turnover ratio, debt-to-equity ratio, debt-to-assets ratio

Thriving in the Digital Enterprise: Distributed Ledgers and Blockchain

[7] **LEARNING OBJECTIVE**
Explain why businesses would be interested in blockchain and other distributed ledger technologies.

If you've explored cryptocurrencies such as bitcoin, you've probably run across the term *blockchain*, which refers to a new way of processing and securing transactions. This section offers a brief look at how this concept is being applied in a variety of business applications.

THE NOT-SO-SIMPLE PROCESS OF RECORDING TRANSACTIONS

As you learned in this chapter, any time a company completes a transaction, it records the event as a debit and credit. In the days before computers, transactions were recorded in books called *ledgers*. Accounting software does the same thing, only replacing the physical ledger book with a database stored on a computer.

When two companies transact, each records the event in its own ledger/database. If the buyer and the seller meet in person and transact using physical currency, it's a simple enough matter to confirm that the buyer received the product and the seller received payment. Each party can update its ledger, and the transaction is complete.

However, transactions are rarely this simple in today's business world. Many buyers and sellers never meet, and sellers may transact with hundreds, thousands, or millions of buyers. With multiple ledgers, there are multiple versions of the truth, which makes the process vulnerable to error and fraud and can require all the parties involved to reconcile their ledgers to make sure their records match. To validate transactions across ledgers, a bank or other financial intermediary often must be involved, sometimes an auditor is required to authenticate transactions, and the identity of the parties in the transaction must be confirmed, all of which make the process slower and more expensive.[29]

In physical supply chains, raw materials and products can move from the field, mine, or factory through multiple stages of transportation and distribution, often across international boundaries, involving mountains of "paperwork" (some of it still on actual paper) and many incompatible and disconnected ledgers.[30] When transactions involve digital products or electronic cash, these units of value can be surreptitiously copied, misdirected, or stolen. Plus, conventional databases are vulnerable to intentional attack or accidental corruption.

RETHINKING THE LEDGER

distributed ledger
Method of verifying and recording transactions that replaces the individual ledgers of market participants with a shared ledger that everyone can access.

blockchain
A type of distributed ledger in which each new transaction is captured in a "block," which is then appended to the previous block in a continuous chain.

With so many points of complexity, inefficiency, and weakness in the conventional approach, it's no wonder that businesses have been looking for better ways to record transactions. A new model emerged in 2008 from an unlikely source: the anonymous programmer or programmers who invented bitcoin. To ensure that this new digital currency could be created, used, and stored safely, bitcoin's creators proposed the idea of a **distributed ledger**, which replaces the individual ledgers of all the participants in a marketplace with a shared ledger that everyone can access (see Exhibit 15.7). *Distributed ledger technology (DLT)* encompasses the ledgers themselves, plus software to handle cryptography, access permissions, and other needs.

The specific type of distributed ledger that bitcoin uses is called **blockchain**, in which each new transaction is captured in a "block" that is appended to the previous block in a continuous chain. All the participants can verify the authenticity of each transaction, and new transactions aren't added to the chain until they have been verified. Once they're added, transactions can't be modified. With this approach, no single entity can control the ledger—or be a point of catastrophic failure—and everyone can see and back-trace every transaction. There are no central banks or other intermediaries in the bitcoin model; the system polices itself.[31]

BUSINESS BENEFITS AND APPLICATIONS OF BLOCKCHAIN

While the eventual impact of bitcoin is still unclear, businesses in a wide range of industries are investing heavily in blockchain technology. Although the concept came from bitcoin, it has spread far beyond cryptocurrency and can be applied to situations involving any kind of tangible or intangible asset.

Blockchains can be *public* or *private* and *permissionless* or *permissioned*. The bitcoin blockchain is both public and permissionless, meaning anyone can join without restriction. This is an elegant approach for freely creating and trading cryptocurrency on a global scale, but it isn't ideal for many other business applications. The blockchains that businesses are investing in are both private and permissioned, meaning participants must be invited and can be granted specific levels of access.[32] By being private, these blockchains allow only identified participants to join and therefore don't require the computationally intensive verification step that gives the bitcoin blockchain a voracious appetite for electricity and that can slow transactions. And the permissioning aspect is vital for most businesses, because it lets them comply with data privacy regulations and other questions of access.[33]

(A quick note to confirm the terminology: *Distributed ledger* is the umbrella concept here; *blockchain* is one type of distributed ledger, and the *bitcoin blockchain* is one specific implementation of the blockchain model.)

Businesses have identified a variety of benefits from blockchain:[34]

- Lower costs
- Fewer errors
- Faster transactions
- Greater transparency
- Simpler auditing procedures
- Tighter data security, including *immutability* (data records cannot be altered once stored)
- Tighter network security, with no single point of attack
- Traceability and greater control over which assets get into the system
- Opportunities to apply big data analytics across an entire business ecosystem

The following sections look at three application areas that illustrate the power of blockchain in business. (In addition to handling transactions, the distributed ledger idea has been expanded to the use of *smart contracts*, which are covered on page 499.)

EXHIBIT 15.7 **Distributed Ledgers and Blockchain**

With distributed ledgers such as blockchain, the individual transaction ledgers of all the participants in a business relationship are replaced with a single shared ledger in which every transaction is verified, stored, and viewable by all participants (depending on their level of access permission). In this simplified model of a food ecosystem, for example, in a matter of seconds anyone in the system can find out where an individual shipment came from, how long it has been in storage, and other important facts.

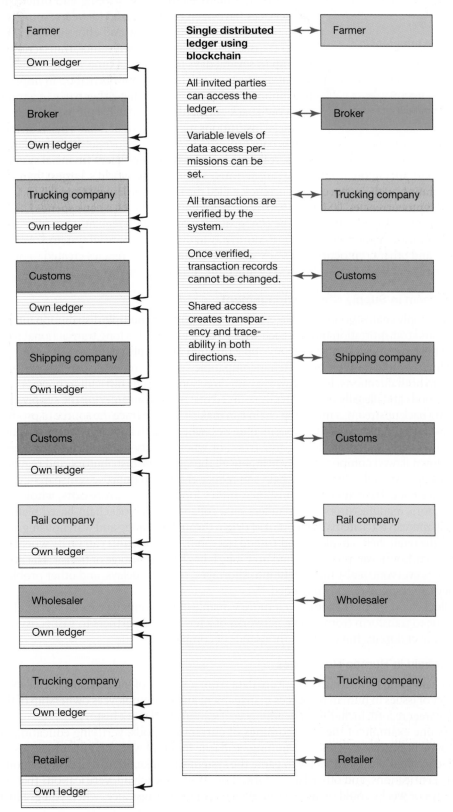

Blockchain in Financial Services

Blockchain is already disrupting financial services, and many banks recognize that they need to adapt before they get cut out of, or *disintermediated*, from many financial transactions (as has already happened with cryptocurrencies, for instance). Because blockchain can be applied whenever tangible or intangible assets are involved, it can potentially be used for everything from leasing equipment to trading derivatives and other financial contracts.

Although many elements of banking and other financial services have been computerized for years, some major aspects are still surprisingly slow and effort-intense. When banks transact with each other, for instance, transactions can take up to several days to finalize, a time window known as *settlement*. During settlement, money is tied up in unproductive limbo, and there is the risk that either party in a transaction could back out. Settlement is such a problem that it costs financial institutions many billions of dollars per year, in fact. Blockchain promises to sharply reduce settlement delays and costs, resulting in a much more efficient financial system.[35]

REAL-TIME UPDATES

Learn More by Reading This Infographic

A simple overview of blockchain

See how blockchain helps companies overcome the limitations of traditional ledgers. Go to **real-timeupdates.com/bia9** and select Learn More in the Students section.

To simplify global banking transactions, some of the world's largest banks are collaborating on their own cryptocurrency, called the Utility Settlement Coin (USC). Unlike other cryptocurrencies, USC is backed by cash holdings, and when a bank spends USC, it is spending its real-world currency. The USC group is working with regulators and the central banks of various nations to integrate it more fully in the global financial system.[36] Whereas bitcoin and other cryptocurrencies are "anti-establishment" currencies created to operate outside regulatory regimes, USC is very much the "establishment" cryptocurrency.

Blockchain in Supply Chain Management

In long supply chains, goods and materials can pass through multiple distribution intermediaries and transportation modes, each with its own ledger. This long transactional path is prone to errors and delays, which can ripple through the supply chain.

Moreover, the multiple and often incompatible systems limit transparency and traceability in both directions. In the downstream direction, it can be difficult to prevent counterfeit goods and illegally or unethically sourced materials from entering the supply chain. Looking back upstream, a multistep chain can make it hard to trace the source of products, such as during outbreaks of foodborne illnesses, when health authorities need to quickly find out where tainted products came from, or when quality-control engineers need to track down flawed components. By bringing all the suppliers, distributors, and regulators onto a single, shared ledger, blockchain can reduce errors and improve transparency.[37]

IBM's Food Trust system, for instance, unites food growers, processors, wholesalers, distributors, manufacturers, and retailers on a collaborative, blockchain-based platform. Participants can track items from point of origin through shipping and warehousing all the way to the retail shelf. Thanks to end-to-end traceability, participants can verify where food came from, how it was processed, and how long it has been in storage or transit. The system also gives everyone real-time insight into shortages, customs delays, and other problems, so they can respond quickly if needed.[38]

Blockchain should become even more valuable in the coming years as supply chains continue to transform from simple networks of a few trusted partners to vast ecosystems that connect dozens, hundreds, or thousands of companies.

Blockchain in Human Resources

Blockchain's ability to securely capture data from a variety of participants could solve a number of issues in human resources management and give employees ownership of their entire career record, including education, certifications, and work history.

As one example of the shortcomings of current methods, verifying education and employment history is a time-consuming headache for employers, and the process is vulnerable to fraud as applicants try to game the system with fake or inflated degrees, nonexistent certifications, and other false information. With blockchain, verifications that now take days or weeks could be done securely in seconds. For instance, when you graduate, your university could submit proof to the blockchain, and each time you are promoted or receive a professional certification such as a CPA, those events could become blocks as well. You would own all your career data and grant access to employers, lenders, and other parties when required. Blockchain isn't nearly as far along in human resources as it is in other functional areas, but within a few years it could dramatically change how companies handle employee information.[39]

✓ CHECKPOINT

LEARNING OBJECTIVE 7: Explain why businesses would be interested in blockchain and other distributed ledger technologies.

SUMMARY: Distributed ledger technologies and blockchain in particular can help businesses overcome the limitations of each party in a business relationship having its own transactional ledger. Working through independent and sometimes incompatible ledgers can be inefficient, and it makes a transactional network vulnerable to errors, delays, and fraud. By accessing a single, shared ledger, parties have one "source of truth" in which transactions are verified by the system before they are accepted, and once accepted they are immutable.

CRITICAL THINKING: How might blockchain help address the problem of spoilage and waste in the food industry?

IT'S YOUR BUSINESS: Would knowing that the fresh foods you buy were tracked in a blockchain affect your purchasing decisions? Why or why not?

KEY TERMS TO KNOW: distributed ledger, blockchain

BEHIND THE SCENES

An American Icon Struggles to Right Itself

The history of American industry and innovation in the 20th century parallels to a striking degree the history of the industrial behemoth General Electric. GE innovations were integral to modern life—in the home, in the office, in the factory, and in the hospital. The company was the pinnacle of the conglomerate model of corporate organization that had its heyday in the latter decades of the century. Its product mix ranged from jet engines, steam turbines, nuclear power plants, and locomotives to light bulbs, home appliances, medical equipment, television broadcasting, and major components of the world's electrical grids. And if customers needed financing to buy a locomotive or a nuclear plant, GE Capital was ready with loans.

Unfortunately, if the first two decades are any indication, the 21st century is not shaping up to be nearly as friendly for GE. There had been rumblings of trouble here and there since 2001, leading to a plan by company management in 2015 to trim down by trying to sell underperforming businesses. Then it all came crashing down in 2017, when GE reported multibillion-dollar losses, cut its famous stock dividend for only the second time since the Great Depression, and watched its stock price drop nearly in half during a year when most stocks were growing like overfertilized weeds. Long-time employees, investors, and the business media were in shock. One former GE executive said, "It's unfathomable. You couldn't possibly dream this up. It's crazy." The headline of a feature story in *Fortune* asked the question that was on many minds: "What the H*** Happened at GE?" (*Fortune* didn't bother with the nicety of asterisks, either.)

That year was shocking indeed, but the troubles didn't come out of nowhere. As another former executive put it, "The wheels came off in 2017, but the lug nuts had been loosening for a long time." Analysts point to two major problems that developed in the years leading up to 2017: culture and capital.

For years, GE was considered by many as a model for how to run a tight, efficient company, with a straight-talking culture that bordered on blunt. From bottom to top, employees were expected to meet their targets, and if they didn't, either improve or find new jobs. A potential downside of such a culture is that people can become afraid to admit they're in trouble or to point out problems. During former CEO Jeffrey Immelt's tenure, from 2001 to mid-2017, some insiders and industry analysts said top executives engaged in "success theater," presenting the company's performance in a positive light when it was actually facing serious challenges.

One example of that came in early 2017, when Immelt told Wall Street analysts that GE Power, the company's huge business unit that sells power-generation equipment, had a "very positive" profit outlook. Two months later, GE announced that the power division's revenues, profits, and outlook were all down. A stock analyst from Deutsche Bank later criticized communication from the company by saying, "There is a credibility gap between what they say and the reality of what is to come."

The reality of what was to come was not pretty, and that had to do with the second major problem: capital—specifically, how the company was allocating its capital during those years. Analysts point to repeated examples of GE acquiring companies at high prices that then proved to be drags on its earnings. Looking at GE Power again, in 2014 the business unit spent $13.5 billion to purchase a large manufacturer of gas turbines, just as demand for fossil-fuel electricity generation was peaking. Bad timing would be bad enough, but in the words of John Flannery, who took over as CEO in late 2017, "We did a poor job running that business."

But wait, there's more. After Flannery stepped in and made sweeping changes in the executive ranks, including having Jamie Miller from GE Transportation take over as CFO, it took GE months to figure out just how bad things were at GE Power. Miller said she was surprised by the "deeper issues" in the power business, issues that significantly affected GE's cash flow. To help get costs in line with revenues, the power unit had to let 12,000 employees go at the end of the year.

Money problems also plague another major business unit, GE Capital. This subsidiary has been offering financing to GE customers since 1938, but over the years it got into a variety of other businesses, including long-term care insurance and subprime mortgages—both of which added to the mountain of woe as 2017 ticked over into 2018. Long-term care insurance, which helps cover the expense of assisted living or in-home care as people age, is proving to be a tough business for many companies as people live longer. In January 2018, GE took a $6 billion write-off for its liabilities in that business, an amount so large it triggered an investigation by the SEC. A month later, the company announced that the U.S. Justice Department was "likely to assert" violations from its lengthy investigation into practices at the subprime mortgage unit, which GE sold way back in 2007. Two months later, GE had to revise its previously reported 2016 and 2017 earnings downward to bring them in line with new GAAP rules for revenue recognition related to its long-term service contracts.

From 2001 through 2017, GE's debt expanded from $1.9 billion to $81.6 billion, its debt ratio jumped from 3.3 percent to 54 percent, its return on capital plunged from 29.6 percent to 6.2 percent, and its GAAP earnings per share dropped from $1.27 to –$0.99. At times, the company was simply spending more money that it was making. From 2015 through 2017, for instance, it spent $75 billion acquiring companies, buying back its own stock, and issuing its famously stable and generous stock dividend—but generated only $30 billion in free cash flow during those years.

Now what? Flannery and Miller are committed to streamlining the company, improving cash flow, and decreasing leverage. The streamlining will focus the company in three business segments: aviation, health care, and power. Miller cautioned investors that it would take a while to sort out GE Power, but for all the trouble power has been, the aviation and health-care units are in good shape. GE Transportation, Miller's former business unit, was sold in 2018. GE Lighting, its most prominent link back to GE's legendary cofounder, light bulb innovator Thomas Edison, had already been put up for sale before Flannery and Miller took over, but as of mid-2018, GE still hadn't found a buyer for it. GE Capital remains a major question mark, with billions in continuing liabilities and, according to an analysis by Bank of America, "zero equity value."

Flannery says everything is under consideration to get the company back on track, including changes in culture, capital allocation, cash management, and communication with investors. In addition to appointing Miller as CFO, he made a number of other changes in the executive team, and the company replaced several members of its board of directors.

Interestingly, one of the new directors is Leslie Seidman, former chair of the FASB (the organization that sets the GAAP rules). Whether that leads to any changes in GE's "notoriously aggressive accounting," in the words of one reporter who follows the company, is yet to be seen, but Seidman would certainly be the person to guide the company in that effort. Speaking of accounting practices, shareholder groups are pressuring the company to fire its outside auditor, KPMG, which GE has been using for more than a century.

In addition to the issues in the various business units, Flannery and Miller need to wrestle with a shortfall of nearly $30 billion in the company's pension program. (As one of the oldest and largest companies in the world, GE has a *lot* of retirees to take care of.) And shareholders have filed multiple lawsuits, with allegations ranging from hiding problems in its insurance business to mismanaging the 401(k) program.

Initial earnings results in 2018 were encouraging, if only slightly. "Baby steps out of the abyss," is how one analyst put it. But after a tumultuous 2017, just seeing some stability was welcome news. One thing is certain: If Flannery, Miller, and the rest of the GE executive team can stabilize the company and get it back into healthy growth mode, they will have pulled off one of the more dramatic corporate turnarounds in U.S. history.[40]

Critical Thinking Questions

15-1. If GE wants to focus attention on its restructuring plan and the solid performance of the business units it intends to keep as it moves forward, isn't it reasonable for it to highlight the performance of those units with a special version of the EPS calculation? Why or why not?

15-2. The U.S. government has at times offered temporary financial support to struggling companies that were deemed significant to the national economy. Looking at GE's portfolio of businesses, should the government consider helping GE? Why or why not?

15-3. If so many companies find non-GAAP calculations useful when communicating with their stakeholders, should the FASB adopt some of them? Why or why not?

Learn More Online

Retrieve GE's latest quarterly and annual reports and scan the financial news for recent items about the company's turn-around plan. How is the company faring now? Has it sold off any additional assets? Have the SEC and Department of Justice investigations and various shareholder lawsuits been resolved? Has the stock price recovered? What is your assessment of the company's future?

End of Chapter

KEY TERMS

accounting (449)
accounting equation (454)
accounts receivable turnover ratio (466)
accrual basis (455)
assets (454)
audit (451)
balance sheet (456)
blockchain (468)
bookkeeping (449)
calendar year (457)
cash basis (455)
certified public accountants (CPAs) (450)
closing the books (456)
controller (450)
cost of goods sold (461)
current assets (459)
current liabilities (459)
current ratio (464)
debt-to-assets ratio (466)
debt-to-equity ratio (466)
depreciation (455)
distributed ledger (468)
double-entry bookkeeping (455)
earnings per share (464)
EBITDA (462)
expenses (460)
external auditors (452)

financial accounting (449)
fiscal year (458)
fixed assets (459)
generally accepted accounting principles (GAAP) (452)
gross profit (461)
income statement (460)
international financial reporting standards (IFRS) (453)
inventory turnover ratio (466)
liabilities (454)
long-term liabilities (459)
management accounting (449)
matching principle (455)
net income (460)
operating expenses (461)
owners' equity (454)
private accountants (450)
public accountants (451)
quick ratio (464)
retained earnings (460)
return on equity (464)
return on sales (464)
Sarbanes-Oxley (453)
statement of cash flows (462)
working capital (464)

TEST YOUR KNOWLEDGE

Questions for Review

15-4. How do the responsibilities of private accountants and public accountants differ?
15-5. What is the Sarbanes-Oxley Act?
15-6. Why do companies sometimes report non-GAAP results?
15-7. What is an audit, and why are audits performed?
15-8. What is the accounting equation?
15-9. What is the matching principle?
15-10. What are the three major financial statements generated by a business?

15-11. What are the two methods used by companies to analyze financial statements?
15-12. What is the value of a statement of cash flows?
15-13. Why are many companies interested in blockchain and other distributed ledger technologies?

Questions for Analysis

15-14. Why were efforts made to converge the GAAP and IFRS standards?

15-15. Could a privately held company benefit from using GAAP accounting, even though it isn't legally required to do so? Why or why not?

15-16. Why are assets listed in order of liquidity?

15-17. Why is EBITDA controversial?

15-18. Why would a bank lending officer be interested in the cash flow statement of a company that is applying for a loan?

15-19. Ethical Considerations. You are preparing a presentation for your company's investors. When discussing your forecasts of next year's revenues and costs, should you use your most optimistic projections, your most pessimistic projections, or your most likely projections. Why?

Questions for Application

15-20. The senior partner of an accounting firm is looking for ways to increase the firm's business. What other services besides traditional accounting can the firm offer to its clients? What new challenges might this additional work create?

15-21. Select a public company of your choice and download its latest annual report. Calculate the profitability ratios and analyze its financial performance. Identify some of the problem areas. If you were advising an investor on whether to buy a significant number of shares in this company, what would you look for in the trend analysis to give you an accurate view of the performance of the company? Should the investor invest in the company? Why or why not?

15-22. If you were asked to lend money to your cousin's clothing store to help her through a slow sales period, would you be more interested in looking at the current ratio or the quick ratio as a measure of liquidity? Why?

15-23. Concept Integration. Your appliance manufacturing company recently implemented a just-in-time inventory system (see Chapter 9) for all parts used in the manufacturing process. How might you expect this move to affect the company's inventory turnover rate, current ratio, and quick ratio?

EXPAND YOUR KNOWLEDGE

Discovering Career Opportunities

The field of accounting is challenging yet highly rewarding. People interested in this field can choose from a wide variety of careers. Visit the page on Accountants and Auditors at **www.bls.gov/ooh** to read more about career opportunities in this field.

15-24. Based on the website, what are the differences between the job responsibilities of a public accountant and an internal auditor?

15-25. What are the common challenges faced by accountants and auditors while performing their duties? Which skills should they acquire to help them overcome these challenges?

15-26. Assume that you have just graduated and have been offered a job in a large and reputable accounting firm. What is the average salary you think you should be offered? Besides pay, what are your other considerations before accepting the job offer?

Intelligent Business Technology: GRC Software

The Sarbanes-Oxley Act's requirement that publicly traded companies regularly verify their internal accounting controls spurred the development of software tools to help companies flag and fix problems in their financial systems. Some software vendors have gone beyond Sarbox compliance to integrate the monitoring of a wide range of legal and financial issues that require management attention. This category of software is generally known as *governance, risk, and compliance (GRC) software*. GRC capabilities can either be built into other software packages (such as accounting and finance software, process management software, or business intelligence software) or be offered as standalone compliance programs. Vendors that offer GRC capabilities include Oracle (**www.oracle.com**), SAP (**www.sap.com**), and IBM (**www.ibm.com**).[41]

Explore one GRC software solution. In a brief email message to your instructor, describe the benefits of using this particular software package.

PRACTICE YOUR SKILLS

Resolving Ethical Dilemmas

You own a magazine-printing company, and for several years, your print machinery has been your most valuable asset. You considered it to be so valuable that you did not depreciate the machinery over the past ten years; hence, your valuation of the business is somewhat inflated. Now that you have decided to sell the business, independent assessors have valued the machinery at around 30 percent less than your estimate, which means that the business is worth considerably less than what you had anticipated. It also means that you will get more money if you dispose of the machinery and sell the empty building for redevelopment than if you sell the business as a going concern. However, there are 22 employees, and the potential owner has offered to retain them if you sell the business to her. If you do not sell the business as a going concern to another owner, your employees will be terminated. Do you have an ethical responsibility to inform your employees of the situation and that their future is at stake? How should you resolve this dilemma?

Growing as a Professional

Making your own personal balance sheet and cash flow statement is a good way to get comfortable with these essential business tools. You can create these reports in Excel or another spreadsheet, you can use a personal finance app, or you can create them on paper. If you are making your own, you can study a variety of formats by search online for "personal balance sheet" and "personal cash flow statement." Maintaining your own financial statements will help you think like a business manager—and get a handle on your personal finances. Also, be sure to check out Appendix D, Personal Finance: Getting Set for Life.

Sharpening Your Communication Skills

Obtain the annual report of a business and examine what the report shows about finances and current operations.

15-27. Consider the statements made by the CEO regarding the past year. Did the company do well, or are changes in operations necessary to its future well-being? What are the projections for growth in sales and profits?

15-28. Examine the financial summaries for information about the fiscal condition of the company. Did the company show a profit?

15-29. Compare the company's annual report from the previous year with the current year's report to see whether past projections were accurate.

15-30. Prepare a brief written summary of your conclusions.

Building Your Team Skills

Divide into small groups and compute the following financial ratios for Jackson and Iles, using the company's balance sheet and income statement. Compare your answers to those of your classmates:

- Profitability ratios: return on sales, return on equity, and earnings per share
- Liquidity ratios: current ratio and quick ratio
- Leverage ratios: debt to equity and debt to total assets

JACKSON AND ILES INCOME STATEMENT YEAR ENDED DECEMBER 31, 2020	
Sales	$5,000
Less: cost of goods sold	$1,200
Gross profit	$3,800
Less: total operating expenses	$1,600
Net operating income before income taxes	$2,200
Less: income taxes	$500
Net Income After Income Taxes	$1,700

JACKSON AND ILES BALANCE SHEET DECEMBER 31, 2020		
ASSETS		
Cash	$4,000	
Accounts Receivable	$900	
Inventory	$1,100	
Current Assets (Cash + AR + Inventory)	$6,000	
Fixed Assets	$2,200	
Total Assets		$8,200
LIABILITIES AND SHAREHOLDERS' EQUITY		
Current liabilities	$6,000	
Long-Term Debts	$1,200	
Shareholders' Equity (100 common shares outstanding valued at $10)	$1,000	
Total Liabilities and Shareholders' Equity		$8,200

Developing Your Research Skills

Select an article from a business journal or newspaper that discusses the quarterly or year-end performance of a company that industry analysts consider notable for either positive or negative reasons.

15-31. Did the company report a profit or a loss for this accounting period? What other performance indicators were reported? Is the company's performance improving or declining?

15-32. Did the company's performance match industry analysts' expectations, or was it a surprise? How did analysts or other experts respond to the firm's actual quarterly or year-end results?

15-33. What reasons were given for the company's improvement or decline in performance?

Writing Assignments

15-34. Should public companies be allowed to publish any non-GAAP performance metrics? Why or why not?

15-35. How could you apply the concept of a balance sheet to your personal financial planning?

ENDNOTES

1. Geoff Colvin, "What the Hell Happened at GE?" *Fortune*, 1 June 2018, fortune.com; Matt Egan, "GE Is Shrinking Its Empire but Not Fixing Its Debt Crisis," *CNN Money*, 24 May 2018, money.cnn.com; General Electric, accessed 22 May 2018, www.ge.com; Rick Clough, "Everyone's Fed Up with GE's Confusing Accounting," *Bloomberg*, 16 October 2017, www.bloomberg.com; Alywin Scott, "GE Still Mulls Breakup, Confirms Distributed Power Unit for Sale," *Reuters*, 20 April 2018, www.reuters.com; David French, "Exclusive: GE Seeking to Shed Troubled Insurance Business—Sources," *Reuters*, 22 May 2018, www.reuters.com; Thomas Gryta and Joann S. Lublin, "GE Overhauls Board, Dumps Longest-Serving Directors, Names Outsiders," *Wall Street Journal*, 26 February 2018, www.wsj.com; Thomas Gryta and Ted Mann, "The Long Shadow of GE Capital Looms over GE," *Wall Street Journal*, 26 March 2018, www.wsj.com; Brooke Sutherland, "No One Said GE's Turnaround Would Be Easy," *Bloomberg*, 23 May 2018, www.bloomberg.com; Matt Egan, "GE Can't Get Rid of Its Light Bulb Business," *CNN Money*, 22 May 2018, money.cnn.com; Matt Egan, "GE Pressured to Fire Auditor After 109 Years," *CNN Money*, 24 April 2018, money.cnn.com; Jim Collins, "3 Long-Term Positive Signs for General Electric: Bonus White Paper," *Real Money*, 20 April 2018, realmoney.thestreet.com; Matt Egan, "Has GE Finally Turned the Corner?" *CNN Money*, 20 April 2018, money.cnn.com; Michael Sheetz, "GE Capital Has 'Zero Equity Value,' Bank of America Says After Deep Dive Analysis," *CNBC*, 12 April 2018, www.cnbc.com; Alwyn Scott, "GE Eyes $4 Billion in Asset Sales, Has No Plans to Sell Stock: CFO," *Reuters*, 21 February 2018, www.reuters.com; Rick Clough and Neil Weinberg, "How a Bad Bet on Power Put a Spotlight on GE's Murky Accounting," *Bloomberg*, 29 January 2018, www.bloomberg.com; Steve Lohr, "G.E. Reports $9.8 Billion Loss and Discloses S.E.C. Accounting Inquiry," *New York Times*, 24 January 2018, www.nytimes.com; Giovanni Bruno, "General Electric CFO Hints 2018 May Be a Throwaway Year," *The Street*, 14 November 2017, www.thestreet.com; Christine Wang, "General Electric Announces Slew of Executive Changes, Including New CFO," *CNBC*, 6 October 2017, www.cnbc.com; Matt Egan, "GE's Legal Troubles Are Mounting," *CNN Money*, 26 February 2018, money.cnn.com.
2. Robert Kemp and Jeffrey Waybright, *Financial Accounting*, 4th ed. (New York: Pearson, 2017), 3.
3. Tracie Miller-Nobles, Brenda Mattison, and Ella Mae Matsumura, *Horngren's Financial & Managerial Accounting*, 6th ed. (New York: Pearson, 2018), 860.
4. "Accountants and Auditors," *Occupational Outlook Handbook*, U.S. Bureau of Labor Statistics, 13 April 2018, www.bls.gov.
5. "Frequently Asked Questions," American Institute of Certified Public Accountants, accessed 23 May 2018, www.aicpa.org.
6. "CMA Certification," Institute of Management Accountants, accessed 23 May 2018, www.imanet.org.
7. "Number of Employees of the Big Four Accounting/Audit Firms Worldwide in 2017," Statista, accessed 23 May 2018, www.statista.com.
8. "Revenue Recognition," Financial Accounting Standards Board, accessed 23 May 2018, www.fasb.org.
9. "About the FASB," Financial Accounting Standards Board, accessed 23 May 2018, www.fasb.org.
10. Lyn M. Fraser and Aileen Ormiston, *Understanding Financial Statements*, 11th ed. (New York: Pearson, 2016), 10.
11. "Earnings Before Interest, Taxes, Depreciation and Amortization—EBITDA," Investopedia.com, accessed 18 November 2013, www.investopedia.com; Jonathan Weil, "Readjusting Black Box's Earnings Adjustments (Adjusted)," *Bloomberg*, 30 January 2013, www.bloomberg.com; Anthony Catanach, "Non-GAAP Metrics: Is It Time to Toss Out the SEC's Reg G?" Grumpy Old Accountants blog, 20 June 2013, grumpyoldaccountants.com.
12. Emily Chasan, "New Benchmarks Crop Up in Companies' Financial Reports," *Wall Street Journal*, 13 November 2012, online.wsj.com.
13. Vincent Ryan, "Former SEC Chair Cox Declares IFRS 'Bereft of Life'," *CFO*, 10 June 2014, www.cfo.com; Paul Pacter, "What Have IASB and FASB Convergence Efforts Achieved?" *Journal of Accountancy*, February 2013, www.journalofaccountancy.com; Tammy Whitehouse, "FASB Looks Inward at Improving GAAP," *Compliance Week*, 1 November 2013, www.complianceweek.com; Anthony Catanach, "The Great IFRS Swindle: Accountants Scamming Accountants," Grumpy Old Accountants blog, 10 November 2013, grumpyoldaccountants.com.
14. Miller-Nobles, Mattison, and Matsumura, *Horngren's Financial & Managerial Accounting*, 381–382; Brian Good, "11 Important Key Points from Each Title of the Sarbanes-Oxley Act," DGK Group, 28 June 2016, www.dgkgrouppc.com; "Summary of SEC Actions and SEC Related Provisions Pursuant to the Sarbanes-Oxley Act of 2002," SEC, accessed 9 May 2004, www.sec.gov.
15. Sarah Johnson, "PCAOB Chairman Mark Olson to Retire," *CFO*, 9 June 2009, www.cfo.com.
16. "The Costs and Benefits of Sarbanes-Oxley," *Forbes*, 10 March 2014, www.forbes.com; "Building Value in Your Sox Compliance Program: Highlights from Protiviti's 2013 Sarbanes-Oxley Compliance Survey," Protiviti, www.protiviti.com; Michael W. Peregrine, "The Law That Changed Corporate America," *New York Times*, 25 July 2012, www.nytimes.com; Kayla Gillan, "It Enhanced Investor Protection," *New York Times*, 25 July 2012, www.nytimes.com.
17. Miller-Nobles, Mattison, and Matsumura, *Horngren's Financial & Managerial Accounting*, 11.
18. Kemp and Waybright, *Financial Accounting*, 105.
19. Miller-Nobles, Mattison, and Matsumura, *Horngren's Financial & Managerial Accounting*, 189, 514; Thayne Forbes, "Valuing Customers," *Journal of Database Marketing & Customer Strategy Management*, October 2007, 4–10.
20. J.B. Maverick, "How Do Intangible Assets Appear on a Balance Sheet?" *Investopedia*, accessed 23 May 2018, www.investopedia.com.
21. Baruch Lev, "Sharpening the Intangibles Edge," *Harvard Business Review*, June 2004, 109–116.
22. Justina Lee, "Bubble-Like Stock Valuations Miss $3.4 Trillion in Hidden Assets," *Bloomberg*, 6 June 2018, www.bloomberg.com.
23. "How to Spot Trouble in Your Financials," *Inc.*, October 2004, 96.
24. Chris Higson, "The Cult of EBITDA," *London Business School Review*, 1 April 2013, www.london.edu; Timothy Green, "How Twitter Tried to Convince Us That It's Doing Really Well," *Money*, 1 May 2015, time.com/money; Ben McClure, "A Clear Look at EBITDA," Investopedia.com, 17 April 2010, www.investopedia.com; "Bobbie Gossage," Cranking Up the Earnings," *Inc.*, October 2004, 54; Lisa Smith, "EBITDA: Challenging the Calculation," Investopedia.com, 20 November 2009, www.investopedia.com.
25. Miller-Nobles, Mattison, and Matsumura, *Horngren's Financial & Managerial Accounting*, 456.
26. "Company Profile: Wal-Mart Stores Inc," MarketLine, 23 November 2017.
27. Fraser and Ormiston, *Understanding Financial Statements*, 218.
28. Fraser and Ormiston, *Understanding Financial Statements*, 218
29. *The Digital Asset Platform*, Digital Asset, 2016, 3; "Blockchain 101," IBM, accessed 24 May 2018, www.ibm.com.
30. "Transform Supply Chain Transparency with IBM Blockchain," IBM, accessed 25 May 2018, www.ibm.com.
31. *Blockchain: IBM Limited Edition* (Hoboken, N.J.: Wiley, 2017), 6–7.

32. *Blockchain: IBM Limited Edition*, 14.

33. Digital Asset,*The Digital Asset Platform*, 5.

34. Maria Wachal, "Blockchain Business Applications Beyond Bitcoin," Software Mill, 28 March 2018, blog.softwaremill .com; Paul Brody, "The Power of a Blockchain-Enabled Supply Chain," *Digitalist*, 30 August 2017, www.digitalistmag.com; *Blockchain: IBM Limited Edition*, 9–10; *Distributed Ledger Technology (DLT) and Blockchain*, World Bank Group, 2017.

35. Hugh Harsono, "Bank-Based Blockchain Projects Are Going to Transform the Financial Industry," *TechCrunch*, 28 January 2018, techcrunch.com; Robert Hackett, "How JPMorgan Chase Learned to Love the Blockchain," *Fortune*, 1 June 2018, fortune .com; Grainne McNamara, "Blockchain Is Poised to Disrupt Trade Finance," PwC, 3 August 2017, usblogs.pwc.com.

36. Jan-Henrik Foerster, "UBS Virtual Currency Group Adds Six More Financial Institutions," Bloomberg, 31August 2017, www.bloomberg.com; "Utility Settlement Coin Concept on Blockchain Gathers Pace," Deutsche Bank, 24 August 2016, www.db.com.

37. Bernard Marr, "How Blockchain Will Transform the Supply Chain and Logistics Industry," *Forbes*, 23 March 2018, www.forbes.com; "Transform Supply Chain Transparency with IBM Blockchain."

38. "Transform Supply Chain Transparency with IBM Blockchain"; "IBM Food Trust," IBM, accessed 25 May 2018, www.ibm.com.

39. Sarah Fister Gale, "Blockchain: The Future of HR?" *Workforce*, 21 May 2018, www.workforce.com.

40. See note 1.

41. Vendors' websites, accessed 24 May 2018.

16 Financial Management and Financial Markets

LEARNING OBJECTIVES   After studying this chapter, you will be able to

1 Identify three fundamental concepts that affect financial decisions, and describe the primary responsibilities of a financial manager.

2 Compare the advantages and disadvantages of debt and equity financing, and explain the two major considerations in choosing from financing alternatives.

3 Identify the major categories of debt financing.

4 Outline the advantages and disadvantages of equity financing.

5 Identify the four most important financial markets for most businesses.

6 Describe four major steps required to become an investor.

7 Explain how businesses can use *smart contracts* to facilitate transactions.

BEHIND THE SCENES   Court Buddy: Looking for a Financial Friend

Court Buddy

After proving the concept behind their automated attorney-client matching system, Court Buddy cofounders James and Kristina Jones faced the challenge of attracting enough investment capital to expand their new venture.

www.courtbuddy.com

You may not view shopping as a skill, but think about the various processes you go through to find and acquire the goods and services you use. Over time, you've learned how to be a smarter shopper when it comes to clothes, for instance. You have developed a better idea of what works for you, deeper insights into which stores and brands offer the value you're looking for, and self-knowledge of which pieces you'll really end up wearing versus buying on a whim and then leaving in the closet until you eventually pass them along to someone else.

Every consumer faces situations in life where past shopping experiences aren't of much help, however. You don't get much practice shopping for colleges, houses, or marriage counselors, for example. For most people, major purchase decisions like these come along only a few times in a person's life—sometimes only once. Unless you become a real estate investor, there's not much opportunity to practice your skills at house buying.

Hiring a lawyer falls into this category—a major decision that few people can prepare for. Even for routine legal matters, many people aren't sure which type of lawyer they need, how to work with an attorney, or how to find an attorney using any method other than a Google search. And when you need a lawyer in a hurry or you're on a tight budget, the process becomes even more stressful.

Florida attorney James Jones, Jr., saw firsthand how this decision was affecting the lives of people appearing in court. Many wound up representing themselves, often with disastrous results, because they believed they couldn't afford an attorney or had no idea how to hire one. He pitched an idea to his wife, Kristina, a freelance art director, about an online matchmaking service for attorneys and potential clients that would help make legal representation more inclusive. Kristina took this idea and added the ability for attorneys to appear for limited representation at flat rates. Her entrepreneurial instincts kicked in and together

they pushed the idea forward until it developed into a new company they called Court Buddy.

They believed in the idea and in themselves and self-funded the idea for two years. However, like most new companies, they needed money to scale at a faster rate. If you were Kristina Jones, how would you go about getting money to launch and expand? Would you try the route many new entrepreneurs try, of relying on friends, relatives, and credit cards to get started? Would you approach banks for a loan? Or would you pitch your business to professional investors?[1]

INTRODUCTION

From start-ups such as Court Buddy (profiled in the chapter-opening Behind the Scenes) to the world's largest corporations, every business enterprise needs cash. In this chapter, you'll learn more about the major financial decisions companies make, starting with the process of developing a financial plan, then creating and maintaining budgets, and finally comparing ways to finance both ongoing operations and growth opportunities.

The Role of Financial Management

Planning for a firm's money needs and managing the allocation and spending of funds are the foundations of **financial management**, or *finance*. In most smaller companies such as Court Buddy, the owner or owners are responsible for the firm's financial decisions, whereas in larger operations, financial management is the responsibility of the finance department. This department, which includes the accounting function, reports to a vice president of finance or a chief financial officer (CFO).

No matter what size the company, decisions regarding company finances must take into account three fundamental concepts (see Exhibit 16.1). First, if the firm spends too much money meeting short-term demands, it won't have enough to make strategic investments for the future, such as building new facilities, developing the next generation of products, or being able to jump on a strategic acquisition. Conversely, if the firm spends too little in the short term, it can lose key employees to better-paying competitors, compromise product quality or customer service, or create other problems with long-term consequences.

Second, most financial decisions involve balancing potential risks against potential rewards, known as a **risk/return trade-off**. Generally speaking, the higher the perceived risk, the higher the potential reward, and vice versa. However, this situation doesn't always hold true. For example, a company with free cash could (a) invest it in the stock market, which offers potentially high returns but at moderate to high risk; (b) put the money in a bank account, which has little to no risk but low returns; or (c) invest in a new facility or a new product, which could yield high returns, moderate returns, or no returns at all. Moreover, the *safest* choice isn't always the *best* choice. For instance, if you're hoarding cash in a safe place while competitors are investing in new products or new stores, you could be setting yourself up for a big decline in revenue.

Third, financial choices can have a tremendous impact on a company's flexibility and resilience. For example, companies that are highly leveraged (that is, carrying a lot of debt) are forced to devote more of their cash flow to debt service and therefore can't spend that money on advertising, staffing, or product development. Heavy debt loads and low cash flow make a company especially vulnerable to economic downturns, too. In contrast, companies with a lot of cash on hand can weather tough times and make strategic moves that their debt-constrained competitors can't make.

financial management
Planning for a firm's money needs and managing the allocation and spending of funds.

risk/return trade-off
The balance of potential risks against potential rewards.

REAL-TIME UPDATES
Learn More by Reading These Articles

Explore careers in finance

This introduction will help you sort out the various career paths in finance. Go to **real-timeupdates.com/bia9** and select Learn More in the Students section.

EXHIBIT 16.1	**Financial Management: Three Fundamental Concepts**

Whether the owner of a small company or the chief financial officer (CFO) of a major corporation, a financial manager must grapple with these three fundamental concepts.

1. Balancing short-term and long-term demands
- Must have ready cash to pay salaries, bills, and taxes
- Needs a financial cushion to ride out rough times
- May need money for acquisitions or other extraordinary expenses
- Must make strategic long-term investments

2. Balancing potential risks and potential rewards
- Every decision involves a risk/reward trade-off
- Higher risks may yield higher rewards
- The safest choices aren't always the best choices

3. Balancing leverage and flexibility
- Can use debt strategically and sometimes out of necessity
- Debt can be a tool, but it can also be a trap
- Highly leveraged companies have far less ability to maneuver and are more vulnerable to setbacks

DEVELOPING A FINANCIAL PLAN

financial plan
A document that outlines the funds needed for a certain period of time, along with the sources and intended uses of those funds.

Successful financial management starts with a **financial plan**, a document that outlines the funds a firm will need for a certain period of time, along with the sources and intended uses of those funds. The financial plan takes its input from three information sources:

- The strategic plan, which establishes the company's overall direction and identifies the need for major investments, expanded staffing, and other activities that will require funds
- The company's financial statements, including the income statement and the statement of cash flows, which tell the finance manager how much cash the company has now and how much it is likely to generate in the near future
- The external financial environment, including interest rates and the overall health of the economy

By considering information from these three sources, managers can identify how much money the company will need and to what extent it will have to rely on external resources to complement its internal resources over the span of time covered by the financial plan (see Exhibit 16.2).

MONITORING CASH FLOW

Overall income, as identified in the income statement, is important, but knowing precisely how much cash is flowing into and out of the company—and when—is critical, because cash is necessary to purchase the assets and supplies a company needs in order to operate, to meet payroll, and to pay dividends to shareholders (for those corporations that pay dividends). Cash flow is generally related to net income; that is, companies with relatively high profits generally have relatively high cash flow, but the relationship is not precise.

Companies that don't keep a close eye on cash flow can find themselves facing a *liquidity crisis*, which means having insufficient cash to meet their short-term needs. In the worst-case scenario, a firm in a liquidity crisis finds itself in a credit crisis, too, meaning it doesn't have the cash it needs and can't borrow any more.

REAL-TIME UPDATES
Learn More by Watching This Video

A simple approach to analyzing cash flow

Understanding cash flow is an essential business skill, and this approach makes it easy. Go to **real-timeupdates.com/bia9** and select Learn More in the Students section.

EXHIBIT 16.2	Finding and Allocating Funds

Financial management involves finding suitable sources of funds and deciding on the most appropriate uses for those funds.

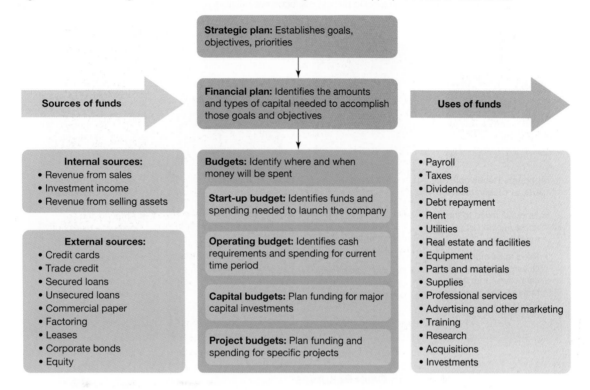

A vital step in maintaining positive cash flow is monitoring *working capital accounts*: accounts receivable, accounts payable, inventory, and cash (see Exhibit 16.3).

Managing Accounts Receivable and Accounts Payable

Keeping an eye on **accounts receivable**—the money owed to a firm by its customers—is one way to manage cash flow effectively. The volume of receivables depends on a financial manager's decisions regarding several issues: who qualifies for credit and who does not, how long customers are given to pay their bills, and how aggressive the firm is in collecting its debts. In addition to setting guidelines and policies for handling these issues, a financial manager analyzes the firm's outstanding receivables to identify patterns that might indicate problems and establishes procedures for collecting overdue accounts.

The flip side of managing receivables is managing **accounts payable**—the bills that the company owes to its suppliers, lenders, and other parties. Here, the objective is generally to postpone paying bills until the last moment, because doing so allows the firm to hold on to its cash for as long as possible. However, a financial manager also needs to weigh the advantages of paying promptly if doing so entitles the firm to cash discounts. In addition, paying on time is essential to maintaining a good credit rating, which lowers the cost of borrowing.

Managing Inventory

Inventory is another area in which financial managers can fine-tune the firm's cash flow. Inventory sitting on the shelf represents capital that is tied up without earning money. Furthermore, the firm incurs expenses for storage and handling, insurance, and taxes. In addition, there is always a risk that inventory will become obsolete before it can be converted into finished goods and sold. Thus, the company's goal is to maintain enough inventory to fill orders in a timely fashion at the lowest cost. To achieve this goal, financial managers work with operations managers and marketing managers to determine the *economic order quantity (EOQ)*: the quantity of materials that, when ordered regularly, results in the lowest ordering and storage costs.

accounts receivable
Amounts that are currently owed to a firm.

accounts payable
Amounts that a firm currently owes to other parties.

| EXHIBIT 16.3 | **Monitoring the Working Capital Accounts** |

The working capital accounts represent a firm's cash on hand as well as economic value that can be converted to cash (inventory) or is expected from customers (accounts receivable), minus what it is scheduled to be paid out (accounts payable).

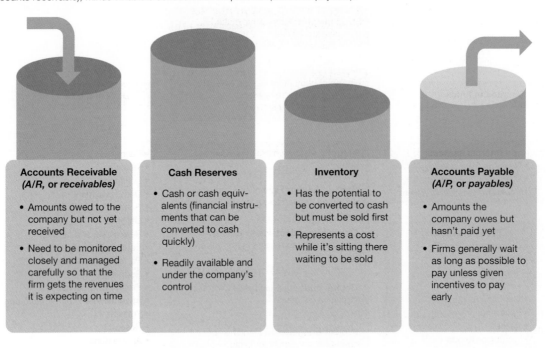

Accounts Receivable (A/R, or receivables)
- Amounts owed to the company but not yet received
- Need to be monitored closely and managed carefully so that the firm gets the revenues it is expecting on time

Cash Reserves
- Cash or cash equivalents (financial instruments that can be converted to cash quickly)
- Readily available and under the company's control

Inventory
- Has the potential to be converted to cash but must be sold first
- Represents a cost while it's sitting there waiting to be sold

Accounts Payable (A/P, or payables)
- Amounts the company owes but hasn't paid yet
- Firms generally wait as long as possible to pay unless given incentives to pay early

Managing Cash Reserves

Financial managers also serve as guardians of a company's cash reserves, whether that cash is from investors who have funded a start-up venture or from profitable product sales in an established company. The nature of this challenge varies widely, depending on the business, the firm's overall financial health, and management's predictions for the economy. For instance, start-ups usually have a finite pool of cash from their investors and need to manage that cash wisely so they don't run out of funds before the new business can start to generate cash on its own.

At the other extreme, an established company with many successful and profitable products can generate more cash than it needs for both ongoing operations and "rainy day" emergency funds. The management team can choose to invest this money, return some of it to shareholders in the form of dividends, or use it to buy back some of the company's stock from the open market. Companies buy back their own stock for several reasons: to reduce the amount of cash they will need to distribute as future dividends, as an investment opportunity if management believes the stock will go up, and to improve financial ratios such as earnings per share (with fewer shares outstanding, earnings per share [EPS] goes up, for example).[2]

THE BUDGETING PROCESS

budget
A planning and control tool that reflects expected revenues, operating expenses, and cash receipts and outlays.

In addition to developing a financial plan and monitoring cash flow, financial managers are responsible for developing a **budget**, a financial guide for a given period, usually the company's fiscal year, or for the duration of a particular project. Like a good personal or household budget, a company budget identifies where and when money will be spent throughout the year. Particularly in larger organizations, budgeting is often a combination of *top-down mandate*, in which top executives specify the amount of money each functional area can have based on the company's total available budget for the year, and *bottom-up requests*, in which individual supervisors and managers add up the amounts they need based on number of employees, project expenses, supplies, and other costs.

Finalizing a budget is usually a matter of negotiation and compromise in which financial managers try to reconcile the top-down and bottom-up numbers. After a budget has been developed, the finance manager compares actual results with projections to discover variances and recommends corrective action, a process known as *financial control*.

Budgeting Challenges

The budgeting process might sound fairly straightforward, but in practice, it can be an exhausting, time-consuming chore that everyone dreads and few managers find satisfactory. Budgeting is a challenge for several reasons (see Exhibit 16.4). First, a company always has a finite amount of money available to spend each year, and every group in the company is fighting for a share of it. Consequently, individual department managers can spend a considerable amount of time making a case for their budgetary needs, and top executives frequently need to make tough choices that won't please everybody.

Second, managers often can't predict with complete accuracy how much revenue will come in or how much the various items included in the budget will cost during the time frame covered by the budget. For instance, some expenses are routine and predictable, but others are variable, and some can be almost impossible to predict. Fixed salaries are easy to predict month to month, but energy costs fluctuate—sometimes wildly. In some cases, companies can try to protect themselves against future price increases by *hedging*, arranging contracts that allow them to buy supplies in the future at designated prices.

Volatile and uncertain situations can make conventional forecasting a dicey proposition because planners often can't make solid assumptions about major factors in their forecasting models. A useful approach in these circumstances is *scenario planning*, in which managers identify two or more possible ways that events could unfold—different scenarios, that is—and have a budgetary response ready for each one. Scenario planning is particularly valuable for long-range planning because the longer the time frame, the harder it is to pin down revenues and costs with any degree of accuracy.

Third, even if they can predict how much revenue will come in or how much various things will cost, managers can't always be sure how much they *should* spend in each part of the budget. A common practice is to take the amounts spent the previous year and raise or lower them by some amount to arrive at this year's budget. This method is simple, but it can produce seriously flawed numbers by ignoring real-world inputs. It also encourages a mentality of "use it or lose it." At the end of the year, managers may hurriedly spend any remaining money in their budgets, even if doing so doesn't make financial sense, because they know that if they don't spend it all, their budgets will be reduced for the next year.

EXHIBIT 16.4	**Budgeting Challenges**

Budgeting can be a tough challenge that requires difficult choices; here are three big issues managers usually face.

1. Every company has a limited amount of money to spend.
- Projects and departments are often in competition for resources.
- Managers need to make tough choices, occasionally taking money from one group and giving it to another.

2. Revenues and costs are often difficult to predict.
- Sales forecasts are never certain, particularly for new products or for sales into new markets.
- Fixed costs are easy to predict, but variable costs can be hard to predict, particularly more than a few months out.

3. It's not always clear how much should be spent.
- With some expenses, such as advertising, managers aren't always sure how much is enough.
- Uncertainty leads to budgeting based on past expenditures, which might be out of line with current strategic needs.

zero-based budgeting
A budgeting approach in which each department starts from zero every year and must justify every item in the budget, rather than simply adjusting the previous year's budget amounts.

A more responsive approach is **zero-based budgeting**, in which each department starts from zero every year and must justify every item in the budget.[3] This approach forces each department to show how the money it wants to spend will support the overall strategic plan. Companies are most likely to succeed with zero-based budgeting if they take a comprehensive, long-term view of cost containment that becomes embedded in the corporate culture and intelligently invest the savings in more-productive areas.[4] Because it forces managers at every level to scrutinize their operations, zero-based budgeting can also identify unproductive organizational habits and other bottlenecks and thereby improve efficiency and effectiveness.[5] One of the biggest complaints about this approach historically has been the amount of time it can take, but modern financial systems with powerful data analytics capabilities can give managers more-detailed insights in less time than ever before.[6]

Types of Budgets

A company can have several types and combinations of budgets:[7]

- The *operating budget* is a detailed financial plan that identifies all the revenues and expenses the company expects to see over a certain time frame. A company may have multiple department or functional budgets that roll up into a combined operating budget.
- A *capital budget* outlines planned purchases of real estate, new facilities, major equipment, and other long-term assets.
- A *cash budget* identifies cash flows using accounts payable and accounts receivable, thereby helping managers monitor cash flow over the course of a month or other time period.
- A *financial budget* includes the cash budget and the *budgeted* income statement and balance sheet (meaning these are forward-looking versions of these statements, not summaries of past amounts).
- The *master budget* incorporates the various other budgets to present a complete and comprehensive view of the company's financial status and plans.

 CHECKPOINT

LEARNING OBJECTIVE 1: Identify three fundamental concepts that affect financial decisions, and describe the primary responsibilities of a financial manager.

SUMMARY: Decisions regarding company finances must consider three fundamental concepts. First, every company has to balance short-term and long-term financial demands. Failure to do so can lead to serious cash flow problems and even bankruptcy. Second, most financial decisions involve a risk/return trade-off in which, generally speaking, the higher the perceived risk, the higher the potential reward, and vice versa. Third, financial choices can have a tremendous impact on a company's flexibility and resilience. Overburdening a company with debt limits its strategic options and makes it vulnerable to economic slowdowns. Financial managers are responsible for developing and implementing a firm's financial plan, monitoring cash flow, managing cash reserves, and overseeing budgets.

CRITICAL THINKING: (1) What role does a company's strategic plan play in the process of financial management? (2) How does zero-based budgeting help a company spend its cash in the most effective ways possible?

IT'S YOUR BUSINESS: (1) What is your financial plan for getting through college? (2) How well do you budget your personal finances? If you don't budget, how do you monitor cash flow to make sure you don't run out of money each month?

KEY TERMS TO KNOW: financial management, risk/return trade-off, financial plan, accounts receivable, accounts payable, budget, zero-based budgeting

Financing Alternatives: Factors to Consider

2 **LEARNING OBJECTIVE**

Compare the advantages and disadvantages of debt and equity financing, and explain the two major considerations in choosing from financing alternatives.

Every firm's need for cash and its ability to get money from various external sources is unique, and it's up to entrepreneurs and financial executives to find the right source or combination of sources. This section explores the factors that finance managers consider when they are looking for outside funds, and the next two sections cover the two major categories of financing: debt and equity.

DEBT FINANCING VERSUS EQUITY FINANCING

The most fundamental decision a company faces regarding financing is whether it will obtain funds by **debt financing**, which is borrowing money, or by **equity financing**, which is selling ownership shares in the company. (And as you'll recall from Chapter 6, crowdfunding can have elements of both approaches, depending on how it is structured.) To meet their changing needs over time, many firms use a combination of debt and equity financing, and many use several kinds of debt financing at the same time for different purposes. A firm's **capital structure** is the overall mix of debt and equity it uses to meet short- and long-term needs. Exhibit 16.5 summarizes the factors that financial managers consider when choosing between debt and equity financing.

Note that business debt usually doesn't have the same negative connotations as consumer debt. Whereas consumers are advised to avoid or minimize most kinds of debt, and being in debt can be a sign of financial trouble or financial mismanagement, robust and well-run businesses of all shapes and sizes use debt as a routine element of financial management. The key difference is that businesses can make money by borrowing money. (Consumers can do so in some cases, such as when investing in real estate or education, but it is a much slower and less certain way to make money.) Of course, companies can get into debt trouble through bad choices and bad luck, just as consumers can, and it's up to financial managers to make smart borrowing choices.

debt financing
Arranging funding by borrowing money.

equity financing
Arranging funding by selling ownership shares in the company, publicly or privately.

capital structure
A firm's mix of debt and equity financing.

REAL-TIME UPDATES
Learn More by Visiting This Website

Looking for money?

This site offers helpful advice for business owners who need short- or long-term funding. Go to **real-timeupdates.com/bia9** and select Learn More in the Students section.

| **EXHIBIT 16.5** | **Debt Versus Equity Financing** |

When choosing between debt and equity financing, companies evaluate the characteristics of both types of funding.

Characteristic	Debt Financing	Equity Financing
Maturity	**Specific:** In most cases, a contract specifies a date by which debt must be repaid.	**N/A:** Equity funding does not need to be repaid.
Claim on income	**Nondiscretionary, usually a recurring cost, and usually fixed:** Debt obligations must be repaid, regardless of whether the company is profitable; payments can be regular (such as monthly), balloon (repaid all at once), or a combination.	**Discretionary cost:** At management's discretion and if company is profitable, shareholders may receive dividends after creditors have been paid; however, company is not required to pay dividends.
Claim on assets	**Priority:** Lenders have priority claims on assets.	**Residual:** Shareholders have claims only after the firm satisfies claims of lenders.
Influence over management	**Usually little:** Lenders usually have no influence over management unless debt vehicles come with conditions or management fails to make payments on time.	**Varies:** As owners of the company, shareholders can vote on some aspects of corporate operations, although in practice only large shareholders have much influence. Private equity holders (such as venture capitalists) can have considerable influence.
Tax consequences	**Deductible:** Debt payments reduce taxable income, lowering tax obligations.	**Not deductible:** Dividend payments are not tax deductible.
Employee benefit potential	**N/A:** Does not create any opportunities for compensation alternatives such as stock options.	**Stock options:** Issuing company shares creates the opportunity to use stock options as a motivation or retention tool.

Of course, not every firm has access to every financing option, and sometimes companies have to take whatever they can get. For instance, only companies that are already public or are prepared to go public (see "Public Stock Offerings" on page 493) can raise funds by selling shares on the open market. Similarly, as you'll read in the section on debt financing, some debt options are not available to small companies.

LENGTH OF TERM

short-term financing
Financing used to cover current expenses (generally repaid within a year).

long-term financing
Financing used to cover long-term expenses such as assets (generally repaid over a period of more than one year).

Financing can be either short term or long term. **Short-term financing** is financing that will be repaid within one year, whereas **long-term financing** is financing that will be repaid in a period longer than one year. The primary purpose of short-term financing is to ensure that a company maintains its liquidity so that it can meet its current liabilities. In contrast, long-term financing is used to acquire long-term assets such as buildings and equipment or to fund expansion, new products, acquisitions, or other strategic moves.

COST OF CAPITAL

cost of capital
The average rate of interest a firm pays on its combination of debt and equity.

In general, a company wants to obtain money at the lowest cost and with the least amount of risk. However, lenders and investors want to receive the highest possible return on their investment, also at the lowest risk. A company's **cost of capital** is the total cost of using its various debt and equity sources. Financial managers compute the cost of each source, then combine those in a weighted total for all the sources.[8]

For any form of financing to make economic sense, the expected returns must exceed the cost of capital. Consequently, financial managers study capital costs carefully in relation to the intended uses of those funds. At the same time, the potential suppliers of external funds, from banks to stock market investors to suppliers who sell on credit, also analyze a company's plans and prospects to determine whether helping the company represents a safe and sensible use of their capital.

Cost of capital depends on three main factors: the perceived risk associated with the company, the prevailing level of interest rates, and opportunity cost.

Risk

Lenders that provide money to businesses expect their returns to be in proportion to the risk they face. Recall from Chapter 2 that lenders offer their *prime rates* to companies with the best credit ratings, because these companies are the least likely to default on their loans. To compensate for the added risk of lending to customers with lower credit ratings, banks often charge higher interest rates. (The same holds true with consumer credit, which is why protecting your credit score is so important.)

Perceived risk can trigger a vicious circle if a company is struggling. As its finances deteriorate, some sources of potential funding can disappear, and those that are left can get more expensive. If the firm opts for an expensive loan, it will pay more in interest, which will drain its finances even further.

Interest Rates

Regardless of how financially solid a company is, its cost of money will vary over time because interest rates fluctuate. Companies must take such interest rate fluctuations and projections into account when making financing decisions. For instance, a project might be economically viable if a company can get funds for it at 3 percent but not at 6 percent. Also, various financing options are available for financial managers who want to hedge against interest rate uncertainty, just as they can hedge against possible changes in material costs. For example, a company might break a loan into several components with staggered lengths and different interest rates, rather than borrowing the entire sum at a single interest rate.[9]

Opportunity Cost

Using a company's own cash to finance its growth has one chief attraction: No interest payments are required. Nevertheless, such internal financing is not free; using money for any particular purpose has an opportunity cost, defined in Chapter 2 as the value of the most appealing alternative from among those that weren't chosen. For instance, a company

EXHIBIT 16.6	**Financial Leverage**

Leverage can be your best friend if investments work out well—or it can be your worst enemy if they don't. Assume that you have $10,000 of your own funds to invest in the stock market or some business venture. You also have the opportunity to borrow an additional $50,000 at 6 percent interest. Should you invest just your own $10,000 or leverage your investment by borrowing the $50,000 so you can invest $60,000 instead? If the investment returns 12 percent after a year, you'll earn a healthy $1,200 if you invest just your own money. But with this leverage, you would earn three and a half times that amount, even after you pay the cost of borrowing the $50,000. However, look at what happens if the investment turns sour: If it loses 12 percent that first year instead, the leveraging will wipe out your entire $10,000.

No leverage; 12% return		5x leverage; 12% return	
Funds	$10,000	Funds	$10,000
Debt	$0	Debt	$50,000
Total to invest	$10,000	Total to invest	$60,000
Annual return (12%)	$1,200	Annual return (12%)	$7,200
Cost of debt	$0	Cost of debt (6%)	($3,000)
Profit (loss)	$1,200	Profit (loss)	$4,200
No leverage; –12% return		5x leverage; –12% return	
Funds	$10,000	Funds	$10,000
Debt	$0	Debt	$50,000
Total to invest	$10,000	Total to invest	$60,000
Annual return (–12%)	($1,200)	Annual return (–12%)	($7,200)
Cost of debt	$0	Cost of debt (6%)	($3,000)
Profit (loss)	($1,200)	Profit (loss)	($10,200)

might be better off investing its excess cash in external opportunities, such as stocks of other companies, and borrowing money to finance its own growth. Doing so makes sense as long as the company can earn a greater return on those investments than the rate of interest paid on borrowed money. This concept is called **leverage** because the loan acts like a lever: It magnifies the power of the borrower to generate profits (see Exhibit 16.6).

However, leverage works both ways: Borrowing may magnify your losses as well as your gains. Because most companies require some degree of external financing from time to time, the issue is not so much whether to use outside money; rather, it's a question of how much should be raised, by what means, and when.

leverage
The technique of increasing the rate of return on an investment by financing it with borrowed funds.

 CHECKPOINT

LEARNING OBJECTIVE 2: Compare the advantages and disadvantages of debt and equity financing, and explain the two major considerations in choosing from financing alternatives.

SUMMARY: Debt financing offers a variety of funding alternatives and is available to a wider range of companies than equity financing. It also doesn't subject management to outside influence in the way equity financing does, and debt payments reduce a company's tax obligations. On the downside, except for trade credit, debt financing always puts a demand on cash flow, so finance managers need to consider whether a company can handle debt payments. The major advantages of equity financing are the fact that the money doesn't have to be paid back and the resulting discretionary drain on cash flow (publicly held companies don't have to pay regular dividends if they choose not to). The major disadvantages are the dilution of management control and the fact that equity financing—public equity financing, in particular—is not available to many firms. The two major considerations in choosing financing alternatives are length of term (the duration of the financing) and cost of capital (the cost to a company of all its debt and equity financing).

CRITICAL THINKING: (1) What factors might lead a company to gain additional funds through debt financing rather than through equity financing? (2) Why does consumer debt have a more negative connotation than business debt?

IT'S YOUR BUSINESS: (1) Do you know your credit score, or have you ever looked at your credit report? To learn more about free credit reports, visit www.ftc.gov/freereports. (2) How should the cost of capital figure into your decisions about attending college, buying cars, and buying housing?

KEY TERMS TO KNOW: debt financing, equity financing, capital structure, short-term financing, long-term financing, cost of capital, leverage

[3] **LEARNING OBJECTIVE**

Identify the major categories of debt financing.

Financing Alternatives: Debt Financing

This section explores the options that entrepreneurs and financial managers have for borrowing money, starting with short-term debt financing.

SHORT-TERM DEBT FINANCING

Depending on the size of the company, financial managers have quite a range of choices when it comes to short-term debt financing, including *credit cards, trade credit, secured loans, unsecured loans, commercial paper,* and *factoring* (see Exhibit 16.7).

EXHIBIT 16.7	Sources of Short-Term Debt Financing

Businesses have a variety of short-term debt financing options, each of which has advantages and disadvantages.

Source	Funding Mechanism	Length of Term	Advantages	Disadvantages and Limitations
Credit cards	Essentially creates a short-term loan every time cardholder makes purchases or gets a cash advance	Revolving (no fixed repayment date)	Widely available; convenient; no external scrutiny of individual purchases	High interest rates; ease of use and lack of external scrutiny can lead to overuse
Trade credit	Allows buyer to make purchases without immediately paying for them	Typically 30 to 90 days	Usually free (no interest) as long as payment is made by due date; enables purchaser to manage cash flow more easily; consolidates multiple purchases into a single payment	Buyer often needs to establish a payment history with seller before credit will be extended; availability and terms vary from seller to seller
Secured loans	Lender provides cash using borrower's assets (such as inventory or equipment) as collateral	Up to 1 year (for short-term loans)	Can provide financing for companies that don't qualify for unsecured loans or other alternatives	More expensive than some other options
Unsecured loans	Lender provides lump sum of cash via a promissory note or on-demand access to cash via a credit line	Up to 1 year (for short-term loans)	Provides cash or access to cash without requiring borrower to pledge assets as collateral	Cost varies according to borrower's credit rating; often not available to customers with unproven or poor credit history
Commercial paper	Participating in the global *money market*, large institutional investors provide unsecured, short-term loans to corporations	Up to 270 days (longer in special cases)	Less expensive and less trouble to get than conventional loans; can generate very large amounts of cash fairly quickly, from $100,000 to many millions	Available only to large corporations with strong credit ratings
Factoring	Third party takes over the process of getting payment from customers, and in the meantime, advances a portion of the accounts payable amounts to the seller	N/A	Frees up working capital; makes cash flow more predictable; can provide some protection from bad debts and customer bankruptcies; often can be arranged more quickly than a loan	Can be expensive, depending on the factoring company's terms

Credit Cards

Credit cards are one of the most expensive forms of financing, but they are sometimes the only form available to business owners, particularly in the early stages of a company's growth. If they are used judiciously and only as a short-term measure, credit cards can be a viable way to provide some of the financing a company needs. However, just as with personal use of cards, funding a company this way can quickly spiral out of control and leave an entrepreneur buried under an avalanche of expensive debt.

Trade Credit

Trade credit is a form of financing in which suppliers provide goods and services to customers without requiring immediate payment. For the seller, these transactions create accounts receivable; for the buyer, they create accounts payable. Trade credit is typically given at no interest for a short period, which can range from 30 to 60 days or longer. Sellers sometimes offer a discount for customers who pay early and charge interest if they pay late, so managing accounts payable carefully is an opportunity for finance managers to minimize their companies' financing costs.[10]

Secured Loans

Secured loans are those backed by something of value, known as **collateral**, which may be seized by the lender in the event the borrower fails to repay the loan. Common types of collateral include property, equipment, accounts receivable, inventories, and securities.

Unsecured Loans

Unsecured loans are loans that require no collateral. Instead, the lender relies on the general credit record and the earning power of the borrower. To increase the returns on such loans and to obtain some protection in case of default, most lenders insist that the borrower maintain some minimum amount of money on deposit at the bank while the loan is outstanding.

A common example of an unsecured loan is a **line of credit**, which is an agreed-on maximum amount of money a bank or other source is willing to lend a business. (For large lines of credit, lenders often require collateral, making this a form of secured loan.) After a line of credit has been established, the financial manager can access it whenever needed, taking cash out up to that maximum amount. A line of credit can provide some welcome flexibility in managing cash flow, such as when some of your accounts receivable are late but you have accounts payable that are due. In a situation like this, when those accounts receivable do come in, you apply that cash to your line of credit to push your outstanding balance back down. Lines of credit are available from banks and from some online financing companies. Banks have more stringent credit requirements but tend to offer lower rates; the alternative lenders are usually less stringent when it comes to qualifying, but their interest rates can be higher, sometimes considerably higher.[11]

Commercial Paper

When businesses need a sizable amount of money for a short period of time, they can issue **commercial paper**—short-term *promissory notes*, or contractual agreements, to repay a borrowed amount by a specified time with a specified interest rate. Commercial paper is usually sold only by major corporations with strong credit ratings, in denominations of $100,000 or more and with maturities of up to 270 days (the maximum allowed by the U.S. Securities and Exchange Commission [SEC] without a formal registration process).[12]

Factoring

Extending trade credit is often a competitive necessity, but it can create cash flow problems for sellers if accounts payable are piling up faster and coming due sooner than accounts receivable are being paid. To close the gap, many companies

trade credit
Credit obtained by a purchaser directly from a supplier.

secured loans
Loans backed up with assets that the lender can claim in case of default, such as a piece of property.

collateral
A tangible asset a lender can claim if a borrower defaults on a loan.

unsecured loans
Loans that require a good credit rating but no collateral.

line of credit
An arrangement in which a financial institution makes money available for use at any time after the loan has been approved.

commercial paper
Short-term *promissory notes*, or contractual agreements, to repay a borrowed amount by a specified time with a specified interest rate.

factoring
Obtaining funding by selling accounts receivable.

rely on **factoring**, in which a third party takes over the process of getting payment from customers and, in the meantime, advances a portion of the accounts payable amounts to the seller.

In a typical factoring arrangement, when an order arrives, the seller ships it to the customer but sends the invoice to the factoring company, who then bills the customer. As soon as the customer receives the order, the factoring company advances a portion of the invoice amount to the seller. When the factoring company collects payment from the customer, it pays the balance of the invoice amount to the seller, minus its factoring fee. With this method, sellers get paid much sooner, often in as little as 24 hours, rather than in the weeks or months it might take without the factoring company's involvement.[13]

LONG-TERM DEBT FINANCING

Although some of them are similar in concept to short-term debt, long-term debt options require a different set of decisions for both borrowers and lenders. The most common long-term debt alternatives are *long-term loans, leases,* and *corporate bonds* (see Exhibit 16.8).

Long-Term Loans

Long-term loans have payback periods longer than a year, sometimes up to 25 years or more. (Long-term loans on real estate are called *mortgages.*) Long-term loans can be an attractive option for borrowers, because such loans can provide substantial capital without the need to sell equity in the company. However, because they tie up a lender's capital for a long period of time and usually involve large sums of money, lending standards tend to be fairly stringent and not all companies can qualify. Lenders usually look at "the five Cs" when considering applications for these loans:[14]

- **Character.** This aspect includes not only the personal and professional character of the company owners but also their experience and qualifications to run the type of business for which they plan to use the loan proceeds.
- **Capacity.** To judge the company's capacity or ability to repay the loan, lenders scrutinize debt ratios, liquidity ratios, and other measures of financial health. For small businesses, the owners' personal finances are also evaluated.

EXHIBIT 16.8   **Sources of Long-Term Debt Financing**

Long-term debt financing can provide funds for major asset purchases and other investments needed to help companies grow.

Source	Funding Mechanism	Length of Term	Advantages	Disadvantages and Limitations
Long-term loans	Bank or other lender provides cash; borrower agrees to repay according to specific terms	From 1 to 25 years	Can provide substantial sums of money without diluting ownership through sale of equity; allows company to make major purchases of inventory, equipment, and other vital assets	Not all companies can qualify for loans at acceptable terms; payments tie up part of cash flow for the duration of the loan; purchases made via loans often require substantial down payments
Leases	Company earns the right to use an asset in exchange for regular payments; arrangement can be directly between lessor and lessee or can involve a third party such as a bank	Typically several years for equipment and vehicles; longer for real estate	Usually require lower down payments than loans; can provide access to essential assets for companies that don't qualify for loans; let company avoid buying assets that are likely to decline in value or become obsolete; often free company from maintenance and other recurring costs	Can restrict how assets can be used; company doesn't gain any equity in return for lease payments, except in the case of lease-to-own arrangements; can be more expensive than borrowing to buy
Corporate bonds	Company sells bonds to investors, with the promise to pay interest and repay the principal according to a set schedule	Typically from 10 to 30 years	Can generate more cash with longer repayment terms than are possible with loans	Available only to large companies with strong credit ratings

- **Capital.** Lenders want to know how well capitalized the company is—that is, whether it has enough capital to succeed. For small-business loans in particular, lenders want to know how much money the owners themselves have already invested in the business.
- **Conditions.** Lenders look at the overall condition of the economy as well as conditions within the applicant's specific industry to determine whether they are comfortable with the business's plans and capabilities.
- **Collateral.** Long-term loans are usually secured with collateral of some kind. Lenders expect to be repaid from the borrower's cash flow, but in case that is inadequate, they look for assets that could be used to repay the loan, such as real estate or equipment.

An old joke about applying for bank loans suggests that the only way to qualify for a loan is to prove you don't need the money. This is an exaggeration, of course, but it is grounded in fact. Before they will part with their capital, responsible lenders want a high degree of assurance that they'll get their money back.

Leases

Rather than borrow money to purchase an asset, a firm may enter into a **lease**, under which the owner of an asset (the *lessor*) allows another party (the *lessee*) to use it in exchange for regular payments. (Leasing is similar to renting; a key difference is that leases fix the terms of the agreement for a specific amount of time.) Leases are commonly used for real estate, major equipment, vehicles, and aircraft. In some cases, the lease arrangement is made directly between the asset owner and the lessee. In other cases, a bank or other financial firm provides leasing services to its clients and takes care of payments to the lessor.

Real estate leases are similar in concept to apartment leases, but they can be much more complicated, with important financial and legal ramifications that business owners need to understand before signing. Lessees can be responsible for damage caused by customers, for instance, and leases in multi-unit buildings often require tenants to pay for shared facilities, even if they rarely use them.[15]

Equipment leasing is also an attractive option used by many companies, particularly when credit rating or cash flow is an issue, because leases are usually easier to get than loans. Equipment leases enable a company to make use of the latest equipment with lower up-front costs and without the long-term commitment of buying. Some leases also include the flexibility to upgrade when new versions of equipment become available. Equipment leases need to be explored as carefully as real estate leases, however. Financial managers should be aware of maintenance and repair clauses, insurance coverage, and the tax implications of leasing versus buying.[16]

lease
An agreement to use an asset in exchange for regular payment; similar to renting.

kozmoat98/E+/Getty Images

Companies can choose to lease equipment to avoid tying up capital through purchasing.

Corporate Bonds

When a company needs to borrow a large sum of money, it may not be able to get the entire amount from a single source. Under such circumstances, it can try to borrow from many individual investors by issuing **bonds**—certificates that obligate the company to repay a certain sum, plus interest, to the bondholder on a specific date. (Note that although bondholders buy bonds, they are acting as lenders.)

Companies issue a variety of bond types. *Secured bonds*, like secured loans, are backed by company-owned property that passes to the bondholders if the issuer does not repay the amount borrowed. The most common types of bonds sold by U.S. companies are unsecured *debentures*, which are backed only by a corporation's promise to pay. Because debentures are riskier than other types of bonds, they pay higher interest rates to attract buyers. *Convertible bonds* can be exchanged for a predefined number of shares of the corporation's common stock.[17]

With most bond issues, a corporation retains the right to pay off the bonds before maturity. Bonds containing this provision are known as *callable bonds*, or *redeemable bonds*. If a company issues bonds when interest rates are high and then rates fall later on, it may want to pay off its high-interest bonds and sell a new issue at a lower rate. To compensate investors for calling the bond early, the bond contract usually specifies a higher payback amount than they would receive if bonds were left to mature.[18]

bonds
A method of funding in which the issuer borrows from an investor and provides a written promise to make regular interest payments and repay the borrowed amount in the future.

CHECKPOINT

LEARNING OBJECTIVE 3: Identify the major categories of debt financing.

SUMMARY: Debt financing can be divided into short-term debts, payable in full in less than a year, and long-term debts, payable over more than one year. The major categories of short-term debt financing are credit cards, trade credit (the option to delay paying for purchases for 30 to 60 days or more), secured loans (loans backed by sellable assets such as land, equipment, or inventory), unsecured loans (loans and lines of credit extended solely on the borrower's creditworthiness), commercial paper (short-term promissory notes issued by major corporations), and factoring (selling a firm's accounts payable to a third-party financer; strictly speaking, not a form of debt financing).

The major categories of long-term debt financing are long-term loans (substantial amounts of capital for major purchases or other needs, on terms from 1 to 25 years, usually secured by assets), leases (similar to renting, conferring the rights to use an asset in exchange for regular payments), and bonds (certificates that obligate the company to repay a specified sum, plus interest, to the bondholder on a specific date).

CRITICAL THINKING: (1) How does getting a secured loan using accounts receivable as collateral differ from factoring? (2) Why would lenders want to see that a business already has some level of capitalization before giving it access to more capital by means of a loan?

IT'S YOUR BUSINESS: (1) Would you launch a new company if the only way to finance it was through the use of your personal credit cards? Why or why not? (2) Which of the debt alternatives identified in this section are available to you as a consumer?

KEY TERMS TO KNOW: trade credit, secured loans, collateral, unsecured loans, line of credit, commercial paper, factoring, lease, bonds

[4] **LEARNING OBJECTIVE**

Outline the advantages and disadvantages of equity financing.

Financing Alternatives: Equity

The most far-reaching alternative for securing funds is to sell shares of ownership in a company. Selling shares can dramatically change the way a company is managed and, in extreme cases, can even lead to outsiders taking control of the company if they can purchase enough shares. Even when owners retain control, equity financing complicates operations by adding new layers of scrutiny, accountability, and government regulations. Moreover, the process of obtaining equity financing is expensive and time-consuming, so even companies that could obtain it don't always choose to do so—and some that sell equity to the public eventually choose to reverse the decision by buying it back.

With all these caveats, why would any company bother with equity financing? There are two key reasons. The first is the tremendous upside potential for the company as a whole and for any individual or organization that owns shares. Equity financing has fueled the growth of most of the major corporations in the world and has given countless small companies the opportunity to grow. The second reason is cash flow: Debt financing puts an immediate and continuing squeeze on cash flow because, in most cases, the company must make regular payments against the debt. Equity financing doesn't require repayment and therefore doesn't affect cash flow in the way debt financing does. (Public equity financing does, however, incur the one-time cost of the initial public offering [IPO] process, recurring payments to the outside auditor, and some increases in fixed costs with any additional staff required for financial accounting and regulatory filings.)

Although public equity financing is available to only a fraction of companies, it is one of the most powerful forms of financing. Moreover, it directly and indirectly plays a huge role in the economy by giving individual and institutional investors the opportunity to increase their own capital by investing in company shares. This section takes a quick look at the private and public varieties of equity financing.

VENTURE CAPITAL AND OTHER PRIVATE EQUITY

Chapter 6 points out that venture capitalists (VCs), as well as angel investors for companies that aren't yet ready for VC funding, are a key source of equity financing for a certain class of start-up companies. As you'll read at the end of the chapter, Court Buddy was able to secure VC funding to expand its attorney-matching service.

VC funding often happens in stages as the company grows. The first round of *seed money* is called Series A. Depending on a company's development needs, it may seek several more rounds of VC funding, each labeled with a letter—Series B, Series C, and so on.

In exchange for a share of ownership, VCs can invest millions of dollars in companies long before those firms qualify for most other forms of financing, so they represent an essential form of funding for high-growth ventures. VCs also provide managerial expertise and industry connections that can be crucial to new companies.

However, VCs are one of the most specialized and least widely available forms of funding, and most firms have no chance of getting venture capital. VCs typically look for privately held firms that are already well established enough to be able to use a significant amount of money and are positioned to grow aggressively enough to give the VCs a good shot at eventually selling their interests at an acceptable profit. Not all VC-backed firms grow enough to pay back their investors, so to compensate for losses from some investments, VCs rely on getting very high returns from a handful of winners.

Venture capital is one form of funding known as **private equity**, which involves any ownership in privately held companies. In common usage, "private equity" usually refers to specialized investment firms that normally get involved after the VC stage and use funds to buy all or part of privately held companies or to buy shares of public companies with the aim of taking them private. Private equity firms often look for underperforming or undervalued companies and invest in them with the aim to turn them around and eventually cash out by reselling their stakes.[19]

These investors sometimes get a reputation as "asset strippers" that sell off anything of value while laying off employees, load up companies with debt during leveraged buyouts, or pressure company boards into short-term mindsets in the attempt to avoid takeover bids. While there certainly have been cases of "slash and burn" takeovers, many private equity firms make substantial, long-term investments that help companies improve their operations and become more stable and profitable. For instance, Vista Equity Partners, the fastest-growing private equity firm in the Unites States, positions itself as a "value-added" investor and backs that up with a staff of more than 100 consultants who help acquired companies run better by applying a "playbook" of best practices that cover every aspect of company management.[20]

> **REAL-TIME UPDATES**
> **Learn More by Visiting This Website**
>
> **Expanding access to new-venture financing**
>
> The Intent Manifesto's mission is "to educate, inform and raise awareness and support for women of color technology start-ups." Go to **real-timeupdates.com/bia9** and select Learn More in the Students section.

private equity
Ownership assets that aren't publicly traded; includes venture capital.

PUBLIC STOCK OFFERINGS

Going public—offering shares of stock to the public through a stock market such as the New York Stock Exchange—can generate millions or even billions of dollars in funding. However, going public is not for the faint of heart. The process of launching an IPO takes months of management time and attention, can cost several million dollars, and exposes the company to rigorous scrutiny (which isn't necessarily a bad thing, of course). Moreover, companies have no assurance that efforts to go public will pay off. Some offerings fail to sell at the hoped-for share price, and some offerings are withdrawn before going public because their backers don't think the market conditions are strong enough. Like the economy as a whole, the market for IPOs runs in cycles, and timing an IPO is one of the key factors for success. Despite the costs and risks, the potential rewards are so high that every year hundreds of companies around the world attempt to go public.[21]

For more on financial management and funding alternatives, visit **real-timeupdates.com/bia9** and select Chapter 16.

Going public with an IPO is an exciting moment for a company, but only a small fraction of companies have access to public equity funding.

✓ CHECKPOINT

LEARNING OBJECTIVE 4: Outline the advantages and disadvantages of equity financing.

SUMMARY: Selling shares of a company, either publicly or privately, can give a firm vital capital without putting a squeeze on cash flow the way debt financing does. The two primary disadvantages are (1) the added complexity of dealing with investors and regulators and (2) diminished control, including in extreme cases the possibility of losing control of the company if outsiders can buy enough shares.

CRITICAL THINKING: (1) High-tech firms tend to dominate IPO filings year after year; why do you suppose this is so? (2) Why does the volume of IPOs tend to track the ups and downs of the stock market?

IT'S YOUR BUSINESS: (1) If you had the choice between working at a company still in the pre-IPO stage, which is offering a lower salary but a share of ownership that will become shares of company stock after the IPO, or a higher-paying job with no stock, what additional information would you need before you would be comfortable making a choice? (2) Choose any business that you might like to start as an entrepreneur. How would you make a compelling pitch to private equity investors to encourage them to invest in your company?

KEY TERM TO KNOW: private equity

---

5 **LEARNING OBJECTIVE**

Identify the four most important financial markets for most businesses.

Financial Markets

To obtain financing and to seek investment opportunities, businesses can interact with a number of financial markets. This section looks at four of the most significant: the stock market, the bond market, the money market, and the derivatives market.

Note that *market* is a potentially confusing financial term that is used in a variety of ways in different contexts. For example, when you hear commentators refer to "the market," with no qualifiers, they are probably referring to the stock market and specifically to one or more stock market indexes. You'll also hear markets referred to by various names. The *equities market* is another name for the stock market, and the *securities market* encompasses the stock, bond, and derivatives markets. Finally, securities markets can be divided into *primary markets*, which handle the IPOs of stocks and bonds, and *secondary markets*, which handle all the public buying and selling after that.

THE STOCK MARKET

stock exchanges
Organizations that facilitate the buying and selling of stock.

Organizations that facilitate the buying and selling of stock are known as **stock exchanges**. Some of these are actual physical facilities, whereas others are primarily computer networks. The most famous of the physical variety is the New York Stock Exchange (NYSE; www.nyse.com). The NYSE, often referred to as the "Big Board," is located just off Wall Street in New York City, leading to the frequent use of "Wall Street" as a metaphor for either the stock market or the larger community of financial companies in the immediate area. Tokyo, London, Frankfurt, Paris, Toronto, Shanghai, Hong Kong, and Montreal also have stock exchanges with national or international importance, and smaller regional exchanges play an important role in buying and selling many lesser-known stocks.

The NYSE's major U.S. competitor is the NASDAQ (pronounced "NAZZ-dack"), a computerized stock exchange originated by the National Association of Securities Dealers (www.nasdaq.com). NASDAQ is home to many high-profile tech stocks such as Amazon, Apple, Facebook, and Microsoft.[22]

Stocks that don't meet the listing requirements of an exchange can be sold *over the counter* (*OTC*). Together, the various stock exchanges around the world and the OTC market make up the overall "stock market."

NASDAQ is home to many high-profile technology stocks.

- **How much will you need—and when?** Identify how much money you'll need for significant events, from major purchases to college education to retirement.
- **How much can you invest?** Make a realistic assessment of how much you can invest now and then every month thereafter. Don't let limited cash hold you back, however—with some personal finance apps you can invest as little as $5.00 at a time.
- **How much risk are you willing to accept?** Identify your tolerance for risk, based on your personality, financial circumstances, and stage in life. As with most everything in finance, risk is inversely related to potential **rate of return**, the gain (or loss) of an investment over time.
- **How much liquidity do you need?** Money that you may need in the short term should not be tied up in long-term investments that are difficult to sell quickly or whose value may fluctuate wildly and leave you facing a loss if you need to sell.
- **What are the tax consequences?** Various investments have different tax ramifications, and some are designed specifically to minimize taxes.

rate of return
The gain (or loss) of an investment over time, expressed as a percentage.

By answering these questions, you'll be able to establish realistic investment objectives that are right for you and your family.

LEARNING TO ANALYZE FINANCIAL NEWS

Knowing how to analyze financial news is essential to making good investment choices. Investors have access to more information than ever before, and much of this information is free (and chances are that your college or community library has subscriptions to many of the sources that aren't free). You can quickly uncover basic information about a company on its website, scan its "financials" on Google Finance (www.google.com/finance) or Yahoo! Finance (finance.yahoo.com), read articles from numerous business periodicals online, judge customer sentiment by reading comments on social commerce sites, catch late-breaking news on 24-hour cable TV channels, and monitor the company and its industry using a variety of newsfeeds and social media.

REAL-TIME UPDATES
Learn More by Visiting This Website

Get started in investing with these free guides

From stocks to mutual funds to real estate, MarketWatch can help you get started as an investor. Go to **real-timeupdates.com/bia9** and select Learn More in the Students section.

Don't get overwhelmed with all the information available to investors these days; some of it is aimed at professional investors, and a lot of it is just noise that won't affect your long-term investment plans.

Matej Kastelic/Shutterstock

Unfortunately, so much information is available that to avoid being overwhelmed, you almost need to take a defensive posture, filtering out information that is irrelevant and keeping a sharp eye for information that is biased or unreliable. This information overload carries the additional risk of prompting investors to make snap decisions based on something they heard on TV or something that just popped up on Twitter.

Fortunately, the vast majority of the information out there won't apply to you and your investments. Much of it is detailed material aimed at financial specialists, and much of it is short-term "noise" that probably won't affect you in the long term. To make the best use of all this information without getting overwhelmed or sidetracked, start on a small scale. Learn the basic language of investing on a site such as Investopedia (www.investopedia.com), a free website with extensive content written by investment professionals.

You'll gradually pick up on the terminology and start to identify the themes you need to care about and which of the many arcane topics you can leave to the specialists. For instance, you'll soon get familiar with the general conditions of the stock market and learn the terms that define its ups and downs. If stock prices have been rising over a long period, for instance, the industry and the media will often describe this situation as a **bull market**. The reverse is a **bear market**, one characterized by a long-term trend of falling prices.

Finally, one more bit of good news: Virtually everything you learn in this course and in other business courses will help you analyze business and financial news and become a more successful investor. When you know what makes companies successful, you can apply this insight to choosing investments with solid growth potential.

bull market
A market situation in which most stocks are increasing in value.

bear market
A market situation in which most stocks are decreasing in value.

Today's digital investment tools allow you to create a personalized investment plan that aligns with your resources, goals, and risk capacity. Ellevest, for example, was created to address the unique financial challenges that women face, including the fact that women's salaries tend to peak much earlier in their careers then do men's salaries.

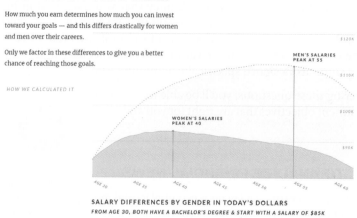

Your Salary Is Different... and Not How You'd Think

How much you earn determines how much you can invest toward your goals — and this differs drastically for women and men over their careers.

Only we factor in these differences to give you a better chance of reaching those goals.

HOW WE CALCULATED IT

MEN'S SALARIES PEAK AT 55

WOMEN'S SALARIES PEAK AT 40

$120K
$110K
$100K
$90K

AGE 30 AGE 35 AGE 40 AGE 45 AGE 50 AGE 55 AGE 60

SALARY DIFFERENCES BY GENDER IN TODAY'S DOLLARS
FROM AGE 30, BOTH HAVE A BACHELOR'S DEGREE & START WITH A SALARY OF $85K

CREATING AN INVESTMENT PORTFOLIO

investment portfolios
Collections of various types of investments.

asset allocation
Management of a portfolio to balance potential returns with an acceptable level of risk.

No single investment provides an ideal combination of income, growth potential, safety, liquidity, and tax consequences. For this reason, investors build **investment portfolios**, or collections of various types of investments (see Exhibit 16.10). Managing a portfolio to balance potential returns with an acceptable level of risk is known as **asset allocation**, dividing investments among *cash instruments* such as money-market mutual funds, *income instruments* such as government and corporate bonds, and *equities* (mainly common stock). In general, younger investors want to focus on *building* capital through equity investments, whereas older investors want to focus on *protecting* capital through income and cash instruments, so they rebalance their portfolios over time.

BUYING AND SELLING SECURITIES

broker
A certified expert who is legally registered to buy and sell securities on behalf of individual and institutional investors.

In most cases, buying and selling securities requires using a **broker**, an expert who has passed a series of formal examinations and is legally registered to buy and sell securities on behalf of individual and institutional investors. You pay *transaction costs* for every order, and these fees vary by the level of service you get. A *full-service broker* advises you on selecting investments, for example, whereas a *discount broker* provides fewer services and generally charges lower commissions as a result.

More-experienced investors can use a number of buying and selling strategies beyond simple cash purchases of stock. With *margin trading*, investors buy stock using a combination of their own cash and money borrowed from their brokers. The appeal of margin trading is leverage, amplifying potential gains by using someone else's money in addition to your own. Margin trading is risky, however, because it also amplifies losses. In fact, with leverage, you can lose more money than you originally invested. And if prices are dropping and you want to hang on until they climb back up, you might not be allowed to. If the stock price drops so low that it violates the maximum leverage allowed in your account, you can be forced to sell immediately.

Most investors buy stock with the anticipation that it will rise in value. However, if you believe that a stock's price is about to drop, you may choose a trading procedure known as *short selling*, or "going short." With this procedure, you sell stock you borrow from a broker in the hope of buying it back later at a lower price. After you return the borrowed stock to the broker, you keep the price difference. However, selling short can be quite risky, because you can lose more than you originally invested. For instance, if the price doubles instead of falling as you anticipated, you can lose twice as much as you invested.

For more information on financial markets and investing, visit **real-timeupdates .com/bia9** and click on Chapter 16.

 CHECKPOINT

LEARNING OBJECTIVE 6: Describe four major steps required to become an investor.

SUMMARY: The first step toward becoming an investor is to establish your investment objectives, based on your financial needs and goals, your tolerance for risk, your liquidity requirements, and tax consequences that apply to you. The second step is learning to analyze financial news; the best way is to start with the basics, gradually accumulate information as you need it, and filter out news that is irrelevant or potentially unreliable. The third step is to plan and create an investment portfolio, using asset allocation to maintain an acceptable balance of risk and potential reward. The fourth step is to engage in buying and selling securities, using a broker of your choice and the right trading strategies for your circumstances.

CRITICAL THINKING: (1) Why is it important to establish objectives before you begin to invest? (2) Why is asset allocation a fundamentally important strategy for investors?

IT'S YOUR BUSINESS: (1) Do you think you currently have the discipline needed to control your spending in order to free up cash for regular investing? If not, what changes could you make? (2) If someone gave you a "hot tip" on a stock, how would you go about researching the opportunity before making an investment decision?

KEY TERMS TO KNOW: rate of return, bull market, bear market, investment portfolios, asset allocation, broker

---

Thriving in the Digital Enterprise: Smart Contracts

 LEARNING OBJECTIVE

Explain how businesses can use *smart contracts* to facilitate transactions.

smart contract
Digital agreement in a distributed ledger such as blockchain that automatically executes when its criteria are fulfilled by incoming data.

Chapter 15's discussion of distributed ledgers and blockchain (see page 467) highlights the benefits of uniting trading parties through a shared ledger. An important emerging application running on blockchain is the **smart contract**, a digital agreement that automatically executes when its criteria are fulfilled by incoming data.

The complicated world of freight and logistics illustrates the potential and value of smart contracts. The transportation of goods and materials is a multitrillion-dollar global industry that grows every year with the continued expansion of world trade. It is also a highly fragmented industry fairly swimming in paperwork. A single international shipment can involve dozens of companies and regulatory bodies that deal with inventory management, insurance, audits, customs inspections, and payments. The ocean-shipping company Maersk says that a container moving from East Africa to Europe needs the approval of up to 30 individuals and passes through more than 200 separate interactions before it reaches its destination.[25] Thanks to this fragmentation, the industry is plagued with inefficiencies, errors, counterfeiting, and theft. In the United States alone, cargo thieves make off with an estimated $30 billion in goods every year.[26]

The fragmented complexity of the global freight and logistics industry makes it a good candidate for automated smart contracts.

As Chapter 15 explained, bringing all these parties together on a distributed ledger would give everyone access to the same records as shipments pass through the transportation network. In addition, using smart contracts at key handoff points could reduce delays, errors, and opportunities for fraud. For example, rather than multiple people physically verifying that a particular container has been offloaded from a ship in port, cleared through customs, and then loaded onto a rail car or truck for the next leg of the journey, a series of smart contracts could collect data from Internet of Things sensors attached to the containers or the goods inside. As the appropriate conditions are met at each stage, each contract can confirm receipt, update tracking systems, send payments, update logistics parties further down the line, and so on. The contracts would be verified and locked into the blockchain, making them visible to everyone and impossible to tamper with or duplicate.

Maersk says that building out the system globally will take several years because of all the parties involved, but it should eventually be able to replace the cumbersome paperwork with a much smoother automated approach.[27] The Blockchain in Transport Alliance (bita.studio), whose members include FedEx, UPS, and many other significant parties in global freight and logistics, is defining technology standards that everyone in the industry can use.[28]

Smart contracts are also being developed for the financial services sector. J.P. Morgan, for example, created an open-source system called Quorum, an enterprise version of the Ethereum blockchain. One of its first uses was selling certificates of deposit (CDs), a type of savings instruments issued by banks. Smart contracts automated every step of the process, from creating the CDs to distributing them through brokers to sending interest payments to investors.[29] As a permissioned blockchain, Quorum can maintain privacy for participants while giving government regulators access to details they need in order to ensure compliance with finance laws.[30]

Business blockchain and smart contracts will no doubt hit some snags as they mature, but given the scope of the problems this technology can solve, the vast investment now under way, and the successful applications already in place, its widespread adoption appears to be more a matter of when, not if.

✔ CHECKPOINT

LEARNING OBJECTIVE 7: Explain how businesses can use *smart contracts* to facilitate transactions.

SUMMARY: Smart contracts are digital agreements that execute if certain predetermined conditions are met. They can replace the slow and error-prone process of manually executing contracts. When used in a blockchain, the agreements are verified and locked into the chain, making them visible and immutable.

CRITICAL THINKING: (1) If a smart contract malfunctions, who should be held liable—the people who developed it or the people using the system? (2) How might the growth of blockchain and smart contracts affect employment in financial services or freight and logistics?

IT'S YOUR BUSINESS: Does the prospect of working with blockchain and related technologies sound appealing? Would you consider pursuing a career in this area?

KEY TERM TO KNOW: smart contract

BEHIND THE SCENES

Landing Venture Capital at Court Buddy

When entrepreneurs, executives, lenders, and investors ponder a company's growth prospects, one of the most important factors they look at is *scalability*: How big and how quickly can this company scale up?

In some industries and with some business models, growth potential is tightly linked to some aspect of physical capacity or human resources. If you launch a diner, for instance, your capacity to grow is limited by the number of tables and how many hours a day you want to stay open. If you want to scale up from there, you'll need to add a second location or perhaps offer takeout or home delivery service. These moves can give you some headroom for growth, but before long you'll be maxed out again, with building yet another diner as the only growth path. Businesses that depend on physical capacity like this can only grow in a *linear* fashion, which can be slow and expensive.

It's no coincidence that venture capitalists focus on a handful of industries, most of which are science- or technology-based: These businesses tend to be much easier to scale up than companies that rely on physical capacity or labor. That's why so many VC-funded businesses are concentrated in digital, online market segments that have the potential to grow *exponentially*.

Imagine if doing a Google search required visiting a Google office, explaining your question to a Google staffer, and then waiting until this person brought you the answer. To handle the trillions of searches that users now make every year, Google would probably need more office space than exists everywhere on Earth, not to mention several billion employees. Fortunately, as a digital business, Google has been able to scale to its mind-boggling size with relative ease.

When Kristina Jones and her cofounder husband, James, contemplated funding for their business, they knew they had digital scalability on their side. The system they designed works by automatically matching the needs of legal clients on one side with the capabilities and availability of attorneys on the other. On the Court Buddy website, people who need legal representation enter their location, the type of service they require, the amount of money they can spend, and their court date, if applicable. The system then finds attorneys who perform the desired legal services, who will work at a flat rate with the client's budget, and who are licensed to practice law in the relevant state. The system doesn't require labor or production capacity beyond computing bandwidth, which is easily scalable these days thanks to cloud computing services. With an unmet market need and a scalable business model, Court Buddy was a prime candidate for venture capital funding.

The approach Jones took is a case study in how to secure venture capital funding, and that started with extensive networking. Unlike applying for a loan from the one bank where you already do business, private equity funding is very much a numbers game—entrepreneurs need to get visibility in front of as many investors as possible. Investors are extremely selective, so to increase the odds of being chosen, entrepreneurs may need to pitch to dozens of investors before getting a bite. Networking, both informally and in organized events, can result in introductions to investors, influential people who know investors, and other industry insiders who might be able to help.

Today's entrepreneurs can take advantage of countless networking opportunities, many focused on helping particular types of businesses or founders. For Jones, an essential networking effort was getting involved with SheWorx (**www.sheworx .com**), a global forum that supports tens of thousands of female entrepreneurs. Networking opportunities such as SheWorx provide another priceless benefit to entrepreneurs, which is advice from people who've been through the process. For instance, Jones learned to start preparing months in advance before approaching investors and to pitch her "star" investors last so that her pitch would be practiced and highly polished. She describes her pitch as a "tight two-minute '$200k in 10 months'" story (indicating that the company had generated $200,000 in sales in its first 10 months).

Business plan competitions and demo days are two other great ways to get visibility, make connections, and build credibility in the eyes of investors. Jones pursued many such opportunities, and Court Buddy has won a string of awards and recognitions, from being named the People's Pick Winner in the *Miami Herald* Business Challenge to winning an American Entrepreneurship Award to being named one of the best new legal tech products in several competitions. *Demo days* are tech industry events in which entrepreneurs demonstrate their products and pitch their business plans to an audience of reporters and investors (including the investment arms of major corporations).

Court Buddy's path to funding started with being admitted to the business accelerator 500 Startups (**500.co**). Recall from Chapter 6 that accelerators are fast-track programs that work with start-ups to refine their business models and products as needed in order to become attractive to investors. (Like SheWorx, 500 Startups is committed to making the start-up ecosystem in general and private equity in particular more inclusive in order to support the full spectrum of aspiring entrepreneurs.)

Court Buddy's next step demonstrated the value of networking and the need to cast a wide net. The Joneses started with a list of more than 100 VCs, spoke to roughly 40 of those, and wound up pitching to about 20. The VC who recognized the company's potential and offered to lead the first round of financing, its Series A seed money, was someone Jones had met earlier at a SheWorx event and who had seen Court Buddy in action at a 500 Startups demo day. Again, it's about numbers and networking.

With development money and the encouragement of a large community of fellow entrepreneurs and supporters, Court Buddy began its growth trajectory and has already served thousands of clients. Kristina Jones would probably be happy with something less than a trillion lawyer-client matches every year, but whatever peak Court Buddy might eventually scale to, it has a solid start thanks to clear business planning and the backing of professional investors.[31]

Critical Thinking Questions

16-1. What other professional service businesses might be able to use an automated matchmaking service like Court Buddy?

16-2. What are the costs (financial and otherwise) of pursuing and accepting VC funding, as Kristina Jones did?

16-3. Would Kristina Jones's entrepreneurial/start-up story be an effective element to include in Court Buddy's marketing efforts? Why or why not? How would this compare with the marketing efforts by someone such as Tata Harper in Chapter 14?

Learn More Online

Visit **www.courtbuddy.com** and explore the latest news from the company. Review its start-up story and the long list of rewards and recognitions. Also, take a look at the SheWorx and 500 Startups websites. How can communities and programs like these help entrepreneurs get vital funding?

End of Chapter

KEY TERMS

accounts payable (481)
accounts receivable (481)
asset allocation (498)
bear market (497)
bond market (495)
bonds (491)
broker (498)
budget (482)
bull market (497)
capital structure (485)
collateral (489)
commercial paper (489)
cost of capital (486)
derivatives (495)
derivatives market (495)
debt financing (485)
equity financing (485)
factoring (490)

financial management (479)
financial plan (480)
investment portfolios (498)
lease (491)
leverage (487)
line of credit (489)
long-term financing (486)
money market (495)
private equity (493)
rate of return (497)
risk/return trade-off (479)
secured loans (489)
short-term financing (486)
smart contract (499)
stock exchanges (494)
trade credit (489)
unsecured loans (489)
zero-based budgeting (484)

TEST YOUR KNOWLEDGE

Questions for Review

16-4. What information sources are used to create a financial plan?

16-5. What is an EOQ?

16-6. What is the difference between accounts payable and accounts receivable?

16-7. What is equity financing?

16-8. What is the difference between a secured loan and an unsecured loan?

16-9. What factors influence a company's cost of capital?

16-10. How can trade credit help companies to manage their cash flow?

16-11. What is a smart contract?

Questions for Analysis

16-12. Would it be wise for a young company that is growing quickly but still hasn't achieved profitability to attempt to issue bonds as a way to expand its working capital? Why or why not?

16-13. Why would a company use zero-based budgeting, given that it requires more time and effort from managers throughout the company?

Services," *Black Enterprise*, 19 June 2017, www.blackenterprise .com; Robert Ambrogi, "This Week in Legal Tech: Startups to Face Off at ABA TECHSHOW," Above the Law, 13 March 2017, abovethelaw.com; Nancy Dahlberg, "Service Brings Access to Legal System to the People," *Miami Herald*, 26 April 2015, www .miamiherald.com; 500 Startups website, accessed 29 May 2018, 500.co; "About SheWorx," SheWorx Facebook page, accessed 29 May 2018, www.facebook.com/pg/sheworx; Danny Sullivan, "Google Now Handles at Least 2 Trillion Searches per Year," *Search Engine Land*, 24 May 2016, searchengineland.com.

2. "Why Would a Company Buy Back Its Own Shares?" *Investopedia*, 30 March 2018, www.investopedia.com.

3. Tracie Miller-Nobles, Brenda Mattison, and Ella Mae Matsumura, *Horngren's Financial & Managerial Accounting*, 6th ed. (New York: Pearson, 2018), 1187.

4. Ronald Falcon, Kyle Hawke, Matthew Maloney, and Mita Sen, "How Absolute Zero (-Based Budgeting) Can Heat Up Growth," McKinsey, January 2018, www.mckinsey.com; Kris Timmermans and Shin Shuda, "Getting Ahead by Cutting Back," Accenture, 2017, www.accenture.com.

5. Kyle Hawke, Matt Jochim, Carey Mignerey, and Allison Watson, "Five New Truths About Zero-Based Budgeting," McKinsey, August 2017, www.mckinsey.com.

6. Hawke, Jochim, Mignerey, and Watson, "Five New Truths About Zero-Based Budgeting."

7. Karen Wilken Braun and Wendy M. Tietz, *Managerial Accounting*, 5th ed. (New York: Pearson, 2018), 511; Miller-Nobles, Mattison, and Matsumura, *Horngren's Financial & Managerial Accounting*, 1187–1190.

8. Raymond M. Brooks, *Financial Management*, 3rd ed. (New York: Pearson, 2016), 324.

9. "Interest Rate Hedging," UBS, accessed 28 May 2018, www.ubs.com.

10. "Trade Credit," *Entrepreneur*, accessed 28 May 2018, www .entrepreneur.com.

11. Steve Nicastro, "Business Line of Credit: How It Works and Best Options," Nerdwallet, 6 February 2017, www.nerdwallet.com.

12. Brooks, *Financial Management*, 365.

13. "Manufacturing Factoring," Interstate Capital, accessed 28 May 2018, www.interstatecapital.com; "What Is Accounts Receivable Factoring?" CIT, 15 March 2018, www.cit.com.

14. "5 C's of Credit: What Are Banks Looking For?" Bank of America, accessed 28 May 2018, www.bankofamerica.com.

15. Clint Gharib, "Negotiating a Commercial Lease? Here's What You Need to Know," *Forbes*, 2 June 2015, www.forbes.com.

16. "The Fundamentals of Leasing Business Equipment," *Entrepreneur*, accessed 29 May 2018, www.entrepreneur.com.

17. Brooks, *Financial Management*, 165.

18. Brooks, *Financial Management*, 166.

19. Kimberly Amadeo, "Private Equity: Firms, Funds, and Role in Financial Crisis," The Balance, 12 March 2018, www.thebalance .com.

20. Nathan Vardi, "How to Best Wall Street and Silicon Valley Simultaneously," *Forbes*, 31 March 2018, 36–50; Vista Equity Partners, accessed 29 May 2018, www.vistaequitypartners.com.

21. Ryan Vlastelica, "IPO Activity Surged in 2017, Thanks to Pickup Among Tech Stocks," *MarketWatch*, 18 December 2017, www.marketwatch.com.

22. NASDAQ, accessed 30 May 2018, www.nasdaq.com.

23. Chizoba Morah, "Why Are Most Bonds Traded on the Secondary Market 'Over the Counter'?" *Investopedia*, 2 April 2018, www.investopedia.com.

24. Hemal Gosai, "Part Two: Fuel Hedging in the Airline Industry," AirlineGeeks, 18 September 2017, airlinegeeks.com.

25. Mariella Moon, "Shipping Giant Tests IBM's Blockchain Tech to Track Cargo," *Engadget*, 7 March 2017, www.engadget.com.

26. Deep Patel, "UPS Bets on Blockchain as the Future of the Trillion-Dollar Shipping Industry," *TechCrunch*, 15 December 2017, www.techcrunch.com.

27. Moon, "Shipping Giant Tests IBM's Blockchain Tech to Track Cargo."

28. Blockchain in Transport Alliance, accessed 30 May 2018, bita.studio.

29. Penny Crosman, "Spinoff Rumors or Not, JPM's Blockchain Unit Is Evolving," *American Banker*, 23 April 2018, www .americanbanker.com.

30. "What Is Quorum?" J.P. Morgan, accessed 30 May 2018, www.jpmorgan.com.

31. See note 1.

Business Law

The U.S. Legal System

Federal, state, and local governments work in numerous ways to protect both individuals and other businesses from corporate wrongdoing. Laws also spell out accepted ways of performing many essential business functions—along with the penalties for failing to comply. Naturally, any U.S. company that does business in other countries must comply with the laws of those countries as well.

SOURCES OF LAW

A *law* is a rule developed by a society to govern the conduct of, and relationships among, its members. The U.S. Constitution, including the Bill of Rights, is the foundation for U.S. laws. Because the Constitution is a general document, laws offering specific answers to specific problems are constantly embellishing its basic principles. However, law is not static; it develops in response to changing conditions and social standards. Individual laws originate in various ways: through legislative action (*statutory law*), through administrative rulings intended to enact and enforce statutory laws (*administrative law*), and through customs and judicial precedents (*common law*). To one degree or another, all three forms of law affect businesses. In situations in which the three forms of law appear to conflict, statutory law generally prevails.

U.S. laws come from three sources: *statutory law* (those passed by legislative bodies), *administrative law* (those created by government agencies in their responsibility to enact and enforce statutory laws), and *common law* (those created by court decisions).

Statutory Law

Statutory law is law written by the U.S. Congress, state legislatures, and local governments. Specific statutory laws are known as *statutes*. One of the most important elements of statutory law that affects businesses is the **Uniform Commercial Code (UCC)**, designed to reconcile numerous conflicts among state laws in order to simplify interstate commerce.[1] For example, the UCC provides a nationwide standard in many issues of commercial law, such as sales contracts, bank deposits, and warranties.

Administrative Law

After statutes have been passed by a state legislature or Congress, an administrative agency or commission typically takes responsibility for enacting and enforcing them. That agency may be called on to clarify a regulation's intent, often by consulting representatives of the affected industry. The administrative agency may then write more specific regulations. The body of laws that govern these administrative agencies is known as **administrative law**.[2]

Administrative agencies also have the power to investigate corporations suspected of breaking administrative laws. A corporation found to be in violation of administrative laws may agree to a **consent order**, or *consent decree*, which allows the company to promise to stop doing something without admitting to any illegal behavior. If an agency cannot get a company to agree with a consent order, it can forward the case to an *administrative law judge* to begin legal proceedings against the company.[3]

Common Law

Common law, which originates in courtrooms and judges' decisions, began in England many centuries ago and was transported to the United States by the colonists. It is applied in all states except Louisiana (which follows a French model). In contrast to laws based on legislative acts and administrative agency regulations, common law is established through custom and the precedents set in courtroom proceedings.[4]

In the United States, common law is applied and interpreted in the system of courts (see Exhibit A.1). The U.S. Supreme Court (or the highest court of a state when state laws are involved) sets precedents for entire legal systems. Lower courts must then abide by those precedents as they pertain to similar cases. Many business cases are heard in

EXHIBIT A.1	**Major Elements of the U.S. Court System**

A legal proceeding may begin in a trial court or an administrative agency. An unfavorable decision may be appealed to a higher court at the federal or state level. (The court of appeals is the highest court in states that have no state supreme court; some other states have no intermediate appellate court.) The U.S. Supreme Court, the country's highest court, is the court of final appeal.

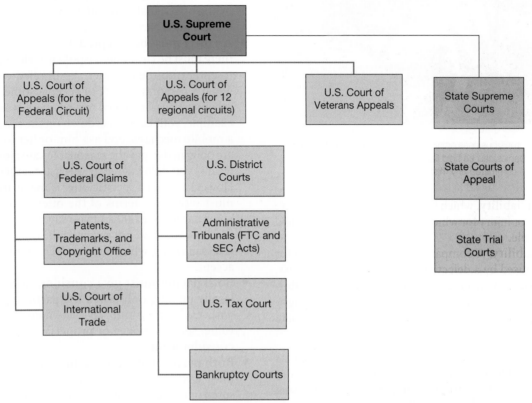

Sources: Henry Cheeseman, *Business Law*, 9th ed. (New York: Pearson, 2016), 23, 29; Nancy K. Kubasek, Bartley A. Brennan, and M. Neil Browne, *The Legal Environment of Business*, 8th ed. (New York: Pearson, 2017), 47; "Court Role and Structure," United States Courts, accessed 15 June 2018, www.uscourts.gov.

standard trial courts, but more than half of U.S. states now have special *business courts* presided over by judges experienced in handling commercial law.[5]

Major Concepts in Business Law

Although businesses must comply with the full body of laws that apply to individuals, a subset of laws can be defined more precisely as **business law**. It includes the elements of law that directly affect business activities. For example, laws pertaining to business licensing, employee safety, and corporate income taxes can all be considered business law. The most important categories of laws affecting business include torts, contracts, agency, property transactions, patents, trademarks, copyrights, negotiable instruments, and bankruptcy.

TORTS

A **tort** is a wrongful act, other than a breach of contract. The victim of a tort is legally entitled to some form of financial compensation, or **damages**, for his or her loss and suffering.

This compensation is also known as a *compensatory damage award*. In some cases, the victim may also receive a *punitive damage award* to punish the wrongdoer if the misdeed is deemed particularly bad. Torts can be classified as *intentional, unintentional,* or *strict liability*:[6]

- **Intentional torts.** An **intentional tort** is a willful act that results in injury. For example, accidentally hitting a softball through someone's window is a tort, but purposely cutting down someone's tree because it obscures your view is an intentional tort. Note that *intent* in this case does not mean the intent to cause harm; it is the intent to commit a specific act. Some intentional torts involve communication of false statements that harm another's reputation. If the communication is published in any permanent form, from a Facebook post to a television program, it is called *libel*. Spoken defamation is referred to as *slander*.[7]

- **Negligence and product liability.** In contrast to intentional torts, torts of **negligence** involve failure to use a reasonable amount of care necessary to protect others from injury.[8] Cases of alleged negligence often involve

William Perugini/Shutterstock

With some dangerous business activities, the doctrine of strict liability means that companies can be held liable for damages even if they are not found to have committed any mistakes.

product liability, which is a product's capacity to cause damages or injury for which the producer or seller is held responsible.

- **Strict liability.** A company may also be held liable for injury caused by a defective product or faulty process, even if it used with all reasonable care. Such **strict liability** makes it possible to assign liability without assigning fault, such as in the case of dangerous but legitimate business activities.[9]

Product liability is one of the most controversial aspects of business law. On one side, advocates for consumers—and particularly patients in the health-care industry—assert that sizable monetary damages in liability cases compensate customers who have been wronged and serve as an incentive for safer products and practices. On the other side, critics of big awards say these payouts lead to higher costs for consumers, stifle innovation, and can reduce the availability of some goods and services. This battle over *tort reform* has been going on for some years and promises to continue in the years ahead.[10]

CONTRACTS

Broadly defined, a **contract** is an exchange of promises between two or more parties that is enforceable by law. Many business transactions—including buying and selling products, hiring employees, purchasing group insurance, and licensing a technology—involve contracts. Most business contracts are **express contracts**, meaning they are articulated in written or spoken language. **Implied contracts** are based on the conduct of the parties, such as when a buyer accepts the seller's price in a transaction and takes the product. This behavior legally obligates the buyer to pay the seller.[11]

Elements of a Contract

The law of contracts deals largely with identifying the exchanges that can be classified as contracts. The following factors must usually be present for a contract to be enforceable and defensible:[12]

- **An offer must be made.** One party must propose that an agreement be entered into. The offer may be oral or written, but it must be firm, definite, and specific enough to make it clear that someone intends to be legally bound by the offer. Finally, the offer must be communicated to the intended party or parties.

- **An offer must be accepted.** For an offer to be accepted, there must be clear intent (spoken, written, or by action) to enter into the contract. An implied contract arises when a person requests or accepts something and the other party has indicated that payment is expected. If, for example, your car breaks down on the road and you call a mobile mechanic and ask him or her to repair it, you are obligated to pay the reasonable value for the services, even if you didn't agree to specific charges beforehand. However, when a specific offer is made, the acceptance must satisfy the terms of the offer. If someone offers you a car for $18,000 and you say you would take it for $15,000, you have not accepted the offer. Your response is a *counteroffer*, which the salesperson may or may not accept.

- **Both parties must give consideration.** A contract is legally binding only when the parties have bargained with each other and have exchanged something of value, such as money or property, which is called the **consideration**.

- **Both parties must give genuine assent.** Both parties must agree to a contract voluntarily, without being pressured or tricked into agreeing. In addition, if both parties made a mistake, such as misjudging the profitability of a business being sold, courts will likely rescind (void) the contract.

- **Both parties must be competent.** The law grants certain classes of people only a limited capacity to enter into contracts. People who were not mentally competent when entering a contract can usually be freed from it, and special rules apply to minors (people who are not of legal age in a specific state).

- **The contract must not involve an illegal act.** Courts will not enforce a promise that involves an illegal act. For example, a drug dealer cannot get help from the courts to enforce a contract to deliver illegal drugs at a prearranged price.

REAL-TIME UPDATES
Learn More by Reading These Articles

Dozens of free articles on business law

Get legal tips on every aspect of starting and running a business. Go to **real-timeupdates.com/bia9** and select Learn More in the Students section.

Contract Performance

A contract normally expires when the agreed-on conditions have been met—that is, when the parties have *performed* the requirements of the contract. However, not all contracts run their expected course. Both parties involved can agree to back out of a contract, for instance.

If one party fails to live up to the terms of the contract, its failure is called a **breach of contract**. The other party may have several options at that point, such as suing for damages (*litigation*) or pursuing *alternative dispute resolution*, including (1) attempting to negotiate and settle the situation privately; (2) entering into *mediation*, in which a neutral third party tries to get the disputing parties to reach a settlement; or (3) entering into *arbitration*, in which the disputing parties agree (or are required by a court) to let a neutral third party decide how the situation should be resolved.[13]

To control the increasing costs of litigation, many companies have turned to mediation and arbitration. For example, the contracts that consumers enter into with banks, credit card companies, and mobile phone carriers often specify *mandatory binding arbitration*, in which the disputing parties agree to be bound by the arbitrator's decision with no recourse to sue if they don't agree with it. Mandatory binding arbitration is controversial, because consumers have no choice whether to enter into these contracts (other than not buying the products or services in question, of course), they lose their right to sue, and many consumers aren't aware of what they are agreeing to.[14]

Warranties

The UCC specifies that sales and lease transactions involving tangible goods are a special kind of contract, even though they may not meet all the exact requirements of regular contracts. A key aspect of this contract is the notion of a **warranty**, a promise that a product being sold (or leased) will meet particular standards of quality and performance. If those standards aren't met, warranties give buyers legal recourse. Warranties can also have promotional value, as they offer some assurance to buyers that products will live up to sellers' claims.[15]

Express warranties are specific written statements. Courts may also enforce *implied warranties* that meet a variety of unwritten expectations, such as the expectation that food products are fit for human consumption.[16]

AGENCY

Individuals and businesses frequently engage others to act on their behalf, creating the legal concept of **agency**. Agency can come in three forms: *employer–employee*, *employer–independent contractor*, and *principal–agent*. Each of these relationships creates a different level of legal authority and responsibility. For example, a company can establish a principal–agent relationship with a corporate officer who is then empowered to enter into contracts on the company's behalf. To enact this type of agency, the principal must give written authority to the agent via a legal document known as *power of attorney*.[17]

PROPERTY TRANSACTIONS

Anyone interested in business must know the basics of property law, and the legal definition of property differs from the common usage of the term. **Property** is a *bundle of rights* conferred on owners, relative to all other persons. In other words, the law gives owners various rights that nonowners don't have, including the right to use, sell, donate, or destroy property.[18]

The law recognizes two distinct types of property: real and personal. **Real property** includes land, buildings and other permanent fixtures, minerals below the surface, plant life and water on the surface, and airspace above the surface. It can also include attached items within buildings, such as cabinetry.[19] **Personal property** is all property that is not real property, and it includes both tangible items (such as furniture, equipment, and jewelry) and intangible items (such as bank accounts, insurance policies, and customer lists).[20]

Two types of documents are important in obtaining real property for factory, office, or store space: a deed and a lease. A **deed** is a legal document by which an owner transfers the *title*, or right of ownership, to real property to a new owner.[21] A **lease** is used for a temporary transfer of the right to possess and use real or personal property in exchange for regular payments.[22]

REAL-TIME UPDATES
Learn More by Visiting This Website

Legal advice for small businesses

The Small Business Administration offers free information on some of the key topics in business law. Go to **real-timeupdates.com/bia9** and select Learn More in the Students section.

PATENTS, TRADEMARKS, AND COPYRIGHTS

Several forms of legal protection are available for **intellectual property (IP)**, which refers to intangible property that is created through mental effort and imagination. IP includes inventions, designs, literary works, artistic works, patents, and logos.[23] Three types of IP of particular concern to business are patents, trademarks, and copyrights.

Patents

A **patent** protects the invention or discovery of a new and useful process, an article of manufacture, a machine, a chemical composition, a new variety of plant, or an improvement on any of these. In the United States, patents are issued by the U.S. Patent and Trademark Office (USPTO). U.S. law grants the owner of a patent the exclusive right to make, use, or sell an invention for a certain number of years, depending on the type of patent and when it was filed.[24] After the specified time, the patented design becomes available for common use.

Patent law attempts to balance the rights of creators with the common good. By giving creators the exclusive right to benefit from their designs for a relatively long period of time, the law encourages people to devise new devices and processes. And by placing a limit on that exclusivity, the law also allows others in society to eventually benefit from and potentially improve upon the original concepts.

Trademarks

A *trademark* is any word, name, symbol, or device used to distinguish the product of one manufacturer from those made by others. A service mark is the same thing for services, although "trademark" is commonly used for both purposes.[25] The McDonald's golden arches and Nike's "swoosh" are two of the most visible modern trademarks. Brand names can also be registered as trademarks.

If properly registered and periodically renewed as required by the USPTO, a trademark generally belongs to its owner forever. However, as Chapter 13 notes, some terms that were once legally protected brand names have become *generic*, meaning that they describe a whole class of products. A brand name trademark can become a generic term if the trademark has been allowed to expire, if it has been incorrectly used by its owner, or if the public comes to equate the name with the class of products.[26] Laws also protect *trade dress*, the general appearance or image of a product, as long as the trade dress is both distinctive and nonfunctional.[27]

Copyrights

Copyrights protect the creators of literary, dramatic, musical, artistic, scientific, and other intellectual works. Any printed, filmed, or recorded material can be copyrighted. The copyright gives its owner the exclusive right to reproduce, sell, or adapt the work he or she has created. The U.S. Copyright Office will issue a copyright to the creator or to whomever the creator has granted the right to reproduce the work. (A book, for example, may be copyrighted by the author or

In addition to trademarks, companies can seek legal protection for trade dress, which can be everything from the shape of containers to the color of packages.

the publisher.) The length of time that copyright protection lasts depends on the circumstances of a work's creation and publication. For example, for works created by an individual after 1978, copyright lasts for the duration of the creator's life plus 70 years.[28]

The ability to reproduce and transmit materials digitally has vastly complicated the interpretation and enforcement of copyright law, and several key laws have been passed in the United States to protect content creators. One of the most important of these laws, the Digital Millennium Copyright Act (DMCA), remains controversial two decades after its passage. Critics of the DMCA, such as the Electronic Frontier Foundation (EFF), say its *digital rights management* provision goes too far, restricting free expression, limiting fair use of purchased rights, and restraining competition and innovation. However, the EFF and others also argue that the DCMA's *safe harbor* provision, which protects internet service providers from legal liability for content posted by users, has enabled the growth of popular services (including YouTube and Google) that millions of people use every day.[29]

REAL-TIME UPDATES
Learn More by Visiting This Website

The EFF's position on the DCMA

See what the Electronic Frontier Foundation has to say about the Digital Millennium Copyright Act. Go to **real-timeupdates.com/bia9** and select Learn More in the Students section.

NEGOTIABLE INSTRUMENTS

A **negotiable instrument** is a transferable document that represents a promise to pay a specified amount. *Negotiable* in this sense means that it can be sold or used as payment of a debt; an *instrument* is simply a written document that expresses a legal agreement. Negotiable instruments include personal and business checks, certificates of deposit, promissory notes, and commercial paper. Negotiable instruments serve several important purposes: substituting for money, extending credit (in some instances), and providing a record of a transaction.[30]

BANKRUPTCY

When individuals or companies are unable to meet their financial obligations, they have the option of pursuing **bankruptcy** protection to gain some measure of relief from creditors. The federal Bankruptcy Code provides for several types of bankruptcies, each of which is identified by the chapter of the code in which it is described. The three most common forms are[31]

- **Chapter 7 bankruptcy.** In this type of bankruptcy, the debtor's *nonexempt* property is sold, and the proceeds are used to repay creditors, whose claims are then permanently settled. Any money that debtors earn after settlement is theirs to keep, even if the settlement does not fully pay off the debt. Debtors can keep a limited amount of *exempt* property, including clothes and items used in a debtor's trade.[32]

- **Chapter 11 bankruptcy.** In this type of bankruptcy, the debtor is allowed a period of time to reorganize and reestablish financial viability. Chapter 11 protection is sought most frequently by companies, rather than individuals, and usually with the intent to modify capital structures in order to lessen the burden of debt payments.

- **Chapter 13 bankruptcy.** In this type of bankruptcy, individuals who have regular incomes but are unable to meet their recurring debt payments can negotiate new payment plans with their creditors.

TEST YOUR KNOWLEDGE

Questions for Review

A-1. What are the three types of U.S. laws, and how do they differ from one another?

A-2. What is the difference between negligence and intentional torts?

A-3. What are the elements of a valid contract?

A-4. What is intellectual property?

A-5. What criteria must an instrument meet to be negotiable?

Questions for Analysis

A-6. What is precedent, and how does it affect common law?

A-7. What does the concept of strict product liability mean to businesses?

A-8. Why is agency important to business?

A-9. How can intellectual property rights help spur innovation?

A-10. **Ethical Considerations.** Should products that can be used in the commission of a crime be declared illegal? For example, DVD burners can be used to make illegal copies of movies pirated from the internet. Why wouldn't the government simply ban such devices?

Writing Assignments

A-11. Should individual employees or managers of a corporation be penalized (through fines or imprisonment) if they are responsible when their companies commit illegal acts? For example, if a company is fined for polluting, should the people who authorized and carried out the pollution be fined as well? Why or why not?

A-12. Would musicians, artists, writers, and inventors continue to create if they had no patent or copyright protection? Explain your answer.

APPENDIX A GLOSSARY

administrative law Rules, regulations, and interpretations of statutory law set forth by administrative agencies and commissions.

agency A business relationship in which one party engages another to act on its behalf; various forms of agency exist.

bankruptcy A legal procedure that grants indebted persons or businesses permanent or temporary relief from debts in order to regain financial viability.

breach of contract Failure to live up to the terms of a contract, with no legal excuse.

business law The elements of law that directly influence or control business activities.

common law Laws based on the precedents established by judges' decisions.

consent order A settlement in which an individual or organization promises to discontinue some illegal activity without admitting guilt.

consideration A negotiated exchange that is necessary to make a contract legally binding.

contract A legally enforceable exchange of promises between two or more parties.

damages Financial compensation to an injured party for loss and suffering.

deed A legal document by which an owner transfers the title, or ownership rights, to real property to a new owner.

express contracts Contracts articulated in written or spoken language.

implied contracts Contracts derived from actions or conduct.

intellectual property (IP) Intangible property that is created through mental effort and imagination; includes inventions, designs, literary works, artistic works, patents, and logos.

intentional tort A willful act that results in injury.

lease A legal document used to temporarily transfer the right to possess and use real or personal property in exchange for regular payments.

negligence A tort in which a party failed to exercise a reasonable amount of care to protect others from risk of injury.

negotiable instrument A transferable document that represents a promise to pay a specified amount.

patent The right granted to inventors to exclusively make, use, or sell an invention or design for a certain number of years; after the patent expires, others may create products using that design.

personal property All property that is not real property.

product liability The capacity of a product to cause harm or damage for which the producer or seller is held accountable.

property A bundle of rights conferred on owners, relative to all other persons.

real property Land, buildings and other permanent fixtures, minerals below the surface, plant life and water on the surface, and airspace above the surface.

statutory law Statutes, or laws, created by legislatures.

strict liability Liability for injury caused by a product or process even when all reasonable care was used in its manufacture, distribution, or sale; no fault is assigned.

tort A noncriminal act, other than breach of contract, that results in injury to a person or to property.

Uniform Commercial Code (UCC) A set of laws designed to standardize business transactions across all 50 states.

warranty A promise that a product being sold (or leased) will meet particular standards of quality and performance.

ENDNOTES

1. Henry Cheeseman, *Business Law*, 9th ed. (New York: Pearson, 2016), 189.
2. "Administrative Law," Cornell Law School, Legal Information Institute, June 2017, www.law.cornell.edu.
3. Nancy K. Kubasek, Bartley A. Brennan, and M. Neil Browne, *The Legal Environment of Business*, 8th ed. (New York: Pearson, 2017), 490.
4. Cheeseman, *Business Law, 10*.
5. Jenni Bergal, "'Business Courts' Take on Complex Corporate Conflicts," Pew Charitable Trusts, 28 October 2015, www.pewtrusts.org.
6. Cheeseman, *Business Law*, 95.
7. Kubasek, Brennan, and Browne, *The Legal Environment of Business*, 309.
8. Kubasek, Brennan, and Browne, *The Legal Environment of Business*, 184.
9. Cheeseman, *Business Law*, 117.
10. Kimberly Kindy, "House GOP Quietly Advances Key Elements of Tort Reform," *Washington Post*, 9 March 2017, www.washingtonpost.com.
11. Cheeseman, *Business Law*, 193–194; Kubasek, Brennan, and Browne, *The Legal Environment of Business, 253.*
12. Kubasek, Brennan, and Browne, *The Legal Environment of Business*, 258–270; Cheeseman, *Business Law*, 188.
13. Kubasek, Brennan, and Browne, *The Legal Environment of Business*, 77.
14. "Mandatory Binding Arbitration," *Investopedia*, accessed 11 June 2018, www.investopedia.com.
15. Kubasek, Brennan, and Browne, *The Legal Environment of Business*, 342; Cheeseman, *Business Law*, 357.
16. Cheeseman, *Business Law*, 358.
17. Cheeseman, *Business Law*, 488–489; Kubasek, Brennan, and Browne, *The Legal Environment of Business*, 413.
18. Kubasek, Brennan, and Browne, *The Legal Environment of Business*, 361.
19. Cheeseman, *Business Law*, 799.
20. Cheeseman, *Business Law*, 783.
21. "Deed," Law.com, accessed 14 June 2018, dictionary.law.com.
22. Cheeseman, *Business Law*, 319.
23. "What Is Intellectual Property?" World Intellectual Property Organization, accessed 14 June 2018, www.wipo.int.
24. "General Information Concerning Patents," U.S. Patent and Trademark Office, October 2015, www.uspto.gov; Cheeseman, *Business Law*, 138.
25. *Protecting Your Trademark*, U.S. Patent and Trademark Office, May 2016.
26. Mary Beth Quirk, "15 Product Trademarks That Have Become Victims of Genericization," *Consumerist*, 19 July 2014, consumerist.com.
27. "Trade Dress Law," *The Fashion Law*, 19 September 2016, www.thefashionlaw.com.
28. "How Long Does Copyright Protection Last?" U.S. Copyright Office, accessed 14 June 2018, www.copyright.gov; Cheeseman, *Business Law*, 139.
29. "Digital Millennium Copyright Act," Electronic Frontier Foundation, accessed 14 June 2018, www.eff.org; Kubasek, Brennan, and Browne, *The Legal Environment of Business*, 400.
30. Cheeseman, *Business Law*, 371.
31. "Bankruptcy Basics," Third Edition, United States Courts, November 2011, www.uscourts.gov.
32. Kubasek, Brennan, and Browne, *The Legal Environment of Business*, 748.

Risk Management

The Business of Risk

All businesses face the risk of loss. Fire, lawsuits, accidents, network hacks, natural disasters, theft, illness, disability, interest rate changes, credit freezes, contract defaults, and the deaths or departures of key employees can devastate any business if it is not prepared. Misjudging or mismanaging risks can damage careers, companies, and entire economies.

UNDERSTANDING RISK AND LOSS EXPOSURE

Although a formal definition of **risk** is the variation in possible outcomes of an event, business managers charged with managing risk often speak in terms of **loss exposure**, defined as "any situation or circumstance in which a loss is possible, regardless of whether a loss actually occurs."[1] This concept is helpful because it explains why people purchase **insurance**, a contractual arrangement whereby one party agrees to compensate another party for losses.

In business, **risk management** is a systematic approach to recognizing, evaluating, and addressing loss exposures to ensure that a company can continue to meet its objectives.[2] The practice of risk management has evolved over the years, and many companies now take a comprehensive view of risk that covers every threat from regulatory changes to economic and political upheaval. This broader view is known as *enterprise risk management*.[3]

Companies face a wide variety of risks, so careful risk management is a vital step in ensuring business continuity.

REAL-TIME UPDATES
Learn More by Visiting This Website

Get the latest news on risk management and career insights
Read *Risk Management* magazine, published by the Risk Management Society. Go to **real-timeupdates.com/bia9** and select Learn More in the Students section.

In many ways, the decisions that risk managers make are similar to the decisions you make in your personal life. Backing up the files on your digital devices, buying health insurance, and putting some money aside in an emergency fund are just a few of the risk-management decisions that you face in your own life. In all these situations, you must decide how to balance the time or money required to minimize your loss exposure with the potential benefits of doing so.

Just as you do, businesses face different types of risk, and these entail different types of risk-management responses. **Speculative risk** refers to exposures that offer the prospect of making a profit or loss—such as spending money to develop new products or investing in stock. **Pure risk**, on the other hand, is the threat of loss without the possibility of gain.[4] Disasters such as an earthquake or a fire at a manufacturing plant are examples of pure risk.

An **insurable risk** is one that meets certain requirements in order for an insurer to provide protection, whereas an **uninsurable risk** is one that an insurance company will not cover (see Exhibit B.1). Generally speaking, most speculative risks are not insurable, but many pure risks are. For example, most insurance companies are unwilling to cover potential losses that can occur from general economic conditions such as a recession (although strategies such as financial hedging might help in such scenarios).

Of course, just because a particular risk is theoretically insurable doesn't mean a firm will be able to get—or afford—insurance coverage for it. Insurers carefully evaluate the nature of specific loss exposures to determine whether insuring against them will be profitable and at what price. Insurance companies are able to stay in business only if the amounts they pay out in **claims** (customer demands to pay for insured losses) are less than the **insurance premiums** (fees paid by customers to get insurance) they collect. As a simple example, a property insurance company can't survive if it takes in $10 million in premiums every year but 20 or 30 customers lose $1 million buildings every year.

curraheeshutter/Shutterstock

EXHIBIT B.1	Insurable and Uninsurable Risk

Some of the risks that businesses and individuals face are insurable, but many others aren't.

Generally Insurable	Generally Uninsurable
Property risks: Uncertainty surrounding the occurrence of loss from perils that cause	**Market risks:** Factors that may result in loss of property or income, such as
1. Direct loss of property	1. Price changes, both seasonal and cyclical
2. Loss of use of or benefits of property	2. Consumer indifference
	3. Style changes
Personal risks: Uncertainty surrounding the occurrence of loss due to	4. Increased competition
1. Premature death	**Political risks:** Uncertainty surrounding the occurrence of
2. Physical disability	1. Overthrow of a government
3. Old age	2. Restrictions imposed on free trade
	3. Unreasonable or punitive taxation
Legal liability risks: Uncertainty surrounding the occurrence of loss arising out of	4. Restrictions of free exchange of currencies
1. Use of automobiles	**Production risks:** Uncertainties surrounding the occurrence of
2. Occupancy of buildings	1. Failure of machinery to function economically
3. Employment	2. Failure to solve technical problems
4. Manufacture of products	3. Exhaustion of raw-material resources
5. Professional misconduct	4. Strikes, absenteeism, and labor unrest
	Personal risks: Uncertainty surrounding the occurrence of
	1. Unemployment
	2. Poverty from factors such as divorce, lack of education or opportunity, and loss of health from military service

ASSESSING RISK

One of the first steps in managing risk is to identify the source of the threat. Some types of exposures are common to all businesses, such as fires, floods, and the death of key personnel. Other risks vary from industry to industry. For example, financial firms must assess *credit risk* (the risk that borrowers will not repay loans), *market risk* (the risk that investments will lose value), and *operational risk* (the risk that anything from computer hackers to hurricanes will disrupt trading operations). Manufacturers have many of these loss exposures as well, plus such added risks as product liability and inventory losses during storage or transportation. Retailers worry about *shrinkage*, the loss of inventory as a result of shoplifting or internal theft. Medical firms face the possibility of lawsuits from *malpractice* claims.

Risk managers also need to understand the breadth or extent of a risk, because this determines how much control they have—if any. Some risks are confined within or are unique to a single company, whereas some are spread across an entire industry or the economy as a whole. For instance, a trucking company with an aging fleet of trucks in poor repair faces a unique degree of risk of service interruptions and accidents, but all trucking companies face the risk of higher fuel costs.

Companies (and individuals) can also be at risk from the actions of other companies. This is a particular concern in the financial sector, where the actions of a single company or group of companies can threaten the entire economy, a condition known as **systemic risk**.[5] During the Great Recession of 2008–2009, for example, the failure of a relatively small number of financial firms helped trigger a global financial crisis that harmed millions of companies and individuals who had nothing to do with risky and arcane financial dealings that brought those companies down.

(A note on terminology: You may encounter different usages of *systemic*. In addition to the sense in the previous paragraph, of a single entity endangering a broader market or economy, *systemic* can refer to financial risk that cannot be reduced by diversifying an investment portfolio.[6] Further complicating the issue, this type of market risk is sometimes called *systematic*, rather than *systemic*.[7])

Finally, managers need to estimate the *probability* that a potential threat could become real and the magnitude of its *impact* if it does become real. For example, chemical spills are much more likely in facilities that use chemicals in processing or manufacturing than in facilities that use chemicals only for cleaning. And the impact of spilling a gallon of cleaning fluid is obviously less severe than the impact of a train derailment that spills the contents of a tanker car.

After managers have characterized a potential for risk, they have three possible responses:

- Accept the risk and go on with business as usual, which can be a reasonable response for low-probability, low-impact risks
- Take steps to control the risk
- Shift some or all of the responsibility for the risk to a third party

Combining the last two steps, controlling and shifting risk, is common.

CONTROLLING RISK

If a risk is controllable and significant enough to warrant attention, managers can use a number of *risk-control techniques* to minimize the organization's losses:[8]

- **Risk avoidance.** A risk manager might try to eliminate the chance of a particular type of loss, such as when a bank chooses not to lend money to new companies that haven't yet proven their ability to sustain profitable sales. The implication of risk avoidance is that it can mean not pursuing particular business opportunities—but that isn't always a bad thing.

- **Loss prevention.** Companies can take steps to reduce the *chances* of particular losses by removing hazards or taking preventive measures. Security guards at banks, warnings on medicines and dangerous chemicals, and safety locks are examples of physical loss-prevention measures. Banks can use tighter lending standards to prevent instances of loan defaults.

- **Loss reduction.** Acknowledging that it's impossible to prevent all losses, companies can take steps to reduce the *severity* of losses that do occur, such as installing fire suppression systems to contain the spread of any fires that may break out.

- **Duplication.** Companies can duplicate key resources in order to keep running in the event that something happens to the primary resources. Examples include keeping backup copies of important records (printed and digital) and installing a second set of production machinery that can be switched over to if the primary set fails.

- **Separation.** Companies can reduce the risk of catastrophic losses by dividing key resources and keeping parts in separate locations. A company might store its products in two separate warehouses, for instance, or spread its cash accounts across several banks.

- **Diversification.** Finally, companies can reduce their reliance on any one source of revenue or capital growth by *diversifying*. For example, a small firm with only a few regular customers is at risk of losing significant revenue if one customer drops out. By diversifying its customer base, it can reduce its reliance on any single customer.

SHIFTING RISK TO A THIRD PARTY

If a company can't prevent or reduce potential losses to an acceptable level, the next option is to *finance* the risk by paying another company to assume part or all of it. You do the same thing when you buy an insurance policy for your car: You're paying an insurance company to hold the risk of losses caused by thefts or accidents. (Companies can shift risk in a variety of ways; this appendix focuses primarily on the use of insurance.)

Insurance companies don't count on making a profit on any particular policy, nor do they count on paying for a single policyholder's losses out of the premium paid by that particular policyholder. Rather, the insurance company pays for

EXHIBIT B.2	Business Risks and Protection

Here are some of the most common types of business insurance.

Risk	Protection
Loss of property	
Due to destruction or theft	Fire insurance Disaster insurance Marine insurance Automobile insurance
Due to dishonesty or nonperformance	Fidelity bonding Surety bonding Credit life insurance Crime insurance
Loss of income	Business interruption insurance Extra-expense insurance
Liability	Comprehensive general liability insurance Automobile liability insurance Workers' compensation insurance Umbrella liability insurance Professional liability insurance
Loss of services of key personnel	Key person insurance

a loss by drawing the money out of the pool of funds it has received from all its policyholders in the form of premiums. In this way, the insurance company redistributes the cost of predicted losses from a single individual or company to a large number of policies. To determine premium amounts, insurers rely on **actuaries**—loss-assessment specialists who compile statistics of losses to determine how much income insurance companies need to generate from premiums in order to pay likely claims over a given period.[9]

The types of insurance that a company needs depend on the nature of the business and its ability to withstand specific types of losses. Most companies protect themselves against the loss of property, loss of income, liability, and loss of services of key personnel (see Exhibit B.2).

Property Insurance

Property insurance covers physical damage, destruction, or theft of company property. Policies vary in how much funding is provided. *Replacement-cost coverage* provides enough money to replace or restore property, without any reductions for depreciation in the property's value since it was put into service. In contrast, *actual cash value coverage* pays only what the property is currently worth, as determined by depreciation, fair market value, or expert evaluation.[10]

Business Interruption Insurance

In addition to the direct losses they inflict, fires, floods, criminal acts, and other events can cause significant indirect losses if they disrupt business operations. To get some level of reimbursement for lost revenue while operations are being restored, companies can often purchase **business interruption insurance**, also known as *business income insurance*. These policies can also cover external events, such as disruptions in raw material shipments from a key supplier.[11]

Liability Insurance

A variety of **liability insurance** policies are available to protect against *liability losses*, financial losses that occur when companies or their employees are found to be responsible for damage or injury to another party (which can include a company's own employees). Here are some of the most common types of liability insurance:

- *Commercial general liability* policies provide financial protection in the event a company is sued for damaging property or causing injury. General liability policies often have exclusions that require companies to purchase additional types of policies if they want comprehensive coverage.[12]

- *Product-liability coverage* provides financial protection in the event that a company's products cause injury, disease, or death. Claims can result from defects in design, packaging, materials, labeling, safety warnings, and user instructions.[13]

- *Professional liability insurance*, sometimes known as *malpractice insurance* or *errors and omissions insurance*, covers people who might be found liable for professional negligence. This insurance applies to specialties such as accounting and medicine, as well as top management in public corporations. To protect corporate officers and members of corporate boards from lawsuits stemming from claims of mismanagement, companies can purchase *directors' and officers' liability insurance*, often called *D&O insurance*.[14]

- Finally, businesses sometimes purchase *commercial umbrella insurance* to get additional coverage beyond the payout limits of their other liability policies.[15]

REAL-TIME UPDATES
Learn More by Visiting This Website

Understand the options for business insurance

Take a look at the most common types of insurance policies used in business risk management. Go to **real-timeupdates.com/bia9** and select Learn More in the Students section.

Key Person Insurance

If an employee or executive is essential to a company's ability to generate revenue, the firm can purchase **key person insurance** to cushion the financial blow of losing that person's services in the event of death, disability, or unexpected departure. Of course, if a person is that essential to the company, the management team should also take steps to have potential replacements ready to step in if needed.[16]

SELF-INSURING AGAINST RISK

Rather than finance risk through a third party, companies sometimes choose to address risk through **self-insurance**, which attempts to replicate at least part of the coverage that would normally be provided by an independent insurer. For instance, most large U.S. employers self-insure their employee health plans, and a smaller but growing percentage of small and midsize firms now do as well.[17]

Companies can self-insure in several ways, including setting aside a portion of each year's income in a risk-management fund or opening a line of credit to be used for risk management.[18] Importantly, self-insurance is not the same as *no* insurance, which occurs when a company either fails to recognize a loss exposure or chooses not to insure against it.

Insuring the Health and Well-Being of Employees

In addition to protecting company property and assets, many businesses look out for the well-being of employees by providing them with health, disability, workers' compensation, and life insurance coverage. Disease and disability may cost employees huge sums of money unless they are insured. In addition, death carries the threat of financial hardship for an employee's family.

HEALTH INSURANCE

Many employers have long offered health insurance as an employee benefit, and the Affordable Care Act now mandates that all companies with 50 or more full-time employees provide some level of health insurance. Most employee health insurance involves *managed plans*, which attempt to balance high-quality care with careful cost management.[19]

Roughly half of employees with employer-sponsored health insurance are in **preferred-provider organizations (PPOs)**, health-care providers that contract with employers, insurance companies, or other third-party payers to deliver health-care services to employees. The "preferred providers" are medical specialists and medical facilities that have opted to join that particular PPO network. Employees generally aren't required to use in-network providers, but they pay more for using out-of-network services.[20]

The second-most common type of managed plans, covering about one-third of U.S. employees who get coverage through work, are **high-deductible health plans**. As their name suggests, these plans carry relatively high *deductibles*, which are the annual costs that employees must pay out of pocket before their insurance coverage kicks in. These plans vary in terms of features and costs, but a feature common to all is a **health savings account (HSA)**, which allows people to save a portion of their earnings in a special account that can be used for major medical expenses when needed. Contributions to HSAs are tax deductible, and any interest or investment gains in an HSA are tax-free as well.[21]

The third most-common type of managed plans are **health maintenance organizations (HMOs)**, which are prepaid group plans in which members pay a set fee and, in return, receive many services as needed either for no additional cost or for a modest copayment. Unlike PPOs, HMOs require patients to use the organization's doctors and facilities, but the trade-off for the loss of flexibility is lower costs. To keep operating costs low, HMOs usually place a high priority on wellness and disease prevention.[22]

DISABILITY INCOME AND WORKERS' COMPENSATION INSURANCE

Two forms of insurance exist to help employees who are temporarily or permanently unable to work. **Disability income insurance** replaces a portion of an employee's income, typically up to 60 or 70 percent. The length and type of coverage vary widely. Some policies are designed only for short-term disabilities, whereas others provide benefits for a number of years. Policies also vary in terms of how they define disability, such as whether your disability prohibits you from continuing in your current profession but does not prevent you from finding employment in a different profession.[23]

In contrast to disability insurance, which can be provided as part of an employer's overall health insurance package or purchased by individuals, **workers' compensation insurance** programs are administered by state governments. The intent of "workers' comp" is to replace some portion of an employee's income and to pay for medical costs if he or she is unable to work as the result of a job-related accident or illness.[24]

LIFE INSURANCE

Life insurance provides financial support to selected beneficiaries (such as spouses and children) in the event of a person's death. Some employers include life insurance in their benefits packages, and many people buy policies on their own as well. The range of life insurance products is quite varied; the two basic categories are *term life* and *whole life*:

- The simplest form of life insurance, **term life insurance**, offers coverage for a specific period of time—the *term* of the policy. Unlike other types of life insurance, term life is insurance only, with no savings or investment components. Term life is usually the least expensive for younger buyers, but it can become prohibitively expensive for older individuals who need significant amounts of coverage. A smart use of term life is investing the money you save (compared to other insurance policies) so that by the time the term is up, you have accumulated enough assets to protect your loved ones without relying on life insurance.[25]
- **Whole life insurance** differs from term in two important ways: It provides coverage until the insured person dies, and part of the premiums paid accumulates in a savings plan. The policyholder can borrow against this amount or cash in the policy, if needed.[26]
- **Universal life insurance** is a combination life insurance and investment product, in which customers purchase an insurance policy and invest additional funds. The combination of insurance and investments gives customers some flexibility in the amount and frequency of premiums and the size of the death benefits.[27]

TEST YOUR KNOWLEDGE

Questions for Review

B-1. What is the difference between pure risk and speculative risk?

B-2. What is risk management?

B-3. What is enterprise risk management?

B-4. What are the three steps to controlling risk?

B-5. What is the difference between workers' compensation insurance and disability income insurance?

Questions for Analysis

B-6. Why might governments be interested in monitoring and managing systemic risk?

B-7. Is self-insurance the same as going without insurance? Why or why not?

B-8. Why is it a good idea to purchase business interruption insurance?

B-9. Does every worker or consumer need life insurance? Why or why not?

B-10. **Ethical Considerations.** Life insurance can be one of the most complex purchases a consumer ever makes. It is also an expensive purchase and often sold by salespeople working on commission, which means they are motivated to make the sale. Whose responsibility is it to make sure purchasers understand the options available to them and understand all the details and ramifications of the specific policies they choose? Why?

Writing Assignments

B-11. Should employers be required to provide some level of health insurance to their employees? If not, how should employees get coverage?

B-12. Is the chance that a new product might fail in the marketplace an insurable risk? Why or why not?

APPENDIX B GLOSSARY

actuaries Risk analysts employed by insurance companies to forecast expected losses and to calculate the cost of premiums.

business interruption insurance Insurance that covers losses resulting from temporary business disruptions.

claims Demands for payments from an insurance company based on the terms in an insurance policy.

disability income insurance Short-term or long-term insurance that replaces some of the income lost when an individual is unable to perform his or her work as a result of illness or injury.

health maintenance organizations (HMOs) Prepaid medical plans in which consumers pay a set fee to receive a full range of medical care from a group of medical practitioners.

health savings account (HSA) Special savings account that allows employees to save a portion of their earnings to use for medical expenses when needed.

high-deductible health plans Health plans that carry relatively high deductibles and are therefore able to offer coverage at lower monthly cost.

insurable risk Risk that an insurance company might be willing to cover.

insurance A contractual arrangement whereby one party agrees to compensate another party for losses.

insurance premiums Fees that insured parties pay insurers for coverage against losses.

key person insurance Insurance that provides a business with funds to compensate for the loss of a key employee by unplanned retirement, resignation, death, or disability.

liability insurance Policies that protect against *liability losses*—financial losses that occur when companies or their employees are found to be responsible for damage or injury to another party.

life insurance Insurance that provides financial support to selected beneficiaries in the event of a person's death.

loss exposure Areas of risk in which a potential for loss exists.

preferred-provider organizations (PPOs) Health-care providers offering reduced-rate contracts to groups that agree to obtain medical care through the providers' organization.

property insurance Insurance that covers physical damage, destruction, or theft of company property.

pure risk Risk that involves the chance of loss only; compare with *speculative risk*.

risk management A systematic approach to recognizing, evaluating, and addressing loss exposures to ensure that a company can continue to meet its objectives.

risk The variation in possible outcomes of an event; risk managers typically think in terms of *loss exposure*.

self-insurance A financial protection strategy in which a company funds its own ability to pay for potential losses on its own, rather than purchasing insurance coverage.

speculative risk Risk that involves the chance of both loss and profit; compare with *pure risk*.

systemic risk Situation in which the actions of a single company or group of companies can threaten the entire economy.

term life insurance Life insurance that provides death benefits for a specified period.

uninsurable risk Risk that few, if any, insurance companies will assume because it cannot be covered profitably.

universal life insurance A combination life insurance and investment product in which customers purchase an insurance policy and invest additional funds.

whole life insurance Insurance that provides both death benefits and savings for the insured's lifetime.

workers' compensation insurance Insurance that partially replaces lost income and that pays for employees' medical costs and rehabilitation expenses for work-related injuries.

ENDNOTES

1. George E. Rejda and Michael J. McNamara, *Principles of Risk Management and Insurance*, 13th ed. (New York: Pearson, 2017), 48.

2. "About Risk Management," Institute of Risk Management, accessed 10 June 2018, www.theirm.org; Rejda and McNamara, *Principles of Risk Management and Insurance*, 48.

3. "What Is ERM?" Risk Management Association, accessed 10 June 2018, www.rmahq.org.

4. Rejda and McNamara, *Principles of Risk Management and Insurance*, 6.

5. Rejda and McNamara, *Principles of Risk Management and Insurance*, 6.

6. "Unique vs. Systemic Risk," NASDAQ, accessed 16 June 2018, www.nasdaq.com.

7. "Systematic and Unsystematic Risk," *Investopedia*, accessed 16 June 2016, www.investopedia.com.

8. Rejda and McNamara, *Principles of Risk Management and Insurance*, 50–51.

9. Rejda and McNamara, *Principles of Risk Management and Insurance*, 109.

10. "Actual Cash Value (ACV)," International Risk Management Institute, accessed 16 June 2018, www.irmi.com.

11. "Business Interruption Insurance: 8 Terms to Help You Understand What Is Covered," Marsh, accessed 16 June 2018, www.marsh.com; "Loss of Income Insurance Helps Pay Bills and Cover Payroll If Your Business Is Interrupted," Nationwide, accessed 16 June 2018, www.nationwide.com.

12. Rejda and McNamara, *Principles of Risk Management and Insurance*, 578.

13. "Product Liability, Recall and Contamination Insurance," Insurance Information Institute, accessed 16 June 2018, www.iii.org.

14. Rejda and McNamara, *Principles of Risk Management and Insurance*, 30.

15. "What Is Commercial Umbrella Insurance?" The Hartford, accessed 16 June 2018, www.thehartford.com.

16. "Key Person Insurance," *Entrepreneur*, accessed 16 June 2018, www.entrepreneur.com.

17. Stephen Miller, "More Small and Midsize Firms Choose to Self-Insure," Society for Human Resource Management, 29 July 2016, www.shrm.org.

18. Rejda and McNamara, *Principles of Risk Management and Insurance*, 51.

19. Rejda and McNamara, *Principles of Risk Management and Insurance*, 335.

20. Les Masterson, "What Is the Difference Between HMO, PPO, HDHP, POS, EPO?" Insurance.com, 24 October 2017, www.insurance.com; "Preferred Provider Organization (PPO)," Cigna, accessed 16 June 2018, www.cigna.com; Rejda and McNamara, *Principles of Risk Management and Insurance*, 335.

21. Masterson, "What Is the Difference Between HMO, PPO, HDHP, POS, EPO?"; Kimberly Lankford, "Know the Facts About Health Savings Plans," *Chicago Tribune*, 27 September 2013, www.chicagotribune.com.

22. Masterson, "What Is the Difference Between HMO, PPO, HDHP, POS, EPO?"; Rejda and McNamara, *Principles of Risk Management and Insurance*, 335.

23. Rejda and McNamara, *Principles of Risk Management and Insurance*, 318.

24. Rejda and McNamara, *Principles of Risk Management and Insurance*, 588.

25. Barbara Marquand, "The Differences Between Term and Whole Life Insurance," NerdWallet, 29 March 2017, www.nerdwallet.com; Rejda and McNamara, *Principles of Risk Management and Insurance*, 212.

26. Marquand, "The Differences Between Term and Whole Life Insurance."

27. Rejda and McNamara, *Principles of Risk Management and Insurance*, 217.

Information Technology

Information Systems

Even before the digital transformation discussed throughout this book began to reshape the practice of business, digital information played a vital role in business operations. As more and more functions rely on big data, analytics, and other data-intensive techniques, companies depend more than ever on information systems—technologies and processes that "create, collect, process, store, and distribute useful data."[1]

In any application, information represents one of the most intriguing challenges you'll face as both an employee and a manager. A company can find itself drowning in an ocean of data but struggling to find real insights that can mean the difference between success and failure.[2]

The first step in turning information into a competitive advantage is understanding the difference between **data** (recorded facts and statistics), **information** (useful knowledge, often extracted from data), and **insight** (a deep level of understanding about a particular situation). The transformation of data into insight requires a combination of technology, information-management strategies, creative thinking, and business experience (see Exhibit C.1). Companies that excel at this transformation have a huge advantage over their competitors. In fact, entire industries can be created when a single person looks at the same data and information that everyone else is looking at but sees things in a new way, yielding insights that no one has ever had before.

Businesses collect data from a wide array of sources—checkout scanners, website clicks, research projects, and Internet of Things sensors, to name just a few. A single customer order can generate hundreds of data points, from a credit card number to production statistics to accounting totals that end up on a tax form. Even a small business can quickly amass thousands or millions of individual data points; large companies generate billions and even trillions of data points.[3]

To keep all these data points under control and to extract useful information from them, companies rely on **databases**, computerized files that collect, sort, and cross-reference data. An ongoing challenge with information systems management is ensuring information quality, which can be defined as being *relevant* (directly pertinent to the recipient's needs), *accurate* (both current and free from errors), *timely* (delivered in time to make a difference), and *cost effective* (costs a reasonable amount of money compared to the value it offers).

HOW BUSINESSES USE INFORMATION

Companies invest heavily in information for the simple reason that they can't live without it. Here's a small sample of the ways managers rely on information:

- **Research and development.** In a sense, the cycle of information use starts with understanding customer needs and then moves to developing new goods and

---

EXHIBIT C.1 | **From Data to Information to Insight**

Businesses generate massive amounts of data, but a key challenge is transforming all those individual data points into useful information and then applying creative thinking (sometimes with the help of computers) to extract deeper insights from the information.

Zippy Motors monthly sales

	Econo Cruiser	Mega Cruiser	Hyper Cruiser	Total sales
Jan	1546	0	1205	2751
Feb	1602	0	1189	2791
Mar	1485	0	1195	2680
Apr	1537	0	1215	2752
May	1285	575	902	2762
Jun	1061	890	854	2805
Jul	804	1140	789	2733
Aug	723	1355	701	2779
Sep	612	1460	675	2747
Oct	495	1832	552	2879
Nov	366	2187	412	2965
Dec	397	2452	323	3172

"We thought the new Mega Cruiser, which we introduced in May, would find a new mid-market group of customers and expand our overall sales. However, it has mostly taken sales away from the Econo Cruiser on the low end and the Hyper Cruiser on the high end. Apparently, we misread customer needs."

Data | **Information** | **Insight**

services to meet those needs. Information is vital at every step, from researching markets to analyzing competitors to testing new products.

- **Planning and control.** Two of the most important functions of management are planning and control—deciding what to do and making sure it gets done. Accounting managers need accurate financial information, sales managers need to know if their teams are meeting their sales goals, human resource managers need to make sure the company has enough of the right kind of employees, and so on.
- **Marketing and sales.** Thanks to technology, marketing and sales have evolved from "gut-feel" activities to more scientific, information-driven functions. "Making Data-Driven Marketing Decisions" on page 358 in Chapter 12 discusses this development in more detail.
- **Communication and collaboration.** Throughout an organization, employees, managers, and teams rely on information to communicate and collaborate. In fact, information technology is changing the very definition of what an organization means, thanks to the internet's ability to connect people from every corner of the globe.

TYPES OF BUSINESS INFORMATION SYSTEMS

Over the years, the collective label for the technologies used to manage information has changed; what used to be called *data processing* is now called either *information systems (IS)* or *information technology (IT)*, depending on the context. The types of information systems used by a company generally fall into two major categories: (1) operational systems and (2) professional and managerial systems. (The specific systems you'll encounter in various companies are likely to have their own names, often arcane acronyms that make no sense to outsiders.) Some systems meet the information needs of people at specific levels in the organization, whereas *enterprise systems* are designed to connect everyone in the organization, giving each person the information he or she needs to meet specific job responsibilities.

Operational Systems

Operational systems are the "frontline" workhorses of IT, collecting and processing the data and information that represent the day-to-day work of the business enterprise. These systems typically support daily operations and decision-making for lower-level managers and supervisors:

- **Transaction processing systems.** Much of the daily flow of data into and out of the typical business organization, particularly regarding sales, is handled by a *transaction processing system (TPS)*, which captures and organizes raw data and converts these data into information.
- **Process and production control systems.** Operational systems are also used to make routine decisions that control operational processes. *Process control systems*

Nyul/Fotolia

Customer relationship management (CRM) systems help companies capture and organize all the interactions they have with their customers and then use that information to foster positive long-term relationships with customers.

monitor conditions such as temperature or pressure change in physical processes. *Production control systems* are used to manage the production of goods and services by controlling production lines, robots, and other machinery and equipment.

- **Office automation systems.** *Office automation systems* address a wide variety of typical office tasks. These systems range from a single personal computer with word-processing software to *collaboration platforms* that help teams and departments collaborate on work projects.
- **Customer relationship management systems.** As Chapter 12 notes, customer relationship management (CRM) systems capture, organize, and capitalize on all the interactions that a company has with its customers, from marketing surveys and advertising through sales orders and customer support. Companies continue to find ways to integrate social media into customer communication, too, such as using Twitter to answer customer support questions and offering coupons and other special deals on their Facebook pages.

Professional and Managerial Systems

In contrast to operational systems, *professional and managerial systems* help with such higher-level tasks as designing new products, analyzing financial data, identifying industry trends, and planning long-term business needs. These systems are used by professionals such as engineers and marketing specialists and by managers up to the top executive and board of directors. An important advance for many professionals is the idea of a *knowledge management (KM) system*, which collects the expertise of employees across an organization.

A **management information system (MIS)** provides managers with information and support for making routine decisions. (Note that *MIS* is sometimes used synonymously with both *IS* and *IT* to describe an overall IT effort.) An MIS takes data from a database and summarizes or restates it into useful information, such as monthly sales summaries, daily inventory levels, product manufacturing schedules, employee earnings, and so on.

Whereas an MIS typically provides structured, routine information for managerial decision-making, a *decision support system (DSS)* assists managers in solving highly unstructured and nonroutine problems through the use of decision models and specialized databases. Many of these now use artificial intelligence to perform predictive analytics and other decision-support tasks. *Business intelligence (BI) systems* constitute a range of research and analysis systems, particularly big data and analytics.

Information Systems Management Issues

As a business manager or entrepreneur, you'll be responsible for a variety of legal, ethical, and administrative issues that stem from the use of digital technologies, starting with the challenge of ensuring privacy and security.

ENSURING SECURITY AND PRIVACY

Linking computers and other devices via networking technology creates enormous benefits for businesses and consumers, but there are significant downsides to connecting everyone everywhere. Managers need to be constantly vigilant to make sure their information systems remain secure and that data on them remain private. In recent years, millions of employee and customer records have been stolen or exposed, and billions of dollars have been lost to damage from computer viruses. The estimated financial damage from computer-based crime is now more than a half-trillion dollars per year.[4]

REAL-TIME UPDATES
Learn More by Visiting This Website

The latest news on IT security

Info Security covers the latest threats and response strategies. Go to **real-timeupdates.com/bia9** and select Learn More in the Students section.

The collection, storage, and use of private information raises a host of legal and ethical issues that managers must consider:

- **Malicious software. Malware**, short for *malicious software*, is the term often applied to the diverse and growing collection of computer code designed to disrupt websites, take over computers and mobile devices, destroy information, or enable criminal activity. These threats go by a variety of names, including *viruses, worms, Trojan horses, spyware,* and *adware*. Criminals can even use the processing power of your computer to mine (create) bitcoin and other cryptocurrencies.[5] One of the nastiest malware is *ransomware*, which takes control of the file storage on a device; criminals then demand ransom payments and threaten to erase all the files unless they are paid.

- **Security breaches.** Any time a device is connected to a wired or wireless network, it becomes vulnerable to security breaches. Given the enormous value of information stored on business information systems, particularly credit card numbers and other personal data that can be used for identity theft, there is financial motivation for outsiders to break in and for insiders to sell out. The billions of Internet of Things devices now connected to home and business networks also represent a massive security risk. For example, in order to keep cost and power consumption down, many of these devices sacrifice security, making them vulnerable to hacking.[6]

- **Unauthorized software, services, and devices.** IT departments in many companies face a constant battle with employee use of unauthorized apps, online services, and personal digital devices. Employees expose their companies to security risks and potential legal liability if they download or transmit inappropriate content on company networks.

- **Social media.** Social media help companies create a more open communication environment for employees, customers, and other communities, but these technologies also create new system vulnerabilities.

- **Poor security planning and management.** Many viruses and worms are able to wreak their havoc and gain intruders access because device owners haven't kept their programs or apps up to date or haven't installed *firewalls*, hardware or software devices that block access to intruders. In other cases, companies commit major design blunders, such as creating easily hacked links between high-security financial systems and lower-security building control systems.

- **Lack of physical control.** Software controls and network security aren't enough. Some of the most egregious security lapses involve the loss or theft of mobile devices that contain sensitive data such as employee or customer records.

- **Employees' personal devices.** IT departments and managers must also have policies and procedures in place when employees want to connect their own computers, smartphones, and tablets to corporate information networks. These devices can present additional security risks because they don't always have the security controls that equipment designed or customized for business use have.

PERIODICALLY MEASURE YOUR PROGRESS

To make sure you're on track to meet your goals, get in the habit of periodically checking your progress. Is your net worth increasing? (It might still be moving up toward zero, but that's progress!) Are your expenses under control? However, don't obsess over your finances. Life's too short, and there are too many other pleasurable and productive ways to spend your time. You don't need to check your stock portfolio a dozen times a day or lie in bed every night dreaming up new ways to squeeze nickels and dimes out of your budget. After a while, you'll get a sense of how often you need to measure your progress to make sure you stay on track toward your goals. In general, check your income and expenses at least once a month to make sure you're staying within budget. For larger assets such as your house, you might want to verify approximate values once or twice a year.

However, don't put off checking your financial health for so long that you don't notice problems such as poorly performing investments or small expenses that have somehow ballooned into big expenses. If you're using a financial planner, don't wait for an annual statement. Find out where you stand at least once a quarter.

ADJUST YOUR GOALS AND PLANS AS NEEDED

At various points in your life, you'll find that your goals or your financial status have changed enough to require adjustments to your plan. Whenever you pass through one of life's major transitions, such as getting married, having children, changing jobs, or buying a house, you'll need to make some revisions. For instance, many first-time home buyers are surprised by the amount of money it takes to maintain a house, particularly a "fixer-upper" that needs a lot of work. To keep your income and expenses in balance, you may find you need to make sacrifices elsewhere in your budget.

If you're like most college students, you'll go through at least four major stages in your financial life: getting through college, establishing a financial foundation, building your net worth and preparing for life's major expenses, and planning for retirement. (If you're back in college after having been in the workforce for a while, your situation might vary.) The following sections give you an overview of the decisions to consider at each major stage in your life.

Life Stage 1: Getting Through College

With tuition and expenses rising rapidly these days, completing your education can be a mammoth struggle, to be sure. Costs are getting so high that some people are even beginning to wonder if the effort is worth it, particularly if you need to borrow heavily. Consider the eye-opening statistics discussed in the following sections and then think about your specific situation.

FINANCING YOUR EDUCATION

On the plus side, according to one survey, workers with a bachelor's degree earn on average more than double what people with only high school educations earn.[6] Over the course of a 40- or 45-year career, this difference can be huge.

However, that doesn't tell the whole story. First, this differential is only an average; a college education increases your chances of making more money, but it is by no means a guarantee. Quite a few people with only high school educations make more than people with college educations, and the income variations among graduates with different majors can be dramatic.[7]

Second, while you're in college, people who went to work right out of high school are already earning wages. By the time you graduate, those full-time workers who didn't go to college might be $100,000 or more ahead of you in cumulative earnings to that point.

Third, you're likely to be saddled with some debt when you graduate, setting you even further behind. With costs continuing to climb, more students are forced to borrow in ever-larger amounts to complete their education. Is it a good idea to borrow money to get through college? From a purely economic perspective, the only honest answer these days is that it depends. For starters, you need to compare education costs with potential income. Yes, a college education is likely to boost your income, and your education should ideally be about more than simply career training, but the reality of the situation is that your education needs to be paid for somehow. If you take on a lot of debt and need many years to pay off your student loans, you need to think about how doing that will affect your life plans.

Fourth, new research shows that many employers require a college degree even when the jobs they are hiring for don't require college-level education and many current employees in those positions don't have degrees.[8] In other words, a degree is becoming a baseline requirement for an increasing number of jobs.

The worst of all possible outcomes is borrowing a lot of money and then not getting your degree. This situation will saddle you with big loan payments *and* the likelihood of lower income. Once you commit to going for your degree, make sure you get it. Ask for advice—and help—if you need it. Many people find doing so uncomfortable or embarrassing, but you're almost guaranteed to regret it later if you don't ask for help now. Talk to a counselor in your school's financial aid office, and make sure you explore every available option for financial assistance. Ask friends and family members for advice. If you have a job, see whether your employer is willing to help with school expenses.

Our intent here isn't to scare you out of school or reduce a life-enhancing experience to mere dollars and cents, but rather to make sure you understand the reality of the situation so that you can make choices that are best for you, your family, and your future.

STAYING OUT OF THE CREDIT CARD BLACK HOLE

Speaking of borrowing, every college student needs to be aware of the dangers of credit card debt. Far too many students dig themselves into giant holes with such debt. If you find yourself in this situation, don't panic—but stop digging any deeper. Your first step to recovery is to recognize that you're at a make-or-break point in both your college career and your life as a whole. No amount of extracurricular fun is worth the damage that a credit card mess can inflict on your life. Excessive credit card debt from college can follow you for decades and severely limit your financial options.

Don't assume that you can easily pay off those balances when you start working, either. Recent graduates entering the workforce are sometimes disappointed to find themselves bringing home less and paying out more than they expected. You'll be facing a host of new expenses, from housing to transportation to a business-quality wardrobe. You can't afford to devote a big chunk of your new salary to paying off your beer and pizza bills—with interest—from the previous four or five years.

Your second step is to compile your income and expense statement, as described previously, so you know where all that borrowed money is going. Do a thorough and honest evaluation of your expenses: How much of your spending is going to nonessentials? At first, it won't seem possible that these small-ticket items can add up to big trouble, but it happens to thousands of college students every year. Most colleges and college towns offer a wide spectrum of free and low-cost entertainment options. With a little effort and creativity, anyone can find ways to reduce nonessential expenses, often by hundreds of dollars a month. A few sacrifices now can make a big difference.

Life Stage 2: Building Your Financial Foundation

Whew, you made it: You scraped by to graduation, with any luck found a decent job, and now are ready to get really serious about financial planning. First, give yourself a pat on the back; it's a major accomplishment in life. Second, dust off that financial plan you put together in college. It's time to update it to reflect your new status in life. Third, don't lose those frugal habits you learned in college. Keep your *fixed expenses*, the bills you have to pay every month no matter what, as low as possible. Some of these expenses are mandatory, such as transportation and housing, but others may not be. Such things as gym memberships and added services on your mobile phone tend to creep into your budget and gradually raise your expenses. Before you know it, you could be shelling out hundreds of dollars a month on these recurring but often nonessential expenses. In addition, if your income temporarily drops, the lower your fixed expenses are, the more easily you can handle the setback.

Some of the important decisions you may need to make at this stage involve paying for transportation and housing, taking steps to maximize your earning power, and managing your cash and credit wisely.

PAYING FOR TRANSPORTATION

Transportation is likely to be one of your biggest ongoing expenses, particularly if that means owning or leasing a vehicle. The *true cost* of owning a vehicle is significantly higher than the price tag. You'll probably have to finance it, you'll definitely need to insure it, and you'll face recurring costs for fuel and maintenance. And, unfortunately, unlike houses, which often *appreciate* in value, cars always *depreciate* in value (except in extremely rare cases, such as with classic cars). In fact, that lovely new ride can lose as much as 20 percent of its value the instant you drive it away from the dealership. If you pay $25,000 for a car, for example, your net worth could drop by $5,000 before you've driven your first mile. And if you took out a five-, six-, or seven-year loan, you'll probably owe more than the car is worth for the first several years.

There is good news, however: Most cars tend not to depreciate much during their second, third, and fourth years, but their value plummets again after about five years. You can take advantage of this effect by looking for a used car that is about a year old, driving it for three years, and then selling it.[9] Automotive websites such as www.edmunds.com offer a wealth of information about depreciation and other costs, including the true cost of owning any given model. Also check with your insurance company before buying any car, as some models cost considerably more to insure.

Negotiating the purchase of a car ranks high on most consumers' list of dreaded experiences. You can level the playing field, at least somewhat, by remembering two important issues. First, most buyers worry only about the monthly payment, which can be a costly mistake. Salespeople usually negotiate with four or even five variables at once, including the monthly payment, purchase price, down payment, value of your trade-in, and terms of your loan. If you don't pay attention to these other variables, you can get a low monthly payment and still get a bad deal. Be sure to negotiate the purchase price separately.[10] If you're not comfortable negotiating, consider using a car-buying service such as CarsDirect (www.carsdirect.com).

Leasing, rather than buying, is a popular option with many consumers, but it's not always a money-smart option. In general, the biggest advantage of leasing is lower monthly payments than with a purchase (or a nicer car for the same monthly payment, depending on how you look at it). However, leases are even more complicated than purchases and often more expensive, so it's even more important to know what you're getting into. Also, leases usually aren't the best choice for consumers who want to minimize their long-term costs.

PAYING FOR HOUSING

Housing also presents you with a lease-versus-buy decision, although purchasing a house has two huge advantages that purchasing a car doesn't have: Houses *can* appreciate in value over the long term, and the interest on a home mortgage is tax deductible. And compared to renting, buying your own place also lets you build *equity*, the portion of the house's value that you own. However, there are times when renting makes better financial sense. The **closing costs** for real estate—the fees and commissions associated with buying or selling a house—can be considerable. Depending on how fast your house's value rises, you may need to stay in it for several years just to recoup your closing costs before selling.

If you think that a job change, an upcoming marriage, or any other event in your life might require you to move in the near future, plug your numbers into a "rent versus buy" calculator to see which option makes more sense. The Real-Time Updates item on this page has links to such a calculator and advice on deciding whether to rent or buy.

REAL-TIME UPDATES

Learn More by Exploring This Interactive Website

Should you rent or buy?

Use this calculator to find out which option is best for you. Go to **real-timeupdates.com/bia9** and select Learn More in the Students section.

When you are ready to buy, take your time. Buying a house is the most complicated financial decision many people will ever make, involving everything from property values in the neighborhood to the condition of the home to the details of the financial transaction. Fortunately, you can learn more about home ownership from a number of sources. Check local lenders and real estate agencies for free seminars. Online sources include the U.S. Department of Housing and Urban Development (**www.hud.gov**) and MSN Real Estate (**www.msn.com/en-us/money/realestate**). Buying your own house can and should be a wonderful experience, but don't let emotional factors lead you to a decision that doesn't make financial sense. Keep in mind that a house is both a home and an investment.

MAXIMIZING YOUR EARNING POWER

Why do some people peak at earning $40,000 or $50,000 a year, while others go on to earn 2 or 3 or 10 times that much? Your salary is likely to be the primary "engine" of your financial success, so this question warrants careful consideration. The profession you choose is one of the biggest factors, of course, but even within a given profession, you'll often find a wide range of income levels. A number of factors influence these variations, including education, individual talents, ambition, location, contacts, and good old-fashioned luck. You can change some of these factors throughout your career, but others you can't change. However, compensation experts stress that virtually everyone can improve his or her earning power by following these tips:

- **Know what you're worth.** The more informed you are about your competitive value in the marketplace, the better chance you have of negotiating a salary that reflects your worth. Several websites offer salary-level information that will help you decide your personal value, including **www.bls.gov**, **www.salary.com**, and **www.salaryexpert.com**. (Some of these sites charge a modest fee for customized reports, but the information might be worth many times what you pay for it.)

- **Be ready to explain your value.** In addition to knowing what other people in your profession make, you need to be able to explain to your current employer or a potential new employer why you're worth the money you think you deserve. Collect concrete examples of how you've helped your company or previous employers earn more or spend less in the past—and be ready to explain how you can do so in the future. Moreover, seek out opportunities that let you increase and demonstrate your worth.

- **Don't overlook the value of employee benefits, performance incentives, and perks.** For instance, even if you can't negotiate the salary you'd really like, maybe you can negotiate extra time off or a flexible schedule that would allow you to run a home-based business on the side. Or perhaps you can negotiate a bonus arrangement that rewards you for higher-than-average performance.

- **Understand the salary structure in your company.** If you hope to rise through the ranks and make $200,000 as a vice president, for instance, but the chief executive officer (CEO) is making only $150,000, your goal is obviously unrealistic. Some companies pay top performers well above market average, whereas others stick closely to industry norms.

- **Study top performers.** Some employees have the misperception that top executives must have "clawed their way" to the top or stepped on others on their way up. However, the employees and managers who continue to rise through an organization often do so because they make people around them successful. Being successful on your own is one thing; helping an entire department or an entire company be successful is the kind of behavior that catches the attention of the people who write the really big paychecks.

MANAGING CASH

When paychecks start rolling in, you'll need to set up a system of **personal cash management**, a system for handling cash and other liquid assets—those that can be quickly and easily converted to cash. You have many alternatives for storing cash you don't need in the near term, including basic savings accounts and a variety of investment funds, but most offer interest rates that are below the average level of inflation. In other words, if you were to keep all your money in such places, your buying power would slowly but surely erode over time. Consequently, the basic challenge of cash management is keeping enough cash or other liquid assets available to cover your near-term needs without keeping so much cash that you lose out on investment growth opportunities or fall prey to inflation. Once again, your budget planning will come to the rescue by showing you how much money you need month to month. Financial experts also recommend keeping anywhere from three to six months' worth of basic living expenses in an *emergency fund* that you can access if you find yourself between jobs or have other unexpected needs. It can take a while to build up such a fund, but it will bring you enormous peace of mind and help you survive setbacks without going into debt.

You can choose from several options for holding cash (see Exhibit D.4 for a summary of their advantages and disadvantages):[11]

- **Checking accounts.** Whether it's a traditional checking account from your neighborhood bank, an online account at an internet bank, or a brokerage account with check-writing privileges, your checking account will serve as your primary cash management tool. A checking account can be either a demand deposit, which doesn't pay interest, or an interest-bearing or *negotiable order of withdrawal (NOW)* account.
- **Savings accounts.** Savings accounts are convenient places to store small amounts of money. Many savings accounts can be linked to a checking account for quick access to your cash. Although they're convenient and safe, savings accounts nearly always offer interest rates below average inflation rates, so the buying power of your account steadily diminishes.
- **Money-market accounts.** Money-market accounts, sometimes called *money-market deposit accounts*, are an alternative to savings accounts; the primary difference is that they have variable interest rates that are usually higher than savings account rates.
- **Money-market mutual funds.** Money-market mutual funds, sometimes called money funds, are similar to stock mutual funds, although they invest in *debt instruments* such as bonds, rather than stocks.
- **Asset management accounts.** Brokerage firms and mutual fund companies frequently offer *asset management accounts* as a way to manage cash that isn't currently invested in stocks or stock mutual funds.
- **Certificates of deposit.** With a certificate of deposit (CD), you are essentially lending a specific amount of money to a bank or another institution for a specific length of time and at a specific interest rate. The length of time can range from a week to several years; the longer the time span and the larger the amount, the higher the interest rate.

No matter which types of accounts you choose, make sure you understand all the associated fees—which might not be clearly labeled as fees. Some accounts charge a fee every month, some charge fees when your balance drops below a certain amount or when you write too many checks, and so on. For accounts with checking capability, **overdraft fees**

EXHIBIT D.4	**Places to Stash Your Cash**

You can find quite a few places to park your cash, but they're not all created equal. Note that banks and credit unions continue to refine their offerings, so you may find options that don't fit neatly into these categories, and various institutions can have different names for the same general types of accounts.

Type of Account	Advantages	Disadvantages
Basic checking account	Convenient; low monthly fees; some have no fees if you maintain a certain minimum balance (or no fees in some cases); some have no minimum balance to open; insured against losses due to bank failure	Does not earn any interest; may have monthly fees if a minimum balance isn't maintained
Interest-bearing checking account (NOW account)	Convenience of a regular checking account, plus you earn interest on your balance; insured against bank failure	Some institutions require a minimum balance to open an account; modest interest rates
Savings account	Slightly higher interest rate than on typical checking account; often linked to a checking account for easy transfers; insured	Lower interest rates than other longer-term cash accounts; somewhat less convenient than checking accounts
Money-market deposit account	Higher interest rates than checking or savings accounts; insured	High minimum balances; limited check writing; fees can limit real returns
Money-market mutual fund	Higher interest rates than many other cash management options	Not insured (but limited exposure to risk); minimum balance requirements; restrictions on check writing
Asset management account	Convenience of having cash readily available for investment purposes; higher interest rates than regular checking or savings accounts; consolidated statements show your cash management and investing activity	Can have high monthly fees, depending on account balance; some have large minimum balances; restrictions on check-writing privileges (such as high minimum amounts) can limit usefulness as regular checking account; not insured against losses
Certificate of deposit (CD)	Higher interest rates that are fixed and therefore predictable; insured	Minimum balance requirements; limited liquidity (your money is tied up for weeks, months, or years); no checking or cash transfer features

Sources: Jeff Madura, *Personal Finance*, 6th ed. (New York: Pearson, 2017), 159–165; Melissa Lambarena, "How to Choose a Bank Account: Seek Low Fees, High Rates," *NerdWallet*, 9 March 2017, www.nerdwallet.com.

can chew up hundreds of dollars if you bounce checks frequently. Also, be sure to verify your account statement every month and **reconcile** your checking account to make sure you and the bank agree on the balance.

MANAGING CREDIT

Even if you never want to use a credit card or borrow money, it's increasingly difficult to get by without credit in today's consumer environment. For instance, car rental companies usually require a credit card before you can rent a car, most hotels require a credit card upon check-in, and landlords want to verify your **credit history**, a record of your mortgages, consumer loans (such as financing provided by a home appliance store), credit card accounts, and bill-paying performance. Banks and other companies voluntarily provide this information to credit rating agencies, businesses that compile **credit reports**. An increasing number of employers are looking at the credit histories of job applicants as well. Moreover, you may find yourself in need of a loan you didn't anticipate, and getting a loan without a credit history is not easy. Consequently, a solid credit history needs to be a part of your lifetime financial plan.

To build a good credit history, apply for a modest amount of sensible credit (a credit card, an auto loan, or a line of credit at a bank, for instance) and use that credit periodically. Also, if you are married or in a domestic partnership where expenses are shared, make sure that at least some credit is being established in your name so that you have an independent credit record. Most important of all is to pay all your bills on time. If you find that you can't pay a particular bill by the due date, call the company and explain your situation. You may get some leniency by showing that you're making a good-faith effort to pay your bill.

Experts also recommend that you verify the accuracy of your credit report at least once a year. Mistakes do creep into credit reports from time to time, and you also need to make sure you haven't been a victim of identity theft, in which someone illegally applies for credit using your name. Actually, you don't have just one credit report. The three major credit reporting agencies in the United States each keep a file on you and provide their own credit reports to lenders, landlords, and others with a valid need to see them. You are entitled to one free credit report every 12 months from each of the three companies; visit www.annual creditreport.com for more information. You can also directly visit the three bureaus: Experian (www.experian .com), TransUnion (www.transunion.com), and Equifax (www.equifax.com). Make sure you type these URLs carefully and don't visit any other website that promises to offer free credit reports. AnnualCreditReport.com is the only website authorized by the federal government to give you access to reports from all three bureaus.

Managing your credit wisely will help you avoid one of the most traumatic events that can befall a consumer: **personal bankruptcy**. You have several options for declaring bankruptcy, but none of them is desirable, and all should be avoided by every means possible. Bankruptcy is not a simple cure-all, as it is sometimes presented. If you are considering bankruptcy, talk to a counselor first. Start with the National Foundation for Credit Counseling (www.nfcc.org). Wherever you turn for advice, make sure you understand it thoroughly and understand why the organization would be motivated to give you that particular advice.

Life Stage 3: Increasing Your Net Worth and Preparing for Life's Major Expenses

With your basic needs taken care of and a solid foundation under your feet, the next stage of your financial life is to increase your net worth and prepare for both expected and unexpected expenses. Some of the major decisions at this stage include investments, taxes, insurance, your children's education, and emergency planning.

INVESTING: BUILDING YOUR NEST EGG

The various cash management options described previously can help you store and protect money you already have, but they aren't terribly good at generating more money. That's the goal of *investing*, in which you buy something with the idea that it will increase in value before you sell it to someone else. You read about the most common financial investment vehicles in Chapter 16: stocks, mutual funds, and bonds. Real estate is the other major category of investment for most people—not only their own homes but also rental properties and commercial real estate. The final category of investments includes precious metals (primarily gold), gems, and collectibles such as sports or movie memorabilia.

The details of successful investing in these various areas differ widely, but six general rules apply to all of them:

- **Don't invest cash that you may need in the short term.** You may not be able to *liquidate* the investment (selling it to retrieve your cash) in time, or the value may be temporarily down, in which case you'll permanently lose money.
- **Don't invest in anything you don't understand or haven't thoroughly evaluated.** If you can't point to specific reasons that the investment should increase in value, you're simply guessing or gambling.
- **Don't invest on emotion.** You might love eating at a certain restaurant chain, shopping at a particular online retailer, or collecting baseball cards, but that doesn't mean any of these is automatically a good investment.
- **Understand the risks.** Aside from a few low-interest investments such as savings bonds, virtually no investment can guarantee that you'll make money or even protect the money you originally invested. You could lose most or all of your money, and in the riskiest investments, you can lose even more than you invested. Risk is nearly

always a component of investing, and to pursue higher gains, you usually need to accept higher levels of risk.

- **Beware of anybody who promises guaranteed results or instant wealth.** Chances are that person will profit more by snaring you into the investment than you'll earn from the investment yourself.
- **Given the risks involved, don't put all your eggs in one basket.** Diversify your investments to make sure you don't leave yourself vulnerable to downturns in a single stock or piece of real estate, for instance.

If you plan to invest in a specific area, take a course about it or commit to learning on your own. Most of the websites mentioned throughout this appendix offer information, and some offer formal courses you can take online. Working with an investment club is an increasingly popular way to learn and pool your resources with other individual investors. In the beginning, don't worry about the details of particular stocks or the intricacies of real estate investment trusts and other more advanced concepts. Focus on the fundamentals: Why do stock prices increase or decrease? What effect do interest rates have on bonds? Why do some houses appreciate in value much faster than others?

As Chapter 16 points out, you can also practice investing without risking any money. This is a smart move early in your career, when you're still getting on your feet and may not have much money to invest yet. After you've learned the basics of stock investing, for instance, set up a "mock portfolio" on one of the many online sites that provide free portfolio tracking. Month by month, monitor the performance of your choices. Whenever you see a big increase or decrease, dig deeper to understand why. By practicing first, you can learn from your mistakes before those mistakes cost you any money.

TAXES: MINIMIZING THE BITE

Taxes will be a constant factor in your personal financial planning. In most states, you pay *sales tax* on many of the products you buy; you pay federal *excise taxes* on certain purchases, such as gasoline and phone service; you pay *property tax* on real estate; and you pay *income tax* on both earned income (wages, salaries, tips, bonuses, commissions, and business profits) and investment income. The total taxes paid by individuals vary widely, but you can safely assume that taxes will consume 30 to 40 percent of your income.

Your personal tax strategy should focus on minimizing the taxes you are required to pay without running afoul of the law. You are expected to pay your fair share of taxes, but no one expects you to pay more than your share.

You can reduce taxes in three basic ways: (1) by reducing your consumption of goods and services that are subject to either sales tax or excise taxes, (2) by reducing your *taxable income*, or (3) by reducing your tax through the use of *tax credits*. Reducing consumption is a straightforward concept, although there are obviously limits to how far you can reduce consumption and therefore this portion of your tax obligation.

Reducing your taxable income (the part of your income that is subject to local, state, or federal income tax, not reducing your overall income level) is more complicated but can have a great impact on your finances. Authorities such as the IRS allow a variety of **deductions**, such as interest paid on home mortgages and the costs associated with using part of your home for office space. Qualifying deductions can be subtracted from your *gross income* to lower your taxable income. A portion of your income is also *exempt* from federal income tax, based on the number of dependents in your household. The more **exemptions** you can legally claim, the lower your taxable income. You can also lower your taxable income by investing a portion of your income in *tax-exempt* or *tax-deferred* investments. With **tax-exempt investments** (which are primarily bonds issued by local governments), you don't have to pay federal income tax on any income you earn from the investment. With **tax-deferred investments**, such as 401(k) plans and individual retirement accounts (IRAs), you can deduct the amount of money you invest every year from your gross income, and you don't have to pay tax on income from the investment until you withdraw money during retirement.

Unlike deductions, which only reduce your taxable income and therefore reduce your tax burden by the amount of your tax rate, **tax credits** reduce your tax obligation directly. In other words, a $100 *deduction* reduces your tax bill by $28 (if you're in the 28 percent tax bracket, for instance), whereas a $100 *credit* reduces your tax bill by $100.

Personal tax software can guide you through the process of finding deductions and credits. For more complex scenarios, though, it's always a good idea to get the advice of a professional tax adviser.

INSURANCE: PROTECTING YOURSELF, YOUR FAMILY, AND YOUR ASSETS

Unfortunately, things go wrong in life, from accidents to health problems to the death of an income provider. Insurance is designed to protect you, your family, and your assets if and when these unpleasant events occur. In a sense, insurance is the ultimate risk/reward trade-off decision. If you had an ironclad guarantee that you would never get sick or injured, you would have no need for health insurance. However, there's a reasonable chance that you will need medical attention at some point, and major injuries and illness can generate many thousands of dollars of unplanned expenses. Consequently, most people consider it a reasonable trade-off to pay for health insurance to protect themselves from catastrophic financial blows. Exhibit D.5 on the next page provides a brief overview of your most significant insurance options.

Another vital step to protecting your loved ones—and one that is often overlooked by younger people—is preparing a **will**, a legal document that specifies what will happen to your assets, who will execute your estate (carry out the terms of your will), and who will be the legal guardian of your children, if you have any, in the event of your death.

EXHIBIT D.5	Understanding Your Insurance Options

You can buy insurance for many loss exposures, from earthquake damage to vacation interruptions, but the most common and most important types include health, disability, auto, homeowner's or renter's, and life insurance.

Category	Highlights
Health insurance	Most plans offer a variety of cost and coverage options—for instance, to lower your monthly costs you can select a higher deductible, which is the amount you have to pay before insurance coverage kicks in; selecting the right plan requires a careful analysis of your needs and financial circumstances; all individuals are now required by law to have health insurance: be sure to check **www.healthcare.gov** or your state's exchange if it doesn't participate in the federal exchange
Disability insurance	Temporarily replaces a portion of your income if you are unable to work; various policies have different definitions of "disability" and restrictions on coverage and payments
Auto insurance	Most states now have *compulsory liability insurance laws*, meaning that you have to prove that you are covered for any damage you might cause as a driver; coverage for your vehicle can be both *collision* (damages resulting from collisions) and *comprehensive* (other damages or theft); you can also buy coverage to protect yourself from illegally uninsured motorists
Homeowner's insurance	Most policies include both *property loss coverage* (to replace or repair the home and its contents) and *liability coverage* (to protect you in case someone sues you); often required by the lender when you have a mortgage
Renter's insurance	Insures against losses of personal property and can provide liability coverage
Life insurance	Primary purpose is to provide for others in the event that your death would create a financial hardship for them; common forms are *term life* (limited duration, less expensive, no investment value), *whole life* (permanent coverage, builds cash value over time, more expensive than term life), and *universal life* (similar to whole life but more flexible)

Life Stage 4: Plan for a Secure, Independent Retirement

Retirement? You're only 25 years old (or 35 or 45). Yes, but as you saw in the discussion of compound interest, it's never too early to start planning for retirement. It's tempting to picture retirement as a carefree time when you can finally ditch your job and focus on hobbies, travel, volunteer work, and the hundreds of other activities you haven't had time for previously in your life. Sadly, the reality for millions of retired people today is much different. Between skyrocketing medical costs and lower-than-expected company pensions in some cases, retirement for many people is a financial struggle, with little hope for improvement.

Perhaps the most important step you can take toward a more positive retirement is to shed some misconceptions and mistaken beliefs that people sometimes have about retirement planning, including the following:

- **I can count on a significant inheritance to help fund my retirement.** Of course, you may have solid personal knowledge that you're in line for a significant inheritance, but a majority of Millennials are counting on an inheritance that they might not receive. Millions of baby boomers now moving into retirement are going to be hard-pressed to fund their own retirements, much less have any significant funds to pass on to their children.[12]
- **My living expenses will drop significantly, so I'll need less money.** Some of your expenses may well drop, but rising health-care costs may swamp any reductions you have in housing, clothing, and other personal costs. To maintain the same standard of living, your monthly expenses in retirement could be as high as 90 percent of what you spent before retirement.[13]
- **Social Security will cover my basic living expenses.** Social Security probably won't cover even your basic requirements, and the entire system is in serious financial trouble. Although it's unlikely that political leaders would ever let Social Security collapse, benefits may well drop in the future. The safest bet is to not count on having Social Security at all during retirement; then what you do receive will provide a financial cushion.
- **My employer will keep funding my pension and health insurance.** Even if your employer's pension plan is insured by the Pension Benefit Guaranty Corporation, the PBGC doesn't have enough funds to cover all potential failures.[14]
- **I can't save much right now, so there's no point in saving anything at all.** If you find yourself thinking this, remind yourself of the magic of compounding. Over time, small amounts grow into large amounts of money. Do whatever it takes to get started now.
- **I have plenty of time to worry about retirement later.** Unfortunately, you don't. The longer you wait, the harder it will become to ensure a comfortable retirement. If you're not prepared, your only option will be to continue working well into your 70s or 80s.

The situation is serious, but it is not hopeless by any means. You control your destiny, and you don't need to abandon all pleasures and comforts now to make it happen. However, you do need to put together a plan and start saving now. Make retirement planning a positive part of your personal financial planning—part of your dream of living the life you want to live.

TEST YOUR KNOWLEDGE

Questions for Review

D-1. What does the *time value of money* mean?

D-2. What is compounding?

D-3. What is the major advantage of using a fee-only financial planner?

D-4. What is credit counseling?

D-5. What is the difference between a tax deduction and a tax credit?

Questions for Analysis

D-6. Should you borrow at any cost to get through college? Explain your answer.

D-7. What are the risks of relying on credit cards for living expenses while in college?

D-8. Why is it essential to keep a close eye on fixed expenses?

D-9. Why do you need to be able to explain your value to potential employers?

D-10. Ethical Considerations. Is it unethical for lenders to get students to sign up for loans that the students may not fully understand? Why or why not?

Writing Assignments

D-11. If you have money to invest but are worried that the stock market could fall soon, is it wise to keep all your investment funds in cash instead? Why or why not?

D-12. Why is it important to understand your risk tolerance before you start investing?

APPENDIX D GLOSSARY

closing costs Fees associated with buying and selling a house.

commission-based planners Financial advisers who are paid commissions on the financial products they sell you, such as insurance policies and mutual funds.

compounding The acceleration of balances caused by applying new interest to interest that has already accumulated.

credit history A record of your mortgages, consumer loans, credit card accounts (including credit limits and current balances), and bill-paying performance.

credit reports Reports generated by credit bureaus, showing an individual's credit usage and payment history.

deductions Opportunities to reduce taxable income by subtracting the cost of a specific item, such as business expenses or interest paid on home mortgages.

exemptions Reductions to taxable income based on the number of dependents in the household.

fee-only planners Financial advisers who charge a fee for their services rather than earning a commission on financial services they sell you.

net worth The difference between your assets and your liabilities.

overdraft fees Penalties charged against your checking account when you write checks that total more than your available balance.

personal bankruptcy A condition in which a consumer is unable to repay his or her debts; depending on the type of bankruptcy, a court will either forgive many of the person's debts or establish a compatible repayment plan.

personal cash management All the planning and activities associated with managing your cash and other liquid assets.

personal income and expense statement A listing of your monthly inflows (income) and outflows (expenses); also called an *income statement*.

reconcile To compare the balance you believe is in your account with the balance the bank believes is in your account.

tax credits Direct reductions in your tax obligation.

tax-deferred investments Investments such as 401(k) plans and IRAs that let you deduct the amount of your investments from your gross income (thereby lowering your taxable income); you don't have to pay tax on any of the income from these investments until you start to withdraw money during retirement.

tax-exempt investments Investments (usually municipal bonds) whose income is not subject to federal income tax.

time value of money The increasing value of money as a result of accumulating interest.

will A legal document that specifies what will happen to your assets, who will execute your estate (carry out the terms of your will), and who will be the legal guardian of your children, if you have any, in the event of your death.

ENDNOTES

1. Jeff Madura, *Personal Finance*, 6th ed. (New York: Pearson, 2017), 67.

2. "Interview Guidelines," WiserAdvisor.com, accessed 17 June 2018, www.wiseradvisor.com.

3. Madura, *Personal Finance*, 16.

4. Lori Hil, "Is Retail Therapy Really Therapeutic? New Data Speaks," *Forbes*, 29 November 2017, www.forbes.com.

5. "The Truth About Money and Relationships," *Dave Ramsey*, accessed 17 June 2018, www.daveramsey.com.

6. "Unemployment Rates and Earnings by Educational Attainment, 2017," U.S. Bureau of Labor Statistics, 27 March 2018, www.bls.gov.

7. "Study Puts Dollar Amounts on Earning Power of College Majors," OregonLive.com, 24 May 2011, www.oregonlive.com; Kathy Kristof, "Crushed by College," *Forbes*, 2 February 2009, 60–65.

8. Joseph Fuller, "Why Employers Must Stop Requiring College Degrees for Middle-Skill Jobs," *Harvard Business School Working Knowledge*, 18 December 2017, hbswk.hbs.edu.

9. "Beat the Depreciation Curve When You Buy Your Next Car," Edmunds.com, accessed 17 June 2018, www.edmunds.com.

10. "Negotiating Car Prices," Edmunds.com, accessed 17 June 2018, www.edmunds.com.

11. Madura, *Personal Finance*, 159–165.

12. Steven Vernon, "Don't Fall for These Retirement Myths," *CBS News*, 21 June 2017, www.cbsnews.com.

13. Dayana Yochim, "Let's Get Real: What an Average Retirement Costs," *NerdWallet*, 28 May 2018, www.nerdwallet.com.

14. "Pension Benefit Guaranty Corporation Insurance Programs," U.S. Government Accountability Office, accessed 18 June 2018, www.gao.gov.

Glossary

360-degree review A multidimensional review in which a person is given feedback from subordinates, peers, superiors, and possibly outside stakeholders such as customers and business partners.

401(k) plan A defined-contribution retirement plan in which employers often match the amount employees invest.

accounting equation The equation stating that assets equal liabilities plus owners' equity.

accounting Measuring, interpreting, and communicating financial information to support internal and external decision-making.

accounts payable Amounts that a firm currently owes to other parties.

accounts receivable turnover ratio A measure of the time a company takes to turn its accounts receivable into cash, calculated by dividing sales by the average value of accounts receivable for a period.

accounts receivable Amounts that are currently owed to a firm.

accrual basis An accounting method in which revenue is recorded when a sale is made and an expense is recorded when it is incurred.

acquisition An action taken by one company to buy a controlling interest in the voting stock of another company.

administrative skills The technical skills necessary to direct an organization, including scheduling, researching, analyzing data, and managing projects.

advertising appeal A creative tactic designed to capture the audience's attention and promote preference for the product or company being advertised.

advertising media Communication channels that companies use to reach target audiences.

advertising The delivery of announcements and promotional messages via time or space purchased in various media.

advisory board A team of people with subject-area expertise or vital contacts who help a business owner review plans and decisions.

affirmative action Activities undertaken by businesses to recruit and promote members of groups whose economic progress has been hindered through either legal barriers or established practices.

agile organization A company whose structure, policies, and capabilities allow employees to respond quickly to customer needs and changes in the business environment.

algorithmic pricing A variety of computational methods used to set price, either in more nuanced ways than simple cost- or competition-based pricing or in dynamic ways that respond in real time to fluctuations in demand and other market conditions.

analytics Computing tools and techniques used to analyze big data; major types include data mining, text mining, and predictive analytics.

angel investors Private individuals who invest money in start-ups, usually earlier in a business's life and in smaller amounts than VCs are willing to invest or banks are willing to lend.

asset allocation Management of a portfolio to balance potential returns with an acceptable level of risk.

assets Any things of value owned or leased by a business.

attribution The contribution a given marketing activity makes to sales and other marketing goals.

audit Formal evaluation of the fairness and reliability of a client's financial statements.

augmented reality (AR) Systems that superimpose visual or textual information on live images of real scenes.

augmented writing Systems that provide real-time advice about the effectiveness of written language.

autocratic leaders Leaders who do not involve others in decision-making.

automated writing The use of AI to to produce finished or near-finished writing.

balance of payments The sum of all payments one nation receives from other nations minus the sum of all payments it makes to other nations, over some specified period of time.

balance of trade Total value of the products a nation exports minus the total value of the products it imports, over some period of time.

balance sheet A statement of a firm's financial position on a particular date; also known as a *statement of financial position*.

balanced scorecard A method of monitoring the performance from four perspectives: finances, operations, customer relationships, and the growth and development of employees and intellectual property.

barriers to entry Resources or capabilities a company must have before it can start competing in a given market.

bear market A market situation in which most stocks are decreasing in value.

behavioral segmentation Categorization of customers according to their relationship with products or response to product characteristics.

benchmarking Collecting and comparing process and performance data from other companies.

benefit corporation A profit-seeking corporation whose charter specifies a social or environmental goal that the company must pursue in addition to profit.

big data The massive data sets that companies collect and analyze to find important trends and insights.

blockchain A type of distributed ledger in which each new transaction is captured in a "block," which is then appended to the previous block in a continuous chain.

board of directors A group of professionals elected by shareholders as their representatives, with responsibility for the overall direction of the company and the selection of top executives.

bond market The collective buying and selling of bonds; most bond trading is done over the counter, rather than in organized exchanges.

bonds A method of funding in which the issuer borrows from an investor and provides a written promise to make regular interest payments and repay the borrowed amount in the future.

bonus A cash payment, in addition to regular wage or salary, that serves as a reward for achievement.

bookkeeping Recordkeeping; the clerical aspect of accounting.

brand communities Formal or informal groups of people united by their interest in and ownership of particular products.

brand equity The value that a company has built up in a brand.

brand extension Applying a successful brand name to a new product category.

brand licensing Agreement in which one company pays to use another company's brand on its products.

brand loyalty The degree to which customers continue to purchase a specific brand.

brand managers Managers who develop and implement the marketing strategies and programs for one or more of a company's products or brands.

brand marks The portion of brands that cannot be expressed verbally.

brand names The portion of brands that can be spoken, including letters, words, or numbers.

brand A name, term, sign, symbol, design, or combination of those used to identify the products of a firm and to differentiate them from competing products.

break-even analysis A method of calculating the minimum volume of sales needed at a given price to cover all costs.

break-even point Sales volume at a given price that will cover all of a company's costs.

broker A certified expert who is legally registered to buy and sell securities on behalf of individual and institutional investors.

budget A planning and control tool that reflects expected revenues, operating expenses, and cash receipts and outlays.

bull market A market situation in which most stocks are increasing in value.

bundling Offering several products for a single price that is presumably lower than the total of the products' individual prices.

business accelerators Organizations that work with existing companies with the primary goal of making them more attractive to investors.

business cycles Fluctuations in the rate of growth that an economy experiences over a period of several years.

business incubators Facilities that help early-stage entrepreneurial teams develop ideas into workable business models and establish company frameworks for commercializing products.

business mindset Adopting an insider's view of business with an appreciation for the decisions to be made and challenges that managers face.

business model A concise description of how a business generates or intends to generate revenue.

business plan A document that summarizes a proposed business venture, its goals, and plans for achieving those goals.

business Any profit-seeking organization that provides goods and services designed to satisfy customers' needs.

calendar year A 12-month accounting period that begins on January 1 and ends on December 31.

capacity planning Establishing the overall level of resources needed to meet customer demand.

capital items More expensive organizational products with a longer useful life, ranging from office and plant equipment to entire factories.

capital structure A firm's mix of debt and equity financing.

capitalism Economic system based on economic freedom and competition.

cash basis An accounting method in which revenue is recorded when payment is received and an expense is recorded when cash is paid.

centralization Concentration of decision-making authority at the top of an organization.

certified public accountants (CPAs) Professionally licensed accountants who meet certain requirements for education and experience and who pass a comprehensive examination.

chain of command A pathway for the flow of authority from one management level to the next.

chief executive officer (CEO) The highest-ranking officer of a corporation.

closing the books Transferring net revenue and expense account balances to retained earnings for the period.

closing The point at which a sale is completed.

co-branding A partnership between two or more companies to closely link their brand names together for a single product.

coaching Helping employees reach their highest potential by meeting with them, discussing problems that hinder their ability to work effectively, and offering suggestions and encouragement to overcome these problems.

code of ethics A written statement that sets forth the principles that guide an organization's decisions.

cognitive automation AI technology that aims to help professionals and managers with complex questions that present some of the most daunting decision scenarios.

cognitive dissonance Tension that exists when a person's beliefs don't match his or her behaviors; a common example is *buyer's remorse*, when someone regrets a purchase immediately after making it.

collateral A tangible asset a lender can claim if a borrower defaults on a loan.

commercial banks Banks that accept deposits, offer various checking and savings accounts, and provide loans; note that this label is often applied to banks that serve businesses only, rather than consumers.

commercial paper Short-term *promissory notes*, or contractual agreements, to repay a borrowed amount by a specified time with a specified interest rate.

commercialization Large-scale production and distribution of a product.

commissions Employee compensation based on a percentage of sales made.

committee A team that may become a permanent part of the organization and is designed to deal with regularly recurring tasks.

communication mix A blend of communication vehicles—advertising, direct response marketing, personal selling, sales promotion, social media, and public relations—that a company uses to reach current and potential customers.

compensation Money, benefits, and services paid to employees for their work.

competition-based pricing A method of setting prices based on what suppliers of similar products are charging.

competition Rivalry among businesses for the same customers.

competitive advantage Some aspect of a product or company that makes it more appealing to target customers.

conceptual skills The ability to understand the relationship of parts to the whole.

conflicts of interest Situations in which competing loyalties can lead to ethical lapses, such as when a business decision may be influenced by the potential for personal gain.

consultative selling An approach in which a salesperson acts as a consultant and adviser to help customers find the best solutions to their personal or business needs.

consumer market Individuals or households that buy goods and services for personal use.

consumer price index (CPI) A monthly statistic that measures changes in the prices of a representative collection of consumer goods and services.

consumerism A movement that pressures businesses to consider consumer needs and interests.

content marketing The tactic of offering helpful, value-added content to potential customers.

contingent employees Nonpermanent employees, including temporary workers, independent contractors, and full-time employees hired on a probationary basis.

controller The highest-ranking accountant in a company, responsible for overseeing all accounting functions.

controlling The process of measuring progress against goals and objectives and correcting deviations if results are not as expected.

convenience products Everyday goods and services that people buy frequently, usually without much conscious planning.

core competencies Activities that a company considers central and vital to its business.

core message The single most important idea an advertiser hopes to convey to the target audience about its products or the company.

corporate governance In a broad sense, all the policies, procedures, relationships, and systems in place to oversee the successful and legal operation of the enterprise; in a narrow sense, the responsibilities and performance of the board of directors specifically.

corporate officers The top executives who run a corporation.

corporate social responsibility (CSR) The idea that business has obligations to society beyond the pursuit of profits.

corporation A legal entity, distinct from any individual persons, that has the power to own property and conduct business.

cost of capital The average rate of interest a firm pays on its combination of debt and equity.

cost of goods sold The cost of producing or acquiring a company's products for sale during a given period.

cost-based pricing A method of setting prices based on production and marketing costs, rather than conditions in the marketplace.

crisis management Procedures and systems for minimizing the harm that might result from some unusually threatening situations.

critical path In a PERT network diagram, the sequence of operations that requires the longest time to complete; the project can't be completed any faster than the critical path.

cross-functional team A team that draws together employees from different functional areas.

cross-training Training workers to perform multiple jobs and rotating them through these various jobs to combat boredom or burnout.

crowdfunding Soliciting project funds, business investment, or business loans from members of the public.

cryptocurrency Currency represented by digital tokens.

cultural pluralism The practice of accepting multiple cultures on their own terms.

culture A shared system of symbols, beliefs, attitudes, values, expectations, and norms for behavior.

current assets Cash and items that can be turned into cash within one year.

current liabilities Obligations that must be met within a year.

current ratio A measure of a firm's short-term liquidity, calculated by dividing current assets by current liabilities.

customer experience The cumulative effect of the customer journey from presales exploration through purchase through product use and ownership.

customer loyalty The degree to which customers continue to buy from a particular retailer or buy the products of a particular manufacturer or service provider.

customer relationship management (CRM) A type of information system that captures, organizes, and capitalizes on all the interactions that a company has with its customers.

customized production The creation of a unique good or service for each customer.

debt financing Arranging funding by borrowing money.

debt-to-assets ratio A measure of a firm's ability to carry long-term debt, calculated by dividing total liabilities by total assets.

debt-to-equity ratio A measure of the extent to which a business is financed by debt as opposed to invested capital, calculated by dividing the company's total liabilities by owners' equity.

decentralization Delegation of decision-making authority to employees in lower-level positions.

decision-making skills The ability to identify a decision situation, analyze the problem, weigh the alternatives, choose an alternative, implement it, and evaluate the results.

deep learning A type of machine learning that uses layers of neural networks to attack problems at multiple levels.

deflation An economic condition in which prices fall steadily throughout the economy.

demand curve A graph of the quantities of a product that buyers will purchase at various prices.

demand Buyers' willingness and ability to purchase products at various price points.

democratic leaders Leaders who delegate authority and involve employees in decision-making.

demographics The study of the statistical characteristics of a population.

departmentalization Grouping people within an organization according to function, division, matrix, or network.

depreciation An accounting procedure for systematically spreading the cost of a tangible asset over its estimated useful life.

deregulation Removing regulations to allow the market to prevent excesses and correct itself over time.

derivatives market A market that includes exchange trading (for futures and some options) and over-the-counter trading (for all other derivatives, at least currently).

derivatives Contracts whose value is derived from some other entity (usually an asset of some kind, but not necessarily); used to hedge against or speculate on risk.

digital enterprise Any company that uses digital systems as one of the foundations of its value-creation processes, regardless of what industry it is in or what products it makes.

digital transformation Process of reimagining a company's business model and operations to become a digital enterprise.

direct response marketing Direct communication with potential customers other than personal sales contacts designed to stimulate a measurable response; also known as direct marketing.

discount rate The interest rate that member banks pay when they borrow funds from the Fed.

discounts Temporary price reductions to stimulate sales or lower prices to encourage certain behaviors such as paying with cash.

discrimination In a social and economic sense, denial of opportunities to individuals on the basis of some characteristic that has no bearing on their ability to perform in a job.

disruptive innovation Development so fundamentally different and far reaching that it can create new professions, companies, or even entire industries while damaging or destroying others.

distributed ledger Method of verifying and recording transactions that replaces the individual ledgers of market participants with a shared ledger that everyone can access.

distribution channels Systems for moving goods and services from producers to customers; also known as marketing channels.

distribution channel An organized network of intermediaries that work together to move goods from producer to customer or to facilitate the delivery of services.

distribution strategy A firm's overall plan for moving products through intermediaries and on to final customers.

diversification Creating new products for new markets.

diversity and inclusion initiatives Programs and policies that help companies support diverse workforces and markets.

diversity All the characteristics and experiences that define each person as an individual.

divisional structure Grouping departments according to similarities in product, process, customer, or geography.

double-entry bookkeeping A method of recording financial transactions that requires a debit entry and credit entry for each transaction to ensure that the accounting equation is always kept in balance.

dumping Charging less than the actual cost or less than the home-country price for goods sold in other countries.

earnings per share A measure of a firm's profitability for each share of outstanding stock, calculated by dividing net income after taxes by the average number of shares of common stock outstanding.

EBITDA Earnings before interest, taxes, depreciation, and amortization.

economic environment The conditions and forces that affect the cost and availability of goods, services, and labor and thereby shape the behavior of buyers and sellers.

economic globalization The increasing integration and interdependence of national economies around the world.

economic indicators Statistics that measure the performance of the economy.

economic system The policies that define a society's particular economic structure; the rules by which a society allocates economic resources.

economics The study of how a society uses its scarce resources to produce and distribute goods and services.

economies of scale Savings from buying parts and materials, manufacturing, or marketing in large quantities.

economy The sum of all economic activity within a given region.

embargo A total ban on trade with a particular nation (a sanction) or of a particular product.

employee assistance program (EAP) A company-sponsored counseling or referral plan for employees with personal problems.

employee benefits Compensation other than wages, salaries, and incentive programs.

employee empowerment Giving employees the power to make decisions that apply to their specific aspects of work.

employee retention Efforts to keep current employees.

employee stock-ownership plan (ESOP) A program that enables employees to become partial owners of a company.

engagement An employee's rational and emotional commitment to his or her work.

enterprise resource planning (ERP) A planning system that addresses the needs of the entire organization, from manufacturing to sales to human resources.

entrepreneurial spirit The positive, forward-thinking desire to create profitable, sustainable business enterprises.

equilibrium price The point at which quantity supplied equals quantity demanded.

equity financing Arranging funding by selling ownership shares in the company, publicly or privately.

equity theory The idea that employees base their level of satisfaction on the ratio of their inputs to the job and the outputs or rewards they receive from it.

ethical dilemma A situation in which more than one side of an issue can be supported with valid ethical arguments.

ethical lapse A situation in which an individual or a group makes a decision that is morally wrong, illegal, or unethical.

ethics The rules or standards governing the conduct of a person or group.

ethnocentrism Judging all other groups according to the standards, behaviors, and customs of one's own group.

etiquette The expected norms of behavior in any particular situation.

exchange process The act of obtaining a desired object or service from another party by offering something of value in return.

exchange rate The rate at which the money of one country is traded for the money of another.

exclusive distribution A market coverage strategy that gives intermediaries exclusive rights to sell a product in a specific geographic area.

expectancy theory The idea that the effort employees put into their work depends on expectations about their own ability to perform, expectations about likely rewards, and the attractiveness of those rewards.

expense items Inexpensive products that organizations generally use within a year of purchase.

expenses Costs created in the process of generating revenues.

experiential marketing Special events that emphasize fun, discovery, or community involvement.

export subsidies A form of financial assistance in which producers receive enough money from the government to allow them to lower their prices in order to compete more effectively in the global market.

exporting Selling and shipping goods or services to another country.

external auditors Independent accounting firms that provide auditing services for public companies.

factoring Obtaining funding by selling accounts receivable.

factors of production Economic resources, including natural resources, human resources, capital, entrepreneurship, and knowledge.

family branding Using a brand name on a variety of related products.

federal funds rate The interest rate that member banks charge each other to borrow money overnight from the funds they keep in their Federal Reserve accounts.

Federal Reserve System The central banking system of the United States; responsible for regulating banks and implementing monetary policy.

fiat money Official currencies issued and maintained through government *fiat*, or proclamation.

financial accounting The area of accounting concerned with preparing financial information for users outside the organization.

financial management Planning for a firm's money needs and managing the allocation and spending of funds.

financial plan A document that outlines the funds needed for a certain period of time, along with the sources and intended uses of those funds.

fintech Technologies with the potential to improve or disrupt financial services.

first-line managers Those at the lowest level of the management hierarchy; they supervise the operating employees and implement the plans set at the higher management levels.

fiscal policy Use of government revenue collection and spending to influence the business cycle.

fiscal year Any 12 consecutive months used as an accounting period.

fixed assets Assets retained for long-term use, such as land, buildings, machinery, and equipment; also referred to as *property, plant, and equipment*.

fixed costs Business costs that remain constant regardless of the number of units produced or number of customers served.

foreign direct investment (FDI) Investment of money by foreign companies in domestic business enterprises.

franchisee A business owner who pays for the rights to sell the products and use the business system of a franchisor.

franchise A business arrangement in which one company (the franchisee) obtains the rights to sell the products and use various elements of a business system of another company (the franchisor).

franchisor A company that licenses elements of its business system to other companies (franchisees).

free trade International trade unencumbered by restrictive measures.

free-market system Economic system in which decisions about what to produce and in what quantities are decided by the market's buyers and sellers.

freemium pricing A hybrid pricing strategy of offering some products for free while charging for others, or offering a product for free to some customers while charging others for it.

functional structure Grouping workers according to their similar skills, resource use, and expertise.

functional team A team whose members come from a single functional department and that is based on the organization's vertical structure.

gamification Applying game principles such as scorekeeping to various business processes.

general partnership A partnership in which all partners have joint authority to make decisions for the firm and joint liability for the firm's financial obligations.

generally accepted accounting principles (GAAP) Standards and practices used by publicly held corporations in the United States and a few other countries in the preparation of financial statements.

geographic segmentation Categorization of customers according to their geographical location.

gig economy Portion of the economy composed of people who work as independent contractors on a series of short-term projects or tasks.

glass ceiling An invisible barrier attributable to subtle discrimination that keeps women and minorities out of the top positions in business.

global strategy A highly centralized approach to international expansion, with headquarters in the home country making all major decisions.

goal-setting theory A motivational theory suggesting that setting goals can be an effective way to motivate employees.

goal A broad, long-range target or aim.

gross domestic product (GDP) The value of all the final goods and services produced by businesses located within a nation's borders; excludes outputs from overseas operations of domestic companies.

gross profit The amount remaining when the cost of goods sold is deducted from net sales; also known as *gross margin*.

groupthink Uniformity of thought that occurs when peer pressures cause individual team members to withhold contrary or unpopular opinions.

Hawthorne effect A supposed effect of organizational research, in which employees change their behavior because they are being studied and given special treatment; the validity of the effect is uncertain, and the Hawthorne studies were richer and more influential than this simple outcome would suggest.

Herzberg's two-factor theory A model that divides motivational forces into satisfiers ("motivators") and dissatisfiers ("hygiene factors").

hidden agenda Private, counterproductive motives in a team setting, such as a desire to take control of the group, to undermine someone else on the team, or to pursue an incompatible goal.

hostile takeover Acquisition of another company against the wishes of management.

human resources (HR) management The specialized function of planning how to obtain employees, oversee their training, evaluate them, and compensate them.

identity theft A crime in which thieves steal personal information and use it to take out loans and commit other types of fraud.

import quotas Limits placed on the quantity of imports a nation will allow for a specific product.

importing Purchasing goods or services from another country and bringing them into one's own country.

inbound marketing Strategy that attracts customers by offering value-added information related to the subjects they are already engaged in and the products that already interest them.

incentives Monetary payments and other rewards of value used for positive reinforcement.

income statement A financial record of a company's revenues, expenses, and profits over a given period of time; also known as a *profit-and-loss statement*.

Industry 4.0 The digital transformation of manufacturing, moving from automated factories to smart factories that emphasize the use of cyber-physical systems.

inflation An economic condition in which prices rise steadily throughout the economy.

information technology (IT) A functional area of business as well as the systems responsible for gathering, processing, and distributing information where needed throughout an organization.

initial public offering (IPO) A corporation's first offering of shares to the public.

insider trading The use of unpublicized information that an individual gains from the course of his or her job to benefit from fluctuations in the stock market.

integrated marketing communications (IMC) A strategy of coordinating and integrating communication and promotion efforts with customers to ensure greater efficiency and effectiveness.

intensive distribution A market coverage strategy that tries to place a product in as many outlets as possible.

international financial reporting standards (IFRS) Accounting standards and practices used in many countries outside the United States.

interpersonal skills Skills required to understand other people and to interact effectively with them.

inventory control Determining the right quantities of supplies and products to have on hand and tracking where those items are.

inventory turnover ratio A measure of the time a company takes to turn its inventory into sales, calculated by dividing cost of goods sold by the average value of inventory for a period.

inventory Goods and materials kept in stock for production or sale.

investment banks Firms that offer a variety of services related to initial public stock offerings, mergers and acquisitions, and other investment matters.

investment portfolios Collections of various types of investments.

ISO 9000 A globally recognized family of standards for quality management systems.

job characteristics model A model suggesting that five core job dimensions influence three critical psychological states that determine motivation, performance, and other outcomes.

job description A statement of the tasks involved in a given job and the conditions under which the holder of a job will work.

job enrichment Making jobs more challenging and interesting by expanding the range of skills required.

job specification A statement describing the kind of person who would be best for a given job—including the skills, education, and previous experience that the job requires.

joint venture A separate legal entity established by two or more companies to pursue shared business objectives.

just-in-time (JIT) Inventory management in which goods and materials are delivered throughout the production process right before they are needed.

labor relations The relationship between organized labor and management (in its role as the representative of company ownership).

labor unions Organizations that represent employees in negotiations with management.

laissez-faire leaders Leaders who leave most decisions up to employees, particularly those concerning day-to-day matters.

layoffs Termination of employees for economic or business reasons.

leading The process of guiding and motivating people to work toward organizational goals.

lean systems Systems (in manufacturing and other functional areas) that maximize productivity by reducing waste and delays.

lease An agreement to use an asset in exchange for regular payment; similar to renting.

legal and regulatory environment Laws and regulations at local, state, national, and even international levels.

leveraged buyout (LBO) Acquisition of a company's publicly traded stock, using funds that are primarily borrowed, usually with the intent of using some of the acquired assets to pay back the loans used to acquire the company.

leverage The technique of increasing the rate of return on an investment by financing it with borrowed funds.

liabilities Claims against a firm's assets by creditors.

licensing Agreement to produce and market another company's product in exchange for a royalty or fee.

limited liability company (LLC) A structure that combines limited liability with the pass-through taxation benefits of a partnership; the number of shareholders is not restricted, nor is members' participation in management.

limited liability A legal condition in which the maximum amount each owner is liable for is equal to whatever amount each invested in the business.

limited partnership A partnership in which one or more persons act as *general partners* who run the business and have the same unlimited liability as sole proprietors.

line of credit An arrangement in which a financial institution makes money available for use at any time after the loan has been approved.

liquidity A measure of how easily and quickly an asset such as corporate stock can be converted into cash by selling it.

logo A graphical and/or textual representation of a brand.

long-term financing Financing used to cover long-term expenses such as assets (generally repaid over a period of more than one year).

long-term liabilities Obligations that fall due more than a year from the date of the balance sheet.

loss-leader pricing Selling one product at a loss as a way to entice customers to consider other products.

machine learning The general capability of computers to learn.

machine translation Any form of computer-based, automated language translation.

management accounting The area of accounting concerned with preparing data for use by managers within the organization.

management by objectives (MBO) A motivational approach in which managers and employees work together to structure personal goals and objectives for every individual, department, and project to mesh with the organization's goals.

management pyramid An organizational structure divided into top, middle, and first-line management.

management The process of planning, organizing, leading, and controlling to meet organizational goals.

market development Selling existing products to new markets.

market environment A company's target customers, the buying influences that shape the behavior of those customers, and competitors that market similar products to those customers.

market penetration Selling more of a firm's existing products in the markets it already serves.

market segmentation The division of a diverse market into smaller, relatively homogeneous groups with similar needs, wants, and purchase behaviors.

market share A firm's portion of the total sales in a market.

marketing analytics A range of analytical tools and techniques that help marketers plan and evaluate marketing activities.

marketing concept An approach to business management that stresses customer needs and wants, seeks long-term profitability, and integrates marketing with other functional units within the organization.

marketing intermediaries Businesspeople and organizations that assist in moving and marketing goods and services between producers and consumers.

marketing mix The four key elements of marketing strategy: product, price, distribution, and customer communication.

marketing research The collection and analysis of information for making marketing decisions.

marketing strategy An overall plan for marketing a product; includes the identification of target market segments, a positioning strategy, and a marketing mix.

marketing The process of creating value for customers and building relationships with those customers in order to capture value back from them.

market A group of customers who need or want a particular product and have the money to buy it.

Maslow's hierarchy A model in which human needs are arranged in a hierarchy, with the most basic needs at the bottom and the more advanced needs toward the top.

mass customization A manufacturing approach in which part of the product is mass produced and the remaining features are customized for each buyer.

mass production The creation of identical goods or services, usually in large quantities.

matching principle The fundamental principle requiring that expenses incurred in producing revenue be deducted from the revenues they generate during an accounting period.

materials requirements planning (MRP) A planning system that works backward from a company's sales forecasts to make sure it has enough of everything required to build those goods or perform those services in a timely manner.

matrix structure A structure in which employees are assigned to both a functional group and a project team (thus using functional and divisional patterns simultaneously).

mentoring A process in which experienced managers guide less experienced colleagues in nuances of office politics, serving as role models for appropriate business behavior and helping to negotiate the corporate structure.

merchant wholesalers Independent wholesalers that take legal title to goods they distribute.

merger An action taken by two companies to combine as a single entity.

microlenders Organizations, often not-for-profit, that lend smaller amounts of money to business owners who might not qualify for conventional bank loans.

micromanaging Overseeing every small detail of employees' work and refusing to give them freedom or autonomy.

middle managers Those in the middle of the management hierarchy; they develop plans to implement the goals of top managers and coordinate the work of first-line managers.

mission statement A brief statement of why an organization exists; in other words, what the organization aims to accomplish for customers, investors, and other stakeholders.

monetary policy Government policy and actions taken by the Federal Reserve Board to regulate the nation's money supply.

money market An over-the-counter marketplace for short-term debt instruments such as Treasury bills and commercial paper.

money supply The amount of money in circulation at any given time.

money Anything generally accepted as a means of paying for goods and services; serves as a medium of exchange, a unit of accounting, a store of value, and a standard of deferred value.

monopolistic competition A situation in which many sellers differentiate their products from those of competitors in at least some small way.

monopoly A situation in which one company dominates a market to the degree that it can control prices.

motivation The combination of forces that drive individuals to take certain actions and avoid other actions.

multidomestic strategy A decentralized approach to international expansion in which a company creates highly independent operating units in each new country.

multinational corporations (MNCs) Companies with operations in more than one country.

national brands Brands owned by manufacturers and distributed nationally.

needs Differences between a person's actual state and his or her ideal state; they provide the basic motivation to make a purchase.

negative reinforcement Encouraging the repetition of a particular behavior (desirable or not) by removing unpleasant consequences for the behavior.

neobanks Banks that provide services entirely through mobile and digital channels.

net income Profit (or loss) incurred by a firm, determined by subtracting expenses from revenues; casually referred to as the *bottom line*.

network structure A structure that coordinates resources inside and outside the company to form a cohesive whole.

new-employee orientation Sessions or procedures for acclimating new employees to the organization.

nongovernmental organizations (NGOs) Not-for-profit groups that provide charitable services or promote social and environmental causes.

norms Informal standards of conduct that guide team behavior.

not-for-profit organizations Organizations that provide goods and services without having a profit motive; also called *nonprofit organizations*.

objective A specific, short-range target or aim.

offshoring Transferring a part or all of a business function to a facility (a different part of the company or another company entirely) in another country.

oligopoly A market situation in which a small number of suppliers, sometimes only two, provide a particular good or service.

omnichannel retailing Strategy in which a company builds an integrated online and offline presence so that consumers have a seamless experience throughout the buying process.

onboarding Programs to help new employees get comfortable and productive in their assigned roles.

operating expenses All costs of operation that are not included under cost of goods sold.

operations management Management of the people and processes involved in creating goods and services.

organization chart A diagram that shows how employees and tasks are grouped and where the lines of communication and authority flow.

organization structure A framework that enables managers to divide responsibilities, ensure employee accountability, and distribute decision-making authority.

organizational culture A set of shared values and norms that support the management system and that guide management and employee behavior.

organizational market Companies, government agencies, and other organizations that buy goods and services either to resell or to use in the creation of their own goods and services.

organizing The process of arranging resources to carry out the organization's plans.

outsourcing Contracting out certain business functions or operations to other companies.

owners' equity The portion of a company's assets that belongs to the owners after obligations to all creditors have been met.

participative management A philosophy of allowing employees to take part in planning and decision-making.

partnership An unincorporated company owned by two or more people.

pension plans Generally refers to traditional, defined-benefit retirement plans.

performance management systems Systems that help companies establish goals for employees and track performance relative to those goals.

performance reviews Periodic evaluations of employees' work according to specific criteria.

permission-based marketing A marketing approach in which firms first ask permission to deliver messages to an audience and then promise to restrict their communication efforts to those subject areas in which audience members have expressed interest.

personal selling One-on-one interaction between a salesperson and a prospective buyer.

philanthropy The donation of money, time, goods, or services to charitable, humanitarian, or educational institutions.

pivoting Adjusting a firm's business model when a better opportunity presents itself.

planned system Economic system in which the government controls most of the factors of production and regulates their allocation.

planning Establishing objectives and goals for an organization and determining the best ways to accomplish them.

point-of-purchase (POP) display Advertising or other display materials set up at retail locations to promote products to potential customers as they are making their purchase decisions.

positioning Managing a business in a way designed to occupy a particular place in the minds of target customers.

positive reinforcement Encouraging desired behaviors by offering pleasant consequences for completing or repeating those behaviors.

press conference An in-person or online gathering of media representatives at which companies announce new information; also called a *news conference.*

press release A brief statement or video program released to the press announcing new products, management changes, sales performance, and other potential news items; also called a *news release.*

price The amount of money charged for a product or service.

prime rate The interest rate a bank charges its best loan customers.

private accountants In-house accountants employed by organizations and businesses other than a public accounting firm; also called *corporate accountants.*

private brands Brands that carry the label of a retailer or a wholesaler rather than a manufacturer.

private corporation A corporation in which all the stock is owned by only a few individuals or companies and is not made available for purchase by the public.

private equity Ownership assets that aren't publicly traded; includes venture capital.

problem-solving team A team that meets to find ways to improve quality, efficiency, and the work environment.

procurement The acquisition of the raw materials, parts, components, supplies, and finished products required to produce goods and services.

producer price index (PPI) A statistical measure of price trends at the producer and wholesaler levels.

product development process A formal process of generating, selecting, developing, and commercializing product ideas.

product development Creating new products for a firm's current markets.

product life cycle Four stages through which a product progresses: introduction, growth, maturity, and decline.

product line A series of related products offered by a firm.

product mix The complete portfolio of products that a company offers for sale.

product placement The paid display or use of products in television shows, movies, and video games.

production and operations management Overseeing all the activities involved in producing goods and services.

productivity The efficiency with which an organization can convert inputs to outputs.

product A bundle of value that satisfies a customer need or want.

professionalism The quality of performing at a high level and conducting oneself with purpose and pride.

profit sharing The distribution of a portion of the company's profits to employees.

profit Money left over after all the costs involved in doing business have been deducted from revenue.

promotion A wide variety of persuasive techniques used by companies to communicate with their target markets and the general public.

prospecting The process of finding and qualifying potential customers.

protectionism Government policies aimed at shielding a country's industries from foreign competition.

prototypes Preproduction samples of products used for testing and evaluation.

proxy A document that authorizes another person to vote on behalf of a shareholder in a corporation.

psychographics Classification of customers on the basis of their psychological makeup, interests, and lifestyles.

public accountants Professionals who provide accounting services to other businesses and individuals for a fee.

public corporation A corporation in which stock is sold to anyone who has the means to buy it.

public relations (PR) Nonsales communication that businesses have with their various audiences (including both communication with the general public and press relations).

pure competition A situation in which so many buyers and sellers exist that no single buyer or seller can individually influence prices.

purpose-driven business A company that aspires to accomplish more than just making money for owners and investors.

quality The degree to which a product or process meets reasonable or agreed-on expectations.

quality assurance A more comprehensive approach of companywide policies, practices, and procedures to ensure that every product meets quality standards.

quality control Measuring quality against established standards after the good or service has been produced and weeding out any defective products.

quality of work life (QWL) An overall environment that results from job and work conditions.

quick ratio A measure of a firm's short-term liquidity, calculated by adding cash, marketable securities, and receivables, then dividing that sum by current liabilities; also known as the *acid-test ratio*.

rate of return The gain (or loss) of an investment over time, expressed as a percentage.

rebates Partial reimbursements of price, offered as a purchase incentive.

recession A period during which national income, employment, and production all fall; often defined as at least six months of decline in the GDP.

recruiting The process of attracting appropriate applicants for an organization's jobs.

regulation Relying more on laws and policies than on market forces to govern economic activity.

reinforcement theory A motivational approach based on the idea that managers can motivate employees by influencing their behaviors with positive and negative reinforcement.

relationship marketing A focus on developing and maintaining long-term relationships with customers, suppliers, and distribution partners for mutual benefit.

research and development (R&D) Functional area responsible for conceiving and designing new products.

retail theater Tactics designed to engage retail consumers in ways that foster store loyalty, keep shoppers in stores longer, and encourage repeat business.

retailers Intermediaries that sell goods and services to individuals for their own personal use.

retained earnings The portion of shareholders' equity earned by the company but not distributed to its owners in the form of dividends.

retirement plans Company-sponsored programs for providing retirees with income.

return on equity The ratio between net income after taxes and total owners' equity.

return on sales The ratio between net income after taxes and net sales; also known as the *profit margin*.

revenue Money a company brings in through the sale of goods and services.

risk/return trade-off The balance of potential risks against potential rewards.

robotic process automation (RPA) A software capability that does for knowledge work what mechanical robots do for manufacturing and other physical processes.

S corporation A type of corporation that combines the capital-raising options and limited liability of a corporation with the federal taxation advantages of a partnership.

salary Fixed cash compensation for work, usually by a yearly amount; independent of the number of hours worked.

sales promotion A wide range of events and activities designed to promote a brand or stimulate interest in a product.

Sarbanes-Oxley The informal name of comprehensive legislation designed to improve the integrity and accountability of financial information.

scalability The potential to increase production by expanding or replicating its initial production capacity.

scarcity A condition of any productive resource that has finite supply.

scientific management A management approach designed to improve employees' efficiency by scientifically studying their work.

secured loans Loans backed up with assets that the lender can claim in case of default, such as a piece of property.

seed money The first infusion of capital used to get a business started.

selective distribution A market coverage strategy that uses a limited number of carefully chosen outlets to distribute products.

self-managed team A team in which members are responsible for an entire process or operation.

seniority The length of time someone has worked for his or her current employer, relative to other employees.

sexual harassment Unwelcome sexual advances, requests for sexual favors, or other verbal or physical conduct of a sexual nature within the workplace.

shareholder activism Activities undertaken by shareholders (individually or in groups) to influence executive decision-making in areas ranging from strategic planning to social responsibility.

shareholders Investors who purchase shares of stock in a corporation.

shopping products Fairly important goods and services that people buy less frequently with more planning and comparison.

short-term financing Financing used to cover current expenses (generally repaid within a year).

Six Sigma A rigorous quality management program that strives to eliminate deviations between the actual and desired performance of a business system.

skills inventory A list of the skills a company needs from its workforce, along with the specific skills that individual employees currently possess.

skim pricing Charging a high price for a new product during the introductory stage and lowering the price later.

small business A company that is independently owned and operated, is not dominant in its field, and employs fewer than 500 people.

smart contract Digital agreement in a distributed ledger such as blockchain that automatically executes when its criteria are fulfilled by incoming data.

social commerce The creation and sharing of product-related information among customers and potential customers.

social communication model An approach to communication based on interactive social media and conversational communication styles.

social customer care The use of social media to listen for complaints or frustrations, to respond to customers who ask for help, and to share useful information with their brand communities.

social environment Trends and forces in society at large.

sole proprietorship A business owned by a single person.

span of management The number of people under one manager's control; also known as span of control.

specialty products Particular brands that the buyer especially wants and will seek out, regardless of location or price.

stakeholders Internal and external groups affected by a company's decisions and activities.

statement of cash flows A statement of a firm's cash receipts and cash payments that presents information on its sources and uses of cash.

statistical process control (SPC) The use of random sampling and tools such as control charts to monitor the production process.

stereotyping Assigning a wide range of generalized and often false attributes to an individual based on his or her membership in a particular culture or social group.

stock exchanges Organizations that facilitate the buying and selling of stock.

stock options A contract that allows the holder to purchase or sell a certain number of shares of a particular stock at a given price by a certain date.

strategic alliance A long-term partnership between companies to jointly develop, produce, or sell products.

strategic CSR Social contributions that are directly aligned with a company's overall business strategy.

strategic marketing planning The process of examining an organization's current marketing situation, assessing opportunities and setting objectives, and then developing a marketing strategy to reach those objectives.

strategic plans Plans that establish the actions and the resource allocation required to accomplish strategic goals; they're usually defined for periods of two to five years and developed by top managers.

subscription pricing A pricing model in which customers are charged a recurring fee for the right to continuing using a product.

succession planning Workforce planning efforts that identify possible replacements for specific employees, usually senior executives.

supply chain management (SCM) The business procedures, policies, and computer systems that integrate the various elements of the supply chain into a cohesive system.

supply chain A set of connected systems that coordinate the flow of goods and materials from suppliers all the way through to final customers.

supply curve A graph of the quantities of a product that sellers will offer for sale, regardless of demand, at various prices.

supply A specific quantity of a product that a seller is able and willing to provide at a particular date at various prices.

sustainable development Operating business in a manner that minimizes pollution and resource depletion, ensuring that future generations will have vital resources.

system An interconnected and coordinated set of elements and processes that converts inputs to desired outputs.

target markets Specific customer groups or segments to whom a company wants to sell a particular product.

tariffs Taxes levied on imports.

task force A team of people from several departments who are temporarily brought together to address a specific issue.

taskbot A software agent that can be assigned to complete a variety of tasks within an app or business system.

tax haven A country whose favorable banking laws and low tax rates give companies the opportunity to shield some of their income from higher tax rates in their home countries or other countries where they do business.

team A unit of two or more people who share a mission and collective responsibility as they work together to achieve a goal.

technical skills The ability and knowledge to perform the mechanics of a particular job.

technological environment Forces resulting from the practical application of science to innovations, products, and processes.

termination The process of getting rid of an employee through layoff or firing.

test marketing A product development stage in which a product is sold on a limited basis to gauge its market appeal.

Theory X A managerial assumption that employees are irresponsible, are unambitious, and dislike work and that managers must use force, control, or threats to motivate them.

Theory Y A managerial assumption that employees enjoy meaningful work, are naturally committed to certain goals, are capable of creativity, and seek out responsibility under the right conditions.

three-needs theory David McClelland's model of motivation that highlights the needs for power, affiliation, and achievement.

top managers Those at the highest level of the organization's management hierarchy; they are responsible for setting strategic goals, and they have the most power and responsibility in the organization.

total quality management (TQM) An approach to quality assurance that encompasses every aspect of a company's operations.

touchpoint Any point of interaction—online, on the phone, or in person—between a company and its current and potential customers.

trade allowances Discounts or other financial considerations offered by producers to wholesalers and retailers.

trade credit Credit obtained by a purchaser directly from a supplier.

trade deficit An unfavorable trade balance created when a country imports more than it exports.

trade promotions Sales promotion efforts aimed at inducing distributors or retailers to push a producer's products.

trade surplus A favorable trade balance created when a country exports more than it imports.

trademarks Brands that have been given legal protection so that their owners have exclusive rights to their use.

trading blocs Organizations of nations that remove barriers to trade among their members and that establish uniform barriers to trade with nonmember nations.

transaction An exchange of value between parties.

transnational strategy A hybrid approach that attempts to reap the benefits of international scale while being responsive to local market dynamics.

transparency The degree to which affected parties can observe relevant aspects of transactions or decisions.

turnover rate The percentage of the workforce that leaves every year.

unemployment rate The portion of the labor force (those ages 16 and older who have or are looking for a job) currently without a job.

unlimited liability A legal condition under which any damages or debts incurred by a business are the owner's personal responsibility.

unsecured loans Loans that require a good credit rating but no collateral.

unstructured organization An organization that doesn't have a conventional structure but instead assembles talent as needed from the open market; the virtual and networked organizational concepts taken to the extreme.

utility The power of a good or service to satisfy a human need.

value chain All the elements and processes that add value as raw materials are transformed into the final products made available to the ultimate customer.

value webs Multidimensional networks of suppliers and outsourcing partners.

value-based pricing A method of setting prices based on customer perceptions of value.

values statement A brief articulation of the principles that guide a company's decisions and behaviors.

variable costs Business costs that increase with the number of units produced or customers served.

venture capitalists (VCs) Investors who provide money to finance new businesses in exchange for a portion of ownership, with the objective of selling their shares at a significant gain.

virtual reality (VR) Computer-generated simulations that create the sensation of being in a real environment.

virtual team A team that uses communication technology to bring together geographically distant employees to achieve goals.

voice of the customer (VoC) Everything that current and potential customers are saying and writing about a company and its products; also refers to efforts to capture all this feedback.

wages Cash payment based on the number of hours an employee has worked or the number of units an employee has produced.

wants Specific goods, services, experiences, or other entities that are desirable in light of a person's experiences, culture, and personality.

whistle-blowing The disclosure by a company insider of information that exposes illegal or unethical behavior by others within the organization.

wholesalers Intermediaries that sell products to other intermediaries for resale or to organizations for internal use.

word of mouth Communication among customers and other parties, transmitting information about companies and products through online or offline personal conversations.

work rules A common element of labor contracts that specifies such things as the tasks certain employees are required to do or are forbidden to do.

work specialization Specialization in or responsibility for some portion of an organization's overall work tasks; also called division of labor.

workforce analytics The application of big data and analytics to workforce management.

working capital Current assets minus current liabilities.

work–life balance Efforts to help employees balance the competing demands of their personal and professional lives.

zero-based budgeting A budgeting approach in which each department starts from zero every year and must justify every item in the budget, rather than simply adjusting the previous year's budget amounts.

Brand, Organization, and Name Index

Subject Index